FHG

The original Farm Holiday Guide to Coast & Country Holidays 2003

England, Scotland, Wales, Ireland & Channel Islands

with
Farms • Hotels • Guest Houses • Self-catering • Caravan & Camping • Activity Holidays • Country Inns •

BOARD/SELF-CATERING

For Contents see Pages 50 & 51
For Index of towns/counties see back of book

Publications Paisley

Part of IPC Country and Leisure Media

ENGLAND and WALES
Counties
NORTH WALES
1. Denbighshire
2. Flintshire
3. Wrexham
SOUTH WALES
4. Swansea
5. Neath and Port Talbot
6. Bridgend
7. Rhondda Cynon Taff
8. Merthyr Tydfil
9. Vale of Glamorgan
10. Cardiff
11. Caerphilly
12. Blaenau Gwent
13. Torfaen
14. Newport
15. Monmouthshire
NORTHUMBERLAND
TYNE & WEAR
DURHAM
CUMBRIA
ISLE OF MAN
NORTH YORKSHIRE
LANCASHIRE
EAST RIDING OF YORKSHIRE
WEST YORKSHIRE
GREATER MANCHESTER
SOUTH YORKSHIRE
MERSEYSIDE
ISLE OF ANGLESEY
CONWY
CHESHIRE
DERBYSHIRE
NOTTINGHAM-SHIRE
LINCOLNSHIRE
GWYNEDD
STAFFORDSHIRE
SHROPSHIRE
LEICESTERSHIRE
RUTLAND
NORFOLK
WEST MIDLANDS
POWYS
CAMBRIDGESHIRE
NORTHAMPTONSHIRE
CEREDIGION
WARWICKSHIRE
WORCESTERSHIRE
SUFFOLK
BEDFORDSHIRE
HEREFORDSHIRE
PEMBROKESHIRE
CARMARTHENSHIRE
BUCKINGHAM-SHIRE
ESSEX
GLOUCESTERSHIRE
HERTFORDSHIRE
OXFORDSHIRE
BRISTOL
GREATER LONDON
BERKSHIRE
WILTSHIRE
SURREY
KENT
SOMERSET
HAMPSHIRE
WEST SUSSEX
E. SUSSEX
DORSET
DEVON
ISLE OF WIGHT
CORNWALL
SCILLY ISLES
©MAPS IN MINUTES™ 2001

SELF-CATERING

St Ives Bay

1st Class S/C Apartments and Bungalows near Beach

Fully equipped for your self catering holiday. Sleeps 2-6 persons. Peaceful location, small friendly site with Play Area, Garden, Free Parking, Dogs Welcome. Open all year. South West coastal path close by.

Weekly from £120 / Short Breaks £90

Tel: 01736 752594

www.sandbank-holidays.co.uk

Sandbank Holidays ST. IVES BAY

MasterCard VISA

SELF-CATERING

CSH ABSOLUTE ESCAPES

LAKE DISTRICT • EDEN VALLEY • NORTH CUMBRIA/SCOTTISH BORDERS • NORTH PENNINES • NORTHUMBERLAND

Excellent and very varied range of self-catering properties in a wide variety of locations from Towns to secluded Country Retreats.

- **Competitive rates**
- **Free brochure**

CSH Absolute Escapes,
1 Little Dockray, Penrith,
Cumbria CA11 7HL

Tel: 01768 868989 - 24hrs
Fax: 01768 865578

e-mail: Shirley.Thompson@csh.co.uk
website: www.csh.co.uk

SELF-CATERING

Country Holidays

BRITAIN'S FAVOURITE COTTAGE HOLIDAYS

Every kind of property for every kind of holiday

With over 3,000 quality graded cottages throughout the UK, catering from two to twenty-two, you're sure to find the right property for you. Many of our properties also accept pets so none of your family need miss out.

Look & Book at: www.country-holidays.co.uk or call 0870 442 5413 for your 2003 brochure.

SELF-CATERING

LOWER KITLEIGH COTTAGE Week St Mary, Near Bude, Cornwall

Pretty, Listed farmhouse in unspoilt country near magnificent coast. Newly renovated with all conveniences, yet retaining its charm, it stands in a peaceful grassy garden with picnic table and own parking. The sitting room has period furniture, inglenook fireplace, free logs and colour TV. The fully equipped kitchen has fridge/freezer, double sink, electric cooker and washer/tumble dryer. Three bedrooms with panoramic views, cots, duvets. Well-controlled dogs allowed. Riding nearby, golf, safe beaches, surfing, Cornish Moors, markets, cliff walks. All electricity inclusive, and central heating ensures a cosy stay throughout the year. Prices from £250 to £475 weekly; reductions for part week. Sleeps seven plus cot.

Mr and Mrs T. Bruce-Dick, 114 Albert Street, London NW1 7NE Tel: 0207-485 8976

BOARD

PENLEAZE is a Victorian farmhouse on a working family farm, situated amidst rolling countryside on the North Cornish coast, which is renowned for its spectacular views, rugged coastline and sandy beaches to explore, also lovely, quaint villages such as Boscastle. One mile to our pretty village and two miles to Bude, also ideally placed for visiting North Devon. We offer three double en suite bedrooms, a twin room with a private bathroom, and a small single room; four-poster and roll-top bath available. An English breakfast, using fresh local produce prepared on the Aga, is served in the dining room. There is a separate sitting room for guests to relax in.

Silver
SILVER AWARD

Penleaze Farmhouse Bed & Breakfast, Marhamchurch, Bude EX23 0ET
Tel & Fax: 01288 381226 • e-mail: liz@penleaze.co.uk
website: www.penleaze.co.uk

BOARD

Trelawne Hotel

Nestling on the coastline between the Helford and Fal rivers in a beautiful and tranquil corner of Cornwall, this fine country house hotel enjoys a magnificent outlook across Falmouth Bay to the Roseland Peninsula. Maenporth beach is a short distance away and there are numerous idyllic coves nearby. The tastefully furnished and centrally heated bedrooms have en suite facilities, as well as colour television, radio, telephone and tea and coffee makers. There is a charming cocktail bar where new friends are easily made, and there is an indoor pool and games room. The cuisine comes high on the list of attractions at this well-run hotel, dishes being prepared by award-winning chefs and backed by an extensive wine list.

Mawnan Smith, Falmouth, Cornwall TR11 5HS
Tel: 01326 250226 • Fax: 01326 250909

SELF-CATERING

Near Perranporth

Greenmeadow Cottages

Highly praised luxury cottages. Sleep 6. Superbly clean, comfortable and spacious. Open all year. Short Breaks out of season. Pets welcome in two of the cottages. Non-smoking available. Ample off-road parking.

For brochure and bookings

Tel: 01872 540483

DISCOVER SUNLAND HOLIDAY VILLAGE AND EXPERIENCE THE DELIGHTS OF CORNWALL!

Sunland Holiday Village overlooks the beautiful coastline of Portreath and virtually all of Cornwall's sights and scenes are within a short drive.

The newly refurbished chalets can sleep up to 6 people, they include a Lounge with TV, fully equipped fitted Kitchen with Dining Area, 2 Bedrooms and Bathroom.

Visit our website and see the exciting new additions at Sunland's for 2003! Or telephone the hotline now!

PETS ARE WELCOME!

HOTLINE: 01209 842354

Sunland Holiday Village Portreath Cornwall TR16 4PE
Telephone: 01209 842354 **Facsimile:** 01209 842365

Check out our website at: www.sunlandholidays.co.uk or email us at: info@sunlandholidays.co.uk

SELF-CATERING

TREMAINE GREEN

for MEMORABLE HOLIDAYS

"A beautiful private hamlet" of 11 traditional cosy **Cornish** craftsmen's cottages between **Looe** and **Polperro.** Clean, comfortable and well equipped, with a warm friendly atmosphere, for pets with 2 to 8 people. Set in lovely grounds, only 12 miles from the **Eden Project** with country & coastal walks nearby. Pets £16 pw, owners from only **£89.**

• Towels, Linen, Central Heating & Hot Water included • Dishwashers in larger cottages • Power shower Baths • Launderette • Games Room • Tennis Court • TV/Videos • Cots & Highchairs available • Pubs & Restaurants in easy walking distance

Mr & Mrs J Spreckley, Tremaine Green Country Cottages, Pelynt, Near Looe, Cornwall PL13 2LT
Tel: 01503 220333 • e-mail: stay@tremainegreen.co.uk • web: www.tremainegreen.co.uk

SELF-CATERING

BOSINVER HOLIDAY COTTAGES

Nestling in a hidden valley near the sea, the Eden Project and Lost Gardens of Heligan, our small farm has friendly animals and ponies. Choose from our 16th Century thatched farmhouse or cottages privately set in their own gardens surrounded by wildflower meadows. Wander down to the fishing lake or village pub, swim in the pool, play tennis, or relax and listen to the birdsong. No pets during Summer school holidays please.

Brochure from: Mrs Pat Smith, Bosinver Farm, Trelowth, St Austell, Cornwall PL26 7DT.
Tel: 01726 72128 • Internet: www.bosinver.co.uk

BOARD

"One of the most beautifully situated hotels in England"

Willapark Manor is a lovely character house in a beautiful setting amidst 14 acre grounds, overlooking Bossiney Bay. Surrounded by woodland, it is secluded and has direct access to the coastal path and beach. It is a family-run hotel with a friendly and informal atmosphere, excellent cuisine and a well stocked cocktail bar. Beautifully appointed bedrooms, all en suite and with colour TV and tea/coffee making facilities. Some four-posters. A warm welcome and a memorable holiday assured.

Willapark Manor Hotel

Bossiney, Tintagel, Cornwall PL34 0BA
Tel: 01840 770782
www.willapark.co.uk

CARAVANS

JOHN FOWLER
HOLIDAY PARKS
Widemouth Bay
Caravan Park
Nr. Bude, Cornwall

Overlooking beautiful Widemouth Bay, our 50 acre Park is only a few minutes from a safe sandy beach.

★ *NEW Tropical Indoor Heated Pool* ★
★ Children's Club ★ Safe Playground
★ Electric Hook-ups ★ Launderette
★ Shop and Takeaway

or write: Dept. CU, John Fowler Holidays Marlborough Road, Ilfracombe North Devon EX34 8PF

FREE
Hot Showers
★★★
Awning Space
★★★
Entertainment
★★★
Licensed Club
★★★
Crazy Golf

Your Stepping Stone to the Cumbrian Lake District

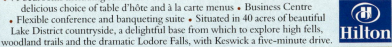

Carrock Cottages are three recently renovated stone built cottages set on the fringe of the Lakeland Fells. A quiet rural location near the lovely villages of Hesket Newmarket with its award-winning brewery, Caldbeck and Greystoke.
Explore the beauty of the Lake District National Park or head North to historic Carlisle and on to Hadrian's Wall.
Fell walking & other activities close to hand as well as excellent restaurants.
A warm welcome guaranteed.

Carrock House, Hutton Roof, Penrith, Cumbria CA11 0XY
Tel: Malcolm or Gillian on 01768 484 111 or Fax: 01768 488 850

WWW.CARROCKCOTTAGES.CO.UK

Lake District - Keswick

Harney Peak

PORTINSCALE, NEAR KESWICK, CUMBRIA

We can offer you the very best in self catering accommodation in our spacious well-equipped apartments in the quiet village of Portinscale – overlooking Derwentwater yet only one mile from Keswick.

- *Hot water and CH included in rental.*
- *Laundry facilities.* • *Ample off-street parking.*
- *Open all year.* • *Dogs welcome*

Various sized apartments makes this an ideal location for couples or families and short breaks are available off season.

website: www.leatheshead.co.uk

For brochure please apply to:
Mr & Mrs Smith, The Leathes Head Hotel,
Borrowdale, Cumbria CA12 5UY
Tel: 017687 77247 • Fax: 017687 77363

Hilton Keswick Lodore

Keswick, Cumbria CA12 5UX
Tel: 017687 77285 • Fax: 017687 77343
Central reservations: 08705 909090

Overlooking Lake Derwentwater the elegant Hilton Keswick Lodore is set in stunning Lake District scenery, yet is less than half an hour from the M6 and Penrith railway station.

• LivingWell Health Club Massage and Beauty Salon • Complimentary midweek golf nearby • 71 bedrooms including suites and Lake View rooms • Lodore Restaurant with delicious choice of table d'hôte and à la carte menus • Business Centre • Flexible conference and banqueting suite • Situated in 40 acres of beautiful Lake District countryside, a delightful base from which to explore high fells, woodland trails and the dramatic Lodore Falls, with Keswick a five-minute drive.

Birthwaite Edge, Windermere

Birthwaite Edge, set in two acres of mature gardens located in an exclusive Windermere area, provides superior self-catering. Spring visitors enjoy rhododendrons in blossom and in summer relax at the poolside. Autumn gives way to views of lake and snow-capped hills.

◇ Ideal for exploring the Lake District and Northern England by car or with public transport and coach tours.

◇ Ten-minute stroll to the lake or village.

◇ Good road and rail connections with major cities and Manchester Airport.

◇ Resident proprietors guarantee comfortable clean apartments.

◇ No smoking, no pets or feathers.

English Tourism Council ★★★ SELF CATERING

Brochure from – Bruce and Marsha Dodsworth, Birthwaite Edge, Birthwaite Road, Windermere, Cumbria LA23 1BS

Tel & Fax: 015394 42861 • e-mail: fhg@lakedge.com • www.lakedge.com

Lane Ends Cottages

Three cottages are situated next to "Fellside" on the edge of Elterwater Common. Two cottages accommodate a maximum of four persons: double bedroom, twin bedded room; fully equipped kitchen/diningroom; bathroom. Third cottage sleeps five: as above plus single bedroom and separate diningroom. Electricity by meters. The cottages provide an ideal base for walking/touring holidays with Ambleside, Grasmere, Hawkshead and Coniston within a few miles. Parking for one car per cottage, additional parking opposite. Open all year; out of season long weekends available. Rates from £175 per week. Brochure on request (SAE please).

Mrs M. E. Rice, "Fellside", Elterwater, Ambleside LA22 9HN • 015394 37678

SANDOWN

Lake Road, Windermere, Cumbria LA23 2JF • Tel: 015394 45275

Superb Bed and Breakfast accommodation. All rooms en suite with colour TV and tea/coffee making facilities. Situated two minutes from Lake Windermere, shops and cafes. Many lovely walks. Open all year. Special out of season rates, also two-day Saturday/Sunday breaks. From £22 to £32 per person, excluding Bank Holidays. Well behaved dogs welcome. Each room has own safe private car parking. SAE or telephone for further details.

Proprietors: Irene and George Eastwood

BOARD

Malcolm & Margaret MacFarlane

Borwick Lodge

Outgate, Hawkshead, Ambleside, Cumbria LA22 0PU
Tel & Fax: Hawkshead (015394) 36332
e-mail: borwicklodge@talk21.com • website: www.borwicklodge.com

Award-winning delightful 17th century house nestling in three acres of secluded gardens. Breathtaking panoramic lake and mountain views. Ideally situated. Close to Hawkshead village with good choice of restaurants and inns. Beautiful en suite rooms with colour televisions and tea-making facilities. King-size four-poster rooms. Somewhere special in this most beautiful corner of England. Ample parking. NON-SMOKING THROUGHOUT. Bed and Breakfast from £30. Residential licence.

See Board Section – Ambleside, Cumbria

CARAVANS

Greenhowe Caravan Park
Great Langdale, English Lakeland.

Greenhowe Caravan Park
Great Langdale, Ambleside,
Cumbria LA22 9JU

Greenhowe is a permanent Caravan Park with Self Contained Holiday Accommodation. Subject to availability Holiday Homes may be rented for short or long periods from 1st March until mid-November. The Park is situated in the Lake District half-a-mile from Dungeon Ghyll at the foot of the Langdale Pikes. It is an ideal centre for Climbing, Fell Walking, Riding, Swimming, Water-Skiing. **Please ask about Short Breaks.**

Winners of the Rose Award 1983-2000. ETC Grading "Very Good".

For free colour brochure

Telephone: (015394) 37231 • Fax: (015394) 37464 • Freephone: 0800 0717231

BOARD

Stybeck Farm, Thirlmere, Keswick, Cumbria CA12 4TN • Tel: 017687 73232

A warm welcome awaits you on this Lakeland working farm, beautifully situated amidst stunning landscape and ideal for touring or walking. Luxury studio also available with four-poster bed. Renowned for good food, and mentioned in national magazines. Six en suite rooms. B&B £20 - £26pp. Open January to December. Sorry, no smoking or pets. Ample parking.

e-mail: stybeckfarm@farming.co.uk
website: http://members.farmline.com/stybeckfarm

SELF-CATERING

CUDDY'S HALL HOLIDAY COTTAGE

A peaceful rural retreat set amidst forest and winding streams in the beautiful Cumbrian/Scottish Borders. Perfect for the great outdoors – walking, cycling, pony trekking. Also a good base to explore – Scotland, the Roman Wall, Kielder Water, the Solway Coast, and the Lake District, to name but a few...

• A good value Quality Country Cottage • Open all year • Sleeps up to 5 guests
• See also advertisement in the main section under Cumbria •

For further details please telephone Mrs Joanna Furness: 016977 48160
or visit our website: www.cuddys-hall.co.uk

BOARD

The Blacksmiths Arms

Talkin Village, Brampton, Cumbria CA8 1LE
Tel: 016977 3452 • Fax: 016977 3396

The Blacksmith's Arms offers all the hospitality and comforts of a traditional country inn. Enjoy tasty meals served in the bar lounges, or linger over dinner in the well-appointed restaurant. The inn is personally managed by the proprietors, Anne and Donald Jackson, who guarantee the hospitality one would expect from a family concern. Guests are assured of a pleasant and comfortable stay. There are five lovely bedrooms, all en suite and offering every comfort. Peacefully situated in the beautiful village of Talkin, the inn is convenient for the Borders, Hadrian's Wall and the Lake District. There is a good golf course, walking and other country pursuits nearby.

SELF-CATERING

Ullswater –Tirril Farm Cottages

Opened in 2001, these tasteful barn conversions are set around a quiet courtyard, some with outstanding views of the fells. Situated in the village of Tirril, two miles from Ullswater and three miles from Penrith, this is an ideal, quiet location for visiting the Lake District and Eden Valley. Tirril is an attractive village with a pub/restaurant and regular bus service. Fully centrally heated cottages with bed linen and towels provided. Large car park and lock-up for cycles. Short breaks welcome. A warm welcome awaits you from the resident proprietors.

For bookings or brochure Tel/Fax: 01768 864767
e-mail: enquiries@tirrilfarmcottages.co.uk
www.tirrilfarmcottages.co.uk

★★★★ SELF CATERING

SELF-CATERING

WOLFSCOTE GRANGE FARM COTTAGES

Hartington, Near Buxton, Derbyshire SK17 0AX
Tel & Fax: 01298 84342

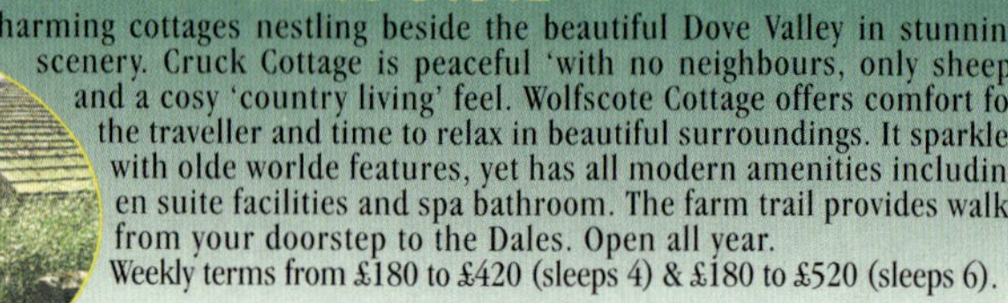

Charming cottages nestling beside the beautiful Dove Valley in stunning scenery. Cruck Cottage is peaceful 'with no neighbours, only sheep' and a cosy 'country living' feel. Wolfscote Cottage offers comfort for the traveller and time to relax in beautiful surroundings. It sparkles with olde worlde features, yet has all modern amenities including en suite facilities and spa bathroom. The farm trail provides walks from your doorstep to the Dales. Open all year.
Weekly terms from £180 to £420 (sleeps 4) & £180 to £520 (sleeps 6).

ETC ★★★★
e-mail: wolfscote@btinternet.com
website: www.wolfscotegrangecottages.co.uk

Field Head Farmhouse Holidays
CALTON

Situated midway between Leek and Ashbourne within the Southern Peak District and the Staffordshire Moorlands

Grade II Listed farmhouse with stables, set within its own grounds with open views. Well equipped, with SKY TV. Sleeps 11 plus campbed and cot. Ample space for family caravan. Set in beautiful secluded surroundings close to Dovedale and the Manifold Valley. Ideal country for the walker, horse rider or cyclist. Alton Towers 15-minute drive. All pets and horses welcome. Open all year. Short winter breaks. Late booking discount.

Contact Janet Hudson

Tel: 01538 308352 • www.field-head.co.uk

SELF-CATERING

Bulleigh Park Farm

Farmhouse accommodation with spectacular country views

The friendly Dallyn Family welcome guests to their spacious farmhouse, set in rural surroundings just four miles from the coast. One en suite bedroom, one with private facilities; both have TV, hairdryer, hospitality trays and toiletries. Pleasant views are afforded from the lounge, conservatory and dining room. Award-winning breakfasts are prepared from local produce; for dinner, the local pub is just a stroll away. No smoking in bedrooms or dining room. Guests enjoy visiting nearby beaches, gardens, antique centres, Paignton Zoo, and Agatha Christie's house (NT).

Tel & Fax: 01803 872254 • e-mail: bulleigh@lineone.net
Bulleigh Park Farm, Ipplepen, Newton Abbot, Devon TQ12 5UA

BOARD

Dart Valley Cottages – South Devon

A fine collection of individual, well-equipped cottages set in the glorious scenery of the River Dart Valley. Sleep 2 – 10. Many properties have stunning views. Wonderful countryside for walking, good beaches close by.

Short Breaks available

For brochure telephone

01803 771127

enquiries@dartvalleycottages.co.uk
www.dartvalleycottages.co.uk

SELF-CATERING

BONEHAYNE FARM
COLYTON, DEVON EX24 6SG

COTTAGE: CARAVAN: BOARD

- Family 250 acre working farm • Competitive prices
- Spectacular views • South facing luxury caravan
- Cottage with four-poster and central heating
- Four miles to the beach • Five minutes from Colyton
- Spacious lawns/gardens • Laundry room, BBQ, picnic tables
- Good trout fishing, woods to roam, walks

Mrs Gould

Tel: 01404 871416/871396

website: www.bonehayne.co.uk • e-mail: gould@bonehayne.co.uk

CARAVANS/SELF-CATERING

BOARD

Dartington Hall

The beautiful 14th century Courtyard at Dartington Hall is the perfect place to relax. Set amidst 1000 acres of farmland and ancient deer park, there are many walks for you to enjoy, through the woodlands, along the River Dart and in the magnificent gardens surrounding the Hall.

Dartington Hall is also an ideal base from which to explore Devon and Cornwall, including Dartmoor, the coast, Eden Project and National Trust properties.

SPECIAL BREAK OFFER

£49.50pppn for Bed, Breakfast and Dinner in our award-winning White Hart Bar & Restaurant.

STAY 5 NIGHTS FOR THE PRICE OF 4!

Min. stay 2 nights. Subject to availability Quote CCH3

The White Hart Bar & Restaurant

Located within the Courtyard, the White Hart Bar offers mouthwatering meals, freshly prepared using the finest local ingredients, including organic produce from Dartington Hall's own market garden.

Open for lunch and dinner.

Dartington Hall, Totnes, South Devon TQ9 6EL

Accommodation and Conference enquiries: 01803 847147

Bar and Restaurant reservations: 01803 847111

www.dartingtonhall.com

Rosette Award for Food – Which? Guide to Country Pubs • 'Pick of the Pubs' recommended – AA Pub Guide 2002 • As featured on Carlton TV's 'Taste of the West' • Gold, Silver & Bronze medals - South Hams Festival 2002.

BOARD

Great Sloncombe Farm

Moretonhampstead Devon TQ13 8QF

Tel: 01647 440595

Share the magic of Dartmoor all year round while staying in our lovely 13th century farmhouse full of interesting historical features. A working dairy farm set amongst peaceful meadows and woodland abundant in wild flowers and animals, including badgers, foxes, deer and buzzards. A welcoming and informal place to relax and explore the moors and Devon countryside. Comfortable double and twin rooms with en suite facilities, TV, central heating and coffee/tea making facilities. Delicious Devonshire suppers and breakfasts with new baked bread.

Open all year~No smoking~Farm Stay UK

e-mail: hmerchant@sloncombe.freeserve.co.uk • website: www.greatsloncombefarm.co.uk

Silver
SILVER AWARD

SELF-CATERING

We have a lovely farm set at the head of the Fuchsia Valley of Lee, with views across the Atlantic. Our four fully furnished cottages and two holiday homes are so popular we have erected a log cabin to accommodate all the visitors who want to keep coming to stay in this peaceful corner of Devon, surrounded by our special animals and the beautiful wildlife - *deer, badgers, geese and buzzards to name but a few*. The beaches of Lee Woolacombe are close by. Meals and cream teas are available, by arrangement, in our conservatory.

Lower Campscott Farm

Lee, Ilfracombe, Devon EX34 8LS

Tel: 01271 863479

e-mail: holidays@lowercampscott.co.uk

website: www.lowercampscott.co.uk

BOARD

Harton Farm

Oakford, Tiverton EX16 9HH (01398 351209)

Come and enjoy a unique rural experience on our traditional non-intensive working farm near Exmoor; peace and quiet for adults, and for the children, a chance to meet the animals. 17th Century stone farmhouse, secluded but accessible, ideal touring centre. Comfortable accommodation in three double bedrooms with washbasin and tea making facilities; luxury bathroom with a view; dining room serving real country cooking with farm-produced additive-free meat and organic vegetables; home baking a speciality; guests' lounge with colour TV. Home spun wool. Garden. Children over four welcome. Pets accepted. Car essential - parking. Open for Evening Meal, Bed and Breakfast from £26; Bed and Breakfast from £18. Reductions for children. Farm walks. Fishing, shooting, riding can be arranged. Vegetarian meals available on request.

e-mail: lindy@hartonfarm.co.uk **web: www.hartonfarm.co.uk**

SELF-CATERING

Hope Barton Barns

Tel: 01548 561393

www.hopebarton.co.uk

★★★★ *Open All Year*

Nestling in its own valley close to the sandy cove, Hope Barton Barns is an exclusive group of 17 stone barns in two courtyards and three luxury apartments in the converted farmhouse. Superbly furnished and fully equipped, accommodation ranges from a studio to four bedrooms, sleeping two to 10. Heated indoor pool, sauna, gym, lounge bar, tennis court, trout lake and a children's play barn. We have 35 acres of pastures and streams. Farmhouse meals. Ample parking. Golf, sailing and coastal walking nearby. A perfect setting for family summer holidays, walking in Spring/Autumn or just a "get away from it all" break. Free range children and well behaved dogs welcome. For full colour brochure please contact: ***Mike or Judy Tromans.***

Hope Cove – Near Salcombe - South Devon – TQ7 3HT

BOARD

Farmhouse Bed & Breakfast • Horwood Barton Farm

Touring North Devon?

Then stay with us on our 400-acre dairy farm. Large impressive farmhouse with stunning views from your bedroom. Breakfast is served in a delightful panelled dining room with 18th century moulded ceiling. Two rooms available: one family/twin room en suite, one double with large private bathroom. TV and tea/coffee facilities in rooms. Private lounge for guests.

Come and go as you please. Welcome to tour farm. Quality assured. 5 miles Bideford, 3 miles RHS Garden Rosemoor, 3 miles Tarka Cycle Trail, 8 miles sandy beaches. Non-smoking. Sorry, no pets. £20pppn.

Mrs Valerie Beer, Horwood Barton Farm, Monkleigh, Bideford, Devon EX39 5LF (01805 623174)

BOARD/SELF-CATERING

Winner of the 2002 Golden Achievement Award of Excellence for Quality and Service, this tastefully refurbished 16th century farmhouse is situated close to the road between Barnstaple and Bideford on the lovely Taw/Torridge estuary, immediately adjacent to the Tarka Trail. Open all year, the rooms are fully modernised, with colour TV and en suite facilities. With courtyard parking, this is an ideal base for touring Devon and Cornwall. It is within a mile of the sandy beach at Instow, and excellent pubs and restaurants. A self-catering cottage (**ETC ★★★**) is also available, and there are many leisure activities close at hand. For details contact:

English Tourism Council ♦♦♦♦ GUEST ACCOMMODATION

2002 Golden Achievement Award of Excellence for Quality and Service

Peter Day, Lower Yelland Farm, Fremington, Barnstaple EX31 3EN

Tel: 01271 860101 / 07803 933642

e-mail: peterday@loweryellandfarm.co.uk

www.loweryellandfarm.co.uk

SELF-CATERING

Northcott Barton Farm Cottage

English Tourism Council ★★★★ SELF CATERING

Beautifully equipped, spotlessly clean three bedroom cottage with large enclosed garden. A walker's and country lover's ideal: for a couple seeking peace and quiet or a family holiday. Very special rates for low season holidays, couples and short breaks. Near golf, riding, Tarka trail and R.H.S. Rosemoor. Character, comfort, beams, log fire, "*Perfick*".

For availability please contact Sandra Gay,
Northcott Barton, Ashreigney, Chulmleigh, Devon EX18 7PR
Tel/Fax: 01769 520259 • E-mail: sandra@northcottbarton.co.uk
Web: www.northcottbarton.co.uk

SELF-CATERING

Parkfield Luxury Apartments have 1, 2 or 3 bedrooms, each fully equipped with TV and video, own patio and lovely views. Parkfield's landscaped grounds accommodate a children's play area, ample parking and kennels for dogs which are welcome.
The tranquil setting is a short drive to beaches, coastal walks, traditional pubs, steam railways and other family attractions.

For more information please phone/fax or write to June or Roy at:
Parkfield Luxury Apartments, Claddon Lane,
Maidencombe, Torquay TQ1 4TB Tel: 01803 328952
website: www.parkfieldapartments.co.uk

Parkfield Holiday Apartments

BOARD/SELF-CATERING

Withill Farm, Walkhampton, West Dartmoor

Relax on our small, secluded farm. Enjoy a friendly welcome and the comfort and good food of our pleasant farmhouse. For self-caterers there is a delightful converted barn. Pets are welcome. Ideal for walking, riding, cycling and touring throughout Devon and Cornwall.

- B&B three bedrooms, including one en suite and one twin, all with TV and tea/coffee facilities. Supper by arrangement. Packed lunches. From £19 per night
- Self-catering. Sleeps 2-4. Central heating, TV, fridge, freezer, washing machine, barbecue. From £158 per week.

Brochure from Pam Kitchin at Withill Farm, Sampford Spiney, Yelverton, Devon PL20 6LN
Tel/Fax: 01822 853992 • e-mail: withillfarm1@aol.com

SELF-CATERING

SELF-CATERING

Wooder Manor

Tel & Fax: 01364 621391

e-mail: angela@woodermanor.com

website: www.woodermanor.com

Widecombe-in-the-Moor
Near Ashburton TQ13 7TR

Cottages and converted coach house, on 150-acre working family farm nestled in the picturesque valley of Widecombe, surrounded by unspoilt woodland, moors and granite tors. Half-a-mile from village with post office, general stores, inn with dining room, church and National Trust Information Centre. Excellent centre for touring Devon with a variety of places to visit and exploring Dartmoor by foot or on horseback. Accommodation is clean and well equipped with colour TV, central heating, laundry room. Children welcome. Large gardens and courtyard for easy parking. Open all year, so take advantage of off-season reduced rates. Short Breaks also available. Two properties suitable for disabled visitors. Brochure available.

SELF-CATERING

WOOLACOMBE COTTAGES

A good selection of cottages, from seafront to farmhouse, including many in private grounds, with excellent golf course and swimming pool. Close to beach, moors and gardens, with riding, surfing, tennis and much more available. Weekly tariff £145 to £1500. Short Breaks from £75.

Ivycott Farm, Woolacombe, Devon EX34 7HL

For further details phone/fax:

01271 870846

www.woolacombe-cottages.co.uk

SELF-CATERING

DEVONCOAST HOLIDAYS

We are an experienced Holiday Letting Agency, with properties ranging from one bedroom flats to three bedroomed houses, all in **Sunny South Devon.** Some have sea views. All are fully equipped with CTV and car parking. Children and pets are welcome. Mini Breaks.

We are open all year. Free brochure & map.

P. O. BOX 14, BRIXHAM, DEVON TQ5 9AB

Tel: 07050 33 8889 www.devoncoast.com

BOARD

This charming old farmhouse was a monastery during the 16th century, restored in 1849 and is now a Listed building. A family-run working dairy farm, 140 acres overlooking the Blackmoor Vale. Accommodation is in three comfortable en suite rooms with colour TV and tea/coffee making facilities. Diningroom with inglenook fireplace, lounge with colour TV, for guests' use at all times. Also garden and lawn. Plenty of reading material and local information provided for this ideal touring area. Bed and Breakfast from £23. Excellent evening meals in all local inns nearby. Situated six miles from Sherborne with its beautiful Abbey and Castle.

AA ♦♦♦♦ Guest Accommodation

SAE for further details. **Mrs Jenny Mayo**

Hermitage, Holnest, Sherborne DT9 6HA

(Tel and Fax: 01963 210296)

Alms House Farm

SELF-CATERING

East Briscoe Farm Cottages

Baldersdale
Barnard Castle
Co. Durham
DL12 9UL

Ann & Peter Wilson

01833 650087

In a beautiful situation central to the North of England.
The six stone-built cottages offer superb accommodation on a stunning riverside estate which offers walks and fishing.
A place to relax and explore the North.
Sleep 2-6. Open all year.
Pets welcome in two of the cottages.
Terms from £120

Winner of the Northumbria TB 'Self-Catering of the Year' 1999

English Tourism Council ★★★★ SELF CATERING

fax: 01833 650027 • e-mail: peter@eastbriscoe.co.uk • www.eastbriscoe.co.uk

SELF-CATERING

The Cottage and Dairy Cottage

Three adjoining self-contained units, two comprising one double and one twin bedroom, kitchen, bathroom and comfortable living area. The third has a double bedroom plus a studio couch in the living area. Colour TV, private garden and patio furniture, heating and linen are all included in the price. We are a working sheep farm just north of the village of Castleside on the A68 heading towards Corbridge and offer easy access to the Roman Wall, Durham City, the Metro Centre, Beamish Museum and lots more. Pass the Fleece Inn Pub on the north side of the village, take a left turn after a short distance, left again down a very steep hill, the road is signposted 'Derwent Grange', follow this and we are the farm on the right. Terms from £175 to £200 Low Season, £200 to £250 High Season.

English Tourism Council ★★-★★★ SELF CATERING

Please contact for further information: Kay Elliot, Derwent Grange Farm, Castleside, Consett DH8 9BN • Tel: 01207 508358 • e-mail: ekelliot@aol.com

SELF-CATERING

Attention All Dog Lovers!

Romantic 18th century cottage in the heart of the beautiful Cotswold Hills. Two double bedrooms, beams, wood-burners, outdoor heated swimming pool, patio heater and all year round, bubbling Hot Tub. Small enclosed garden plus a further 20 acres of woodland. Two dogs in the cottage, but a spacious private kennel will accommodate loads more for free!
Weekends from £108 and 4 night mid-week breaks from £102. Full weeks £183 – £542. Colour brochure from Ros Smith.
2nd cottage available for larger family groups or available separately from £140pw – £354.

The Old Coach House

Edgecombe House, Toadsmoor Road, Brimscombe, Stroud GL5 2UE • Tel: 01453 883147

BOARD

A warm and friendly welcome awaits you at our completely refurbished 15th century Grade II Listed farmhouse, in the heart of this beautiful village. Spacious beamed rooms, inglenook fireplace in dining room where a full English breakfast is served. Large private car park at rear. All bedrooms are en suite and have coffee/tea making facilities, TV, radio and hairdryer.

Accommodation comprises one double, two twin and one family suite consisting of a single and a double room en suite.
Sorry no pets allowed in the house.
Non-smoking
***Terms per night**: £55 per double bedded suite, 2 persons sharing. More than two nights £50. Twin-bedded rooms are £50 or single occupancy £40. Family room for 3 persons sharing £80.*

Veronica Stanley, Home Farm House, Ebrington, Chipping Campden GL55 6NL
Tel & Fax: 01386 593309
e-mail: willstanley@farmersweekly.net • website: www.homefarminthecotswolds.co.uk

BOARD

POOL FARM

Bath Road, Wick, Bristol BS30 5RL
Tel: 0117 937 2284

Welcome to our 350 year old Grade II Listed farmhouse on a working farm. On A420 between Bath and Bristol and a few miles from Exit 18 of M4, we are on the edge of the village, overlooking fields, but within easy reach of pub, shops and golf club. We offer traditional Bed and Breakfast in one family and one twin room with tea/coffee facilities and TV; guest lounge. Central heating. Ample parking. Open all year except Christmas. Terms from £20.

BOARD

Longwood Dean, Near Winchester SO21 1JS
Tel: 01962 777486 & Fax: 01962 777747

Twelve minutes' drive from Winchester, (the eleventh century capital city of England), Mays Farm is set in rolling countryside on a lane which leads from nowhere to nowhere. The house is timber framed, originally built in the sixteenth century and has been thoroughly renovated and extended by its present owners, James and Rosalie Ashby. There are three guest bedrooms, (one double, one twin and one either), each with a private bathroom or shower room. A sitting room with log fire is usually available for guests' use. Ducks, geese, chickens and goats make up the two acre "farm". Prices from £23 per person per night for Bed and Breakfast.

Booking is essential • Please telephone or fax for details

BOARD

Felton House

Felton, Near Hereford HR1 3PH • Tel/Fax: (01432) 820366
e-mail: bandb@ereal.net
websites: www.SmoothHound.co.uk/hotels/felton.html
www.herefordshirebandb.co.uk

A country house of immense character, hidden away in a haven of tranquil gardens only 20 minutes from Hereford, Leominster, Bromyard and Ledbury. A warm welcome on arrival, with home-baked refreshments. Excellent evening meals of fine local produce at nearby inns. Sleep soundly in a four-poster or antique bed. Awake refreshed to enjoy, in a superb Victorian dining room, a wide selection of Herefordshire dishes sourced from fresh local ingredients. Felton House is Highly Commended by the AA, with a 'Top British Breakfast' award, and by the English Tourism Council, with a Gold Award for excellence of service and hospitality. Non-smoking. Winners of 'Flavours of Herefordshire' Breakfast Award 2001/2002.

B&B £27 per person, with en suite or private bathroom.

SELF-CATERING

Mainoaks Farm Cottages

Goodrich, Ross-on-Wye

Six units sleeping two, four, six and seven. Mainoaks is a 15th century listed farm which has been converted to form six cottages of different size and individual character. It is set in 80 acres of pasture and woodland beside the River Wye in an area of outstanding natural beauty and an SSSI where there is an abundance of wildlife. All cottages have exposed beams, pine furniture, heating throughout, fully equipped kitchen with microwave, washer/dryer etc, colour TV. Private gardens, barbecue area and ample parking. Linen and towels provided. An ideal base for touring the local area with beautiful walks, fishing, canoeing, pony trekking, golf, bird-watching or just relaxing in this beautiful tranquil spot. Open throughout the year. Short breaks available. Pets by arrangement. Brochure on request.

Mrs P. Unwin, Hill House, Chase End, Bromsberrow, Ledbury, Herefordshire HR8 1SE
Telephone 01531 650448 ETC ★★★ to ★★★★ Highly Commended

SELF-CATERING

Spring Head Farm Cottages

Hellifield Road, Bolton-by-Bowland, Near Clitheroe, Lancashire BB7 4LU
Contact : Mrs S M D Lund – Tel: 01200 447245

Three charming, cosy, comfortable cottages in the beautiful Ribble Valley. Furnished to a very high standard. Sleep 4 to 8. Enjoy the bird song and peace of the countryside. Views to Pendle Hill. *Open all year.*

Ideal base for visiting Yorkshire Dales, Lake District, West Coast and many market towns. Ground floor of Mallard suitable for wheelchair users. Non- smoking. Brochure available. *Rates from £180 - £475.*

BOARD/SELF-CATERING

Rakefoot Farm

ETC ◆◆◆◆
ETC ★★★/★★★★

Chaigley, Near Clitheroe BB7 3LY
Tel: (Chipping) 01995 61332 or 07889 279063 • Fax: 01995 61296
e-mail: info@rakefootfarm.co.uk • website: www.rakefootfarm.co.uk

Family farm peacefully situated in the beautiful countryside of the Ribble Valley in the Forest of Bowland, with panoramic views. Ideally placed for touring Coast, Dales and Lakes. 8 miles M6 Junction 31a. Superb walks, golf and horse riding nearby, or visit pretty villages and factory shops. Warm welcome whether on holiday or business, refreshments on arrival. **BED AND BREAKFAST or SELF-CATERING** in 17th century farmhouse and traditional stone barn conversion. Wood-burning stoves, central heating, exposed beams and stonework. Most bedrooms en suite, some ground floor. Excellent home cooked meals, pubs/restaurants nearby. Indoor/outdoor play areas, gardens and patios. Dogs by arrangement. Laundry. **NWTB Award for Self-catering Holiday of the Year 2000.**

B&B (some with own lounge) £17.50-£25 S/C properties (3 can be internally interlinked) £80-£507 per property per week. Short Breaks available.

SELF-CATERING

Woodside & Parkside

ETC ★★★★ SELF CATERING

High Bentham, Lancaster LA2 7BN • Contact: Thomas & Jane Marshall
Tel/Fax: 015242 62163 • www.riversidecaravanpark.co.uk

Large stone barn converted into two properties with interconnecting doors so they can be let separately for 6 and 8, or let together to accommodate 14. Mainly en suite bathrooms.

Parkside has a ground floor bedroom and bathroom. Set in beautiful countryside yet within walking distance of the market town. Colour brochure. Open all year. Pets welcome. Terms from £200.

SELF-CATERING

It's great here!

The Chestnuts

FARM & COUNTRY COTTAGES WITH PRIVATE FISHING
Wainfleet Road, Burgh Le Marsh, Lincs PE24 5AH
Tel/Fax: 01754 810904
e-mail: mack@freenetname.co.uk
www.thechestnutsfarm.co.uk

Farm • Fishing • Friendly • Fun

Stay on a real farm on the edge of the village of Burgh le Marsh, only 5 miles from Skegness.

- Children's play area, farm animals.
- Cottages have their own private fishing waters.
- Tennis court, plenty of space, ample parking, gardens.

Short Breaks out of season as little as £70. Phone for current price list

For a very quiet rural holiday, visit Chestnuts Country Cottages, only one mile from the farm.

- **Full colour brochure available.**
- **2, 3 and 4 bedroom cottages.**

Mrs Anne Harrison-Smith
Midstone Farmhouse, Southorpe, Stamford PE9 3BX
Tel: 01780 740136 • Fax: 01780 749294
e-mail: midstonehouse@yahoo.co.uk
www.SmoothHound.co.uk/stamford

Farmhouse situated in a quiet village close to Stamford and Peterborough. Centrally heated, with all modern facilities while retaining original features. Close to nature reserve with many wild flowers and butterflies. Ideal location for exploring Lincolnshire, Cambridgeshire and Norfolk – we can arrange a holiday itinerary for you. Brochure on request.

Weekly rates from £250 – £450

3 night breaks available Spring and Autumn

B&B also available – ETC ◆◆◆◆ Silver Award

Rose Cottage

Claythorpe, Alford, Lincs

A small cottage set in farmland ¼ mile from the road.

GROUND FLOOR: large living room with colour TV • small kitchen with fridge/freezer, microwave • room with single bed • bathroom
UPSTAIRS: one double and two single rooms
Electricity incl.• bed linen and towels can be hired
• no smoking indoors • gas-fired central heating plus open fire
• dogs allowed if under strict control • pub within 4 miles

Details from Mrs D. Stovin,
Aby Grange, Aby, Alford, Lincs LN13 0DG
• Tel: 01507 450367 • Fax: 01507 450771
• e-mail: danddstovin@amserve.net

Short breaks from £95, weekly rates from £175 to £245

WOODTHORPE HALL COUNTRY COTTAGES

Very well appointed luxury one and three bedroomed cottages, overlooking the golf course, all with central heating, colour TV, microwave, washer, dryer, dishwasher and fridge freezer. Woodthorpe is situated approximately six miles from the coastal resort of Mablethorpe and offers easy access to the picturesque Lincolnshire Wolds. Adjacent facilities include golf, fishing, garden centre, aquatic centre, snooker, pool and restaurant with bar and family room. ETC ★★★★. For further details contact:

Woodthorpe Hall, Woodthorpe, Near Alford, Lincs LN13 0DD • Tel: 01507 450294
Fax: 01507 450885 • e-mail: enquiries@woodthorpehall.com • www.woodthorpehall.com

Beautiful old red brick and pantile barn conversion with gardens and stables. Tastefully decorated with modern facilities and overlooking open countryside. Both cottages are spacious, with fully fitted kitchens, lounge/dining rooms with colour TV and video. Bicycles available for hire. Babysitting and evening meals by arrangement.

Terms: £175 to £350 per week.
3-night short breaks available all year

No.1	*No.2*
April-Sep £120	*April-Sep £200*
Oct-Mar £100	*Oct-Mar £180*

e-mail: jmerivale@aol.com • www.thegables-hatton.co.uk

Bookings: **Mrs Julia Merivale, The Gables, Hatton Hall, Hatton, Market Rasen, Lincs LN8 5QG**
01673 858862/07702 271041
07801 282529

BOARD

Earsham Park Farm

Harleston Road, Earsham, Bungay NR35 2AQ
Tel: 01986 892180 • Fax: 01986 894796

Escape into the beautiful East Anglian countryside in this family-run quiet and friendly farmhouse surrounded by lovely gardens and farm walks. Superbly set on a hill overlooking the gorgeous Waveney Valley. The rooms are all spacious and beautifully furnished, but with comfort as a priority. Two large doubles (one with four-poster), and one twin room, all en suite. All rooms have extensive facilities, including easy chairs, colour TV, tea tray, radio, etc., whilst thick fluffy towels and embroidered linen add to your comfort. The farm's own produce is used in the excellent breakfasts. The famous Earsham Otter Trust is at the bottom of the drive. Your hosts have a wealth of local knowledge. FHB Member. A non-smoking house. B&B from £25 per person, based on two sharing.

e-mail: bobbie@earsham-parkfarm.co.uk
website: www.earsham-parkfarm.co.uk

SELF-CATERING

THE OLD MILL

The Old Mill in the heart of Norfolk has been tastefully converted to provide peaceful holidays, away from the rush of modern living. Standing in the owners' delightful grounds, it has one round Victorian style double bedroom with French doors overlooking the paddock. Lounge/diner with TV, kitchen, bathroom, scullery with fridge and microwave. Linen and towels provided. Electricity with £1 coin meter. Village has a surgery, chemist, bakery, butcher, P.O. etc. Market town of Dereham four miles, Norwich 12. Convenient for Sandringham and the Broads. Your privacy respected. Warm welcome. Sorry no smoking or pets. Open all year. Terms on request.

Margaret & Don Fisher,
Ivydene, Mill Road, Mattishall, Dereham NR20 3RL
Tel: 01362 850312

BOARD

4B&B STRENNETH

Country Bed and Breakfast

Airfield Road, Fersfield, Diss, Norfolk IP22 2BP

STRENNETH is a well-established, family-run business, situated in unspoiled countryside just a short drive from Bressingham Gardens and the picturesque market town of Diss. Offering first-class accommodation, the original 17th Century building has been carefully renovated to a high standard with a wealth of exposed oak beams and a newer single storey courtyard wing. There is ample off-road parking and plenty of nice walks nearby. All seven bedrooms, including a Four-Poster and an Executive, are tastefully arranged with period furniture and distinctive beds. Each having remote colour television, hospitality trays, central heating and full en suite facilities. The establishment is smoke-free and the guest lounge has a log fire on cold winter evenings. There is an extensive breakfast menu using local produce. Ideal touring base. Pets most welcome at no extra charge. Outside kennels with runs if required. Bed and Breakfast from £25.00.

Telephone: 01379 688182 • Fax: 01379 688260
E-mail: pdavey@strenneth.co.uk • Website: www.strenneth.co.uk

CARAVANS

Cable Gap Holiday Park, Coast Road, Bacton, Norfolk NR12 0EW

Tel: 01692 650667 • Fax: 01692 651388
e-mail: cablegap@freenet.co.uk • www.visitbritain.co.uk

Cable Gap Holiday Park is a friendly, family-run caravan park that takes pride in providing first-class facilities. Our caravans have achieved the highest Tourist Board grading and the coveted Rose Award for many years. We have also achieved a Silver David Bellamy Conservation Award. You can have a carefree and relaxing time in one of our wide choice of quality caravans, sited only a stone's throw from the beach. We take pride in offering you a choice of 2 & 3 bedroom caravans, both 12ft and 10ft wide. All caravans are equipped to a high standard, and include background heating in the main bedroom. Our De Luxe range caravans are centrally heated and double glazed. There are also some caravans on the front row with a beach view. A one-bedroom caravan is also available. Well-behaved pets are welcome in a selected number of caravans.

We are situated just a few minutes' walk from Bacton village centre, with local shops, public houses, restaurant & tea rooms, a Post Office, an amusement arcade and a fish & chip shop. Bacton Woods is only a few minutes' drive away, an excellent place for a picnic, walking or cycling.

★★★★★ HOLIDAY PARK

BOARD

Shrublands Farm

Burgh St Peter, Near Beccles, Suffolk NR34 0BB (Tel & Fax: 01502 677241)

A warm and friendly welcome at this attractive, homely farmhouse, surrounded by one acre of garden and lawn on the Norfolk/Suffolk border. The River Waveney flows through the 550 acres of mixed working farmland; opportunities for bird-watching. Ideal base for touring Norfolk and Suffolk; Beccles, Lowestoft, Great Yarmouth and Norwich are all within easy reach. Two double rooms with en suite facilities and one twin-bedded room with private bathroom, shower room and toilet. All have satellite colour TV and tea/coffee making facilities; diningroom, lounge with colour satellite TV. Non-smoking rooms. No pets. Car essential, ample parking. Tennis court available. Swimming pool and food at River Centre nearby.

Silver
SILVER AWARD

Open all year except Christmas.
Bed and Breakfast from £21 per person.
Reductions for longer stays. SAE please.

SELF-CATERING

Enjoy a break on the Northumberland Coast

Choose from twelve family-owned and managed cottages along the Northumberland coast. Three-day short breaks from £70 per cottage during low season. Beautiful rugged coastline, fishing villages little changed in 100 years, golden beaches, historic castles, wildlife, walks, cycling, fishing, golf, National Park, Kielder Water and Forest.

For details and bookings contact: Heritage Coast Holidays, Unit 6 Greensfield Court, Alnwick, Northumberland NE66 2DE
• 01670 787864 24-hour enquiry line • Tel: 01665 606022 (office hours)
• Fax: 01670 787336 • e-mail: pault@marishal.co.uk

Visit our website• www.northumberland-holidays.com

BOARD

Comfortable farmhouse accommodation on working mixed farm situated on the Heritage Coast between the villages of Craster and Howick. Ideal base for walking, golfing, bird-watching or exploring the coast, moors and historic castles. The Farne Islands, famous for their colonies of seals and seabirds, and Lindisfarne (Holy Island) are within easy driving distance. Accommodation is in two double rooms with washbasins. Guests have their own TV lounge/dining room with full central heating. Bed and Breakfast from £19.00. Open Easter to November. Non-smoking.

Craster, Alnwick NE66 3SU
Tel & Fax: 01665 576665
e-mail: stay@howickscar.co.uk
website: www.howickscar.co.uk

BOARD

Moss Kennels

Housesteads, Hexham NE47 6NL
e-mail: Tim.mosskennels@virgin.net

A spacious farmhouse offering a friendly and relaxed atmosphere. Set in a large garden. Situated on Hadrian's Wall; magnificent scenery with many interesting places to visit and lovely walks. Only half-a-mile east of Housesteads and half-an-hour from the Metro Centre. All rooms are spacious, comfortable and en suite, with colour TV and tea/coffee making facilities. Open all year. Bed and Breakfast from £20, Evening Meal £12.50.

Mrs E. Reed
Tel: 01434 344016
Fax: 01434 344016

BOARD

West Wharmley

Hexham, Northumberland NE46 2PL
Tel & Fax: 01434 674227

We offer a warm welcome to our well-appointed accommodation on a 400 acre working farm, with outstanding views over the South Tyne Valley. The 18th century farmhouse has a self-contained wing which is decorated to a high standard and has full central heating. A large private sittingroom, complete with open fire, oak beams and colour TV, provides a homely retreat for the evenings. Two large bedrooms, both en suite, have colour TV and tea/coffee making facilities. Ideal for families. Close to Hadrian's Wall and very accessible to Northumberland's many attractions. Bed and Breakfast from £20 to £25.

SELF-CATERING

Anita's Holiday Cottages
Banbury, Oxfordshire

'The Shippon' • 'The Byre' • 'The Stables'

Top quality barn conversions sleep 2 to 8. Superbly finished to a high standard. Fitted kitchen, microwave, cooker, washing machine, dishwasher; fully heated; linen included. Suits couples or larger groups. Central for Cotswolds, Oxford, Stratford or just enjoying the surrounding countryside. Walk to village pub. Non-smoking. No pets and sorry, no under 5s. Ample parking. Close to M40 Junction 12. Short breaks available during low season.

★★★ and ★★★★ rating

Contact Mrs Jeffries, The Yews, Mollington, Banbury OX17 1AZ
Telephone: 01295 750731 or 07966 171959

BOARD

HARPER ADAMS UNIVERSITY COLLEGE

Harper Adams is situated close to the north Shropshire / Staffordshire border in the village of Edgmond, three miles from the market town of Newport. The upper west wing of the magnificent main building is given over to eight charming guest suites, each with its own individual character. These suites are served by a private lounge and bathrooms and have superb views across Harper Adams' gardens and fields. Supplementing these suites are 180 en suite bedrooms, as well as 160 bedrooms with shared bathroom facilities. Guests are never more than a short walk away from numerous on-site facilities. Our team of domestic staff will be pleased to assist you in any way possible during your stay, and will ensure that rooms are serviced on a daily basis.

Edgmond, Newport, Shropshire TF10 8NB • Tel: 01952 820280 • Fax: 01952 814783
e-mail: info@harper-adams.ac.uk • website: www.harper-adams.ac.uk

BOARD

Malt House Farm

Lower Wood, Church Stretton, Shropshire SY6 6LF
Prop. Mrs Lyn Bloor
Tel: (01694) 751379
AA ◆◆◆

Olde worlde beamed farmhouse situated amidst spectacular scenery at the lower slopes of the Long Mynd Hills. We are a working farm producing beef cattle and sheep. One double bedroom and one twin, both with en suite bathroom, colour TV, hairdryer and tea tray. Good farmhouse cooking is served in the dining room. Private guests' sitting room. Non-smoking. Regret no children or pets. Now fully licensed.

Bed and Breakfast from £20pppn • Evening Meal from £15.00pp.

BOARD

Red House Farm

Red House Farm is a late Victorian farmhouse in Longdon-on-Tern, a small village noted for the aqueduct built by Thomas Telford in 1796 to carry the Shropshire Union Canal over the River Tern.

- Friendly welcome • Spacious rooms
- Home comforts • Families welcome
- Local pubs serving good food
- Bed & Breakfast from £20 per person

Visit the world famous Ironbridge Gorge with its industrial museums

Tel: 01952 770245

Contact Mrs Mary Jones, Red House Farm, Longdon-on-Tern, Wellington, Telford, Shropshire TF6 6LE
website: www.virtual-shropshire.co.uk/red-house-farm • e-mail: rhf@virtual-shropshire.co.uk

BOARD

PASSION PERFECT

Overlooking Porlock Weir, where Exmoor meets the sea, is a restaurant with rooms where every meal is an experience; where each room is individual; and where pets are just as welcome as their owners. Discover the perfect break on Exmoor at Andrews.

Porlock Weir, Porlock, Somerset
Tel: 01643 863300 Fax: 01643 863311
www.andrewsontheweir.co.uk

BOARD

Barrow is a dairy farm of 146 acres. The house is 15th century and of much character, situated between Wells, Glastonbury and Shepton Mallet. It makes an excellent touring centre for visiting Somerset's beauty spots and historic places, for example, Cheddar, Bath, Wookey Hole and Longleat. Near Bath and West Showground. Guest accommodation consists of two double rooms, one family room, one single room and one twin-bedded room, each with washbasin, TV and tea/coffee making facilities. Bathroom, two toilets; two lounges, one with colour TV; diningroom with separate tables. Guests can enjoy farmhouse fare in generous variety, home baking a speciality. Bed and Breakfast, with optional four-course Dinner available. Car essential; ample parking. Children welcome; cot and babysitting available. Open all year except Christmas. Sorry, no pets. Bed and Breakfast from £18. Dinner £12.

AA ◆◆◆ Guest Accommodation

Barrow Farm

North Wootton, Near Glastonbury BA4 4HL
Tel & Fax: 01749 890245

BOARD

The Castle Hotel

Porlock, Somerset TA24 8PY
Tel & Fax: 01643 862504

The Castle Hotel is a small, fully licensed family-run hotel in the centre of the lovely Exmoor village of Porlock. It is an ideal holiday location for those who wish to enjoy the grandeur of Exmoor on foot or by car. The beautiful villages of Selworthy and Dunster with its castle are only a short distance away. There are 13 en suite bedrooms, all fully heated, with colour TV and tea/coffee making facilities.The Castle Hotel has a well-stocked bar with Real Ale. Draught Guinness and Cider. A full range of Bar Meals is available at lunchtimes and evenings or dine in our Restaurant.Children and pets are most welcome. Family room available. Darts, pool and skittles.

✤✤ Special Breaks available ✤ Extremely low rates ✤✤

SELF-CATERING

Leigh Farm

Pensford, Near Bristol BS39 4BA

Telephone or Fax: 01761 490281

Leigh Farm is situated in the old mining village of Pensford (Bristol 7 miles and Bath 8 miles). Overlooking the floodlit pool – a 3-bedroomed cottage sleeping 6 plus baby. Terraced bungalow conversion built tastefully in natural stone with original oak beams. One or two bedroomed, with shower room, WC and basin. TV. Night storage heating. Bed linen is not supplied but can be hired. Cot and high chair available. Wander round the ponds where duck and moorhen nest. Park and Ride for both cities near, and plenty of tourist information for your use. Safe floodlit car park.

Open all year. No pets. £170-£400 weekly. B&B available. *For brochure contact Josephine Smart.*

BOARD

NORTH DOWN FARM

Pyncombe Lane, Wiveliscombe, Taunton TA4 2BL

Tel & Fax: 01984 623730

e-mail: jennycope@tiscali.co.uk

In tranquil secluded surroundings on the Somerset/Devon border. Traditional working farm set in 100 acres of natural beauty with panoramic views of over 40 miles. M5 motorway seven miles and Taunton 10 miles. All rooms tastefully furnished to high standard include en suite, TV, and tea/coffee making facilities. Family room, double or single available. Dining room and lounge with log fires for guests' comfort; centrally heated and double glazed. Drying facilities. Delicious home produced food a speciality. Fishing, golf, horse riding and country sports nearby. Dogs welcome.

Bed and Breakfast from £23 per person per night. Weekly rates B&B and Evening Meal £185pp.

North Down Break: three nights Bed and Breakfast and Evening Meal £85 per person. **ETC ◆◆◆◆ Silver Award**

BOARD

Exmoor ★★★ South West Tourism

Idyllic location for a self-catering holiday in the National Trust village of Allerford alongside the shallow River Aller, overlooking the famous Pack Horse Bridge. Immediate access to Exmoor and the beautiful surrounding countryside.

Variety of well equipped apartments and family cottage arranged around a pretty courtyard. Sleeping two - six. Pets welcome. Stabling available. Ample private parking. Local amenities - Post office, stores, additional restaurants/pubs etc in nearby Porlock.

Terms: £200 – £450 per week. Open all year. Short breaks available.

The Pack Horse, Allerford, Near Minehead, Somerset TA24 8HW **Tel & Fax: 01643 862475**

e-mail: holidays@thepackhorse.freewire.co.uk • website: www.thepackhorse.net

SELF-CATERING

CHEDDAR – SUNGATE HOLIDAY APARTMENTS

Church Street, Cheddar, Somerset BS27 3RA

Delightful apartments in Cheddar village, each fully equipped. Sleep 2/4. Laundry facilities. Private parking. Family, disabled, and pet friendly.

Contact: Mrs. M.M. Fieldhouse for brochure

Tel: 01934 842273/742264

Fax: 01934 844994

BOARD

Offley Grove Farm, Adbaston, Eccleshall, Staffs ST20 0QB

Tel/Fax: 01785 280205

You'll consider this a good find! Quality accommodation and excellent breakfasts. Small traditional mixed farm surrounded by beautiful countryside. The house is tastefully furnished and provides all home comforts. Whether you are planning to book here for a break in your journey, stay for a weekend or take your holidays here, you will find something to suit all tastes among the many local attractions. Situated on the Staffordshire/ Shropshire borders we are convenient for Alton Towers, Stoke-on-Trent, Ironbridge, etc. Reductions for children. Play area for children. Open all year. Bed and Breakfast all en suite from £23pp. Many guests return. Self-catering cottages available.

Brochure on request.

e-mail: accomm@offleygrovefarm.freeserve.co.uk

website: www.offleygrovefarm.co.uk

SELF-CATERING

Knights Holiday Homes

at Kessingland on the Suffolk Heritage Coast

THE BEST OF BRITISH SELF-CATERING HOLIDAYS

at the 'Seaview' and 'Alandale' Holiday Parks on the peaceful Suffolk Coast

CHILDREN AND PETS WELCOME

OPEN ALL YEAR

Welcome to a place where you can hear yourself think...

'Kessingland: Most easterly village in the United Kingdom. First to greet the sun. Once known as the richest village in England because of its prolific fishing. Now known for its peaceful, pleasant surroundings, its beautiful spacious beach and its Suffolk countryside, where you can relax in peace and watch the boats sail by on the North Sea's Herring Pond.'

Seaview Bungalows

These bungalows are situated on a quiet, attractive estate set in nine acres of lawns overlooking the sea. There is a made-up roadway round the estate and parking near your door. Your bungalow has three bedrooms, bathroom and toilet, kitchen and lounge with a sun door opening onto the lawns. A walkway leads immediately from the estate to the promenade and the beach.

SHOPS ARE APPROXIMATELY 450 YARDS AND BUS STOP 300 YARDS.

THE BUNGALOWS

- 1-6 persons
- Colour Television
- Bed linen supplied • Fully equipped kitchens
- Full size cookers and refrigerators
- Cots and Highchairs are available
- Electrically heated - no meters • Parking

THE VILLAGE

- Clean Beach Award
- Mother Hubbard's Cupboard – Kessingland Art Centre and Gift Shop
- Suffolk Wildlife Park
- Shops • Pubs
- Restaurants • Cafes • Bus Service

BROCHURE ◆ CALENDAR ◆ OFFER LETTER ◆ BOOKING FORM from

Knights Holiday Homes, 198 Church Road, Kessingland, Suffolk NR33 7SF Freephone 0800 269067

VISA

BOARD

JEAKE'S HOUSE

Mermaid Street, Rye, East Sussex TN31 7ET

Telephone: 01797 222828 Fax: 01797 222623

E-mail: jeakeshouse@btinternet.com • Website: www.jeakeshouse.com

Dating from 1689, this beautiful Listed Building stands in one of England's most famous streets. Oak-beamed and panelled bedrooms overlook the marsh to the sea. Brass, mahogany or four-poster beds with linen sheets and lace; honeymoon suite. En suite facilities, TV, radio, telephone. Book-lined Bar. Traditional and vegetarian breakfast served. £35.00–£56.00pp. Private car park. Access, Visa and Mastercard accepted.

PREMIER SELECTED

Sparkling Diamond & Warm Welcome Award

Good Hotel Guide César Award

Church Farm Country Cottages

Seven single-storey cottages, formerly old cow byres, tastefully converted, with exposed beams and vaulted ceilings.
Heated indoor swimming pool and games room - new for 2003!
Countryside location in an Area of Outstanding Natural Beauty.

Three cottages sleep 2 and four cottages sleep 4/5 on working farm with sheep and horses. Enclosed garden with patio furniture. Ample parking. Pub/shop 500m. Bath 5 miles. Close to Longleat, Lacock, Stonehenge and many National Trust properties. Kennet & Avon Canal ¾ mile for boating, cycling and walking. Regular buses. Welcome cream tea. Short Breaks when available. Also 20-pitch rural caravan/campsite with many facilities.

Church Farm Country Cottages, Winsley, Bradford-on-Avon, Wiltshire BA15 2JH
e-mail: stay@churchfarmcottages.com • website: www.churchfarmcottages.com
Tel & Fax: 01225 722246

Lovett Farm

Little Somerford, Near Malmesbury, Wiltshire SN15 5BP
Tel & Fax: 01666 823268 • mobile: 07808 858612

Enjoy traditional hospitality at our delightful farmhouse just three miles from the historic town of Malmesbury with its wonderful Norman Abbey and gardens. Central for Cotswolds, Bath, Stratford, Avebury and Stonehenge. Two attractive en suite bedrooms with delightful views, each with tea/coffee making facilities, colour television and radio. Delicious full English breakfast served in our cosy diningroom/lounge. Central heating throughout.

Bed and Breakfast from £23.50. Non-smoking accommodation. Open all year. Credit cards accepted.

e-mail: lovettfarm@btinternet.com • website: www.lovettfarm.co.uk

BRICKBARNS, a 200-acre mixed farm, is situated two miles from Great Malvern at the foot of the Malvern Hills, 300 yards from the bus service and one-and-a half miles from the train. The house, which is 300 years old, commands excellent views of the Malvern Hills and guests are accommodated in one double, one single and one family bedrooms with washbasins; two bathrooms, shower room, two toilets; sittingroom and diningroom. Children welcome and cot and babysitting offered. Central heating. Car essential, parking. Open Easter to October for Bed and Breakfast from £16 nightly per person. Reductions for children and Senior Citizens. Birmingham 40 miles, Hereford 20, Gloucester 17, Stratford 35 and the Wye Valley is just 30 miles.

Mrs J.L. Morris, Brickbarns Farm, Hanley Road, Malvern Wells WR14 4HY
Tel: 016845 61775 • Fax: 01886 830037

Come and enjoy our luxury B&B, in a 17th century Cotswold stone farmhouse peacefully located just 5 minutes from Broadway. We farm 1800 acres of cereals and sheep and all our rooms have panoramic views over the Cotswold Hills.

The luxury rooms are spacious and elegantly furnished, with king-size bed or twin beds. All have en suite bathrooms, colour TV, tea and coffee making facilities, clock radios and hairdryers etc. One room is situated on the ground floor for those who find the stairs difficult, whilst another has a king-size bed and a single and is suitable for a family room. An extra bed and a cot are available for a larger family.

A three-course evening meal with coffee may be taken by arrangement or there is a wealth of excellent eating houses nearby. Guidance will be given with pleasure, and reservations may be easily made by us on your behalf.

Ewes and lambs, horses and ponies all form part of the scene. An ideal location for regenerating the batteries or just relaxing. Self-catering cottage also available.

Lower Field Farm
Willersey, Broadway, Worcs WR11 5HF

Tel: Jane Organ on 01386 858273 or 07703 343996• Fax: 01386 854608
e-mail: info@lowerfield-farm.co.uk

SELF-CATERING

With delightful views overlooking the Yorkshire Wolds, ideally situated for touring the East Coast, Bridlington, Scarborough, Moors and York, this secluded and private four-bedroomed farmhouse is set in its own acre of woodland lawns and orchard, with garden furniture, summerhouse and children's play area. Games room in converted Granary in the main farm area 200 yards away. Clean and comfortable and very well equipped including dishwasher, microwave, automatic washing machine and dryer; two bathrooms, payphone, TV and video. Fully centrally heated. Beds are made up for your arrival; cots and high chair available. Three miles to the nearest village of Kilham with Post Office, general stores, garage and public houses. Available all year. Terms per week from £270 to £380 (low season), from £380 to £505 (high season). Brochure on request.

Mrs P.M. Savile, Raven Hill Farm, Kilham, Driffield YO25 4EG
Tel: 01377 267217

BOARD

Browson Bank Farmhouse Accommodation

A newly converted granary set in 300 acres of farmland. The accommodation consists of three very tastefully furnished double/twin rooms all en suite, tea and coffee making facilities, colour TV and central heating. A large, comfortable lounge is available to relax in. Full English breakfast served. Situated six miles West of Scotch Corner (A1). Ideal location to explore the scenic countryside of Teesdale and the Yorkshire Dales and close to the scenic towns of Barnard Castle and Richmond. Terms from £19.00 per night.

Browson Bank Farmhouse, Browson Bank, Dalton, Richmond DL11 7HE
Tel: (01325) 718504 or (01325) 718246

BOARD

Furnace Farm

Fryup, Lealholm, Whitby, North Yorkshire YO21 2AP
Tel/Fax: 01947 897271
E-Mail: furnacefarm@hotmail.com

A warm Yorkshire welcome to our working family farm in the peaceful Esk Valley. Close to Moors and Coast, an ideal base for walking and touring. Stone-built farmhouse – comfortable, spacious rooms, lounge/dining room with TV and video. Two family rooms – one en suite, one with private bathroom, both with TV and tea/coffee facilities and double/single beds. Cot available. Use of large garden.

B&B £22.50 - £25.00 • Open February to October • Contact: Peter & Jane Dowson

BOARD

High Gaterley enjoys a unique position, located within the boundaries of Castle Howard's magnificent country estate. It is ideally situated for easy access to the City of York, East Coast and the North Yorkshire Moors renowned for ruined abbeys and castles. The tranquil ambience with panoramic views over the Howardian Hills make it a perfect location for a peaceful and relaxing stay in a comfortable well-appointed farmhouse with the option of fine cuisine. En suite facilities with tea and coffee in all rooms, log fire in the drawing room, TV, non-smoking, dogs by prior arrangement. Open all year.

Bed and Breakfast from £20.
Optional evening meal and special diets by arrangement.

Sandie and Peter Turner, High Gaterley Farm, Near Welburn, York YO60 7HT • Tel & Fax: 01653 694636
e-mail: relax@highgaterley.com • website: www.highgaterley.com

SELF-CATERING

Hill House Farm Cottages

Julie & Jim Griffith
Hill House Farm
Little Langton, Northallerton DL7 0PZ
Tel: 01609 770643 Fax: 01609 760438
e-mail: info@Hillhousefarmcottages.com

These former farm buildings sleeping 2/4 have been converted into 4 well-equipped cottages, retaining original beams. Cosily heated for year-round appeal. Peaceful setting with magnificent views. Centrally located between Dales and Moors with York, Whitby and Scarborough all within easy driving distance. Pets welcome. Exercise Field. Weekly rates from £150 incl. all linen, towels, heating and electricity. Short Breaks available.

• Pub food 1 mile • Golf 2 miles • Shops 3 miles

For a free colour brochure please call 01609 770643

SELF-CATERING

New Close Farm

A supa dupa cottage on New Close Farm in the heart of Craven Dales with panoramic views over the Aire Valley. Excellent area for walking, cycling, fishing, golf and touring.

- Two double and one single bedrooms; bathroom.
- Colour TV and video.
- Full central heating and double glazing.
- Bed linen, towels and all amenities included in the price.
- Sorry, no young children, no pets.
- Non-smokers preferred.
- From £250-£300. Winter Short Breaks available.

The weather can't be guaranteed but your comfort can

Kirkby Malham, Skipton BD23 4DP
Tel: 01729 830240 • Fax: 01729 830179
e-mail: brendajones@newclosefarmyorkshire.co.uk
website: www.newclosefarmyorkshire.co.uk

SELF-CATERING

Panoramic views, waterfalls, wild birds and tranquillity

Stone farmhouse with panoramic views, high in the Yorkshire Dales National Park (Herriot family's house in 'All Creatures Great and Small' on TV). Three bedrooms (sleeps 6-8), sitting and dining rooms with wood-burning stoves, kitchen, bathroom, WC. House has electric storage heating, cooker, microwave, fridge, washing machine, colour TV, telephone. Garden, large barn, stables. Access from lane, private parking, no through traffic. Excellent walking from front door, near Wensleydale. Pets welcome. Self-catering from £400 per week.

Westclose House (Allaker),
West Scrafton, Coverdale, Leyburn, North Yorks DL8 4RM
For bookings telephone 020 8567 4862
e-mail: ac@adriancave.com • www.adriancave.com/allaker

SELF-CATERING

Summerwine Cottages

Shepley, Near Holmfirth, Huddersfield, West Yorkshire

www.summerwinecottages.co.uk

★★★ SELF CATERING

Set in 6 acres of Pennine farmland, deep in the heart of 'Summer Wine' country. The 3 self-contained cottages, ***Granary*** (1 double room), ***Harvest*** (1 double, 1 twin) and ***Winnow*** (1 double, 1 twin), can accommodate up to 4 adults. Each has central heating and double glazing, as well as ample off-road parking and telephone. Furnishings and decor are of a high standard, with TV, video, washer/dryer and microwave. Cot, high chair etc available on request. Pubs, restaurants and shops are only a short walk; surrounding villages well served by public transport. Open all year; minimum let two nights. Terms from £150 to £325 per week.

Details from Mrs S. Meakin, West Royd Farm, Marsh Lane, Shepley, Huddersfield HD8 8AY
01484 602147/07711 000233 • Fax: 01484 609427 • e-mail: summerwinecottages@lineone.net

SELF-CATERING

Open all year including for Short Breaks.

BROCHURE SENT WITH PLEASURE.

BRYN BRAS CASTLE

LLANRUG, Near CAERNARFON, NORTH WALES LL55 4RE
Tel & Fax: Llanberis (01286) 870210

This romantic neo-Romanesque Castle is set in the gentle Snowdonian foothills near North Wales' mountains, beaches, resorts and heritage. Built in 1830, on an earlier structure, the Regency castle reflects peace not war - it stands in 32 acres of tranquil gardens, with views. Bryn Bras offers distinctive and individual Apartments, for 2-4 persons, within the castle, each having spacious rooms radiating comfort, warmth and tranquillity and providing freedom and independence. All highest grade. ***Many inns and restaurants nearby. This welcoming castle, still a family home, particularly appeals to romantic couples.***

BOARD

FRON HEULOG COUNTRY HOUSE

Betws-y-Coed, North Wales LL24 0BL
Tel: 01690 710736 • Fax: 01690 710920
e-mail: jean&peter@fronheulog.co.uk
website: www.fronheulog.co.uk

Jean & Peter Whittingham welcome house guests

"The Country House in the Village !"

Betws-y-Coed – "Heart of Snowdonia"

You are invited to enjoy real hospitality at Fron Heulog; an elegant Victorian stone-built house with excellent non-smoking accommodation, comfortable bedrooms, all with en suite bathrooms, spacious lounges, a pleasant dining room, and full central heating. Enjoy the friendly atmosphere with hosts' local knowledge and home cooking. Sorry, no small children; no pets.

From the centre of Betws-y-Coed turn off busy A5 road over picturesque Pont-y-Pair bridge (B5106), then immediately turn left. Fron Heulog is 150 yards up ahead facing south, in quiet, peaceful, wooded, riverside scenery. Bed and breakfast £22-£30 pppn. ***Welcome – Croeso!***

"The longer you stay – pay less each day!"

RAC ◆◆◆◆ Hospitality Quality Awards AA ◆◆◆◆

WTB Tourism Award. In "Which?"

BOARD

Warwick Hotel

56 Church Walks,
Llandudno LL30 2HL
Tel: 01492 876823

Friendly family-run licensed hotel, 14 en suite guest bedrooms with colour TV and hospitality trays. Family accommodation available. Open all year. Victorian building, originally a doctor's house. Pleasant garden and sun terrace. The dining room overlooks the garden and the hotel's proprietor is happy to cater for special diets or children's menus. 5 minutes walk to town centre and pier. Pets welcome free of charge.

Your Host: Mrs Nerys E. George

Directions: Drive along the Promenade to the pier, turn left. B&B is 300/400 yards on the right just past the tram station.

RAC ★★

BOARD

East Hook FARM

Howard and Jen welcome you to their Georgian Farmhouse surrounded by beautiful countryside, four miles from the coastline and three miles from Haverfordwest. Double, twin and family suite available, all en suite. Pembrokeshire produce used for dinner and breakfast. Dinner £14 per person. Bed and Breakfast from £20 to £22 per person.

Mr and Mrs Patrick, East Hook Farm,
Portfield Gate, Haverfordwest, Pembroke SA62 3LN
01437 762211 • www.easthookfarmhouse.co.uk

SELF-CATERING

Two charming cottages privately situated and ideally located for exploring Pembrokeshire. The resorts of Saundersfoot and Tenby are close at hand with the seaside resort of Amroth and the coastal path just minutes away. Each cottage sleeps four to five adults, cots and high chairs also provided. All facilities including fully fitted kitchens, central heating, colour televisions are included. There is ample private parking plus a lawned garden area and patio with garden furniture provided.

CRUNWERE & HAYLOFT COTTAGES

WTB ★★★★★

Contact: John & Carol Lloyd, East Llanteg Farm, Llanteg, Amroth SA67 8QA
Tel: 01834 831336

e-mail: john@pembrokeshireholiday.co.uk • website: www.pembrokeshireholiday.co.uk

SELF-CATERING

Stable Cottage & Granary Cottage, Amroth

The impressive position of these cottages, the wonderful views and beautiful setting, together with an imaginative conversion of an exceptionally high standard, make these properties outstanding. From the cottages and grounds, some nine acres, it is possible to see for many miles.

Stable Cottage sleeps 6 • 3 bedrooms • WTB Grade 5 • Terms from £251.
Granary Cottage sleeps 4 • 2 bedrooms • WTB Grade 5 • Terms from £235

Details from **Mrs Green, Furzewood Farm, Amroth, Pembrokeshire SA67 8NQ**
Tel: 01834 814674 • www.coastalcottages.co.uk

SELF-CATERING

Gwarmacwydd

Gwarmacwydd is a country estate of over 450 acres, including two miles of riverbank. See a real farm in action, the hustle and bustle of harvest, newborn calves and lambs. Children are welcomed. On the estate are five character stone cottages, Tourist Board Grade Four. Each cottage has been lovingly converted from traditional farm buildings, parts of which are over 200 years old. Each cottage is fully furnished and equipped. All electricity and linen included. All cottages are heated for year-round use. Colour brochure available.

Tel: 01437 563260 Fax: 01437 563839
e-mail: info@a-farm-holiday.org
website: www.a-farm-holiday.org

Mrs Angela Colledge, Llanfallteg, Whitland, Pembrokeshire SA34 0XH

SELF-CATERING

St Bride's Bay COTTAGES

Cosy cottages and farmhouses near superb beaches and coastal path, around beautiful St.Brides Bay in Pembrokeshire. WTB graded. Sleeps 2-11. Pet welcome.

www.stbridesbaycottages.com

Tel: 0870 7572270

BOARD

Tastefully restored Tudor farmhouse on working farm in peaceful location. En suite bedrooms with breathtaking views over fields and woods, colour TV, beverage trays. Two lounges with log fires. Renowned for excellent food. Wonderful area for wildlife, walking, cycling, near Red Kite feeding station. Safe parking. Brochure on request.

Bed, Breakfast and Evening meal weekly from £215 to £240. Bed and Breakfast from £22 to £26 per day.

Mrs Ruth Jones, Holly Farm, Howey, Llandrindod Wells LD1 5PP
Tel & Fax: 01597 822402 • Taste of Wales Tourism Award • Farm Stay UK Member

SELF-CATERING

OAK WOOD LODGES
Llwynbaedd, Rhayader, Powys LD6 5NT

SELF CATERING LOG CABINS

Luxurious Norwegian log cabins situated at approximately 1000ft above sea level with spectacular views of the Elan Valley and Cambrian Mountains. Enjoy pursuits such as walking, pony trekking, mountain biking, fishing, and bird watching in the most idyllic of surroundings. Excellent touring centre. Dogs welcome. Short breaks as well as full weeks. Open all year round.

For more information and brochure call
01597 811422

★★★★

BOARD

THE Grange

Penrhos, Raglan, Monmouthshire NP15 2LQ

Organic mixed farm (115 acres) off the beaten track. Enjoy our peace and space and breathtaking views. Lots of places to visit, and several good local golf courses (The Rolls of Monmouth is 3 miles). The country is ideal for walking, and we are on Offa's Dyke Path. We welcome families, dogs and horses – we have an arena, stabling and farm jumps.

Come and share this beautiful place.

Large en suite rooms and superb home-cooked evening meals if required.
Bed & Breakfast from £20 to £25.

Mrs J.E. Thom 01600 780202

SELF-CATERING

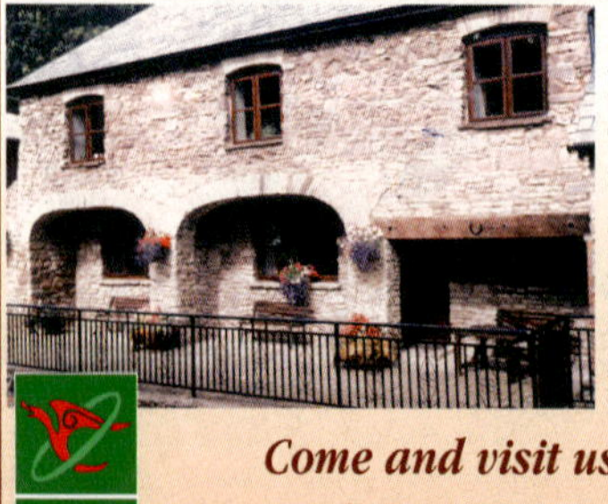

The Granary and Coach House in beautifully converted barn, midway between Abergavenny and Monmouth. Ideal family self-catering holiday accommodation. Each unit has three bedrooms (2 twin and 1 double), lounge, diner/kitchen with full electric cooker, microwave, refrigerator and toaster. Bathroom has shower over bath. Colour TV in lounge. Bed linen, towels and electricity included in price. Cot and high chair available. Patio and children's play area. Barbecue. Ample parking. Pets by arrangement only. Superb country area for walking, birdwatching or visiting interesting market towns and local castles.

Come and visit us to relax and explore. Colour brochure.

★★★★ Mrs Ann Ball, Upper Cwm Farm, Brynderi, Llantilio Crossenny, Abergavenny NP7 8TG
Tel/Fax: 01873 821236 • e-mail: uppercwm@btopenworld.com • www.downourlane.co.uk/3htm

 Please mention Farm Holiday Guide when enquiring

SCOTLAND
Counties

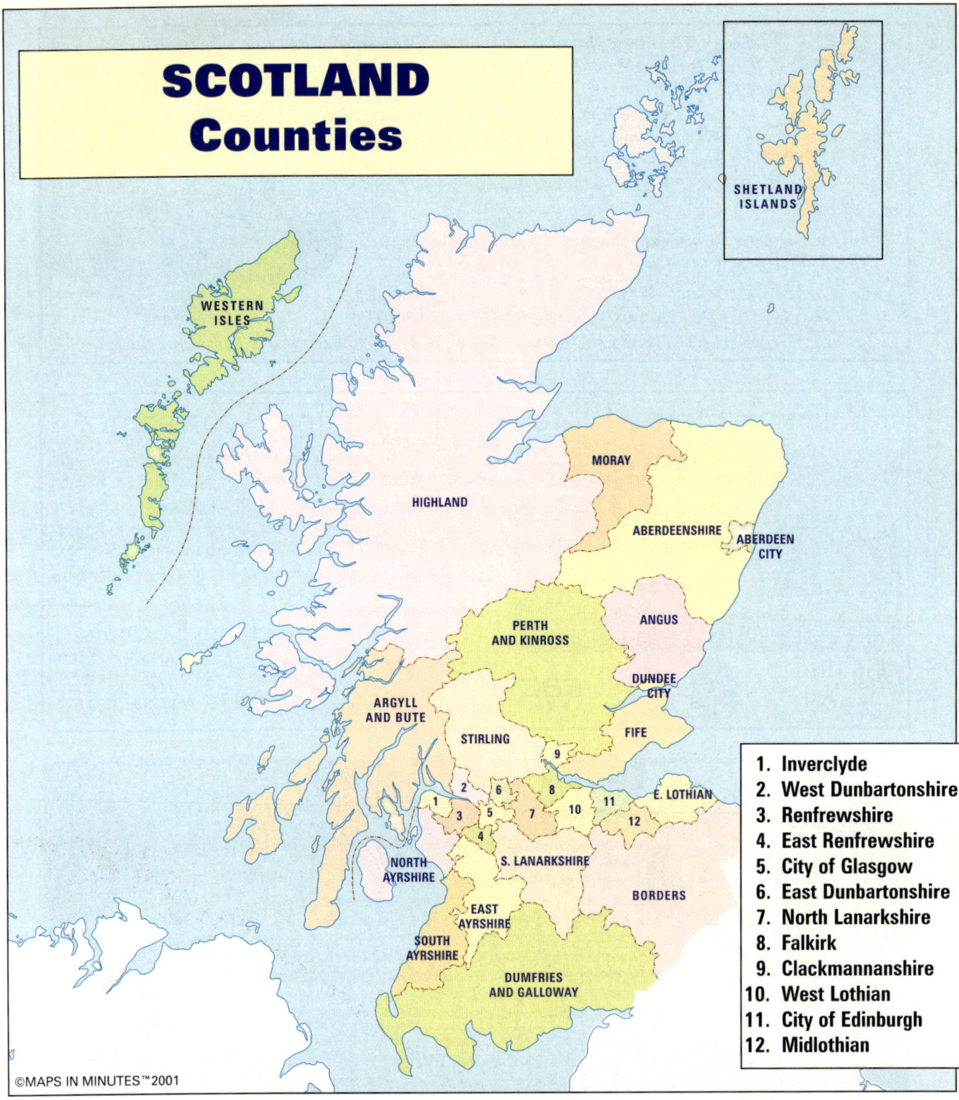

SHETLAND ISLANDS
WESTERN ISLES
HIGHLAND
MORAY
ABERDEENSHIRE
ABERDEEN CITY
ANGUS
PERTH AND KINROSS
DUNDEE CITY
FIFE
ARGYLL AND BUTE
STIRLING
E. LOTHIAN
S. LANARKSHIRE
NORTH AYRSHIRE
BORDERS
EAST AYRSHIRE
SOUTH AYRSHIRE
DUMFRIES AND GALLOWAY

1. Inverclyde
2. West Dunbartonshire
3. Renfrewshire
4. East Renfrewshire
5. City of Glasgow
6. East Dunbartonshire
7. North Lanarkshire
8. Falkirk
9. Clackmannanshire
10. West Lothian
11. City of Edinburgh
12. Midlothian

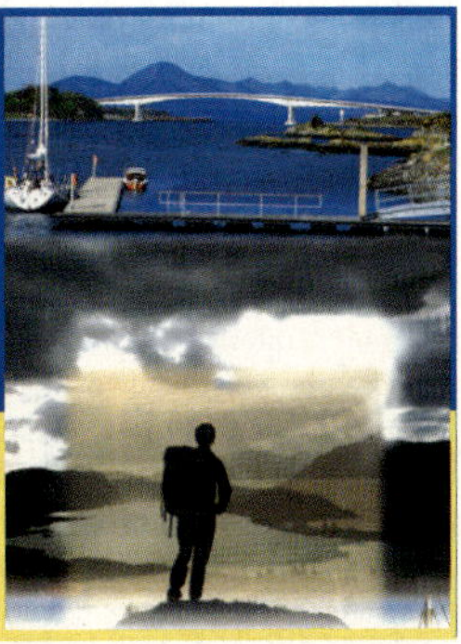

SELF-CATERING

SELF-CATERING

The Estate lies along the beautiful Deveron River and our traditional stone cottages nestle in individual seclusion. Visitors can explore one of the ancient baronies of Scotland. The sea is only nine miles away, and the market town of Turriff only two miles, with its golf course, swimming pool, etc. Places of interest including the Cairngorms, Aviemore, picturesque fishing villages and castles, all within easy reach on uncrowded roads. See our Highland cattle. 6 miles of own walks.

Terms: from £149 weekly. Special Winter lets. 10 cottages sleeping 6-9. Children and reasonable dogs welcome. STB Inspected.

For a brochure contact: ***Mrs P. Bates, Holiday Cottages, Forglen Estate, Turriff, Aberdeenshire AB53 4JP***
Tel: 01888 562918/562518 • Fax: 01888 562252 • Web: www.forglen.co.uk

BOARD/SELF-CATERING

Raemoir House Hotel – Self-Catering Apartments

Raemoir House Hotel is part of an idyllic 3,500 acre estate, situated on Royal Deeside and within easy reach of Aberdeen. Timeless and beautiful the hotel is recognised as the finest in the area. The food is divine. Also self-catering cottages in the grounds with one, two or three bedrooms sleeping up to 8 people – A wonderful welcome for you and your pets.

Raemoir House Hotel, Raemoir, Banchory, Kincardineshire AB31 4ED
Tel: 01330 824884 • Fax: 01330 822171

AA ★★★ · Scottish Tourist Board ★★★★ HOTEL · RAC ★★★

SELF-CATERING

ARDTUR COTTAGES

Two adjacent cottages in secluded surroundings on promontory between Port Appin and Castle Stalker. Ideal for hill walking, climbing, pony trekking, boating and fly-fishing. (Glencoe and Ben Nevis half-hour drive). Tennis court by arrangement. Direct access across the field to sea (Loch Linnhe). First cottage is suitable for up to 8 people in one double and three twin-bedded rooms, large dining/sittingroom/kitchenette and two bathrooms. Second cottage is suitable for 6 people in one double and two twin-bedded rooms, dining/sittingroom/kitchenette and bathroom. Everything provided except linen. Shops one mile; sea 200 yards. Pets allowed. Car essential, parking. Open March/October. Terms from £165 to £375 weekly.

SAE, please for details to Mrs J. Pery, Ardtur, Appin PA38 4DD (01631 730223 or 01626 834172)
e-mail: pery@eurobell.co.uk

SELF-CATERING

ELERAIG HIGHLAND LODGES

near Oban, Argyll, gateway to the Highlands and Islands

Scottish Tourist Board ★★ SELF CATERING

In the breathtaking scenery of a private glen within 1800-acre working sheep farm. The chalets are ideal for a holiday with dogs (& cats). Widely spaced, sleeping four to seven. Parking by each chalet. Cots and high chairs available. By Loch Tralaig. Free fishing and boating. Peace and tranquillity are features of this walkers' and birdwatchers' paradise. Riding, golf, watersports and evening entertainment available locally. Open March to January.

Terms from £205 per week.
Colour brochure from resident owners:

Anne and Robin Grey, Eleraig Highland Lodges
Kilninver, by Oban, Argyll PA34 4UX
Tel/Fax: 01852 200225 • Web: www.scotland2000.com/eleraig

The Highland Estate of

- PEACE
- SECLUSION
- VARIETY OF INTERESTS
- FREEDOM
- HISTORY
- OUTSTANDING SCENERY

Ellary

and Castle Sween

This 15,000 acre Highland Estate lies in one of the most beautiful and unspoilt areas of Scotland and has a wealth of ancient historical associations within its bounds.

There is St Columba's Cave, probably one of the first places of Christian Worship in Britain, also Castle Sween, the oldest ruined castle in Scotland, and Kilmory Chapel where there is a fascinating collection of Celtic slabs.

There is a wide range of accommodation, from small groups of cottages, many of the traditional stone-built estate type, to modern holiday chalets, super luxury and luxury caravans at Castle Sween.

Most of the cottages accommodate up to six, but one will take eight.

All units fully equipped except linen. Television reception is included.

Ellary is beautiful at all times of the year and is suitable for windsurfing, fishing, swimming, sailing and the observation of a wide variety of wildlife; there are paths and tracks throughout the estate for the visitor who prefers to explore on foot, and guests will find farmers and estate workers most helpful in their approach.

For further details, brochure and booking forms, please apply to:

ELLARY ESTATE OFFICE, by LOCHGILPHEAD, ARGYLL PA31 8PA

Tel: 01880 770232/770209 or 01546 850223

Fax: 01880 770386

e-mail: info@ellary.com • website: www.ellary.com

SELF-CATERING

Situated on beautiful Seil Island with wonderful views of surrounding countryside. These lovingly restored cottages (one detached and one attached to the main croft house) retain their traditional character while incorporating all modern facilities. The cottages are near to each other and ideal for two families on holiday together. Seil is one of the most peaceful and tranquil spots in the West Highlands, with easy access to neighbouring Isles of Luing and Easdale.

Oban, the hub for trips to Mull and Iona, is half an hour's drive away over the famous 18th century " Bridge Over The Atlantic". Wonderful area for hillwalking, cycling, fishing and bird watching.

Short breaks from £35.00 per day.

Kilbride Cottage

Kilbride Croft

Balvicar, Isle of Seil, Argyll PA34 4RD
Contact: Mary & Brian Phillips
Tel: 01852 300475
e-mail: kilbridecroft@aol.com
web: www.kilbridecroft@fsnet.co.uk

Croft Cottage

BOARD

Rockhill Waterside Country House

Ardbrecknish, By Dalmally, Argyll PA33 1BH Tel: 01866 833218

17th century guest house in spectacular waterside setting on Loch Awe with breathtaking views to Ben Cruachan, where comfort, peace and tranquillity reign supreme. Small private Highland estate breeding Hanoverian competition horses. 1200 metres free trout fishing. Five delightful rooms with all modern facilities. First-class highly acclaimed home cooking with much home-grown produce. Wonderful area for touring the Western Highlands, Glencoe, the Trossachs and Kintyre. Ideal for climbing, walking, bird and animal watching. Boat trips locally and from Oban (30 miles) to Mull, Iona, Fingal's Cave and other islands. Dogs' Paradise! Also Self-Catering Cottages.

website: www.rockhillhanoverianstud.co.uk

SELF-CATERING

Scoor House Self-Catering Holidays

Bunessan, Isle of Mull

Scoor House is a former farmhouse, restored and converted to provide four self-catering apartments, with adjoining cottage plus a detached cottage nearby. All have stunning views to the sea and the Hebrides. Each property has a spacious lounge/dining area with kitchenette. There is a utility room with washing machine, tumble dryer and deep freeze. Payphone on premises; cots can be provided. Dogs allowed but must be kept under control. All domestic equipment and bed linen provided. Electricity by meter reading. Open all year. Terms from £100 to £380. *Details from Manageress:*

Rosie Burgess, Kintra, Fionnphort, Isle of Mull PA66 6BT • Tel & Fax: 01681 700509
e-mail: info@scoorhouse.f9.co.uk • www.scoorhouse.f9.co.uk

BOARD

Welcome to Dunduff Farm where a warm, friendly atmosphere awaits you. Situated just south of Ayr at the coastal village of Dunure, this family-run beef and sheep unit of 600 acres is only 15 minutes from the shore providing good walks and sea fishing and enjoying close proximity to Dunure Castle and Park. Accommodation is of a high standard yet homely and comfortable. Bedrooms have washbasins, radio alarm, tea/coffee making facilities, central heating, TV, hair dryer and en suite facilities (the twin room has private bathroom). There is also a small farm cottage available sleeping two/four people. Bed and Breakfast from £23 per person; weekly rate £130. Cottage £250 per week. Colour brochure available.

Mrs Agnes Gemmell, Dunduff Farm, Dunure, Ayr KA7 4LH
01292 500225 • www.gemmelldunduff.co.uk

AA ♦♦♦♦ Guest Accommodation
RAC ♦♦♦♦♦ Guest Accommodation
Scottish Tourist Board ★★★★ B&B

SELF-CATERING

Edenmouth Farm, Near Kelso TD5 7QB
Tel: 01890 830391

Unique, quality cottages, recently converted from a traditional farm steading. Magnificent views across the Tweed Valley. Ideal base for fishermen, golfers, walkers, families and couples wanting a relaxing break. Comfortable, well-equipped cottages on ground level. All bedrooms have en suite bathrooms. Central heating, linen, towels and electricity included in rates. Large grass garden, games room, laundry/drying room, bicycle lock-up. Pets by arrangement. Open all year. Cottages sleep 1-8. Parties of up to 18 catered for.

Weekly lets from £160-£420. Short Breaks – 3 nights for 2 people £100. B&B £20pppn.
Mrs Geraldine O'Driscoll, Edenmouth Farm, Kelso, Scottish Borders TD5 7QB
e-mail: edenmouth.odris@virgin.net • www.edenmouth.co.uk

BOARD

Castle Douglas, Kirkcudbrightshire DG7 3HU

Working farm. Family-run 18th century farmhouse. All bedrooms en suite. Billiard room. Lovely oak-panelled dining room offering Cordon Bleu cooking using local produce such as venison, pheasant and salmon. Trout fishing, walking, and golfing available. Winner of the Macallan Taste of Scotland 2001.

Little Gem Award

AA ◆◆◆◆◆ Guest Accommodation

Premier Award

Tel and Fax: 01556 650233
www.craigadam.com

SELF-CATERING

Self-Catering Holiday Cottages by the Sea in Galloway, South-West Scotland

Four houses – **Craig Cottage** (sleeps 5), **Milnecroft Cottage** (sleeps 2/4), **Braeview Cottage** (sleeps 6) and **Barlocco House** (sleeps 10) – in a stunning coastal location. Borgue two miles, Kirkcudbright and Gatehouse-of-Fleet (7 miles) Beaches within walking distance; good sea fishing, walking, golf. Babysitting, cooking, bike and boat hire are all available by prior arrangement.

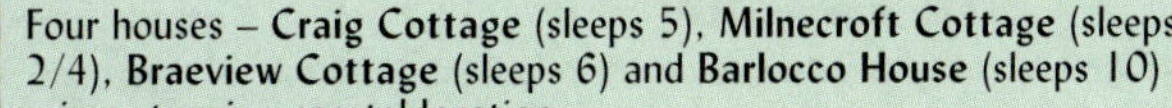

Details from: Lindsey Brown, Roberton, Borgue, Kirkcudbright DG6 4UB
Tel: 01557 870217
e-mail: cottages@roberton.sol.co.uk

STB ★★/★★★★ Self-Catering

SELF-CATERING

Hunter Holiday Cottages

Thornton Farm, Rosewell, Edinburgh EH24 9EF
Tel: 0131 448 0888 • Fax: 0131 440 2082
e-mail: info@edinburghcottages.com
website: www.edinburghcottages.com

Hunter Holiday Cottages offer a range of cottages in beautiful countryside only eight miles from Edinburgh City Centre. These superior cottages are recently renovated, have all modern facilities and sleep four to ten plus. They provide the ideal base for the perfect Scottish holiday from their location in Midlothian's historic countryside. There is easy access to Scotland's capital and the major routes to the rest of Scotland.

For more information visit our website • Also B&B £25 per night • Contact Margot Crichton.

SELF-CATERING

Crubenbeg
Holiday Cottages

Rural self-catering cottages in the central Highlands where one can relax and stroll from the doorstep or take part in the choice of many sporting activities in the area. We have a children's play area, a Games Room, Pond stocked with trout for fishing and a barbecue. Pets welcome.

Newtonmore, Inverness-shire PH20 1BE

Tel: 01540 673566 • Fax: 01540 673509

E-mail: enquiry@crubenbeg.com • Website: www.crubenbeg.com

BOARD

Glenmarkie Guest House
Health Spa & Riding Centre

Glenisla, Perthshire PH11 8QB • 01575 582295

www.glenmarkie.freeserve.co.uk

Quietly situated within one of the most beautiful glens in Perthshire, nestling on the edge of the forest. Our traditional licensed Scottish Guest House is cosy; all bedrooms are en suite, with tea/coffee making facilities.

Enjoy bird watching, walking, wildlife, riding lessons, hacks and trekking in breathtaking scenery. Treat yourself to a hot spa or use the beauty facilities offering top-to-toe beauty therapy. Brochures and price list available on request.

BOARD

Newmill Farm

STB ★★★ B&B

Mrs Ann Guthrie, Newmill Farm, Stanley, Perthshire PH1 4QD
Telephone: (01738) 828281 e-mail:guthrienewmill@sol.co.uk
website: www.newmillfarm.co.uk

Newmill Farm is situated only six miles from Perth, in 330 acres of lovely farmland. Twin and double en suite rooms available and a family room with private bathroom; lounge, sittingroom, diningroom; bathroom, shower room and toilet. The many castles and historic ruins around Perth are testimony to Scotland's turbulent past. Situated at the "Gateway to the Highlands" the farm is ideally placed for those seeking some of the loveliest unspoilt scenery in Western Europe. Many golf courses and trout rivers nearby. Bed and Breakfast from £19, Evening Meal on request. Reductions and facilities for children. Pets welcome.

• Hawthorn Cottage •
Luxury Self-Catering Accommodation

Hawthorn Cottage was purpose-built in 2001 to the highest standard. The cottage can sleep up to six people plus a baby and is suitable for the disabled. Prices range from £330 to £510.
Also available at West Drip is a brand new for 2003 residential caravan which sleeps up to 8. Prices from £170 to £230 per week.
Both cottage and caravan are located at West Drip farm (3 miles north of Stirling) and have a quiet and peaceful setting with panoramic views. Sorry no pets.

For bookings contact: Eleanor Graham, West Drip Farm, By Stirling FK9 4UJ
Tel: 01786 472523 • e-mail: enquiries@westdripfarm.com
www.westdripfarm.com

Scottish
TOURIST BOARD
★★★★
SELF CATERING

Selected Self-Catering Holidays in Scotland

Members of the ASSC are committed to high and consistant standards in self catering. Contact your choice direct and be assured of an excellent holiday.

Brochures: 0990 168 571 • Web site: www.assc.co.uk

Owner-Operators ready to match our standards and interested in joining are requested to contact our Secretary for information – 0990 168 571

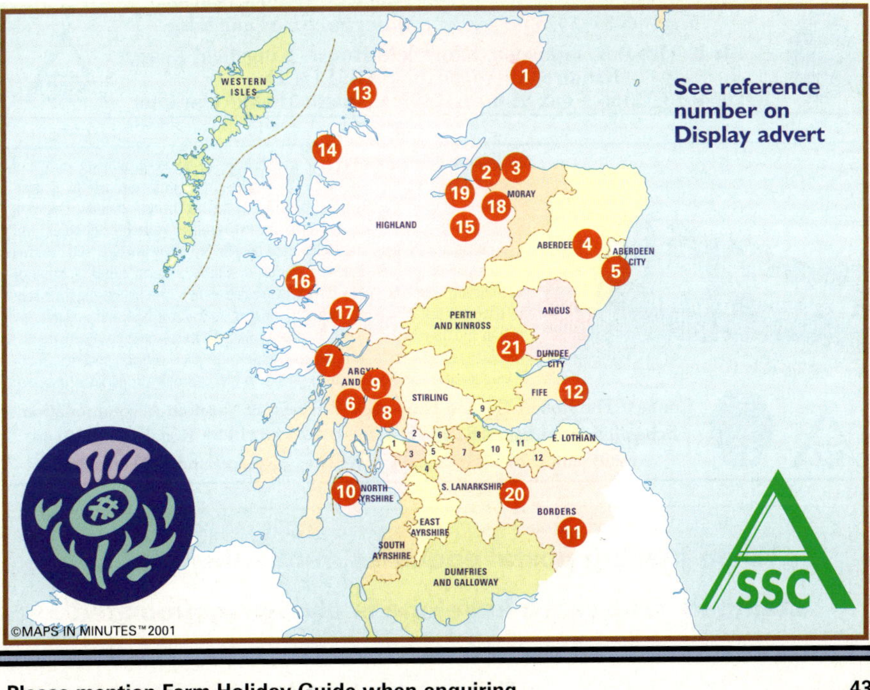

See reference number on Display advert

WESTERN ISLES
HIGHLAND
MORAY
ABERDEEN
ABERDEEN CITY
ANGUS
PERTH AND KINROSS
DUNDEE CITY
FIFE
ARGYLL AND
STIRLING
E. LOTHIAN
NORTH AYRSHIRE
S. LANARKSHIRE
BORDERS
EAST AYRSHIRE
SOUTH AYRSHIRE
DUMFRIES AND GALLOWAY

ASSC

©MAPS IN MINUTES™2001

1

ABERDEEN • Holiday Flat to suit couple or small family. Clean, comfortable and conveniently located for Aberdeen city centre and attractions. Lounge, double bedroom, bathroom with shower, fully equipped galley kitchen. Heating, lighting and all bedding included. Regular bus service to city centre. No smoking and no pets. **STB ★★★**

WICK – *A Quality Home for Your Quality Time* Sleeps up to 6. Close to airport, bus and rail stations. Lounge with DVD, SKY TV, Playstation; dining kitchen, bathroom, en suite double bedroom, twin/double and single/twin; ground floor single. Fully equipped.

ASSC

Details of both properties from **Donald Campbell, The Old Schoolhouse, Ulbster, Lybster, Caithness KW2 6AA (Tel & Fax: 01955 651297) • e-mail: ulbster@ntlworld.com • www.visit.ourflat.co.uk • www.assc.co.uk**

2

Tulloch Lodges • *Peace, Relaxation and Comfort in Beautiful Natural Surroundings*
One of the loveliest self-catering sites in Scotland. Modern, spacious, attractive and beautifully equipped Scandinavian lodges for up to 6 in glorious woodland/water setting. Perfect for the Highlands and Historic Grampian, especially the Golden Moray Coast and the Golf, Castle and Malt Whisky Trails. £235-£675 per week. Brochure:
Tulloch Lodges, Rafford, Forres, Moray IV36 2RU • Tel: 01309 673311
Fax: 01309 671515 • web: www.tullochlodges.co.uk • STB ★★★★ *Self-Catering*

ASSC

3

Sheriffston Farm Chalet *Near Elgin*

One 'A' frame chalet on working farm. 'Habitat' furnished, fully equipped for two – six people, colour TV, bed linen, duvets. Beautiful rural location in Moray – famous for flowers – district of lowlands, highlands, rivers, forests, lovely beaches, historic towns, welcoming people. Excellent local facilities. Moray golf tickets available. *From £180–£300 (January-December)*
Contact: Mrs. J. M. Shaw, Sheriffston, Elgin, Moray IV30 8LA
Tel & Fax: 01343 842695 • e-mail: jennifer_m_shaw@hotmail.com

ASSC

Scottish Tourist Board ★★ Self Catering

4

THE GREENKNOWE

A comfortable, detached, renovated cottage in a quiet location at the southern edge of the village of Kintore. Ideally situated for touring castles and pre-historic sites or for walking, fishing and golfing. The cottage is on one level with large sittingroom facing south and the garden. Sleeps four.

• Walkers Welcome Scheme •

Terms £275–£475 per week including electricity and linen.

Mr & Mrs P. A. Lumsden, Kingsfield House, Kingsfield Road, Kintore, Aberdeenshire AB51 OUD
Tel: 01467 632366 • Fax 01467 632399 • e-mail: kfield@clara.net

5

The Robert Gordon University in the heart of Aberdeen offers a variety of accommodation in the city centre to visitors from June through to August. Aberdeen is ideal for visiting Royal Deeside, castles and historic buildings, playing golf or touring the Malt Whisky Trail. The city itself is a place to discover, and Aberdonians are friendly and welcoming people. We offer Two Star self-catering accommodation for individuals or groups at superb rates, in either en suite or shared facility flats. Each party has exclusive use of their own flat during their stay. The flats are self-contained, centrally heated, fully furnished and suitable for children and disabled guests. All flats have colour TV, microwave, bed linen, towels, all cooking utensils, and a complimentary 'welcome pack' of basic groceries. There are laundry and telephone facilities on site as well as ample car parking spaces.

Contact: The Robert Gordon University, Business & Vacation Accommodation, Schoolhill, Aberdeen AB10 1FR • Tel: 01224 262134 • Fax: 01224 262144
e-mail: p.macinnes@rgu.ac.uk • website: www.scotland2000.com/rgu

When making postal enquiries, remember that a stamped, addressed envelope is always appreciated

BRALECKAN HOUSE. A mid19th century stone building carefully restored to provide two comfortable houses. Situated on private upland farm. Each comprises sitting room, fully fitted kitchen, two bedrooms, bathroom and shower room. Both are completely private, or suitable for two families wishing to holiday together. Large parking area and garden. Children most welcome, but regretfully no pets. Contact **Mr & Mrs Crawford, Brenchoille Farm, Inveraray, Argyll PA23 8XN • Tel: 01499 500662**

SSC

Scottish Tourist Board ★★★ Self Catering

6

Cologin
Country Chalets
Oban

All Scottish Glens have their secrets: let us share ours with you – and your pets !

Call now for our colour brochure and find out more

Open all year round. Rates from £160 to £495 per week. Autumn Gold breaks and mid-week deals also available

MRS LINDA BATTISON, COLOGIN FARMHOUSE, LERAGS GLEN, BY OBAN, ARGYLL PA34 4SE Tel: (01631) 564501 • Fax: (01631) 566925
e-mail: cologin@west-highland-holidays.co.uk
web: www.west-highland-holidays.co.uk

STB ★★★ to ★★★★ Self Catering

7

West Loch Tarbert, Argyll – Dunmore Court

Five cottages in architect design conversion of home farm on the estate of Dunmore House. Spacious accommodation for 2-8 persons. All have stone fireplaces for log fires. Bird-watching, fishing and walking. Easy access to island ferries. Pets welcome. Open all year. Colour brochure. From £175-£490. STB ★★

8

Telephone: 01880 820654
e-mail: dunmorecourtsc@aol.com
www.dunmorecourt.com

Contact: Amanda Minshall, Dunmore Court, Kilberry Road, Near Tarbert, Argyll PA29 6XZ

Mr & Mrs E. Crawford

Blarghour Farm

Loch Awe-side, by Dalmally, Argyll PA33 1BW
Tel: 01866 833246 • Fax: 01866 833338
e-mail: blarghour@aol.com
www.self-catering-argyll.co.uk

At Blarghour Farm one may choose from four centrally heated and double glazed holiday homes sleeping from two to six people, all enjoying splendid views of lovely Loch Awe. Kitchens are well appointed, lounges tastefully decorated and furnished with payphone, TV and gas fire, beds are made up and towels supplied while the two larger houses have shower rooms in addition to bathrooms, all with shaver point. The two larger houses are suitable for children and have cots and high chairs. No pets are allowed. Open all year. Centrally situated for touring. Illustrated brochure on request.

9

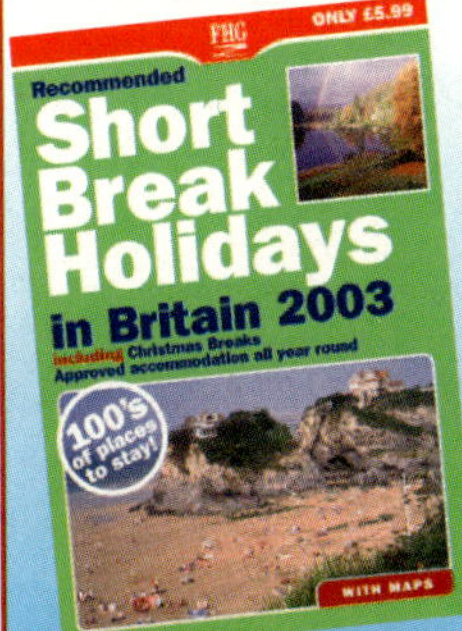

Recommended

Short Break Holidays in Britain 2003

Specifically designed to cater for the most rapidly growing sector of the holiday market in the UK. Illustrated details of hotels offering special "Bargain Breaks" throughout the year.

Available from bookshops and larger newsagents for £5.99

FHG PUBLICATIONS LTD

Abbey Mill Business Centre, Seedhill, Paisley, Scotland PA1 1TJ

www.holidayguides.com

ArranHideAways
www.arran-hideaways.co.uk
Arran's Local Accommodation Booking Service

Properties throughout the Island
All villages – all dates
STB Quality Assured*
Short Breaks available
Major credit cards accepted

SSC

10 Please ask for our brochure – One Call Does It All
Weekdays/Office Hours: 01770 302303/302310
Evenings & Weekends: 01770 860 556
www.arran-hideaways.co.uk • on-line booking & availability
Invercloy House, Brodick, Isle of Arran KA27 8AJ

* All our properties have applied for grading under the STB Quality Assurance Scheme

11 **Mill House, Letterbox & Stockman's Cottages** – Three recently renovated, quality Cottages, each sleeping four, on a working farm three miles from Jedburgh. All ideal centres for exploring, sporting holidays or getting away from it all. Each cottage has two public rooms (ground floor available). Minimum let two days. Terms £190–£330. Open all year. Bus three miles, airport 54 miles.

Scottish Tourist Board ★★★★ Self Catering

Mrs A. Fraser, Overwells, Jedburgh, Roxburghshire TD8 6LT
Telephone: 01835 863020 • Fax: 01835 864334
e-mail: abfraser@btinternet.com • www.overwells.co.uk

SSC

The Old Bank House Restaurant and Apartments

12 In an enviable position overlooking its own beach just west of the harbour in Anstruther. Four letting apartments, sleeping 2-11 persons, all en suite, with telephone, central heating and fully equipped kitchens. Double occupancy rate from £20 pppn.
Ricardo Sparrow, Old Bank House, 23-25 High St, Anstruther, FIFE KY10 3DQ • Tel: 01333 310189 • E-mail:ricardosrest@hotmail.com • www.undiscoveredscotland.co.uk/anstruther/oldbank/

SSC

13 **Clashmore Holiday Cottages** Our three croft cottages at Clashmore, are the ideal base for a holiday in the Highlands. They are cosy and fully equipped, with linen provided. Nearby there are sandy beaches, mountains and lochs for wild brown trout fishing. Children welcome but sorry no pets. Open all year, sleeping two-five £160-£340 per week.

Contact Mr and Mrs H. Mackenzie, Lochview,
216 Clashmore, Stoer, Lochinver, Sutherland IV27 4JQ
Tel & Fax: 01571 855226 • e-mail: clashcotts@supanet.com

SSC

Scottish Tourist Board ★★★ Self Catering

14 **Innes Maree Bungalows, Poolewe IV22 2JU**
Only a few minutes' walk from the world-famous Inverewe Gardens in magnificent Wester Ross. A purpose-built complex of six superb modern bungalows, all equipped to the highest standards of luxury and comfort. Each bungalow sleeps six with main bedroom en suite. Children and pets welcome. Terms from £190 to £425 inclusive of bed linen and electricity. Brochure available. **Tel & Fax 01445 781454**
E-mail: fhg@poolewebungalows.com • Website: www.poolewebungalows.com

SSC

STB ★★★★

Loch Insh Log Chalets, Kincraig, Inverness-shire PH21 1NU
Tel: 01540 651272
e-mail: office@lochinsh.com
website: www.lochinsh.com

SUMMER WATERSPORTS AND WINTER SKIING

Just six miles south of Aviemore these superb log chalets are set in 14 acres of woodland in the magnificent Spey Valley, surrounded on three sides by forest and rolling fields with the fourth side being half a mile of beach frontage. Free watersports hire for guests, 8.30-10am/4-5.30pm daily. Sailing, windsurfing, canoeing, salmon fishing, archery, dry ski slope skiing. Hire/instruction available by the hour, day or week mid April to end October. Boathouse Restaurant on the shore of Loch Insh offering coffee, home-made soup, fresh salads, bar meals, children's meals and evening à la carte. Large gift shop and bar. New Children's Adventure Areas, 3km Lochside/Woodland Walk/Interpretation Trail, Ski Slope, Mountain Bike Hire and Stocked Trout Lochan are open all year round. Ski, snowboard hire, and instruction available December-April. 15

SSC

Arisaig House Cottages – *luxurious secluded accommodation in mature woodland*

Achnahanat

- ACHNAHANAT in the grounds of Arisaig House, sleeps up to 8
- THE BOTHY set at the end of the walled gardens, sleeps up to 8
- THE COURTYARD self-contained apartment on first floor, sleeps 2
- FAGUS LODGE set in mature gardens, sleeps up to 6
- GARDENER'S COTTAGE set in gardens off small courtyard, sleeps up to 3
- ROSHVEN overlooks walled gardens of Arisaig House, sleeps up to 4

SSC 16

Set in an area of breathtaking coastal and hill scenery, and wonderful sandy beaches. Mountain bike hire, clay pigeon shooting, and fishing on Loch Morar can be arranged. Golf 7 miles, swimming pool 13 miles. Day trips to the Small Isles and to Skye.

Details from: **Andrew Smither, Arisaig House, Beasdale, Arisaig, Inverness-shire PH39 4NR**
Tel/Fax: 01687 450399
e-mail: enquiries@arisaighouse-cottages.co.uk • www.arisaighouse-cottages.co.uk

Cuilcheanna Cottages

Onich, Fort William
Inverness-shire PH33 6SD

A small peaceful site for self catering with three cottages and eight caravans (6 x 2003 models). Situated in the village of Onich, 400 yards off the main road. An excellent centre for touring and hill walking in the West Highlands.

For further details please phone 01855 821526 or 01855 821310

17

BLACKPARK FARM Westhill, Inverness IV2 5BP

This newly built holiday home is located one mile from Culloden Battlefield with panoramic views over Inverness and beyond. Fully equipped with many extras to make your holiday special, including oil fired central heating to ensure warmth on the coldest of winter days. Ideally based for touring the Highlands including Loch Ness, Skye etc. Extensive information is available on our website. 18

A Highland welcome awaits you.

Tel: 01463 790620 • Fax: 01463 794262 • e-mail: i.alexander@blackpark.co.uk • website: www.blackpark.co.uk

SSC

Visit the FHG website www.holidayguides.com
for details of accommodation featured in the full range of FHG titles

The Farm Holiday Guide to

Coast & Country Holidays in

England, Scotland, Wales & Ireland

• Farms, guest houses and country hotels •
• cottages, flats and chalets • caravans and camping •
• activity holidays • country inns •

CONTENTS

ENGLAND

BOARD

SELF-CATERING

CONTENTS

SCOTLAND

BOARD

SELF-CATERING

WALES

BOARD

SELF-CATERING

REPUBLIC OF IRELAND

COUNTRY INNS

The Original Farm Holiday Guide to
Coast & Country Holidays 2003

On seeing the words FARM HOLIDAY GUIDE in the title, you could be forgiven for thinking that all the properties listed here are situated on farms, as was the case when the guide was first published 56 years ago. Indeed, many are genuine farm holidays, and most are in the country or by the sea. However, in this edition, you will also find details of accommodation in small hotels, guest houses and B&Bs in towns and villages, as well as self-catering properties and caravans, and a small selection of country inns and activity holidays. Something for everyone in fact, and all with something in common, the FHG tradition of country hospitality – a warm and friendly welcome, clean, comfortable accommodation and good wholesome food, if provided. All the entries are well described and generally give an indication of rates. There is generally some information about the area to help you plan your outings, and by using the Readers' Offer Vouchers at the front of the book you may even save some money.

Anne Cuthbertson
Editor

ISBN 185055 341 6

Cover photographs:
Ivan J. Belcher
Cover design: Focus Network

Typeset by FHG Publications Ltd, Paisley.
Printed and bound in Great Britain by Polestar Wheatons Ltd, Exeter, Devon

Distribution. Book Trade: Plymbridge House, Estover Road, Plymouth PL6 7PY
Tel: 01752 202300; Fax: 01752 202333
News Trade: Market Force (UK) Ltd, 5th Floor Low Rise, King's Reach Tower,
Stamford Street, London SE1 9LS
Tel: 0207 633 3450; Fax: 0207 633 3572

Published by FHG Publications Ltd., Abbey Mill Business Centre,
Seedhill, Paisley PA1 ITJ (Tel: 0141-887 0428; Fax: 0141-889 7204).
e-mail: fhg@ipcmedia.com

US ISBN 1-58843-325-0
Distributed in the United States by
Hunter Publishing Inc., 130 Campus Drive, Edison, N.J. 08818, USA

The Original Farm Holiday Guide to Coast & Country Holidays is an FHG publication, published by
IPC Country & Leisure Media Ltd, part of IPC Media Group of Companies.

Ratings You Can Trust

ENGLAND

The English Tourism Council (formerly the English Tourist Board) has joined with the **AA** and **RAC** to create a new, easily understood quality rating for serviced accommodation, giving a clear guide of what to expect.

HOTELS are given a rating from One to Five **Stars** – the more Stars, the higher the quality and the greater the range of facilities and level of services provided.

GUEST ACCOMMODATION, which includes guest houses, bed and breakfasts, inns and farmhouses, is rated from One to Five **Diamonds**. Progressively higher levels of quality and customer care must be provided for each one of the One to Five Diamond ratings.

HOLIDAY PARKS, TOURING PARKS and CAMPING PARKS are now also assessed using **Stars**. Standards of quality range from a One Star (acceptable) to a Five Star (exceptional) park.

Look out also for the new **SELF-CATERING** Star ratings. The more **Stars** (from One to Five) awarded to an establishment, the higher the levels of quality you can expect. Establishments at higher rating levels also have to meet some additional requirements for facilities.

SCOTLAND

Star Quality Grades will reflect the most important aspects of a visit, such as the warmth of welcome, efficiency and friendliness of service, the quality of the food and the cleanliness and condition of the furnishings, fittings and decor.

THE MORE STARS, THE HIGHER THE STANDARDS.

The description, such as Hotel, Guest House, Bed and Breakfast, Lodge, Holiday Park, Self-catering etc tells you the type of property and style of operation.

WALES

Places which score highly will have an especially welcoming atmosphere and pleasing ambience, high levels of comfort and guest care, and attractive surroundings enhanced by thoughtful design and attention to detail.

STAR QUALITY GUIDE FOR

HOTELS, GUEST HOUSES AND FARMHOUSES

SELF-CATERING ACCOMMODATION (Cottages, Apartments, Houses)

CARAVAN HOLIDAY HOME PARKS (Holiday Parks, Touring Parks, Camping Parks)

Exceptional quality
Excellent quality
Very good quality
Good quality
Fair to good quality

In England, Scotland and Wales, all graded properties are inspected annually by Tourist Authority trained Assessors.

FHG Diploma Winners 2002

Each year we award a small number of diplomas to holiday proprietors whose services have been specially commended by our readers. The following were our FHG Diploma Winners for 2002.

England

DEVON

Woolacombe Bay Holiday Park,
Woolacombe, North Devon
EX34 7HW (01271 870343).

LANCASHIRE

Mrs Holdsworth,
Broadwater Hotel,
356 Marine Road, East Promenade
Morecambe, Lancashire LA4 5AQ
(01524 411333).

Peter & Susan Bicker,
Kelvin Private Hotel,
Reads Avenue, Blackpool,
Lancashire FY1 4JJ
(01253 620293).

LINCOLNSHIRE

Sue Phillips & John Lister,
Cawthorpe Farm, Cawthorpe
Bourne, Lincolnshire PE10 0AB
(01778 426697).

OXFORDSHIRE

Liz Roach, The Old Bakery,
Skirmett, Nr Henley on Thames
Oxfordshire RG9 6TD
(01491 638309).

SOMERSET

Pat & Sue Weir, Slipper Cottage,
41 Bishopston, Montacute,
Somerset TA15 6UX
(01935 823073)

Scotland

ARGYLL & BUTE

David Quibell,
Rosneath Castle Caravan Park
Near Helensburgh,
Argyll & Bute G84 0QS
(01436 831208)

DUNDEE & ANGUS

Carlogie House Hotel,
Carlogie Road, Carnoustie,
Dundee DD7 6LD
(01241 853185)

EDINBURGH & LOTHIANS

Geraldine Hamilton,
Crosswoodhill Farm, West Calder
Edinburgh & Lothians EH55 8LP
(01501 785205)

FIFE

Mr Alastair Clark,
Old Manor Country House Hotel,
Lundin Links, Nr St Andrews
Fife KY8 6AJ
(01333 320368)

HIGHLANDS

N & J McCallum, The Neuk
Corpach, Fort William PH33 7LE
(01397 772244)

HELP IMPROVE BRITISH TOURISM STANDARDS

Why not write and tell us about the holiday accommodation you have chosen from one of our popular publications? Complete a nomination form giving details of why you think YOUR host or hostess should win one of our attractive framed diplomas and send it to:

FHG Publications, Abbey Mill Business Centre, Seedhill, Paisley PA1 1TJ

READERS' OFFER 2003

Leighton Buzzard Railway

Page's Park Station, Billington Road,
Leighton Buzzard, Bedfordshire LU7 4TN
Tel: 01525 373888
e-mail: info@buzzrail.co.uk • website: www.buzzrail.co.uk

One free adult/child with full-fare adult ticket

valid from 16/3/03 – 29/10/03

NOT TO BE USED IN CONJUNCTION WITH ANY OTHER OFFER

READERS' OFFER 2003

Bekonscot Model Village

Warwick Road, Beaconsfield, Buckinghamshire HP9 2PL
Tel: 01494 672919 • e-mail: Bekonscot@dial.pipex.com
website: www.bekonscot.com

One child FREE when accompanied by full-paying adult

valid February to Octber 2003

NOT TO BE USED IN CONJUNCTION WITH ANY OTHER OFFER

READERS' OFFER 2003

Buckinghamshire Railway Centre

Quainton Road Station, Quainton, Aylesbury HP22 4BY
Tel & Fax: 01296 655720
website: www.bucksrailcentre.org.uk

One child FREE with each full paying adult

not valid for for special events

NOT TO BE USED IN CONJUNCTION WITH ANY OTHER OFFER

FHG

READERS' OFFER 2003

Tamar Valley Donkey Park

St Ann's Chapel, Gunnislake, Cornwall PL18 9HW
Tel: 01822 834072
e-mail: info@donkeypark.com • website: www.donkeypark.com

50p OFF per person, up to six persons

valid from Easter until the end of October 2003

NOT TO BE USED IN CONJUNCTION WITH ANY OTHER OFFER

FHG

READERS' OFFER 2003

Cars of the Stars Motor Museum

Standish Street, Keswick, Cumbria CA12 5HH
Tel: 017687 73757
e-mail: cotsmm@aol.com • website: www.carsofthestars.com

One child free with two paying adults

Valid 2003

NOT TO BE USED IN CONJUNCTION WITH ANY OTHER OFFER

A 65-minute journey into the lost world of the English narrow gauge light railway. Features historic steam locomotives from many countries.

PETS MUST BE KEPT UNDER CONTROL AND NOT ALLOWED ON TRACKS

Open: Sundays and Bank Holiday weekends 16 March to 29 October. Additional days in summer.

Directions: On A4146 towards Hemel Hempstead, close to roundabout junction with A505.

FHG PUBLICATIONS, ABBEY MILL BUSINESS CENTRE, PAISLEY PA1 1TJ

Be a giant in a magical miniature world of make-believe depicting rural England in the 1930's. "A little piece of history that is forever England."

Open: 10am to 5pm daily 15th February to 26th October.

Directions: Junction 16 M25, Junction 2 M40.

FHG PUBLICATIONS, ABBEY MILL BUSINESS CENTRE, PAISLEY PA1 1TJ

A working steam railway centre. Steam train rides, miniature railway rides, large collection of historic preserved steam locomotives, carriages and wagons.

Open: Sundays and Bank Holidays April to October, plus Wednesdays in June, July and August 10.30am to 5.30pm.

Directions: off A41 Aylesbury to Bicester Road, 6 miles north west of Aylesbury.

FHG PUBLICATIONS, ABBEY MILL BUSINESS CENTRE, PAISLEY PA1 1TJ

Cornwall's only Donkey Sanctuary set in 14 acres overlooking the beautiful Tamar Valley. Donkey rides, rabbit warren, goat hill, children's playgrounds, cafe and picnic area.

Open: Easter to end of October and February half-term - daily from 10am to 5.30pm. November to March open weekends. Closed January.

Directions: Just off A390 between Callington and Gunnislake at St Ann's Chapel.

FHG PUBLICATIONS, ABBEY MILL BUSINESS CENTRE, PAISLEY PA1 1TJ

A collection of cars from film and TV, including Chitty Chitty Bang Bang, James Bond cars, Del Boy's van, Fab1 and many more.

PETS MUST BE KEPT ON LEAD

Open: Daily 10am-5pm. Closed February half term. Weekends only in December.

Directions: In centre of Keswick close to car park.

FHG PUBLICATIONS, ABBEY MILL BUSINESS CENTRE, PAISLEY PA1 1TJ

FHG READERS' OFFER 2003

Eskdale Historic Water Mill

Mill Cottage, Boot, Eskdale, Cumbria CA19 1TG

Tel: 019467 23335 • website: www.eskdale.com

e-mail: eskdalemill@supanet.com

Two children FREE with two adults

valid during 2003

NOT TO BE USED IN CONJUNCTION WITH ANY OTHER OFFER

FHG READERS' OFFER 2003

Windermere Steamboat Museum

Rayrigg Road, Windermere, Cumbria LA23 1BN

Tel: 015394 45565 • website: www.steamboat.co.uk

Two for the price of one (adults) OR 25% off family ticket

valid March to October 2003

NOT TO BE USED IN CONJUNCTION WITH ANY OTHER OFFER

FHG READERS' OFFER 2003

Blue-John Cavern

Castleton, Hope Valley, Derbyshire S30 2WP

Tel: 01433 620642 • website: www.bluejohn.gemsoft.co.uk

One child free with every paying adult

Valid until end 2003

NOT TO BE USED IN CONJUNCTION WITH ANY OTHER OFFER

FHG READERS' OFFER 2003

Crich Tramway Village

Crich, Matlock, Derbyshire DE4 5DP

Tel: 0870 7587267 • Fax: 01773 852326

e-mail: info@tramway.co.uk • website: www.tramway.co.uk

One child FREE with every full paying adult

valid during 2003

NOT TO BE USED IN CONJUNCTION WITH ANY OTHER OFFER

FHG READERS' OFFER 2003

Treak Cliff Cavern

HOME OF BLUE JOHN STONE

Castleton, Hope Valley, Derbyshire S33 8WP

Tel: 01433 620571

e-mail: treakcliff@bluejohnstone.com • website: www.bluejohnstone.com

10% discount (not valid on Special Events days)

valid during 2003

NOT TO BE USED IN CONJUNCTION WITH ANY OTHER OFFER

England's oldest working watermill, milling oatmeal daily

DOGS ON LEADS

Open: 11am to 5pm April to September (may be closed Mondays).

Directions: Near inland terminus of Ravenglass & Eskdale Railway or over Hardknott Pass.

FHG PUBLICATIONS, ABBEY MILL BUSINESS CENTRE, PAISLEY PA1 1TJ

World's finest steamboat collection and premier all-weather attraction. Swallows and Amazons exhibition, model boat pond, tea shop, souvenir shop. Free guided tours. Model boat exhibition.

Open: 10am to 5pm 3rd weekend in March to last weekend October.

Directions: on A592 half-a-mile north of Bowness-on-Windermere.

FHG PUBLICATIONS, ABBEY MILL BUSINESS CENTRE, PAISLEY PA1 1TJ

Large range of natural water-worn caverns featuring mining equipment, stalactites and stalagmites, and fine deposits of Blue-John stone, Britain's rarest semi-precious stone.

DOGS MUST BE KEPT ON LEAD

Open: 9.30am to 5.30pm.

Directions: Situated 2 miles west of Castleton; follow brown tourist signs.

FHG PUBLICATIONS, ABBEY MILL BUSINESS CENTRE, PAISLEY PA1 1TJ

A superb family day out in the atmosphere of a bygone era. Explore the recreated period street and fascinating exhibitions. Unlimited tram rides are free with entry. Play areas, shops, tea rooms, pub, restaurant and lots more.

Open: daily April to October 10 am to 5.30pm, weekends in winter.

Directions: Eight miles from M1 Junction 28, follow brown and white signs for "Tramway Museum".

FHG PUBLICATIONS, ABBEY MILL BUSINESS CENTRE, PAISLEY PA1 1TJ

An underground wonderland of stalactites, stalagmites, rocks, minerals and fossils. Home of the unique Blue John stone – see the largest single piece ever found. Suitable for all ages.

Open: Opens 10am. Enquire for last tour of day and closed days.

Directions: Half-a-mile west of Castleton on A6187 (old A625)

FHG PUBLICATIONS, ABBEY MILL BUSINESS CENTRE, PAISLEY PA1 1TJ

READERS' OFFER 2003

Coldharbour Mill Visitor Centre & Museum

Coldharbour Mill, Uffculme, Cullompton, Devon EX15 3EE

Tel: 01884 840960 • e-mail: coldharbour@lineone.net
website: www.coldharbourmill.org.uk

TWO adult tickets for the price of ONE

valid during 2003

NOT TO BE USED IN CONJUNCTION WITH ANY OTHER OFFER

READERS' OFFER 2003

The Gnome Reserve & Wild Flower Garden

West Putford, Near Bradworthy, Devon EX22 7XE

Tel: 01409 241435 • e-mail: info@gnomereserve.co.uk
website: www.gnomereserve.co.uk

One FREE child with full paying adult

Valid during 2003

NOT TO BE USED IN CONJUNCTION WITH ANY OTHER OFFER

READERS' OFFER 2003

Devonshire Collection of Period Costume

Totnes Costume Museum,
Bogan House, 43 High Street, Totnes TQ9 5NP

FREE child with a paying adult with voucher

valid from end of May to end of Sept 2003

NOT TO BE USED IN CONJUNCTION WITH ANY OTHER OFFER

FHG

READERS' OFFER 2003

Killhope Lead Mining Museum

Cowshill, Upper Weardale, Co. Durham DL13 1AR

Tel: 01388 537505

e-mail: killhope@durham.gov.uk • website: www.durham.gov.uk/killhope

One child FREE with full-paying adult (not valid for Park Level Mine)

valid April to October 2003

NOT TO BE USED IN CONJUNCTION WITH ANY OTHER OFFER

READERS' OFFER 2003

Barleylands Farm

Barleylands Road, Billericay, Essex CM11 2UD

Tel: 01268 290229 • e-mail: info@barleylandsfarm.co.uk
website: www.barleylandsfarm.co.uk

FREE adult ticket when accompanied by one child

Valid 1st March to 31st October. Not special event days

NOT TO BE USED IN CONJUNCTION WITH ANY OTHER OFFER

A picturesque 200-year old woollen mill with machinery that spins yarn and weaves cloth. Mill machinery, restaurant, shop and gardens in a waterside setting and the largest stiched embroidery in the world.

Open: March to December daily 10.30am to 5pm.

Directions: Two miles from Junction 27 M5; follow signs to Willand (B3181) then brown tourist signs to Museum

FHG PUBLICATIONS, ABBEY MILL BUSINESS CENTRE, PAISLEY PA1 1TJ

Visit 1000+ gnomes and pixies in two acre beech wood. Gnome hats are loaned free of charge - so the gnomes think you are one of them - don't forget your camera! Also 2-acre wild flower garden with 250 labelled species.

Open: Daily 10am to 6pm 21st March to 31st October.

Directions: Between Bideford and Bude; follow brown tourist signs from A39/A388/A386.

FHG PUBLICATIONS, ABBEY MILL BUSINESS CENTRE, PAISLEY PA1 1TJ

Themed exhibition, changed annually, based in a Tudor house. Collection contains items of dress for women, men and children from 17th century to 1980s, from high fashion to everyday wear.

Open: Open from May 27th to end of September. 11am to 5pm Monday to Friday.

Directions: Centre of town, opposite Market Square. Mini bus up High Street stops outside.

FHG PUBLICATIONS, ABBEY MILL BUSINESS CENTRE, PAISLEY PA1 1TJ

Britain's best preserved lead mining site – and a great day out for all the family, with lots to see and do. Underground Experience – Park Level Mine now open.

Open: April 1st to September 30th 10.30am to 5pm daily. Weekends and half term in October

Directions: Alongside A689, midway between Stanhope and Alston in the heart of the North Pennines.

FHG PUBLICATIONS, ABBEY MILL BUSINESS CENTRE, PAISLEY PA1 1TJ

Farm Centre with animals, museum, blacksmith, glassblowing, miniature railway (Sundays and August), craft shops, tea room and licensed restaurant.

DOGS MUST BE KEPT ON LEAD

Open: 1st March to 31st October.

Directions: M25, A127 towards Southend. Take A176 junction off A127, 3rd exit Wash Road, 2nd left Barleylands Road.

FHG PUBLICATIONS, ABBEY MILL BUSINESS CENTRE, PAISLEY PA1 1TJ

FHG READERS' OFFER 2003

Cider Museum and King Offa Distillery

21 Ryelands Street, Hereford HR4 0LW

Tel: 01432 354207 • Fax: 01432 371641

e-mail: info@cidermuseum.co.uk • website: www.cidermuseum.co.uk

50p reduction on entry fee

valid during 2003

NOT TO BE USED IN CONJUNCTION WITH ANY OTHER OFFER

FHG READERS' OFFER 2003

Verulamium Museum

St Michael's, St Albans, Herts AL3 4SW

Tel: 01727 751810

e-mail: a.coles@stalbans.gov.uk • website: www.stalbansmuseums.org.uk

"Two for One"

valid from 1/8/03 until 31/12/03

NOT TO BE USED IN CONJUNCTION WITH ANY OTHER OFFER

FHG READERS' OFFER 2003

Museum of Kent Life

Lock Lane, Sandling, Maidstone ME14 3AU

Tel: 01622 763936 • Fax: 01622 662024

e-mail: enquiries@museum-kentlife.co.uk • website: www.museum-kentlife.co.uk

Two tickets for the price of one (cheapest ticket FREE)

valid from March to November 2003

NOT TO BE USED IN CONJUNCTION WITH ANY OTHER OFFER

FHG READERS' OFFER 2003

Docker Park Farm

Arkholme, Carnforth, Lancashire LA6 1AR

Tel & Fax: 015242 21331

e-mail: lindsay.abbott@dockerparkfarm.fsnet.co.uk

website: www.dockerparkfarm.co.uk

One FREE child per one paying adult (one voucher per child)

valid from January to December 2003

NOT TO BE USED IN CONJUNCTION WITH ANY OTHER OFFER

FHG READERS' OFFER 2003

DONINGTON GRAND PRIX COLLECTION

DONINGTON PARK

Castle Donington, Near Derby, Leics DE74 2RP

Tel: 01332 811027 • e-mail: enquiries@donington.co.uk

website: www.doningtoncollection.com

One child FREE with each full-paying adult

valid until 01/01/04

NOT TO BE USED IN CONJUNCTION WITH ANY OTHER OFFER

Discover the fascinating history of cider making. There is a programme of temporary exhibitions and events plus free samples of Hereford cider brandy.

Open: April to Oct
10am to 5.30pm (daily)
Nov to Dec 11pm to 3pm (daily)
Jan to Mar 11am to 3pm (Tues to Sun)
Directions: situated west of Hereford off the A438
Hereford to Brecon road.

FHG PUBLICATIONS, ABBEY MILL BUSINESS CENTRE, PAISLEY PA1 1TJ

The museum of everyday life in Roman Britain. An award-winning museum with re-created Roman rooms, hands-on discovery areas, and some of the best mosaics outside the Mediterranean.

Open: Monday to Saturday
10am-5.30pm
Sunday 2pm-5.30pm.

Directions: St Albans.

FHG PUBLICATIONS, ABBEY MILL BUSINESS CENTRE, PAISLEY PA1 1TJ

Kent's award-winning open air museum is home to a collection of historic buildings which house interactive exhibitions on life over the last 150 years.

Open: Seven days a week from March to November.
10am to 5.30pm.

Directions: Junction 6 off M20, follow signs to Aylesford.

FHG PUBLICATIONS, ABBEY MILL BUSINESS CENTRE, PAISLEY PA1 1TJ

We are a working farm, with lots of animals to see and touch. Enjoy a walk round the Nature Trail or refreshments in the tearoom. Lots of activities during school holidays.

Open: Summer: daily
10.30am to 5pm
Winter: daily except Tuesdays
10.30am to 4pm.
Directions: Junction 35 off M6, take B6254 towards Kirkby Lonsdale, then follow the brown signs.

FHG PUBLICATIONS, ABBEY MILL BUSINESS CENTRE, PAISLEY PA1 1TJ

The world's largest collection of Grand Prix racing cars – over 130 exhibits within five halls, including McLaren Formula One cars.

Open: Daily 10am to 5pm
(last admission 4pm).
Closed Christmas/New Year.

Directions: 2 miles from M1 (J23a/24) and M42/A42; to north-west via A50.

FHG PUBLICATIONS, ABBEY MILL BUSINESS CENTRE, PAISLEY PA1 1TJ

FHG READERS' OFFER 2003

Snibston Discovery Park

Ashby Road, Coalville, Leicestershire LE67 3LN

Tel: 01530 278444 • Fax: 01530 813301

e-mail: snibston@leics.gov.uk • website: www.leics.gov.uk/museums

One FREE child with every full paying adult

valid until June 2003

NOT TO BE USED IN CONJUNCTION WITH ANY OTHER OFFER

FHG READERS' OFFER 2003

Butterfly & Wildlife Park

Long Sutton, Spalding, Lincs PE12 9LE

Tel: 01406 363833

e-mail: butterflypark@hotmail.com • website: www.butterflyandwildlifepark.co.uk

One FREE child with one full-paying adult

valid April to October 2003 (Not Bank Holiday weekends)

NOT TO BE USED IN CONJUNCTION WITH ANY OTHER OFFER

FHG READERS' OFFER 2003

Skegness Natureland Seal Sanctuary

North Parade, Skegness, Lincolnshire PE25 1DB

Tel: 01754 764345

e-mail: natureland@fsbdial.co.uk • website: www.skegnessnatureland.co.uk

Free entry for one child when accompanied by full-paying adult.

Valid during 2003

NOT TO BE USED IN CONJUNCTION WITH ANY OTHER OFFER

FHG READERS' OFFER 2003

PLEASURELAND

Marine Drive, Southport, Merseyside PR8 1RX

Tel: 08702 200204 • Fax: 01704 537936

e-mail: mail@pleasurelandltd.freeserve.co.uk • website: www.pleasureland.uk.com

3 for 2, if two all day wristbands purchased, third provided FREE
• offer not valid on Bank Holiday Weekends

valid from March to November 2003

NOT TO BE USED IN CONJUNCTION WITH ANY OTHER OFFER

FHG READERS' OFFER 2003

Southport Zoo and Conservation Trust

Princes Park, Southport, Merseyside PR8 1RX

Tel: 01704 548894 • Tel & Fax: 01704 538102

e-mail: info@southportzoo.co.uk • website: www.southportzoo.co.uk

FREE Zoo Pack per family

valid during 2003 except Bank Holidays

NOT TO BE USED IN CONJUNCTION WITH ANY OTHER OFFER

Located in 100 acres of landscaped grounds, Snibston is a unique mixture, with historic mine buildings, outdoor science play areas, wildlife habitats and an exhibition hall housing five hands-on galleries. Cafe and gift shop.

Open: Seven days a week 10am to 5pm.

Directions: Junction 22 from M1, Junction 13 from M42. Follow Brown Heritage signs.

FHG PUBLICATIONS, ABBEY MILL BUSINESS CENTRE, PAISLEY PA1 1TJ

Large wildlife park with Reptile Land, Tropical House, Insectarium, Birds of Prey Centre, farm animals, wallaby enclosure, llamas; adventure playground, tea room and gift shop.

Open: Daily from 10am April to 28th October 2003

Directions: Off A17 at Long Sutton.

FHG PUBLICATIONS, ABBEY MILL BUSINESS CENTRE, PAISLEY PA1 1TJ

Well known for rescuing and rehabilitating orphaned and injured seal pups found washed ashore on Lincolnshire beaches. Also: penguins, aquarium, pets' corner, reptiles, Floral Palace (tropical birds and butterflies etc).

Open: Daily from 10am. Closed Christmas/Boxing/New Year's Days.

Directions: At the north end of Skegness seafront.

FHG PUBLICATIONS, ABBEY MILL BUSINESS CENTRE, PAISLEY PA1 1TJ

Over 100 rides and attractions, including the Traumatizer - the UK's tallest, fastest suspended looping coaster and the new Lucozade Space Shot.

Open: March to November, times vary.

FHG PUBLICATIONS, ABBEY MILL BUSINESS CENTRE, PAISLEY PA1 1TJ

Lions, snow leopards, chimpanzees, otters, reptiles, aquarium and lots more, set amidst landscaped gardens. Gift shop, cafe and picnic areas.

Open: all year round from 10am

Directions: on the coast 16 miles north of Liverpool; follow the brown and white tourist signs

FHG PUBLICATIONS, ABBEY MILL BUSINESS CENTRE, PAISLEY PA1 1TJ

FHG READERS' OFFER 2003

Sacrewell Farm & Country Centre

Sacrewell, Thornhaugh, Peterborough PE8 6HJ

Tel & Fax: 01780 782254

e-mail: wsatrust@supanet.com • website: www.sacrewell.org.uk

One child FREE with one full paying adult

valid from March 1st to October 1st 2003

NOT TO BE USED IN CONJUNCTION WITH ANY OTHER OFFER

FHG READERS' OFFER 2003

Chesters Walled Garden

Chollerford, Hexham NE46 4BQ

Tel: 01434 681483

website: www.chesterswalledgarden.co.uk

One FREE adult with one paying adult

valid Easter to end of August 2003

NOT TO BE USED IN CONJUNCTION WITH ANY OTHER OFFER

FHG READERS' OFFER 2003

The New Metroland

39 Garden Walk, Metrocentre, Gateshead NE11 9XY

Tel: 0191 4932048 • Fax: 0191 4932904

e-mail: enquiries@metroland.uk.com• website: www.metroland.uk.com

TWO all day unlimited ride passes for the price of ONE

valid until 31/12/03 except Bank Holiday Weekends

NOT TO BE USED IN CONJUNCTION WITH ANY OTHER OFFER

FHG READERS' OFFER 2003

The Caves of Nottingham

Drury Walk, Broadmarsh Centre, Nottingham NG1 7LS

Tel: 0115 924 1424 • e-mail: info@cavesofnottingham.co.uk

One child free when accompanied by two full paying adults

Valid during 2003 except Bank Holidays and August.

NOT TO BE USED IN CONJUNCTION WITH ANY OTHER OFFER

FHG READERS' OFFER 2003

Galleries of Justice

Shire Hall, High Pavement, Lace Market, Nottingham NG1 1HN

Tel: 0115 9520555 • Fax: 0115 9939828

e-mail: info@galleriesofjustice.org.uk • website: www.galleries of justice.org.uk

TWO for ONE with full paying adult one free visit per voucher

Valid from Jan to Dec 2003, not Bank Holidays

NOT TO BE USED IN CONJUNCTION WITH ANY OTHER OFFER

Farm animals, 18th century watermill and farmhouse, farm artifacts, caravan and camping, children's play area. Restaurant and gift shop.

Open: all year 9.30am to 5pm.

Directions: signposted off both A47 and A1.

FHG PUBLICATIONS, ABBEY MILL BUSINESS CENTRE, PAISLEY PA1 1TJ

Beautiful walled garden with famous collections of herbs and herbaceous plants, including Roman Garden, National Thyme and Marjoram Collections. There is also a woodland walk. Gift shop.

Open: From Easter to the end of October 10am to 5pm daily.

Directions: Six miles north of Hexham off B6318 next to Chesters Roman Fort.

FHG PUBLICATIONS, ABBEY MILL BUSINESS CENTRE,PAISLEY PA1 1TJ

Europe's largest indoor family funfair, with exciting rides like the new rollercoaster, disco dodgems and swashbuckling pirate ship. There's something for everyone whatever the weather!

Open: Open daily except Christmas Day. 10am to 8pm Monday to Saturday, 11am to 6pm Sunday. (Open from 12 noon Monday to Friday during term time).

Directions: Signposted from the A1

FHG PUBLICATIONS, ABBEY MILL BUSINESS CENTRE, PAISLEY PA1 1TJ

750-year old man-made cave system beneath a modern day shopping centre. Discover how the caves were used with a unique 40-minute audio tour.

Open: Daily Mon-Sat 10am to 4.15pm, Sundays 11am to 4pm

Directions: In Nottingham city centre, inside Broadmarsh Shopping Centre on upper level

FHG PUBLICATIONS, ABBEY MILL BUSINESS CENTRE, PAISLEY PA1 1TJ

Journey with us through 300 years of Crime and Punishment on this unique atmospheric site. Witness a real trial in the authentic Victorian courtroom. Prisoners and gaolers act as guides as you becomepart of history.

Open: Tuesday to Sunday 10am to 5pm peak season 10am to 4pm off-peak.

Directions: from Nottingham city centre follow the brown tourist signs.

FHG PUBLICATIONS, ABBEY MILL BUSINESS CENTRE, PAISLEY PA1 1TJ

FHG READERS' OFFER 2003

Newark Air Museum

The Airfield, Winthorpe, Newark, Nottinghamshire NG24 2NY

Tel: 01636 707170

e-mail: newarkair@lineone.net • website: www.newarkairmuseum.co.uk

Party rate discount for every voucher (50p per person off normal admission).

Valid during 2003

NOT TO BE USED IN CONJUNCTION WITH ANY OTHER OFFER

FHG READERS' OFFER 2003

The White Post Modern Farm Centre

Farnsfield, Nottingham NG22 8HL

Tel: 01623 882977 • e-mail: tim@whitepostfarmcentre.co.uk

Fax: 01623 883499 • website: www.whitepostfarmcentre.co.uk

10% off entry to the farm with voucher

valid during 2003

NOT TO BE USED IN CONJUNCTION WITH ANY OTHER OFFER

FHG READERS' OFFER 2003

The Tales of Robin Hood

30 - 38 Maid Marion Way, Nottingham NG1 6GF

Tel: 0115 9483284 • Fax: 0115 9501536

e-mail: robinhoodcentre@mail.com • website: www.robinhood.uk.com

One FREE child with full paying adult per voucher

valid from January to December 2003

NOT TO BE USED IN CONJUNCTION WITH ANY OTHER OFFER

FHG

READERS' OFFER 2003

Cogges Manor Farm Museum

Church Lane, Witney, Oxfordshire OX28 3LA

Tel: 01993 772602

Two for the price of one

Valid April to end of November 2003

NOT TO BE USED IN CONJUNCTION WITH ANY OTHER OFFER

FHG READERS' OFFER 2003

Avon Valley Railway

Bitton Station, Bath Road, Bitton, Bristol, BS30 6HD

Tel: 0117 932 5538

e-mail: enquiries@avonvalleyrailway.co.uk • website: www.avonvalleyrailway.co.uk

Up to two FREE child tickets with every fare-paying adult
(Not valid for "Day out with Thomas Events")

valid from May to September 2003

NOT TO BE USED IN CONJUNCTION WITH ANY OTHER OFFER

A collection of 61 aircraft and cockpit sections from across the history of aviation. Extensive aero engine and artefact displays.

Open: Daily from 10am (closed Christmas period).

Directions: Follow brown and white signs from A1, A46, A17 and A1133.

FHG PUBLICATIONS, ABBEY MILL BUSINESS CENTRE, PAISLEY PA1 1TJ

A modern working farm with displays indoors and outdoors designed to help visitors listen, feel and learn whilst having fun. Daily baby animal holding sessions plus a large indoor play barn.

Open: Daily 10am to 5pm.

Directions: 12 miles from Nottingham on A614 or follow Robin Hood signs from J27 of M1.

FHG PUBLICATIONS, ABBEY MILL BUSINESS CENTRE, PAISLEY PA1 1TJ

Travel back in time to the dark and romantic world of intrigue and adventure of Medieval England's most endearing outlaw - Robin Hood. Story boards, exhibitions and a film show all add interest to the story.

Open: 10am -6pm, last admission 4.30pm.

Directions: Follow the brown and white tourist information signs whilst heading towards the city centre.

FHG PUBLICATIONS, ABBEY MILL BUSINESS CENTRE, PAISLEY PA1 1TJ

Historic manor house and farm with traditional animals. Baking in the Victorian kitchen every afternoon.

Open: April to 2nd December: Tuesday to Friday 10.30am to 5.30pm. Saturday and Sunday 12-5.30pm.

Directions: Just off A40 Oxford to Cheltenham road at Witney.

FHG PUBLICATIONS, ABBEY MILL BUSINESS CENTRE, PAISLEY PA1 1TJ

The Avon Valley Railway offers a whole new experience for some, and a nostalgic memory for others. Steam trains operate every Sunday May to September, plus Bank Holidays and Christmas.

PETS MUST BE KEPT ON LEADS AND OFF TRAIN SEATS

Open: Steam trains operate every Sunday May to Sept plus Bank Holidays and Christmas

Directions: On the A431 midway between Bristol and Bath at Bitton

FHG PUBLICATIONS, ABBEY MILL BUSINESS CENTRE, PAISLEY PA1 1TJ

FHG READERS' OFFER 2003

The Helicopter Museum

The Heliport, Locking Moor Road, Weston-Super-Mare BS24 8PP

Tel: 01934 635227 • Fax: 01934 645230

e-mail: office@helimuseum.fsnet.co.uk • website: www.helicoptermuseum.co.uk

One child FREE with each full-paying adult

valid from April to October 2003

NOT TO BE USED IN CONJUNCTION WITH ANY OTHER OFFER

FHG READERS' OFFER 2003

Wookey Hole Caves & Papermill

Wookey Hole, Wells, Somerset BA5 1BB

Tel: 01749 672243

e-mail: witch@wookey.co.uk • website: www.wookey.co.uk

£1 per person OFF full admission price (up to max. 5 persons)

valid during 2003

NOT TO BE USED IN CONJUNCTION WITH ANY OTHER OFFER

FHG READERS' OFFER 2003

Royal Doulton Visitor Centre

Nile Street, Burslem, Stoke-on-Trent, Staffs ST6 2AJ

Tel: 01782 292434 • Fax: 01782 292424

e-mail: visitor@royal-doulton.com • website: www.royal-doulton.com

Two admissions for the price of one – does not apply to factory tours

valid during 2003

NOT TO BE USED IN CONJUNCTION WITH ANY OTHER OFFER

FHG READERS' OFFER 2003

Easton Farm Park

Easton, Near Wickham Market, Ipswich, Suffolk IP13 0EQ

Tel: 01728 746475 • e-mail: easton@eastonfarmpark.co.uk

website: www.eastonfarmpark.co.uk

£1 per person off for up to 4 full paying admissions

Valid until end 2003

NOT TO BE USED IN CONJUNCTION WITH ANY OTHER OFFER

FHG READERS' OFFER 2003

New Pleasurewood Hills

Leisure Way, Corton, Lowestoft, Suffolk NR32 5DZ

Tel: 01502 508200 • Fax: 01603 567393

e-mail: info@pleasurewoodhills.com • website: www.pleasurewoodhills.com

'3 for 2' One FREE adult/child with two full paying adults

valid during 2003, except special events and at Christmas

NOT TO BE USED IN CONJUNCTION WITH ANY OTHER OFFER

The world's largest helicopter collection - over 60 exhibits, includes two royal helicopters, Russian Gunship and Vietnam veterans plus many award-winning exhibits. Cafe, shop. Flights.

PETS MUST BE KEPT UNDER CONTROL

Open: Wednesday to Sunday 10am to 6pm. Daily during school and public holidays. (10am to 4pm November to March)

Directions: Junction 21 off M5 then follow the propellor signs.

FHG PUBLICATIONS, ABBEY MILL BUSINESS CENTRE, PAISLEY PA1 1TJ

** Britain's most spectacular caves*
** Traditional paper-making*
** Penny Arcade*
** Magical Mirror Maze **

Open: Summer 10am to 5pm last tour; Winter 10.30am to 4.30pm last tour. Closed 17-25 Dec.

Directions: From M5 J22 follow brown-and-white signs via A38 and A371. Two miles from Wells.

FHG PUBLICATIONS, ABBEY MILL BUSINESS CENTRE, PAISLEY PA1 1TJ

Extensive displays of Royal Doulton products both past and present including figures, giftware, tableware and crystal. Live demonstrations, museum area, restaurant and shop. Factory Tours by prior booking weekdays only.

Open: Monday to Saturday 9.30am to 5pm; Sundays 10.30am to 4.30pm Closed Christmas/New Year period.

Directions: From M6 Junction 15/16; follow A500 to exit for A527. Follow signs for about one mile.

FHG PUBLICATIONS, ABBEY MILL BUSINESS CENTRE, PAISLEY PA1 1TJ

Lots of baby animals. FREE pony rides, face painting, green trail, 'pat-a-pet', indoor children's soft play area; gift shop, tearoom, pets' paddocks

DOGS MUST BE KEPT ON LEADS

Open: March to October 10.30am to 6pm

Directions: Follow brown tourist signs off A12 and other roads

FHG PUBLICATIONS, ABBEY MILL BUSINESS CENTRE, PAISLEY PA1 1TJ

With over forty rides, shows and attractions set in fifty acres of parkland - you'll have everything you need for a brilliant day out. The mixture of old favourites and exciting new introductions are an unbeatable combination.

Open: From 10am. Closing time varies depending on season.

Directions: Off A12 between Great Yarmouth and Lowestoft.

FHG PUBLICATIONS, ABBEY MILL BUSINESS CENTRE, PAISLEY PA1 1TJ

FHG READERS' OFFER 2003

Buckley's Yesterday's World

High Street, Battle, East Sussex TN33 0AQ

Tel: 01424 775378 e-mail: info@yesterdaysworld.co.uk

website: www.yesterdaysworld.co.uk

50p off each admission

Valid until end 2003

NOT TO BE USED IN CONJUNCTION WITH ANY OTHER OFFER

FHG READERS' OFFER 2003

PARADISE PARK & GARDENS

Avis Road, Newhaven, East Sussex BN9 0DH

Tel: 01273 512123 • Fax: 01273 616000

e-mail: enquiries@paradisepark.co.uk • website: www.paradisepark.co.uk

Admit one FREE adult or child with one adult paying full entrance price

valid during 2003

NOT TO BE USED IN CONJUNCTION WITH ANY OTHER OFFER

FHG READERS' OFFER 2003

Wilderness Wood

Hadlow Down, Near Uckfield, East Sussex TN22 4HJ

Tel: 01825 830509• Fax: 01825 830977

e-mail: enquiries@wildernesswood.co.uk • website: www.wildernesswood.co.uk

TWO for the price of ONE

valid during 2003

NOT TO BE USED IN CONJUNCTION WITH ANY OTHER OFFER

FHG READERS' OFFER 2003

Wildfowl & Wetlands Trust

District 15, Washington, Tyne & Wear NE38 8LE

Tel: 0191 416 5454

e-mail: wetlands@euphony.net • website: www.wwt.org.uk

One FREE admission with full-paying adult

valid from 1st Jan 2003 to 30th Sep 2003

NOT TO BE USED IN CONJUNCTION WITH ANY OTHER OFFER

FHG READERS' OFFER 2003

The Shire Horse Centre

Clifford Road, Stratford-Upon-Avon CV37 8HW

Tel: 01789 2415274

e-mail: shire.horse@virgin.net • website: www.shirehorsecentre.co.uk

£1 per person off entry with voucher

valid during 2003

NOT TO BE USED IN CONJUNCTION WITH ANY OTHER OFFER

The past is brought to life at the top attraction in the South East 2002 (England for Excellence Awards). Step back in time and wonder through over 30 shop and room settings.

PETS NOT ALLOWED IN CHILDREN'S PLAY AREA

Open: 9.30am to 6pm (last admission 4.45pm, one hour earlier in winter).

Directions: Just off A21 in Battle High Street opposite the Abbey.

FHG PUBLICATIONS, ABBEY MILL BUSINESS CENTRE, PAISLEY PA1 1TJ

A plant lover's paradise with outstanding themed gardens and extensive Museum of Natural History. Conservatory gardens contain a large and varied collection of the world's flora. Sussex History Trail. Dinosaur Museum. Rides and amusements.

Open: Open daily, except Christmas Day and Boxing Day.

Directions: Signposted off A26 and A259.

FHG PUBLICATIONS, ABBEY MILL BUSINESS CENTRE, PAISLEY PA1 1TJ

Wilderness Wood is a unique family-run working woodland in the Sussex High Weald. Explore trails and footpaths, enjoy local cakes and ices, try the adventure playground. Many special events and activities. Parties catered for.

Open: daily 10am to 5.30pm or dusk if earlier.

Directions: On the south side of the A272 in the village of Hadlow Down. Signposted with a brown tourist sign.

FHG PUBLICATIONS, ABBEY MILL BUSINESS CENTRE, PAISLEY PA1 1TJ

100 acres of parkland, home to hundreds of duck, geese, swans and flamingos. Discovery centre, cafe, gift shop; play area.

Open: Every day except Christmas Day

Directions: Signposted from A19, A195, A1231 and A182.

FHG PUBLICATIONS, ABBEY MILL BUSINESS CENTRE, PAISLEY PA1 1TJ

Shire horses and rare breeds, country village exhibition, indoor and outdoor playground, snackbar and gift shop, tours or parades at 11.15am and 2pm.

DOGS MUST BE KEPT ON LEADS AT ALL TIMES

Open: Easter to Early Sept
10am to 5pm
Saturday to Wednesday, except school holidays when open every day.

FHG PUBLICATIONS, ABBEY MILL BUSINESS CENTRE, PAISLEY PA1 1TJ

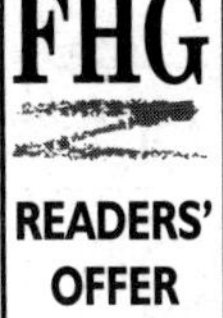

FHG READERS' OFFER 2003

Cholderton Rare Breeds Farm Park

Aylesbury Road, Cholderton, Wiltshire SP4 0EW

Tel: 01980 629438

e-mail: sales@rabbitworld.co.uk • website: www.choldertonfarm.co.uk

One person FREE with two paying adults
(not valid on Public Holidays or weekends during July and August)

valid June to November 3rd 2003

NOT TO BE USED IN CONJUNCTION WITH ANY OTHER OFFER

FHG READERS' OFFER 2003

Avoncroft Museum

Stoke Heath, Bromsgrove, Worcestershire B60 4JR

Tel: 01527 831363 • Fax: 01527 876934

e-mail: avoncroft1@compuserve.com • website: www.avoncroft.com

One FREE child with one full paying adult

valid from March to November 2003

NOT TO BE USED IN CONJUNCTION WITH ANY OTHER OFFER

FHG READERS' OFFER 2003

Museum of Rail Travel

Ingrow Railway Centre, Near Keighley, West Yorkshire BD22 8NJ

Tel: 01535 680425

e-mail: admin@vintagecarriagestrust.org • website: www.vintagecarriagestrust.org

"ONE for ONE" free admission

Valid during 2003 except during special events (ring to check)

NOT TO BE USED IN CONJUNCTION WITH ANY OTHER OFFER

FHG READERS' OFFER 2003

The Grassic Gibbon Centre

Arbuthnott, Laurencekirk, Aberdeenshire AB30 1PB

Tel: 01561 361668 • e-mail: lgginfo@grassicgibbon.com
website: www.grassicgibbon.com

TWO for the price of ONE entry to exhibition (based on full adult rate only)

Valid during 2003 (not groups)

NOT TO BE USED IN CONJUNCTION WITH ANY OTHER OFFER

FHG READERS' OFFER 2003

Argyll Wildlife Park

By Inveraray, Argyll PA32 8XT

Tel: 01499 302264 • website: www.argyllwildlifepark.co.uk
e-mail: animals@argyllwildlifepark.co.uk

One child (3-16) with 2 full paying adults

Valid Easter to 31/10/2003

NOT TO BE USED IN CONJUNCTION WITH ANY OTHER OFFER

Lovely rural farm with 50 breeds of rabbit, and several breeds of poultry, pig, sheep, goat, horses and ponies. Cafe, craft shop, events throughout holidays, famous pig races, nature trail, indoor and outdoor play.

Open: 10.30am to 6pm in season, weekends 10am to 4pm in winter.

Directions: Near Stonehenge, just off the A303 at the intersection with A338 Salisbury/Swindon Road.

FHG PUBLICATIONS, ABBEY MILL BUSINESS CENTRE, PAISLEY PA1 1TJ

A fascinating world of historic buildings covering seven centuries, rescued and rebuilt on an open-air site in the heart of the Worcestershire countryside.

Directions: A38 south of Bromsgrove, near Junction 1 of M42, Junction 5 of M5.

FHG PUBLICATIONS, ABBEY MILL BUSINESS CENTRE, PAISLEY PA1 1TJ

A fascinating display of railway carriages and a wide range of railway items telling the story of rail travel over the years.

ALL PETS MUST BE KEPT ON LEADS

Open: Daily 11am to 4.30pm

Directions: Approximately one mile from Keighley on A629 Halifax road. Follow brown tourist signs

FHG PUBLICATIONS, ABBEY MILL BUSINESS CENTRE, PAISLEY PA1 1TJ

Visitor centre dedicated to the much-loved Scottish writer Lewis Grassic Gibbon. Exhibition, cafe, gift shop. Outdoor children's play area. Disabled access throughout.

Open: Daily April to October 10am to 4.30pm. Groups by appointment including evenings.

Directions: On the B967, accessible and signposted from both A90 and A92.

FHG PUBLICATIONS, ABBEY MILL BUSINESS CENTRE, PAISLEY PA1 1TJ

45-acre natural wildlife park, with nature trails. On view are fallow deer, raccoons, wallabies, Scottish wild cats, foxes, monkeys, birds of prey, deer and much more. Small cafe and gift shop.

Open: Easter weekend to October 31st. Open 10am, last admission 5pm.

Directions: A82 Glasgow-Tarbet, then A83 Campbeltown. One mile south of Inveraray village.

FHG PUBLICATIONS, ABBEY MILL BUSINESS CENTRE, PAISLEY PA1 1TJ

FHG READERS' OFFER 2003

Oban Rare Breeds Farm Park

Glencruitten, Oban, Argyll PA34 4QB

Tel: 01631 770608

e-mail: info@obanrarebreeds.com • website: www.obanrarebreeds.com

10% DISCOUNT on all admissions

valid during 2003

NOT TO BE USED IN CONJUNCTION WITH ANY OTHER OFFER

FHG READERS' OFFER 2003

Dunaskin Heritage Centre

Waterside, Patna, Ayrshire KA6 7JF

Tel: 01292 531144

e-mail: dunaskin@btconnect.com • website: www.dunaskin.org.uk

TWO for the price of ONE

valid from 1st May to 31st October 2003

NOT TO BE USED IN CONJUNCTION WITH ANY OTHER OFFER

FHG READERS' OFFER 2003

Kelburn Castle & Country Centre

Fairlie, Near Largs, Ayrshire KA29 0BE

Tel: 01475 568685 • e-mail: info@kelburncountrycentre.com
website: www.kelburncountrycentre.com

One child FREE for each full paying adult

Valid until October 2003

NOT TO BE USED IN CONJUNCTION WITH ANY OTHER OFFER

FHG READERS' OFFER 2003

Scottish Maritime Museum

Harbourside, Irvine KA12 8QE

Tel: 01294 278283 • e-mail: smm@tildesley.fsbusiness.co.uk
website: www.scottishmaritimemuseum.org • Fax: 01294 313211

TWO for the price of ONE

Valid from January to December 2003

NOT TO BE USED IN CONJUNCTION WITH ANY OTHER OFFER

FHG READERS' OFFER 2003

CREETOWN GEM ROCK MUSEUM

Chain Road, Creetown, Near Newton Stewart, Kirkcudbrightshire DG8 7HJ

Tel: 01671 820357 • e-mail: gem.rock@btinternet.com
website: www.gemrock.net

10% off admission prices

valid during 2003

NOT TO BE USED IN CONJUNCTION WITH ANY OTHER OFFER

Rare breeds of farm animals, pets' corner, conservation groups, tea room, woodland walk in beautiful location

Open: 10am to 6pm mid-March to end October

Directions: two-and-a-half miles from Oban along Glencruitten road

FHG PUBLICATIONS, ABBEY MILL BUSINESS CENTRE, PAISLEY PA1 1TJ

Set in the rolling hills of Ayrshire, Europe's best preserved ironworks. Guided tours, audio-visuals, walks with electronic wands. Restaurant/coffee shop.

Open: April to October daily 10am to 5pm.

Directions: A713 Ayr to Castle Douglas road, 12 miles from Ayr, 3 miles from Dalmellington.

FHG PUBLICATIONS, ABBEY MILL BUSINESS CENTRE, PAISLEY PA1 1TJ

The historic home of the Earls of Glasgow. Waterfalls, gardens, famous Glen, unusual trees. Riding school, Falconry Centre stockade, play areas, exhibitions, shop, cafe and The Secret Forest.

PETS MUST BE KEPT ON LEAD

Open: daily 10am to 6pm Easter to October.

Directions: On A78 between Largs and Fairlie, 45 mins drive from Glasgow.

FHG PUBLICATIONS, ABBEY MILL BUSINESS CENTRE, PAISLEY PA1 1TJ

Scotland's seafaring heritage is among the world's richest and you can relive the heyday of Scottish shipping at the Maritime Museum.

Open: all year except Christmas and New Year Holidays. 10am - 5pm

Directions: Situated on Irvine harbourside and only a 10 minute walk from Irvine train station.

FHG PUBLICATIONS, ABBEY MILL BUSINESS CENTRE, PAISLEY PA1 1TJ

Worldwide collection of gems, minerals, crystals and fossils
•Erupting Volcano•Audio Visual•
•Crystal Cave•Unique Giftshop•
•Relax in our themed tea room•
•Internet Cafe

Open: Open daily Easter to 30th November; December to February – weekends only.

Directions: 7 miles from Newton Stewart, 11 miles from Gatehouse of Fleet; just off A75 Carlisle to Stranraer road.

FHG PUBLICATIONS, ABBEY MILL BUSINESS CENTRE, PAISLEY PA1 1TJ

FHG READERS' OFFER 2003

Almond Valley Heritage Centre

Millfield, Livingston, West Lothian EH54 7AR

Tel: 01506 414957

e-mail: info@almondvalley.co.uk • website: www.almondvalley.co.uk

Free child with adult paying full admission

Valid during 2003

NOT TO BE USED IN CONJUNCTION WITH ANY OTHER OFFER

FHG READERS' OFFER 2003

Edinburgh Crystal Visitor Centre

Eastfield, Penicuik, Midlothian EH26 8HB

Tel: 01968 675128 • Fax: 01968 674847

e-mail: VisitorCentre@edinburgh-crystal.co.uk • website: www.edinburgh-crystal.com

TWO adults for the price of ONE

valid during 2003

NOT TO BE USED IN CONJUNCTION WITH ANY OTHER OFFER

FHG READERS' OFFER 2003

MYRETON MOTOR MUSEUM

Aberlady, East Lothian EH32 0PZ

Tel: 01875 870288

One child FREE with each paying adult

valid during 2003

NOT TO BE USED IN CONJUNCTION WITH ANY OTHER OFFER

FHG READERS' OFFER 2003

Deep Sea World

North Queensferry, Fife KY11 1JR

Tel: 01383 411880 / 0906 941 0077 (24hr info line, calls cost 10p per minute)

info@deepseaworld.com • www.deepdseaworld.com

One child FREE with a full-paying adult

valid until end 2003

NOT TO BE USED IN CONJUNCTION WITH ANY OTHER OFFER

FHG READERS' OFFER 2003

Highland and Rare Breeds Farm

Elphin, Near Ullapool, Sutherland IV27 4HH

Tel: 01854 666204

One FREE adult or child with adult paying full entrance price

valid May to September 2003

NOT TO BE USED IN CONJUNCTION WITH ANY OTHER OFFER

An innovative museum exploring the history and environment of West Lothian on a 20-acre site packed full of things to see and do, indoors and out.

Open: Daily (except Christmas and New Year) 10am to 5pm.

Directions: 15 miles from Edinburgh, follow "Heritage Centre" signs from A899.

FHG PUBLICATIONS, ABBEY MILL BUSINESS CENTRE, PAISLEY PA1 1TJ

Watch the craftsmen, feel the passion and discover the history of the UK's favourite crystal on tours of the glasshouse. Plus great shopping.

Open: Monday to Saturday 10am to 5pm, Sundays 11am to 5pm. Closed Christmas and New Year fortnight

Directions: 30 minutes south of Edinburgh city centre. From city bypass, take A701 to Peebles, following the signs for Penicuik.

FHG PUBLICATIONS, ABBEY MILL BUSINESS CENTRE, PAISLEY PA1 1TJ

On show is a large collection, from 1899, of cars, bicycles, motor cycles and commercials. There is also a large collection of period advertising, posters and enamel signs.

Open: Daily Easter to September 11am to 4pm;
October to Easter: Sundays 1pm to 3pm or by special appointment.

Directions: Off A198 near Aberlady. Two miles from A1.

FHG PUBLICATIONS, ABBEY MILL BUSINESS CENTRE, PAISLEY PA1 1TJ

Scotland's award-winning aquarium where you can enjoy a spectacular diver's eye view of our marine environment through the world's longest underwater safari. New 'Amazing Amphibians' display, (Cayman crocodile), behind the scenes tours. Aquamazing entertainment for all the family

Open: Daily except Christmas Day.

Directions: From Edinburgh follow signs for Forth Road Bridge, then signs through North Queensferry. From North, follow signs through Inverkeithing and North Queensferry.

FHG PUBLICATIONS, ABBEY MILL BUSINESS CENTRE, PAISLEY PA1 1TJ

Highland croft open to visitors for "hands-on" experience with over 30 different breeds of farm animals "stroke the goats and scratch the pigs". Farm information centre and old farm implements. For all ages, cloud or shine!

Open: July and August 10am to 5pm.

Directions: On A835 15 miles north of Ullapool

FHG PUBLICATIONS, ABBEY MILL BUSINESS CENTRE, PAISLEY PA1 1TJ

FHG READERS' OFFER 2003

Highland Folk Museum

Aultlarie Crofthouse, Newtonmore, Inverness-shire PH20 1AY

Tel: 01540 661307 • Fax: 01540 661631

e-mail: highland.folk@highland.gov.uk • website: www.highlandfolk.com

One child FREE with each adult paying full admission price

valid from May to October 2003

NOT TO BE USED IN CONJUNCTION WITH ANY OTHER OFFER

FHG READERS' OFFER 2003

Landmark Forest Heritage Park

Carrbridge, Inverness-shire PH23 3AJ

Tel: 01479 841613 • Freephone 0800 731 3446

e-mail: landmarkcentre@compuserve.com • website: www.landmark.centre.co.uk

10% DISCOUNT for pet owners. Free admission for pets!
Maximum of four persons per voucher

Valid during 2003

NOT TO BE USED IN CONJUNCTION WITH ANY OTHER OFFER

FHG READERS' OFFER 2003

Speyside Heather Garden & Visitor Centre

Speyside Heather Centre, Dulnain Bridge, Inverness-shire PH26 3PA

Tel: 01479 851359 • Fax: 01479 851396

e-mail: enquiries@heathercentre.com • website: www.heathercentre.com

FREE entry to 'Heather Story' exhibition

valid during 2003

NOT TO BE USED IN CONJUNCTION WITH ANY OTHER OFFER

FHG READERS' OFFER 2003

New Lanark World Heritage Site

New Lanark Mills, New Lanark. Lanarkshire ML11 9DB

Tel: 01555 661345• Fax: 01555 665738

e-mail: development@newlanark.org • website: www.newlanark.org

One FREE child with every full price adult

valid until 31st October 2003

NOT TO BE USED IN CONJUNCTION WITH ANY OTHER OFFER

FHG READERS' OFFER 2003

Finlaystone Country Estate

Langbank, Renfrewshire PA14 6TJ

Tel & Fax: 01475 540285

e-mail: info@finlaystone.co.uk • website: www.finlaystone.co.uk

Two for the price of one

valid until April 03

NOT TO BE USED IN CONJUNCTION WITH ANY OTHER OFFER

300 years of history has been recreated in a thriving township from the 1700s, a working Highland farm with old breed horses, cattle, ducks, farm machinery and and an old tin school where the teacher rules!

Open: Mid-April to October. Check for opening times.

Directions: Follow signs from A9 to Newtonmore. North end of Newtonmore on A86.

FHG PUBLICATIONS, ABBEY MILL BUSINESS CENTRE, PAISLEY PA1 1TJ

Great day out for all the family. Wild Water Coaster, Microworld exhibition, Forest Trails, Viewing Tower, Climbing Wall*, Tree Top Trail, Steam powered Sawmill*, Clydesdale Horse*. Shop, restaurant and snackbar. (* Easter to October)*

DOGS MUST BE KEPT ON LEADS

Open: Daily except Christmas Day.

Directions: 20 miles south of Inverness at Carrbridge, just off the A9.

FHG PUBLICATIONS, ABBEY MILL BUSINESS CENTRE, PAISLEY PA1 1TJ

Award-winning attraction with unique 'Heather Story' exhibition, extensive giftshop. Large garden centre selling 300 different heathers, antique shop, children's play area and famous Clootie Dumpling restaurant.

Open: All year except Christmas Day.

Directions: Just off A95 between Aviemore and Grantown-on-Spey.

FHG PUBLICATIONS, ABBEY MILL BUSINESS CENTRE, PAISLEY PA1 1TJ

A beautifully restored cotton mill village close to the Falls of Clyde. Explore the fascinating history of the village, try the 'New Millennium Experience', a magical chair ride which takes you back in time to discover what life used to be like.

Open: 11am to 5pm daily. Closed Christmas and New Year.

FHG PUBLICATIONS, ABBEY MILL BUSINESS CENTRE, PAISLEY PA1 1TJ

Colourful gardens, imaginative woodland play areas and tumbling waterfalls. The Estate combines history with adventure in a fun day out for the family, where your dog can run freely. Step back in time and uncover its secrets.

Open: Daily 10.30am to 5pm

Directions: Off A8 west of Langbank

FHG PUBLICATIONS, ABBEY MILL BUSINESS CENTRE, PAISLEY PA1 1TJ

FHG READERS' OFFER 2003

Bala Lake Railway

The Station, Llanuwchllyn, Gwynedd LL23 7DD

Tel: 01678 540666 • Fax: 01678 540535

website: www.bala-lake-railway.co.uk

One child FREE with each full fare paying adult

valid from Easter to September 2003

NOT TO BE USED IN CONJUNCTION WITH ANY OTHER OFFER

FHG READERS' OFFER 2003

Llanberis Lake Railway

Gilfach Ddu, Llanberis, Gwynedd LL55 4TY

Tel: 01286 870549 • e-mail: info@lake-railway.co.uk

website: www.lake-railway.co.uk

One pet travels free with each full fare paying adult

Valid Easter to October 2003

NOT TO BE USED IN CONJUNCTION WITH ANY OTHER OFFER

FHG READERS' OFFER 2003

Alice in Wonderland Centre

3/4 Trinity Square, Llandudno, Conwy, North Wales LL30 2PY

Tel: 01492 860082 • e-mail: alice@wonderland.co.uk

website: www.wonderland.co.uk

One child FREE with two paying adults. Guide Dogs welcome

valid during 2003

NOT TO BE USED IN CONJUNCTION WITH ANY OTHER OFFER

FHG READERS' OFFER 2003

National Cycle Collection

Automobile Palace, Temple Street, Llandrindod Wells, Powys LD1 5DL

Tel: 01597 825531

e-mail: cycle.museum@care4free.net • website: www.cyclemuseum.org.uk

TWO for the price of ONE

Valid during 2003 except Special Event days

NOT TO BE USED IN CONJUNCTION WITH ANY OTHER OFFER

FHG READERS' OFFER 2003

Rhondda Heritage Park

Lewis Merthyr Colliery, Coed Cae Road, Trehafod, Near Pontypridd CF37 7NP

Tel: 01443 682036 • e-mail: info@rhonddaheritagepark.com

website: www.rhonddaheritagepark.com

Two adults or children for the price of one

Valid until end 2003 for full tours only. Not valid on special event days.

NOT TO BE USED IN CONJUNCTION WITH ANY OTHER OFFER

Take a trip along this narrow gauge steam railway, passing by the largest natural lake in Wales.

Open: Easter to the end of September, except some Mondays and Fridays.

Directions: Off the A494 at Llanuwchllyn.

FHG PUBLICATIONS, ABBEY MILL BUSINESS CENTRE, PAISLEY PA1 1TJ

A 40-minute ride along the shores of beautiful Padarn Lake behind a quaint historic steam engine. Magnificent views of the mountains from lakeside picnic spots.

DOGS MUST BE KEPT ON LEAD AT ALL TIMES ON TRAIN

Open: Most days Easter to October. Free timetable leaflet on request.

Directions: Just off A4086 Caernarfon to Capel Curig road at Llanberis; follow 'Country Park' signs.

FHG PUBLICATIONS, ABBEY MILL BUSINESS CENTRE, PAISLEY PA1 1TJ

Walk through the Rabbit Hole to the colourful scenes of Lewis Carroll's classic story set in beautiful life-size displays. Recorded commentaries and transcripts available in several languages.

Open: 10am to 5pm daily (closed Sundays Easter to November); closed Christmas/Boxing/New Year's Days.

Directions: situated just off the main street, 250 yards from coach and rail stations.

FHG PUBLICATIONS, ABBEY MILL BUSINESS CENTRE, PAISLEY PA1 1TJ

Journey through the lanes of cycle history and see bicycles from Boneshakers and Penny Farthings up to modern Raleigh cycles. Over 250 machines on display

PETS MUST BE KEPT ON LEADS

Open: 1st March to 1st November daily 10am onwards.

Directions: AA signs to car park. Town centre attraction.

FHG PUBLICATIONS, ABBEY MILL BUSINESS CENTRE, PAISLEY PA1 1TJ

Make a pit stop whatever the weather! Join an ex-miner on a tour of discovery, ride the cage to pit bottom and take a thrilling ride back to the surface. Multi-media presentations, period village street, children's adventure play area, restaurant and gift shop. Full disabled access.

Open: Open daily 10am to 6pm (last tour 4.30pm). Closed Mondays October to Easter, also Christmas/Boxing days.

Directions: Exit Junction 32 M4, signposted from A470 Pontypridd. Trehafod is located between Pontypridd and Porth.

FHG PUBLICATIONS, ABBEY MILL BUSINESS CENTRE, PAISLEY PA1 1TJ

ENGLAND

Board Accommodation

BEDFORDSHIRE

SANDY

Mrs Anne Franklin, Village Farm, Thorncote Green, Sandy SG19 1PU (01767 627345). Village Farm is a family-run working farm, mixed arable with a flock of 1000 free range laying hens, plus turkeys and geese for Christmas trade. Accommodation comprises one double bedroom, two twin/family rooms, both en suite. Full farmhouse breakfast plus beverages in room. Thorncote Green is a picturesque hamlet within easy reach of many interesting places: Shuttleworth Collection, Swiss Gardens, RSPB headquarters, Greensand Ridge walk, Woburn Abbey, Wimpole Hall and Cambridge. Bed and Breakfast from £25 per person per night. **ETC ◆◆**

SANDY

Mrs M. Codd, Highfield Farm, Great North Road, Sandy SG19 2AQ (01767 682332; Fax: 01767 692503). Tranquil welcoming atmosphere on attractive arable farm. Set well back off A1 giving quiet, peaceful seclusion yet within easy reach of the RSPB, the Shuttleworth Collection, the Greensand Ridge Walk, Grafham Water and Woburn Abbey. Cambridge 22 miles, London 50 miles. All rooms have tea/coffee making facilities, most have bathroom en suite and two are on the ground floor. There is a separate guests' sitting room with TV. Family room. Dogs welcome by arrangement. No smoking. Most guests return! Prices from £27.50 per person per night. **ETC ◆◆◆◆◆** *SILVER AWARD, GUESTACCOM "GOOD ROOM" AWARD. BEST ETC B&B REGIONAL WINNER FOR EASTERN COUNTIES.*
e-mail: margaret@highfield-farm.co.uk

Terms quoted in this publication may be subject to increase if rises in costs necessitate

CAMBRIDGESHIRE

CAMBRIDGE

Mrs Jean Wright, White Horse Cottage, 28 West Street, Comberton, Cambridge CB3 7DS (01223 262914). A 17th century cottage with all modern conveniences situated in a charming village four miles south-west of Cambridge. Junction 12 off M11 – A603 from Cambridge, or A428 turn-off at Hardwick turning. Accommodation includes one double room, twin and family rooms. Own sitting room with colour TV; tea/coffee making facilities. Full central heating; parking. Golfing facilities nearby. Excellent touring centre for many interesting places including Cambridge colleges, Wimpole Hall, Anglesey Abbey, Ely Cathedral, Imperial War Museum at Duxford, and many more. Bed and Breakfast from £22.50 per person sharing a double. Children welcome.

ELY

Mrs Linda Peck, Sharps Farm, Twenty Pence Road, Wilburton, Ely CB6 3PX (01353 740360). Between Ely (six miles) and Cambridge (12 miles) our modern farmhouse offers guests a warm welcome and a relaxed atmosphere. All rooms have en suite or private bathroom, central heating, colour TV, radio alarm, tea/coffee making facilities, hair dryer and views over surrounding countryside. Breakfast is served in the Conservatory, with home-made preserves and free range eggs. Special diets catered for. Disabled facilities. Ample parking. No smoking. Bed and Breakfast from £22.00 per person. Short Breaks available.
e-mail: sharpsfarm@yahoo.com

CHESHIRE

CONGLETON

Mrs Sheila Kidd, Yew Tree Farm, North Rode, Congleton CW12 2PF (01260 223569; Fax: 01260 223328). Discover freedom, relaxation, wooded walks and beautiful views. Meet a whole variety of pets and farm animals on this friendly working farm. One double and one triple room, both en suite. Your comfort is our priority and good food is a speciality. Generous scrummy breakfasts and traditional evening meals. A true taste of the countryside – just for you! Bed and Breakfast £22 to £27; optional Evening Meal £12. Brochure on request. **ETC ◆◆◆◆**
e-mail: yewtreebb@hotmail.com
website: www.yewtreebb.co.uk

HYDE (near Manchester)

Mrs Charlotte R. Walsh, Needhams Farm, Uplands Road, Werneth Low, Gee Cross, Near Hyde SK14 3AQ (0161 368 4610; Fax: 0161-367 9106). Working farm. A cosy 16th century farmhouse set in peaceful, picturesque surroundings by Werneth Low Country Park and the Etherow Valley, which lie between Glossop and Manchester. The farm is ideally situated for holidaymakers and businessmen, especially those who enjoy peace and quiet, walking and rambling, golfing and riding, as these activities are all close by. At Needhams Farm everyone, including children and pets, receives a warm welcome. Good wholesome meals available in the evenings. Residential licence and Fire Certificate held. Open all year. Bed and Breakfast from £22 single minimum to £36 double maximum; Evening Meal £7. **ETC/AA ◆◆◆**
e-mail: charlotte@needhamsfarm.co.uk **website: www.needhamsfarm.co.uk**

KNUTSFORD

Virginia Brown, Pickmere House, Park Lane, Pickmere, Knutsford WA16 0JX (Tel & Fax: 01565 733433; Mobile 07867 533508). A Listed Georgian farmhouse in rural village close to Arley Hall and Tatton Park, two miles west of M6 Junction 19 on B5391 giving swift access to airport and all major north west towns and tourist attractions. Spacious en suite rooms with TV, tea/coffee trays and hairdryers, overlooking farmlands. Parking at rear. No smoking policy. Bed and Breakfast £22.50 to £32.50 single, £48 double/twin; Evening Meal by arrangement. Minibus groups by negotiation. AA Approved. Also Mews Cottage (two bedrooms, two bathrooms) available for self-catering lets.

MACCLESFIELD

Susan Brocklehurst, Hill Top Farm, Wincle, Macclesfield SK11 0QH (01260 227257). Working farm. Overlooking the beautiful Dane Valley in this unspoilt region of the East Cheshire countryside, Hill Top is a working dairy and sheep farm situated in the tiny village of Wincle. Pretty bedrooms, a cosy television lounge and separate diningroom, together with good food and a friendly service make this the ideal base from which to explore the Peak District National Park, either by car or as a walker. Bed and Breakfast from £22 per person. Evening meal also available. **ETC ◆◆◆◆**

e-mail: a.brocklehurst@talk21.com

NANTWICH

Mrs Jean E. Callwood, Lea Farm, Wrinehill Road, Wybunbury, Nantwich CW5 7NS (01270 841429; Fax: 01270 841030). Charming farmhouse set in landscaped gardens, where peacocks roam, on 150 acre dairy farm. Working farm, join in. Spacious bedrooms, colour TVs, electric blankets, radio alarm and tea/coffee making facilities. Centrally heated throughout. Family, double and twin bedrooms, en suite facilities. Luxury lounge, dining room overlooking gardens. Pool/snooker; fishing in well stocked pool in beautiful surroundings. Bird watching. Children welcome, also dogs if kept under control. Help feed the birds and animals and see the cows being milked. Near to Stapeley Water Gardens, Bridgemere Garden World. Also Nantwich, Crewe, Chester, the Potteries and Alton Towers. Bed and Breakfast from £20 per person. Children half price. Weekly terms available. **AA ◆◆◆**

e-mail: contactus@leafarm.co.uk

NANTWICH

Mrs West, Stoke Grange Mews, Stoke Grange Farm, Chester Road, Nantwich CW5 6BT (01270 625525). Comfortable canal-side farmhouse B&B with en suite rooms, colour TV, tea/coffee facilities plus a four-poster bed. Balcony giving panoramic views of canal and countryside. Log burning fire in diningroom and wonderful antique tapestry in the lounge. We also have a four-bedroomed self-catering cottage with all mod cons in a converted barn across from the farmhouse. Shared garden. Pets' corner. Meals can be obtained from two pubs in the village of Barbridge only a ten minute walk away along the canal or road. Bed and Breakfast from £30 single, £25 if more than three nights. Self-catering from £225 to £495 per week. **ETC ◆◆◆◆**

CORNWALL

BODMIN

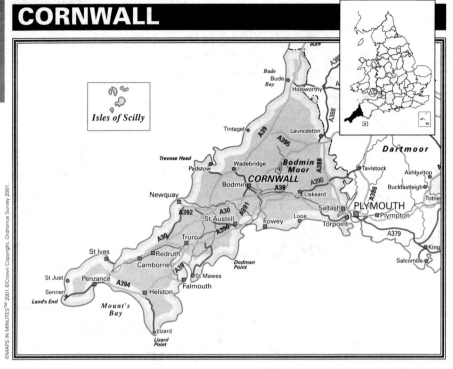

Mrs Joy Rackham, High Cross Farm, Lanivet, Near Bodmin PL30 5JR (01208 831341). Working farm. Traditional Victorian granite farmhouse on a working farm in the village of Lanivet, the geographical centre of Cornwall. Ideal for the north and south coasts, the moor and central for touring. The exciting new Eden Project is close by, The Lost Gardens of Heligan and Lanhydrock to name but a few. Lanivet is the half way mark for walking the Saints Way. There is the Camel Trail for walking, cycling or horseriding; fishing and golf are available in the area. High Cross offers quiet off road parking and modern facilities for guests. Rooms have hot/cold, shaver points, one room en suite, separate dining room and lounge for guests. Full English breakfast and optional evening meal. Bed and Breakfast from £20.

BODMIN

Mrs Margaret Oliver, Tremeere Manor, Lanivet, Near Bodmin PL30 5BG (01208 831513). Tremeere is a 17th Century Manor House set in a 240-acre dairy farm in mid-Cornwall on the halfway mark for the Saints Way, 15 minutes' drive from the Eden Project. There are spacious comfortable rooms comprising two double en suite bedrooms and one twin-bedded room, with lovely views of the surrounding countryside. Central heating, tea/coffee making facilities and a comfortable guests' lounge with TV. Prices are from £22 per person. No smoking. Nearby is Bodmin town with its ancient Gaol and Steam Railway. Lanhydrock House (NT), The Lost Gardens of Heligan or walking on Bodmin Moor and visiting the famous Jamaica Inn. Coastal walks and beaches are within easy reach as well as walking the Camel Trail.

BOSCASTLE

Mrs Cheryl Nicholls, Trerosewill Farm, Paradise, Boscastle PL35 0BL (01840 250545). Working farm. Luxurious Bed and Breakfast accommodation in modern farmhouse on working farm, only a short walk from the picturesque village of Boscastle. Rooms have spectacular coastal and rural views, all en suite with tea making facilities. Mineral water and bath-robes provided. Licensed. Centrally heated. Seasonal log fires. Large gardens. Traditional farmhouse fayre. Superb coastal and countryside walks. One-way walks arranged. Packed lunches available. Spring and Autumn breaks. Bed and Breakfast from £23. Strictly no smoking. **ETC ◆◆◆◆◆** *SILVER AWARD; FHG DIPLOMA AWARD; GOOD FOOD AWARD WINNER OF FARMHOUSE BED AND BREAKFAST FOR CORNWALL 2000, 2001, 2002, WINNER SOUTH-WEST 2002.*

BOSCASTLE

Mrs P. E. Perfili, Trefoil Farm, Camelford Road, Boscastle PL35 0AD (01840 250606). Set in its own tranquil grounds with ample parking. Trefoil offers non-smoking, centrally heated, en suite accommodation with tea and coffee making facilities and colour TV. Overlooking Boscastle village, with views of the coast and Lundy Island. Trefoil is ideally positioned to explore Cornwall. Two minutes' walk leads you to a local 16th century Inn with real ales and good food. Terms from £21pppn. **ETC ◆◆◆**

BUDE

Margaret and Richard Heard, Trencreek Farmhouse, St Gennys, Bude EX23 0AY (01840 230219). Comfortable farmhouse which offers a homely and relaxed family atmosphere. Situated in quiet and peaceful surroundings yet within easy reach of Crackington Haven. Well placed for easy access to coastal and countryside walks. Family, double and twin-bedded rooms, most en suite, all with tea and coffee making facilities. Two comfortable lounges. Games room. Separate dining room. Generous portions of home-cooked farmhouse food are always freshly prepared. Children welcome, special rates for under twelves. Spring and Autumn breaks available. Non-smoking. Sunday lunches and midday lunches optional.

BUDE

Mrs Sylvia Lucas, Elm Park, Bridgerule, Holsworthy EX22 7EL (01288 381231). Elm Park is a 205 acre dairy, beef and sheep farm. Six miles from surfing beaches at Bude and ideal for touring Devon/Cornwall. Children are especially welcomed, with pony rides. Games room available with snooker, table skittles, darts, etc, and golf putting. There are spacious family rooms (two en suite) and a twin-bedded room, all with colour TV and tea/coffee making facilities. Ample four-course dinners with freshly produced fare and delicious sweets. Bed, Breakfast and Evening Meal, reasonable terms. Reductions for children and everyone is made welcome and comfortable. Brochure available.

BUDE

Mrs Christine Nancekivell, Dolsdon Farm, Boyton, Launceston PL15 8NT (01288 341264). Dolsdon was once a 17th century coaching inn, now modernised, situated on the Launceston to Bude road within easy reach of sandy beaches, surfing, Tamar Otter Park, leisure centre with heated swimming pool, golf courses, fishing, tennis and horse riding and is ideal for touring Cornwall and Devon. Guests are welcome to wander around the 260-acre working farm. All bedrooms have washbasins, televisions and tea making facilities (en suite family room and double room available). Comfortably furnished lounge has colour TV. Plenty of good home cooking assured – full English breakfast. Parking. Bed and Breakfast from £17.50; reductions for children. Brochure available.

ENGLAND

See also Colour Display Advertisement

BUDE

Mrs E. Turner, Penleaze Farmhouse B&B, Marhamchurch, Bude EX23 0ET (Tel & Fax: 01288 381226). Penleaze is a Victorian farmhouse on a working family farm situated amidst rolling countryside on the North Cornish Coast, renowned for its spectacular views, rugged coastline and sandy beaches to explore, also lovely quaint villages such as Boscastle. One mile to our pretty village and two miles to Bude, also ideally placed for visiting North Devon. We offer three double en suite bedrooms, a twin with private bathroom and a small single; four-poster, roll top bath available. An English breakfast using fresh local produce prepared on the Aga is served in the dining room, separate sitting room for guests to relax. B&B £19.50 to £25pppn. **ETC ◆◆◆◆** *SILVER AWARD.*

e-mail: liz@penleaze.co.uk **website: www.penleaze.co.uk**

BUDE

Mrs Pearl Hopper, West Nethercott Farm, Whitstone, Holsworthy (Devon) EX22 6LD (01288 341394). Working farm, join in. Personal attention and a warm welcome await you on this dairy and sheep farm. Watch the cows being milked, help with the animals. Free pony rides, scenic farm walks. Short distance from sandy beaches, surfing and the rugged North Cornwall coast. Ideal base for visiting any part of Devon or Cornwall. We are located in Cornwall though our postal address is Devon. The traditional farmhouse has washbasins and TV in bedrooms; dining room and separate lounge with colour TV. Plenty of excellent home cooking. Access to the house at anytime. Bed and Full English Breakfast from £16, Evening Meal and pack lunches available. Children under 12 years reduced rates. Weekly terms available.

e-mail: pearl@westnethercott.fsnet.co.uk

See also Colour Display Advertisement

FALMOUTH

Trelawne Hotel, Mawnan Smith, Falmouth TR11 5HS (01326 250226; Fax 01326 250909). Nestling on the coastline between the Helford and Fal rivers in a beautiful and tranquil corner of Cornwall, this fine country house hotel enjoys a magnificent outlook across Falmouth Bay to the Roseland Peninsula. The tastefully furnished and centrally heated bedrooms have en suite facilities, as well as colour television, radio, telephone and tea and coffee makers. There is a charming cocktail bar and an indoor pool and games room. The cuisine, prepared by award-winning chefs, comes high on the list of attractions at this well-run hotel and is backed by an extensive wine list. **AA/ETC ★★★**, *SILVER AWARD.*

FOWEY

Mrs S.C. Dunn, Menabilly Barton, Par PL24 2TN (01726 812844). Working farm. Menabilly Barton is a secluded farmhouse set in a wooded valley leading to a quiet sandy beach. Spacious dining room, lounge with TV, peaceful garden open during the day. Good traditional farmhouse food. Three large bedrooms, en suite available. Bathroom with shower, two toilets. Facilities for making drinks and microwave if required. Coastal walks, National Trust properties, Heligan Gardens and The Eden Project all nearby. Local village pub serves good food. Historic port of Fowey three miles, North Coast only 40 minutes' drive. Bed and full English Breakfast. Reductions for children. Colour brochure on request.

Readers are requested to mention this guidebook when seeking accommodation (and please enclose a stamped addressed envelope).

HELSTON

Mrs P. Roberts, Hendra Farm, Wendron, Helston TR13 0NR (01326 340470). Hendra Farm, just off the main Helston/Falmouth road, is an ideal centre for touring Cornwall; three miles to Helston, eight to both Redruth and Falmouth. Safe sandy beaches within easy reach – five miles to the sea. Two double, one single, and one family bedrooms with washbasins and tea-making facilities; bathroom and toilets; sittingroom and two diningrooms. Cot, babysitting and reduced rates offered for children. No objection to pets. Car necessary, parking space. Enjoy good cooking with roast beef, pork, lamb, chicken, genuine Cornish pasties, fish and delicious sweets and cream. Open all year except Christmas. Evening Dinner, Bed and Breakfast from £140 per week which includes cooked breakfast, three course evening dinner, tea and home-made cake before bed. Bed and Breakfast only from £15 per night also available.

LAUNCESTON

Hurdon Farm, Launceston PL15 9LS (01566 772955). Elegant Listed 18th century farmhouse, idyllically tucked away amidst our 500 acre mixed working farm. Centrally positioned on Devon/Cornwall border, it is ideally located for exploring the many attractions in both counties. Near the Eden Project. Six luxurious and spacious en suite bedrooms, all with colour TV, radio, tea/coffee facilities and central heating. Comfortable guests' lounge. Superb English breakfasts and delicious four-course dinners, freshly prepared and cooked, are served at separate tables in the dining room. Open May till November. Bed and Breakfast from £21. **AA/RAC ◆◆◆◆**

LAUNCESTON

Mary Rich, "Nathania", Altarnun, Launceston PL15 7SL (01566 86426). A warm welcome awaits you, for accommodation on a small farm on Bodmin Moor within easy reach of coast, moors, towns, lakes and fishing. Visit King Arthur country – Tintagel, Dozmary Pool, the famous Jamaica Inn, Wesley Cottage and cathedral of the moors. One mile from A30, very quiet, ideal for overnight stop for West Cornwall. Double room en suite, twin rooms with bathroom adjoining. Tea making facilities and TV. Payphone. Conservatory and lounge for quiet relaxation. We look forward to meeting you for one night, or why not book your holiday with us and tour Cornwall. You will enjoy the quiet, happy, relaxing atmosphere. Prices from £10.50 per person per night. Please telephone, or write, for details – SAE, thank you.

LISKEARD

Mrs Stephanie Rowe, Tregondale Farm, Menheniot, Liskeard PL14 3RG (Tel & Fax: 01579 342407). Working farm, join in. Feeling like a break near the coast? Come and relax, join our family with the peace of the countryside - breathtaking in Spring - on a 200 acre mixed farm, situated near Looe between A38 and A390. See pedigree South Devon cattle and sheep naturally reared, explore the new woodland farm trail amidst wildlife and flowers. This stylish, characteristic farmhouse, which dates back to the Domesday Book, has featured in the Daily Telegraph, and is a Cream of Cornwall member, provides exceptional comfort with en suite suite bedrooms all with colour TV, tea/coffee making facilities, lounge/diningroom with log fires. A conservatory to enjoy each day's warmth capturing a beautiful view over the farm, set in an original walled garden including picnic table, tennis court and play area. Special activities can be arranged — golf, fishing, cycling and walking. Home and local produce a speciality, full English Breakfast; try our delicious optional Evening Meal from £13.50. Bed and Breakfast from £25. Open all year. Self-catering character cottage also available (**ETC ★★★★**). A warm welcome awaits you to discover the beauty of Cornwall. Please phone for a brochure and discuss your requirements. **ETC/AA ◆◆◆◆** *SILVER AWARD.*

e-mail: tregondale@connectfree.co.uk website: www.tregondalefarm.co.uk

ENGLAND

LOOE

Mrs Angela Eastley, Little Larnick Farm, Pelynt, Looe PL13 2NB (01503 262837). Little Larnick is situated in a sheltered part of the West Looe river valley. Walk to Looe from our working dairy farm and along the coastal path to picturesque Polperro. The character farmhouse and barn offers twin, double and family en suite rooms. The bedrooms are superbly equipped and decorated to a high standard. The family room is in a downstairs annexe overlooking the garden. Our newly renovated barn offers three self-contained bedrooms with their own lounge areas. Cycling shed, drying room and ample parking. No pets. No smoking. Bed and Breakfast from £20 to £25. Open all year. **ETC ◆◆◆◆**

LOOE

Mrs D. Eastley, Bake Farm, Pelynt, Looe PL13 2QQ (01503 220244). Working farm. This is an old farmhouse, bearing the Trelawney Coat of Arms (1610), situated midway between Looe and Fowey. The two double en suite bedrooms and the family room with private bathroom are all decorated to a high standard and have tea/coffee making facilities and TV. Sorry, no pets, no smoking. Open from March to October. A car is essential for touring the area, ample parking. There is much to see and do here – horse riding, coastal walks, golf, National Trust properties, the Eden Project and Heligan Gardens are within easy reach. The sea is only five miles away and there is shark fishing at Looe. Bed and Breakfast from £20-£24. Cleanliness guaranteed. Brochure available on request. **ETC ◆◆◆**

MEVAGISSEY

Mrs Dawn Rundle, Lancallan Farm, Mevagissey, St Austell PL26 6EW (Tel & Fax: 01726 842284). Lancallan is a large 17th century farmhouse on a working 700 acre dairy and beef farm in a beautiful rural setting, one mile from Mevagissey. We are close to Heligan Gardens, lovely coastal walks and sandy beaches, and are well situated for day trips throughout Cornwall. Also six to eight miles from the Eden Project (20 minutes' drive). Enjoy a traditional farmhouse breakfast in a warm and friendly atmosphere. Accommodation comprises one twin room and two double en suite rooms (all with colour TV and tea/coffee facilities); bathroom, lounge and diningroom.Terms and brochure available on request. SAE please.

e-mail: dawn@lancallan.fsnet.co.uk

MULLION

Mrs Joan Hyde, Campden House, The Commons, Mullion TR12 7HZ (01326 240365). Campden House offers comfortable accommodation in a peaceful setting with large gardens and a beautiful sea view. It is within easy reach of Mullion, Polurrian and Poldhu Coves, and is ideally situated for exploring the beautiful coast and countryside of the Lizard. Mullion golf course is less than one mile away. All eight bedrooms have handbasin with hot and cold water and comfortable beds; some rooms have en suite shower. There is a large sun lounge, TV lounge with colour TV and a large dining room and bar. Guests have access to the lounges, bedrooms and gardens at all times. Children and pets welcome. Bed and Breakfast from £16.50.

NEWQUAY

Ms Jill Brake, Bre-Pen Farm, Mawgan Porth, Newquay TR8 4AL (01637 860420). A warm Cornish welcome awaits you from Rod and Jill in a friendly farmhouse on a working farm. The National Trust Coastal Path skirts the farm, making it an ideal walking area. The beaches of Mawgan Porth and Watergate Bay are within easy walking distance, both ideal for surfing. A short drive east takes you to the historic fishing port of Padstow, Bedruthan Steps and many glorious sandy beaches. Ideally situated for visiting the many attractions of Cornwall. Horse riding, stabling and kennels available; recently constructed cross-country course on the farm. Double en suite rooms, twin and family suite, all with tea/coffee facilities and colour TV. Traditional farmhouse breakfast; vegetarians catered for. **ETC ◆◆◆◆**

NEWQUAY

Mrs B. L. Harvey, Shepherds Farm, Fiddlers Green, St Newlyn East, Newquay TR8 5NW (01872 540502). Working farm. A warm welcome awaits you on our family-run 600 acre mixed working farm. Come and share our warm and friendly atmosphere with first class service in affordable quality accommodation. Cleanliness guaranteed. All rooms en suite and have colour TV and tea making facilities. Large garden. Central location, ideal for touring. The farm is set in rural, small hamlet of Fiddlers Green three miles from beautiful Cornish coastline, five miles from Newquay; 20 minutes from south coast. Glorious sandy beaches, ideal for surfing, little rivers for the very young. Beautiful breathtaking views and walks along scenic clifftops. One-and-a-half miles from National Trust property of Trerice. Good pub food close by. Come and join us! Discounted golf. Bed and Breakfast from £20 to £22. **ETC ◆◆◆◆**

PADSTOW

Carole and Tony Webb, Trevone Bay Hotel, Trevone, Near Padstow PL28 8QS (01841 520243; Fax: 01841 521195). On arrival relax with a pot of tea, then stroll through the tranquil village to the beautiful sandy bay. Follow the coast path along the rocky bay, then back across the fields to your comfortable hotel. Does this tempt you? How about an excellent home-cooked meal, coffee watching the sunset and an evening socialising in the bar. Our hotel is non-smoking throughout. All bedrooms en suite. Ideal for walking, touring, bird watching or relaxing on the beach. From £30 Bed and Breakfast, four-course Evening Meal £14.95. Open February half-term to end of October and for Christmas breaks. If this sounds like your sort of holiday, write or phone for brochure. **ETC ◆◆◆◆**
e-mail: webb@trevonebay.demon.co.uk

PADSTOW

Mrs Sandra May, Trewithen Farm, St Merryn, Near Padstow PL28 8JZ (01841 520420). Trewithen farmhouse is a newly renovated Cornish Roundhouse, set in a large garden and situated on a working farm enjoying country and coastal views. The picturesque town of Padstow with its pretty harbour and narrow streets with famous fish restaurants is only three miles away. St Merryn Parish boasts seven beautiful sandy beaches and bays. Also coastal walks, golf, fishing and horse riding on neighbouring farm. Hire a bike or walk along the Camel Trail cycle and footpath - winding for 18 miles along the River Camel. The accommodation has been tastefully decorated to complement the exposed beams and original features. All bedrooms are en suite or have private facilities, TV and hot drinks tray. Parking. Full English breakfast. Evening Meal optional. TV lounge. Bed and Breakfast from £23 per person per night. Weekly rates and Winter weekend breaks available. **ETC ◆◆◆◆**

ENGLAND

Linda & Alan Sunderland

KERRIS MANOR FARM

Kerris, Penzance TR19 6UY
Tel: 01736 731198

Peaceful, relaxing surroundings and a warm welcome on our working farm three miles from Penzance off the B3315. Ideal for exploring Mousehole, Land's End, Sennen or Newlyn. Excellent beaches nearby. Clay pigeon shooting available with tuition if required. Guest lounge and dining room with wood burner. Two well-equipped double bedrooms and separate guest bathroom. Bed and hearty farmhouse breakfast.

Sorry, no smoking. Open all year. But regret we are unable to accommodate children or pets.

PENZANCE

Mrs Rosalind Wyatt, South Colenso Farm, Goldsithney, Penzance TR20 9JB (01736 762290). Working farm. South Colenso Farm is a 76 acre working arable farm. The spacious Georgian style farmhouse is set in beautiful unspoilt countryside, peaceful and secluded, yet not isolated. Ideally situated between Marazion and Praa Sands, a perfect location for touring both coasts of Cornwall, with sandy beaches and pretty coves nearby. The large en suite bedrooms (two double and one family rooms) have colour TV, tea/coffee making facilities and a lovely country view. Relax in our comfortable lounge with colour television and log fire. Full English Breakfast is served in our sunny dining room with separate tables. Ample private parking. Non-smoking. Please write or call for terms.

See also Colour Display Advertisement

PENZANCE

Mr Wilson, Boscean Country Hotel, St Just, Penzance TR19 7QP (Tel & Fax: 01736 788748). The Boscean Country Hotel, located amidst some of the most dramatic scenery in West Cornwall, is somewhere very special just waiting to be discovered. This country house offers a wonderful combination of oak panelled walls, a magnificent oak staircase and open log fires. The natural gardens, extending to nearly three acres, are a haven for wildlife including foxes and badgers. Situated on the heritage coast in an Area of Outstanding Natural Beauty close to Cape Cornwall and the coastal footpath, this is an ideal base from which to explore the Land's End Peninsula. The moors of Penwith are rich in Iron and Bronze Age relics dating back to 4000 BC. Penzance, St Michael's Mount, St Ives, Land's End and the Minack Theatre are all a short distance away. Twelve en suite rooms, centrally heated throughout, licensed bar. Excellent home cooking using fresh local produce. Open all year. Bed and Breakfast £23. Dinner, Bed and Breakfast £36. **ETC ◆◆◆◆**

e-mail: Boscean@aol.com **website: www.bosceancountryhotel.co.uk**

PENZANCE

Mrs M.D. Olds, Mulfra Farm, Newmill, Penzance TR20 8XP (01736 363940). Near Mulfra Quiot this hill farm, with cows and calves, high on the edge of the Penwith Moors, offers superb accommodation which attracts many of our guests to return year after year. The 17th century stone-built, beamed farmhouse has far reaching views, is attractively decorated and furnished, and offers two double en suite bedrooms with tea and coffee making facilities, TV, shaver socket; comfortable lounge with inglenook fireplace, diningroom with separate tables and conservatory. Car essential, ample parking. Warm friendly atmosphere, good food, beautiful walking country, ideal centre for exploring west Cornwall. Bed and Breakfast from £20 per person per night. Evening Meal by arrangement. Further details with pleasure. **CTB** *APPROVED.*

PENZANCE (near Porthcurno)

Mrs P. M. Hall, Treen Farmhouse, Treen, St Levan, Penzance TR19 6LF (01736 810253). Situated just off the South-West coastal footpath, Treen Farm is a family-run organic dairy farm set in 80 acres of pastureland on the cliffs beside the world famous Minack Theatre and the historic Logan Rock. Lands End four miles. Visitors are welcome to use the gardens, walk around the farm and watch the milking (children supervised please). Pub, shop, cafe, campsite, bus stop and beaches nearby. Ideal for walking, relaxing and sightseeing. Comfortable farmhouse Bed and Breakfast accommodation, twin and double (en suite) rooms with tea/coffee making facilities, garden/sea views and some with TV. Traditional English Breakfast served. Guests' lounge with open fire and television. Private parking. Pets welcome. Reductions for children. Sorry, no smoking. Bed and Breakfast from £15.00. Self-catering also available for two people from £120 per week.
e-mail: paulachrishall@treenfarm.fsnet.co.uk

PORT ISAAC

Chris and Liz Bolton, Trewetha Farm, Port Isaac PL29 3RU (01208 880256). 18th century traditional farmhouse in Betjeman country in an area designated as outstanding natural beauty. Spectacular views over the sea and surrounding countryside. Pet the miniature Shetland ponies, help feed the hens or watch the sheep graze. Ideal location for sandy beaches, walking, cycling and all water sports. The double and twin en suite rooms are tastefully decorated and centrally heated. Each has colour TV and tea/coffee making facilities. ENQUIRE ABOUT OUR COASTAL WALKING BREAKS: full English breakfast, packed lunch, three-course dinner and transport to the start of the walk. Self-catering cottages also available.

ROSELAND PENINSULA

Mrs Shirley E. Pascoe, Court Farm, Philleigh, Truro TR2 5NB (01872 580313). Working farm. Situated in the heart of the Roseland Peninsula, undoubtedly one of the loveliest parts of Cornwall with safe, unspoilt beaches on the seaward side, and the beautiful River Fal on the other. The traditionally run farm extends to about 250 acres, 50 of which border the upper reaches of the estuary, providing superb walking and bird watching, while down river is excellent for sailing, fishing, water skiing etc. The spacious old farmhouse, with over an acre of garden and plenty of parking space, lies in the quiet little village of Philleigh with its lovely old Norman Church and 17th century 'Roseland Inn'. There are plenty of good pubs and restaurants within a few miles. For horse owners who fancy a riding holiday we specialise in providing first class facilities for you and your horse(s). There is also a 6-bed cottage available for holiday letting. Please write or phone for brochure and terms.

ST AUSTELL

Mrs Liz Berryman, Polgreen Farm, London Apprentice, St Austell PL26 7AP (Tel & Fax: 01726 75151). Polgreen is a family-run dairy farm nestling in the Pentewan Valley in an area of outstanding natural beauty. One mile from the coast and four miles from the picturesque fishing village of Mevagissey. A perfect location for a relaxing holiday in the glorious Cornish countryside. Centrally situated, Polgreen is ideally placed for touring all of Cornwall's many attractions. Cornish Way Leisure Trail adjoining farm. Within a few minutes' drive of the spectacular Eden Project and Heligan Gardens. All rooms with private facilities, colour TV, tea/coffee making facilities, guest lounge, children welcome. Terms from £21 per person per night. **ETC ◆◆◆◆**
e-mail: polgreen.farm@btclick.com

ST IVES

Mrs N.I. Mann, Trewey Farm, Zennor, St Ives TR26 3DA (01736 796936). Working farm. On the main St Ives to Land's End road, this attractive granite-built farmhouse stands among gorse and heather-clad hills, half-a-mile from the sea and five miles from St Ives. The mixed farm covers 400 acres, with Guernsey cattle and fine views of the sea; lovely cliff and hill walks. Guests will be warmly welcomed and find a friendly atmosphere. Five double, one single and three family bedrooms (all with washbasins); bathroom, toilets; sittingroom, diningroom. Cot, high chair and babysitting available. Pets allowed. Car essential – parking. Open all year. Electric heating. Bed and Breakfast only. SAE for terms, please.

ST MAWES/TRURO

Mrs A. Palmer, Trenestrall Farm, Ruan High Lanes, Truro TR2 5LX (01872 501259). Working farm, join in. A tastefully restored 200 year old barn, now a farmhouse offering comfortable accommodation on a 300 acre mixed working farm. Situated on beautiful Roseland Peninsula, within easy reach of St Mawes and Truro and amenities such as Heligan Gardens and the Eden Project, at the same time not being too far from attractions further west. Close to safe beaches and beautiful Fal estuary for sailing, bird watching etc. Accommodation consists of double, family or twin rooms all en suite, with tea/coffee facilities; sittingroom with TV. Amenities include private fishing lake and snooker room, table tennis and pony riding. Pride taken with presentation of food using home produce whenever possible. Children welcome, babysitting service. Pets accepted. Phone or write for details of Bed and Breakfast from £20 per person per night.

See also Colour Display Advertisement

TINTAGEL

Willapark Manor Hotel, Bossiney, Tintagel PL34 0BA (01840 770782). Willapark Manor is a lovely character house in a beautiful setting amidst 14 acre grounds, overlooking Bossiney Bay. Surrounded by woodland, it is secluded and has direct access to the coastal path and beach. It is a family-run hotel with a friendly and informal atmosphere, excellent cuisine and a well stocked cocktail bar. Beautifully appointed bedrooms, all en suite and with colour TV and tea/coffee making facilities. Some four-posters. A warm welcome and a memorable holiday assured. One of the most beautifully situated hotels in England. **ETC ★★**
website: www.willapark.co.uk

WADEBRIDGE

Mrs E. Hodge, Pengelly Farm, Burlawn, Wadebridge PL27 7LA (01208 814217). A Listed Georgian farmhouse situated in a quiet location on a 150 acre farm overlooking wooded valleys, approximately one-and-a-half miles from Wadebridge. Ideal location for touring or walking and cycling close to the Camel Trail. There are a number of beaches plus sailing, golf, horse riding and much more within 20 minutes' drive. Large garden for relaxing or for children to play. Two prettily decorated bedrooms with own vanity units, tea/coffee making facilities, colour TV, and hair dryers. Traditional English breakfast or special requests by prior arrangement. Lounge with colour TV. Children welcome - cot and highchair available, babysitting on request. Bed and Breakfast £20. **ETC ◆◆◆◆**, *CORNWALL TOURIST BOARD REGISTERED*.

Visits & Attractions

The Eden Project, Near St Austell, Cornwall • 01726 811911
website: www.edenproject.com

A gateway into the fascinating interaction of plants and people. Two gigantic geodesic conservatories - the Humid Tropics Biome and the Warm Temperate Biome - set amidst landscaped outdoor terraces.

Goonhilly Earth Station, Helston, Cornwall • 01326 221333
website: www.goonhilly.bt.com

Explore the wonders of pioneering technology at one of the most important communication stations in the world. Scan the skies by operating an IV dish aerial yourself.

A useful index of towns and counties appears at the back of this book on pages 379-382. Refer also to Contents Pages 50/51.

ENGLAND

CUMBRIA

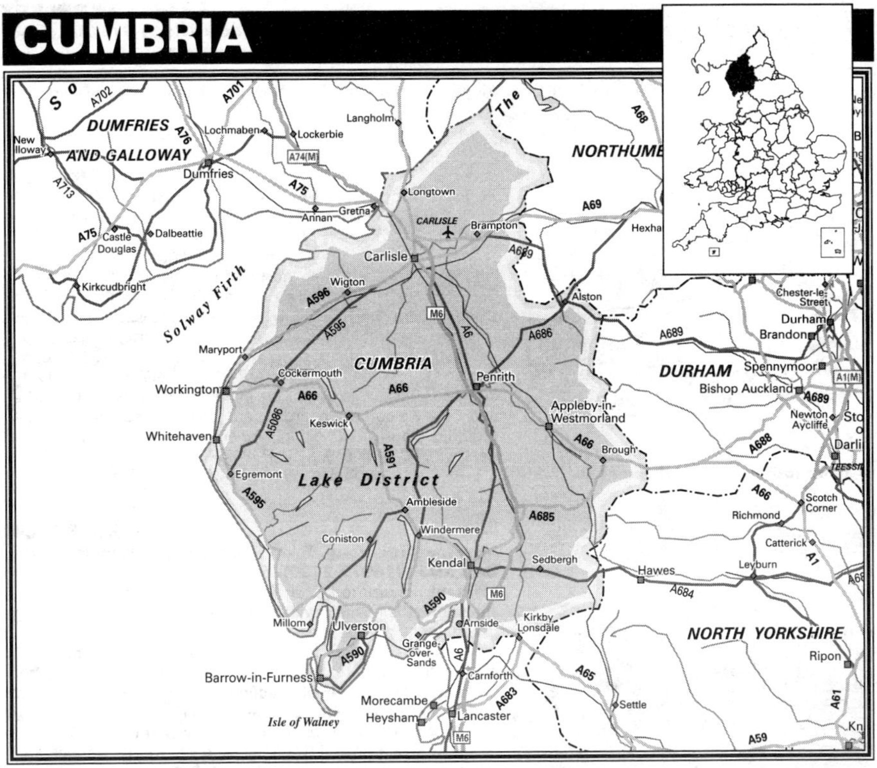

Malcolm & Margaret MacFarlane

Borwick Lodge

Outgate, Hawkshead, Ambleside, Cumbria LA22 0PU
Tel & Fax: Hawkshead (015394) 36332
e-mail: borwicklodge@talk21.com • website: www.borwicklodge.com

Silver
SILVER AWARD

Award-winning delightful 17th century house nestling in three acres of secluded gardens. Breathtaking panoramic lake and mountain views. Ideally situated. Close to Hawkshead village with good choice of restaurants and inns. Beautiful en suite rooms with colour televisions and tea-making facilities. King-size four-poster rooms. Somewhere special in this most beautiful corner of England. Ample parking. NON-SMOKING THROUGHOUT. Bed and Breakfast from £30. Residential licence.

See Board Section – Hawkshead, Cumbria

See also Colour Advertisement

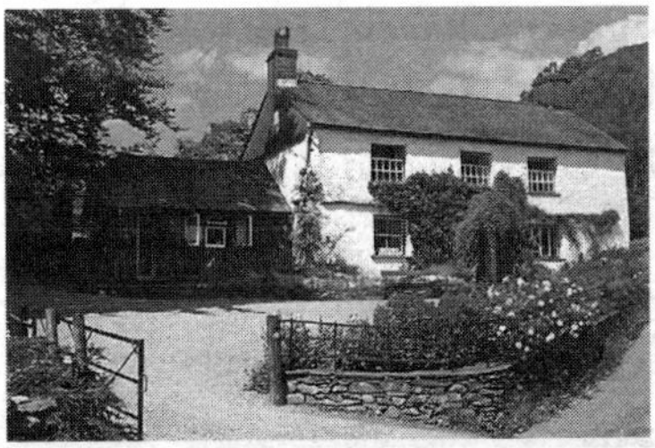

AMBLESIDE

Mrs D.E. Wrathall, The Oaks, Loughrigg, Ambleside LA22 9HQ (015394 37632). Set in the secluded Loughrigg Valley in the heart of the Lake District, this 18th century farmhouse is the property of the National Trust. Accommodation is offered in two family rooms and one double, all with washbasins; two bathrooms; sitting room with TV; dining room. Central heating in bedrooms during colder months. Bed and breakfast. Good food served in a friendly atmosphere. Reductions for children sharing parents' room. Open February to November. Car essential, parking. SAE for terms.

APPLEBY

Mrs C. Jackson, Wickerslack Farm, Crosby Ravensworth, Penrith CA10 3LN (01931 715236). A very warm welcome awaits you on our family-run working farm. Peaceful rural setting with superb views, ideal base for walking and touring holidays or just to relax. Beautifully decorated, spacious accommodation with three rooms, two en suite. Guests' lounge with TV and log fire which is accessible all day. Light suppers available. For bookings or further details contact: Christine Jackson.

BAMPTON

Elaine Goodwin, Lodfin Farm, Morebath, Bampton EX16 9DD (Tel & Fax: 01398 331400). The calming ambience of this beautiful 17th century Devon farmhouse offers everything to relax and unwind. Lodfin Farm is situated on the edge of Exmoor National Park, one mile north of the historic floral town of Bampton and nestles in a secluded valley, of which five acres is a natural woodland habitat, with a stream and lake, for our guests to enjoy. Accommodation is spacious, comfortable and inviting with log fires and interesting artefacts. Three pretty bedrooms, two en suite, with tea making facilities and television. Hearty Aga cooked breakfast served in the inglenook dining room. Children and pets welcome. Separate pets' accommodation available if required. Sorry, no smoking. Bed and Breakfast from £22 per person. **ETC ◆◆◆◆** *SILVER AWARD.*

e-mail: lodfin.farm@eclipse.co.uk

website: www.lodfinfarm.com

BRAMPTON

Mrs Una Armstrong, Town Head Farm, Walton, Brampton CA8 2DJ (016977 2730). Town Head offers comfortable and pleasant accommodation. Our 100 acre beef/sheep farm is situated in the peaceful village of Walton overlooking the village green and commanding scenic views of the Pennines and Lakeland hills. An ideal base for touring the Lakes, Hadrian's Wall and Scottish Borders; three miles from Brampton, 10 miles from Carlisle – leave the M6 at Junction 43. One double, one twin or family bedrooms with tea making facilities and TV; lounge/ diningroom. Children welcome. Open all year except Christmas and New Year. Bed and Breakfast from £17 to £18. Reduced rate for children and Short Breaks. **ETC ◆◆◆**

CALDBECK

Mr and Mrs A. Savage, Swaledale Watch, Whelpo, Caldbeck CA7 8HQ (Tel & Fax: 016974 78409). Ours is a mixed farm of 300 acres situated in beautiful countryside within the Lake District National Park. Central for Scottish Borders, Roman Wall, Eden Valley and Lakes. Primarily a sheep farm (everyone loves lambing time). Visitors are welcome to see farm animals and activities. Many interesting walks nearby or roam the peaceful northern fells. Enjoyed by many Cumbrian Way walkers. Very comfortable accommodation with excellent home cooking. All rooms have private facilities. Central heating. Tea making facilities. We are a friendly Cumbrian farming family and make you very welcome. Bed and Breakfast from £19 to £25; Evening Meal from £12 to £15, Tuesday, Wednesday, Thursday and Saturday only. **ETC/AA ◆◆◆◆**

e-mail: nan.savage@talk21.com

Terms quoted in this publication may be subject to increase if rises in costs necessitate

CARLISLE

Mrs Dorothy Nicholson, Gill Farm, Blackford, Carlisle CA6 4EL (01228 675326; mobile: 07808 571586). In a delightful setting on a beef and sheep farm, this Georgian style farmhouse dated 1740 offers a friendly welcome to all guests breaking journeys to or from Scotland or having a holiday in our beautiful countryside. Near Hadrian's Wall, Gretna Green and Lake District. Golf, fishing, swimming and large agricultural auction markets all nearby; also cycle path passes our entrance. Accommodation is in one double room en suite, one family and one twin/single bedrooms. All rooms have washbasins, shaver points and tea/coffee making facilities. Two bathrooms, shower; lounge with colour TV; separate diningroom. Open all year. Reductions for children; cot provided. Central heating. Car essential, good parking. Pets permitted. Bed and Breakfast from £18. Telephone for further details or directions.

CARLISLE

Mrs Georgina Elwen, New Pallyards, Hethersgill, Carlisle CA6 6HZ (01228 577308). Working farm. Farmhouse filmed for BBC TV. Relax and see beautiful North Cumbria and the Borders. A warm welcome awaits you in our country farmhouse tucked away in the Cumbrian countryside, yet easily accessible from M6 Junction 44. In addition to the surrounding attractions there is plenty to enjoy, including hill walking, peaceful forests and sea trout/salmon fishing or just nestle down and relax with nature. Bed and Breakfast: Two double en suite, two family en suite rooms and one twin/single bedroom, all with tea/coffee making equipment. Bed and Breakfast from £21 per person, Dinner £13; Dinner, Bed and Breakfast weekly rates from £160 to £170. Menu choice. Self-catering offered. Disabled facilities. We are proud to have won a National Salon Culinaire Award for the "Best Breakfast in Britain". **ETC ◆◆◆◆** *GOLD AWARD WINNER.*

e-mail: info@newpallyards.freeserve.co.uk **website: www.newpallyards.freeserve.co.uk**

See also Colour Display Advertisement

HAWKSHEAD

Malcolm & Margaret MacFarlane, Borwick Lodge, Outgate, Hawkshead, Ambleside LA22 0PU (015394 36332). A leafy driveway entices you to the most enchantingly situated house in the Lake District, a very special 17th century country lodge with magnificent panoramic lake and mountain views, quietly secluded in beautiful gardens. Ideally placed in the heart of the Lakes and close to Hawkshead village with its good choice of restaurants and inns. Beautiful en suite bedrooms with colour TV and tea/coffee facilities including "Special Occasions" and "Romantic Breaks" two king-size four-poster rooms. Malcolm and Margaret welcome you to their "haven of peace and tranquillity" in this most beautiful corner of England. Ample parking. NON-SMOKING. Bed and Breakfast from £30. May we send our brochure? **ETC ◆◆◆◆** *SILVER AWARD.*

e-mail: borwicklodge@talk21.com **website: www.borwicklodge.com**

Visits & Attractions

Rheged Discovery Centre, Off M6 Junction 40, A66 • 01768 868000
website: www.rheged.com

The Lake District's most spectacular attraction. Six-storey high cinema screen takes you on a journey through 2000 years of Cumbria's history, myths and legends.

Cumberland Pencil Museum, Keswick, Cumbria • 017687 73626
website: www.pencils.co.uk

The fascintating history of the humble pencil, from the discovery of Borrowdale graphite to present day manufacture. See the world's largest colouring pencil, Shop.

ETC ◆◆◆◆

Hollin Root Farm

Garth Row, Skelsmergh, Kendal, Cumbria LA8 9AW
Tel: 01539 823638
e-mail: b-and-b@hollin-root-farm.freeserve.co.uk
website: www.hollinrootfarm.co.uk

Dating from 1844 Hollin Root Farm is a typical Lakeland farmhouse set in beautiful open countryside with land down to the river. Tranquil settings and large gardens make this an ideal place for longer stays and a good base from which to explore the Lake District. There are many footpaths near the farm including the 84 mile Dales Way. Accommodation consists of three en suite rooms all with colour TV and tea/coffee making facilities. Excellent breakfasts. Packed lunches available. Private car park, safe cycle storage. Children and vegetarians welcome.

Open all year. Non-Smoking establishment. B&B from £22 to £28 pppn.

Mrs Betty Fishwick, Stock Bridge Farm, Staveley, Kendal LA8 9LP (01539 821580). A comfortable, well appointed 17th century farmhouse on edge of by-passed village, just off A591 Kendal-Windermere Road. Situated at the foot of the Kentmere Valley. Ideal for walking. All bedrooms have fitted washbasins with shaver points. Bathroom with shower and toilet, plus separate toilet. Cosy lounge/diningroom with open fire, colour TV. Fire Certificate held. Full central heating. Full English Breakfast served at separate tables; friendly personal service. Good off-road parking facilities. Three good village pubs within walking distance of the farm. Excellent stop-off for England-Scotland routed through beautiful English Lakeland. Terms from £17.50pppn.

KESWICK

Lyndhurst Guest House, 22 Southerby Street, Keswick CA12 4EF (01767 72303). Well-established Bed and Breakfast for non-smokers, two minutes' walk from town centre and ideally situated for local walks. All rooms are fully en suite and have colour TV, central heating and tea/coffee making facilities. Family, twin and double rooms available. Children and groups welcome; child discount applies. Cyclists welcome and cycle storage available. Packed lunches available. Bed and full English Breakfast £19.50 per person, two or more nights £18.50.

See also Colour Display Advertisement

KESWICK

Hilton Keswick Lodore, Keswick CA12 5UX (017687 77285; Central Reservations: 08705 909090). Overlooking Derwentwater, this elegant hotel is set in stunning Lake District scenery, yet less than half an hour from the M6. Facilities include 71 bedrooms, including suites and Lake view rooms, a health club with swimming pools, solarium, sauna and fitness suite, massage and beauty salon, games room, and children's play area. The Lodore Restaurant offers a delicious choice of table d'hôte and à la carte menus. Situated in 40 acres of beautiful countryside, this hotel offers a delightful base from which to explore fells and woodland trails. **ETC ★★★★**

KESWICK

Colin and Lesley Smith, Mosedale House, Mosedale, Mungrisdale CA11 0XQ (017687 79371). Traditional 1862 built, lakeland farmhouse. A smallholding with donkeys and hens. It enjoys a magnificent position, nestling at the foot of Carrock Fell, overlooking the river Caldew, three-and-a-half miles from the A66 Keswick to Penrith road. Four-course dinners, licensed, vegetarians welcome. Home-baked bread, our own free-range eggs. Packed Lunches. No smoking. En suite rooms. Attractive lounge. Bed and Breakfast £25. Dinner £14.50. Delightful two bedroomed self-catering cottage. Peaceful location, fell-walking from the door. Abundant wildlife. Visit us on our website below. Grade One facilities for disabled guests. **ETC ◆◆◆◆**

e-mail: mosedale@northlakes.co.uk **website: www.mosedalehouse.co.uk**

ENGLAND

KESWICK

Mrs M. M. Beaty, Birkrigg Farm, Newlands, Keswick CA12 5TS (017687 78278). Working farm. Birkrigg is a working beef and sheep farm, very pleasantly and peacefully situated, with an excellent outlook in the lovely Newlands Valley. Five miles from Keswick between Braithwaite and Buttermere. Being in a beautiful mountainous area makes this an ideal place to stay especially for those wishing to walk or climb. Centrally located for touring the many beauty spots in the Lake District. Clean, comfortable accommodation awaits you. A good Breakfast is offered at 8.30am, Evening Tea at 9.30pm. Packed Lunches available. Sorry, no Evening Meals. Local inns all provide good food, two to four miles away. Open March to November. **ETC ◆◆**

NEAR SAWREY

Mrs Elizabeth Mallett, Esthwaite How Farmhouse, Near Sawrey, Ambleside LA22 0LB (015394 36450). A warm and friendly welcome awaits you at Esthwaite How Farmhouse, situated in this lovely village where Beatrix Potter wrote her books. Beautiful views of the countryside and the lake (where part of the television film about her life was made) can be seen from bedrooms and the diningroom. Ideal for walking, fishing and touring. Accommodation comprises two double rooms, one en suite, and one twin bedded room. Dining/sitting room with open log fire, central heating. Children welcome; babysitting can be arranged. Open all year. Car essential, parking for two cars. Bed and Breakfast from £16; Bed, Breakfast and Evening Meal from £24. Half rates for children sharing room.

NEAR SAWREY

Miss Gillian Fletcher, High Green Gate Guest House, Near Sawrey, Ambleside LA22 0LF (015394 36296). The Guest House is a converted 18th century farmhouse in the quiet hamlet where Beatrix Potter lived and wrote. Her house, owned by the National Trust, is close by and open to the public. The area abounds with pleasant easy walks and is a good centre for the Southern Lakes. Open from March to October. Good food and service under the personal attention of the owner. Spacious diningroom, lounge and separate TV lounge. All bedrooms have hot and cold water and individual heating in addition to central heating. Rooms with private facilities available. Reduced rates for children sharing with parents. Cot and highchair are available and babysitting can be arranged. Dogs welcome. A car is desirable and there is parking for seven cars. Bed and Breakfast from £25 per night; Bed, Breakfast and Evening Meal from £36 per night (£230 weekly). **ETC/AA/RAC ◆◆◆**
e-mail: highgreengate@amserve.net

NEWBIGGIN ON LUNE

Mrs Brenda Boustead, Tranna Hill, Newbiggin on Lune, Kirkby Stephen CA17 4NY (015396 23227 or 07989 892368). Tranna Hill offers a relaxing and friendly atmosphere in a non-smoking environment. Five miles from M6 Junction 38, ideal base for all activities with Howgill Fells Nature Reserve, fish farm and golf course only minutes away. Well placed for breaking your journey or touring the Lakes and Dales. Private parking and large gardens. En suite rooms furnished to a high standard with TV, refreshment trays, central heating and beautiful views. Delicious breakfasts. All for £20pppn. **ETC ◆◆◆◆**
e-mail: trannahill@hotmail.com

PENRITH

Mrs Brenda Preston, Pallet Hill Farm, Penrith CA11 0BY (017684 83247). Pallet Hill Farm is pleasantly situated two miles from Penrith on the Penrith-Greystoke-Keswick road (B5288). It is four miles from Ullswater and has easy access to the Lake District, Scottish Borders and Yorkshire Dales. There are several sports facilities in the area - golf club, swimming pool, pony trekking. Good farmhouse food and hospitality with personal attention. An ideal place to spend a relaxing break. Double, single and family rooms; TV lounge and dining room. Children welcome, cot, high chair. Sorry, no pets. Car essential, parking. Open Easter to November. Bed and Breakfast £14 (reduced weekly rates), reduced rates for children.

ENGLAND

SANDOWN

Lake Road, Windermere, Cumbria LA23 2JF • Tel: 015394 45275

Superb Bed and Breakfast accommodation. All rooms en suite with colour TV and tea/coffee making facilities. Situated two minutes from Lake Windermere, shops and cafes. Many lovely walks. Open all year. Special out of season rates, also two-day Saturday/Sunday breaks. From £22 to £32 per person, excluding Bank Holidays. Well-behaved dogs welcome. Each room has own safe private car parking. SAE or telephone for further details

Proprietors: Irene and George Eastwood

See also Colour Advertisement

PENRITH

Mrs Sheila Robinson, Skygarth Farm, Temple Sowerby, Penrith CA10 1SS (01768 361300). A working farm on the outskirts of Temple Sowerby in the beautiful Eden Valley, ideal for a stopover en route to or from Scotland. A warm and friendly welcome awaits all guests arriving at our spacious 17th century farmhouse. Relax and watch TV in our comfortable guest sitting room, which has tea/coffee making facilities, or sit in the garden and savour the quiet tranquillity of the Eden Valley. We have two spacious family rooms which look out over the garden, with central heating, TV, and tea/coffee facilities. A hearty farmhouse breakfast starts your day. **AA ◆◆◆**
e-mail: enquire@skygarth.co.uk
website: www.skygarth.co.uk

TROUTBECK

Mrs Maureen Dix, Greenah Crag, Troutbeck, Penrith CA11 0SQ (017684 83233). Enjoy a relaxing break at Greenah Crag, a 17th century former farmhouse peacefully located in the Lake District National Park, just 10 miles from Keswick and only eight miles from the M6 motorway. Ideal for exploring Northern Lakes, Eden Valley, Carlisle, Hadrian's Wall and the Western Pennines. Accommodation is in two double bedrooms with bathroom en suite, and one twin-bedded room with washbasin, all with tea/coffee making facilities. The guests' sittingroom with TV and woodburning stove is a cosy place on the coldest days! A full breakfast is served in the oak-beamed diningroom. Pub/ restaurant three-quarters-of-a-mile. Regret no pets or smoking in the house. Bed and Breakfast from £16.50 per person. Please telephone for brochure.

Two children FREE with two adults at

Eskdale Historic Water Mill

See our READERS' OFFER VOUCHER for details.

Two for the price of one (adults) or 25% off family tickets at

Windermere Steamboat Museum

See our READERS' OFFER VOUCHER for details.

The FHG Directory of Website Addresses

on pages 349–378 is a useful quick reference guide for holiday accommodation with e-mail and/or website details

DERBYSHIRE

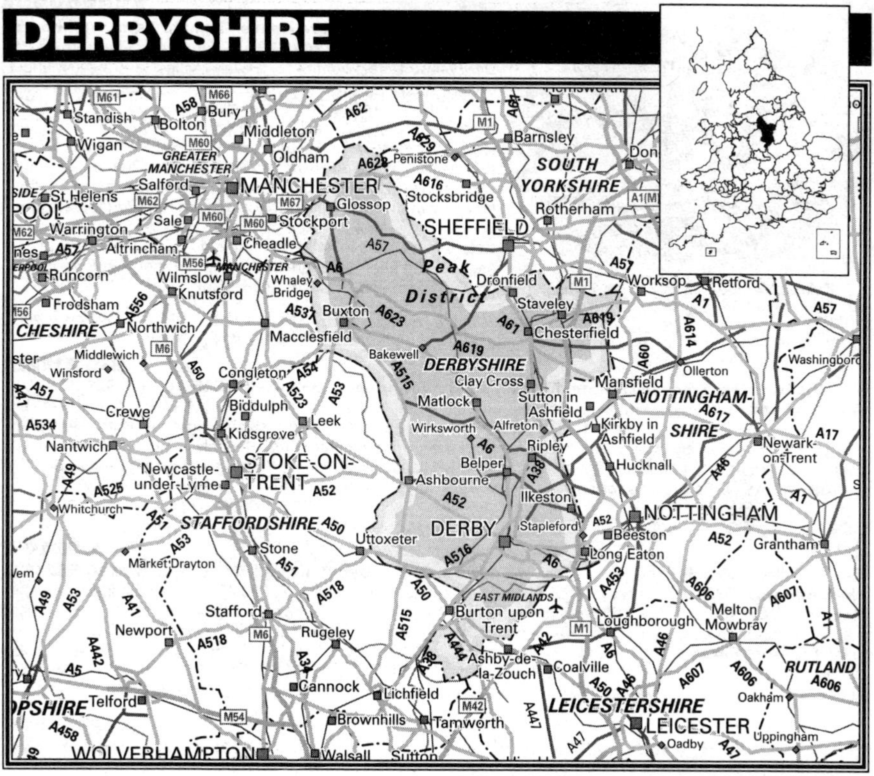

ASHBOURNE

The Courtyard, Dairy House Farm, Alkmonton, Longford, Ashbourne DE6 3DG (Tel & Fax: 01335 330187). Grazing farm. Victorian cowshed tastefully converted and furnished to a very high standard.Tranquil location, yet within easy reach of Alton Towers (eight miles), Chatsworth House, Calke Abbey and many other historic houses. The Potteries are close to hand, as is the American Adventure Theme Park. We are surrounded by beautiful countryside which includes Dovedale and the many other lovely Dales which make up the Derbyshire Dales. A newly opened 18 hole, par-three golf course is only four miles away. Good farmhouse fare served on our 18 acre farm. Stay in one of our seven rooms – five double, one twin and one family, all with en suite facilities. Category 1 Wheelchair Access. Children welcome. Regret, no pets. Bed and Breakfast from £24 to £30; Winter breaks October 20–March 20: Dinner, Bed and Breakfast £34 per person per night, minimum two nights. **ETC/AA ◆◆◆◆**

e-mail: andy@dairyhousefarm.org.uk **website: www.dairyhousefarm.org.uk**

ASHBOURNE

Mrs M. Richardson, Throwley Hall Farm, Ilam, Ashbourne DE6 2BB (01538 308202 or 308243). Situated on a working beef and sheep farm in quiet countryside near the Manifold Valley, on the public road from Ilam to Calton. Within easy reach of Dovedale and Alton Towers, also stately homes. Accommodation comprises two double and two twin rooms, two rooms en suite, all with washbasins and TVs. Dining/sitting room with colour TV. Full central heating, also open fire. Tea/coffee making facilities. Bed and Breakfast from £25. Reduced rates for children, cot and high chair available.

ASHBOURNE

Mrs E.M. Smail, New House Organic Farm, Ashbourne DE6 1JL (01335 342429). Organic family farm in the Derbyshire Dales, central to "Peak Practice" and near Matlock, Bakewell, Dove Dale; one mile from Carsington Watersports Centre. There are free range animals, a farm trail and shop selling organic produce. We serve organic, free-range and fair-traded foods. Vegetarians and other diets are catered for. Pets, horses, bicycles and children welcome. Six-berth mobile home to rent at £10 per night, a 1960's gypsy caravan which sleeps two to four, two caravans sleeping two to four, space for three tourers and a field for individual or group camping. Bed and Breakfast or Self-Catering available in holiday cottage, decorated to be suitable for asthma and allergy sufferers. We also arrange FREE WORKING HOLIDAYS. Members of ECEAT and affiliated to the Environmental Tourism Association.

BAKEWELL

Mrs Alison Yates, Smerrill Grange, Middleton, By Youlgreave, Bakewell DE45 1LQ (01629 636232). Working farm. Traditional bed and breakfast on beef cattle and sheep farm. Beautiful setting in heart of Peak District. Very old farmhouse. Many tourist attractions within short driving distance, eg Chatsworth House and Haddon Hall. Bakewell and Matlock six miles. Glorious walks in Derbyshire Dales. Double en suite, double and twin bedrooms with private bathroom. Tea/coffee making facilities. Private guests' sitting and dining rooms. Bed and Breakfast from £17. Reductions for children. Dogs by arrangement.

BASLOW

Mrs S. Mills, Bubnell Cliff Farm, Wheatlands Lane, Baslow, Bakewell DE45 1RH (01246 582454). Working farm. A 300 acre working farm situated half-a-mile from the village of Baslow in the beautiful Derbyshire Peak District. Guests can enjoy, from their bedroom window, breathtaking views of Chatsworth Park and surrounding area. Chatsworth House, the majestic home of the Duke of Devonshire, medieval Haddon Hall and the traditional market town of Bakewell (famous for its puddings), are all close by. Accommodation comprises two double rooms, guests' lounge/dining room with TV and log fires in the winter. NON-SMOKERS ONLY. Bed and Breakfast from £17.50 per person with shared bathroom. Reductions for children. Varied breakfast menu.

CHINLEY (near Buxton)

Mrs Barbara Goddard, Moseley House Farm, Maynestone Road, Chinley, High Peak SK23 6AH (01663 750240). Enjoy a stay on our farm set in a special landscaped area in the lovely Peak District. We offer comfort and hospitality in spacious family/twin and double rooms, some en suite. Colour TV, central heating. Delicious breakfasts. Children welcome. Village half a mile away. Open all year except Christmas. Also newly-built self-catering cottage suite designed for two plus sofa bed. Fabulous views. Weekly lets or short breaks. Bed and Breakfast from £20 to £23. **ETC ◆◆◆**

e-mail: moseleyhouse@supanet.com

DOVEDALE

Mrs Joan Wain, Air Cottage Farm, Ilam, Ashbourne DE6 2DB (01335 350475). Working farm, join in. Holidaymakers to the Peak District will enjoy staying at Air Cottage Farm situated at the edge of Dovedale with picturesque views of Thorpe Cloud and Dovedale Valley.The famous Stepping Stones are just 10 minutes away and it is an ideal base for touring the Peak District National Park, stately homes and many other places of local historic interest. Unlimited walks in the Manifold Valley and the Tissington Nature Trail and scenic routes for motorists. Within easy reach of Alton Towers and Carsington Reservoir for water sports. Activities available include swimming, squash and horse riding, all within easy reach. Two double bedrooms and one single (sleeping two); bathroom, two toilets; sittingroom; dining room. Cot and high chair provided for children. Open March to November. A car essential – parking. Terms and further details on request.

GLOSSOP

Graham and Julie Caesar, Windy Harbour Farm Hotel, Woodhead Road, Glossop SK13 7QE (01457 853107). Situated in the heart of the Peak District on the B6105, approximately one mile from Glossop town centre and adjacent to the Pennine Way. Our 10-bedroom hotel with outstanding views of Woodhead and Snake Passes and the Longdendale Valley is an ideal location for all outdoor activities. A warm welcome awaits you in our licensed bar and restaurant serving a wide range of excellent home-made food. Bed and Breakfast from £25 per night.

GLOSSOP

Margaret Child, Rock Farm, Monks Road, Glossop SK13 6JZ (01457 861086). Delightful secluded farmhouse, with panoramic views all round, set in the beautiful scenery of the Dark Peak, yet only 40 minutes from Manchester. Warm, friendly, atmosphere makes for a very relaxing stay. Plenty of good walks from the doorstep, with many local pubs nearby offering excellent, good-value meals. Tastefully decorated bedrooms each have beamed ceilings, colour TV, radio and tea/coffee making trays. South-facing guest lounge can be used throughout the day if the weather lets you down. Centrally heated throughout. Bed and Breakfast from £20 pppn. Top twenty finalist in last two AA Landlady of the Year Awards. **AA ◆◆◆◆**
website: www.rockfarm99.freeserve.co.uk

KIRK LANGLEY

Mrs Diane Buxton, New Park Farm, Lodge Lane, Kirk Langley DE6 4NX (01332 824262). Working farm. An early 19th century farmhouse situated seven miles from Ashbourne and four miles from Derby, within easy reach of Alton Towers and The American Adventure Park, Dovedale, Carsington Water, two miles from Kedleston Hall. Hotels and pubs are only a few miles away where good food is served. Accommodation consists of one double bedroom, one family bedroom and one twin bedroom, all with TV and tea/coffee making facilities. Parking is off road, close by the house. Situated in peaceful surroundings overlooking Kirk Langley Village and countryside. Bed and Breakfast from £14 per person. Reductions for children. Self-catering flat also available. Open all year. Write or telephone for details.

MATLOCK

Mrs Linda Lomas, Middlehills Farm Bed and Breakfast, Grange Mill, Matlock DE4 4HY (01629 650368). We know the secret of contentment - we live in the most picturesque part of England. Share our good fortune, breathe the fresh air, absorb the peace, feast your eyes on the beautiful scenery that surrounds our small working farm, with our pot bellied pig who just loves to have her ears scratched, and Bess and Ruby who are ideal playmates for children of all ages. Retire with the scent of honeysuckle and waken to the aroma of freshly baked bread and sizzling bacon then sample the delights of the Peak District and Derbyshire Dales such as Dovedale, Chatsworth and Haddon Hall.

MATLOCK

Mrs D. Wootton, Old School Farm, Uppertown Lane, Uppertown, Ashover, Near Chesterfield S45 0JF (01246 590813). Working farm, join in. This working farm in a small hamlet on the edge of the Peak District enjoys unspoilt views. Ashover is three miles away and mentioned in the Domesday Book; Chatsworth House, Haddon Hall, Hardwick Hall, Matlock Bath and Bakewell all within seven miles. Accommodation comprises two family rooms with en suite facilities, one double, one single rooms. Washbasin in two of the rooms; shared bathroom for guests' use only. Plenty of hot water; fitted carpets; large livingroom/diningroom with colour TV. Car essential. No smoking in bedrooms. NO PETS. Disabled guests welcome. Children welcome. Open from April to October. Bed and Breakfast from £22 per person per night; Bed, Breakfast and Evening Meal £30 per person per night. Evening meal minimum two persons. Reductions for children. Take the B5057 Darley Dale Road off the A632 Chesterfield to Matlock main road. Take second left. Keep on this road for approximately one mile. Old School Farm is on left opposite the stone water trough. **ETC/RAC ◆◆◆◆** *SPARKLING DIAMOND AWARD*.

MELBOURNE (near)

Mrs Mary Kidd, Ivy House Farm, Stanton-by-Bridge, Near Melbourne DE73 1HT (Tel & Fax: 01332 863152). Working farm, join in. Ivy House Farm is a 400 acre arable farm with horses at livery. The farmhouse, converted in 2000, has three en suite double rooms and we have also converted some cowsheds into chalets, all of which are en suite with tea/coffee making facilities and TV. Each chalet has a theme – Cowshed, Sheep Pen, Stable and Pigsty. The area has lots to do and see, such as Calke Abbey, ski slopes, Alton Towers, motor racing at Donington Park. There are also lots of places to eat. Children are welcome, but we are strictly non-smoking. Ample off-road parking. Bed and Breakfast from £25. **ETC** *SILVER AWARD*.
e-mail: mary@guesthouse.fsbusiness.co.uk
website: www.ivy-house-farm.com

DEVON

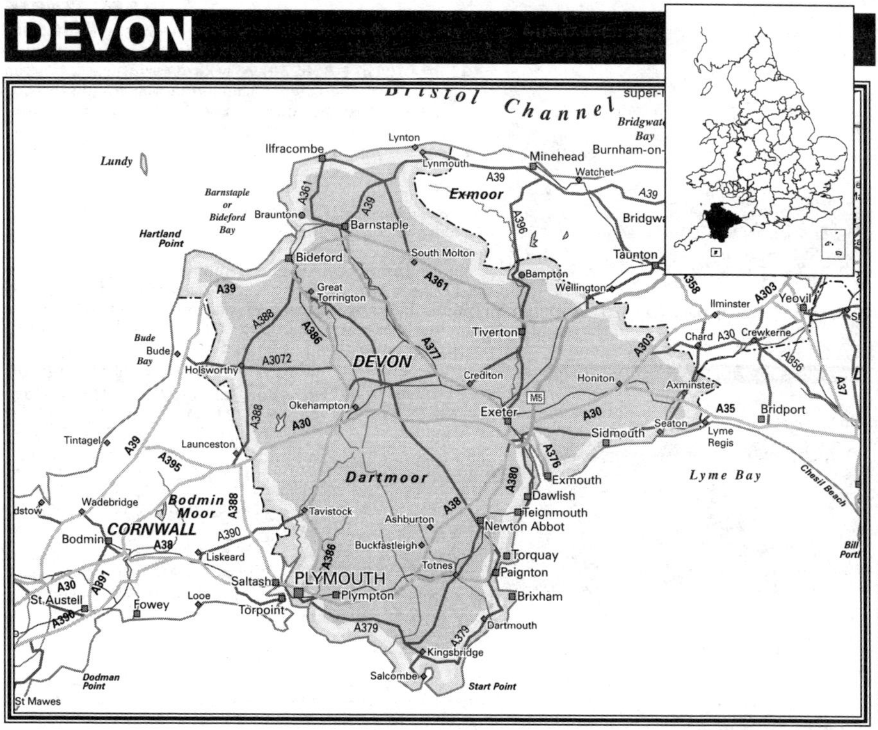

ASHBURTON

Chris and Annie Moore, Gages Mill, Buckfastleigh Road, Ashburton TQ13 7JW (Tel & Fax: 01364 652391). Relax in the warm and friendly atmosphere of our lovely 14th century former wool mill, set in over an acre of gardens on the edge of the Dartmoor National Park. Eight delightful en suite rooms, one on the ground floor; all with tea and coffee making facilities, central heating, hairdryers, radio and alarm clocks. We have a large comfortable lounge with corner bar and granite archways leading to the dining room and a cosy sittingroom with colour TV. Home cooking of a very high standard. Licensed. Ample car parking. Being one mile from the centre of Ashburton, this is an ideal base for touring South Devon or visiting Exeter, Plymouth, Dartmouth, the many National Trust properties and other places of interest. Children over 12 years welcome. Sorry no pets. Bed, Breakfast and Evening Meal or Bed and Breakfast only. **ETC/AA ◆◆◆◆, ETC** *SILVER AWARD FOR EXCELLENCE*

e-mail: gagesmill@aol.com

See also Colour Display Advertisement

BAMPTON

Mrs Lindy Head, Harton Farm, Oakford, Tiverton EX16 9HH (01398 351209). Working farm, join in. Come and enjoy a unique rural experience on our traditional non-intensive farm near Exmoor. Peace and quiet for adults, and for children, a chance to meet the animals. 17th century stone farmhouse, secluded but accessible, ideal touring centre. Comfortable accommodation in three double bedrooms with washbasin and tea making facilities; luxury bathroom with a view; dining room serving real country cooking with farm-produced additive-free meat and organic vegetables; home baking a speciality; guests' lounge with colour TV. Home spun wool. Garden. Children over four welcome. Pets accepted. Car essential - parking. Open for Evening Meal, Bed and Breakfast from £26; Bed and Breakfast from £18. Reductions for children. Farm walks. Fishing, shooting, riding can be arranged. Vegetarian meals available on request.

e-mail: lindy@hartonfarm.co.uk **website: www.hartonfarm.co.uk**

ENGLAND

BARNSTAPLE (near)

Mrs J. Ley, West Barton, Alverdiscott, Near Barnstaple EX31 3PT (01271 858230). Working farm. Our family-run working farm of 250 acres is situated in a small rural village between Barnstaple and Torrington on the B3232. Ideal base for your holiday within easy reach of Exmoor or visiting our rugged coastline of many sandy beaches. Also Dartington Glass, RHS Rosemoor Gardens, Clovelly and many other beauty spots. West Barton farmhouse is situated beside the B3232 with panoramic views of the beautiful North Devon countryside. Children welcome with reductions. Comfortable accommodation, family room, twin beds, single and double rooms available. Visitors' own lounge with colour TV. Dining room. Good farmhouse cooking including a variety of our own produce when available. Basic Food Hygiene Certificate. Regret no pets. Bed and Breakfast from £16; Evening Meal optional. Weekly terms on request.

See also Colour Display Advertisement

BIDEFORD

Mrs Valerie Beer, Horwood Barton Farm, Monkleigh, Bideford EX39 5LF (01805 623174). Touring North Devon? Then stay with us on our 400-acre family dairy farm. Large impressive farmhouse with stunning views from your bedroom. Breakfast is served in a delightful panelled dining room with 18th century moulded ceiling. Two rooms available: one family/twin room en suite, one double with large private bathroom. TV, tea/coffee facilities in rooms. Private lounge for guests. Come and go as you please. Welcome to tour farm. Quality assured. Five miles to Bideford, three miles to RHS Garden Rosemoor, three miles Tarka cycle trail, eight miles to sandy beaches. Non-smoking. Sorry, no pets. £20 per person per night.

BIDEFORD

Lynne Pirrie, The Pines at Eastleigh Hotel & Cottages, Eastleigh, Near Bideford EX39 4PA (01271 860561). A Georgian country house set in seven hilltop acres with magnificent views over the Torridge estuary to Lundy Island. Log fires, king-size beds, garden room bar with library, maps and a warm welcome await our guests. Breakfasts use home produce and prize-winning locally sourced ingredients. There are ground floor rooms set around the courtyard garden with easy access. All rooms en suite and have teletext television, well-stocked hospitality tray with tea and coffee making facilities, telephones and hairdryers. Bed and Breakfast from £29. Two cottages offer self-catering from £206 for four. No smoking. Selected by the AA as "One of Britain's Best in 2003." **AA ◆◆◆◆**

e-mail: pirrie@thepinesateastleigh.co.uk **website: www.thepinesateastleigh.co.uk**

BIDEFORD (near)

Mrs Yvonne Heard, West Titchberry Farm, Hartland Point, Near Bideford EX39 6AU (Tel & Fax: 01237 441287). Situated on the rugged North Devon coast, West Titchberry is a traditionally run stock farm, half a mile from Hartland Point. The South West coast path skirts around the farm making it an ideal base for walkers. The three guests' rooms comprise an en suite family room; one double and one twin room both having wash basins. All rooms have colour TV, radio, hairdryer, tea/coffee making facilities; bathroom/toilet and separate shower room on the same floor. Outside, guests may take advantage of a sheltered walled garden and a games room for the children. Hartland village is three miles away, Clovelly six miles, Bideford and Westward Ho! sixteen miles and Bude eighteen miles. Bed and Breakfast from £18 pppn. Evening meal £9. Children welcome at reduced rates for under 12s. Open all year except Christmas. Sorry, no pets.

When making enquiries or bookings, a stamped addressed envelope is always appreciated

BRAUNTON

Mrs Roselyn Bradford, "St. Merryn", Higher Park Road, Braunton EX33 2LG (01271 813805). Set in beautiful, sheltered garden of approximately one acre, with many peaceful sun traps. Ros extends a warm welcome to her guests. Rooms (£20–£22 per person) include single, double and family rooms, with washbasin, central heating, colour TV and tea/coffee making facilities. All rooms either en suite or with private bathrooms. Evening meal (£12) may be served indoors or out. Guests may bring own wine. Guest lounge with colour TV, patio door access to garden. Swimming pool, fish ponds, hens and thatched summerhouse plus excellent parking. Self-catering flat also available. Please send for brochure.

See also Colour Display Advertisement

COLYTON

Mrs Ruth Gould, Bonehayne Farm, Colyton EX24 6SG. (01404 871396). Working farm. Bonehayne Farm, situated in beautiful Coly Valley, set amidst 250 acres dairy farmland on banks of the River Coly, where daffodils are a feature in springtime, and Mallard duck and Kingfishers are a common sight. Trout fishing freely available. Woodlands to explore. Visitors welcome to participate in some farm activities and make friends with the animals. One family, one double bedrooms, with washbasins; bathroom, toilet. Spacious, homely lounge with inglenook fireplace, TV. A good English breakfast. Lawn and play area for children with extended large lawn overlooking surrounding countryside. Reduced rates, cot, high chair. Parking. Farway Country Park, riding school, Honiton Golf Course, coastal area, all within four-and-a-half miles. Open April to October. Bed and Breakfast; Evening Meal. Terms on request.

e-mail: gouldrl@hotmail.com **website: www.bonehayne.co.uk**

COLYTON

Mrs Norma Rich, Sunnyacre, Northleigh, Colyton EX24 6DA (01404 871422). Working farm, join in. A warm and friendly welcome awaits you. Come and enjoy a relaxing holiday on our working farm, which is set in an area of outstanding natural beauty amongst the rolling hills of East Devon. Children may help with animal feeding, includes calves, chickens, ducks, lambs etc., and collect the free range eggs for their breakfast (adults are welcome to help as well!). There is a Full English Breakfast. Fresh and mainly homegrown produce is used to make excellent and varied Evening Meals. Sweets are all homemade and served with clotted cream. Early Morning Tea. Evening drinks. Three bedrooms with washbasin, separate w.c. TV in lounge, games room, sun room, Wendy house, sandpit. Cot and high chair available. Please enquire for reasonable rates.

CREDITON

Mrs M Reed, Hayne Farm, Cheriton Fitzpaine, Crediton EX17 4HR (01363 866392). Guests are welcome to our 17th century working beef and sheep farm, situated between Cadeleigh and Cheriton Fitzpaine. Exeter nine miles, Tiverton eight miles. South and North coast, Exmoor and Dartmoor within easy reach. Three local pubs nearby. Good farm fayre. Fishing lake; summer house overlooking duck pond. Bed and Breakfast from £18, reduction for children.

CROYDE

Audrey Isaac, Crowborough B&B, Georgeham, Braunton EX33 1JZ (01271 891005). OPEN ALL YEAR. Peaceful Georgian farmhouse only two miles from Croyde. Ideal location for easy access to the sandy beaches of Croyde (two miles); Putsborough (one mile); Woolacombe (four miles); Saunton (four miles) and Saunton Championship Golf Course. Five minutes' walk to the village and friendly local Inn. Exmoor National Park is only 45 minutes' drive away and there are many places of interest to visit eg: Lundy Island, Arlington Court (National Trust), Clovelly, many gardens (including RHS Rosemoor) etc. Accommodation comprises two double and one twin rooms; breakfast/sitting room with TV, beverage tray and woodburner in winter. Ideal for a family or group. Bed and Breakfast from £20 per person per night.
e-mail: amisaac@aol.com

CULLOMPTON

Mrs Margaret Chumbley, Oburnford Farm, Cullompton EX15 1LZ (01884 32292). Working farm, join in. Treat yourself to a "special break" and enjoy our welcoming friendly family atmosphere. Mentioned in the Domesday Book, Oburnford is a dairy farm where guests may watch the milking and the making of clotted cream. The Listed Georgian farmhouse is set in large gardens, and is ideally situated for the coasts, Exmoor, Dartmoor, coarse fishing and several National Trust properties. Cullompton (M5 J28) two-and-a-half miles. The spacious en suite bedrooms all have tea/coffee facilities; the guest lounge has a colour television; separate dining room. Generous farmhouse hospitality, licensed, full menu, four-course evening meals and fresh clotted cream all make for a perfect relaxing break at anytime of the year. Special diets welcome. Bed and Breakfast £20. Bed, Breakfast and Evening Meal £199 per week. Phone now "free wine". Pets welcome. Open all year.

EXETER

Karen Williams, Stile Farm, Starcross, Exeter EX6 8PD (Tel & Fax: 01626 890268). Enjoy a peaceful break in beautiful countryside. Close to the Exe Estuary and only two miles to the nearest sandy beach. Take a stroll to the village (only half a mile) to discover many eating places, or a little further to some specially recommended ones. Birdwatching, golf, fishing, racing, etc. all nearby, and centrally situated for exploring all the lovely countryside and coastline in the area. Good shopping in Exeter. Comfortable rooms, guests' lounge, English breakfast. Nice garden. Plenty of parking. NON- SMOKING. Personal service and a 'home from home' atmosphere guaranteed. Bed and Breakfast from £18 per person per night.
website: www.stile-farm.co.uk

EXETER

Mrs Sally Glanvill, Rydon Farm, Woodbury, Exeter EX5 1LB (01395 232341). Working farm. Come, relax and enjoy yourself in our lovely 16th century Devon longhouse. We offer a warm and friendly family welcome at this peaceful dairy farm. Three miles from M5 Junction 30 on B3179. Ideally situated for exploring the coast, moors and the historic city of Exeter. Only 10 minutes' drive from the coast. Inglenook fireplace and oak beams. All bedrooms have central heating, private or en suite bathrooms, hair dryers and tea/coffee making facilities. One room with romantic four-poster. A traditional farmhouse breakfast is served with free range eggs and there are several excellent pubs and restaurants close by. Pets by arrangement. Open all year. Colour brochure available. Bed and Breakfast from £26 to £35. **ETC/AA ◆◆◆◆**, *FARM STAY UK MEMBER*.

HARTLAND

Mrs A. Heard, Greenlake Farm, Hartland, Bideford EX39 6DN (01237 441251). Greenlake is a mixed farm set in approximately 250 acres of unspoilt countryside, just two miles from Hartland on the North Devon coast. While the farmhouse retains its original character with features such as oak beams in some of the rooms, it also offers every facility for your comfort. Some accommodation offers en suite facilities, while all rooms have fitted carpets, TV and tea/coffee equipment. There is a television lounge and a separate dining room. Guests are welcome to watch the farm work in progress. Ideally situated for touring North Devon and North Cornwall; the popular sandy beaches of Bude and Westward Ho! are only a short drive away, as are the market towns of Bideford and Holsworthy.

IVYBRIDGE

Mrs P. Stephens, Venn Farm, Ugborough, Ivybridge PL21 0PE (01364 73240). Enjoy a rural retreat at Venn, yet only three miles from dual carriageway. We are 20 minutes from beaches and South Dartmoor is visible from the farm. We have two family bedrooms, and a separate garden cottage which has two twin ground floor bedrooms overlooking a large pond. We also have self-catering for eight, four and two persons, again with ground floor bedrooms. Brochure on request from: **Pat Stephens (01364 73240). ETC ◆◆◆** (★★★★ *SELF-CATERING*), *DISABLED CATEGORY 2 ACCESSIBILITY.*
website: www.SmoothHound.co.uk/hotels/vennfarm

IVYBRIDGE (near)

Mrs Susan Winzer, Higher Coarsewell Farm, Ugborough, Near Ivybridge PL21 0HP (01548 821560). Working farm. Higher Coarsewell Farm is part of a traditional family-run dairy farm situated in the heart of the peaceful South Hams countryside, near Dartmoor and local unspoilt sandy beaches. It is a very spacious bungalow with beautiful garden and meadow views. One double room with bathroom en suite and one en suite family room. Guest lounge/dining room. Good home cooked food, full English breakfast served. Children welcome - cot, high chair and babysitting available. Bed and Breakfast from £17 daily; optional Evening Meal extra. Open all year. A3121 turn-off from the main A38 Exeter to Plymouth road.

KINGSBRIDGE

Mrs Angela Foale, Higher Kellaton Farm, Kellaton, Kingsbridge TQ7 2ES (Tel & Fax 01548 511514). Working farm. Smell the fresh sea air, delicious Aga-cooked breakfast in the comfort of this lovely old farmhouse. Nestled in a valley, our farm with friendly animals welcomes you. Spacious, well-furnished rooms, en suite, colour TVs, tea/coffee making facilities, own lounge, central heating and log fires. Flexible meal times. Attractive walled garden. Safe car parking. Situated between Kingsbridge and Dartmouth. Visit Salcombe by ferry. One-and-a-half miles to the lost village of Hallsands and Lanacombe Beach. Beautiful, peaceful, unspoilt coastline with many sandy beaches, paths, wild flowers and wildlife. Ramblers' haven. Good pubs and wet-weather family attractions. Open Easter to October. Non-smoking. Bed and Breakfast from £18.50. **ETC ◆◆◆**
e-mail: higherkellatonfarm@agriplus.net website: www.welcometo/higherkellaton

KINGSBRIDGE

Anne Rossiter, Burton Farm, Galmpton, Kingsbridge TQ7 3EY (01548 561210). Working farm in South Huish Valley, one mile from the fishing village of Hope Cove, three miles from famous sailing haunt of Salcombe. Walking, beaches, sailing, windsurfing, bathing, diving, fishing, horse-riding – facilities for all in this area. We have a dairy herd and two flocks of pedigree sheep. Guests are welcome to take part in farm activities when appropriate. Traditional farmhouse cooking and home produce. Country restaurant on site serving freshly cooked meals using local produce. Lunches, cream teas, dinner, children's meals. Access to rooms at all times. Tea/coffee making facilities and TV in rooms, all of which are en suite. Games room. Non-smoking. Open all year, except Christmas. Warm welcome assured. Self-catering cottages also available. Dogs by arrangement. Details and terms on request. Bed and Breakfast from £30 to £35 per person.

e-mail: anne@burtonfarm.co.uk **website: www.burtonfarm.co.uk**

KINGSBRIDGE (near)

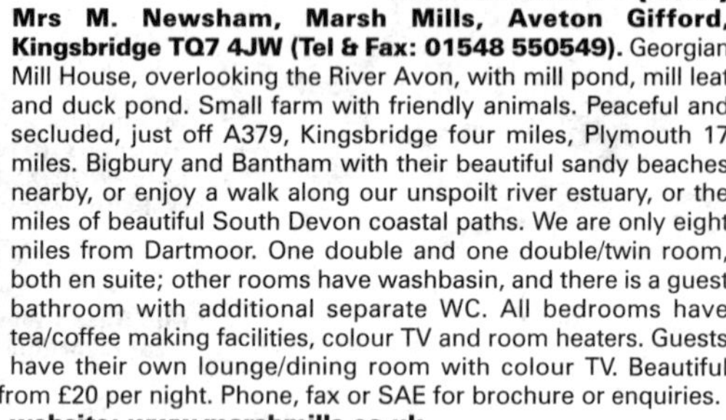

Mrs M. Newsham, Marsh Mills, Aveton Gifford, Kingsbridge TQ7 4JW (Tel & Fax: 01548 550549). Georgian Mill House, overlooking the River Avon, with mill pond, mill leat and duck pond. Small farm with friendly animals. Peaceful and secluded, just off A379, Kingsbridge four miles, Plymouth 17 miles. Bigbury and Bantham with their beautiful sandy beaches nearby, or enjoy a walk along our unspoilt river estuary, or the miles of beautiful South Devon coastal paths. We are only eight miles from Dartmoor. One double and one double/twin room, both en suite; other rooms have washbasin, and there is a guest bathroom with additional separate WC. All bedrooms have tea/coffee making facilities, colour TV and room heaters. Guests have their own lounge/dining room with colour TV. Beautiful gardens, ample car parking. Bed and Breakfast from £20 per night. Phone, fax or SAE for brochure or enquiries.

e-mail: newsham@marshmills.co.uk **website: www.marshmills.co.uk**

LYNMOUTH

Tricia and Alan Francis, Glenville House, 2 Tors Road, Lynmouth EX35 6ET (01598 752202). Idyllic riverside setting for our delightful Victorian house built in local stone, full of character and lovingly refurbished, at the entrance to the Watersmeet Valley. Picturesque village, enchanting harbour and unique water-powered cliff railway nestled amidst wooded valleys. Beautiful area where Exmoor meets the sea. Breathtaking scenery, riverside, woodland and magnificent coastal walks with spectacular views to the heather-clad moorland. Peaceful, tranquil, romantic - a very special place. Tastefully decorated bedrooms, most with pretty en suites. Elegant lounge overlooking river. Enjoy a four-course breakfast in our attractive dining room. Non-smoking. Licensed. Bed and Breakfast from £24 per person per night. **AA ◆◆◆◆**

e-mail: tricia@glenvillelynmouth.co.uk **website: glenvillelynmouth.co.uk**

See also Colour Display Advertisement

MORETONHAMPSTEAD

Mrs T. M. Merchant, Great Sloncombe Farm, Moretonhampstead TQ13 8QF (01647 440595). Working farm. Share the magic of Dartmoor all year round while staying in our lovely 13th century farmhouse full of interesting historical features. A working dairy farm set amongst peaceful meadows and woodland abundant in wild flowers and animals, including badgers, foxes, deer and buzzards. A welcoming and informal place to relax and explore the moors and Devon countryside. Comfortable double and twin rooms with en suite facilities, TV, central heating and coffee/tea making facilities. Delicious Devonshire suppers and breakfasts with new baked bread. Open all year. No smoking. **ETC ◆◆◆◆** *SILVER AWARD*, **AA ◆◆◆◆**, *FARM STAY UK MEMBER.*

e-mail: hmerchant@sloncombe.freeserve.co.uk
website: www.greatsloncombefarm.co.uk

Bulleigh Park Farm

Farmhouse accommodation with spectacular country views

The friendly Dallyn Family welcomes guests to their spacious farmhouse, set in rural surroundings just four miles from the coast. One en suite bedroom, one with private facilities; both have TV, hairdryer, hospitality trays and toiletries. Pleasant views are afforded from the lounge, conservatory and dining room. Award-winning breakfasts are prepared from local produce; for dinner, the local pub is just a stroll away. No smoking in bedrooms or dining room. Guests enjoy visiting nearby beaches, gardens, antique centres, Paignton Zoo, and Agatha Christie's house (NT).

Tel & Fax: 01803 872254 • e-mail: bulleigh@lineone.net
Bulleigh Park Farm, Ipplepen, Newton Abbot, Devon TQ12 5UA

See also Colour Advertisement

PLYMOUTH

Mrs Margaret MacBean, Gabber Farm, Down Thomas, Plymouth PL9 0AW (01752 862269). Working farm. Come and join us on this 120 acre working farm in an area of outstanding natural beauty with lovely walks on the farm and coastline. It is ideally situated for touring and near the historic city of Plymouth. Good food and a warm welcome are assured with Bed and Breakfast or Bed, Breakfast and Evening Meal available. One double and one family room en suite, one single, one twin and one family room with washbasins. All have tea/coffee making facilities, TV and clock radio. Iron, ironing board, hairdryer available. TV lounge, dining room. Fire Certificate. Bed and Breakfast from £18 to £20. Special rates for Senior Citizens and children. Brochure available on request.

SIDMOUTH

Kerstin Farmer, Higher Coombe Farm, Tipton St John, Sidmouth EX10 0AX (Tel & Fax: 01404 813385). Find a warm, friendly welcome and comfortable, fully equipped rooms in our Victorian farmhouse, family-owned since 1913. We offer total relaxation and a superb breakfast, using local produce. After exploring East Devon's towns and villages, rolling countryside and beaches, take tea on the patio overlooking mature garden. Ideal for families. Easily reached, four miles inland from Sidmouth seafront. One family, one single and two double rooms (one with en suite shower). Bed & Breakfast £19 to £23 per person per day, half price for children in family room. Open March to December. **ETC** ◆◆◆

e-mail: KerstinFarmer@farming.co.uk
website: www.SmoothHound.co.uk/hotels/higherco

SIDMOUTH

Mrs Elizabeth Tancock, Lower Pinn Farm, Peak Hill, Sidmouth EX10 0NN (01395 513733). Working farm. Lower Pinn is in an area of outstanding natural beauty, two miles west of the unspoilt coastal resort of Sidmouth and one mile to the east of the pretty village of Otterton. Comfortable, spacious en suite rooms with colour TV, hot drink facilities, electric blankets and central heating. Guests have their own keys and may return at all times throughout the day. Ample parking. Substantial breakfast served in dining room. Local inns and restaurants nearby provide excellent evening meals. Children and pets welcome. Open all year. Bed and Breakfast from £22 to £25. Full details on request. **ETC** ◆◆◆◆

e-mail: liz@lowerpinnfarm.co.uk
website: www.lowerpinnfarm.co.uk

SOUTH MOLTON (near)

Hazel Milton, Partridge Arms Farm, Yeo Mill, West Anstey EX36 3NU (01398 341217; Fax: 01398 341569). Now a working farm of over 200 acres, four miles west of Dulverton, "Partridge Arms Farm" was once a coaching inn and has been in the same family since 1906. Genuine hospitality and traditional farmhouse fare await you. Comfortable accommodation in double, twin and single rooms, some of which have en suite facilities. There is also an original four-poster bedroom. Children welcome. Animals by arrangement. Residential licence. Open all year. Fishing and riding available nearby. Bed and Breakfast from £22 to £27; Evening Meal from £10.50. *FARM HOLIDAY GUIDE DIPLOMA WINNER.*

STOKE-IN-TEIGNHEAD

Mrs R. Wilkinson, Deane Thatch Accommodation, Stoke-in-teignhead, Near Torquay TQ12 4QU (Tel & Fax: 01626 873724; mobile: 0778 6060302). A charming thatched Devonshire cob cottage, and thatched cob Linhay. Situated in a secluded rural spot enjoying uninterrupted views of farmland with an atmosphere of total tranquillity. Half-a-mile from the village of Stoke-in-teignhead and just one mile from the sea. Ideally situated for Torquay (the English Riviera) and Dartmoor National Park. All rooms have colour TV, private bathroom, shower or bidet and tea/coffee making facilities; king-size bed in Linhay. Children welcome, reduced rates and babysitting available. Open all year. Bed and Breakfast from £24, discounts for weekly rate. Brittany Ferries recommended. **ETC ◆◆◆**

e-mail: enquiries@deanethatch.co.uk **website: http://www.deanethatch.co.uk**

TAVISTOCK

Hilary Tucker, Beera Farm, Milton Abbot, Tavistock PL19 8PL (Tel & Fax: 01822 870216). Beera is a working farm on the river Tamar, providing an ideal base for touring Devon and Cornwall. Visit the north and south coasts with rugged cliffs, sandy beaches and quaint fishing villages, Saltram House where 'Sense and Sensibility' was filmed and many other National Trust properties nearby. Play golf, walk the Tamar Trail and the farm and admire the beautiful scenery; off-road driving, archery, clay pigeon shooting can be arranged. Enjoy excellent evening meals using local and home grown produce. Packed lunches available. Two doubles, one twin all en suite with tea/coffee, central heating, clock/radios, hair dryers. Brochure available. Children welcome. Open all year. Bed and Breakfast from £22, Evening Meal from £14. **ETC ◆◆◆◆**

e-mail: robert.tucker@farming.co.uk **website: www.beera-farm.co.uk**

TEIGN VALLEY

S. and G. Harrison-Crawford, Silver Birches, Teign Valley, Trusham, Newton Abbot TQ13 0NJ (01626 852172). A warm welcome awaits you at Silver Birches, a comfortable bungalow at the edge of Dartmoor. A secluded, relaxing spot with two acre garden running down to river. Only two miles from A38 on B3193. Exeter 14 miles, sea 12 miles. Car advisable. Ample parking. Excellent pubs and restaurants nearby. Good centre for fishing, bird watching, forest walks, golf, riding; 70 yards salmon/trout fishing free to residents. Centrally heated guest accommodation with separate entrance. Two double bedded rooms, one twin bedded room, all with own bath/shower, toilet. Guest lounge with colour TV. Dining room, sun lounge overlooking river. Sorry, no children under eight. Terms including tea on arrival - Bed and full English Breakfast from £25 per person per night, £168 weekly. Evening Meal optional. Open all year. Self catering caravans also available from £135.

See also Colour Advertisement

TORQUAY

Ann and Joe Lazenby, Whitburn Guest House, St Luke's Road North, Torquay TQ2 5PD (01803 296719). We welcome you to our family-run guesthouse close to town centre and seafront. Our comfortable rooms are pleasantly decorated with en suite or private facilities, colour TV, radio/alarm clock, beverage-making facilities and central heating. Full English breakfast served daily at your table. Torquay, on the coastal footpath from Bournemouth to Land's End has a modern shopping centre, department stores, cinemas, theatres and all facilities, including beaches, modern marina, 10-pin bowling and leisure centre. Dartmoor (30 minutes' drive) has splendid scenery, peaceful open spaces, great for long or short walks all year. Bed and Breakfast per person from £15. **ETC ◆◆◆**
e-mail: joe@lazenby15.freeserve.co.uk

TOTNES

Mrs Anne Torr, Downe Lodge, Broadhempston, Totnes TQ9 6BY (01803 812828). Centrally situated for Dartmoor and the coast, in a peaceful location with woodland walking from the doorstep, Downe Lodge is a perfect place for those seeking a 'homebase' to explore the numerous attractions of this area. Miles of quiet lanes for easy cycling. Three-quarters of a mile from an excellent 15th century village pub with fabulous food. Four miles from the fascinating historic towns of Totnes and Ashburton. Registered Dartmoor ponies, rare breed chickens and ducks. Children welcome to collect eggs, join in etc. One family unit consisting of a double room and a bunk room with own full bathroom (rooms available separately). Tea-making facilities, central heating, TV, highchair. Holiday cottage also available with one/three bedrooms, one/two bathrooms. Please phone for information.

TOTNES

As seen on BBC TV's Holiday Programme

Christine Hillier & David Miller, The Old Forge at Totnes, Seymour Place, Totnes TQ9 5AY (01803 862174). A charming 600-year-old stone building, delightfully converted from blacksmith and wheelwright workshops and coach houses, complete with blacksmith's prison cell. We have our own bit of "rural England" close to the town centre. Very close to the River Dart steamer quay, shops and station (also steam train rides). Ideally situated for touring most of Devon including Dartmoor and Torbay coasts. A day trip from Exeter, Plymouth and Cornwall. Elizabethan costume markets on Tuesdays in Summer (May to September). Double, twin and family rooms, all en suite. Ground floor rooms suitable for some disabled guests. All rooms have colour TV, telephone, beverage tray (fresh milk on request). Central heating. Licensed lounge and patio. Conservatory-style leisure lounge with whirlpool spa. No smoking indoors. Parking, walled gardens. Excellent choice of breakfast menu including vegetarian and special diets. Evening meals available by prior arrangement. Children welcome but sorry, no pets. Bed and Breakfast from £27 to £37 per person (en suite). Cottage suite for two to six persons, suitable for disabled visitors. **ETC ◆◆◆◆** *SILVER AWARD,* **AA ◆◆◆◆**

ENGLAND

See also Colour Display Advertisement

WEST DARTMOOR

Withill Farm, Walkhampton, West Dartmoor. Relax on our small, secluded farm. Enjoy a friendly welcome and the comfort and good food of our pleasant farmhouse. For self-caterers there is a delightful converted barn. Pets are welcome. Ideal for walking, riding, cycling and touring throughout Devon and Cornwall. B&B three bedrooms, including one en suite and one twin, all with TV and tea/coffee facilities. Supper by arrangement. Packed lunches. Terms from £19 per night. Self-catering, sleeps 2-4. Central heating, TV, fridge, freezer, washing machine, barbecue. Terms from £158 per week. Brochure from **Pam Kitchin, Withill Farm, Sampford Spiney, Yelverton, Devon PL20 6LN (Tel & Fax: 01822 853992).**
e-mail: withillfarm1@aol.com

WOOLACOMBE

Dave and Chris Ellis, Crossways Hotel, The Seafront, Woolacombe EX34 7DJ (Tel & Fax: 01271 870395). Cosy, family-run, licensed hotel, situated in one of the finest sea front positions in Woolacombe, overlooking the pretty Combesgate beach and Lundy Island and being surrounded by National Trust land. Bathing and surfing from hotel and ideally situated for golf, horse riding and beautiful walks. Menu choice for breakfast and evening dinner, and children's menu. Varied bar snacks available at lunchtime. All bedrooms individually refurbished to a high standard, many en suite and with fabulous sea views. Colour TV and tea/coffee making facilities in all rooms. Children half-price or Free. Non-smoking establishment. Pets welcome. Free on-site parking. Why not find out why many of our guests return year after year? **ETC/AA/RAC ★**, **ETC** *SILVER AWARD*. **RAC** *DINING AWARD*.

YELVERTON

Ruth Gozzard, Stokehill Farmhouse, Stokehill Lane, Crapstone, Yelverton PL20 7PP (Tel & Fax: 01822 853791). The small hamlet of Stokehill consists of seven houses and is situated between Plymouth and Tavistock on the edge of Dartmoor National Park. Ideally situated for the West Country, it is within reach of both the north and south coasts of Devon and Cornwall. Accommodation comprises two double bedrooms and one twin-bedded room, all with views over gardens and countryside. One bedroom is en suite, the other two have private bathrooms. All rooms have colour TV and tea/coffee making facilities. Non-smoking. Children welcome over 10 years. Sorry, no pets. Ample off-road parking. Terms from £35 single per night, £55 double per night, reductions for three nights or more.
e-mail: enquirires@stokehillfarmhouse.co.uk **website: www.stokehillfarmhouse.co.uk**

DORSET

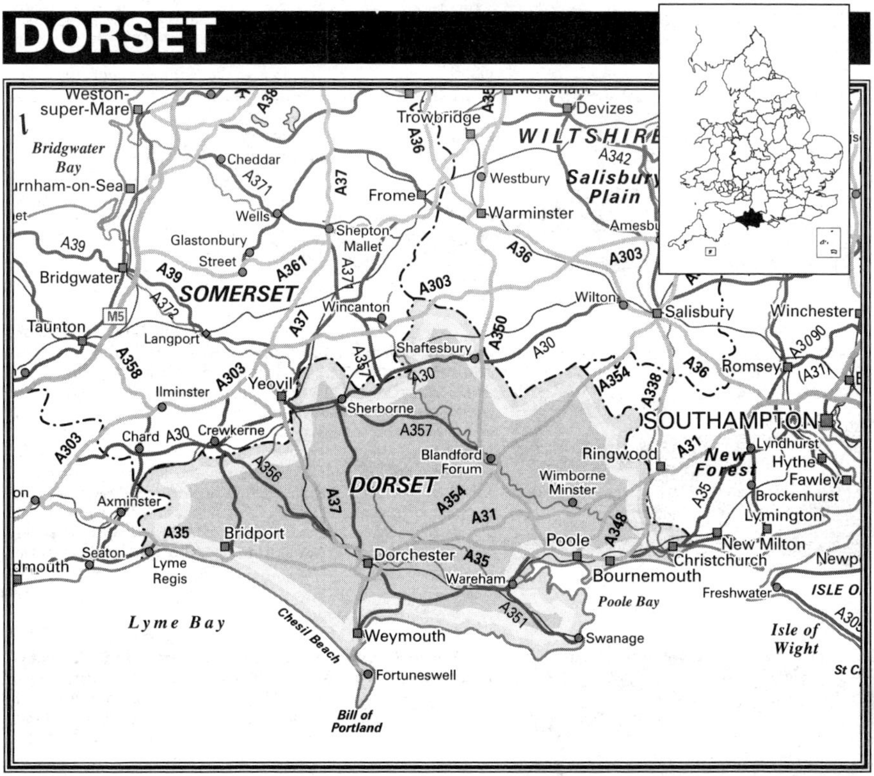

BLANDFORD FORUM

Mrs C.M.Old, Manor House Farm, Ibberton, Blandford Forum DT11 0EN (01258 817349). Working farm, dairy and sheep. Situated nine miles west of Blandford Forum. Small 16th century manor house, now a farmhouse, surrounded by large colourful garden in a quiet unspoilt village which at one time was given to Katherine Howard by Henry VIII. The oak beams and nail studded doors confirm its centuries-old past. One double bedroom, one double or twin (both en suite), and one twin bedroom (separate bathroom); all with tea making facilities. Bathroom and toilet; lounge with TV, diningroom with separate tables. Children welcome, cot and high chair provided. Bed and Breakfast from £17 to £20. Open all year. No evening meal. Good food at Crown Inn nearby. Self catering accommodation also available.

BRIDPORT

Jane Greening, New House Farm, Mangerton Lane, Bradpole, Bridport DT6 3SF (Tel & Fax: 01308 422884). Stay in a modern, comfortable farmhouse on a small working farm set in the rural Dorset hills and become one of the family. A large wild garden where you are welcome to sit or stroll round. Two large rooms available, both en suite, both with lovely views over the surrounding countryside, both with television and tea/coffee making facilities. We are near to Bridport and the seaside, golf courses, fossil hunting, beautiful gardens, wonderful walking, coarse fishing lake - lots to do. Simple traditional farmhouse evening meals can be provided, subject to booking. Bed and Breakfast from £22. **ETC ◆◆◆**

BRIDPORT

Mrs D.P. Read, The Old Station, Powerstock, Bridport DT6 3ST (01308 485301). Peacefully situated deep in the glorious Dorset countryside, one mile south east of Powerstock, in two-and-a-half acres of garden, this former railway station enjoys beautiful views. Conveniently situated for drives into neighbouring counties; many rural walks; can be reached by public transport. Two double bedrooms, one single, all with washbasins and tea-making facilities; bathroom, three toilets; central heating. Daytime access. Off road parking; tennis, fun golf. Hearty English breakfast prettily served (vegetarian breakfast by previous arrangement). Open March through October, from £17. Badger watching possible most evenings from house. SAE, please, for details. Sorry no children or pets. No smoking.

BRIDPORT (near)

Mrs Sue Norman, Frogmore Farm, Chideock, Bridport DT6 6HT (01308 456159). Working farm. Set in the rolling hills of West Dorset, enjoying splendid sea views, our delightful 17th century farmhouse offers comfortable, friendly and relaxing accommodation. An ideal base from which to ramble the many coastal and country footpaths of the area (nearest beach Seatown one-and-a-half miles) or tour by car the interesting places of Dorset and Devon. Bedrooms with en suite shower rooms, TV and tea making facilities. Guests' dining room and cosy lounge with woodburner. Well behaved dogs welcome. Open all year; car essential. Bed and Breakfast from £17. Brochure and terms free on request.

CERNE ABBAS

Mrs T. Barraclough, Magiston Farm, Sydling St Nicholas, Dorchester DT2 9NR (01300 320295). Working farm. Magiston is a 400 acre working farm with a comfortable 17th century cob and brick farmhouse set deep in the heart of Dorset. Large garden with river. Half-an-hour's drive from coast and five miles north of Dorchester. The farmhouse comprises double, twin and single bedrooms including a twin on the ground floor. Delicious evening meals served. Children over 10 years and pets welcome. Central heating. Open January to December. Bed and Breakfast from £18.50 per person per night. Please write or telephone for further details. **ETC ◆◆◆**

CHARMOUTH

See also Colour Display Advertisement

Mrs S. M. Johnson, Cardsmill Farm, Whitchurch Canonicorum, Charmouth, Bridport DT6 6RP (Tel & Fax: 01297 489375). Working farm, join in. A Grade II Listed comfortable quiet farmhouse in the picturesque Marshwood Vale, three miles from Charmouth. Ideal location for touring, safe beaches, fossil hunting, golf and walking the coastal path. See the farm animals, pets and crops. Family and double en suite rooms available, each with CTV, shaver points, tea/coffee trays. Cot available. Full central heating and double glazed windows throughout. Lounge with Inglenook fireplace, woodburning stove, oak beams, colour TV, games and books. Dining area with separate tables. English and varied breakfasts. Access at all times. Children and well behaved pets welcome. Large garden with patio, picnic table and seats. Bed and Breakfast from £21 to £26 per person per night. Open February till end of November. Brochure available. Also two self-catering farmhouses to sleep 11 and 16 plus cots, for long or short stays all year. **ETC ◆◆◆**

e-mail: cardsmill@aol.com **website: www.farmhousedorset.com**

A useful index of towns and counties appears at the back of this book on pages 379-382. Refer also to Contents Pages 50/51.

DORCHESTER

Mrs V.A. Bradbeer, Nethercroft, Winterbourne Abbas, Dorchester DT2 9LU (01305 889337). This country house with its friendly and homely atmosphere welcomes you to the heart of Hardy's Wessex. Central for touring the many places of interest that Dorset has to offer, including Corfe Castle, Lyme Regis, Dorchester, Weymouth, Lulworth Cove, etc. Lovely country walks and many local attractions. Two double rooms, one single, washbasins or en suite. Separate bathroom, shower and toilets. TV lounge, dining room. Large garden. Open all year. Central heating. Car essential, ample parking. Bed and Breakfast from £18. Take A35 from Dorchester, we are the last house at the western edge of the village.
e-mail: vbradbeer@ukonline.co.uk

DORCHESTER

Mrs Jane Rootham, The Old Post Office, Martinstown, Dorchester DT2 9LF (01305 889254). Situated in the Winterbourne Valley, The Old Post Office is a stone and slate Georgian cottage used as the village post office until 1950. It is part of a row of cottages that are all listed buildings. Winterbourne St Martin (Martinstown) is in the heart of Hardy country, two miles from the Neolithic Hill Fort of Maiden Castle, Hardy's monument and the town of Dorchester. The coast and beach are five miles away and it is an ideal walking and touring base. The bedrooms all have washbasins, tea/coffee making facilities and some have TV. Pets and children welcome. Bed and Breakfast from £15 to £25.

DORCHESTER

Michael and Jane Deller, Churchview Guest House, Winterbourne Abbas, Near Dorchester DT2 9LS (Tel & Fax: 01305 889296). Our 17th century guest house, noted for warm hospitality, delicious Breakfasts and Evening Meals, makes an ideal base for touring beautiful West Dorset. Our character bedrooms are all comfortable and well appointed. Meals, served in our beautiful dining room, feature local produce, with relaxation provided by two attractive lounges and licensed bar. Your hosts Jane and Michael Deller are pleased to give every assistance with local information to ensure a memorable stay. NON-SMOKING. Terms: Dinner, Bed and Breakfast £39 to £48; Bed and Breakfast £25 to £35 Short breaks available. **ETC/AA ◆◆◆◆**
e-mail: stay@churchview.co.uk
website: www.churchview.co.uk

FURZEHILL

Mrs King, Stocks Farm, Furzehill, Wimborne BH21 4HT (Tel & Fax: 01202 888697). Stocks Farm is a family-run farm and nursery situated in peaceful countryside just one-and-half miles from the lovely country town of Wimborne Minster, off the B3078. Surrounded by lovely Dorset countryside and pretty villages; coastline, beaches and New Forest within easy reach. Bed and Breakfast accommodation consists of one double en suite bedroom and one twin bedroom with private bathroom, both on ground level. Disabled guests are very welcome. Tea and coffee making facilities in both rooms. All accommodation is non-smoking. Situated in secluded garden with patio for guests to enjoy breakfast outside. Local pubs and restaurants offer varied menus. Bed and Breakfast from £20 per person per night.

When making enquiries or bookings, a stamped addressed envelope is always appreciated

Fyrnhams • Sheila and David Taylor

A spacious and non-smoking guesthouse, in quiet and unspoilt surroundings with gardens and grounds of about seven acres, with lovely views. Situated about three miles from Lyme Regis and Charmouth, ideal for touring, beaches, fishing, golf course and fossil hunting. Private parking. Access to house all day. A warm and friendly welcome awaits in a real home from home. Excellent accommodation in a comfortable, and well furnished bungalow with one double room with en suite bathroom, one double room with king size and single bed with private facilities, bathroom including a shower. All rooms have CTV, tea/coffee making facilities, clock/radio, hairdryer, towels, heating. Lounge with widescreen TV/ video, overlooks rear patio and gardens. Dining area – we serve a good English farmhouse breakfast. Nearby pub for evening meals. *B&B from £20.*

Raymonds Hill, Near Axminster EX13 5SZ

Tel/Fax: 01297 33222 or e-mail: sheilataylor@fyrnhams.fsnet.co.uk

POOLE

Mrs Stephenson, Holly Hedge Farm, Bulbury Lane, Lytchett Matravers, Poole BH16 6EP (01929 459688). Built in 1892, Holly Hedge Farm is situated next to Bulbury Woods Golf Course, set in 11 acres of wood and grassland adjacent to lake. We are just 15 minutes away from the Purbecks, the beach and the forest. The area is ideal for walking or cycling and Poole Quay and Harbour are also nearby. Accommodation comprises two double/family rooms, one twin and one single, all with en suite showers, colour TV, tea/coffee making facilities, radio alarms and central heating. Prices for a single room £25 to £30, double £46 per night. Open all year round for summer or winter breaks. Full English or Continental breakfast served.

SHAFTESBURY

Mrs G. Gosney, Kington Manor Farm, Church Hill, Kington Magna, Near Gillingham SP8 5EG (01747 838371). Working farm. Attractive farmhouse situated in a quiet, pretty village, with splendid views over the pastoral Blackmore Vale. Near the historic towns of Shaftesbury and Sherborne; Stourhead National Trust house and gardens and stately home of Longleat and Safari Park nearby. Bath 45 minutes' drive away. TV in all bedrooms. Bed and Breakfast £25 per person per night. Reductions for children. Excellent pub food nearby. Outdoor swimming pool. Pets welcome. **ETC ◆◆◆◆**

SHERBORNE

See also Colour Display Advertisement

Mrs J. Mayo, Alms House Farm, Hermitage, Holnest, Sherborne DT9 6HA (Tel & Fax: 01963 210296). This charming old farmhouse was a monastery during the 16th century, restored in 1849 and is now a Listed building. A family-run working dairy farm, it is surrounded by 140 acres overlooking the Blackmoor Vale, just one mile off the A352. Accommodation is in three comfortable en suite rooms with colour TV and tea/coffee making facilities. Diningroom with inglenook fireplace, lounge with colour TV, for guests' use at all times. Also garden and lawn. Plenty of reading material and local information provided for this ideal touring area. Bed and Breakfast from £23. Excellent evening meals in all local inns nearby. Situated six miles from Sherborne with its beautiful Abbey and Castle. SAE for further details. **ETC/AA ◆◆◆◆, ETC** *GOLD AWARD.*

SHILLINGSTONE

Mrs Rosie Watts, Pennhills Farm, Sandy Lane, off Lanchards Lane, Shillingstone, Blandford DT11 0TF (01258 860491). Pennhills Farmhouse set in 100 acres of unspoiled countryside, is situated one mile from the village of Shillingstone in the heart of the Blackmore Vale, an ideal peaceful retreat, short break or holiday. It offers spacious comfortable accommodation for all ages; children welcome, pets by arrangement. One downstairs bedroom. All bedrooms en suite with TV and tea/coffee making facilities, complemented by traditional English breakfast with home produced bacon and sausages. Vegetarians catered for. Good meals available locally. Brochure sent on request. A warm and friendly welcome is assured from your host Rosie Watts. From £18 per person.

SWANAGE

Mrs Rosemary Dean, Quarr Farm, Valley Road, Swanage BH19 3DY (01929 480865). Quarr is a working family farm steeped in history dating back to the Domesday Book. Animals kept naturally – cows, calves, horses, poultry. Bring your children to feed ducks, chickens, peacocks and watch steam trains passing through our meadows. Accommodation in family room with en suite bathroom, own sitting room with colour TV, real log fire, tea making facilities. Old Dairy, low beamed ceilings, small windows, double room with en suite shower, sittingroom with colour TV, kitchen. Bed and Breakfast. Cot available. Easy reach high class restaurants, pubs; sea three miles. Studland, sandy beach just five miles away. Ideal for walking, cycling, coastal path, RSPB Reserves, golf courses, riding. Please telephone for further details and terms.

SWANAGE

Mrs Justine Pike, Downshay Farm, Haycrafts Lane, Harmans Cross, Swanage BH19 3EB (01929 480316). Working dairy farm in the heart of beautiful Isle of Purbeck, midway between Corfe Castle and Swanage. This Victorian Purbeck stone farmhouse has family room en suite and one double with private shower room close by. Both rooms have colour TV and tea/coffee making facilities. Steam railway within walking distance, coastal path and sandy beaches three miles away. Excellent pubs and restaurants to be found locally. Open Easter to October for Bed and Breakfast from £20 per person. **e-mail: downshayfarm@tiscali.co.uk**

WIMBORNE

Mrs A. C. Tory, Hemsworth Manor Farm, Witchampton, Wimborne BH21 5BN (01258 840216; Fax: 01258 841278). Our lovely old Manor Farmhouse which is mentioned in the Domesday Book, is situated in an exceptionally peaceful location, yet is only half-an-hour's drive from Salisbury, Dorchester, Poole, Bournemouth and the New Forest. Hemsworth is a working family farm of nearly 800 acres, providing some lovely walks. The farm is mainly arable, but is also home to cattle, sheep, pigs, horses, ponies and various domestic pets. We have three fully equipped en suite bedrooms, and one double room with private bathroom. All have colour TV. Separate lounge for guests' use. There are excellent pubs locally. Brochure available. **ETC ◆◆◆◆**

WINTERBORNE ZELSTON

Mrs R. Kerley, Brook Farm, Winterborne Zelston, Blandford DT11 9EU (Tel & Fax: 01929 459267). A warm welcome awaits you at Brook Farm, a friendly working farm situated in a pretty, peaceful hamlet overlooking the River Winterborne, between Wimborne and Dorchester. Central for visiting the many attractions of Dorset. Two large double/twin en suite rooms and one twin room with private facilities. Colour TV, beverage making facilities, hairdryer etc. in all rooms. Guests have own keys, plenty of parking space. Hearty English breakfasts are served with our free-range eggs and home-made marmalade. Excellent food at the local country inns. Open all year except Christmas. Children over 10 years welcome, regret no pets or smoking. Terms from £20 to £22 per person per night, (extra for single occupancy) with reductions for three or more nights and favourable weekly terms. **ETC ◆◆◆**

DURHAM

BISHOP AUCKLAND

Newlands Hall, Frosterley in Weardale, Bishop Auckland DL13 2SH (01388 529233). Working farm. Secluded farmhouse with panoramic views set in the beautiful scenery of Weardale - an area of outstanding natural beauty. Yet only 18 miles from the cathedral city of Durham. Rich in wildlife the farm is at the centre of a network of local footpaths. Ideal for exploring Weardale, Teesdale and the North Pennines. Within easy travelling distance of Beamish Open Air Museum, Metro Centre, Hexham and Hadrian's Wall. Accommodation comprises double/family room with private bathroom, tea/coffee making facilities, TV, hairdryer, radio alarm and central heating. Sorry no pets and no smoking. Bed and Breakfast from £20. Open Easter to October.
e-mail: carol.oulton@ukonline.co.uk

CHESTER LE STREET

e-mail: lowurpeth@hotmail.com

Mrs H. Johnson, Low Urpeth Farm, Ouston, Chester Le Street DH2 1BD (0191 4102901; Fax: 0191 4100088). Superb farmhouse accommodation, spacious rooms, well furnished in a very traditional style. Beverage facilities, TV and comfortable chairs. Our large square stone farmhouse is within easy distance of county cricket at Chester-le-Street, Beamish Museum, Durham Cathedral (a World Heritage site), Durham Dales and Castles and coastline of Northumberland. Directions: leave A1M at Junction 63, follow A693, one-and-a-half miles turn right to Ouston, continue a further one-and-a-half miles, down hill, over roundabout, turning left at "Trees Please", sign into Low Urpeth. Bed and Breakfast from £22.50. Closed Christmas and New Year. Self Catering also available. **ETC ◆◆◆◆**
website: www.lowurpeth.co.uk

ESSEX

BRAINTREE

Mrs A. Butler, Brook Farm, Wethersfield, Braintree CM7 4BX (01371 850284). Beautiful Listed farmhouse, parts dating back to 13th century, on a 100-acre mixed farm set on the edge of a picturesque village. Essex can offer many picturesque places to visit and the Suffolk villages of Long Melford, Lavenham and Dedham, as well as Constable Country, are all within easy reach. Warm, spacious and comfortable rooms, guests' lounge, safe parking. Thirty minutes from Stansted Airport. Camping also available. Open all year. Prices from £20 to £25pp in double, twin or family rooms; from £25 to £30 single. **ETC ◆◆◆**

COLCHESTER

Mrs Jill Tod, Seven Arches Farm, Chitts Hill, Lexden, Colchester CO3 9SX (01206 574896). Working farm. Georgian farmhouse set in large garden close to the ancient town of Colchester. The farm extends to 100 acres and supports both arable crops and cattle. Private fishing rights on the River Colne, which runs past the farmhouse. This is a good location for visits to North Essex, Dedham and the Stour Valley which have been immortalised in the works of John Constable, the landscape painter. Children and pets welcome. Open all year. Bed and Breakfast from £25; Evening Meal from £5. Twin room £40; family room en suite. Static caravan on caravan site also available.

GLOUCESTERSHIRE

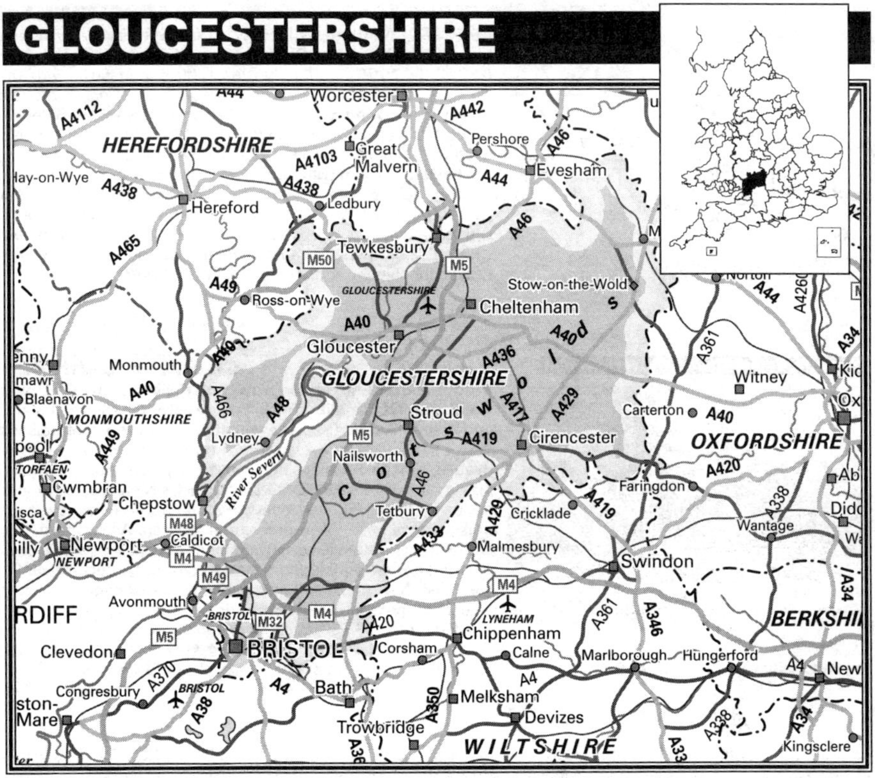

See also Colour Display Advertisement

BATH (near)

Mrs Pam Wilmott, Pool Farm, Bath Road, Wick, Bristol BS30 5RL (0117 937 2284). Welcome to our 350 year old Grade II Listed farmhouse on a working farm. On A420 between Bath and Bristol and a few miles from Exit 18 of M4, we are on the edge of the village, overlooking fields, but within easy reach of pub, shops and golf club. We offer traditional Bed and Breakast in one family and one twin room with tea/coffee facilities and TV. Guest lounge. Central heating. Ample parking. Open all year except Christmas. Terms from £20.

BRISTOL

Marilyn and Bob Downes, Box Hedge Farm, Coalpit Heath, Bristol BS36 2UW (01454 250786). Box Hedge Farm is set in 200 acres of beautiful rural countryside on the edge of the Cotswolds. Local to M4/M5, central for Bristol and Bath and the many tourist attractions in this area. An ideal stopping point for the South West and Wales. We offer a warm, friendly atmosphere with traditional farmhouse cooking. All bedrooms have colour TV and tea/coffee making facilities. Bed and Breakfast £25 single standard, £30 single en suite, £40 double standard, £46 double en suite. Family rooms - prices on application. All prices include VAT. Self-catering accommodation also available.
website: www.boxhedgefarmbandb.co.uk

CHELTENHAM

Mrs Carole M. Rand, "Cleevely", Wadfield Farm, Corndean Lane, Winchcombe, Cheltenham GL54 5AL (Tel & Fax: 01242 602059). A family-run arable/sheep farm with the Cotswold Way running through. Half-timbered Cotswold stone house overlooking Sudeley and Winchcombe Valley. Splendid views. Excellent base for exploring the Cotswolds. Winter breaks, log fires, TV lounge. Traditional farmhouse cuisine. Twin en suite, double/family room with private bathroom, both with tea/coffee making facilities. Ample parking. Twin en suite from £24 per person per night, Double/family room (maximum four people) with private bathroom from £60. Three course Evening Meal from £10 to £12 per person. Vegetarian and special diets catered for. Packed lunches by arrangement. **ETC ◆◆◆◆**

See also Colour Display Advertisement

CHIPPING CAMPDEN

Veronica Stanley, Home Farm House, Ebrington, Chipping Campden GL55 6NL (Tel & Fax: 01386 593309). A warm and friendly welcome awaits you at our completely refurbished 15th century Grade II Listed farmhouse, in the heart of this beautiful village. Spacious beamed rooms, inglenook fireplace in dining room where a full English breakfast is served. Large private car park at rear. All bedrooms are en suite and have coffee/tea making facilities, TV, radio and hairdryer. Accommodation comprises one double, two twin and one family suite consisting of a single and a double room en suite. Sorry, no pets allowed in the house. Non-smoking. Terms per night: £55 per double bedded suite, two persons sharing; more than two nights £50. Twin bedded rooms are £50, or single occupancy £40. Family room for three persons sharing, £80. **ETC ◆◆◆◆**

e-mail: willstanley@farmersweekly.net
website: www.homefarminthecotswolds.co.uk

COTSWOLD COUNTRY
BED AND BREAKFAST

CHIPPING CAMPDEN

Mrs Gené Jeffrey, Brymbo, Honeybourne Lane, Mickleton, Chipping Campden GL55 6PU (01386 438890; Fax: 01386 438113). A warm and welcoming farm building conversion with large garden in beautiful Cotswold countryside, ideal for walking and touring. Close to Stratford-upon-Avon, Broadway, Chipping Campden and with easy access to Oxford and Cheltenham. All rooms are on the ground floor, with full central heating. The comfortable bedrooms all have colour television and tea/coffee making facilities. Sitting room with open log fire. Breakfast room. Children and dogs welcome. Parking. Maps and guides to borrow. Sample menus from local hostelries for your information. Home-made preserves a speciality. FREE countryside tour of area offered to three-night guests. Rooms: two double, two twin, one family. Bathrooms - three en suite, two shared. B&B: single £24-£38, double £38-£50. Brochure available. Credit cards accepted. **ETC ◆◆◆◆**

e-mail: enquiries@brymbo.com
website: www.brymbo.com

FAIRFORD

Suzie Paton, Milton Farm, Fairford GL7 4HZ (01285 712205; Fax: 01285 711349). Located in the picturesque Cotswolds, Milton Farm has an impressive Georgian farmhouse with very spacious, individual en suite bedrooms and a comfortable guest lounge with large open fireplace. Warm hospitality and breakfast with locally sourced, quality produce, ensure a memorable stay. Quiet, pleasant outlook on edge of most attractive Cotswold market town with numerous beautiful walks from the farm, across meadowland beside the River Coln. Family, twin and double rooms available with comfortable furniture, remote-controlled TV, tea/coffee making facilities, central heating. All rooms are non-smoking. Fishing can be arranged. Stables available for horse guests. **ETC ◆◆◆◆**

e-mail: milton@farmersweekly.net
website: www.milton-farm.co.uk

ENGLAND

Aston House, Broadwell, Moreton-In-Marsh GL56 0TJ

Aston House is a chalet bungalow overlooking fields in the peaceful village of Broadwell, one-and-a-half miles from Stow-on-the-Wold. It is centrally situated for all the Cotswold villages, while Blenheim Palace, Warwick Castle, Oxford, Stratford-upon-Avon, Cheltenham, Cirencester and Gloucester are within easy reach. Accommodation comprises a twin-bedded and a double/twin room, both en suite on the first floor, and a double room with private bathroom on the ground floor. All rooms have tea/coffee making facilities, radio, colour TV, hairdryer and electric blankets for the colder nights. Bedtime drinks and biscuits are provided. Guests and children over ten years, are welcomed to our home from March to October. No smoking. Car essential, parking. Pub within walking distance. Bed and good English breakfast from **£24** to **£26** per person daily; weekly from **£172.50** per person.

RAC ◆◆◆◆ Warm Welcome Award, Sparkling Diamond Award **ETC** ◆◆◆◆ Silver Award

Telephone: 01451 830475 • E-mail: fja@netcomuk.co.uk
Website: www.netcomuk.co.uk/~nmfa/aston_house.html

GLOUCESTER (near)

S.J. Barnfield, "Kilmorie Smallholding", Gloucester Road, Corse, Staunton, Gloucester GL19 3RQ (Tel & Fax: 01452 840224). Quality all ground floor accommodation. "Kilmorie" is Grade II Listed (c1848) within conservation area in a lovely part of Gloucestershire, deceptively spacious yet cosy, and tastefully furnished. Double, twin, family or single bedrooms, all having tea tray, colour TV, radio, mostly en suite. Very comfortable guests' lounge, traditional home cooking is served in the separate diningroom overlooking large garden where there are seats to relax, watch our free range hens (who provide excellent eggs for breakfast!) or the wild birds and butterflies we encourage to visit. Perhaps walk waymarked farmland footpaths which start here. Children may "help" with our child's pony, and hens. Rural yet ideally situated to visit Cotswolds, Royal Forest of Dean, Wye Valley and Malvern Hills. Children over five years. Bed, full English Breakfast and Evening Dinner from £26; Bed and Breakfast from £18. Ample parking. **ETC ◆◆◆◆**
e-mail: sheila-barnfield@supanet.com

STOW-ON-THE-WOLD

Robert Smith and Julie-Anne, Corsham Field Farmhouse, Bledington Road, Stow-on-the-Wold GL54 1JH (01451 831750). A traditional farmhouse with spectacular views of Cotswold countryside. Quiet location one mile from Stow. Ideally situated for exploring all Cotswold villages including Bourton-on-the-Water, Broadway, Burford and Chipping Campden. Within easy reach of Cheltenham, Oxford and Stratford-upon-Avon; also places of interest such as Blenheim Palace, Warwick Castle and many National Trust houses and gardens. Family, twin and double bedrooms; mostly en suite. TV, tea tray and hairdryer in all rooms. Relaxing guest lounge/dining room. Pets and children welcome. Open all year for Bed and Full English Breakfast from £22 (reductions for children). Excellent pub food five minutes' walk away.

STOW-ON-THE-WOLD

Graham and Helen Keyte, The Limes, Evesham Road, Stow-on-the-Wold GL54 1EN (01451 830034/831056; Fax: 01451 830034). Over the last 30 years this guesthouse has established a reputation for its homely and friendly atmosphere. It is just four minutes' walk from the town centre; central for visiting Stratford-upon-Avon, Burford, Bourton-on-the Water, Cirencester, Cheltenham, etc. The Limes overlooks fields and has an attractive large garden with ornamental pool and waterfall. Double, twin and family rooms with washbasins. Four rooms en suite, one four-poster and family room; other doubles. All rooms have tea/coffee making facilities and colour TV; hairdryers available. Central heating. TV lounge. Dining room. Children welcome, cot. Pets welcome. Car park. Fire Certificate held. Bed and full English Breakfast from £20 to £25 per person per night. Reductions for children. Vegetarians catered for. Open all year except Christmas. **AA ◆◆◆, RAC.**

The FHG Directory of Website Addresses
on pages 349–378 is a useful quick reference guide for holiday accommodation with e-mail and/or website details

ENGLAND

STROUD

Mrs Salt, Beechcroft, Brownshill, Stroud GL6 8AG (01453 883422). Our Edwardian house is quietly situated in a beautiful rural area with open views, about four miles from Stroud. The house is set in an attractive garden with mature trees, shrubs and herbaceous borders. We are in the midst of good walking country, for which we can lend maps and guides. We provide a full cooked breakfast or fruit salad and rolls with home-made bread and preserves. We welcome the elderly and small children. We are within easy reach of Cheltenham, Gloucester, Cirencester and Bath, also Berkeley Castle, Slimbridge and the North Cotswolds. We are a non-smoking establishment. Evening meal by prior arrangement. Bed and Breakfast from £18 to £22.

TEWKESBURY

Michael and Pippa Cluer, Lampitt House, Lampitt Lane, Bredon's Norton, Tewkesbury GL20 7HB (01684 772295). Lampitt House is situated in a large informal garden on the edge of a quiet village at the foot of Bredon Hill. Splendid views across to the Malverns. Ideal for visiting the Cotswolds, Stratford, Worcester, Cheltenham, Gloucester and the Forest of Dean. All rooms are furnished to a high standard and have private bathrooms, central heating, colour TV and tea/coffee making facilities. Ground floor room available. Children are welcome. Ample parking. No smoking. Open all year. Hill and riverside walks. Arrangements can be made for windsurfing and riding. Double room Bed and Breakfast £50.

TEWKESBURY

Mrs Bernadette Williams, Abbots Court, Church End, Twyning, Tewkesbury GL20 6DA (Tel & Fax: 01684 292515). Working farm. A large, quiet farmhouse set in 350 acres, built on the site of monastery between the Malverns and Cotswolds, half a mile M5-M50 junction. Six en suite bedrooms with colour TV and tea making facilities. Centrally heated. Open all year except Christmas. Large lounge with open fire and colour TV. Spacious diningroom. Licensed bar. Good home cooked food in large quantities, home produced where possible. Children's own TV room, games room and playroom. Tennis lawn. Play area and lawn. Cot and high chair available. Laundry facilities. Ideally situated for touring with numerous places to visit. Swimming, tennis, sauna, golf within three miles. Coarse fishing available on the farm. Bed and Breakfast from £19 to £21. Reduced rates for children and Senior Citizens. **ETC ◆◆◆**
e-mail: bernie@abbotscourt.fsbusiness.co.uk

HAMPSHIRE

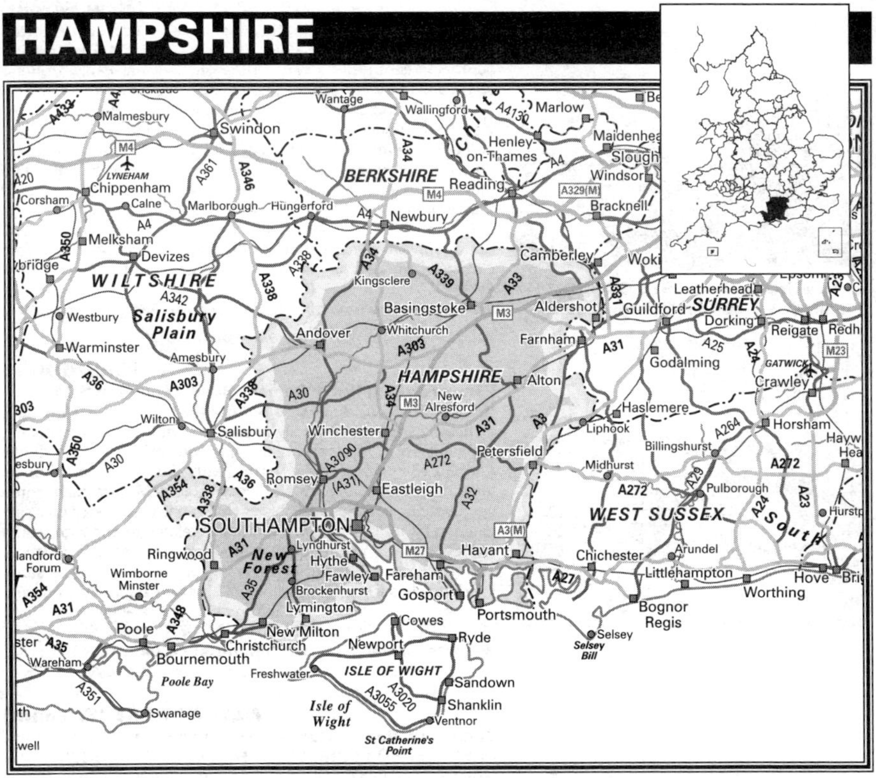

ANDOVER

Mrs J. Fergusson, Carinya Farm, Cattle Lane, Abbots Ann, Andover SP11 7DR (01264 710269). Modern farmhouse accommodation with traditional values. Home-made produce, large patio and garden with wildlife pond. Play area for small children. Local country pub serving meals daily. Friendly welcome for happy farm stay. Open all year. Bed and Breakfast from £20 to £25. **ETC ◆◆◆**

e-mail: carinya.farm@virgin.net

website: www.carinyafarm.co.uk

ASHLEY HEATH

Mrs Jan Hodges, Lions Hill Farmhouse B&B, Ashley Heath, Ringwood BH24 2EX (01425 472115). Set in 13 acres of farmland, adjacent to a walking, cycling and riding track, Lions Hill Farmhouse is just 12 miles from Bournemouth and a short journey by car from the New Forest. Accommodation is available in two cottage bedrooms with shared bathroom and washing machine, ideal for families; and a spacious double room with en suite bathroom. Heated outdoor swimming pool. There is stabling for guests' own horses, with adjacent grazing and a large yard for trailer/lorry parking. Direct access from farm gate to forest tracks. There are two pubs within a short walk, and many good restaurants in the local area. Well-behaved pets are welcome. B&B from £25 per person per night.

ENGLAND

BROCKENHURST (New Forest)

Mrs Pauline Harris, Little Heathers, Whitemoor Road, Brockenhurst SO42 7QG (01590 623512; Fax: 01590 624255; Mobile: 07775 715584). Reg and Pauline offer a warm and friendly welcome at their spacious bungalow, in a quiet location on the outskirts of Brockenhurst, just a few minutes' walk from open forest. Ideal location for touring, walking, cycling and horse riding. Golf courses nearby. Ground floor double/twin en suite bedrooms with TV, hairdryer, beverage facilities and other extras. Multi-choice breakfasts, special diets can be catered for. Lymington Yacht Haven with the ferry to the Isle of Wight. Beaulieu Motor Museum, Exbury Gardens, Bournemouth and Southampton all just a short drive away. Bed and Breakfast from £24 pppn. Stay six nights, seventh night free, other Short Breaks available. NO SMOKING. **ETC ◆◆◆◆** *SILVER AWARD.*

e-mail: little_heathers@hotmail.com **website: www.newforest.demon.co.uk/littleheathers.htm**

LYNDHURST

Penny Farthing Hotel, Romsey Road, Lyndhurst SO43 7AA (023 8028 4422; Fax: 023 8028 4488). The Penny Farthing is a cheerful small Hotel ideally situated in Lyndhurst village centre, the capital of "The New Forest". The Hotel offers en suite single, double, twin and family rooms with direct-dial telephones, tea/coffee tray, colour TV and clock radios. We also have some neighbouring cottages available as Hotel annexe rooms or on a self-catering basis. These have been totally refitted, much with "Laura Ashley" decor, and offer quieter, more exclusive accommodation. The hotel has a licensed bar, private car park and bicycle store. Lyndhurst has a charming variety of shops, restaurants, pubs and bistros and "The New Forest Information Centre and Museum". All major credit cards accepted. **AA/ RAC/ ETC ◆◆◆◆**

website: www.pennyfarthinghotel.co.uk

NEW FOREST (Fritham)

John and Penny Hankinson, Fritham Farm, Fritham, Lyndhurst SO43 7HH (Tel & Fax: 023 8081 2333). Lovely farmhouse on working farm in the heart of the New Forest. Dating from the 18th century, all three double/twin bedrooms have en suite facilities and provision for tea/coffee making. There is a large comfortable lounge with TV and log fire. Fritham is in a particularly beautiful part of the New Forest, still largely undiscovered and with a wealth of wildlife. It is a wonderful base for walking, riding, cycling and touring. Non-smoking. Children 10 years and over welcome. Come and enjoy peace and quiet in this lovely corner of England. Bed and Breakfast from £21.50 to £23.00 per person. **ETC/AA ◆◆◆◆**

WINCHESTER (near)

See also Colour Display Advertisement

Mays Farm, Longwood Dean, Near Winchester SO21 1JS (01962 777486; Fax 01962 777747). Twelve minutes' drive from Winchester, (the eleventh century capital city of England), Mays Farm is set in rolling countryside on a lane which leads from nowhere to nowhere. The house is timber framed, originally built in the sixteenth century and has been thoroughly renovated and extended by its present owners, James and Rosalie Ashby. There are three guest bedrooms, (one double, one twin and one either), each with a private bathroom or shower room. A sitting room with log fire is usually available for guests' use. Ducks, geese, chickens and goats make up the two acre "farm". Prices from £23 per person per night for Bed and Breakfast. Booking is essential. Please telephone or fax for details.

When making enquiries or bookings, a stamped addressed envelope is always appreciated

HEREFORDSHIRE

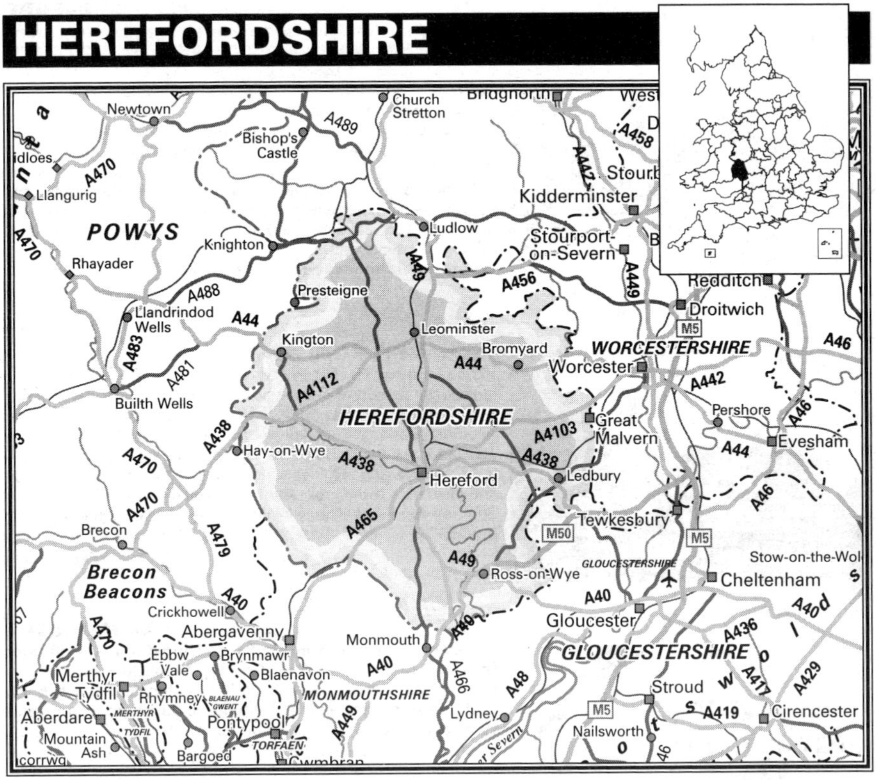

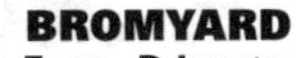

BROMYARD

Sheila and Roger Steeds, Linton Brook Farm, Bringsty, Bromyard WR6 5TR (Tel & Fax: 01885 488875). An historic, comfortable and spacious home, tastefully renovated. We offer two large double bedrooms with en suite facilities and TV, and a smaller twin-bedded room with private bathroom. All have central heating and tea/coffee making facilities. The dining room has an open inglenook fire place and the large sittingroom has an inviting wood burner. Wide range of country pubs, inns and hostelries nearby. Children are most welcome; dogs can be accommodated in an adjacent building. There are plenty of nearby places of interest, as well as golf, fishing, bowls, tennis, horse racing and cricket, wonderful walks and wildlife. Ample car parking; transport service available.

HEREFORD

David Jones, Sink Green Farm, Rotherwas, Hereford HR2 6LE (01432 870223). Working farm. Warm and friendly atmosphere awaits your arrival at this 16th century farmhouse, on the banks of the River Wye. Three miles south of the cathedral city of Hereford, with Ross-on-Wye, Leominster, Ledbury, Malvern and the Black Mountains within easy reach. All rooms en suite, tea/coffee making facilities and colour TV. One room with four-poster, family room by arrangement. Guests' own lounge. Pets by arrangement. Bed and Breakfast from £20 per person.

HEREFORD

Mrs Diana Sinclair, Holly House Farm, Allensmore, Hereford HR2 9BH (01432 277294; Fax: 01432 261285; mobile 07885 830223). Spacious luxury farmhouse and over 10 acres of land with horses, situated in beautiful and peaceful open countryside. Bedrooms en suite or with private bathroom, central heating, TV and tea/coffee making facilities. We are only five miles south-west of Hereford city centre. Ideal base for Welsh Borders, market towns, Black Mountains, Brecon and Malvern Hills and the Wye Valley. We have a happy family atmosphere and pets are welcome. Brochure on request. From £22 per person per night and with our delicious English Breakfast you will be fit for the whole day!
e-mail: hollyhousefarm@aol.com

LEDBURY

Mrs C. Gladwin, Hill Farm, Eastnor, Ledbury HR8 1EF (01531 632827). HILL FARM is a 300-year-old stone and brick farmhouse surrounded by woodland at the foot of the Malvern Hills, one mile from Ledbury and one mile from Eastnor Castle. Accommodation comprises one twin room and two family rooms also used as twin/double rooms all with washbasin, TV and tea/coffee making facilities. Guests own sittingroom with log fire and the dining room look out onto a large garden and rural views. Bed and Breakfast from £17.50. Evening Meal by arrangement from £10.00.

LEOMINSTER

Mrs Jenny Davies, Holgate Farm, Kingsland, Leominster HR6 9QS (01568 708275). Working farm. Guests will receive a warm welcome at this attractive 17th century farmhouse. Enjoy a delicious breakfast in the well-furnished diningroom and relax in the comfortable sittingroom which greets you with a cosy fire on chilly evenings. The old elm staircase leads to two spacious, well appointed bedrooms, both with tea/coffee trays. Guests have their own bathroom and the house is centrally heated. This is a working family-run farm and the River Lugg, designated as an area of Special Scientific Interest, runs through most of the land. The local countryside is ideal for walking and exploring, or visit the historic town of Ludlow, the busy market town of Leominster, Hereford Cathedral and the Mappa Mundi exhibition. Also nearby are churches, castles, black and white villages, gardens, National Trust Properties and the Bulmers Cider museum. Many local inns offer a wide range of delicious restaurant and bar meals. We are a non-smoking house. Bed and Breakfast from £19 per person. Reductions for children. £1 single supplement.

ROSS-ON-WYE

Mrs M. E. Drzymalska, Thatch Close, Llangrove, Ross-on-Wye HR9 6EL (01989 770300). Secluded, peaceful, comfortable Georgian farmhouse, yet convenient for A40 and M4, M50. Our three lovely bedrooms, each with its own bathroom (two en suite), have magnificent views over the unspoilt countryside. Relax in the visitors' lounge or sit in the shade of mature trees in our garden. You may be greeted by our dog or free-flying parrot. Telephone or e-mail for brochure. **ETC ◆◆◆◆**
website: www.thatchclose.com

Readers are requested to mention this guidebook when seeking accommodation (and please enclose a stamped addressed envelope).

ISLE OF WIGHT

See also Colour Advertisement

NEWPORT

Alvington Manor Farm, Manor Farm Lane, Carisbrooke, Newport PO30 5SP (01983 523463). Alvington Manor is a 17th century manor farmhouse, situated in the centre of the Isle of Wight, near Carisbrooke Castle and the start of the Tennyson Trail. We have five en suite bedrooms, four with bathrooms, one with a shower room. All rooms have televisions and tea/coffee making facilities. There is a guest sitting room, gardens and car parking. Good food pubs nearby. We are open all year round. Prices from £20 per person per night, inclusive of full English breakfast. Children welcome, price on application. **ETC ◆◆◆** For ferry booking from Portsmouth and Lymington phone 01990 827744; from Southampton phone 01703 334010.

KENT

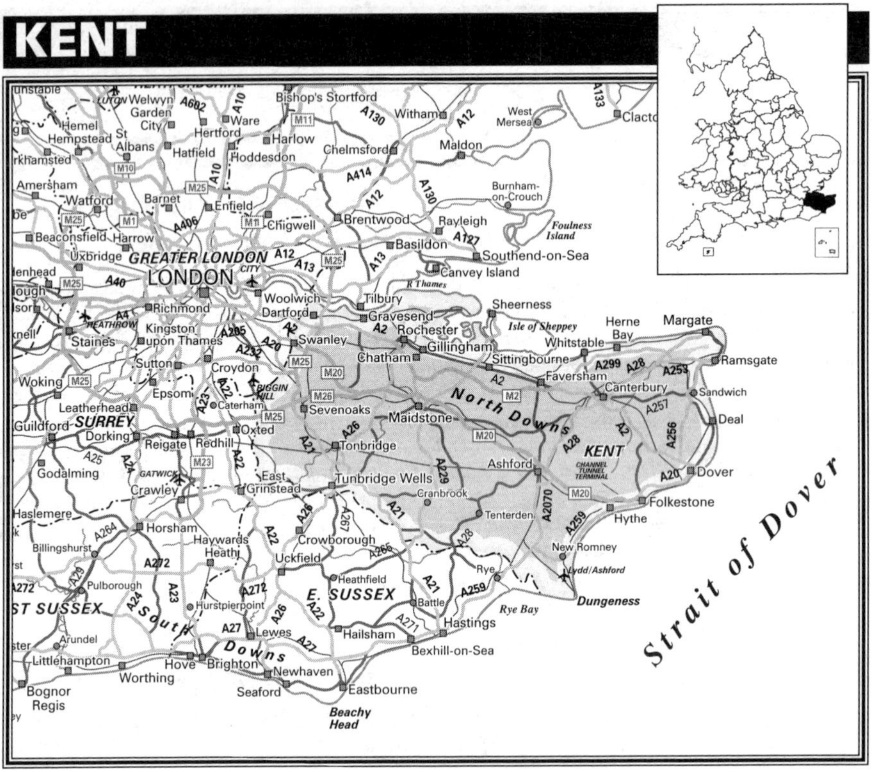

ASHFORD

Mrs Janet Feakins, Old Farm House, Soakham Farm, Whitehill, Bilting, Ashford TN25 4HB (01233 813509). Soakham is a working farm situated on the North Downs Way between Boughton Aluph and Chilham and adjoining Challock Forest. It is ideally located both for walking and visiting many places in the South East area. Canterbury and Ashford are ten miles and five miles respectively. The farmhouse was originally a Hall House and Grade II Listed with much exposed woodwork. It offers the following accommodation; two double rooms including one with a four-poster bed and a twin-bedded room. Prices are from £18 per person for Bed and Breakfast. Ample parking is available and we are open all year round.

ASHFORD (near)

Pam and Arthur Mills, Cloverlea, Bethersden, Ashford TN26 3DU (Tel & Fax: 01233 820353; mobile: 07711 739690). A warm welcome awaits in a spacious country bungalow in a lovely peaceful location. Breakfast is served in a new sun-room overlooking the large garden, fields and woods. Ideal for Ashford International Station (10 minutes), Folkestone, Eurotunnel (half-an-hour), visiting Canterbury, Rye, Sissinghurst and Leeds Castles, and many gardens of interest. Superb accommodation, one twin room with private bathroom and one king size/family room, en suite. Both have colour TV, tea/coffee making facilities, hair dryer, radio and biscuits. Central heating. Excellent breakfasts, home produced bread and eggs. Ample safe parking. Good pub food three-quarters of a mile. Bed and Breakfast from £20. Reductions for children under 10. Non-smoking. **ETC ◆◆◆**

e-mail: Pam.mills@amserve.net

ENGLAND

BLERIOT'S

47 Park Avenue, Dover, Kent CT16 1HE Telephone (01304) 211394

A Victorian Residence set in a tree-lined avenue, in the lee of Dover Castle. Within easy reach of trains, bus station, town centre, Hoverport and docks. Channel Tunnel approximately 10 minutes' drive. Off-road parking. We specialise in one night 'stop-overs' and Mini Breaks. Single, Double, Twin and Family rooms with full en suite. All rooms have colour TV, tea and coffee making facilities, and are fully centrally heated. Full English Breakfast served from 7am. Reduced rates for room only. Open all year.

Rates: Bed & Breakfast: £20 to £25 per person per night.
Mini-Breaks: January-April and October-December £19 per person per night.
Mastercard and Visa Accepted ETC ◆◆◆

CANTERBURY

Mr and Mrs R. Linch, Upper Ansdore, Duckpit Lane, Petham, Canterbury CT4 5QB (01227 700672; Fax: 01227 700840). Beautiful secluded Listed Tudor farmhouse with various livestock, situated in an elevated position with far-reaching views of the wooded countryside of the North Downs. The property overlooks a Kent Trust Nature Reserve, it is five miles south of the cathedral city of Canterbury and only 30 minutes' drive to the ports of Dover and Folkestone. The accommodation comprises three double and one twin bedded room, and a family room. All have shower, WC en suite and tea-making facilities. Dining/ sittingroom, heavily beamed with large inglenook. Car essential. Bed and Full English Breakfast from £22.50 per person. Credit Cards accepted. **AA ◆◆◆**

CANTERBURY

Mrs Lewana Castle, Great Field Farm, Canterbury CT4 6DE (01227 709223). Situated in beautiful countryside, our spacious farmhouse is about eight miles from Canterbury and Folkestone, 12 miles from Dover and Ashford. We are a working farm with some livestock including friendly ponies and chickens. We provide a friendly and high standard of accommodation with full central heating and double glazing, traditional breakfasts cooked on the Aga, courtesy tray and colour TV in each of our suites/bedrooms. Our annexe suite has a private staircase, lounge, kitchen, double bedroom and bathroom and is also available for self-catering holidays. Our cottage suite has its own entrance, stairs, lounge, bathroom and twin-bedded room. Our large double/family bedroom has en suite bathroom and air-bath. There is ample off-road parking and good pub food nearby. Bed and Breakfast from £25 per person; reductions for children. Non-smoking establishment. **ETC ◆◆◆◆** *SILVER AWARD.*

CANTERBURY

Mrs A. Hunt, Bower Farmhouse, Stelling Minnis, Near Canterbury CT4 6BB (01227 709430). Anne and Nick Hunt welcome you to Bower Farm House, a traditional 17th century Kentish farmhouse situated in the midst of Stelling Minnis, a medieval common of 125 acres of unspoilt trees, shrubs and open grassland; seven miles south of the cathedral city of Canterbury and nine miles from the coast; the countryside abounds in beauty spots and nature reserves. The house is heavily beamed and maintains its original charm. The accommodation comprises a double room and a twin bedded room, both with private facilities. Full traditional English breakfast is served with home-made bread, marmalade and fresh free-range eggs. Children welcome; pets by prior arrangement. Open all year (except Christmas). Car essential. Excellent pub food five minutes away. Bed and Breakfast from £22.50 per person. **ETC ◆◆◆◆** *SILVER AWARD.*

e-mail: book@bowerbb.freeserve.co.uk **website: www.kentac.co.uk/bowerfm**

ENGLAND

FOLKESTONE/ASHFORD

Bolden's Wood, Fiddling Lane, Stowting, Near Ashford TN25 6AP (Tel & Fax: 01303 812011). Between Ashford/ Folkestone. Friendly atmosphere – modern accommodation (one double/twin, two singles) on our smallholding, set in unspoilt countryside. No smoking throughout. Log-burning stove in TV lounge. Full English breakfast. Country pubs (meals) nearby. Children love the old-fashioned farmyard, free-range chickens, friendly sheep and cattle...and llamas! Treat yourself to a llama-led picnic trek to our private, secluded woodland and downland, and enjoy watching the birdlife, rabbits, foxes, badgers and, occasionally, deer. You could round off your trip by booking a short sightseeing or fishing trip on our Folkestone Fishing Boat. Easy access to the Channel Tunnel and Ferry Ports.
Bed and Breakfast £21 per person per night.
e-mail: StayoverNight@aol.com

TUNBRIDGE WELLS

Manor Court Farm B&B and Camping. Georgian farmhouse on a working 350-acre sheep and arable farm priding itself on its warm and friendly atmosphere, spacious rooms and lovely views of Medway Valley. Various animals such as dogs, cats, horses, guinea fowl, chickens etc. Tennis and swimming available by arrangement. Large secluded garden with ponds and orchard area. Secluded space for tents and caravans with new facilities. Excellent base for walking, cycling and touring the south east of England. Chartwell, Leeds Castle, Sissinghurst, Hever etc, are all within easy reach and London 45 minutes by train from Tonbridge. Bed and Breakfast from £24 per person per night (three rooms available), camping from £5 per person per night. Children welcome. Pets by arrangement. You will find us on the A264 road, five miles west of Tunbridge Wells at Stone Cross. Contact: **Julia Soyke or Becky Masey (01892 740279; Fax: 01892 740919). ETC ◆◆◆**
e-mail: jsoyke@jsoyke.freeserve.co.uk **website: www.manorcourtfarm.co.uk**

LANCASHIRE

BACUP

Ann Isherwood, Pasture Bottom Farm, Bacup OL13 9UZ (Tel & Fax: 01706 873790). Pasture Bottom Farm is situated at the head of the Rossendale Valley on the Lancashire–Yorkshire border. It is set in an elevated position with panoramic views. It is a working beef farm. We are within a short distance from the main road on a private lane with no passing traffic. All rooms are centrally heated. Two twin rooms, one en suite, one with private bathroom, and one double room en suite. TV in each room and tea/coffee facilities. Tariff from £18 per person per night. **ETC ◆◆◆**

e-mail: ha.isherwood@zen.co.uk

website: www.SmoothHound.co.uk/hotels/pasture.html

CARNFORTH

Mrs Vera Casson, Galley Hall Farm, Shore Road, Carnforth LA5 9HZ (01524 732544). A 17th century farmhouse on a stock rearing farm on the North Lancashire coast, near Junction 35 M6, close to Leighton Moss RSPB, historic Lancaster; ideal base for touring the Lake District or the coastal resorts. Double, twin and single rooms; tea/coffee, washbasin and radio in all rooms; TV available. Sorry, no pets or smoking. Central heating, log fires. Lounge with TV. Evening meals on request. Good golf courses and fishing in the area. We offer a homely and friendly atmosphere. Open all year except Christmas. Bed and Breakfast from £20 per person. **ETC ◆◆◆◆**

ENGLAND

See also Colour Display Advertisement

CLITHEROE

Rakefoot Farm, Chaigley, Near Clitheroe BB7 3LY (Chipping 01995 61332; mobile: 07889 279063; Fax: 01995 61296). Family farm peacefully situated in the beautiful countryside of the Ribble Valley in the Forest of Bowland, with panoramic views. Ideally placed for touring Coast, Dales and Lakes. Eight miles from M6 Junction 31a. Superb walks, golf and horse riding nearby, or visit pretty villages and factory shops. Warm welcome whether on holiday or business, refreshments on arrival. Bed and Breakfast or Self Catering in 17th century farmhouse and traditional stone barn conversion. Wood-burning stoves, central heating, exposed beams and stonework. Most bedrooms en suite, some ground floor. Excellent home-cooked meals, laundry; pubs/restaurants nearby. Indoor/outdoor play areas, garden and patios. Dogs by arrangement. Bed and Breakfast £17.50 to £25.00 sharing double/twin room; some rooms available with own lounge. Four self-catering properties, three can be internally interlinked. £80 to £507 per property per week. Short breaks available. **ETC ◆◆◆◆** *GUEST ACCOMMODATION*; **ETC ★★★/★★★★** *SELF-CATERING. NWTB SILVER AWARD FOR SELF CATERING HOLIDAY OF THE YEAR 2000.*

e-mail: info@rakefootfarm.co.uk **website: www.rakefootfarm.co.uk**

ORMSKIRK

Mrs A. Mercer, The Meadows, New Sutch Farm, Sutch Lane, Ormskirk L40 4BU (01704 894048). Lovely 17th century farmhouse situated down a private country lane. Relaxed and friendly atmosphere. Three pretty en suite ground floor bedrooms with all home comforts. Both lounge and diningroom overlook beautiful gardens. Enjoy a hearty breakfast whilst listening to the birdsong. Welcome pot of tea. M6, 15 minutes, A59 five minutes. Bed and Breakfast from £19.50. Open all year.

SOUTHPORT

Mrs Wendy E. Core, Sandy Brook Farm, 52 Wyke Cop Road, Scarisbrick, Southport PR8 5LR (Tel & Fax: 01704 880337). Bill and Wendy Core offer a homely, friendly atmosphere at Sandy Brook, a small working farm situated three-and-a-half miles from the seaside resort of Southport and five miles from the historic town of Ormskirk. Motorways are easily accessible, and the Lake District, Trough of Bowland, Blackpool and North Wales are within easy reach. Six en suite bedrooms with colour TV and tea/coffee making facilities. Central heating throughout. Sittingroom with colour TV; diningroom. High chairs and cots available. Room available for wheelchair/disabled guests. Open all year round, except Christmas. Bed and Breakfast from £18. Reductions for children. Weekly terms on request. **ETC ◆◆◆**, *NWTB SILVER AWARD WINNER "PLACE TO STAY" FARMHOUSE CATEGORY.*

LEICESTERSHIRE

BELTON-IN-RUTLAND (near Uppingham)

The Old Rectory, Belton-in-Rutland, Oakham LE15 9LE (01572 717279; Fax: 01572 717343). Guest accommodation. Victorian country house and guest annexe in charming village overlooking Eyebrook valley and rolling Rutland countryside. Comfortable and varied selection of rooms, mostly en suite, with direct outside access. Prices from £20 per person per night including breakfast. Small farm environment (horses and sheep) with excellent farmhouse breakfast. Public House 100 yards. Lots to see and do: Rutland Water, castles, stately homes, country parks, forestry and Barnsdale Gardens. Non-smoking. Self catering also available. **RAC ◆◆◆**
e-mail: bb@iepuk.com
website: www.rutnet.co.uk/orb

LINCOLNSHIRE

ALFORD (near)

Nev and Jill Brown, Wellbeck Farmhouse, Well, Near Alford LN13 9LT (Tel & Fax: 01507 462453). Nev and Jill welcome you to their farmhouse, set in a large peaceful garden within easy reach of the beautiful Lincolnshire Wolds and the superb beaches. Lincoln 35 miles, Alford 1½ miles. There are two family rooms and one single, with tea and coffee making facilities and colour TV. Full English breakfast is served. Pets by arrangement. Ample parking. £18 per person; reductions for children.

BROXHOLME

Peter & Catrin Fieldson, Manor Farm Stables, Broxholme LN1 2NG (01522 704220; mobile: 07890 812323). We have converted a characterful old Listed barn into a comfortable family home and invite you to join us in our self-contained, four diamond-rated Bed and Breakfast suite, where you can enjoy privacy along with the comfort and style of this beautiful building. The suite consists of a large, double, beamed bedroom along with private lounge/dining room and Victorian-style bathroom and shower. Free fishing and bicycles available for guests. There is a view of Lincoln Cathedral which stands illuminated and majestic in the distance and creates a beautiful backdrop to the hamlet of Broxholme, just ten minutes away from two thousand years of history. **ETC ◆◆◆◆**
e-mail: pfieldson@lineone.net

HOLBEACH

Mrs M. Biggadike, Cackle Hill House, Cackle Hill Lane, Holbeach PE12 8BS (01406 426721; Fax: 01406 424659; mobile: 07930 228755). A warm welcome awaits you at our comfortable farmhouse. One double and one twin en suite, one twin with private bathroom. All rooms are tastefully furnished and have tea/coffee making facilities. One mile north of Holbeach on B1168. Prices from £22 to £28. Non-smoking. Short break rates. **ETC ◆◆◆◆** *SILVER AWARD*, **RAC ◆◆◆◆** *SPARKLING DIAMOND AWARD, WELCOME HOST*

HORNCASTLE

Mrs C.E. Harrison, Baumber Park, Baumber, Near Horncastle LN9 5NE (01507 578235; Fax: 01507 578417). Spacious elegant farmhouse of character in quiet parkland setting on a mixed farm. Large gardens, wildlife pond and grass tennis court. Fine bedrooms with lovely views, period furniture and log fires. Central in the county and close to the Lincolnshire Wolds, this rolling countryside is little known and quite unspoilt. Bridleways and lanes ideal for walking, cycling or riding: stabling for horses available. Two championship golf courses at nearby Woodhall Spa. Well located for historic Lincoln, interesting market towns and many antique shops. Single, double en suite and twin with private bathroom. Bed and Breakfast from £20. A warm welcome awaits. **ETC ◆◆◆◆**

website: http://uk.geocities.com/baumberpark/thehouse

LANGWORTH

Mr & Mrs Fleetwood, Ferry House Farm, Low Barlings, Langworth, Lincoln LN3 5DG (01522 751939; Fax: 01522 751959). 18th century farmhouse set in peaceful countryside next to Barlings Abbey, on the Viking Way. Accommodation comprises one single, one double and one twin room, all with central heating, TV and tea/coffee facilities. Horseriding, walking, cycling available. Ideal for Lincoln Showground and the Wolds. Lincoln seven miles, Wragby five miles. Children and pets welcome. Non-smoking. Prices range from £20 to £24 single and £40 to £48 twin/double. Short breaks available.

e-mail: ifleet@barlings.demon.co.uk

MARKET RASEN

Mrs Marlene Burton, Little Owls, Northend Farm, Thornton Road, North Owersby, Market Rasen LN8 3PP (Tel & Fax: 01673 828116; mobile: 07816 209645). Find peace and relaxation. Set around a charming paved courtyard, colourful with flowers and an ornamental fish pond, Little Owls is a group of farm buildings which has been ingeniously converted into attractive and comfortable bed and breakfast accommodation. Formerly a cattle shed and waggon house, the buildings are part of North End Farm, and are surrounded by more than 12 acres of garden and paddocks which guests are free to enjoy. Guest rooms, all on the ground floor, have en suite and private facilities, and are tastefully furnished and decorated, with full central heating. Convenient for the Viking Way and the Hull to Harwich cycle route. Secure parking for cars and bicycles.

website: www.littleowls.com

THORPE FENDYKES

Mrs S. Evans, Willow Farm, Thorpe Fendykes, Wainfleet, Skegness PE24 4QH (01754 830316). In the heart of the Lincolnshire Fens, Willow Farm is a working smallholding with free range hens, goats, horses and ponies. Situated in a peaceful hamlet with abundant wildlife, ideal for a quiet retreat - yet only 15 minutes from the Skegness coast, shops, amusements and beaches. Bed and Breakfast is provided in comfortable en suite rooms from £17 per person per night, reductions for children (suppers and sandwiches can be provided in the evening on request). Rooms have tea and coffee making facilities and a colour TV and are accessible to disabled guests. Friendly hosts! Ring for brochure.

website: www.willowfarmholidays.fsnet.co.uk

NORFOLK

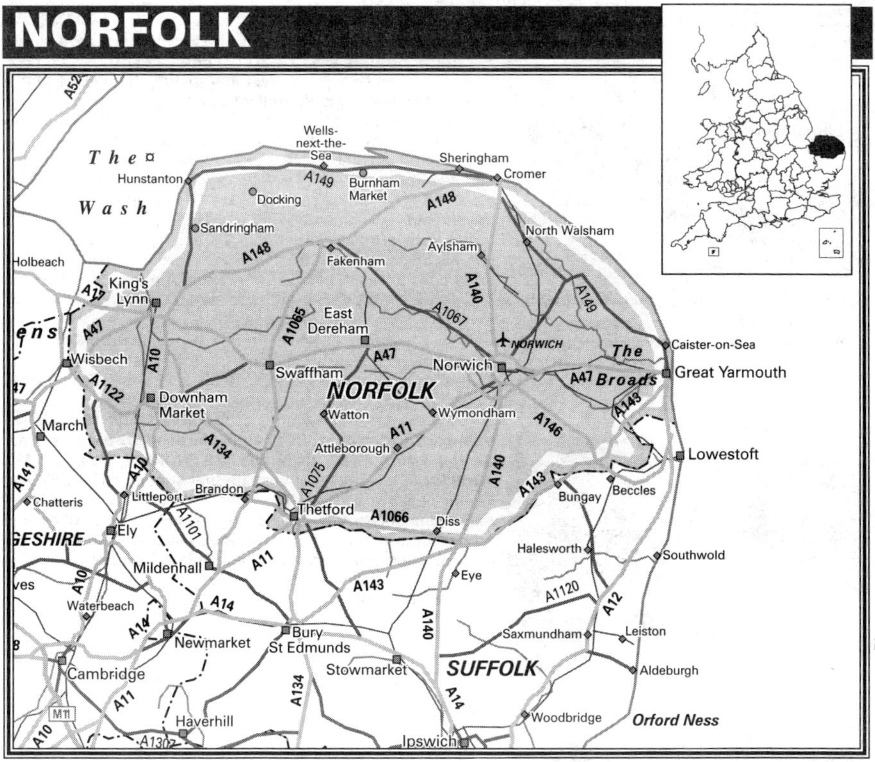

ATTLEBOROUGH

Hill House Farm, Deopham Road, Great Ellingham, Attleborough NR17 1AQ (01953 453113; Fax: 01953 451582). A working farm in quiet rural setting situated within easy reach of all local attractions. We offer our guests a warm welcome, children welcome, pets by arrangement only. Attractions include Banham Zoo, world famous Butterfly Gardens, Snetterton Racing Circuit and fishing lakes are close by; seaside resorts and Norfolk Broads are approximately 40 miles distant. Comfortable rooms with washbasins, tea/coffee facilities and colour TV. Ample parking. Open all year. Awarded Good Food Hygiene Certificate. Terms from £20 per person per night, reduced rates for children under 10 years. Walkers and Cyclists welcome, clothes drying facilities and packed lunches available.

e-mail: maureenray@talk21.com **website: www.SmoothHound.co.uk/hotels/hillhousefarm.html**

See also Colour Display Advertisement

BECCLES (near)

Mrs Rachel Clarke, Shrublands Farm, Burgh St Peter, Near Beccles, Suffolk NR34 0BB (Tel & Fax: 01502 677241). This attractive homely farmhouse, offering a warm and friendly welcome, is peacefully situated in the Waveney Valley on the Norfolk/Suffolk border, and surrounded by one acre of garden and lawns. The River Waveney flows through the 550 acres of mixed working farmland; opportunities for bird-watching. Ideal base for touring Norfolk and Suffolk; Beccles, Lowestoft, Great Yarmouth and Norwich are all within easy reach. The house has two double rooms with en suite facilities and one twin-bedded room with private bathroom, shower room and toilet. All have satellite colour TV and tea/coffee making facilities; dining room, lounge with colour satellite TV. Non-smoking rooms. No pets. Car essential, ample parking. Tennis court available. Swimming pool and food at River Centre nearby. Open all year except Christmas. Bed and Breakfast from £21 per person. Reductions for longer stays. SAE please. **ETC ◆◆◆◆** *SILVER AWARD*.

See also Colour Display Advertisement

BUNGAY

Mrs B. Watchorn, Earsham Park Farm, Harleston Road, Earsham, Bungay NR35 2AQ (01986 892180; Fax: 01986 894796). This family-run quiet and friendly farmhouse with a relaxed atmosphere is surrounded by lovely gardens and farm walks. Superbly set on a hill overlooking the gorgeous Waveney valley. The rooms are all spacious and beautifully furnished, but with comfort as a priority. Two large doubles (one four poster) and one twin room, all en suite. All rooms have extensive facilities, including easy chairs, colour TV, tea tray, radio etc. Thick fluffy towels and embroidered linen also add to your comfort. The farm's own produce is used in the excellent breakfasts. The famous Earsham Otter Trust is at the bottom of the drive. Your hosts have a wealth of local knowledge. A non-smoking house. Bed and Breakfast from £25 per person (based on two sharing). **ETC ◆◆◆◆** *GOLD AWARD*, **AA ◆◆◆◆**, *FARM STAY UK MEMBER.*

e-mail: bobbie@earsham-parkfarm.co.uk **website: www.earsham-parkfarm.co.uk**

BURNHAM MARKET

Valerie Southerland, Whitehall Farm, Burnham Thorpe, King's Lynn PE31 8HN (01328 738416; Fax: 01328 730937). Situated about two miles from the North Norfolk coast, Whitehall Farm is a working arable farm with a friendly family atmosphere. Comfortable rooms offering TV, tea/coffee and private bathrooms. Ample parking available and use of the garden. Valerie and Barry Southerland look forward to ensuring your stay is an enjoyable experience that you will want to repeat. Children and pets welcome. Open all year. **ETC ◆◆◆◆**

See also Colour Display Advertisement

DISS

4B&B Strenneth Country Bed & Breakfast, Airfield Road, Fersfield, Diss IP22 2BP (01379 688182; Fax: 01379 688260). Well-established, family-run businesss, situated in unspoiled countryside, a short drive from Bressingham Gardens and the picturesque market town of Diss. Offering first-class accommodation, the original 17th century building has been renovated to a high standard with exposed oak beams and a newer single storey courtyard wing. There is ample off-road parking and plenty of nice walks nearby. All seven bedrooms, including a four-poster and an executive, are tastefully furnished, each having colour TV, hospitality trays, central heating and full en suite facilities. The establishment is smoke-free and the guest lounge has a log fire on cold winter evenings. Extensive breakfast menu using local produce. Ideal touring base. Pets most welcome at no extra charge. Outside kennels with runs if required. Bed and Breakfast from £25. **ETC ◆◆◆◆**

e-mail: pdavey@strenneth.co.uk **website: www.strenneth.co.uk**

HOLT

Mrs Lynda Mack, Hempstead Hall, Holt NR25 6TN (01263 712224). Working farm. Enjoy a relaxing holiday with a friendly atmosphere in our 18th century flint farmhouse, beautifully set on a 300 acre arable farm with ducks, donkeys and large gardens. Close to the north Norfolk coast and its many attractions. Take a ride on the steam train or a boat trip to Blakeney Point Seal Sanctuary. Spot the wild deer or the barn owl on the circular walk through our conservation award-winning farm to Holt Country Park. Large en suite family room (children over 8 years only please), double with private bathroom. Colour TV, tea/coffee facilities. Large lounge with log burning stove. Non-smoking. Sorry, no pets indoors. Bed and Breakfast from £22 per person. Children's reductions. **ETC ◆◆◆◆**, *FARM STAY UK MEMBER.*

website: www.broadland.com/hempsteadhall

MUNDESLEY

Mrs Christine Thrower, Whincliff Bed & Breakfast, Cromer Road, Mundesley NR11 8DU (01263 721554). Situated upon the picturesque 'whin gorse' covered cliffs, overlooking the sea. Near beautiful unspoilt beaches, with the lively entertainment centre of Great Yarmouth also close by. Ideal for exploring the Norfolk Broads, with its wealth of wildlife or for visiting the historic city of Norwich. Family, twin and single rooms available, some en suite, all with colour TV and tea/coffee making facilities. Fine selection of food and real ales available at the neighbouring Ingleside Hotel. Off-road parking available. Non-smoking. B&B £16 single/twin, £18 en suite, £50 family en suite. Pets welcome at no extra charge.

e-mail: whincliff@freeuk.com
website: www.whincliff.freeuk.com

NORFOLK BROADS (Neatishead)

Alan and Sue Wrigley, Regency Guest House, The Street, Neatishead, Near Norwich NR12 8AD (Tel & Fax: 01692 630233). An 18th century guest house in picturesque, unspoilt village in heart of Broadlands. Personal service top priority - same owners for 25 years. Long established name for very generous English Breakfasts. 20 minutes from medieval city of Norwich and six miles from coast. Ideal base for touring East Anglia - a haven for wildlife, birdwatching, cycling and walking holidays. Number one centre for Broads sailing, fishing and boating. Guesthouse, holder of "Good Care" award for high quality services, has five bedrooms, individually Laura Ashley-style decorated and tastefully furnished. Rooms, including two king-size doubles, and family room have TV and tea/coffee making facilities and most have en suite bathrooms. Two main bathrooms. Separate tables in beamed ceiling breakfast room. Guests' sittingroom. Cot, babysitting. Reduced rates on stays of more than one night. Pets welcome. Parking. Open all year. Fire Certificate held. There are two good eating places within walking distance of guest house. Bed and Breakfast from £22. **AA/ETC ◆◆◆◆**

e-mail: regencywrigley@btopenworld.com **website: www.norfolkbroads.com/regency**

WYMONDHAM

Mrs Joy Morter, Home Farm, Morley, Wymondham NR18 9SU (01953 602581). Comfortable accommodation set in four acres, quiet location, secluded garden. Conveniently situated off A11 between Attleborough and Wymondham, an excellent location for Snetterton and only 20 minutes from Norwich and 45 minutes from Norfolk Broads. Accommodation comprises two double rooms and one twin-bedded room, all with TV, tea/coffee facilities and central heating. Children over five years old welcome, but sorry no animals and no smoking. Bed and Breakfast from £20 per person per night.

NORTHAMPTONSHIRE

KETTERING

Mrs A. Clarke, Dairy Farm, Cranford St Andrew, Kettering NN14 4AQ (01536 330273). Enjoy a holiday in our comfortable 17th century farmhouse with oak beams and inglenook fireplaces. Four-poster bed now available. Peaceful surroundings, large garden containing ancient circular dovecote. Dairy Farm is a working farm situated in a beautiful Northamptonshire village just off the A14, within easy reach of many places of interest or ideal for a restful holiday. Good farmhouse food and friendly atmosphere. Open all year, except Christmas. Bed and Breakfast from £22 to £35 (children under 10 half price); Evening Meal from £14. **ETC ◆◆◆◆** *SILVER AWARD.*

NORTHUMBERLAND

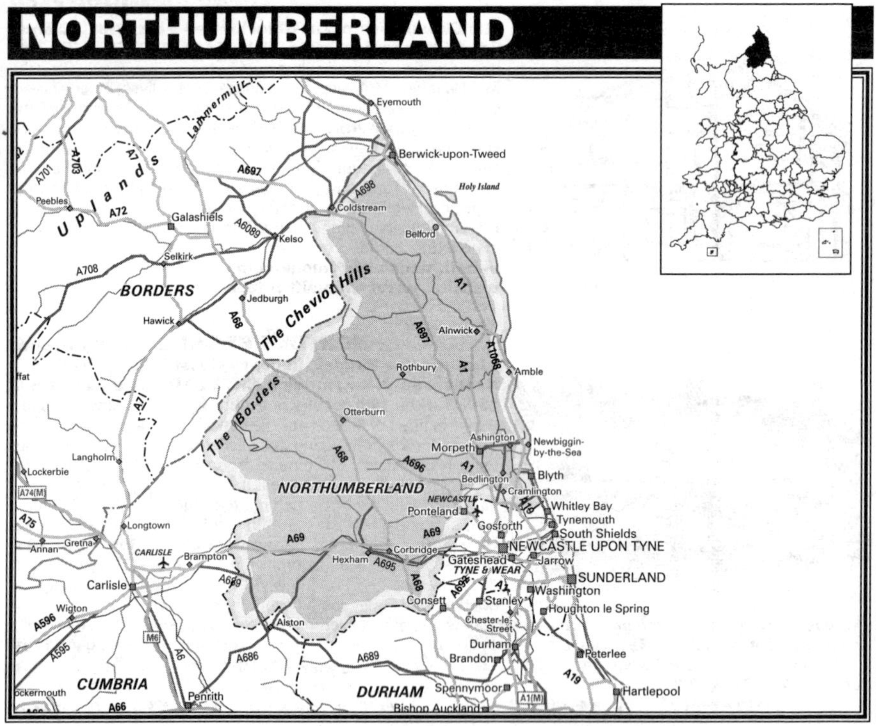

ALNMOUTH

Mrs A. Stanton, Mount Pleasant Farm, Alnmouth, Alnwick NE66 3BY (01665 830215). Mount Pleasant is situated on top of a hill on the outskirts of the seaside village of Alnmouth, with spectacular views of the surrounding countryside. We offer fresh air, sea breezes, green fields, beautiful beaches, country roads and peace and quiet. There are two golf courses and a river meanders around the farm with all its bird life. There are castles, Holy Island, the Farnes and the Cheviots to explore. Farmhouse has large rooms, TV, tea making and en suite facilities. Ample parking. SELF-CATERING AVAILABLE.

See also Colour Display Advertisement

ALNWICK (near)

Mrs Celia Curry, Howick Scar Farm House, Craster, Alnwick NE66 3SU (Tel & Fax: 01665 576665). Comfortable farmhouse accommodation on working mixed farm situated on the Heritage Coast between the villages of Craster and Howick. Ideal base for walking, golfing, bird-watching or exploring the coast, moors and historic castles. The Farne Islands famous for their colonies of seals and seabirds, and Lindisfarne (Holy Island) are within easy driving distance. Accommodation is in two double rooms with washbasins. Guests have their own TV lounge/dining room with full central heating. Non-smoking. Bed and Breakfast from £19. Open Easter to November. **ETC ◆◆◆**, *FARM STAY UK.*
e-mail: stay@howickscar.co.uk
website: www.howickscar.co.uk

ENGLAND

BERWICK-UPON-TWEED

Mrs E. Dobson, Tweed View House, East Ord, Berwick-upon-Tweed TD15 2NS (Tel & Fax: 01289 332378). In the village of East Ord, not far from the A1 and one mile from the historic town of Berwick-upon-Tweed, within easy touring distance of many other Border towns and attractions. A family-run B&B business, we look forward to welcoming you to our home for a short break or longer stay. There are two double/family rooms and a single room, all with en suite shower, television and tea and coffee making facilities. Ample parking space; garage available for motorcycle and bicycle parking. Dogs welcome by prior arrangement. Non-smoking establishment. Prices from £20pppn, special rates for children. Reduced rates for three nights or more.
e-mail: khdobson@aol.com
website: www.tweedview.8k.com

HEXHAM

Mrs Ruby Keenleyside, Struthers Farm, Catton, Allendale, Hexham NE47 9LP (01434 683580). Struthers Farm offers a warm welcome in the heart of England, with many splendid local walks from the farm itself. Panoramic views. Situated in an area of outstanding beauty. Double/twin rooms, en suite, central heating. Good farmhouse cooking. Ample safe parking. Come and share our home and enjoy beautiful countryside. Children welcome, pets by prior arrangement. Open all year. Bed and Breakfast from £20; Evening Meal from £10. *FARM STAY UK MEMBER*.

HEXHAM

Mr & Mrs D Maughan, Greencarts Farm, Humshaugh, Hexham NE46 4BW (01434 681320; mobile: 07752 697355). Greencarts is a working farm situated in Roman Wall country, ideally placed for exploring by car, bike or walking. It has magnificent views of the Tyne Valley. It is warm and homely with central heating and log fires. Home cooked food is provided. En suite accommodation with safe car/bike parking. Convenient for Hexham Racecourse. Fishing available locally. All welcome. Bed and Breakfast from £20 to £22. Open all year
e-mail: Sandra.Maughan2@200m.co.uk.

HEXHAM

Mrs I Wallace, Bridgeford Farm, Bellingham, Hexham NE48 2HU (01434 220940). Working farm. Come to Bridgeford Farm to relax and unwind in peaceful surroundings, in the North Tyne Valley. Spacious farmhouse consisting of two double and one twin bedrooms, all en suite, with colour TV, tea/coffee making facilities. Separate dining room and lounge. Excellent area for walking and cycling. Kielder Water and Hadrian's Wall nearby. Children welcome. Non-smoking. B&B from £22 to £25 pppn. **ETC ◆◆◆◆** *WELCOME HOST.*

Visits & Attractions

Grace Darling Museum, Bamburgh, Northumberland • 01668 214465

Commemorates the rescue by Grace and her father of the nine survivors of the wreck of the Forfarshire. Many relics, including the cable used in the rescue, plus books, paintings etc.

See also Colour Display Advertisement

HEXHAM

Mrs E. Reed, Moss Kennels, Housesteads, Haydon Bridge, Hexham NE47 6NL (Tel & Fax: 01434 344016). A spacious farmhouse offering a friendly and relaxed atmosphere. Set in a large garden. Situated on Hadrian's Wall; magnificent scenery with many interesting places to visit and lovely walks. Only half-a-mile east of Housesteads and half-an-hour from the Metro Centre. All rooms are spacious, comfortable and en suite, with colour TV and tea/coffee making facilities. Open all year. Bed and Breakfast from £20, evening meal £12.50. **ETC ◆◆◆◆**
e-mail: Tim.mosskennels@virgin.net

See also Colour Display Advertisement

HEXHAM

Ros Johnson, West Wharmley, Hexham NE46 2PL (Tel & Fax: 01434 674227). Set on a 400 acre working farm. We offer a warm welcome to our well-appointed accommodation which has outstanding views over the South Tyne Valley. The 18th century farmhouse has a self-contained wing which is decorated to a high standard and has full central heating. A large private sittingroom, complete with open fire, oak beams and colour TV, provides a homely retreat for the evenings. Two large bedrooms, both en suite, have colour TVs and tea/coffee making facilities. Ideal for families. Close to Hadrian's Wall and very accessible to Northumberland's many attractions. Bed and Breakfast from £20 to £25. **ETC ◆◆◆◆**

NOTTINGHAMSHIRE

EDWINSTOWE (near Mansfield)

Robin Hood Farmhouse B&B, Rufford Road, Edwinstowe NG21 9JA (Tel & Fax: 01623 824367). Traditional Olde English farmhouse in Robin Hood's village in the middle of Sherwood Forest. We are in close proximity to Clumber and Rufford Country Parks and adjacent to Center Parcs and South Forest Leisure Complex. Easy access to Nottingham and Lincoln. The farmhouse, which is set in extensive gardens, is open and centrally heated all year round. Accommodation comprises double/family and twin room, colour TV, tea/coffee making facilities in all rooms. Tariff from £17.50 per person per night. Reductions for children and extra nights. Pets and special requirements available on request. Ample secure parking.
e-mail: robinhoodfarm@aol.com

MANSFIELD

Mrs L. Palmer, Boon Hills Farm, Nether Langwith, Mansfield NG20 9JQ (01623 743862). This is a stone-built farmhouse, standing 300 yards back from A632 on edge of village. It is on a 155-acre mixed farm with dogs, cats, goats, chicks, calves. Situated on the edge of Sherwood Forest, six miles from Visitors' Centre, eight miles from M1, 10 miles from A1. Chatsworth House, Newstead Abbey, Hardwick Hall and Creswell Crags all within easy reach. One double en suite, one double and one twin shared bathroom; toilet; fitted carpets throughout. Open fires. Background central heating for comfort all year round. Large sittingroom/diningroom with colour TV. Children welcome and babysitting. No Pets. Car essential - parking. Bed and Breakfast from £18 per night, which includes bedtime drink. Evening Meal available nearby. Non-smokers only. Rates reduced for children. Open March to October inclusive.

STANTON-ON-THE-WOLDS

Mrs V. Moffat, Laurel Farm, Browns Lane, Stanton-on-the-Wolds, Nottingham NG12 5BL (0115 9373488). Laurel Farm is an old farmhouse in approximately three acres of land. All rooms are spacious, with en suite or private facilities. Teatrays, TV, hair dryer and bath robes for non en suite room. Laurel Farm is on a quiet lane with easy access from M1, A46 and A606. Convenient for tourist attractions. Breakfast is served in a spacious dining room and only local produce and our own free-range eggs used. Laurel Farm rooms are for non-smokers only and are therefore 'asthma friendly'. Double/twin from £22.50 per person per night, single occupancy from £37.50 per person per night. **ETC ◆◆◆**

OXFORDSHIRE

BANBURY (near)

Mrs E. J. Lee, The Mill Barn, Lower Tadmarton, Near Banbury OX15 5SU (01295 780349). Tadmarton is a small village, three miles south-west of Banbury. The Mill, no longer working, was originally water powered and the stream lies adjacent to the house. The Mill Barn has been tastefully converted, retaining many traditional features such as beams and exposed stone walls, yet it still has all the amenities a modern house offers. Two spacious en suite bedrooms, one downstairs, are available to guests in this comfortable family home. Base yourself here and visit Stratford, historic Oxford, Woodstock and the beautiful Cotswolds, knowing you are never farther than an hour's drive away. Open all year for Bed and Breakfast from £25, reductions for children. Weekly terms available.

FARINGDON

Mrs Pat Hoddinott, Ashen Copse Farm, Coleshill, Faringdon SN6 7PU (01367 240175; Fax: 01367 241418). Working farm. Perfect place to tour or relax. Our 650 acre National Trust farm is set in wonderful, peaceful countryside, teeming with wildlife. The quiet, comfortable accommodation is a great centre for walking or visiting Cotswolds, Vale of the White Horse, Oxford, Bath, Stratford and all little places in between! So much to see and do. Facilities locally for fishing, golfing, riding, boating and swimming. Many places to eat out nearby. Open all year. One family en suite, one twin and one single bedroom. Bed and Breakfast from £25. No smoking please. **ETC ◆◆◆**
e-mail: pat@hodd.demon.co.uk
website: www.hodd.demon.co.uk

HENLEY-ON-THAMES

The Old Bakery, Skirmett, Near Henley-on-Thames RG9 6TD (01491 638309; Fax: 01491 638086). This welcoming family house is situated on the site of an old bakery, seven miles from Henley-on-Thames and Marlow; half-an-hour from Heathrow and Oxford; one hour from London. It is in the Hambleden Valley in the beautiful Chilterns, with many excellent pubs selling good food nearby. Excellent village pub in Skirmett within easy walking distance. One double en suite, one twin-bedded room and one double with use of own bathroom. All with TV and tea making facilities. Open all year. Parking for five cars (car essential). Children and pets welcome. Bed and Breakfast from £30 single; £60 double, £75 en suite.
e-mail: liz.roach@enphony.net

LONG HANBOROUGH

Mrs I.J. Warwick, The Close Guest House, Witney Road, Long Hanborough OX8 8HF (01993 882485). We offer comfortable accommodation in house set in own grounds of one-and-a-half acres. Two family rooms, one double room; all are en suite and have colour TV and tea/coffee making facilities. Lounge. Full central heating. Use of garden and car parking for eight cars. Close to Woodstock, Oxford and the Cotswolds. Babysitting. Open all year except Christmas. Bed and Breakfast from £20.

MINSTER LOVELL

Mrs Katharine Brown, Hill Grove Farm, Crawley Road, Minster Lovell OX29 0NA (01993 703120; Fax: 01993 700528). Hill Grove is a mixed family-run 300 acre working farm situated in an attractive rural setting overlooking the Windrush Valley. Ideally positioned for driving to Oxford, Blenheim Palace, Witney (Farm Museum) and Burford (renowned as the Gateway to the Cotswolds and for its splendid Wildlife Park). New golf course one mile. Hearty breakfasts. One double/private shower, one twin/double en suite bedrooms. Children welcome. Open all year except Christmas. Bed and Breakfast from £24 per person per night for double/private shower; £26 per person per night for double/twin en suite. Non-smoking. **ETC ◆◆◆◆**
e-mail: kbrown@eggconnect.net

WOODSTOCK

The Leather Bottel, East End, North Leigh, Near Witney OX8 6PY (01993 882174). Joe and Nena Purcell invite you to The Leather Bottel guest house situated in the quiet hamlet of East End near North Leigh, convenient for Blenheim Palace, Woodstock, Roman Villa, Oxford and the Cotswolds. Breathtaking countryside walks. Two double en suite bedrooms, one family room with own bathroom, one single bedroom, all with colour TV and tea/coffee making facilities. Bed and Breakfast £30 per night for single room, from £45 for double. Children welcome. Open all year. Directions: follow signs to Roman Villa off A4095. **ETC ◆◆◆**

SHROPSHIRE

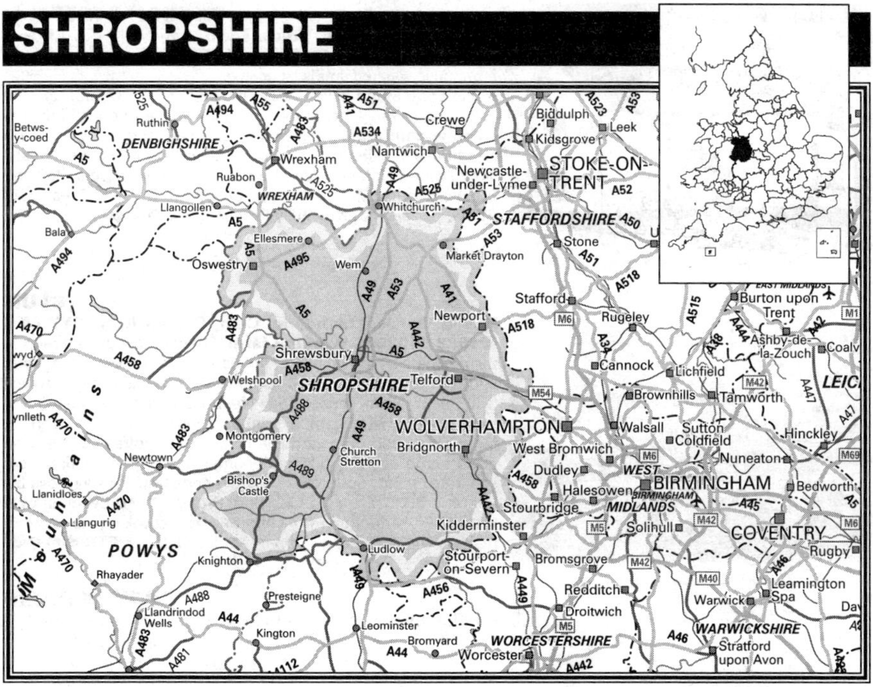

CHURCH STRETTON

Mrs Mary Jones, Acton Scott Farm, Acton Scott, Church Stretton SY6 6QN (01694 781260; Fax: 0870 129 4591). Working farm. Lovely 17th century farmhouse in peaceful village amidst the beautiful hills of South Shropshire, an area of outstanding natural beauty. The house is full of character; the rooms, which are all heated, are comfortable and spacious. Bedrooms have washbasin and tea/coffee making facilities; en suite or private bathroom. Colour TV lounge. Children welcome, pets accepted by arrangement. We are a working farm, centrally situated for visiting Ironbridge, Shrewsbury and Ludlow, each easily reached within half-an-hour. Visitors' touring and walking information available. Bed and full English Breakfast from £19 per person. Non-smoking. Open all year excluding November, December and January. **ETC ◆◆◆**, *FARM STAY UK MEMBER*.

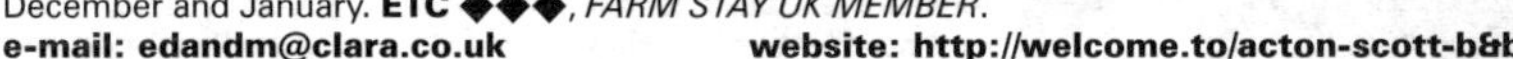

e-mail: edandm@clara.co.uk **website: http://welcome.to/acton-scott-b&b**

CHURCH STRETTON

Mrs J. Brereton, Brereton's Farm, Woolston, Church Stretton SY6 6QD (Tel & Fax: 01694 781201). Working farm. Peace, tranquillity and unforgettable views of rambling countryside (including working of sheep dogs) can be enjoyed from extensive gardens surrounding our elegant red brick farmhouse; an ideal base for visiting Ludlow, Ironbridge, Shrewsbury and Powis Castle, or walk onto the Long Mynd from our working farm. Twin and two double bedrooms (one with pine four-poster), all en suite, with tea making facilities and fresh milk. Residents' lounge with log burner. Hearty English Breakfast. Bed and Breakfast from £21. **ETC ◆◆◆**

e-mail: joanna@breretonhouse.f9.co.uk

website: www.breretonhouse.f9.co.uk

ENGLAND

See also Colour Display Advertisement

CHURCH STRETTON

Mrs Lyn Bloor, Malt House Farm, Lower Wood, Church Stretton SY6 6LF (01694 751379). Olde worlde beamed farmhouse situated amidst specatular scenery on the lower slopes of the Long Mynd hills. We are a working farm producing beef cattle and sheep. One double and one twin bedrooms, both with en suite bathrooms, colour TV, hairdryer and tea tray. Good farmhouse cooking is served in the dining room. Private guests' sitting room. Non-smoking. Regret no children or pets. Bed and Breakfast from £20 per person per night; Evening Meal from £15.00 per person. Now fully licensed. **AA ◆◆◆**

CLUN

Mrs M. Jones, Llanhedric, Clun, Craven Arms SY7 8NG (01588 640203). Working farm. Put your feet up and relax in the recliners as the beauty of the garden, the trickle of the pond, and the views of Clun and its surrounding hills provide solace from the stress of modern day life. Receive a warm welcome at this traditional oak-beamed farmhouse set back from the working farm. Three bedrooms, double en suite, tea/coffee facilities and good home cooking. Visitors' lounge with inglenook fireplace; separate dining room. Walks, history and attractions all close by. Bed and Breakfast from £20, Bed, Breakfast and Evening Meal from £30. Reductions for children. Non-smoking household. Regret no dogs in house. Open April to October. **ETC ◆◆◆◆**

CRAVEN ARMS

Mrs I.J. Evans, Springhill Farm, Clun, Craven Arms SY7 8PE (Tel & Fax: 01588 640337). Springhill Farm is a working farm in an idyllic situation on the Offa's Dyke footpath in glorious South Shropshire countryside with panoramic views over hills and valleys. Walks from the front door. This is a place to relax and unwind away from the pressures of life. Close by are Ludlow, Church Stretton, Ironbridge. All rooms en suite. Evening meals are provided. For reservations contact **Ingrid Evans.**

DORRINGTON

Ron and Jenny Repath, Meadowlands, Lodge Lane, Frodesley, Dorrington SY5 7HD (Tel & Fax: 01694 731350). Former farmhouse set in eight acres of gardens, paddocks and woodland. Pleasant woodland trail for guests' use. Quiet location in a delightful hamlet seven miles south of Shrewsbury. The guest house lies on a no-through road to a forested hill rising to 1000ft. Meadowlands features panoramic views over open countryside to the Stretton Hills. Guest accommodation includes en suite facilities and every bedroom has a colour TV, drink-making facilities and a silent fridge. Guests' lounge with maps and guides for loan. Central heating. Plenty of parking space. Strictly no smoking. Bed and Breakfast from £20; Evening Meal from £12 by arrangement. Brochure available. **ETC ◆◆◆**

e-mail: meadowlands@talk21.com **website: www.meadowlands.co.uk**

See also Colour Display Advertisement

NEWPORT

Harper Adams University College, Edgmond, Newport TF10 8NB (01952 820280; Fax: 01952 814783). Harper Adams is situated close to the north Shropshire/Staffordshire border in the village of Edgmond, three miles from the market town of Newport. The upper west wing of the magnificent building is given over to eight charming guest suites, each with its own individual character. These suites are served by a private lounge and bathrooms and have superb views across Harper Adams' gardens and fields. Supplementing these suites are 180 en suite bedrooms, as well as 160 bedrooms with shared bathroom facilities. Guests are never more than a short walk away from numerous on-site facilities. Our team of domestic staff will be pleased to assist you in any way possible during your stay, and will ensure that rooms are serviced on a daily basis.

e-mail: info@harper-adams.ac.uk **website: www.harper-adams.ac.uk**

ENGLAND

LYTHWOOD HALL

BAYSTON HILL
SHREWSBURY SY3 0AD

Quality Bed and Breakfast accommodation in a comfortable, spacious Georgian house. Enjoy the peaceful rural surroundings, our beautiful gardens or the log fire in winter. Relax in the guests' lounge, visit our spotted horses or walk on the Shropshire Way.

We are centrally placed for guests to tour Shropshire and the Welsh Borders. The medieval town of Shrewsbury is just three miles away and we are within easy reach of several excellent golf courses. Shropshire also has a great range of garden centres and specialist nurseries for keen gardeners to visit. There is easy access to all main routes, e.g. A5, A49, M54, M6. We are open all year. Kennel and run available for dogs. Bed and Breakfast £25, double room £45. Evening meal £14. Home-grown produce, vegetarians welcome.

Tel: 01743/07074 874747 • Fax: 01743 874747 • e-mail: lythwoodhall@amserve.net

OSWESTRY

Mrs Margaret Jones, Ashfield Farmhouse, Maesbury, Near Oswestry SY10 8JH (Tel & Fax: 01691 653589; mobile 07989 477414). Scented roses and scarlet creepers ramble this delightful 16th century coaching-house and Georgian farmhouse, ONE MILE FROM OSWESTRY, NESTLING IN THE ENGLISH/WELSH BORDERS. From the farmhouse it is a five minute walk to the canalside inn and excellent Warehouse restaurant. Visit this beautiful area overflowing with castles, lakes, mountains and woodlands; Chester, Llangollen or Shrewsbury, all half-an-hour away. Exceptionally pretty, cosy and spacious rooms, one has a connecting family room. En suites and private luxury bath/shower room. All rooms fully equipped with TV, hostess tray etc. Many original features including olde worlde dining and sitting rooms. Period decor and oak furnishings, oak staircase, ship's stove and fresh flowers all add to the character and warm appeal. Bed and Breakfast from £21 per person per night. Discounts available for weekly and short breaks (brochure available). **ETC ◆◆◆◆** *SILVER AWARD.*

e-mail: marg@ashfieldfarmhouse.co.uk **website: www.ashfieldfarmhouse.co.uk**

See also Colour Display Advertisement

TELFORD

Mrs Mary Jones, Red House Farm, Longdon-on-Tern, Wellington, Telford TF6 6LE (01952 770245). Red House Farm is a late Victorian farmhouse in the small village of Longdon-on-Tern, noted for its aqueduct, built by Thomas Telford in 1796. Two double bedrooms have private facilities, one family room has its own separate bathroom. All rooms are large and comfortable. Excellent Breakfast. Farm easily located, leave M54 Junction 6, follow A442, take B5063. Central for historic Shrewsbury, Ironbridge Gorge museums or modern Telford. Several local eating places. Open all year. Families most welcome, reductions for children. Pets also welcome. Bed and Breakfast from £20.

e-mail: rhf@virtual-shropshire.co.uk
website: www.virtual-shropshire.co.uk/red-house-farm

Visits & Attractions

Acton Scott Historic Working Farm, Church Stretton • 01694 781306

A fascinating working farm using heavy horses and 19th century techniques, designed to show agricultural life from years past. Daily demonstrations of farming, butter making and traditional crafts.

Readers are requested to mention this guidebook when seeking accommodation (and please enclose a stamped addressed envelope).

SOMERSET

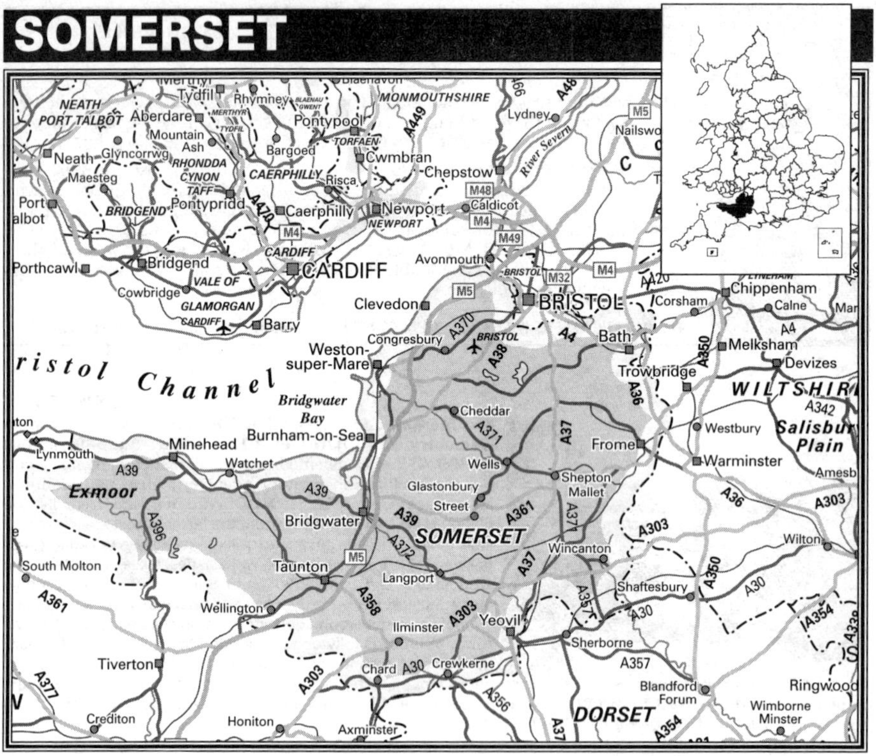

ASHBRITTLE

Mrs Ann Heard, Lower Westcott Farm, Ashbrittle, Wellington TA21 0HZ (01398 361296). On Devon/Somerset borders, 230 acre family-run farm with cattle, sheep, poultry and horses. Ideal for walking, touring Exmoor, Quantocks, both coasts and many National Trust properties. Pleasant farmhouse, tastefully modernised but with olde worlde charm, inglenook fireplaces and antique furniture, set in large gardens with lawns and flower beds in peaceful, scenic countryside. Two family bedrooms with private facilities and tea/coffee making. Large lounge, separate dining room offering guests every comfort. Noted for relaxed, friendly atmosphere and good home-cooking. Brochure by request. Bed and Breakfast from £20; Dinner £12 per person. Reductions for children. **ETC ◆◆◆**
e-mail: lowerwestcott@aol.com

BATH (near)

Mrs P Foster, Pennsylvania Farm, Newton-St-Loe, Bath BA2 9JD (01225 314912) Pennsylvania Farm is set in 280 acres of land close to Bath, Bristol, Cheddar and Wells. The farmhouse is a Listed 17th century building which is well appointed, warm and comfortable. It has three bedrooms, two with en suite bathrooms (power showers), one with private bathroom; a cosy dining room and a pleasant sunny sitting room with log fire. Wonderful farmhouse breakfasts; lunches and evening meals available. Adjacent to the farmhouse is a lovely converted cottage with two bedrooms and its own kitchen and lounge (sleeps four). **ETC ◆◆◆◆**
website: www.pennsylvaniafarm.co.uk

See also Colour Advertisement

BRISTOL

Mrs M. Hasell, The Model Farm, Norton Hawkfield, Pensford, Bristol BS39 4HA (01275 832144). Working farm. Model Farm is situated two miles off the A37 in a peaceful hamlet, nestling under the Dundry Hills. A working arable and beef farm in easy reach of Bristol, Bath, Cheddar and many other interesting places. The spacious accommodation is in two en suite rooms, one family and one double, with tea/coffee facilities. Separate dining room and lounge with colour TV for visitors. Private parking. Open all year (except Christmas and New Year). Bed and Breakfast from £20. **ETC ◆◆◆**

DULVERTON

Mrs Carole Nurcombe, Marsh Bridge Cottage, Dulverton TA22 9QG (01398 323197). This superb accommodation has been made possible by the refurbishment of this Victorian former ex-gamekeeper's cottage on the banks of the River Barle. The friendly welcome, lovely rooms, delicious (optional) evening meals using local produce, and clotted cream sweets are hard to resist! Open all year, and in autumn the trees that line the river either side of Marsh Bridge turn to a beautiful golden backdrop. Just off the B3223 Dulverton to Exford road, it is easy to find and, once discovered, rarely forgotten. From outside the front door footpaths lead in both directions alongside the river. Fishing available. Terms from £18 per person Bed and Breakfast or £33 per person Dinner, Bed and Breakfast.

DULVERTON

Mrs P. Vellacott, Springfield Farm, Ashwick Lane, Dulverton TA22 9QD (Tel & Fax: 01398 323722). At Springfield we offer you wonderful hospitality and delicious food. We farm 270 acres within the Exmoor National Park rearing sheep and cattle. Peacefully situated a one-and-a-half mile walk from the famous beauty spot of Tarr Steps, four miles from the market town of Dulverton (film location of 'The Land Girls'). Much wildlife including red deer can be seen on the farm. An ideal base for walking or touring Exmoor and North Devon coastal resorts. Riding and fishing nearby. One double room with private WC and shower, one twin/family en suite and one double en suite - all with drinks making facilities. Guests' lounge with TV, spacious dining room leading to patio and large garden. Access to rooms at all times. Ample parking (garage by request). Pets by arrangement. No smoking in farmhouse, please. Bed and Breakfast from £22.50 to £25 per person per night. Evening meals (with 24 hours notice) £15.75. Reductions for stays of three nights or more. **ETC ◆◆◆◆**

e-mail: info@springfieldfarms.co.uk **website: www.springfieldfarms.co.uk**

FROME (near)

Mrs Barbara Keevil, Eden Vale Farm, Mill Lane, Beckington, Near Frome BA11 6SN (01373 830371). Eden Vale Farm nestles down in a valley by the River Frome. Enjoying a picturesque location, this old watermill offers a selection of rooms including en suite facilities, complemented by an excellent choice of full English or continental breakfasts. Beckington is an ideal centre for visiting Bath, Longleat, Salisbury, Cheddar, Stourhead and many National Trust Houses including Lacock Village. Only a ten minute walk to the village pub, three-quarters of a mile of river fishing. Local golf courses and lovely walks. Very friendly animals. Dogs welcome. Please phone or write for more information. Open all year. **ETC ◆◆◆**

See also Colour Display Advertisement

GLASTONBURY (near)

Mrs M. White, Barrow Farm, North Wootton, near Glastonbury BA4 4HL (Tel & Fax: 01749 890245). Working farm. Barrow is a dairy farm of 146 acres. The house is 15th century and of much character, situated between Wells, Glastonbury and Shepton Mallet. It makes an excellent touring centre for visiting Somerset's beauty spots and historic places, for example, Cheddar, Bath, Wookey Hole and Longleat. Guest accommodation consists of two double rooms, one family room, one single room and one twin-bedded room, each with washbasin, TV and tea/coffee making facilities. Bathroom, two toilets; two lounges, one with colour TV; dining room with separate tables. Guests can enjoy farmhouse fare in generous variety, home baking a speciality. Bed and Breakfast, with optional four-course Dinner available. Car essential; ample parking. Children welcome; cot and babysitting available. Open all year except Christmas. Sorry, no pets. Bed and Breakfast from £18. Dinner, Bed and Breakfast from £30. **AA ◆◆◆**

ILMINSTER

Mrs G. Phillips, `Hermitage', 29 Station Road, Ilminster TA19 9BE (01460 53028). Enjoy the friendly atmosphere of a lovely Listed 17th century house with beams and inglenook. Four-poster beds. Two acres of delightful gardens, woods and hills beyond. Twin or double rooms with washbasin; en suite available. Lounge with log fire and colour TV. Tea or coffee with homemade biscuits on arrival. Full English breakfast. Traditional inns nearby for evening meals. Ideal touring centre for Quantock Hills, Wells, Glastonbury, Lyme Regis and many picturesque villages. Several National Trust properties, gardens and historic houses within a few miles. Ten miles from M5, one mile from A303. Bed and Breakfast £39 for two people, double/twin; £45 en suite, double/twin. **ETC ◆◆◆**
website: home.freeuk.net/hermitage

NORTH PETHERTON

Mrs Sue Milverton, Lower Clavelshay Farm, North Petherton, Near Bridgwater TA6 6PJ (01278 662347). Working farm. 17th century farmhouse on a working dairy farm set in its own peaceful valley on the edge of the beautiful Quantock Hills. Off the beaten track but within easy reach of the many attractions in Somerset. Only 10 minutes from Junction 24 of the M5 and 15 minutes from Taunton. Two en suite double bedrooms and one family room with private bathroom. Experience simple pleasures - beautiful countryside, long walks, fresh air, wildlife, wild flowers, log fires, starry nights, comfy beds, peace and tranquillity, good food, good books and good humour. Bring your family and your horse! Stables available - wonderful riding on the doorstep. Horse heaven! All meals with fresh local produce - our own where possible. Doubles £22 per person per night; family room £50 per night. Evening Meals on request (£10 adult, £5 child). **AA ◆◆◆**

The Castle Hotel

Porlock, Somerset TA24 8PY
Tel & Fax: 01643 862504

The Castle Hotel is a small, fully licensed family-run hotel in the centre of the lovely Exmoor village of Porlock. It is an ideal holiday location for those who wish to enjoy the grandeur of Exmoor on foot or by car. The beautiful villages of Selworthy and Dunster with its castle are only a short distance away. There are 13 en suite bedrooms, all fully heated, with colour TV and tea/coffee making facilities.The Castle Hotel has a well-stocked bar with Real Ale. Draught Guinness and Cider. A full range of Bar Meals are available at lunchtimes and Evenings or dine in our Restaurant. Children and pets are most welcome. Family room available, cots available on request. Pool, darts and skittles.

✤ ✤ ***Special Breaks available*** ✤ ***Extremely low rates*** ✤✤

See also Colour Advertisement

PORLOCK

Margery and Henry Dyer, West Porlock House, West Porlock, Near Minehead TA24 8NX (01643 862880). Imposing country house in Exmoor National Park on the wooded slopes of West Porlock commanding exceptional sea views of Porlock Bay and countryside. Set in five acres of beautiful woodland gardens unique for its variety and size of unusual trees and shrubs and offering a haven of rural tranquillity. The house has large spacious rooms with fine and beautiful furnishings throughout. Two double, two twin and one family bedrooms, all with en suite or private bathrooms, TV, tea/coffee making facilities, radio-alarm clock and shaver point. Licensed. Non-smoking. Private car park. Bed and Breakfast from £27 to £29.50 per person. Credit Cards accepted. Sorry, no pets. **ETC ◆◆◆◆**

See also Colour Display Advertisement

PORLOCK

Andrews on the Weir, Porlock Weir, Porlock TA24 8PB (01643 863300; Fax: 01643 863311). Overlooking Porlock Weir where Exmoor meets the sea, is a restaurant with rooms where every meal is an experience, where each room is individual and where pets are just as welcome as their owners. Discover the perfect break on Exmoor at Andrews.
website: www.andrewsontheweir.co.uk

SHERBORNE (near)

Mrs Sue Stretton, Beech Farm, Sigwells, Charlton Horethorne, Near Sherborne, Dorset DT9 4LN (Tel & Fax: 01963 220524). Comfortable, spacious farmhouse with relaxed atmosphere on our 137 acre dairy farm, also carrying beef and horses in an area with wonderful views, particularly from Corton Beacon. Located on the Somerset/Dorset border, six miles from Wincanton, four miles from Sherborne and just two miles off the A303. A centrally heated farmhouse with a double room en suite, a twin bedroom and a single bedroom with guest bathroom, all with tea/coffee trays. Pets and horses welcome by arrangement. Bed and Breakfast £17 per person. Less 10% for three or more nights. Open all year.

TAUNTON

Mrs Hayes, Hall Farm Guest House, Stogumber, Taunton TA4 3TQ (01984 656321). Nestled in the centre of Stogumber, a pretty character village surrounded by the Quantocks and Exmoor. It is within easy reach of the sea at Minehead, Blue Anchor, Watchet and St Audries Bay. For the energetic there is walking, riding and fishing all available nearby. We have three double, one family, one twin and one single room - all except the single (which has a washbasin) include full en suite facilities. Breakfast is served from 8am. A car is essential and there is ample parking available. Children and well-behaved dogs are welcome. Bed and Breakfast from £20. Please telephone for further details.

WASHFORD

Mrs Sarah Richmond, Hungerford Farm, Washford, Watchet TA23 0JZ (01984 640285). Hungerford Farm is a comfortable 13th century farmhouse on a 350-acre mixed farm, three-quarters of a mile from the West Somerset Steam Railway, quarter-of-a-mile from Cleeve Abbey and Washford Mill offering local arts and crafts. Situated in beautiful countryside on the edge of the Brendon Hills and Exmoor National Park. Within easy reach of the North Devon coast, two-and-a-half miles from the Bristol Channel and Quantock Hills. Marvellous country for walking, riding, and fishing on the reservoirs. Family room and twin-bedded room, both with colour TV; own bathroom, shower. Breakfast room with TV and open fire on colder days. Children welcome at reduced rates, cot and high chair. Pets by arrangement. Bed and Breakfast from £20, evening drink included, reduced rates for longer stays. Open all year.
e-mail: sarah.richmond@virgin.net

See also Colour Display Advertisement

WIVELISCOMBE

Jenny Cope, North Down Farm, Pyncombe Lane, Wiveliscombe, Taunton TA4 2BL (Tel & Fax: 01984 623730). In tranquil, secluded surroundings on the Somerset/Devon Border. Traditional working farm set in 100 acres of natural beauty with panoramic views of over 40 miles. M5 motorway seven miles and Taunton ten miles. All rooms tastefully furnished to high standard include en suite, TV, and tea/coffee facilities. Family room, double or single available. Dining room and lounge with log fires for our guests' comfort; central heating and double glazed. Drying facilities. Delicious home produced food a speciality. Fishing, golf, horse riding and country sports nearby. Dogs welcome. Bed and Breakfast from £23 per person. Weekly rates BB&EM £185pp North Down Break: three nights Bed and Breakfast and Evening Meal £85 per person. **ETC ◆◆◆◆** *SILVER AWARD.*
e-mail: jennycope@tiscali.co.uk

Visits & Attractions

Wookey Hole Caves, Wells, Somerset • 01749 672243
website: www.wookey.co.uk

Spectacular showcaves with ancient history and legends. Victorian papermill with traditional papermaking, magical mirror maze, old penny arcade, caves museum

West Somerset Railway, Bishops Lydeard (near Taunton) to Minehead • 01643 704996

Enjoy 20 miles of glorious Somerset countryside as the steam train gently rolls back the years. Break your journey at any one of ten restored stations along the route. For 24hr talking timetable call 01643 707650.

STAFFORDSHIRE

ALBRIGHTON

Mrs Margaret Shanks, Parkside Farm, Holyhead Road, Albrighton, Near Wolverhampton WV7 3DA (01902 372310; Fax: 01902 375013). Whether on business or visiting tourist attractions, Parkside Farm offers comfortable accommodation in a friendly atmosphere, overlooking picturesque countryside. It is a working arable farm with three bedrooms all with private facilities, TV and tea/coffee making. Family rooms are also available. It is located within easy distance of the A41, A5, M54 Junctions 3 and 4, Bridgnorth, Wolverhampton and Telford. There are plenty of pubs, bars and restaurants, the nearest within two minutes' walking distance. No dogs allowed in rooms, no smoking on premises; open parking available. Bed and Breakfast from £27 per person per night. **ETC ◆◆◆◆** *SILVER AWARD,* **AA ◆◆◆◆**

e-mail: jmshanks@farming.co.uk **website: www.parksidefarm.com**

See also Colour Display Advertisement

ECCLESHALL

M. Hiscoe-James, Offley Grove Farm, Adbaston, Eccleshall ST20 0QB (01785 280205). You'll consider this a good find! Quality accommodation and excellent breakfasts. Small traditional mixed farm surrounded by beautiful countryside. The house is tastefully furnished and provides all home comforts. Whether you are planning to book here for a break in your journey, stay for a weekend or take your holidays here, you will find something to suit all tastes among the many local attractions. Situated on the Staffordshire/Shropshire borders we are convenient for Alton Towers, Stoke-on-Trent, Ironbridge, etc. Just 15 minutes from M6 and M54; midway between Eccleshall and Newport, four miles from the A519. Reductions for children. Play area for children. Open all year. Bed and Breakfast all en suite from £23. Many guests return. Self-catering cottages available. Brochure on request. **RAC ◆◆◆◆** *WARM WELCOME AWARD AND SPARKLING DIAMOND AWARD.*

e-mail: accomm@offleygrovefarm.freeserve.co.uk **website: www.offleygrovefarm.co.uk**

KINGSLEY

Mrs Jane S. Clowes, The Church Farm, Holt Lane, Kingsley, Stoke-on-Trent ST10 2BA (Tel & Fax: 01538 754759). The famous Alton Towers is just five and a half miles from our farm. The Churnet Valley, with steam railway, wildlife park, narrowboat trips, Nick Williams Pottery and a maze of footpaths, is a fifteen minute walk; truly a hidden paradise! The Potteries and Peak District are within eight miles. Having visited all of these, come and unwind in our spacious cottage garden or with a book by the log fire in winter. Enjoy our beautifully furnished period farmhouse built in 1700 with many thoughtful additions for your comfort. Breakfast menu using own and local produce. Totally non-smoking. **ETC ◆◆◆◆**. *"WHICH? GOOD BED & BREAKFAST GUIDE"*

Visits & Attractions

Tamworth Castle, Tamworth, Staffordshire • 01827 709629

website: www.tamworth.gov.uk

This dramatic Norman castle is reputedly haunted by lady ghosts.
Lots of hands-on activities for children.

SUFFOLK

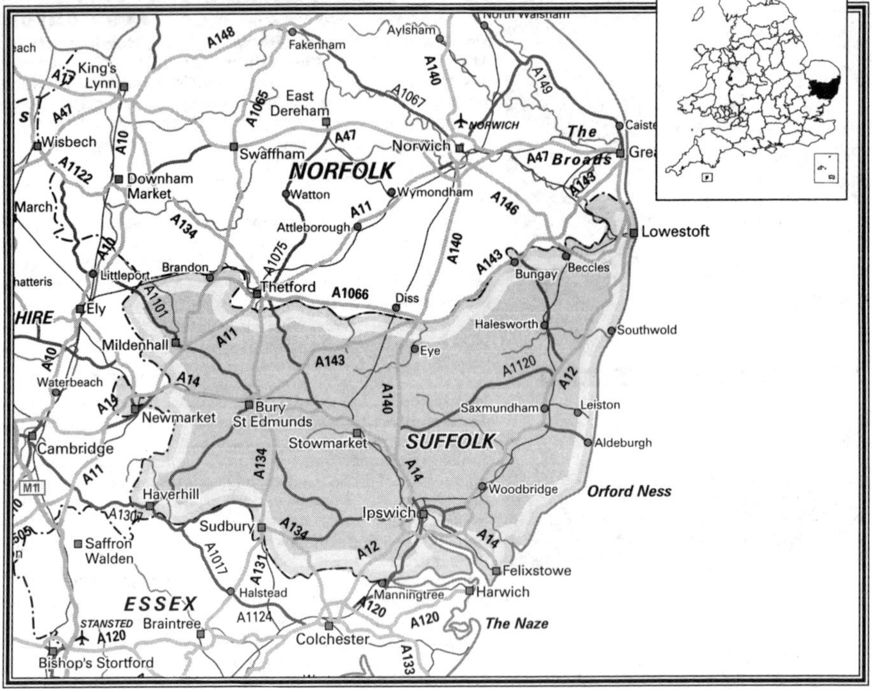

FRAMLINGHAM

Mr and Mrs Kindred, High House Farm, Cransford, Framlingham, Woodbridge IP13 9PD (01728 663461; Fax: 01728 663409). Working farm. Beautifully restored 15th Century Farmhouse on family-run arable farm, featuring exposed oak beams and inglenook fireplaces, with spacious and comfortable accommodation. One double room, en suite and one large family room with double and twin beds and private adjacent bathroom. A warm welcome awaits all, children's cots, high chairs, books, toys, and outside play equipment available. Attractive semi-moated gardens, farm and woodland walks. Explore the heart of rural Suffolk, local vineyards, Easton Farm Park, Framlingham and Orford Castles, Parham Air Museum, Saxtead Windmill, Minsmere, Snape Maltings, Woodland Trust and the Heritage Coast. Bed and Breakfast from £22.50. Reductions for children and stays of three nights or more. Self-catering available in three-bed Gamekeeper's house set in woodland. **ETC ◆◆◆**

e-mail: b&b@highhousefarm.co.uk **website: www.highhousefarm.co.uk**

FRAMLINGHAM

Mrs Anne Bater, Church Farm, Kettleburgh, Woodbridge IP13 7LF (01728 723532). Working farm. In a wonderful country setting overlooking the Deben valley, with duck ponds, flocks of geese and the backdrop of the village church, this spacious house offers much tranquillity and comfort. We are two miles from the historic town of Framlingham and close to Aldeburgh and Snape (music) and Minsmere (birdwatching). The large well-equipped bedrooms each with basins, offer an excellent standard of decor and furnishings. With a large fireplace and woodburning stove, lots of beams and little personal touches, the large lounge is very attractive and cosy. Delightful home cooked food is served in the separate diningroom. Colour TV in lounge. Children and pets welcome. Unlimited parking. Bed and Breakfast from £23 to £25, en suite available. *"WHICH?" RECOMMENDED,* **AA ◆◆◆**

FRAMLINGHAM

Mrs Jennie Mann, Fiddlers Hall, Cransford, Near Framlingham, Woodbridge IP13 9PQ (01728 663729). Working farm, join in. Signposted on B1119, Fiddlers Hall is a 14th century, moated, oak-beamed farmhouse set in a beautiful and secluded position. It is two miles from Framlingham Castle, 20 minutes' drive from Aldeburgh, Snape Maltings, Woodbridge and Southwold. A Grade II Listed building, it has lots of history and character. The bedrooms are spacious; one has en suite shower room, the other has a private bathroom. Use of lounge and colour TV. Plenty of parking space. Lots of farm animals kept. Traditional farmhouse cooking. Bed and Breakfast terms from £23 per person.

FRAMLINGHAM

Brian and Phyllis Collett, Shimmens Pightle, Dennington Road, Framlingham, Woodbridge IP13 9JT (01728 724036). Shimmens Pightle is situated in an acre of landscaped garden, surrounded by farmland, within a mile of the centre of Framlingham, with its famous castle and church. Ideally situated for the Heritage Coast, Snape Maltings, local vineyards, riding, etc. Cycles can be hired locally. Many good local eating places. Double and twin bedded rooms, with washbasins, on ground floor. Comfortable lounge with TV overlooking garden. Morning tea and evening drinks offered. Sorry, no pets or smoking indoors. Bed and traditional English Breakfast, using local cured bacon and home made marmalade. Vegetarians also happily catered for. SAE please. Open mid March to November. Bed and Breakfast from £23.50 per person. Reduced weekly rates. **ETC** 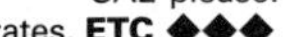

FRAMLINGHAM

Mrs J. R. Graham, Woodlands Farm, Brundish, Near Framlingham, Woodbridge IP13 8BP (01379 384444). Woodlands Farm has a cottage-type farmhouse set in quiet Suffolk countryside. Near historic town of Framlingham with its castle and within easy reach of coast, wildlife parks, Otter Trust, Easton Farm Park and Snape Maltings for music lovers. Open all year. Twin room with en suite shower, washbasin and WC; two double bedrooms with bathroom en suite. Dining room and sittingroom with inglenook fireplaces with log fires in cold weather. Good home-cooked food assured. Full central heating. Car essential, good parking. Sorry, no pets. Bed and Breakfast from £21 to £27.50. SAE or telephone. **AA ◆◆◆◆**, *FARM STAY UK MEMBER.*

The FHG Directory of Website Addresses

on pages 349-378 is a useful quick reference guide for holiday accommodation with e-mail and/or website details

ENGLAND

SURREY

See also Colour Display Advertisement

KINGSTON-UPON-THAMES

Chase Lodge, 10 Park Road, Hampton Wick, Kingston-upon-Thames KT1 4AS (020 8943 1862; Fax: 020 8943 9363). An award-winning hotel with style and elegance, set in tranquil surroundings at affordable prices. Easy access to Kingston town centre and all major transport links; 20 minutes from Heathrow Airport; Full English breakfast and à la carte menus; licensed bar. Ideal for wedding receptions. Various golf courses within easy reach. Major credit cards accepted. From £35.50 per person Bed and Breakfast; from £50 per person Dinner, Bed and Breakfast. Full details on request. **LTB/AA/RAC ★★★**, *LES ROUTIERS.*
e-mail: info@chaselodgehotel.com
website: www.chaselodgehotel.com

LINGFIELD

Mrs Vivienne Bundy, Oaklands, Felcourt Road, Lingfield RH7 6NF (01342 834705). Oaklands is a spacious country house of considerable charm dating from the 17th century. It is set in its own grounds of one acre and is about one mile from the small town of Lingfield and three miles from East Grinstead, both with rail connections to London. It is convenient to Gatwick Airport and is ideal as a "stop-over" or as a base to visit many places of interest in south east England. Dover and the Channel Ports are two hours' drive away whilst the major towns of London and Brighton are about one hour distant. One family room en-suite, one double and one single bedrooms with washbasins; three bathrooms, two toilets; sittingroom; diningroom. Cot, high chair, babysitting and reduced rates for children. Gas central heating. Open all year. Parking. Bed and Breakfast from £23; Evening Meal by arrangement.

LINGFIELD

Mrs Vanessa Manwill, Stantons Hall Farm, Eastbourne Road, Blindley Heath, Lingfield RH7 6LG (01342 832401). Stantons Hall Farm is an 18th century farmhouse set amidst 18 acres of farmland and adjacent to Blindley Heath Common. Family, double and single rooms, most with toilet, shower and washbasin en suite. Separate bathroom. All rooms have colour TV, tea/coffee making facilities and are centrally heated. There are plenty of parking spaces. We are conveniently situated within easy reach of M25 (London Orbital), Gatwick Airport (car parking facilities for travellers) and Lingfield Park Racecourse. Enjoy a traditional English Breakfast in our large farmhouse kitchen. Bed and Breakfast from £23.50 per person, reductions for children sharing. Cot and high chair available. Well behaved dogs welcome by prior arrangement.

Visits & Attractions

Brooklands Museum, Weybridge, Surrey • 01932 857381
website: www.motor-software.co.uk

Set on 30 acres of the original motor racing circuit. Racing cars, motorcycles and bikes, and the new 'Fastest on Earth' exhibition.

Terms quoted in this publication may be subject to increase if rises in costs necessitate

SUSSEX

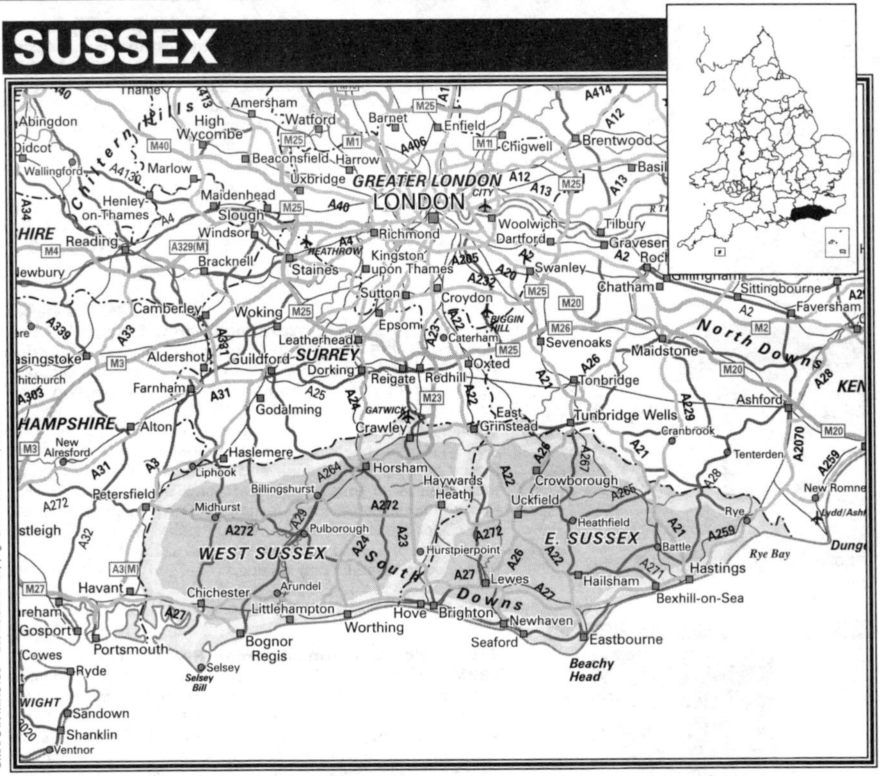

EAST SUSSEX

BURWASH

Mrs E. Sirrell, Woodlands Farm, Burwash, Etchingham TN19 7LA (Tel & Fax: 01435 882794). Woodlands Farm stands one-third-of-a mile off the road, surrounded by fields and woods. This peaceful and beautifully modernised 16th century farmhouse offers comfortable and friendly accommodation. Sitting/dining room; two bathrooms, one en suite, double or twin-bedded rooms (one has four-poster bed) together with excellent farm fresh food. This is a farm of 108 acres with a variety of animals, and is situated within easy reach of 20 or more places of interest to visit and half-an-hour from the coast. Open all year. Central heating. Literature provided to help guests. Children welcome. Dogs allowed if sleeping in owner's car. Parking. Evening Meal optional. Bed and Breakfast from £22 (single) to £48 (double). Non-smoking. Telephone or SAE, please.

e-mail: liz_sir@lineone.net **website: www.SmoothHound.co.uk/hotels/woodlands.html**

HAILSHAM (near)

David and Jill Hook, Longleys Farm Cottage, Harebeating Lane, Hailsham BN27 1ER (Tel & Fax: 01323 841227). Situated in quiet private country lane one mile north of the market town of Hailsham with its excellent amenities including modern sports centre and leisure pool, surrounded by footpaths across open farmland. Ideal for country lovers. Dogs and children welcome. The coast at Eastbourne, South Downs, Ashdown Forest and 1066 country are all within easy access. The non-smoking accommodation comprises one twin room, double room en suite; family room en suite and tea/coffee making facilities. Bed and Breakfast from £19. Reductions for children. **ETC ◆◆◆**

HASTINGS

Mr and Mrs S. York, Westwood Farm, Stonestile Lane, Hastings TN35 4PG (Tel & Fax: 01424 751038). Working farm. Farm with pet sheep, chickens, etc. Quiet rural location off country lane half a mile from B2093 approximately two miles from seafront and town centre. Golf course nearby. Central position for visiting places of interest to suit all ages. Elevated situation with outstanding views over Brede Valley. Double, twin, family rooms with en suite and private facilities. Colour TV, tea/coffee in all rooms, two bedrooms on ground floor. Full English breakfast. Off-road parking. Bed and Breakfast from £19 to £27 per person for two persons sharing. Reduced rates for weekly booking. Also available six-berth self catering caravan – details on request. **ETC ◆◆◆**

See also Colour Display Advertisement

RYE

Jeake's House, Mermaid Street, Rye TN31 7ET (01797 222828; Fax: 01797 222623). Dating from 1689, this beautiful Listed building stands in one of England's most famous streets. Oak-beamed and panelled bedrooms overlook the marsh to the sea. Brass, mahogany or four-poster beds with linen sheets and lace; honeymoon suite. En suite facilities, TV, radio, telephone. Book-lined bar. Traditional and vegetarian breakfast served. Terms from £35 to £56 per person. Private car park. Visa and Mastercard accepted. Pets welcome. **ETC ◆◆◆◆** *SILVER AWARD,* **AA ◆◆◆◆◆** *PREMIER SELECTED,* **RAC ◆◆◆◆◆** *SPARKLING DIAMOND & WARM WELCOME AWARD, GOOD HOTEL GUIDE, CÉSAR AWARD.*

WARWICKSHIRE

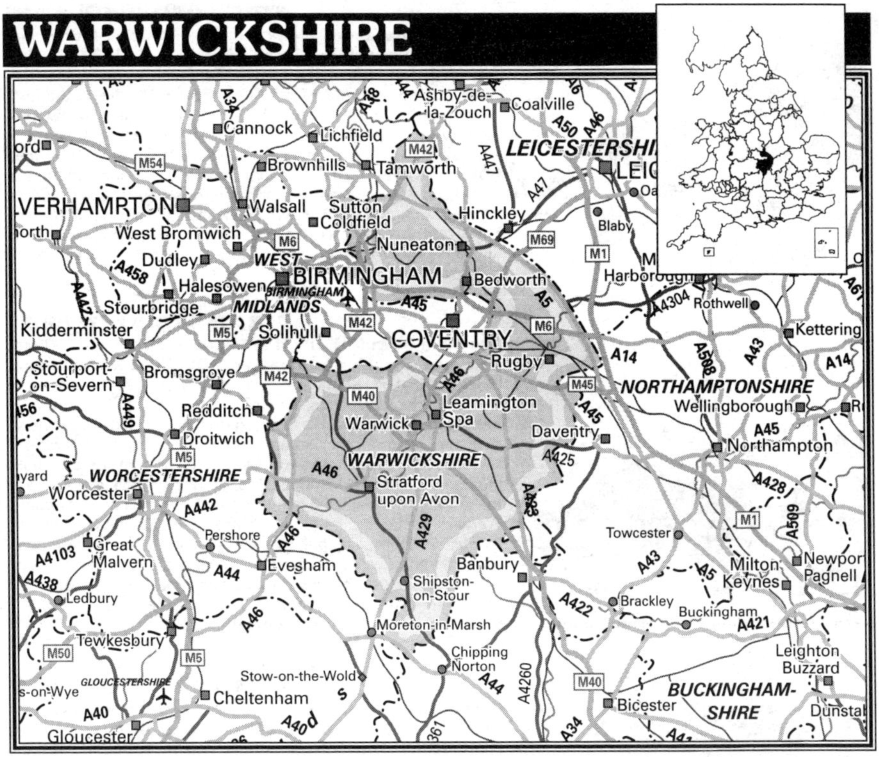

VICKI GARLAND'S B&B

ETC ◆◆◆◆ AA Rated

Elegant farmhouse with spacious interior and attractive bedrooms, set in attractive countryside in the heart of the Midlands. Within 30 minutes' drive of Drayton Manor Park, NEC, Birmingham, Coventry and Leicester. Close to Twycross Zoo, Atherstone, Tamworth, Nuneaton and Hinckley.

Beautiful riverside views and walks with interesting things to see on this working farm. A warm welcome guaranteed.

All bedrooms de luxe en suite. Singles: £20 -£35, Twins/Doubles: £40 - £60; Family rooms from £65.

Mythe Farm, Pinwall Lane, Sheepy Magna, Atherstone Warwickshire CV9 3PF

Tel: 01827 712367 • Mobile: 07751 801508

e-mail: bosworth/advertising@connectfree.co.uk
website: www.mythe-farm.co.uk

COVENTRY

Mrs Sandra Evans, Camp Farm, Hob Lane, Balsall Common, Near Coventry CV7 7GX (01676 533804). Camp Farm is a farmhouse 150 to 200 years old. It is modernised but still retains its old world character. Nestling in the heart of England in Shakespeare country, within easy reach of Stratford-upon-Avon, Warwick, Kenilworth, Coventry with its famous Cathedral, and the National Exhibition Centre, also the National Agricultural Centre, Stoneleigh. Camp Farm offers a warm homely atmosphere and good English food, service and comfortable beds. The house is carpeted throughout. Dining room and lounge with colour TV. Bedrooms – three double rooms or three single rooms, all with washbasin. The house is suitable for partially disabled guests. All terms by letter or telephone.

STRATFORD-UPON-AVON

Mrs R.M. Meadows, Monk's Barn Farm, Shipston Road, Stratford-upon-Avon CV37 8NA (01789 293714; Fax: 01789 205886). Working farm. Two miles south of Stratford-upon-Avon on the A3400 is Monk's Barn, a 75 acre mixed farm welcoming visitors all year. The farm dates back to the 16th century, although the pretty house is more recent. The double, single and twin rooms, most with en suite facilities, are provided in the main house and the cleverly converted milking parlour. The two ground floor rooms are suitable for some disabled guests. Visitors' lounge. Beautiful riverside walk to the village. Tea/coffee making facilities and colour TV in rooms. Sorry, no pets. Non-smokers preferred. Details on request. Bed and Breakfast from £18 to £20. **AA ◆◆◆◆**

STRATFORD-UPON-AVON

Mrs Julia Downie, Holly Tree Cottage, Birmingham Road, Pathlow, Stratford-upon-Avon CV37 0ES (Tel & Fax: 01789 204461). Period cottage dating back to 17th century, with beams, antiques, tasteful furnishings and friendly atmosphere. Large picturesque gardens with extensive views over the countryside. Situated three miles north of Stratford towards Henley-in-Arden on A3400, convenient for overnight stops or longer stays, and ideal for theatre visits. Excellent base for touring Shakespeare country, Heart of England, Cotswolds, Warwick Castle and Blenheim Palace. Well situated for National Exhibition Centre. Double, twin and family accommodation with en suite and private facilities; TV and tea/coffee in all rooms. Full English Breakfast. Restaurant and pub meals nearby. Bed and Breakfast from £25. Telephone for information.

e-mail: john@hollytree-cottage.co.uk **website: www.hollytree-cottage.co.uk**

STRATFORD-UPON-AVON

Penryn Guest House, 126 Alcester Road, Stratford-upon-Avon CV37 9DP (01789 293718; Fax: 01789 266077). Penryn Guest House is personally run by Anne and Robert Dawkes, who provide a comfortable and friendly environment. All bedrooms en suite with colour TV, hairdryer and tea/coffee making facilities. Situated one mile from the town centre, convenient for all major Shakespearean attractions, with Warwick Castle and Cotswolds villages within easy reach. Private car park. Full English or Continental breakfast served. All major credit cards accepted. Strictly Non-Smoking. **ETC/RAC ◆◆◆◆**

e-mail: penrynhouse@btinternet.com

website: www.penrynguesthouse.co.uk

Visits & Attractions

Heritage Motor Centre, Gaydon, Warwickshire • 01926 641188

website: www.heritage.org.uk

The largest collection of British cars in the world. 4-wheel drive demonstration circuit, children's roadway, cafe and gift shop.

Hatton Country World, Hatton, Warwickshire • 01926 843411

website: www.hattonworld.com

Rural crafts, farm park and shopping village. Craft gifts and antiques, plus factory outlets and speciality foods. Displays of traditional farming methods and lots of animals.

WILTSHIRE

CORSHAM

Kate Waldron, Park Farm Barn, Westrop, Corsham SN13 9QF (01249 715911; mobile: 07976 827083; Fax: 01249 701107). Recently converted 18th century tithe barn with newly constructed Cotswold style bed and breakfast accommodation close by. Park Farm Barn has three en suite bedrooms which are light and spacious with apex ceilings and beams. Colour TV and tea/coffee making facilities in each room. Central heating throughout. Breakfast is served in the dining room. Park Farm Barn is an ideal base for the many interesting and historic places in and around Corsham, situated in the delightful hamlet of Westrop, one mile from Corsham and seven miles from junction 17 on the M4. The National Trust village of Lacock is only a short drive away with a number of excellent pubs for evening meals. Castle Combe and Bradford-upon-Avon only 20 minutes, Bath ten miles. Children welcome, cot and highchair available. No smoking. Parking. Terms from £30 pppn single, £22.50 pppn double/twin. **ETC ◆◆◆◆**, *FARM STAY UK MEMBER.*

e-mail: thewaldrons@lineone.net **website: www.parkfarmbarn.co.uk**

See also Colour Display Advertisement

MALMESBURY

Mrs Susan Barnes, Lovett Farm, Little Somerford, Near Malmesbury SN15 5BP (Tel & Fax: 01666 823268; mobile: 07808 858612). Working farm. Enjoy traditional hospitality at our delightful farmhouse just three miles from the historic town of Malmesbury with its wonderful Norman Abbey and gardens and central for Cotswolds, Bath, Stratford, Avebury and Stonehenge. Two attractive en suite bedrooms with delightful views, each with tea/coffee making facilities, colour television and radio. Delicious full English breakfast served in our cosy diningroom/lounge. Central heating throughout. Bed and Breakfast from £23.50. Non-smoking accommodation. Open all year. Farm Holiday Bureau Member. Credit cards accepted. **ETC/AA ◆◆◆◆**, *FARM STAY UK MEMBER.*

e-mail: lovettfarm@btinternet.com
website: www.lovettfarm.co.uk

MARLBOROUGH

Mrs Maggie Vigar-Smith, Wernham Farm, Clench Common, Marlborough SN8 4DR (01672 512236). This working farm is set in picturesque countryside on Wansdyke, off the A345. It is close to Marlborough, Avebury, Pewsey and the Kennet & Avon Canal. Accommodation is available in two family bedrooms, on en suite and one with private bathroom. Terms: £30 single, £44 double. **ETC ◆◆◆**. Five caravan and camping pitches are also available.

e-mail: margglvsf@aol.com

MELKSHAM

FRYING PAN FARM

Barbara Pullen, Frying Pan Farm, Broughton Gifford, Melksham SN12 8LL (01225 702343; Fax: 01225 793652). A warm welcome awaits you at our cosy farmhouse overlooking meadowland. We are situated to the east of Bath making us an ideal base for visiting the city or touring the surrounding countryside with Bradford-on-Avon, Lacock, Stonehenge and numerous National Trust properties within easy driving distance. The accommodation consists of two en suite rooms, one double and one twin, with beverage trays and TV. Good pub food available in the village - one mile. Closed Christmas and New Year. Prices: £27 single; £46 double.
website: www.fryingpanfarm.dial.pipex.com

WARMINSTER

Mrs M. Hoskins, Spinney Farmhouse, Chapmanslade, Westbury BA13 4AQ (01373 832412). Working farm. Off A36, three miles west of Warminster; 16 miles from historic city of Bath. Close to Longleat, Cheddar and Stourhead. Reasonable driving distance to Bristol, Stonehenge, Glastonbury and the cathedral cities of Wells and Salisbury. Pony trekking and fishing available locally and an 18 hole golf course within walking distance. Washbasins, tea/coffee-making facilities and shaver points in all rooms. Family room available. Guests' lounge with colour TV. Central heating. Children and pets welcome. Ample parking. Open all year. Enjoy farm fresh food in a warm, friendly family atmosphere. Bed and Breakfast from £19 per night. Reduction after two nights. Evening Meal £11.

WORCESTERSHIRE

Lower Field Farm

For enquiries, bookings or a free colour brochure contact:

Jane Organ, Lower Field Farm, Willersey, Broadway, Worcs WR11 5HF

Tel: 01386 858273
or 07703 343996
Fax: 01386 854608
e-mail: info@lowerfield-farm.co.uk
website: www.lowerfield.farm.co.uk

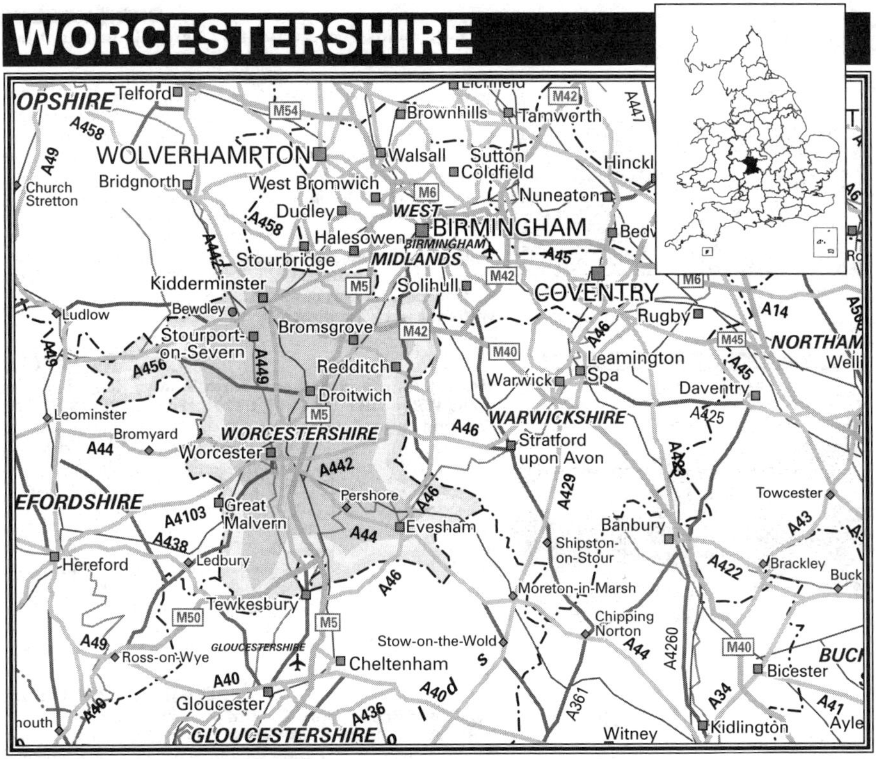

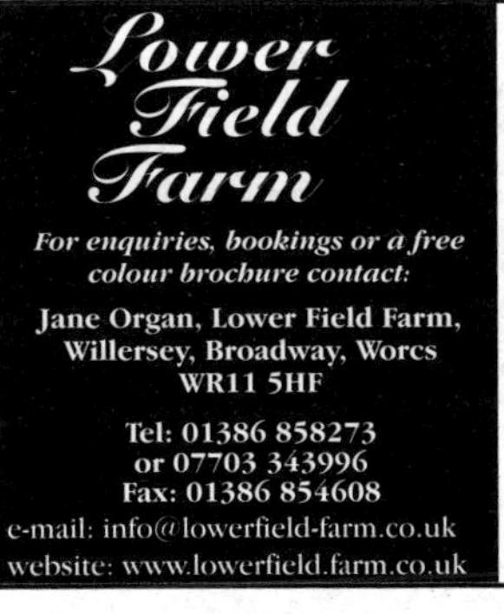

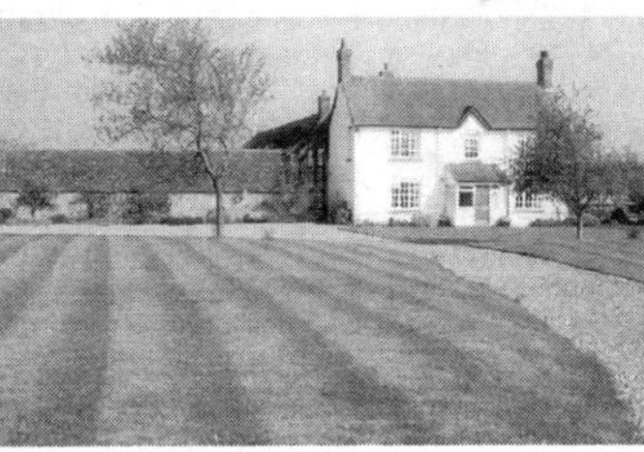

Come and enjoy our luxury B&B, in a 17th Century Cotswold stone farmhouse on our working farm peacefully located just 5 minutes from Broadway. All our spacious and elegantly furnished rooms have panoramic views over the Cotswold Hills with en suite bathrooms, colour TV, tea/coffee making facilities, clock radios and hairdryers etc. A three-course evening meal with coffee may be taken by arrangement.

Walking, cycling, horse riding and golf, with interesting places to visit, all nearby. An ideal location for regenerating the batteries or just relaxing.

See also Colour Advertisement

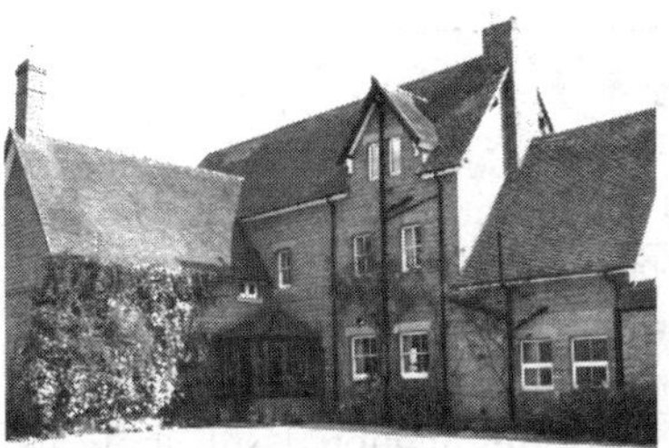

BROADWAY

Mrs Helen Perry, Mount Pleasant Farm, Childswickham, Broadway WR12 7HZ (01386 853424). Working farm. Large Victorian farmhouse set in 850 acres of mixed farm with cattle and horses. Excellent views. Open all year round, guests are offered a warm welcome and a good, traditional farmhouse breakfast. An ideal centre for touring the Cotswolds - three miles from Broadway, 15 miles from Stratford-upon-Avon, within easy reach of Warwick, Oxford, Cheltenham, Burford and many other attractions. All the bedrooms are en suite with TV, tea/coffee facilities and central heating. Bed and Breakfast from £25 per person. Superior self- catering accommodation also available in converted barns sleeping two to eight persons. **ETC/AA ◆◆◆◆**
e-mail: helen@mount/pleasant.fslife.co.uk

BROMSGROVE

Mrs C. Gibbs, Lower Bentley Farm, Lower Bentley, Bromsgrove B60 4JB (01527 821286; Fax: 01527 821193). An attractive Victorian farmhouse with modern comforts on a dairy and beef farm is an ideal base for a holiday, Short Break or business stay. Overlooking peaceful countryside, we are situated five miles away from M5 and M42 between Redditch, Bromsgrove and Droitwich. The accommodation comprises spacious double, two twin rooms with en suite or private bathroom, colour TV and tea/coffee making facilities. The comfortable lounge and separate dining room overlook the large garden. Young children are welcome. We are ideally situated for visits to Stratford-upon-Avon, Warwick, Worcester, Stourbridge, Birmingham, the Black Country, the NEC and International Convention Centre. Prices from £22.50 per person.
website: www.lowerbentleyfarm.co.uk

See also Colour Display Advertisement

MALVERN WELLS

Mrs J.L. Morris, Brickbarns Farm, Hanley Road, Malvern Wells WR14 4HY (016845 61775; Fax: 01886 830037). Working farm. Brickbarns, a 200-acre mixed farm, is situated two miles from Great Malvern at the foot of the Malvern Hills, 300 yards from the bus service and one-and-a half miles from the train. The house, which is 300 years old, commands excellent views of the Malvern Hills and guests are accommodated in one double, one single and one family bedrooms with washbasins; two bathrooms, shower room, two toilets; sittingroom and diningroom. Children welcome and cot and babysitting offered. Central heating. Car essential, parking. Open Easter to October for Bed and Breakfast from £16 nightly per person. Reductions for children and Senior Citizens. Birmingham 40 miles, Hereford 20, Gloucester 17, Stratford 35 and the Wye Valley is just 30 miles.

WORCESTER (near)

Sylvia and Brian Wynn, The Old Smithy, Pirton, Worcester WR8 9EJ (01905 820482). A 17th century half-timbered country house set in peaceful countryside with many interesting walks. Centrally situated, within easy reach of Stratford-upon-Avon, Cotswolds, Warwick Castle, Malvern Hills, Worcester Cathedral and Royal Worcester Porcelain. Four-and-a-half miles from Junction 7 of the M5 Motorway. Private guest facilities include lounge with inglenook log fireplace, colour TV and video, bathroom/dressing room and toilet, laundry, tea/coffee, central heating, gardens. One double bedroom and one twin bedroom. Ample parking. Bed and English Breakfast from £20; three-course Evening Meal optional extra £9.95. Fresh local produce and home cooking. Sorry, no pets or children under 12 years. Craft Workshop (Harris Tweed and knitwear). **ETC ◆◆◆◆**
website: www.SmoothHound.co.uk/hotels/oldsmith.html

PLEASE NOTE

All the information in this book is given in good faith in the belief that it is correct. However, the publishers cannot guarantee the facts given in these pages, neither are they responsible for changes in policy, ownership or terms that may take place after the date of going to press. Readers should always satisfy themselves that the facilities they require are available and that the terms, if quoted, still apply.

YORKSHIRE

©MAPS IN MINUTES™ 2001.©Crown Copyright, Ordnance Survey 2001.

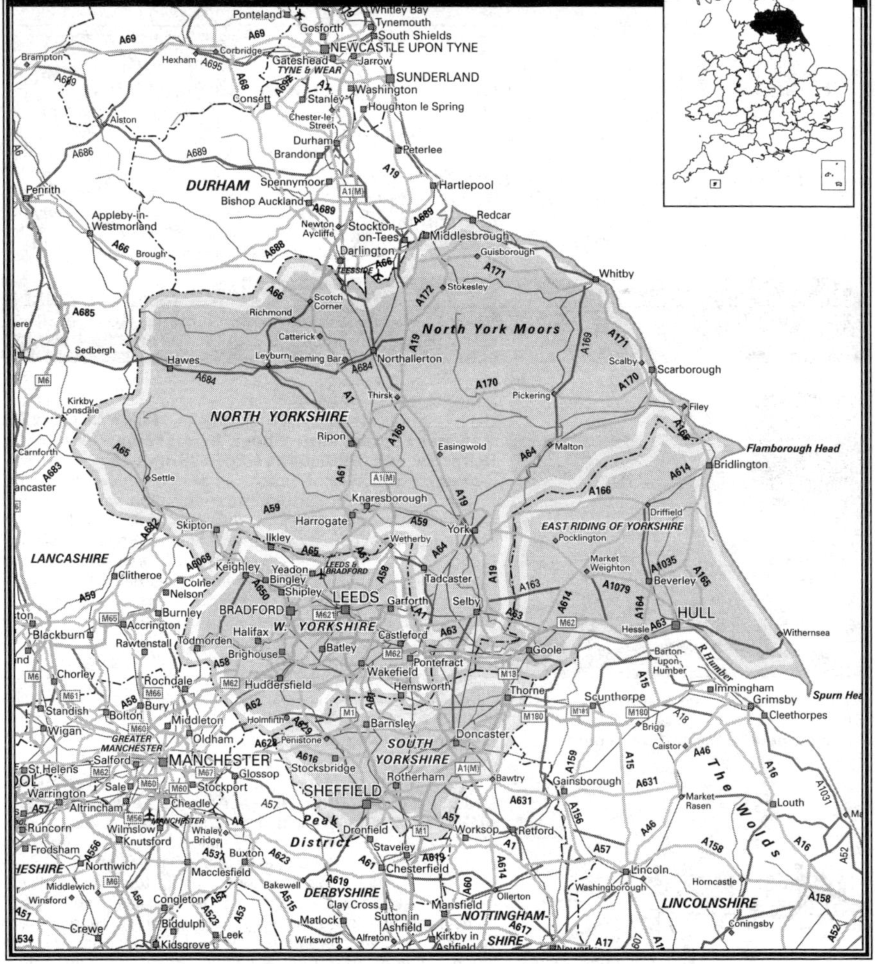

EAST YORKSHIRE

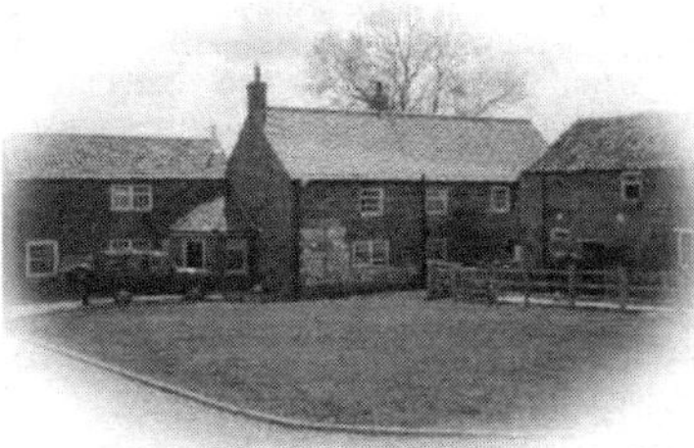

RUDSTON

Mrs Bowden, Eastgate Farm Cottage, Rudston YO25 4UX (Tel & Fax: 01262 420150). Friendly 18th century cottage with superb views nestling on the edge of a medieval village with its own monolith. Ideally located for moor and coastal exploration. Freshwater and sea fishing nearby. RSPB and rural walks in beautiful countryside. Horse trekking available locally. En suite bedrooms with central heating and delightful brass and iron beds. Aga-cooked dinners available. Open all year. Bed and Breakfast from £25. **ETC ◆◆◆**, *FARM STAY UK MEMBER.*

e-mail: ebrudston@aol.com

website: www.eastgatefarmcottage.com

ENGLAND

NORTH YORKSHIRE

AMPLEFORTH

Annabel Lupton, Carr House Farm, Ampleforth, Near Helmsley YO6 4ED (01347 868526 or 07977 113197). Working farm. 'Which?' Guide; Sunday Observer recommends "Fresh air fiends' dream – good food, good walking, warm welcome". In idyllic 16th century farmhouse, sheltered in Herriot/Heartbeat countryside, half an hour to York, ideal to enjoy Moors, Dales, National Parks, coasts, famous abbeys, castles and stately homes. Romantics will love four-poster bedrooms en suite and medieval-styled bedroom in comfortable relaxing home, with large garden. Enjoy full Yorkshire Breakfasts, hearty Evening Meals – own produce used whenever possible and served in oak-panelled, beamed dining room with flagstoned floor, inglenook and original brick bread oven. Aromatherapy beauty treatments and massage available on site. No children under seven, no smoking and no pets. Bed and Breakfast £20. Evening meal from £12.50. Open all year. **ETC ◆◆◆**, *FARM STAY UK MEMBER.*

e-mail: ampleforth@hotmail.com **website: www.guestaccom.co.uk/912.htm**

ASKRIGG

Mrs B. Percival, Milton House, Askrigg, Leyburn DL8 3HJ (01969 650217). Askrigg is situated in the heart of Wensleydale and is within easy reach of many interesting places – Aysgarth Falls, Hardraw Falls, Bolton Castle. Askrigg is one of the loveliest villages in the dale. This is an ideal area for touring or walking. Milton House is a lovely spacious house with all the comforts of home, beautifully furnished and decor to match. All bedrooms are en suite with colour TV and tea/coffee making facilities. Visitors' lounge, dining room. Central heating. Private parking. Milton House is open all year for Bed and Breakfast. Good pub food nearby. You are sure of a friendly welcome and a homely atmosphere. Please write or phone Mrs Beryl Percival for details and brochure. **ETC ◆◆◆◆**

COVERDALE

Mrs Julie A. Clarke, Middle Farm, Woodale, Leyburn DL8 4TY (01969 640271). Middle Farm is a peacefully situated traditional Dales farmhouse, with adjoining stable block for guests' accommodation. Situated on the unclassified road linking Wensleydale and Wharfedale. Ideal place to escape the 'madding crowd'. Good base for walking and touring any of the Dales' many beauty spots. Noted for excellent home cooking, offering Bed and Breakfast with optional Dinner. Two double and one twin-bedded rooms all en suite. Separate lounge, diningroom. Guests' privacy assured. Pets and children welcome. Ample private off-road parking. Open all year round. Brochure available on request. Directions – 5 miles Kettlewell, 10 miles Leyburn, unclassified road.

e-mail: julie-clarke@amserve.com

DANBY

Mrs B. Tindall, Rowan Tree Farm, Danby, Whitby YO21 2LE (01287 660396). Working farm, join in. Rowan Tree Farm is situated in the heart of the North Yorkshire Moors and has panoramic moorland views. Ideal walking area and quiet location just outside the village of Danby. Accommodation comprises one twin-bedded room and one family room all with washbasin and full oil-fired central heating. Residents' lounge with colour TV. Two residents' bathrooms. Children welcome – cot provided if required. Babysitting available. Pets accepted. Good home cooking. Bed and Breakfast from £17; Evening Meals provided on request £8 each. Ample car parking space. **ETC ◆◆◆**

GLAISDALE

e-mail: spashettredhouse@aol.com

Tom and Sandra Spashett, Red House Farm, Glaisdale, Near Whitby YO21 2PZ (Tel & Fax: 01947 897242). Listed Georgian farmhouse featured in "Houses of the North York Moors". Completely refurbished to the highest standards, retaining all original features. Bedrooms have bath/shower/toilet, central heating, TV and tea making facilities. Excellent walks straight from the doorstep. Friendly farm animals – a few cows, horses, geese and pretty free-roaming hens. One-and-a-half acres of gardens, sitting-out areas. Magnificent views. Interesting buildings – listed barns now converted to two holiday cottages. Games room with snooker table. Eight miles from seaside/Whitby. Village pubs within walking distance. Stabling available for horses/dogs. Non-smoking. Please phone Tom or Sandra for more information.

website: www.redhousefarm.net

HARROGATE

e-mail: neil.clarke@virgin.net

Mrs Sue Clarke, Brimham Lodge, Brimham Rocks Road, Burnt Yates, Harrogate HG3 3HE (01423 771770; Fax: 01423 770370). Working farm, join in. The Lodge, built in 1661, was extensively refurbished in 1999 but the farmhouse retains all its original character. Our accommodation offers two twin/double rooms with private facilities. All rooms have central heating, beverage tray, hairdryer, colour TV and clock radio. There is a large sitting room with a blazing fire set in a large inglenook, with television, video and games available. A hearty farmhouse breakfast is served in the oak panelled dining room. Brimham Lodge Farm is situated in the heart of Nidderdale, with many sites of interest within a short walk or car journey. Bed and Breakfast from £20 to £25 per person. **ETC ◆◆◆◆**

website: www.farmhousesbedandbreakfast.com

HARROGATE

Mrs Judy Barker, Brimham Guest House, Silverdale Close, Darley, Harrogate HG3 2PQ (01423 780948). The family-run guest house is situated in the centre of Darley, a quiet village in unspoilt Nidderdale. All rooms en suite and centrally heated with tea/coffee making facilities and views across the Dales. Full English breakfast served between 7am and 9am in the dining room; a TV lounge/conservatory is available for your relaxation. Off street parking. Central for visits to Harrogate, York, Skipton and Ripon, or just enjoying drives through the Dales and Moors where you will take in dramatic hillsides, green hills, picturesque villages, castles and abbeys. Children welcome. Bed and Breakfast from £20 per person per night double, £22 per person twin or £25 single room, reductions for three nights or more. Yorkshire in Bloom Winner. **ETC ◆◆◆◆**

The FHG Directory of Website Addresses

on pages 349–378 is a useful quick reference guide for holiday accommodation with e-mail and/or website details

MALHAM (Yorkshire Dales National Park)

Mr C. Sharp, Miresfield Farm, Skipton BD23 4DA (01729 830414). Miresfield is situated on the edge of the village of Malham in the Yorkshire Dales National Park. An ideal centre for exploring the Dales or for visiting the City of York, Settle and Skipton. Within walking distance is Malham Cove, Gordale Scar with its spectacular waterfalls, and Malham Moor with the famous Field Centre and home of Charles Kingsley's "Water Babies". Miresfield is set in a well-kept garden and offers accommodation in 11 bedrooms, all with private facilities. There are two well furnished lounges with TV, one has open fire; conservatory. Good, old-fashioned farmhouse cooking is served in the large, beamed diningroom. Bed and Breakfast from £24 per person per night. **ETC ◆◆◆**

OTLEY

Mrs C. Beaumont, Paddock Hill, Norwood, Otley LS21 2QU (01943 465977). Converted farmhouse on B6451 south of Bland Hill. Open fires, lovely views, in the heart of the countryside. Within easy reach of Herriot, Bronte and Emmerdale country and with attractive market towns around – Skipton, Knaresborough, Otley and Ripon. Walking, bird- watching and fishing on the nearby reservoirs. Residents' lounge with TV. Comfortable bedrooms. Non-smoking accommodation available. Children welcome. Pets by arrangement. Bed and Breakfast £17, en suite £22. **ETC ◆◆**

See also Colour Display Advertisement

RICHMOND

Browson Bank Farmhouse Accommodation, Browson Bank Farmhouse, Browson Bank, Dalton, Richmond DL11 7HE (01325 718504; Fax: 01325 718246). A newly converted granary set in 300 acres of farmland. The accommodation consists of three very tastefully furnished double/twin rooms, all en suite; tea and coffee making facilities, colour TV and central heating. A large, comfortable lounge is available to relax in. Full English breakfast served. Situated six miles west of Scotch Corner (A1). Ideal location to explore the scenic countryside of Teesdale and the Yorkshire Dales, and close to the scenic towns of Barnard Castle and Richmond. Terms from £19 per night.

ROBIN HOOD'S BAY

Mrs B. Reynolds, 'South View', Sledgates, Fylingthorpe, Whitby YO22 4TZ (01947 880025). Pleasantly situated, comfortable accommodation in own garden with sea and country views. Ideal for walking and touring. Close to the moors, within easy reach of Whitby, Scarborough and many more places of interest. There are two double rooms, lounge and dining room. Bed and Breakfast from £18, including bedtime drink. Parking spaces. Phone for further details.

SCARBOROUGH

Mrs V. Henson, Brinka House, 2 Station Square, Ravenscar, Scarborough YO13 0LU (01723 871470). Brinka House Bed and Breakfast is situated in Ravenscar – midway between Scarborough and Whitby. It has stunning views across to Robin Hood's Bay and is surrounded by the moors. The village boasts a variety of walks, cycle tracks, golf course, pony and llama trekking and a bus service that runs from the front door into town. A warm welcome and tasty breakfast awaits everyone, vegetarians and special diets are catered for. We have a romantic double room with a large corner bath en suite and a twin/family room en suite. All rooms have TV, drinks facilities and sea views. £19 per person per night, £25 single supplement.

Readers are requested to mention this guidebook when seeking accommodation (and please enclose a stamped addressed envelope).

ENGLAND

SCARBOROUGH

Sue and Tony Hewitt, Harmony Country Lodge, Limestone Road, Burniston, Scarborough YO13 0DG (0800 2985840). DISTINCTIVELY DIFFERENT. Peaceful and relaxing retreat, octagonal in design and set in two acres of private grounds overlooking the National Park and sea. Two miles from Scarborough and within easy reach of Whitby, York and the beautiful North Yorkshire countryside. Comfortable en suite centrally heated rooms with colour TV and all with superb views. Attractive dining room, guest lounge and relaxing conservatory. Traditional English breakfast, optional evening meal, including vegetarian. Fragrant massage available. Bed and Breakfast from £22.50 to £30.00. Non-smoking, licensed, private parking facilities. Personal service and warm, friendly Yorkshire hospitality. Spacious five-berth caravan also available for self-catering holidays. Open all year. Please telephone or write for brochure. Children over 7 years welcome. **ETC ♦♦♦♦**

e-mail: harmonylodge@cwcom.net **website: www.harmonylodge.net**

SCARBOROUGH

Simon and Val Green, Killerby Cottage Farm, Killerby Lane, Cayton, Scarborough YO11 3TP (01723 581236; Fax: 01723 585465). Simon and Val extend a warm Yorkshire welcome and invite you to share their charming farmhouse in the pleasant countryside between Scarborough and Filey. All our bedrooms are tastefully decorated and have en suite facilities, colour TV, and well-stocked beverage trays. Hearty breakfasts that will keep you going all day are served in the conservatory overlooking the lovely garden. Our 350-acre farm has diversified and we now have the Stained Glass Centre and tearoom which are open to visitors. Cayton offers easy access to Scarborough, Filey, Whitby, the North York Moors, and York. **ETC ♦♦♦♦**

e-mail: val@green-glass.demon.co.uk

SCARBOROUGH

Mrs M. Edmondson, Plane Tree Cottage Farm, Staintondale, Scarborough YO13 0EY (01723 870796). This small mixed farm is situated off the beaten track, with open views of beautiful countryside and the sea. We have sheep, hens, two ginger cats and special sheep dog "Bess". This very old beamed cottage, small but homely, has one twin with bathroom and two double en suite rooms with tea maker. Meals of very high standard served with own fresh eggs and garden produce as available. Staintondale is about half-way between Scarborough and Whitby and near the North York Moors. Pretty woodland walks nearby. Car essential. Bed and Breakfast from £21 per person per night. Also six-berth caravan available. SAE please for details, or telephone. **ETC ♦♦♦**

SKIPTON

Mrs Rosie Lister, Bushey Lodge Farm, Starbotton, Upper Wharfedale BD23 5HY (01756 760424). Bushey Lodge is a traditional working hill farm of over 2000 acres set in the heart of the Yorkshire Dales. The lovely old farmhouse nestles on the edge of Starbotton village and has been sympathetically restored to create a haven of peace and tranquillity. Each bedroom has en suite bathroom, TV, hairdryer and tea/coffee facilities. Bed and Breakfast from £22.50 per person. **ETC ♦♦♦♦** *SILVER AWARD. WHICH? GOOD BED AND BREAKFAST GUIDE.*

website: www.yorkshirenet.co.uk/stayat/busheylodgefarm

SKIPTON

Mrs Heather Simpson, Low Skibeden Farmhouse, Harrogate Road, Skipton BD23 6AB (07050 207787/01756 793849; Fax: 01756 793804). Detached 16th century farmhouse in private grounds one mile east of Skipton off the A59/A65 gateway to the Dales, eg Bolton Abbey - Malham, Settle. Luxury bed and breakfast with fireside treats in the lounge. All rooms are quiet, spacious, have panoramic views, washbasins, tea facilities and electric overblankets. Central heating October to May. All guests are warmly welcomed and served tea/coffee and cakes on arrival, bedtime beverages are served from 9.30pm. Breakfast is served from 7am to 8.45am in the dining room. No smoking. No pets and no children under 12 years. Safe parking. New arrivals before 10pm. Quality and value guaranteed. Bed and Breakfast from £22 per person per night sharing for standard room with shared hot and cold facilities; two piece en suite from £24 per person per night; single occupancy from £30 to £48. Full en suite from £26 per person per night. Farm cottage sometimes available. (**ETC ★★★**). A deposit secures a room. Open all year. Credit Cards accepted. **AA ◆◆◆◆**, *"WELCOME HOST", "WHICH?".*

e-mail: skibhols.yorksdales@talk21.com **website: www.yorkshirenetco.uk/accgde/lowskibeden**

SUTTON-ON-THE-FOREST

Susan Rowson, Goose Farm, Eastmoor, Sutton-on-the-Forest, York YO61 1ET (Tel & Fax: 01347 810577). Sleeps six. 150 year old farmhouse situated five miles from York Minster in open countryside off the B1363 and within easy access of Herriot Country and the Yorkshire coast. Large rooms, all en suite with TV and tea/coffee making facilities. Central heating throughout and as warm as the welcome to yourselves. Open all year. Bed and Breakfast from £20 to £26. Children and pets welcome. **ETC ◆◆◆**

THIRSK

Mrs M. Fountain, Town Pasture Farm, Boltby, Thirsk YO7 2DY (01845 537298). Working farm, join in. A warm welcome awaits on a 180 acre mixed farm in beautiful Boltby village, nestling in the valley below the Hambleton Hills, in the midst of Herriot country and on the edge of the North York Moors National Park. An 18th century stone-built farmhouse with full central heating, comfortable en suite bedrooms (one family, one twin) with original old oak beams, and tea/coffee facilities; spacious guests' lounge with colour TV. Children and pets welcome. Good home cooking, hearty English breakfast and evening meals by arrangement. Ideal walking country and central for touring the Dales, York and East Coast. Pony trekking in village. Bed and Breakfast from £20. **ETC ◆◆◆**

THIRSK

Joyce Ashbridge, Mount Grace Farm, Cold Kirby, Thirsk YO7 2HL (01845 597389; Fax: 01845 597872). A warm welcome awaits you on this working farm surrounded by beautiful open countryside with magnificent views. Ideal location for touring or exploring the many walks in the area. Luxury en suite bedrooms with tea/coffee facilities. Spacious guests' lounge with colour TV. Garden. Enjoy delicious, generous helpings of farmhouse fayre cooked in our Aga. Children from 12 years plus. No smoking. No pets. Bed and Breakfast from £27; weekly rates available. Open all year except Christmas.

e-mail: joyce@mountgracefarm.com
website: www.mountgracefarm.com

WHITBY

Mr and Mrs Richardson, Egton Banks Farm, Glaisdale, Whitby YO21 2QP (01947 897289). Beautiful old farmhouse situated in a lovely valley close to quiet roadside. Set in 120 acres of pastureland and woods. Centre of National Park. Warm and friendly atmosphere. Separate diningroom and lounge for guests with TV and books. Close to river, one mile from Glaisdale village and mainline railway, eight miles to Whitby and four miles to the steam railway and Heartbeat country. All bedrooms have pretty decor. One double/twin room and one family room, both en suite. Full Yorkshire Breakfast. Packed lunches. All diets catered for. No smoking. **ETC ◆◆◆◆**
e-mail: egtonbanksfarm.@agriplus.net
website: www.egtonbanksfarm.agriplus.net

See also Colour Display Advertisement

WHITBY

Peter and Jane Dowson, Furnace Farm, Fryup, Lealholm, Whitby YO21 2AP (Tel & Fax: 01947 897271). A warm Yorkshire welcome to our working family farm in peaceful Esk Valley, close to moors and coast. Ideal base for walking and touring. Stone built farmhouse, comfortable, spacious rooms, lounge/diningroom with TV and video. Two family rooms, one en suite, one with private bathroom, both with TV and tea/coffee making facilities and double/single beds. Cot available. Use of large garden. Sleeps six. Bed and Breakfast £22.50 to £25. Open February to October. Map Ref: P13. **ETC ◆◆◆**, *FARM STAY UK MEMBER.*
e-mail: furnacefarm@hotmail.com

WHITBY (near)

Mrs Pat Beale, Ryedale House, Coach Road, Sleights, Near Whitby YO22 5EQ (Tel & Fax: 01947 810534). Exclusive to non-smokers, welcoming Yorkshire house of character at the foot of the Moors, National Park "Heartbeat" country, three-and-a-half miles from Whitby. Magnificent scenery, moors, dales, picturesque harbours, cliffs, beaches, scenic railways, superb walking - it's all here! Highly commended beautifully appointed rooms with private facilities, many extras. Guests' lounge; breakfast room with views over Esk Valley. Enjoy the large south-facing terrace and landscaped gardens. Extensive traditional and vegetarian breakfast choice. Local inns and restaurants (two within short walk). Parking available, also public transport. Bed and Breakfast double £21.50 to £22.50, single £20.00 to £24.00. Minimum stay two nights. Weekly reductions and Monday to Friday offers available. Regret no pets or children. **ETC ◆◆◆◆**

YORK

Virginia Collinson, Hall Farm, Gilling East, York YO62 4JW (01439 788314). Come and stay with us at Hall Farm. A beautifully situated 400 acre working stock farm with extensive views over Ryedale. Completely away from all the traffic, we are half-a-mile away from the road, as you drive up to the farm you may see cows with their calves and in the spring and early summer ewes with their lambs. We offer a friendly, family welcome with home-made scones on arrival. A ground floor double en suite room is available and includes hospitality tray with home-made biscuits. Sittingroom with TV and open fire on chilly evenings, diningroom with patio doors to conservatory. You will be the only guests so the breakfast time is up to you. Full English Breakfast includes home-made bread and preserves with our own free-range eggs. There are lots of excellent places to eat in the evenings in the historic market town of Helmsley and nearby villages. York, Castle Howard and the North York Moors within half-an-hour drive. Terms from £20pp.
e-mail: virginia@collinson2.fsnet.co.uk

YORK

Mrs Diana Susan Tindall, Newton House, Neville Street, Haxby Road, York YO31 8NP (01904 635627). Diana and John offer all their guests a friendly and warm welcome to their Victorian End Town House, a few minutes' walk from the City Centre, York's beautiful Minster, the City Walls and museums. Situated near an attractive park with good bowling greens. York is an ideal base for touring Yorkshire Moors, Dales and coastline. Three double/twin en suite rooms, colour TV, tea/coffee tray, central heating, car park. Non-smoking. Fire certificate, Electrical Installation Certificate. Terms from £25 per person.

See also Colour Display Advertisement

YORK (near Castle Howard)

Sandie and Peter Turner, High Gaterley Farm, Near Welburn, York YO60 7HT (Tel & Fax: 01653 694636). High Gaterley enjoys a unique position, located within the boundaries of Castle Howard's magnificent country estate. It is ideally situated for easy access to the City of York, East Coast and the North Yorkshire Moors renowned for ruined abbeys and castles. The tranquil ambience with panoramic views over the Howardian Hills make it a perfect location for a peaceful and relaxing stay in a comfortable well-appointed farmhouse with the option of fine cuisine. En suite facilities with tea and coffee in all rooms, log fire in the drawing room, TV, non-smoking, dogs by prior arrangement. Open all year. Bed and Breakfast from £20. Optional evening meal and special diets by arrangement. **ETC ◆◆◆◆**
e-mail: relax@highgaterley.com
website: www.highgaterley.com

Why Yorkshire?

With ruined abbeys and castles, great houses and gardens framed by high moors and wooded hills, Yorkshire is a place of great natural beauty. This beauty is conserved in three national parks: the Yorkshire Dales, the Peak District and the North York Moors. In contrast to nature, Yorkshire is also home to The West Yorkshire Playhouse, The Yorkshire Sculpture Park and The National Museum of Photography, Film & Television. The Millennium Galleries, the new multimillion MAGNA and The Deep all make it a worthwhile place to visit.
For further information contact the Yorkshire Tourist Board,
Tel: **01904 707070** or visit **www.yorkshirevisitor.com**

ENGLAND

Self-catering Accommodation

ENGLAND

See also Colour Display Advertisement

LAKE DISTRICT, EDEN VALLEY, NORTH CUMBRIA/SCOTTISH BORDERS, NORTH PENNINES AND NORTHUMBERLAND.

Excellent and very varied range of self-catering properties in a wide variety of locations from Towns to secluded Country Retreats. Competitive rates – Free Brochure. **CSH Absolute Escapes, 1 Little Dockray, Penrith, Cumbria CA11 7HL (01768 868989 24hrs; Fax: 01768 865578).**
e-mail: Shirley.Thompson@csh.co.uk
website: www.csh.co.uk

See also Colour Display Advertisement

Country Holidays (0870 442 5413). BRITAIN'S FAVOURITE COTTAGE HOLIDAYS. Every kind of property for every kind of holiday. With over 3,000 quality graded cottages throughout the UK, catering from two to twenty-two, you're sure to find the right property for you. Many of our properties also accept pets so none of your family need miss out. Please telephone for your 2003 brochure.
website: www.country-holidays.co.uk

• • *Some Useful Guidance for Guests and Hosts* • •

Every year literally thousands of holidays, short breaks and ovemight stops are arranged through our guides, the vast majority without any problems at all. In a handful of cases, however, difficulties do arise about bookings, which often could have been prevented from the outset.

It is important to remember that when accommodation has been booked, both parties – guests and hosts – have entered into a form of contract. We hope that the following points will provide helpful guidance.

GUESTS:

- When enquiring about accommodation, be as precise as possible. Give exact dates, numbers in your party and the ages of any children.
- State the number and type of rooms wanted and also what catering you require – bed and breakfast, full board etc. Make sure that the position about evening meals is clear – and about pets, reductions for children or any other special points.
- Read our reviews carefully to ensure that the proprietors you are going to contact can supply what you want. Ask for a letter confirming all arrangements, if possible.
- If you have to cancel, do so as soon as possible. Proprietors do have the right to retain deposits and under certain circumstances to charge for cancelled holidays if adequate notice is not given and they cannot re-let the accommodation.

HOSTS:

- Give details about your facilities and about any special conditions. Explain your deposit system clearly and arrangements for cancellations, charges etc. and whether or not your terms include VAT.
- If for any reason you are unable to fulfil an agreed booking without adequate notice, you may be under an obligation to arrange suitable alternative accommodation or to make some form of compensation.

While every effort is made to ensure accuracy, we regret that FHG Publications cannot accept responsibility for errors, omissions or misrepresentations in our entries or any consequences thereof. Prices in particular should be checked because we go to press early. We will follow up complaints but cannot act as arbiters or agents for either party.

CORNWALL

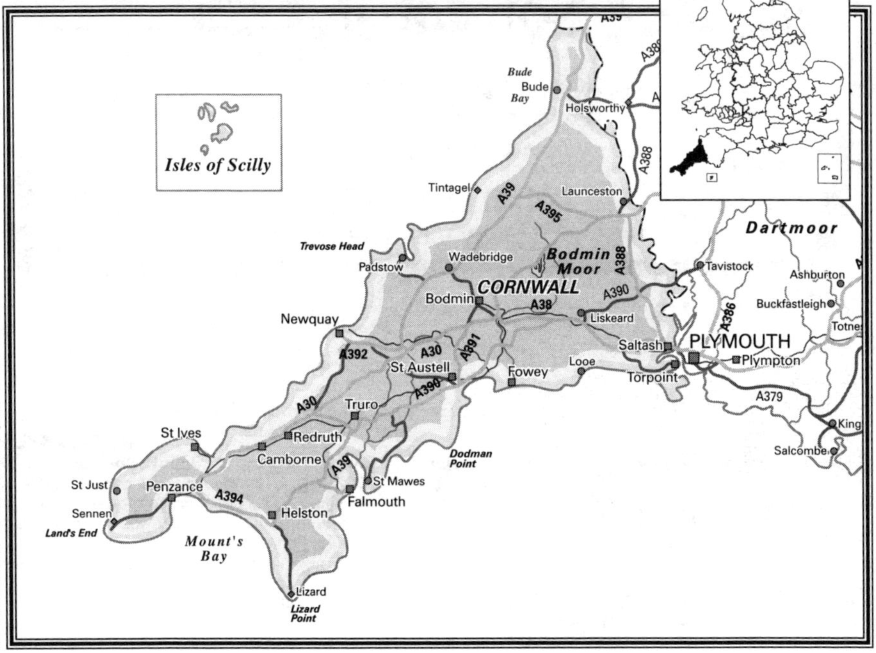

Historic Cornwall

As well as having sun, sea and sand, Cornwall is also home to a collection of interesting historic sites. Tintagel Castle, Pendennis Castle, St Mawes Castle, Launceston Castle, Restormel Castle and Chysauster Ancient Village are scattered throughout Cornwall and are all under English Heritage care. For more information tel: **0870 333 1181** or visit **www.english-heritage.org.uk**

BOSCASTLE

Mrs Harding, Ringford Farm, St. Juliot, Boscastle PL35 0BX (01840 250306). A two-bedroomed centrally heated converted barn sleeping up to six persons comfortably. Set on a 25 acre farm, the accommodation is fully equipped and has magnificent sea views. Pure spring water. Ideally situated for touring Devon and Cornwall, many footpaths to explore. Children and pets welcome. Weekly terms from £120 to £450. Short Breaks available (minimum two nights).

See also Colour Display Advertisement

BUDE

Lower Kitleigh Cottage, Week St Mary, Near Bude. Pretty Listed farmhouse in unspoilt country near magnificent coast. Newly renovated with all conveniences, yet retaining its charm, it stands in a peaceful grassy garden with picnic table and own parking. The sitting room has period furniture, inglenook fireplace, free logs and colour TV. The fully equipped kitchen has fridge/freezer, double sink, electric cooker and washer/tumble dryer. Three bedrooms with panoramic views, cots, duvets. Well-controlled dogs allowed. Riding nearby, golf, safe beaches, surfing, Cornish Moors, markets, cliff walks. All electricity inclusive, and central heating ensures a cosy stay throughout the year. Prices from £250 to £475 weekly, reductions for part week. Sleeps seven plus cot. **Mr & Mrs T. Bruce-Dick, 114 Albert Street, London NW1 7NE (0207 485 8976)**

COVERACK

Polcoverack Farm Cottages, Coverack, Helston TR12 6SP (01326 281021; Fax: 01326 280683). A cluster of delightful stone built cottages approached via a private lane and set within a coastal farm providing a glorious rural setting. Coverack, one of Cornwall's most picturesque fishing villages, is within a ten minute walk. Here you will fine a sandy beach, inn, general stores and restaurants. Each cottage offers comfortable, well-equipped accommodation sleeping two to seven. They include colour television, video recorder, microwave oven, full-sized cooker, refrigerator, cafetiere, hairdryer and all bed linen. Cot and high chair if required. We also provide a laundry room, plus large games room, and ample parking. Phone for a free colour brochure. **website: www.polcoverack.co.uk**

CUSGARNE (near Truro)

Joyce and George Clench, Saffron Meadow, Cusgarne, Near Truro TR4 8RW (01872 863171). Sleeps 2. A cosy single-storey, clean, detached dwelling with own enclosed garden, within grounds of Saffron Meadow, in quiet hamlet five miles west of Truro. Secluded and surrounded by wooded pastureland. Bedroom (double bed) with twin vanity unit. Fully tiled shower/WC and LB. Comprehensively equipped kitchen/diner. Compact TV room. Storage room. Hot water galore and gas included. Metered electricity. Automatic external safety lighting. Your own ample parking space in drive. Inn, good food, a short walk. Central to Truro, Falmouth and North and South coasts. Dogs welcome. Terms from £140 to £210 per week.

FALMOUTH (near Helford River)

Mrs Anne Matthews, Boskensoe Farm, Mawnan Smith, Falmouth TR11 5JP (Tel & Fax: 01326 250257). Sleeps 6/8. BOSKENSOE FARM HOLIDAY BUNGALOW. Situated in picturesque village of Mawnan Smith, Falmouth five miles, one-and-a-half miles from lovely Helford River famous for beautiful coastal walks, gardens and scenery. Several quiet, safe beaches for bathing, also excellent sailing and fishing facilities. Bungalow has three bedrooms, colour TV, electric cooker, fridge/freezer, washing machine and microwave. Fitted with storage heaters and electric fires. Spacious garden and ample parking for cars and boats. Terms from £150 to £425. Brochure on request.

HELFORD ESTUARY

Mrs S. Trewhella, Mudgeon Vean Farm, St Martin, Helston TR12 6DB (01326 231341). Leave the hustle and bustle of town life. Come and enjoy the peace and tranquillity of the Helford Estuary. Three homely cottages sleep four/six, equipped to a high standard. Open all year for cosy winter breaks. Open fires/heating. Set amidst a small 18th century organic working farm with magnificent views across an extensive valley area, surrounded by fields and woodland - a walk through the woods takes you to the Helford River. A superb location in an area of outstanding natural beauty with the rugged coastline of the Lizard Peninsula and beaches only a short drive away. Children and pets welcome. From £115 to £390 per week

e-mail: mudgeonvean@aol.com

website: www.cornwall-online.co.uk/mudgeon-vean/ctb.html

Readers are requested to mention this guidebook when seeking accommodation (and please enclose a stamped addressed envelope).

LAUNCESTON

Mrs Heather French, Higher Scarsick, Treneglos, Launceston PL15 8UH (01566 781372) Working farm. Nestled amongst the peace and tranquillity of unspoilt Cornish countryside, this well furnished and comfortable cottage is the ideal retreat for both couples and families. Very convenient for exploring the many beaches and coves on the North Cornwall Coast yet within easy driving distance of Bodmin Moor, Dartmoor and all leisure pursuits. The accommodation has three bedrooms, two double and one twin bedded, bathroom with separate shower cubicle, a fully equipped large farmhouse kitchen, lounge with open fireplace. Tariff: £120–£450 includes bed linen, night storage heaters, electricity and a very warm welcome. Short breaks from £75. No Pets.

See also Colour Display Advertisement

LAUNCESTON

Hollyvag Farmhouse, Lewannick, Near Launceston PL15 7QH. Sleeps 5. Part of a cosy 17th century Listed farmhouse in 80 acres of fields and woods. Working farm with rare breed sheep, horses, geese, dogs and cats. Central to North and South coasts, Bodmin Moor and the fabulous Eden Project with an abundance of wildlife in the area. Golf and riding nearby. All modern conveniences including electric cooker, microwave, fridge, TV and video; laundry service FOC. Terms from £180. Also available is a luxury mobile home (sleeps four) in private idyllic location. Contact: **Mrs Anne Moore (01566 782309)**

LAUNCESTON

Mrs Kathryn Broad, Lower Dutson Farm, Launceston PL15 9SP (Tel & Fax: 01566 776456). Working farm. Sleeps 2/6. Enjoy a holiday on our traditional working farm. A warm welcome awaits you at our 17th century farmhouse. Historic Launceston with its Norman Castle (even Tescos!) is two miles away. Centrally situated for visiting National Trust houses and gardens, Dartmoor, Bodmin Moor and the beaches and harbours of Devon and Cornwall. Walk or fish along our stretch of the River Tamar for salmon and trout or try your skills at our coarse fishing lake. Well equipped cottage with three bedrooms (plus cot), two bathrooms. Enjoy the 'suntrap' just outside the front door. Children are welcome. Pet by arrangement. Terms £140 to £450. **ETC ★★★**

e-mail: francis.broad@btclick.com **website: www.farm-cottage.co.uk**

LISKEARD

Mrs Cotter, Trewalla Farm Cottages, Trewalla Farm, Minions, Liskeard PL14 6ED (Tel & Fax: 01579 342385). Sleeps 3/4 plus cot. Our small, traditionally-run farm on Bodmin Moor has rare breed pigs, sheep, hens and geese, all free-range and very friendly. The three cottages are beautifully furnished and very well equipped. Their moorland setting offers perfect peace, wonderful views, ideal walking country and a good base for exploring both coastlines, or visiting the Eden Project – if you can tear yourself away! Linen and electricity included. Open March to December and New Year. **ETC ★★★★**
e-mail: cotter.trewalla@virgin.net

THE COTTAGES AT *Trefanny Hill* Nr. LOOE

Cottages for Romantics

Discover the magic of Trefanny Hill!

Old world charm, log fires, antiques ~ beautifully furnished with the comforts of home, private gardens, spectacular views, peace ~ for families, friends & couples to enjoy. Nestling on a south facing hillside, near coast ~ heated pool, tennis, badminton, lake, shire horses, etc. Enchanting 70 acre estate with bluebell wood, walking, fishing & wildlife. Delicious fare also available by candlight 'at home' or in our tiny inn.

F. Slaughter, Trefanny Hill, Duloe, Near Liskeard, Cornwall PL14 4QF

Tel.: 01503 220 622 • E-mail: enq@trefanny.co.uk • Website: www.trefanny.co.uk

A Country lover's paradise ~ with an abundance of country walks from your garden gate and coastal walks only four miles away.

LISKEARD

Mrs C.Copplestone, Trethevy Farm, Darite, Liskeard PL14 5JX (01579 343186). Working farm. Sleeps 9. Come and unwind and enjoy a holiday on our traditional dairy farm. A warm welcome and a Cornish cream tea awaits you at our Listed 16th century cottage. Peace and tranquillity in the heart of unspoilt countryside on the edge of Bodmin Moor, within easy reach of the south coast. Eden Project 35 minutes, local pub five minutes' walk. Close to many places of historic interest. Cottage comprises four bedrooms, fitted kitchen, diningroom, living room with large granite fireplace, wood burner, beamed ceilings, own private garden and parking. Prices from £150. Farmhouse Bed and Breakfast also available. Details on request.

LOOE

Bocaddon Holiday Cottages, Bocaddon Farm, Lanreath, Looe PL13 2PG. Here in South East Cornwall a friendly welcome awaits you on our farm at Bocaddon. We have 350 acres, set in beautiful surroundings, the farm occupying our working hours. There are three cottages converted from little used barns/cow sheds and dairy, and these are superbly constructed with an added advantage of being equipped to high standards for disabled persons. Our first conversion, "Katies", was completed in 1997, and visitors have 'queued' to return, thus our two new cottages opened in 2001. Public transport connections and village shops and Post Office are at Pelynt, two miles away, and Lanreath village also serves your needs close by. There are many tiny backwaters, wonderful sandy beaches, smugglers' coves, and historic gems to explore, and for those wishing to venture further into Cornwall, easy access to major routes. Sorry, no pets allowed. Prices vary throughout the year from £160 in December to £470 in August. **ETC ★★★★**. *ACCESSIBILITY CATEGORY 3.* Contact: **Mrs Alison Maiklem (Tel & Fax: 01503 220192).**

See also Colour Display Advertisement

LOOE

Mr & Mrs J. Spreckley, Tremaine Green Country Cottages, Pelynt, Near Looe PL13 2LT (01503 220333). Sleep 2-8. Tremaine Green for memorable holidays. 'A beautiful private hamlet' of 11 traditional cosy craftsmen's cottages, between Polperro and Looe. Clean, comfortable and well-equipped, with a warm and friendly atmosphere. Set in lovely grounds with country and coastal walks and The Eden Project nearby. Towels, linen, central heating and hot water included. Dishwashers in larger cottages. Power shower baths. Launderette, games room and tennis court. TV/videos. Cot and highchair available. Pubs and restaurants within easy walking distance. Terms from £89. Pets welcome. **ETC ★★★**

e-mail: stay@tremainegreen.co.uk

website: www.tremainegreen.co.uk

LOOE VALLEY

Mr & Mrs R. A. Brown, Badham Farm, St Keyne, Liskeard PL14 4RW (Tel & Fax: 01579 343572). Once part of a Duchy of Cornwall working farm, now farmhouse and farm buildings converted to a high standard to form a six cottage complex around former farmyard. Sleeping from two to ten. All cottages are well furnished and equipped and prices include electricity, bed linen and towels. Most cottages have a garden. Five acre grounds, set in delightful wooded valley, with tennis, putting, children's play area, fishing lake, animal paddock, games room with pool and table tennis. Separate bar. Laundry. Barbecue. Railcar from Liskeard to Looe stops at end of picnic area. Have a 'car free' day out. Children and well behaved dogs welcome. Prices from £115 per week. **ETC ★★★**, *GREEN TOURISM AWARD.*

website: www.looedirectory.co.uk/badhamcottages.htm

MARAZION (near)

Mrs W. Boase, Trebarvah Farm, Perranuthnoe, Penzance TR20 9NG (01736 710361). TREBARVAH FARM COTTAGES. Three cottages, two sleeping four people, one sleeping six people, with magnificent views across Mount's Bay and St Michael's Mount. Just east of Marazion, Perranuthnoe is easily accessible on foot or by car and has a sandy beach. Accommodation: TUE BROOK - one double and two twin-bedded rooms, one en suite, kitchen/diner, lounge and large conservatory. TAIRUA - one double and one twin-bedded room and living room. KERIKERI COTTAGE - one twin room and a double sofa bed in the living room. All properties include duvets, pillows and blankets but no linen or towels. Kitchens are electric and power is through a pre-payment £1 coin meter. Colour TV. Rates from £140-£450 per week. Short breaks available out of summer season.

e-mail: jaybee@trebarvah.freeserve.co.uk **website: www.trebarvahfarmcottages.co.uk**

PADSTOW

The Brewer Family, Carnevas Farm Holiday Park, Carnevas Farm, St Merryn, Padstow PL28 8PN (01841 520230). Bungalow/Chalets sleep 4/6. Situated only half a mile from golden sandy beach, fishing, golf, sailing etc. Quaint harbour village of Padstow only four miles. Bungalows/chalets sleep four/six, have two bedrooms, bathroom, kitchen/diner, airing cupboard, colour TV. Caravans six-berth or eight berth, all have showers, toilets, fridge, colour TV (also separate camping and caravan facilities). Newly converted barns now available, sleep four/six persons, furnished to a high standard. Brochure on request. **ETC ★★★★** *ROSE AWARD PARK 2001. AA THREE PENNANT SITE.*

Visits & Attractions

Goonhilly Earth Station, Helston, Cornwall • 01326 221333

website: www.goonhilly.bt.com

Explore the wonders of pioneering technology at one of the most important communication stations in the world. Scan the skies by operating an IV dish aerial yourself.

NORTH CORNISH COAST

Welcome to the Green Door

Eight comfortably renovated beamed character cottages, sleeping 2/6 persons; each with central heating throughout; spacious lounge with log burner, completely equipped fitted kitchen, colour TV, telephone, free parking; enclosed sheltered garden. Two large flats to sleep eight. Elevated position on cliff, overlooking the Cove. Central heating / Washing machine /Tumble dryer/ Dishwasher / Colour TV / Direct-dial telephone. No meters, everything included in price. Port Isaac half-a-mile; beach 50 yards. Golf, fishing, sailing, riding nearby. Cornish Coastal Path passes the door.

OPEN ALL YEAR.

For Brochure write to Midge Ross,
Green Door Cottages,
Near Port Isaac PL29 3SQ
Tel: 01208 880293 Fax: 01208 880151

DISCOVER SUNLAND HOLIDAY VILLAGE AND EXPERIENCE THE DELIGHTS OF CORNWALL!

Sunland Holiday Village overlooks the beautiful coastline of Portreath and virtually all of Cornwall's sights and scenes are within a short drive. The newly refurbished chalets can sleep up to 6 people, they include a Lounge with TV, fully equipped fitted Kitchen with Dining area, 2 Bedrooms and Bathroom.

Visit our website and see the exciting new additions at Sunland's for 2003! Or telephone the hotline now!

HOTLINE:01209 842354 NOW!

Sunland Holiday Village Portreath Cornwall TR16 4PE
Telephone:01209 842354 **Facsimile:**01209 842365

Check out our website at: www.sunlandholidays.co.uk
or email us at: info@sunlandholidays.co.uk

See also Colour Advertisement

ENGLAND

PENZANCE

Mrs Catherine Wall, Trenow, Relubbus Lane, St Hilary, Penzance TR20 9EA (01736 762308). Mini bungalow sleeps two within the grounds of an old country house. Lovely garden, surrounding rural area. Lounge/ diner with cooking area, fridge, cooker, colour TV etc; shower room. Linen not provided. Beaches within easy reach, sporting activities, bird watching. No pets. Off-road Parking. Terms from £100 per week. Available all year. Please write or phone for further details.

PENZANCE

Mrs James Curnow, Barlowenath, St Hilary, Penzance TR20 9DQ (01736 710409). Working farm. Cottages sleep 4/5. These two cottages are on a dairy farm, in a little hamlet right beside St Hilary Church, with quiet surroundings and a good road approach. A good position for touring Cornish coast and most well-known places. Beaches are two miles away; Marazion two-and-a-half miles; Penzance six miles; St Ives eight; Land's End 16. Both cottages have fitted carpets, lounge/diner with TV; modern kitchen (fridge, electric cooker, toaster, iron); bathroom with shaver point. Electricity by £1 meter, night storage heaters extra. One cottage sleeps five in three bedrooms (one double, twin divans and one single). The second cottage sleeps four in two bedrooms (twin divans in both). Linen not supplied, can be but hired by arrangement. Cot by arrangement. Available all year. £95 to £350 weekly, VAT exempt.

See also Colour Display Advertisement

PERRANPORTH

Greenmeadow Cottages, Near Perranporth. Sleep 6. Highly praised luxury cottages. Superbly clean, comfortable and spacious. Open all year. Short Breaks available out of season. Pets welcome in two of the cottages. Non-smoking available. Ample off-road parking. Please telephone for brochure and bookings. Contact: **01872 540483.**

PORT ISAAC

The Dolphin, Port Isaac. Sleeps 10. This delightful house, originally an inn, is one of the most attractive in Port Isaac. Fifty yards from the sea, shops and pub. Five bedrooms, three with washbasin. Two bathrooms and WCs. Large diningroom. Cosy sittingroom. Spacious and well-equipped kitchen with electric cooker, gas-fired Aga, dishwasher, washing machine. Sun terrace. Port Isaac is a picturesque fishing village with magnificent coastal scenery all round. Nearby attractions include surfing, sailing, fishing, golf, tennis, pony trekking. Reduced rates offered for smaller families and off-peak season. Weekly terms: £400 to £700 inclusive. SAE for details to **Emily Glentworth, 150 Hammersmith Grove, London, W6 7HE (020 8741 2352)**

PORT ISAAC

The Lodge, Treharrock, Port Isaac. Sleeps 6. Pleasant, south-facing and convenient bungalow, set in its own small, natural garden and surrounded by fields and woodland with streams. About two miles inland from Port Isaac, a sheltered, secluded spot at the end of driveway to Treharrock Manor. Rugged North Cornish cliffs with National Trust footpaths and lovely sandy coves in the vicinity. Excellent sandy surfing beach at Polzeath (five miles), also pony trekking, golf etc. in the area. South-facing sun room leads on to terrace; TV. Accommodation for six plus baby. Bathroom, toilet; sittingroom; kitchen/diner. Open all year. Linen extra. Sorry, no pets. Car essential – parking. Terms from £200 to £500 per week (heating included). SAE to **Mrs E. A. Hambly, Willow Mill, St Kew, Bodmin, Cornwall PL30 3EP (01208 841806).**

ENGLAND

PORTSCATHO

Trewince Manor, Portscatho, Near Truro TR2 5ET. Peter and Liz Heywood invite you to take your self-catering or touring holiday at their Georgian Manor House Estate in this undiscovered and peaceful corner of Cornwall. Luxury lodges and small touring site available. Spectacular sea views; our own quay and moorings. Indoor pool, spa bath, sauna. Relaxing lounge bar and restaurant. Launderette and games rooms. Superb walking and sailing. Abundance of wildlife in the area. Dogs welcome. Please write of telephone for further information. **Freephone: 0800 0190289.**
e-mail: bookings@trewince.com.uk

See also Colour Display Advertisement

ST AUSTELL

Bosinver Holiday Cottages. Nestling in a hidden valley near the sea, the Eden Project and Lost Gardens of Heligan, our small farm has friendly animals and ponies. Choose from our 16th Century thatched farmhouse or cottages privately set in their own gardens surrounded by wildflower meadows. Wander down to the fishing lake or village pub, swim in the pool, play tennis, or relax and listen to the birdsong. No pets during Summer school holidays please. **ETC ★★★★**. Brochure from: **Mrs Pat Smith, Bosinver Farm, Trelowth, St Austell, Cornwall PL26 7DT (01726 72128).**
website: www.bosinver.co.uk

ST AUSTELL

Anita Treleaven, Trevissick Manor, Trevissick Farm, Trenarren, St Austell PL26 6BQ (Tel & Fax: 01726 72954). Sleeps 2/4. The east wing of the manor farmhouse on our coastal mixed farm is situated between St Austell and Mevagissey Bays. Spectacular views across the gardens down the valley to the sea. Ideal for a couple or family. Meet the animals, view the milking, or take the farm trail to Hallane Cove. Close to sandy beaches, sailing, watersports, cycling, 18 hole golf. Heligan Gardens and Eden Project nearby. Open all year. Terms from £150 to £500. **ETC ★★★**

ST COLUMB

Mrs J.V. Thomas, Lower Trenowth Farm, St. Columb TR9 6EW (01637 880308). Sleeps 6. This accommodation is part of a large farmhouse, all rooms facing south. Situated in the beautiful Vale of Lanherne, four miles from the sea, eight miles from the holiday resort of Newquay. Golf, horse riding, etc all within easy reach. One double room, one twin-bedded room and one single room with bunk beds, all with washbasins. Bed linen provided. Bathroom. Large lounge with colour TV and video. Fully equipped kitchen/diner. Electricity included in tariff. Large lawn. Ample parking. Dogs accepted if kept under control. SAE for further details please.

St Ives Bay

Ist Class S/C Apartments and Bungalows near Beach

Fully equipped for your self catering holiday. Sleeps 2-6 persons. Peaceful location, small friendly site with Play Area, Garden, Free Parking, Dogs Welcome. Open all year. South West coastal path close by.
Weekly from £120 / Short Breaks £90

Sandbank Holidays
ST. IVES BAY

Tel: 01736 752594
www.sandbank-holidays.co.uk

MasterCard VISA

See also Colour Advertisement

TAMAR VALLEY

Mr and Mrs B.J. Howlett, Deer Park Farm, Luckett, Callington PL17 8NW (Tel & Fax: 01579 370292). Sleeps 4/5. Three character cottages – traditional barn conversions – situated in the delightful rural setting of the Tamar Valley, well away from the traffic. Kit Hill Country Park, Tamar Trail both within one mile, Morwellham Quay, Cotehele House nearby. Free exclusive/private fishing on the farm – carp/roach; also nature and Heritage Trails. St Mellion Golf Club six miles. Also available locally, riding schools, pony trekking, swimming, sports centre, south Cornwall beaches and the quaint fishing villages of Looe and Polperro within easy reach, making this an excellent base for Cornwall, Dartmoor and South Devon. Prices from £175 to £325. Regret no pets. *CTB INSPECTED*

TINTAGEL

Mrs Gillian Sanders, Fentafriddle Farm, Trewarmett, Tintagel PL34 0EX (01840 770580). Fentafriddle overlooks Trebarwith and Port Isaac Bay with lovely sea views and sunsets. A spacious flat occupies the first floor of our farmhouse, with its own entrance, garden and picnic table. There are four bedrooms: one large double, one family and two singles. A cottage adjoins the house and has two bedrooms: one large double and one twin, to sleep two adults plus two/three children. Equipped with dishwasher, electric cooker, microwave, fridge freezer, colour TV, iron and ironing board and night storage heating. Washer/dryer in cottage only. Bed linen provided. We are ideally situated for walking the coastal footpath, surfing and swimming at Trebarwith, Polzeath and Daymer Bay, cycling the Camel Trail, golf at Bowood Park, Camelford, The Eden Project at St Austell, Tintagel Castle and exploring Bodmin Moor. No pets and no smoking.

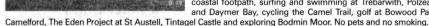

CUMBRIA

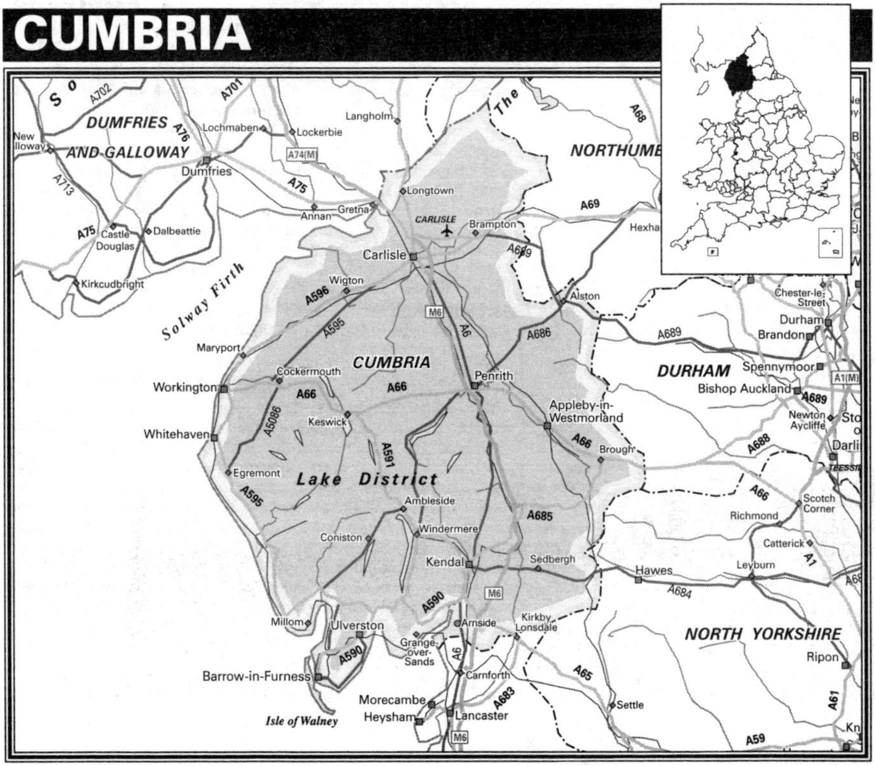

AMBLESIDE

Mr Evans, Ramsteads Coppice, Outgate, Ambleside LA22 0NH (015394 36583). Six timber lodges of varied size and design set in 15 acres of mixed woodland with wild flowers, birds and native wild animals. There are also 11 acres of rough hill pasture. Three miles south west of Ambleside, it is an ideal centre for walkers, naturalists and country lovers. No pets. Children welcome. Open March to November.

AMBLESIDE

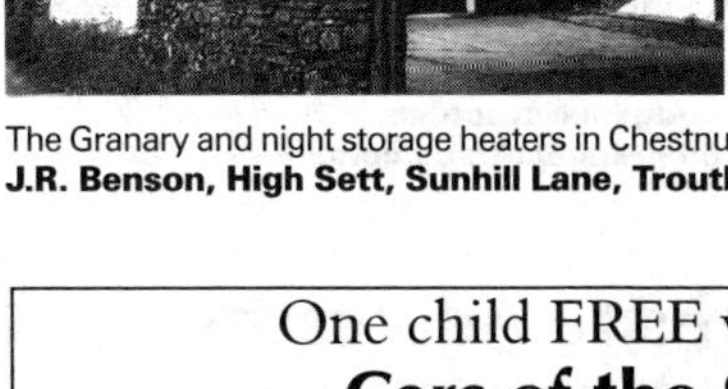

Chestnuts, Beeches & The Granary, High Wray, Ambleside. Sleep 6. Two charming cottages and one delightful bungalow converted from a former 18th century house and cornstore/tack room. Set in idyllic surroundings overlooking Lake Windermere with magnificent panoramic views of the Langdale Pikes, Coniston Old Man and the Troutbeck Fells, making this an ideal base for walking and touring. All three properties have large lounges with satellite TV and video. The Granary has a separate kitchen/diner. Chestnuts and Beeches have balconies overlooking Lake Windermere and dining areas in the large lounges. All properties have bathrooms with bath, shower, fitted kitchens with electric cooker, microwave, washing machine, fridge, freezer and tumble dryer. Included in the cost of the holiday is the oil central heating in The Granary and night storage heaters in Chestnuts and Beeches. Lighting and bed linen included in all three. **Contact J.R. Benson, High Sett, Sunhill Lane, Troutbeck Bridge, Windermere LA23 1HJ (015394 42731).**

AMBLESIDE

Mrs Clare Irvine, Hole House, High Wray. HOLE HOUSE is a charming detached 17th century Lakeland cottage set in idyllic surroundings overlooking Blelham Tarn with magnificent panoramic views of the Langdale Pikes, Coniston Old Man, the Troutbeck Fells and Lake Windermere. High Wray is a quiet unspoilt hamlet set between Ambleside and Hawkshead making this an ideal base for walking or touring. This charming cottage which once belonged to Beatrix Potter has the original oak beams and feature stone staircase. It has recently been restored to provide very comfortable accommodation without losing its olde worlde charm. Accommodation consists of one double and two twin bedrooms; bathroom with shower; large spacious lounge with Sky TV and video; fitted kitchen with microwave oven, fridge, tumble dryer, automatic washing machine and electric cooker. Play area. Ample parking. Please write, or phone, for further details: **Mrs Clare Irvine, Tock How Farm, High Wray (015394 36106).**

e-mail: info@tock-how-farm.com **website: www.tock-how-farm.com**

APPLEBY-IN-WESTMORLAND

Mrs Edith Stockdale, Croft House, Bolton, Appleby-in-Westmorland CA16 6AW (Tel & Fax: 017683 61264). Sleep 2/5 and 10. Three cosy cottages recently converted from an old Westmorland style barn adjoining the owner's house. With an abundance of open stone work and oak beams and many original features. An excellent base for fell and country walking, horse-riding or as a touring base for the Lake District, beautiful Eden Valley, Scottish Borders, Hadrian's Wall and North Yorkshire Dales. Bed linen, towels, electricity and heating included in rent. Facilities include electric cooker, washing machine, fridge-freezer, microwave, colour TV, video, hi-fi and dishwasher. Stabling provided for anyone wishing to bring pony on holiday. Weekly terms from £160. Farmhouse available, sleeps 11. Brochure.

website: www.crofthouse-cottages.co.uk

BOWNESS-ON-WINDERMERE

43A Quarry Rigg, Bowness-on-Windermere. Sleeps 4. Ideally situated in the centre of the village close to the Lake and all amenities, the flat is in a new development, fully self-contained, and furnished and equipped to a high standard for owner's own comfort and use. Lake views, ideal relaxation and touring centre. Accommodation is for two/four people. Bedroom with twin beds, lounge with TV and video; convertible settee; separate kitchen with electric cooker, microwave and fridge/freezer; bathroom with bath/shower and WC. Electric heating. Parking for residents. Sorry, no pets. Terms from £125 to £250. Weekends and Short Breaks also available. SAE, please, for details to **E. Jones, 45 West Oakhill Park, Liverpool, Merseyside L13 4BN (Tel & Fax: 0151-228 5799).**

CARLISLE

Mrs Sarah Hodgson, Grange Cottages, Drumburgh, Wigton, Carlisle CA7 5DW (01228 576551). Relax in this traditional style cottage with open fire and exposed beams - Located in this rural hamlet of Drumburgh in an area of outstanding natural beauty, with views across the Solway Firth. Hadrian's Wall National Trail, Campfield RSPB Reserve and English Nature Reserves are nearby. Electric storage heaters. Bed and Breakfast available. Sleeps two to four people. Children and pets welcome. Non-smoking.Prices from £180 - £280. Please telephone for brochure. **ETC ★★★ – ★★★★**

e-mail: messrs.hodgson@tesco.net

website: www.thegrangecottage.co.uk

Fisherground Farm *Eskdale, Cumbria*

Fisherground is a lovely traditional hill farm, offering accommodation in two stone cottages and three pine lodges, which share an acre of orchard. Ideal for walkers, nature lovers, dogs and children, there is space, freedom, peace and tranquillity here. Eskdale is walking country, with scores of riverside, fell or high mountain walks straight from the farm. Good pubs nearby serve excellent bar meals. ETC ★★★

Phone for a colour brochure: 01946 723319 or try our website: www.fisherground.co.uk and e-mail: holidays@fisherground.co.uk

CONISTON (near)

Mrs J. Halton, "Brookfield", Torver, Near Coniston LA21 8AY (015394 41328). Sleeps 2/4. "Brookfield" is a large attractive modern bungalow property in a rural setting with lovely outlook and extensive views of the Coniston mountains. The bungalow stands in its own half-acre of level garden and grounds. The inside is made into two completely separate self-contained units (semi-detached). The holiday bungalow accommodation consists of large sitting/dining room, kitchen, utility room, two good bedrooms (one twin and one double), bathroom. Good parking. Well-equipped. Linen hire available. Lovely walking terrain. Two village inns with restaurant facilities approximately 300 yards. Ideally situated for visiting any part of the Lake District or the lovely Cumbrian coast. Terms from £190 to £275 weekly. Short breaks available. Special rates for two persons. Further details on request with SAE please.

See also Colour Display Advertisement

ELTERWATER

Lane Ends Cottages, Elterwater. Three cottages are situated next to "Fellside" on the edge of Elterwater Common. Two cottages accommodate a maximum of four persons: double bedroom, twin bedded room; fully equipped kitchen/diningroom; bathroom. Third cottage sleeps five: as above plus single bedroom and separate diningroom. Electricity by meters. The cottages provide an ideal base for walking/touring holidays with Ambleside, Grasmere, Hawkshead and Coniston within a few miles. Parking for one car per cottage, additional parking opposite. Open all year; out of season long weekends available. Rates from £175 per week. Brochure on request (SAE please). **Mrs M. E. Rice, "Fellside", Elterwater, Ambleside LA22 9HN (015394 37678).**

GRIZEDALE FOREST

High Dale Park Barn, High Dale Park, Satterthwaite, Ulverston LA12 8LJ. Delightfully situated south-facing barn, newly converted, attached to owners' 17th century farmhouse, with wonderful views down secluded, quiet valley, surrounded by beautiful broadleaf woodland. Oak beams, log fires, full central heating, patio. Grizedale Visitor Centre (three miles), award-winning sculpture trails, gallery and unique sculptured playground. Grizedale Forest is one of the Lake District's richest areas of wildlife. Accommodation in two self contained units, one sleeping six, the other two plus baby; available separately or as one unit at a reduced rate. Hawkshead three miles, Beatrix Potter's home three miles. Contact: **Mr P. Brown, High Dale Park Farm, High Dale Park, Satterthwaite, Ulverston LA12 8LJ (01229 860226). ETC ★★★**

HAWESWATER/ULLSWATER/EDEN VALLEY

Goosemire Cottages. Over 30 traditional self-catering holiday homes in size from one to four bedrooms, at sensible prices. Most are rustic 17th or 18th Century Lakeland cottages or lovely barn conversions, where antiquity and modern comforts have been beautifully combined. The majority of our holiday cottages are set on, or very near to Lake Ullswater (the Lake District's second largest lake), or near Haweswater. We also have a nice selection of properties in the peaceful Eden Valley. An ideal base for walking, fishing, sailing, bird watching, touring or just relaxing in a beautiful and peaceful setting. Local pubs and post office/shop nearby. Furnished and equipped to a high standard. Log fires and central heating. Majority include heating, electricity and bed linen in tariff. Pets welcome. Open all year. Short Breaks available. Details and brochure: **Goosemire Cottages, Bateman Fold Barn, Crook, Near Kendal, Cumbria LA23 3JD (015395 68102; Fax: 015395 68104). ETC** up to ★★★★

e-mail:goosemirecottage@aol.com **website: www.goosemirecottages.co.uk**

KENDAL

Mrs E. Bateman, High Underbrow Farm, Burneside, Kendal LA8 9AY (01539 721927). Working farm. Sleeps 4. The cottage adjoins the 17th century farmhouse in a sunny position with wonderful views. Ideal spot for touring the Lake District and Yorkshire Dales, with many pleasant walks around. There are two bedrooms (one with double bed, the other with two singles). Children are welcome and a cot is available. Bathroom with bath, shower, toilet and washbasin. Large livingroom/kitchen with colour TV, fitted units, fridge and cooker. Electricity by £1 coin meter. Storage heaters 50p meter. Understairs store. Fitted carpets throughout. Own entrance porch. Sorry, no pets. Shops at Burneside two miles away, Kendal four miles, Windermere eight miles. Linen provided. Car essential – parking. Terms from £160 weekly. There is also a six-berth holiday caravan to let from £155 per week. Dogs allowed in caravan.

KENDAL

The Barns, Field End, Patton, Kendal. Two detached barns converted into five spacious architect-designed houses. The Barns are situated on 200 acres of farmland, four miles north of Kendal. A quiet country area with River Mint passing through farmland and lovely views of Cumbrian Hills, many interesting local walks with the Dales Way Walk passing nearby. Fishing is available on the river. The Barns consist of four houses with four double bedrooms and one house with three double bedrooms. Each house fully centrally heated for early/late holidays; lounge with open fire, diningroom; kitchen with cooker, fridge, microwave and washing machine; bathroom, downstairs shower room and toilet. Many interesting features include oak beams, pine floors and patio doors. Central to Lakes and Yorkshire Dales, National Parks. Terms from £140 to £415. Electricity at cost. Pets welcome. **ETC** ★★★. For brochure of The Barns apply to **Mr and Mrs E.D. Robinson, 1 Field End, Patton, Kendal LA8 9DU (01539 824220 or 07778 596863; Fax: 01539 824464.**

e-mail: robinson@fieldendholidays.co.uk **website: www.fieldendholidays.co.uk**

KESWICK

Keswick Cottages, Kentmere, How Lane, Keswick CA12 5RS (017687 73895). Superb selection of cottages and apartments in and around Keswick. All of our properties are well maintained and thoroughly clean. From a one bedroom cottage to a four bedroom house we have something for everyone. Contact us for a free colour brochure. Some properties suitable for disabled guests. Pets welcome.

e-mail: info@keswickcottages.co.uk

website: www.keswickcottages.co.uk

A useful index of towns and counties appears at the back of this book on pages 379-382. Refer also to Contents Pages 50/51.

See also Colour Display Advertisement

KESWICK

Harney Peak, Portinscale, Near Keswick. We can offer you the very best in self-catering accommodation in our spacious well-equipped apartments in the quiet village of Portinscale - overlooking Derwentwater yet only one mile from Keswick. We have various sized apartments and this makes an ideal location for couples and families. Hot water and central heating included in rental. Laundry facilities. Ample off-street parking. Open all year. Dogs welcome. Short breaks are available off season. For brochure please apply to: **Mr & Mrs Smith, The Leathes Head Hotel, Borrowdale, Cumbria CA12 5UY (017687 77247; Fax: 017687 77363).**
website: www.harneypeak.co.uk

KESWICK (near)

Mrs A.M. Trafford, Bassenthwaite Hall Farm Cottage Holidays, Bassenthwaite Village, Near Keswick CA12 4QP (Tel & Fax: 017687 76393). Working farm. By a stream with ducks! Delightful cottages charmingly restored and cared for in this attractive hamlet near Keswick. Two cosy old world farmhouses sleep 8-10 each; cottage for four/five and cute stable flat for two/three. Open all year. Storage heaters in all properties and log fires in larger properties. Special off-peak rates; weekend and mid-week breaks; farmhouse B&B. Ideally situated just two miles from Skiddaw and Bassenthwaite Lake and six miles from Keswick and Cockermouth. Mid-week and weekend breaks from £80 to £250.Weekly £120-£750. Open all year.
website: www.holidaycottageslakedistrict.co.uk

KIRKBY LONSDALE (near)

Mrs M. Dixon, Harrison Farm, Whittington, Kirkby Lonsdale, Carnforth, Lancashire LA6 2NX (015242 71415). Properties sleep 2/8. Near Hutton Roof, three miles from Kirkby Lonsdale and central for touring Lake District and Yorkshire Dales. Coast walks on Hutton Roof Crag, famous lime stone pavings. Sleeps eight people, one room with double and single bed and one room with double and cot, while third bedroom has three single beds. Bathroom. Sittingroom, diningroom and kitchen. Everything supplied but linen. Parking space. Pets permitted. Other cottages available for two to eight people. Electric cooker, fridge, kettle, iron, immersion heater and TV. Electricity and coal extra. Terms from £200 per week. SAE brings quick reply.

KIRKOSWALD

Liz Webster, Howscales, Kirkoswald, Penrith CA10 1JG (01768 898666; Fax: 01768 898710). Sleeps 2/4. COTTAGES FOR NON-SMOKERS. Howscales was originally a 17th century farm. The red sandstone buildings have been converted into five self-contained cottages, retaining many original features. Set around a cobbled courtyard, the cosy, well-equipped cottages for two/four, are surrounded by gardens and open countryside. Shared laundry facilities. Well-behaved pets welcome by arrangement. Open all year, short breaks available. Colour brochure. Non-smoking. Cared for by resident owner. Ideal base from which to explore The Eden Valley, Lakes, Pennines and Hadrian's Wall. Please ring, write or see our website for details. **ETC ★★★★.** *NATIONAL ACCESSIBILITY SCHEME: CATEGORY 2.*

e-mail: liz@howscales.fsbusiness.co.uk **website: www.eden-in-cumbria.co.uk/howscales**

KIRKOSWALD

Crossfield Cottages with Leisure Fishing. Tranquil quality cottages overlooking fishing lakes amidst Lakeland's beautiful Eden Valley countryside. Only 30 minutes' drive from Ullswater, North Pennines, Hadrian's Wall and the Scottish Borders. You will find freshly made beds for your arrival, tranquillity and freedom to roam. Good coarse and fly fishing, for residents, on your doorstep. Cottages are clean, well-equipped and maintained. Laundry area. Pets very welcome. Exceptional wildlife and walking area. Escape and relax to your home in the country. **ETC ★★★.** SAE to **Crossfield Cottages, Kirkoswald, Penrith CA10 1EU (Tel & Fax: 01768 898711 6pm-10pm for bookings, 24hr Brochure Line).**
e-mail: info@crossfieldcottages.co.uk
website: www.crossfieldcottages.co.uk

ENGLAND

Carrock Cottages Your Stepping Stone to The Cumbrian Lake District

Carrock Cottages are three recently renovated stone built cottages set on the fringe of the Lakeland Fells. A quiet rural location near the lovely villages of Hesket Newmarket with its award-winning brewery, Calbeck and Greystoke. Explore the beauty of the Lake District National Park or head north to historic Carlisle and on to Hadrian's Wall. Fell walking and other activities close to hand as well as excellent restaurants. A warm welcome guaranteed.

Telephone Malcolm or Gillian on 01768 484111 or Fax: 01768 488850

website: www.carrockcottages.co.uk

See also Colour Advertisement

LOWESWATER

Mrs M. Vickers, Askhill Farm, Loweswater, Cockermouth CA13 0SU (01946 861640). Sleeps 6. Askhill Farm is a family run farm which has beef and sheep. The single sited 28ft caravan is situated on the hillside overlooking Loweswater Lake. The view from the lounge window is of the surrounding fells. The area is ideal for fellwalking; there are plenty of walks to suit everyone's ability (high fells or low walks). The western lakes - Crummock Water, Buttermere and Ennerdale are within easy reach. Accommodation consists of double bedroom, bunkroom and dining area which becomes a double bed. The bathroom has toilet, wash basin and shower. Well-equipped kitchen. Electric fire in lounge. Terms from £220 per week, including electricity, based on four people sharing.

See also Colour Display Advertisement

NEWCASTLETON

Cumbrian/Scottish Borders. Sleeps up to 5. A three bedroomed country cottage. Centrally heated throughout, and decorated, furnished to a high standard. Own garden, patio, seating, barbecue, and lockable shed for cycles. Set amidst the beautiful Kershope Forest (part of Kielder Forest Park) with its winding streams, and miles of forest walks right from your door. Pony trekking, fishing and golf, are all nearby. Also a good base to explore Scotland, Cumbria (the Lake District), and Northumberland. Bed linen, towels, electricity, heating and 'welcome food pack' inclusive. Car essential. Ample parking by door. Open all year. Terms from £225 to £330 per week. Short breaks also available. Children seven years and over welcome. Non-smoking. Sorry, no pets. Colour brochure available from: **Mrs Joanna Furness, 2 Cuddy's Hall, Bailey, Newcastleton, Roxburghshire TD9 OTP (Tel & Fax: 016977 48160). ETC ★★★**
website: www.cuddys-hall.co.uk

PENRITH

Skirwith Hall Cottages. Escape to Eden! Get away from it all in one of two comfortable well-equipped cottages on dairy farm in the Eden Valley between the Lake District and the Pennine Dales. Set on the edge of the village of Skirwith in the shadow of Crossfell, the highest mountain in the Pennine range, the properties are maintained to the highest standard with every modern convenience. Accommodating two/four and five/eight people both cottages have riverside gardens and open fires. Well behaved children and pets welcome. **ETC ★★★**. Please contact for brochure. **Mrs L. Wilson, Skirwith Hall, Skirwith, Penrith CA10 1RH (Tel & Fax: 01768 88241).**
e-mail: idawilson@aol.com
website: www.eden-in-cumbria.co.uk/skirwith

When making enquiries or bookings, a stamped addressed envelope is always appreciated

STAVELEY

Margaret and William Beck, Brunt Knott Farm, Staveley, Kendal LA8 9QX (01539 821030; Fax: 01539 821221). Sleep 2/5. Four cosy cottages sympathetically converted from stone barn and stables on small secluded 17th century hill farm set above Staveley, midway between Kendal and Windermere (five miles). Retained beams/stone features. Peaceful hillside setting. Superb panoramic views over Lakeland Fells. Excellent base for walking, touring Lakes/Dales, relaxing in delightful surroundings. Walks/cycling on doorstep. Ample private parking. Laundry facilities. Resident owners. Well-equipped fitted kitchens. Duvets, bed linen provided. Oil central/electric heating. Woodburner/open fire in three cottages. Gardens with tables and benches. Children and pets welcome. Village and shops one and a half miles. Low season Short Breaks. Terms from £185 to £390 per week. Brochure. **ETC ★★★**

e-mail: margaret@bruntknott.demon.co.uk **website: www.bruntknott.demon.co.uk**

See also Colour Display Advertisement

THIRLMERE

Fisher-Gill Camping Barn, Stybeck Experience, Stybeck Farm, Thirlmere, Keswick CA12 4TN (017687 73232). Situated at the foot of the Helvellyn range of mountains near to "Sticks Pass" being part of Stybeck Farm, with stunning views, walks and tourist attractions nearby. This is a single storey traditional Lakeland barn built of stone and slate, comprising two rooms, cooking/seating area with sink, fridge, microwave and electric hotplate. The sleeping area consists of bunk beds with mattresses for 10 persons, groups or individuals. Toilet and electric shower (electricity by meter). Price per night £4.00 to £5.00 per person. Sorry, no smoking inside building. Patio area outside. Ample parking. Open all year.

e-mail: stybeckfarm@farming.co.uk

website: http://members.farmline.com/stybeckfarm

ULLSWATER

The Estate Office, Patterdale Hall Estate, Glenridding, Penrith CA11 0PJ (Tel & Fax: 017684 82308 24 hours). Our range includes three very comfortable large Coach Houses, two stone-built Cottages with open fires, three three-bedroomed pine Lodges, six two-bedroomed cedar Chalets, a unique, detached, converted Dairy, and two converted Bothies which make ideal, low cost accommodation for two people. All set in a private 300 acre Estate between Lake Ullswater and Helvellyn and containing a working hill-farm, a Victorian waterfall wood, private lake foreshore for Guests to use for boating and fishing, and 100 acres of designated ancient woodland for you to explore. Children welcome. Dogs by appointment in some of the accommodation. Colour TV, central heating, launderette, payphone. Day time electricity metered. Linen hire available. Terms from £139 to £452. Please phone for full brochure. **ETC ★★/★★★** *CATEGORY 3 ACCESSIBILITY.*

e-mail: welcome@phel.co.uk **website: www.phel.co.uk**

See also Colour Display Advertisement

ULLSWATER

Tirril Farm Cottages. Opened in 2001 these tasteful barn conversions are set around a quiet courtyard, some with outstanding views of the fells. Situated in the village of Tirril two miles from Ullswater and three miles from Penrith, this is an ideal, quiet location for visiting the Lake District and Eden Valley. Tirril is an attractive village with pub/restaurant and regular bus service. Fully centrally heated cottages with bed linen and towels provided. Large car park and lock-up for cycles. Short Breaks welcome. A warm welcome awaits you from the resident proprietors. For brochure/bookings **Tel or Fax: 01768 864767. ETC ★★★★**

e-mail: enquiries@tirrilfarmcottages.co.uk

website: www.tirrilfarmcottages.co.uk

Birthwaite Edge, Windermere

Situated in extensive grounds in one of the most exclusive areas of Windermere, 10 minutes from village and Lake, this is the perfect all year round holiday base. 10 self catering apartments for two to six people. Resident proprietors personally ensure the highest standards of cleanliness and comfort. Swimming pool open May to September. Colour TV. Well equipped kitchens. Hot water included. Coin metered electricity for lighting, cooking and electric fires. Background central heating during winter. Duvets and linen provided. High chairs and cots extra. Ample car parking. Regret, no smoking and no pets. Terms from £205 to £505.

Brochure from: **Bruce and Marsha Dodsworth, Birthwaite Edge, Birthwaite Road, Windermere LA23 1BS • Tel & Fax: 015394 42861**
e-mail: fhg@lakedge.com • website: www.lakedge.com.

See also Colour Advertisement

WIGTON

Mr & Mrs E. and J. Kerr, Fox Gloves, Greenrigg Farm, Westward, Wigton CA7 8AH (016973 42676). A spacious well-equipped, comfortable cottage on a working farm. Superlative setting and views, large kitchen/dining room, Aga, lounge, open fire, TV/video, three bedrooms, bathroom, separate shower room. Linen, towels, electricity, logs and coal inclusive. Children and pets very welcome. Extensive garden. Storage heaters, washing machine. Easy reach Lake District, Scottish Borders and Roman Wall. Sleeps two to eight people. Prices from £160–£425. Available all year. Short breaks by arrangement.

WINDERMERE

Mrs R. Dodgson, Cragg Farm, Bowston, Burneside, Kendal LA8 9HH (01539 821249). Cragg Farm Cottage adjoins our farmhouse and is set in quiet rural surroundings, with ample parking space, giving the opportunity to walk in the countryside. Three-quarters-of-a-mile from the main Kendal to Windermere Road (A591) it is in an ideal position for visiting the Lakes and Windermere (15 minutes away) and Kendal, four miles away. The villages of Staveley and Burneside are just two miles away. The cottage is comfortable, clean and well-equipped. Lounge/diningroom with colour TV, fully equipped kitchen, one double and one twin-bedded room and bathroom. Gas fire and central heating, electricity on £1 meter. Bed linen provided. Details on request.

Visits & Attractions

Rheged Discovery Centre, Off M6 Junction 40, A66 • 01768 868000
website: www.rheged.com

The Lake District's most spectacular attraction. Six-storey high cinema screen takes you on a journey through 2000 years of Cumbria's history, myths and legends.

Cumberland Pencil Museum, Keswick, Cumbria • 017687 73626
website: www.pencils.co.uk

The fascintating history of the humble pencil, from the discovery of Borrowdale graphite to present day manufacture. See the world's largest colouring pencil, Shop.

DERBYSHIRE

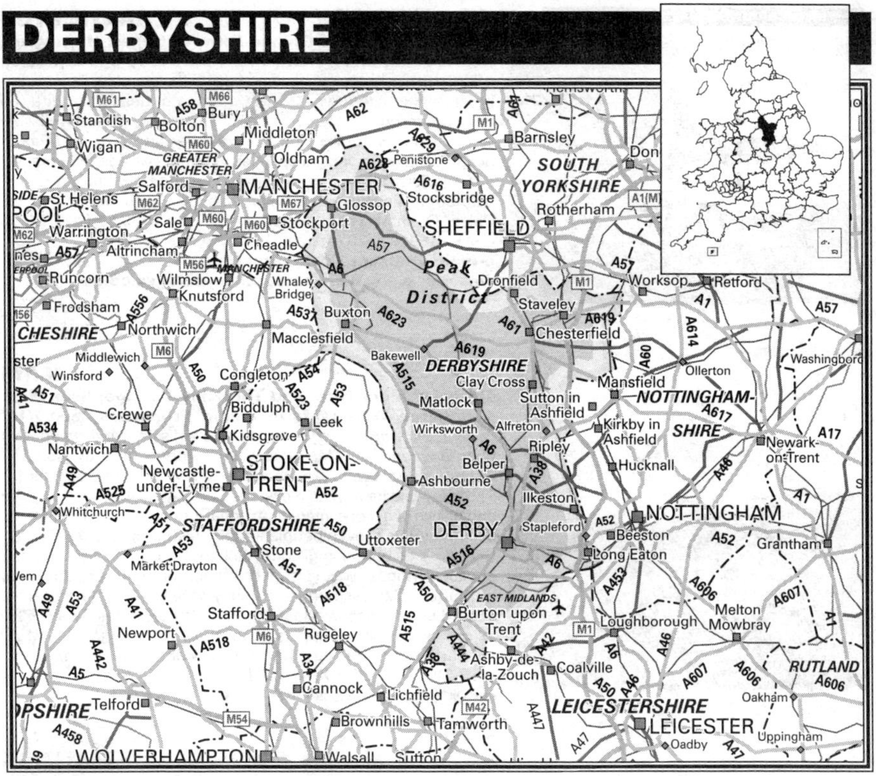

BARLOW

Mr and Mrs R. Ward, Barlow Trout, Mill Farm, Barlow, Dronfield S18 7TJ (0114 289 0543). Units sleeps 2/6. Mill Farm Holiday Cottages are situated in a conservation area with Post Office and pub/bar meals just 300 yards away; bus stop at gate. Coarse and fly fishing is available on site (free with cottage). Children and pets welcome. Central heating. Four-poster bed in three of the five units. Weekly terms from £109 to £210. Linen provided free of charge. Short break bookings accepted October – April. Please write or phone for full details. **ETC ★★/★★★**

HARTINGTON

P. Skemp, Cotterill Farm, Biggin by Hartington, Buxton SK17 0DJ (01298 84447; Fax: 01298 84664). Three stone cottages, two sleeping four, and one sleeping two. Exposed beams, two-person cottage has galleried bedroom, log burner, five-piece suite in bathroom and more. High and tasteful specification. Patio, substantial garden area, wild flower meadows and barbecue. Laundry room. Phone. Glorious location in rolling countryside. Excellent views with privacy. Half-a-mile from village and pub. Tissington Trail three-quarters of a mile, two other cycle/footpath trails within three miles, nature reserve on our land leading after one-and-a-half miles to River Dove, four miles down river is Dovedale. Footpaths/bridleways surround our farm. Highly praised, personalised information pack in each cottage giving loads of advice on attractions, walks, etc. Terms from £180 to £390 per week. **ETC ★★★★**

e-mail: enquiries@cotterillfarm.co.uk **website: www.cotterillfarm.co.uk**

See also Colour Display Advertisement

HARTINGTON

J. Gibbs, Wolfscote Grange Farm Cottages, Hartington, Near Buxton SK17 0AX (Tel & Fax: 01298 84342). Sleep 4/6. Charming cottages nestling beside the beautiful Dove Valley in stunning scenery. Cruck Cottage is peaceful 'with no neighbours, only sheep' and a cosy 'country living' feel. Wolfscote Cottage offers comfort for the traveller and time to relax in beautiful surroundings. It sparkles with olde worlde features, yet has modern amenities including en suite facilities and spa bathroom. The farm trail provides walks from your doorstep to the Dales. Open all year. Weekly terms from £180 to £420 (sleep four); £180 to £520 (sleep six). **ETC ★★★★**
e-mail: wolfscote@btinternet.com
website: www.wolfscotegrangecottages.co.uk

ILAM

Throwley Moor Farm and Throwley Cottage, Ilam, Near Ashbourne. Working farm, join in. Properties sleep 7/12. Self-catering farmhouse and cottage on this beef and sheep farm near Dovedale and Manifold Valley. Approached by A52/A53 Ashbourne to Leek road, then via Calton and follow signs for Throwley and Ilam. Within easy reach of Alton Towers, cycle hire and places of historic interest. An ideal touring centre. The cottage accommodates seven people and the two farmhouses sleep 12. Sittingrooms and diningroom (kitchen/diner in cottage). Electric cookers; fridges; washing machine and dryer. Pay phone. Pets permitted. Car essential – parking. Available all year; terms according to season. Nearest shops three miles away. **ETC**

★★★/★★★★. SAE, please, for further details to **Mrs M.A. Richardson, Throwley Hall Farm, Ilam, Near Ashbourne DE6 2BB (01538 308 202/243).**
e-mail: throwleyhall@talk21.com

MATLOCK

Honeysuckle, Jasmine and Clematis Cottages, Middlehills Farm, Grange Mill, Matlock DE4 4HY (01629 650368). Relax, unwind, enjoy the peace and tranquillity in one of our warm, welcoming cottages or static caravan. JASMINE - two bedroomed, and HONEYSUCKLE - three bedroomed, are full of character – stone mullions, enclosed south-facing patios. CLEMATIS - two bedroomed, Accessible Category 2, is on one level and especially converted for less-able and wheelchair users. Large bathroom with support rails, wheel-in shower with shower seat. Also fully equipped static caravan for bargain breaks. Meet our friendly pot-bellied pig, and Bess and Ruby are ideal playmates for children of all ages.

ENGLAND

PEAK DISTRICT

Shatton Hall Farm Cottages, Peak District. Sleep 4-6. THREE COTTAGES, INCL. £250–£425 PER WEEK. We offer a quiet and peaceful setting on this Elizabethan farmstead, in the centre of a superb walking, climbing and caving area. We have extensive gardens, way-marked field and woodland farm walks, a trout lake and hard tennis court on the farm. Each of our three stone cottages has individual character, beamed livingroom, open gas fire or wood burning stove, well set out new kitchen and bathroom with shower. Ample parking, safe play areas and a visitors laundry. TOWNFIELD BARN is a newly converted facility for Group Activities such as Creative Art, Craft, Nature Study (Programme 2002) and for specialist groups to hire with our cottage accommodation. This beautifully situated barn has a kitchen, toilet, cloakroom and two large rooms with a wood burning stove, opening to superb views. Tariff and course details on application. **ETC ★★★★. Angela Kellie, Shatton Hall Farm, Bamford, Hope Valley S33 0BG (01433 620635; Fax: 01433 620689).**
e-mail: ahk@peakfarmholidays.co.uk website: www.peakfarmholidays.co.uk

See also Colour Display Advertisement

PEAK DISTRICT

Field House Farmhouse Holidays, Calton. Situated midway between Leek and Ashbourne within the Southern Peak District and the Staffordshire Moorlands. Set in beautiful secluded surroundings close to Dovedale and the Manifold Valley, ideal country for the walker, horse rider or cyclist. Alton Towers is a 15 minute drive away. Grade II Listed farmhouse with stables within its own grounds and with open views. Farmhouse is well-equipped and has Sky TV. Sleeps 11 plus campbed and cot. Also ample space for family caravan. All pets and horses welcome. Open all year. Short winter breaks. Late booking discount. **ETC ★★★★. Contact: Janet Hudson (01538 308352).**
e-mail: info@field-head.co.uk
website: www.field-head.co.uk

DEVON

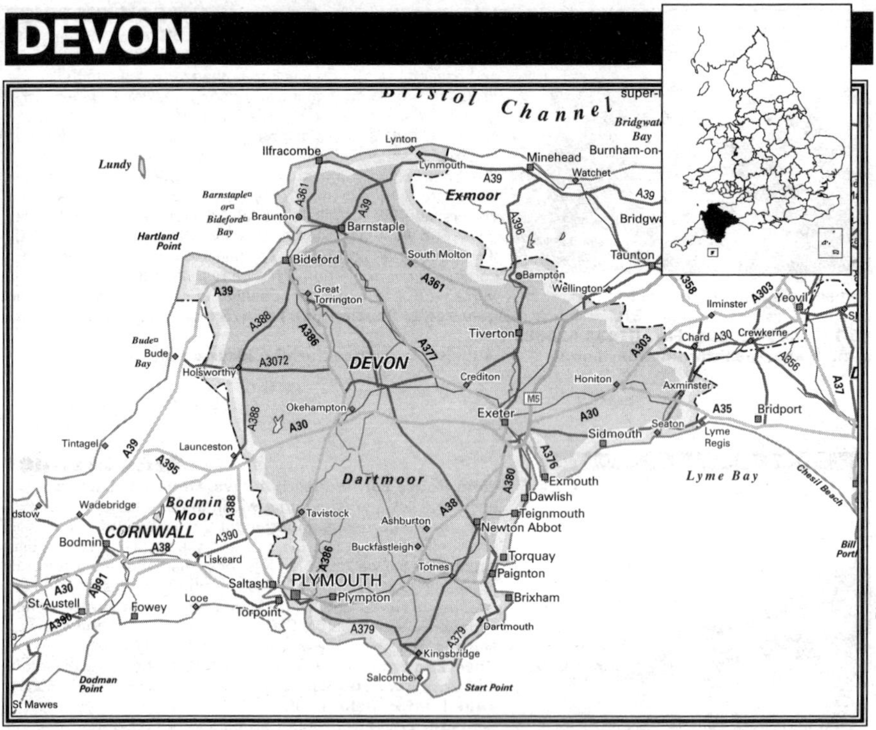

See also Colour Display Advertisement

NORTH DEVON

North Devon Holiday Homes, 19 Cross Street, Barnstaple EX31 1BD (01271 376322 24-hour brochure service; Fax: 01271 346544). With our Free Colour Guide and unbiased recommendation and booking service, we can spoil you for choice in the beautiful unspoilt region around Exmoor and the wide sandy beaches and coves of Devon's beautiful National Trust Coast. Choose from 400 selected properties including thatched cottages, working farms, beachside properties with swimming pools, luxury manor houses, etc. From only £98 to £980 per week. First class value assured.
e-mail: info@northdevonholidays.co.uk
website: www.northdevonholidays.co.uk

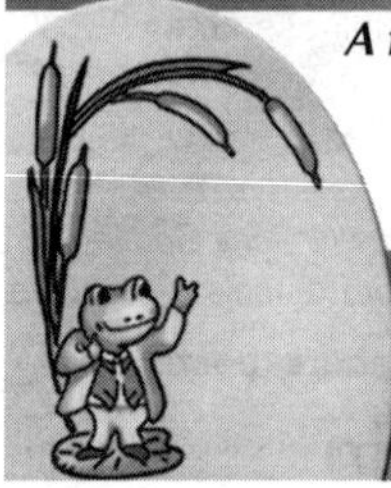

APPLEDORE

Sea Birds Cottage, Appledore. Sea edge, pretty Georgian cottage facing directly out to the open sea. Sea Birds is a spacious cottage with large lounge, colour TV; dining room with French windows onto garden; modern fitted kitchen; three double bedrooms; bathroom, second WC downstairs; washing machine. Lawned garden at back overlooking the sea with garden furniture. Own parking. Dog welcome. Sea views from most rooms and the garden is magnificent; views of the open sea, boats entering the estuary, sunset, sea birds. Appledore is still a fishing village - fishing trips from the quay, restaurants by the water. Area has good cliff and coastal walks, stately homes, riding, swimming, golf, surfing, excellent beaches. Off peak heating. From £95. Other sea edge cottages available. Send SAE for colour brochure to **F. S. Barnes, 140 Bay View Road, Northam, Bideford EX39 1BJ (or phone 01237 473801 for prices and dates).** Photo shows view of sea from garden.

FREE child with a paying adult with voucher at

Devonshire Collection of Period Costume

See our READERS' OFFER VOUCHER for details.

Readers are requested to mention this guidebook when seeking accommodation (and please enclose a stamped addressed envelope).

See also Colour Display Advertisement

ASHBURTON

Mrs Angela Bell, Wooder Manor, Widecombe-in-the-Moor, Near Ashburton TQ13 7TR (01364 621391). Cottages and converted coach house, on 150 acre working family farm nestled in the picturesque valley of Widecombe, surrounded by unspoilt woodland, moors and granite tors. Half-a-mile from village with Post Office, general stores, inn with diningroom, church and National Trust Information Centre. Excellent centre for touring Devon, with a variety of places to visit, and exploring Dartmoor by foot or on horseback. Accommodation is clean and well equipped with colour TV, central heating, laundry room. Children welcome. Large gardens and courtyard for easy parking. Open all year, so take advantage of off-season reduced rates. Short Breaks also available. Two properties suitable for disabled visitors. Brochure available. **ETC ★★★**

e-mail: angela@woodermanor.com **website: www.woodermanor.com**

See also Colour Display Advertisement

BARNSTAPLE

Lower Yelland Farm Cottages, Barnstaple. Winner of the 2002 Golden Achievement Award of Excellence for the Devon Retreat of the Year, this delightfully modernised, comfortable and quiet farm cottage is situated close to the road between Barnstaple and Bideford on the lovely Taw/Torridge estuary, immediately adjacent to the Tarka Trail. Set in its own private lawned gardens with ample courtyard parking, the cottage is ideal for family holidays and as a base for touring. It is within a mile of the sandy beach at Instow and excellent pubs and restaurants. B&B is also available and there are many leisure activities close at hand. **ETC ★★★** *SELF-CATERING*, **◆◆◆◆** *B&B*. Contact: **Mr Peter Day, Lower Yelland Farm, Fremington, Barnstaple EX31 3EN (01271 860101; mobile: 07803 933642).**

e-mail: peterday@loweryellandfarm.co.uk **website: www.loweryellandfarm.co.uk**

BIDEFORD

Yapham Cottages, Hartland, Bideford. Sleep 2-4. Three beautifully furnished and equipped, centrally heated, quality cottages in an Area of Outstanding Natural Beauty with marvellous views, breathtaking coastal scenery, wonderful clifftop walks and secluded beaches. Each has cooker, microwave, fridge, washing machine, colour TV, video, radio, duvets with linen, garden furniture, barbecue and own garden/sitting out area; laundry room. Ample car parking space. Set down our own private drive, the location offers complete tranquillity yet is perfect for visiting nearby tourist attractions: Hartland Abbey and Clovelly; the Tarka Trail for cyclists; Lundy Island for naturalists and the South West Coastal Path for walkers. Pets most welcome. Cream teas on arrival. **ETC ★★★★**. Please contact: **Jane and Jimmy Young, Yapham Farm, Hartland, Bideford, Devon EX39 6AN (01237 441916).**

e-mail: jane.yapham@virgin.net **website: www.yaphamcottages.com**

BIGBURY (near)

Miss C.M. Hodder, Bennicke Farm, Modbury, Ivybridge PL21 0SU (01548 830265). Sleeps 8. Main part of Bennicke Farmhouse(self-contained) in peaceful situation reached by lane, quarter of a mile from road. Large garden. Three bedrooms sleeping eight. Also small bungalow with garden situated on Plymouth/Kingsbridge main road, near Modbury. Sleeps six. Both properties five miles from sandy beach of Bigbury Bay. Within easy reach of Cornwall (15 miles) and Dartmoor(10 miles). Both have mains water, electricity and colour TV. Linen is not provided. Terms from £210 to £295 weekly. No VAT. S.A.E. for details.

ENGLAND

BOVEY TRACEY

John and Helen Griffiths, Lookweep Farm, Liverton, Newton Abbot TQ12 6HT (01626 833277; Fax: 01626 834412). Sleeps 5. Lookweep Farm is set within Dartmoor National Park and is perfectly placed for exploration of Dartmoor, the stunning coastline, charming villages and towns of South Devon. Shippen and Dairy cottages are two attractive, well-equipped stone cottages surrounded by open farmland and woods in this tranquil setting near Bovey Tracey and just a two mile drive from Haytor. Own gardens, ample parking, heated pool and outstanding walks right on your doorstep. Children welcome (high chairs and cots available). Pets also welcome. Short breaks available. Mastercard and Visa accepted. Please phone or write for brochure. **ETC ★★★**

e-mail: holidays@lookweep.co.uk **website: www.lookweep.co.uk**

BRADWORTHY

Mrs L Lewin, Lake House Cottages and B&B, Lake Villa, Bradworthy EX22 7SQ (01409 241962; Fax: 01409 241579). Come and stay in one of our four cosy, character cottages in peaceful countryside, half-a-mile from Bradworthy village square in this hidden corner of Devon. Perfectly situated to explore the spectacular coastline of North Devon and Cornwall as well as the West Country moors. There are also several gardens within reach (Rosemoor, Eden Project) and other places of interest. The cottages sleep six, four, three and two and are well-furnished and fitted with everything you will need for a great cottage holiday. There are also two B&B rooms available in our own home. Tennis court and gardens. Pets welcome.

e-mail: info@lakevilla.co.uk **website: www.lakevilla.co.uk**

See also Colour Display Advertisement

BRIXHAM

Devoncoast Holidays. We are a highly experienced holiday letting agency on Devon's sunny south coast. We have numerous properties on our books ranging from one-bedroom flats to large three bedroomed houses, all in sunny South Devon. We have personally inspected all of our properties and all of the accommodation is of a high standard and comes fully equipped with colour TV, microwave, full cooker and car parking. Our properties are available all year round, for mini breaks or for full week lettings. Pets and children are welcome. Many have a flat access. All of our properties are within easy reach of the coast, some have sea views. We accept all credit cards. Please telephone for a free brochure and map - 24 hour operation. **Devoncoast Holidays, P.O. Box 14. Brixham, Devon TQ5 8AB (Tel & Fax: 07050 338889).**

website: www.devoncoast.com

CHULMLEIGH

Fiona Lincoln-Gordon, Bridleway Cottages, Golland Farm, Burrinton, Umberleigh EX37 9JP (01769 520263). Sleep 2/8. Country lovers' retreat. Two cottages converted from a stone barn on small mixed, organic farm. Overlooking Taw Valley, offering exclusive fishing on coarse and trout ponds. 160 miles of Tarka Trail for cyclists and walkers 10 minutes away. The cottages have been sensitively restored to offer all home comforts. Heating and woodburners for cosy winter breaks. Many original wood features. Organic vegetables from our Veg Box Scheme. A traditional rural country base between Dartmoor and Exmoor. Country pubs. RHS Rosemoor and Trust gardens nearby; Eden Project within one-and-a-half hours. Pets welcome. Open all year. Terms from £170 to £560 per week. Short breaks welcome. Residential courses on greenwood working, basket-making and art. **ETC ★★★**

website: www.golland.btinternet.co.uk **or** **www.artandcraftcourses.co.uk**

Terms quoted in this publication may be subject to increase if rises in costs necessitate

---

ENGLAND

Little Farm

Southleigh
Near Colyton
Devon EX24 6JE

The Studio at Little Farm is set in a glorious and idyllic location in a wooded valley between Seaton (5 miles) and Sidmouth (9 miles). The property has use of a heated swimming pool and its views over the valley make a superb holiday setting. The property is completely secluded, set in 52 acres - perfect for getting away from it all. Totally unspoilt, an animal lover's dream. Bird/Nature reserve on the doorstep!

The accommodation comprises master bedroom en suite, twin room, shower room, kitchen, lounge/diner, luxuriously furnished to a very high standard. In the lounge is a pull-down double bed secreted behind a wall unit. All linen, towels, electricity, gas, water included in the price. Any pets very welcome, kept under control. Grazing available. Open all year.

Please phone for more details - 01404 871361

• *e-mail: littlefarmhols@madasafish.com* • *web: www.littlefarmonline.co.uk*

See also Colour Display Advertisement

CHULMLEIGH

Sandra Gay, Northcott Barton Farm Cottage, Northcott Barton, Ashreigney, Chulmleigh EX18 7PR (Tel & Fax: 01769 520259). Beautifully equipped, spotlessly clean three bedroom cottage with large enclosed garden. A walker's and country lover's ideal: for a couple seeking peace and quiet or a family holiday. Very special rates for low season holidays, couples and short breaks. Near golf, riding, Tarka trail and RHS Rosemoor. Character, comfort, beams, log fire, "Perfick". Please contact for availability. **ETC ★★★★**

e-mail: sandra@northcottbarton.co.uk **website: www.northcottbarton.co.uk**

See also Colour Display Advertisement

COLYTON

Mrs R. Gould and Mrs S. Gould, Bonehayne Farm, Colyton EX24 6SG (01404 871396 or 01404 871416). Bonehayne Farm cottage welcomes you with many olde worlde features. Spacious, fully-furnished with four-poster, microwave, laundry facilities and central heating. Family-run dairy farm on the banks of the river Coly, in a beautiful, picturesque sheltered valley. Large garden, good trout fishing, woodlands to roam and plenty of walks. Coast is only 10 minutes away.

e-mail: gould@bonehayne.co.uk

website: www.bonehayne.co.uk

See also Colour Display Advertisement

DARTMOUTH

Dart Valley Cottages, South Devon. Sleep 2 – 10. A fine collection of individual, well-equipped cottages set in the glorious scenery of the River Dart Valley. Many properties have stunning views. Wonderful countryside for walking, good beaches close by. Short breaks available. For brochure telephone **01803 771127.**

e-mail: enquiries@dartvalleycottages.co.uk

website: www.dartvalleycottages.co.uk

Visits & Attractions

Quince Honey Farm, South Molton, Devon • 01769 572401

The world's largest living honey bee exhibition, where the hives can be viewed in complete safety. Ideal for all ages, with fascinating videos and well-stocked shop.

THE SALTER FAMILY WELCOMES YOU

HALDON LODGE FARM

Kennford, Near Exeter, Devon

20 minutes from Dawlish and Teignmouth Beaches

Freedom and safety for all the family

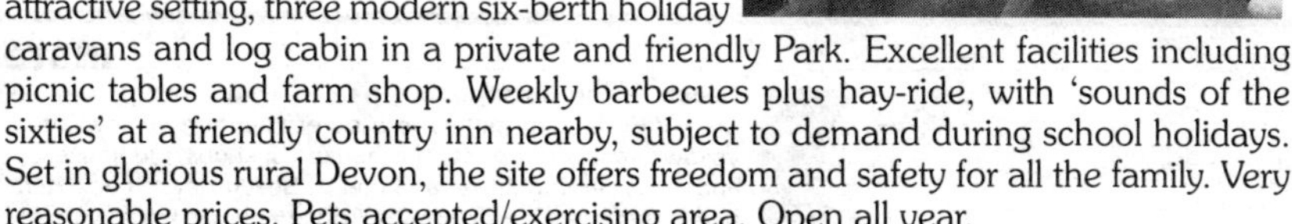

Central for South Devon coast and Exeter in an attractive setting, three modern six-berth holiday caravans and log cabin in a private and friendly Park. Excellent facilities including picnic tables and farm shop. Weekly barbecues plus hay-ride, with 'sounds of the sixties' at a friendly country inn nearby, subject to demand during school holidays. Set in glorious rural Devon, the site offers freedom and safety for all the family. Very reasonable prices. Pets accepted/exercising area. Open all year.

Relax and enjoy the scenery or stroll along the many forest lanes. Famous country inns nearby. Three coarse fishing lakes close to the Park and the attraction of ponies and horse riding at a nearby farm.

Large six-berth caravans, two bedrooms, lounge with TV, bathroom/toilet (H/C); rates from £70 to £195 High Season.

Personal attention and welcome by David & Betty Salter.

For brochure telephone 01392 832312.

See also Colour Display Advertisement

HOPE COVE

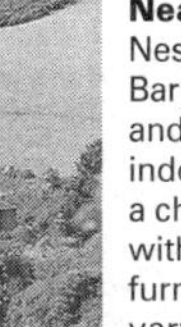

Mike and Judy Tromans, Hope Barton Barns, Hope Cove, Near Salcombe TQ7 3HT (01548 561393). Sleep 2/10. Nestling in its own valley, close to the sandy cove, Hope Barton Barns is an exclusive group of 17 stone barns in two courtyards and three luxury apartments in the converted farmhouse. Heated indoor pool, sauna, gym, lounge bar, tennis court, trout lake and a children's play barn. We have 35 acres of pastures and streams with sheep, goats, pigs, chickens, ducks and rabbits. Superbly furnished and fully-equipped, each cottage is unique and they vary from a studio to four bedrooms, sleeping two to ten. Farmhouse meals from our menu. Ample parking. Golf, sailing and coastal walks nearby. Open all year. A perfect setting for family Summer holidays, a week's walking in Spring/Autumn or just a "get away from it all" break. Free range children and well behaved dogs welcome. For a colour brochure and rental tariff, please contact Mike or Judy. Open all year. ★★★★

website: www.hopebarton.co.uk

ILFRACOMBE

Robin Downer, Middle Lee Farm, Berrynarbor, Ilfracombe EX34 9SD (Tel & Fax: 01271 882256). Sleep 2/6. Middle Lee Farm is an 18th century Devon long-house set at the foot of the Sterridge Valley (an Area of Outstanding Natural Beauty) and a few minutes' walk from the award-winning Berrynarbor village. The original farm outbuildings and the west wing of the farmhouse have been converted into seven individual, self-catering holiday cottages sleeping from two to six. The cottages are in a courtyard setting with a central laundry room and a covered play area for darts and table tennis. Sea one mile, golf one-and-a-half miles, Exmoor three miles. Open all year. Terms from £110 to £425. Dogs welcome. **ETC ★★★/★★★★**

e-mail: middleleefarm@hotmail.com

website: www.middleleefarm.co.uk

ENGLAND

See also Colour Display Advertisement

ILFRACOMBE (near)

Lower Campscott Farm, Lee, Near Ilfracombe EX34 8LS (01271 863479). We have a lovely farm set at the head of the Fuchsia Valley of Lee, with views across the Atlantic. Our four fully furnished cottages and two holiday homes are so popular we have erected a log cabin to accommodate all the visitors that want to keep coming to stay in this peaceful corner of Devon, surrounded by our special animals and the beautiful wildlife - Deer, Badgers, Geese and Buzzards to name a few. The beaches of Lee and Woolacombe are close by. Meals and cream teas are available, by arrangement, in our conservatory.
e-mail: holidays@lowercampscott.co.uk
website: www.lowercampscott.co.uk

INSTOW

Beach Haven Cottage. Sleeps 5. Seafront cottage overlooking the sandy beach. Instow is a quiet yachting village with soft yellow sands and a pretty promenade of shops, old houses, pubs and cafes serving drinks and meals. Beach Haven has extensive beach and sea views from the house and garden, own parking, gas fired central heating, colour TV, washing machine. Lawned garden overlooking sea with terrace and garden furniture. Coastal walks and cycle trails, boat to Lundy Island. Dog welcome. Please send SAE for colour brochure of this and other sea edge cottages to **F. I. Barnes, 140 Bay View Road, Northam, Bideford EX39 1BJ (or phone 01237 473801 for prices and dates).** Photo shows view from balcony of beach and sea.

KINGSBRIDGE (near)

Mrs J. Tucker, Mount Folly Farm, Bigbury-on-Sea, Near Kingsbridge TQ7 4AR (01548 810267). Working farm. Sleeps 2/6. A delightful family farm, situated on the coast, overlooking the sea and sandy beaches of Bigbury Bay. Farm adjoins golf course and River Avon. Lovely coastal walks. Ideal centre for South Hams and Dartmoor. The spacious wing comprises half of the farmhouse, and is completely self-contained. All rooms attractively furnished. Large, comfortable lounge with bay windows overlooking the sea; TV and video. There are three bedrooms – one family, one double and a bunk bed; two have washbasins. The kitchen/diner has a fridge/freezer, electric cooker, microwave, washing machine and dishwasher. There is a nice garden, ideal for children. Cot and babysitting available. Sorry no smoking. Reduction for two people staying in off peak weeks. Please write or telephone for a brochure.

OKEHAMPTON

East Hook Cottages, Okehampton. Sleeps 2/6. An oustanding location in the heart of Devon, with a beautiful panoramic view of the Dartmoor National Park, on the Tarka Trail and Devon Coast to Coast Cycle Route. Three comfortably furnished country cottages with exposed beams, log fire and full of character. Quiet and peaceful, set in own large grounds with garden furniture. Ample parking. Very accessible, one mile from Okehampton, less than two miles from Dartmoor, three miles from the A30. The most central point for leisure in the West Country. Children and pets welcome. Open all year. Flexible short breaks. Terms £145 to £395 per week. Guests return yearly!
Mrs M.E. Stevens, West Hook Farm, Okehampton EX20 1RL (01837 52305).
e-mail: marystevens@westhookfarm.fsnet.co.uk

SOUTH MOLTON

Mike and Rose Courtney, West Millbrook, Twitchen, South Molton EX36 3LP (01598 740382). Properties sleep 2/8. Adjoining Exmoor. Two fully-equipped bungalows and one farmhouse annexe in lovely surroundings bordering Exmoor National Park. Ideal for touring North Devon and West Somerset including moor and coast with beautiful walks, lovely scenery and many other attractions. North Molton village is only one mile away. All units have electric cooker, fridge/freezer, microwave and colour TV; two bungalows also have washing machines. Children's play area; cots and high chairs available free. Linen hire available. Games room. Car parking. Central heating if required. Electricity metered. Out of season short breaks. Weekly prices from £70 to £365. Colour brochure available. **ETC ★★/★★★**
website: www.visitsouthmolton.co.uk

SOUTH MOLTON (near)

Court Green, Bishop's Nympton, Near South Molton. Sleeps 5. A most attractive well-equipped, south-facing cottage with large garden, on edge of the village of Bishop's Nympton, three miles from South Molton. Ideal holiday centre, within easy reach of Exmoor, the coast, sporting activities and places of interest. Three bedrooms, one double, one twin-bedded with washbasin and one single. Two bathrooms with toilet. Sitting and diningrooms, large kitchen. Central heating, electric coal/wood effect fires, TV. One mile sea trout/trout fishing on River Mole. Well behaved pets welcome. Terms April to October £180 to £220. **Mrs J. Greenwell, Tregeiriog, Near Llangollen, North Wales LL20 7HU (01691 600672).**

See also Colour Display Advertisement

TORQUAY

Parkfield Luxury Holiday Apartments have 1, 2 or 3 bedrooms, each fully equipped with TV, video and own patio, and most have panoramic views over the Devonshire countryside. Parkfield's landscaped grounds accommodate a children's play area, ample parking and kennels for dogs, which are welcome. The tranquil setting is a short drive to beaches, coastal walks, traditional pubs, steam railways and other family attractions. Short Breaks available by arrangement. **ETC ★★★**. For more information please phone/fax or write to **Roy and June, Parkfield Luxury Holiday Apartments, Claddon Lane, Maidencombe, Torquay TQ1 4TB (Tel & Fax: 01803 328952).**
e-mail: enquiries@parkfieldapartments.co.uk
website: www.parkfieldapartments.co.uk

PLEASE NOTE

All the information in this book is given in good faith in the belief that it is correct. However, the publishers cannot guarantee the facts given in these pages, neither are they responsible for changes in policy, ownership or terms that may take place after the date of going to press. Readers should always satisfy themselves that the facilities they require are available and that the terms, if quoted, still apply.

Flear Farm Cottages

Discover ten superb cottages set in 75 acres of a beautiful South Devon valley - just five miles from the sea. As well as peace and quiet, we offer a 40ft indoor heated swimming pool, sauna, all weather tennis court, large indoor and outdoor play areas.

Non-smokers only. Children and dogs welcome. Log fires and full central heating - perfect for off-season breaks.

ETC ★★★★/★★★★★

Flear Farm Cottages
East Allington, Totnes,
South Devon
TQ9 7RF

Website: www.flearfarm.co.uk

Phone (01548) 521227 or Fax (01548) 521600 For our Colour Brochure

TOTNES

J. and E. Ball, Higher Well Farm and Holiday Park, Stoke Gabriel, Totnes TQ9 6RN (01803 782289). A quiet secluded farm park welcoming tents, motor caravans and touring caravans. It is less than one mile from the riverside village of Stoke Gabriel and within four miles of Torbay beaches. Central for touring South Devon. Facilities include new toilet/shower block with dishwashing and family rooms. Electric hook-ups and hard standings. Launderette, shop and payphone. Also static caravans to let from £120 per week or £17 per night. **ETC ★★★★**

WOOLACOMBE

Mrs B.A. Watts, Resthaven Holiday Flats, The Esplanade, Woolacombe EX34 7DJ (01271 870248). Situated on the sea front opposite the beautiful Combesgate Beach, with uninterrupted views of the coastline. Two self-contained flats – ground floor sleeps five, first floor sleeps nine. Family, double and single bedrooms, all with washbasins. Comfortable lounges with sea views, colour TV and videos. Fully equipped electric kitchens. Bathrooms have bath and shower. Electricity by £1 meter. Payphone. Free lighting, parking, hot water and laundry facility. Terms from £160 to £800 per week. Please write, or phone, for brochure.

See also Colour Display Advertisement

WOOLACOMBE

Woolacombe Cottages. A good selection of cottages, from seafront to farmhouse, including many in private grounds, with excellent golf course and swimming pool. Close to beach, moors and gardens, with riding, surfing, tennis and much more available. Weekly tariff £145 to £1500. Short Breaks from £75. Please telephone or fax for further details. Contact: **Ivycott Farm, Woolacombe, Devon EX34 7HL (01271 870846).**
website: www.woolacombe-cottages.co.uk

DORSET

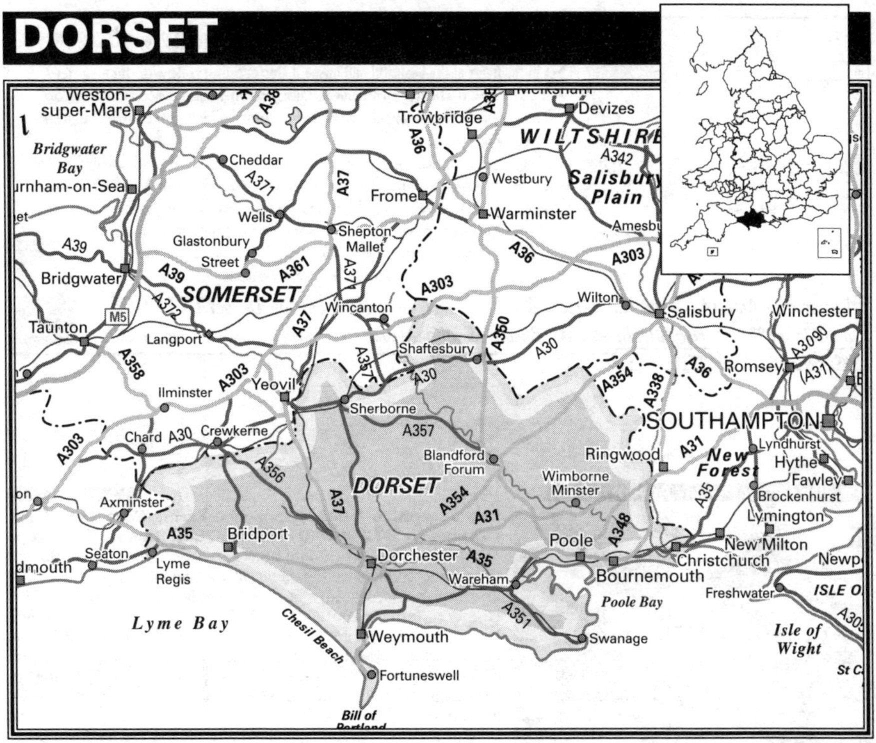

ABBOTSBURY (near)

Character Farm Cottages, Langton Herring. Sleep 2-8. Working farm. Four character farm cottages situated in the villages of Langton Herring and Rodden, nestling on the coastline between picturesque Abbotsbury and Weymouth. This unique part of Dorset's Heritage Coast is ideal for walking, touring, bird-watching and fishing with the added attractions of Abbotsbury's world famous Swannery, The Fleet and Weymouth's safe sandy beaches. The four cottages are all comfortably furnished with features such as open fires, beams, inglenooks, walled gardens and ample parking. Pets and children welcome. Logs and linen available. Prices from £145. Enquiries: **Mrs J. Elwood, Lower Farmhouse, Langton Herring, Weymouth DT3 4JB (01305 871187; Fax: 01305 871347). ETC ★★★★**

e-mail: jane@mayo.fsbusiness.co.uk **website: www.characterfarmcottages.co.uk**

BEAMINSTER

33A St Mary Well Street, Beaminster. Sleeps 7. Delightful two-bedroom bungalow, peacefully located in a small town, nestling in the rolling hills of West Dorset. Each bedroom has a wash hand basin, one has a double bed and the second has two single divans. Z-bed and cot available, settee also converts into a double bed in the lounge. Bathroom and toilet are separate. Well furbished kitchen/dining room. Spacious lounge overlooking patio/garden. Separate utility room. Car parking on private drive. Ideal for walking, fishing and fossil hunting with the stunning Dorset coastline only seven miles away with picturesque harbours, beaches and coastal path. West Bay, Lyme Regis, Hardy's Cottage, Cricket St Thomas, Forde Abbey all nearby. No pets. Terms from £140 to £330. For brochure please send SAE to **Mrs L. Watts, 53 Hogshill Street, Beaminster, Dorset DT8 3AG (01308 863088).**

Superior Self-Catering Holiday Cottages

Set in the heart of the beautiful and unspoilt Dorset countryside with stunning views and a peaceful, traffic-free environment. Luccombe offers quality accommodation for 2-8 people in a variety of converted and historic farm buildings, with original timbers and panelling.

Well-equipped kitchens. Large shower or bath. Cosy lounge/dining with colour TV. Bed linen, duvets, towels provided. Laundry room. Children and well-behaved pets welcome. Ample parking. Disabled access. Riding, tennis, and new for 2003, indoor swimming pool and gymnasium/games room. Clay pigeon shooting and fishing nearby. Post office and village stores in local village. Open throughout the year. Group/family enquiries welcome. Short breaks available.

Luccombe Country Holidays

Murray and Amanda Kayll, Luccombe, Milton Abbas, Blandford Forum, Dorset DT11 OBE

Tel: (01258) 880558 Fax: (01258) 881384 E-mail: mkayll@aol.com Web: www.luccombeholidays.co.uk

See also Colour Advertisement

See also Colour Display Advertisement

BEXINGTON

Mrs Josephine Pearse, Tamarisk Farm, West Bexington, Dorchester DT2 9DF (01308 897784). Sleep 4/6. On slope overlooking Chesil Beach between Abbotsbury and Burton Bradstock. Three large (one suitable for Disabled Category 1 - M3) and two small cottages and two secluded chalets (not ETC Graded). Terms from £105 to £620. Each one stands in own fenced garden. Glorious views along West Dorset and Devon coasts. Lovely walks by sea and inland. Mixed organic farm with arable, sheep, cattle, horses and market garden – vegetables available. Sea fishing, riding in Portesham; lots of tourist attractions and good markets in Bridport (six miles), Dorchester, Weymouth and Portland (all 13 miles). Good centre for touring Thomas Hardy's Wessex. Safe for children, and pets can be quite free. **ETC ★★★/★★★★**

BLANDFORD

Orchard Cottage, Deverel Farm, Milborne St Andrew, Blandford. Sleeps 6. In the midst of Hardy Country, less than one mile from Milborne St Andrew, with Post Office, shop. pub and garage, and just two miles from the picturesque village of Milton Abbas, the cottage is within easy reach of the coast. Situated at the edge of the farmyard, 150 yards from the A354, this modern three bedroom semi-detached cottage has a large, well-fenced garden and views of rolling countryside. Children welcome. Open all year. Weekly terms from £150 to £450 including electricity, heating, bed linen, towels and welcome pack. **ETC ★★★**. Contact: **Charlotte Martin, Deverel Farm, Milborne St Andrew, Blandford DT11 0HX (01258 837195).**

e-mail: deverel@dialstart78.fsnet.co.uk **website: www.oas.co.uk/ukcottages/orchard cottage/**

BRIDPORT (near)

Court Farm Cottages, Askerswell, Dorchester DT2 9EJ (01308 485668). A Grade II Listed barn has been converted into delightful holiday cottages, fully equipped with all modern conveniences to make your holiday as relaxing as possible. Wheatsheaf and Haywain sleep four and feature king-sized four-poster beds. Threshers has three bedrooms and sleeps five. South Barn has four bedrooms and two bathrooms and sleeps seven. A games room and large garden are provided for guests. Askerswell is an idyllic village in an Area of Outstanding Natural Beauty just four miles from the coast. Perfect for walking and touring holidays. Open all year. Low season short breaks available. From £210 to £690 per week. **ETC ★★★★/★★★★★**

e-mail: courtfarmcottages@eclipse.co.uk

website: www.eclipse.co.uk/CourtFarmCottages/WEBPG2

ENGLAND

BRIDPORT (near)

Mrs S. Norman, Frogmore Farm, Chideock, Bridport DT6 6HT (01308 456159). Working farm. Sleeps 6. Delightful farm cottage on ninety acre grazing farm set in the rolling hills of West Dorset. Superb views over Lyme Bay, ideal base for touring Dorset and Devon or rambling the many coastal and country footpaths of the area. This fully equipped self-catering cottage sleeps six. Three bedrooms. Bed linen supplied. Cosy lounge with woodburner and colour TV, French doors to a splendid columned sun verandah. Children and well behaved dogs welcome. Car essential. Open all year. Short breaks available, also Bed and Breakfast in the 17th century farmhouse. Brochure and terms free on request.

DORCHESTER (near)

PITT COTTAGE

Pitt Cottage, Ringstead Bay, Near Dorchester. Sleeps 6. An attractive thatched stone cottage, surrounded by farmland and situated on the edge of a small wood about a quarter mile from the sea, commanding outstanding views of Ringstead Bay on the Dorset Heritage Coast. The cottage is equipped to sleep six; three bedrooms (two beds in each), two bathrooms, sitting room with open fire and large kitchen/dining area. Cot/high chair; washing machine; TV; night storage heaters/electric radiators in all rooms. Car essential. Available from £200 per week. For details please send SAE (reference FHG) to: **Mrs S.H. Russell, 49 Limerston Street, London SW10 0BL or telephone 0207 351 9919.**

LYME REGIS (near)

Mrs Debby Snook, Westover Farm Cottages, Wootton Fitzpaine, Bridport DT6 6NE (01297 560451). Working farm. Sleeps 6/7. Immerse yourself in rural tranquillity. Set in an area of outstanding natural beauty, Wootton Fitzpaine nestles amidst rolling Dorset farmland. Within walking distance of the beaches and shops of Charmouth, world famous for its fossils, and three miles from the renowned Cobb at Lyme Regis. Golf, water sports and riding close by. We have two spacious, comfortable, well-furnished three-bedroomed cottages with open fires, inglenooks, heating and all amenities. Also large secluded, secure gardens with furniture, barbecues, parking. Open all year. Pets and children welcome. Logs and linen available. Guests are welcome to walk our farm. Terms from £170 to £565 per week, winter breaks available. **ETC ★★★**

e-mail: wfcottages@aol.com **website: www.lymeregis.com/westover-farm-cottages**

Visits & Attractions

Sherborne Castle, Sherborne, Dorset • 01935 813182
website: www.sherbornecastle.com

Built by Sir Walter Raleigh in 1594 and home to the Digby family since the early 17th century. Splendid collection of art, furniture and porcelain.

Abbotsbury Swannery, Near Bridport, Dorset • 01305 871858

Up to 600 free-flying swans – help feed them twice daily. Baby swans hatch May/June. AV show, coffee shop and gift shop.

Terms quoted in this publication may be subject to increase if rises in costs necessitate

LANCOMBES HOUSE HOLIDAY COTTAGES

Carol & Karl Mansfield
West Milton
Bridport DT6 3TN

Tel: 01308 485375

website:
www.lancombeshouse.co.uk

Lancombes House is a 200-year-old stone barn built 300 feet above sea level set in 10 acres; there are tame animals for children to play and help with including horses, ponies, goats and ducks. Farm has panoramic views to the sea only four miles away. There are four superbly converted cottages, each with its own sitting-out area, barbecue and garden furniture. They have spacious open plan living areas, most with wood burning stoves. Modern fitted kitchens, double and twin-bedded rooms. Electric central heating, shared laundry. Deep in the heart of Hardy country, this is a delightful area to explore whether on foot or horseback. There are many things to do and pets and children are very welcome. Prices start at £120 for mini-breaks; open all the year round.

★★★ SELF CATERING

SHERBORNE

Mrs J. Warr, Trill Cottages, Trill House, Thornford, Sherborne DT9 6HF (01935 872305). Two cottages situated in the Blackmore Vale only five miles from both Sherborne and Yeovil, and one mile from the villages of Yetminster and Thornford. Ideally placed for exploring the wonderful counties of Dorset and Somerset, where there is so much to see and do. The cottages are comfortably furnished, accommodation in each comprising three bedrooms (one double bed and four singles); lounge with colour TV and dining-room; well equipped kitchen with fridge and microwave; shower and toilet, and bathroom and toilet. Laundry room. A cot and high chair are available on request. Electricity by £1 slot meter. Storage heating. Quiet, peaceful and safe for children. We regret that we do not allow pets. Terms from £130 to £325 **ETC ★★★**
e-mail: trill.cottages@ic24.net

STURMINSTER NEWTON

Mrs Sheila Martin, Moorcourt Farm, Moorside, Marnhull, Sturminster Newton DT10 1HH (Tel & Fax: 01258 820271). Working farm. Sleeps four. Ground floor flat with own entrance and front door key. It is part of the farmhouse, kept immaculately clean and furnished to the highest order. We are a 117 acre dairy farm in the middle of the Blackmore Vale. Guests are welcome to wander round, watch the farm activities and laze in the large garden - we have some garden loungers for your use. We are very central for touring with easy access to New Forest, Longleat Wildlife Park, Cheddar, Stonehenge and the lovely Dorset coast. Accommodation for four people in two double bedrooms, one with a double bed, the other with twin beds. Bathroom, separate toilet. Sittingroom with colour TV and door leading straight onto the back garden. Well equipped kitchen/diner, with fridge/freezer, microwave and washing machine; all utensils colour co-ordinated, matching crockery, etc. Beds made up with fresh linen on arrival. Towels, tea towels, etc provided. Electric heaters in all rooms. Electricity payable by meter, units to be read at the start and finish of your holiday. Sheila creates a friendly atmosphere here "down on the farm" and does her best to make your holiday an enjoyable one. Open April to November. Car essential. Sorry, no pets. Weekly terms from £190 to £295. SAE please.

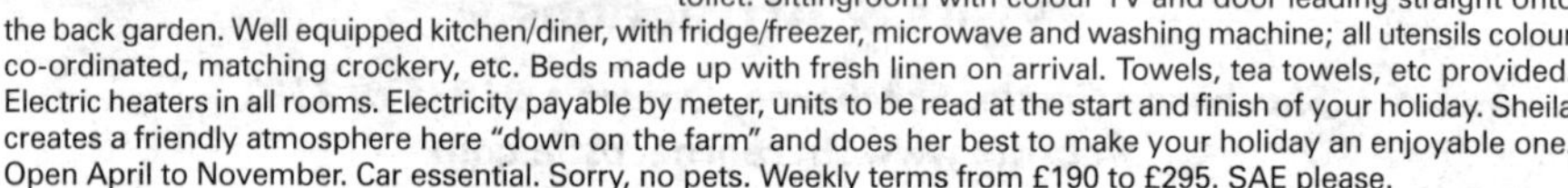

WAREHAM (near)

Mrs M. J. M. Constantinides, "Woodlands", Hyde, Near Wareham BH20 7NT (01929 471239). Secluded house, formerly Dower-House of Hyde Estate, stands alone on a meadow of the River Piddle in four-and-a-half acres in the midst of "Hardy Country". THE MAISONETTE comprises upstairs lounge with colour TV; one bedroom (two single beds); downstairs large kitchen/diner, small entrance hall, bathroom; electric cooker, refrigerator. Independent side entrance. Extra bedroom (two single beds) on request at £35 per week. Visitors are welcome to use house grounds; children can fish or play in the boundary stream. Pleasant walks in woods and heath nearby. Golf course half-a-mile, pony trekking/riding nearby. All linen included, beds ready made and basic shopping arranged on arrival day. Ideal for a quiet holiday far from the madding crowd. Cot and high chair available and children welcome to bring their pets. SAE, please, for terms and further particulars.

Terms quoted in this publication may be subject to increase if rises in costs necessitate

DURHAM

See also Colour Display Advertisement

BARNARD CASTLE

East Briscoe Farm Cottages, Baldersdale, Barnard Castle DL12 9UL (01833 650087; Fax: 01833 650027). Winner of the Northumbria Tourist Board Self-Catering of the Year 1999. In a beautiful situation central to the north of England. The six stone built cottages, sleeping two to six, offer superb accommodation on a stunning riverside estate, which offers walks and fishing. A place to relax and explore the North. Terms from £120. Open all year. Pets welcome in two of the cottages. Contact: **Ann and Peter Wilson. ETC ★★★★**, *FARM STAY UK MEMBER.*
e-mail: peter@eastbriscoe.co.uk
website: www.eastbriscoe.co.uk

See also Colour Display Advertisement

CONSETT

The Cottage and Dairy Cottage. Three adjoining self-contained units, two comprising one double and one twin bedroom, kitchen, bathroom and comfortable living area. The third has a double bedroom plus a studio couch in the living area. Colour TV, private garden and patio furniture, heating and linen are all included in the price. We are a working sheep farm just north of the village of Castleside on the A68 heading towards Corbridge and offer easy access to the Roman Wall, Durham City, the Metro Centre, Beamish Museum and lots more. Pass the Fleece Inn Pub on the north side of the village, take a left turn after a short distance, left again down a very steep hill, the road is signposted 'Derwent Grange', follow this and we are the farm on the right. Terms from £175 to £200 Low Season, from £200 to £250 High Season. **ETC ★★/★★★**. Please contact for further information: **Kay Elliot, Derwent Grange Farm, Castleside, Consett DH8 9BN (01207 508358).**
e-mail: ekelliot@aol.com

LANCHESTER

Mrs Ann Darlington, Browney Cottage, Hall Hill Farm, Lanchester, Durham DH7 0TA (01207 521476; Tel & Fax: 01388 730300). Two country cottages. Well equipped and comfortable. Both cottages have one double and one twin room - sleeps up to four people. Downstairs is a livingroom and large kitchen/diningroom, upstairs two bedrooms and bathroom. Kitchen contains washing machine/tumble dryer, microwave and fridge/freezer. Linen and towels are provided. Both cottages are heated. The cottages are in an ideal location for Durham City and Beamish Museum. You will have a free pass for the week to visit our own open farm. Prices from £160 per week. Children welcome. Sorry no pets. Please write or telephone for brochure. **ETC ★★★**
e-mail: hhf@freenetname.co.uk
website: www.hallhillfarm.co.uk

MIDDLETON-IN-TEESDALE

Mrs Scott, Westfield Cottage, Laithkirk, Middleton-in-Teesdale, Barnard Castle DL12 0PN (01833 640942; Fax: 01833 640560). Sleeps 6. Westfield Cottage is a Grade II Listed building very recently renovated and furnished to a high standard. Situated on a working farm in beautiful Teesdale which is excellent touring, cycling and walking country with the Pennine and Teesdale Ways close by. The Cumbrian border is about six miles away. Ample parking area; free fishing. About half a mile from the local village. Open all year. From £185-£380. **ETC ★★★★**

GLOUCESTERSHIRE

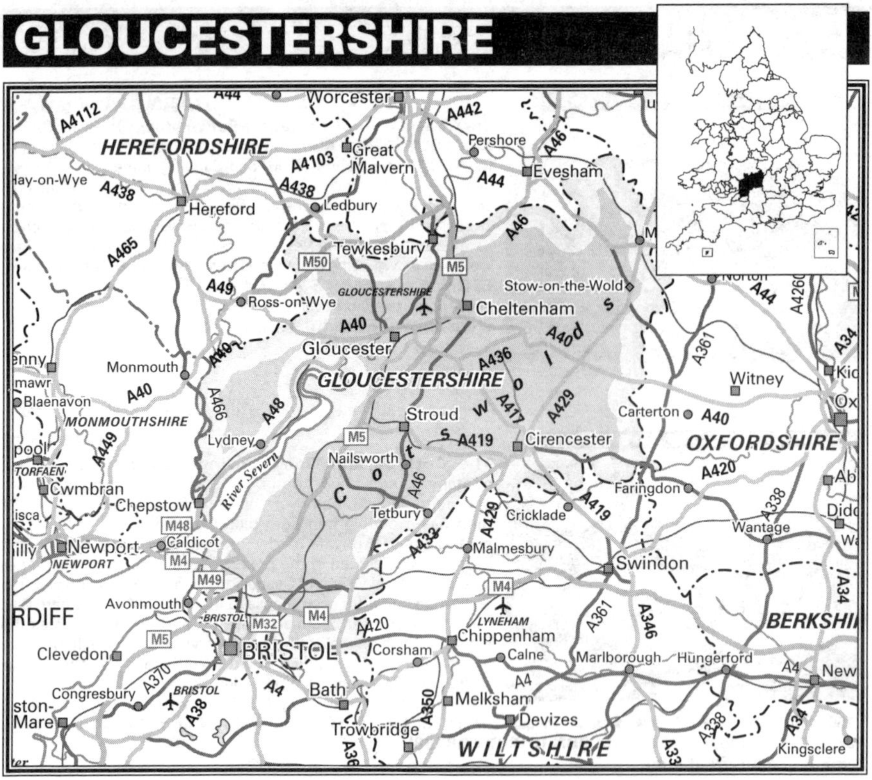

CHELTENHAM

Mr & Mrs J. Close, Coxhorne Farm, London Road, Charlton Kings, Cheltenham, Gloucestershire GL52 6UY (01242 236599). Cosy, well-equipped. Non-smoking. Self-contained apartment with open aspects, attached to the farmhouse of a 100 acre livestock farm. Situated on the eastern outskirts of Cheltenham, on the edge of the Cotswold Escarpment. Comfortably furnished, with full central heating, payphone and plenty of parking space. Electricity and bed linen included in rental. Ideal position for visiting the lovely Regency town of Cheltenham and the mellow villages of the Cotswolds. Sorry, no pets allowed. Terms £140 to £200 per week. **ETC ★★★**

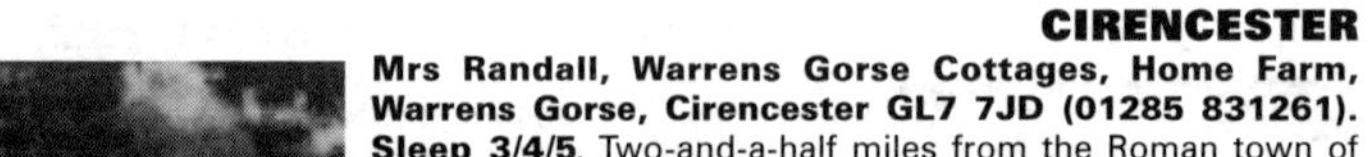

CIRENCESTER

Mrs Randall, Warrens Gorse Cottages, Home Farm, Warrens Gorse, Cirencester GL7 7JD (01285 831261). Sleep 3/4/5. Two-and-a-half miles from the Roman town of Cirencester, these attractive cottages, personally attended by the owners, are ideally situated for touring the Cotswolds, Lying near the farmhouse in a hamlet surrounded by fields on the 100 acre farm of cattle and sheep, the cottages, each with its own garden, are well equipped and comfortably furnished. Easy parking, golf club and water sports nearby. From £160 to £220. Open April to October. **ETC ★★**

DURSLEY

"Two Springbank", 37 Hopton Road, Upper Cam GL11 5PD. Sleeps 4 plus cot. Fully restored mid-terraced cottage in pleasant village opposite 14th century church with open fields to rear and about one mile from Dursley, where the amenities include a swimming pool and sports centre. Superb base for Cotswold Way, touring the Severn Vale and Forest of Dean. Close to Slimbridge Wildfowl Trust, Berkeley Castle and Westonbirt Arboretum, and within easy reach of Gloucester, Bristol, Bath and Cirencester. The ground floor accommodation comprises comfortable sitting room with TV/video and electric fire, dining area with multi-fuel stove and fitted kitchen with fridge/freezer, electric cooker and microwave. A utility room with washing machine gives access to a rear lawn. On the first floor are two bedrooms (one double, one twin) and a bathroom. There are fitted stairgates. Linen and towels included, also cot and high-chair if required. Sorry, no pets or smoking. Electricity, including night storage heaters, charged extra by meter readings. Rates from £132 to £219 per week. Off-peak breaks (three nights) £85 – £125. **ETC ★★★. Mrs F.A. Jones, Everlands, Cam, Dursley GL11 5NL (01453 543047).**

See also Colour Display Advertisement

STROUD

The Old Coach House, Edgecombe House, Toadsmoor Road, Brinscombe, Stroud GL5 2UE (01453 883147). Attention All Dog Lovers! Romantic 18th century cottage in the heart of the beautiful Cotswold Hills. Two double bedrooms, beams, wood-burners, outdoor heated swimming pool, patio heater and all year round, bubbling Hot Tub. Small enclosed garden plus a further 20 acres of woodland. Two dogs in the cottage, but a spacious private kennel will accommodate loads more for free! Weekends from £108 and four-night mid-week breaks from £102. Full weeks £183 – £542. Second cottage available for larger family groups or available separately from £92pw – £286. Colour brochure from Ros Smith.

HAMPSHIRE

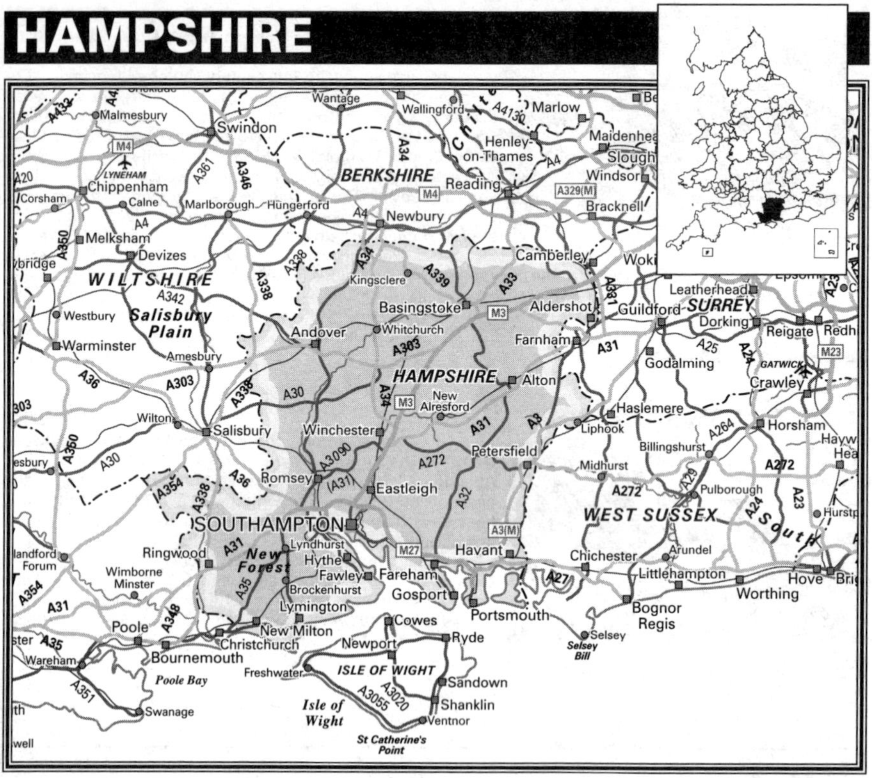

LYNDHURST

Penny Farthing Hotel, Romsey Road, Lyndhurst SO43 7AA (02380 284422; Fax: 02380 284488). We have some neighbouring cottages available as hotel annexe rooms or on a self-catering basis. These have been totally refitted, much with "Laura Ashley" and offer quieter, more exclusive accommodation. The Penny Farthing is a cheerful small Hotel ideally situated in Lyndhurst village centre, the capital of the "New Forest". The hotel offers en suite single, double, twin and family rooms with direct dial telephones, tea/coffee tray, colour TV and clock radios. The hotel has a licensed bar, private car park and bicycle store. Lyndhurst has a charming variety of shops, restaurants, pubs and bistros and the "New Forest Information Centre and Museum". **ETC ★★★**

website: www.pennyfarthinghotel.co.uk

Visits & Attractions

Marwell, Near Winchester, Hants

07626 943163 • website: www.marwell.org.uk

World famous for its dedication to the conservation of endangered species.

Nearly 1000 animals in acres of beautiful parkland.

When making enquiries or bookings, a stamped addressed envelope is always appreciated

HEREFORDSHIRE

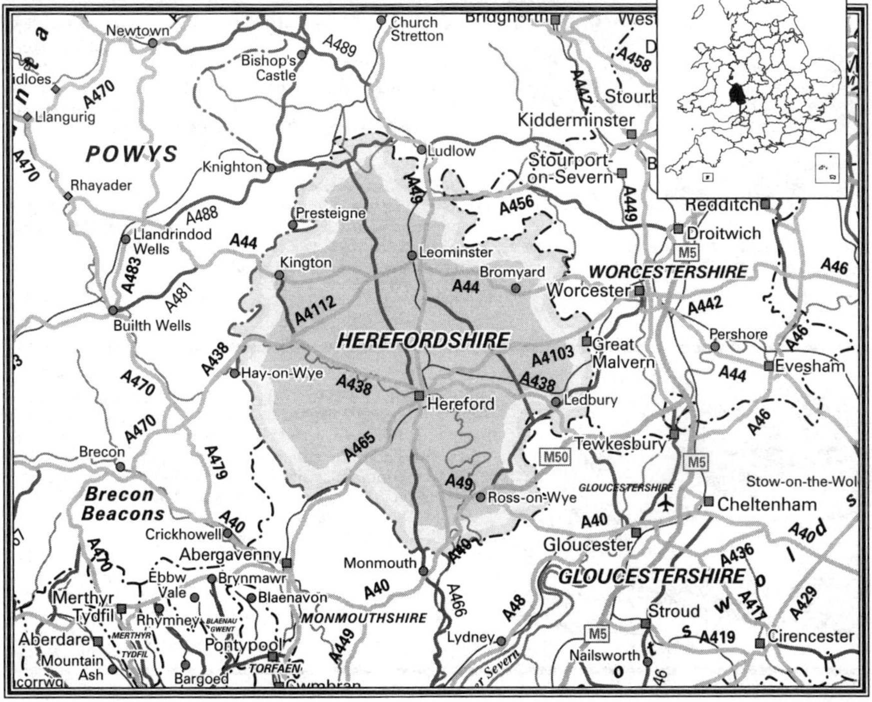

See also Colour Display Advertisement

FELTON

Marjorie and Brian Roby, Felton House, Felton, Herefordshire HR1 3PH (Tel & Fax: 01432 820366). The Lodge is a spotlessly clean, cosy, restful cottage in the beautiful grounds of Felton House, the former rectory, just off A417 between Hereford, Leominster and Bromyard. The Lodge has been restored to its Victorian character but with the convenience of electric heating, a modern kitchen, two shower rooms, a diningroom and a sittingroom with TV. Guests are accommodated in one double, one twin and one single bedroom and a cot is available. Linen may be hired. Children, and pets with responsible owners are most welcome. Private parking, patio and garden. Weekly terms £150 to £275 exclusive of electricity. Brochure available.
websites: www.SmoothHound.co.uk/hotels/felton.html www.herefordshirebandb.co.uk

50p reduction on entry fee at

Cider Museum and King Offa Distillery

See our READERS' OFFER VOUCHER for details.

The FHG Directory of Website Addresses

on pages 349–378 is a useful quick reference guide for holiday accommodation with e-mail and/or website details

See also Colour Display Advertisement

GOODRICH

Mainoaks Farm Cottages, Goodrich, Ross-on-Wye. Six units sleeping 2,4,6 & 7. Mainoaks is a 15th century Listed farm which has been converted to form six cottages of different size and individual character. It is set in 80 acres of pasture and woodland beside the River Wye in an area of outstanding natural beauty and an SSSI where there is an abundance of wildlife. All cottages have exposed beams, pine furniture, heating throughout, fully equipped kitchens with microwaves, washer/dryer etc., colour TV. Private gardens, barbecue area and ample parking. Linen and towels provided. An ideal base for touring the local area with beautiful walks, fishing, canoeing, pony trekking, golf, bird-watching or just relaxing in this beautiful tranquil spot. Open throughout the year. Short breaks available. Pets by arrangement. Brochure on request. **ETC ★★★/★★★★. Mrs P. Unwin, Hill House, Chase End, Bromsberrow, Ledbury, Herefordshire HR8 1SE (01531 650448).**
e-mail: mainoaks@lineone.net **website: www.mainoaks.co.uk**

HEREFORD

Mrs S. Dixon, Swayns Diggins, Harewood End, Hereford HR2 8JU (01989 730358). This highly recommended small first floor flat is completely self-contained at one end of the main house. The bedroom, sitting room and private balcony all face south with panoramic views over farmland towards Ross and Symonds Yat. The well-equipped kitchen overlooks the garden with grand views towards Orcop Hill and the Black Mountains. Open all year, rental from £130 to £140 per week includes electricity, linen, heating, colour TV. Ideal base for exploring the beautiful Wye Valley, Herefordshire, Gloucestershire and the historic Welsh Marches. There is much to see and do in the area. Write or phone for further particulars.

HEREFORD

Carey Dene and Rock House, Hereford. Sleeps 4/8 + cot. Working farm. Two oak-beamed cottages on traditional farm overlooking River Wye. Beautiful area between Hereford and Ross-on-Wye, for a peaceful holiday or a short break. Access to the river, two minutes' walk to pub serving meals. Washing machine, microwave, colour TV, central heating. Electricity and linen included in charge. Open all year. Pets and children welcome. Non-smoking. Prices from £200 to £450. Please contact: **Mrs Milly Slater, Ruxton Farm, Kings Caple, Hereford HR1 4TX (Tel & Fax: 01432 840493).**
e-mail: milly@ruxton.co.uk
website: www.wyevalleycottages.com

LEOMINSTER

Mrs E. Thomas, Woonton Court Farm, Leysters, Leominster HR6 0HL (Tel & Fax: 01568 750232) Enjoy traditional hospitality and experience authentic country life at our working family farm. The Mill House Flat, a comfortably converted former cider house, provides the freedom of self-catering for up to five guests. (We also offer Bed and Breakfast in our Tudor farmhouse). The flat's master bedroom has one large double bed and one single, with washbasin, and the second bedroom has twin beds (suitable for one adult or two children) with adjacent bathroom. The characterful sittingroom has a television and a kitchen area with all facilities. Central heating, linen and electricity included. Laundry, cot, highchair, babysitting and groceries available. Patio garden and ample parking. We welcome you walking the farm (strong footwear advised); observe the animals; enjoy free-range eggs and local produce; and appreciate the peace and tranquillity of the local scenery. Terms from £180 to £260 per week. Brochure on request. **ETC ★★★**

LEOMINSTER

Nicholson Farm Holidays. Self-catering properties on a working dairy farm. Beautiful views. Wide choice of restaurants and bar meals in the area. Supermarket 10 minutes. Excellent walking, golf, riding, carp fishing available on the farm, swimming and tennis 10 minutes. Dogs are welcome but must not remain in during the owner's absence. Non- smoking. Contact: **Mrs J. Brooke, Brimstone Cottage, Docklow, Leominster HR6 0SL (01568 760346).**

SYMONDS YAT

Mrs J. Rudge, Hilltop, Llangrove, Near Ross-on-Wye (01600 890279). Sleeps 4. Chalet bungalow with magnificent views over surrounding countryside. One mile off A40 dual carriageway and within easy reach of Forest of Dean, Monmouth and Black Mountains. The chalet stands in the gardens of a seven-acre smallholding, enjoying peace and quiet, yet close to local shops, public houses and the local attractions. Livingroom with TV. Kitchen and bathroom with all amenities. Two bedrooms, one with two single beds and one with double bed. Patio, sun lounge, garden. Children welcome. No pets. Accommodation particularly suitable for the elderly. No linen supplied. £1 meter. Terms from £175 to £225. SAE, please.

ISLE OF WIGHT

ISLE OF WIGHT

Island Cottage Holidays. Sleep 1/14. Charming individual cottages in lovely rural surroundings and close to the sea. Over 45 cottages situated throughout the Isle of Wight. Beautiful views, attractive gardens, delightful country walks. All equipped to a high standard and graded for quality by the Tourist Board. Terms from £132 to £1195 per week. Short breaks available in low season from £89 to £395 (three nights). For a brochure please contact: **Mrs Honor Vass, The Old Vicarage, Kingston, Wareham, Dorset BH20 5LH (01929 480080; Fax: 01929 481070). ETC ★★★/★★★★★**
e-mail: enq@islandcottageholidays.com
website: www.islandcottageholidays.com

ISLE OF WIGHT

SEE ALSO FULL PAGE COLOUR DISPLAY AND HALF PAGE DISPLAY IN BOARD SECTION FOR THE ISLE OF WIGHT FARM AND COUNTRY HOLIDAY GROUP.

TOTLAND BAY

3 Seaview Cottages, Broadway, Totland Bay. Sleeps 5. This well-modernised cosy old coastguard cottage holds the Farm Holiday Guide Diploma for the highest standard of accommodation. It is warm and popular throughout the year. Four day winter break from £42; a week in summer £250. Located close to two beaches in beautiful walking country near mainland links. It comprises lounge/dinette/ kitchenette; two bedrooms (sleeping five); bathroom/toilet. Well furnished, fully heated, TV, selection of books and other considerations. Another cottage is also available at Cowes, Isle of Wight. Non-smokers only. **Mrs C. Pitts, 11 York Avenue, New Milton, Hampshire BH25 6BT (01425 615215).**

KENT

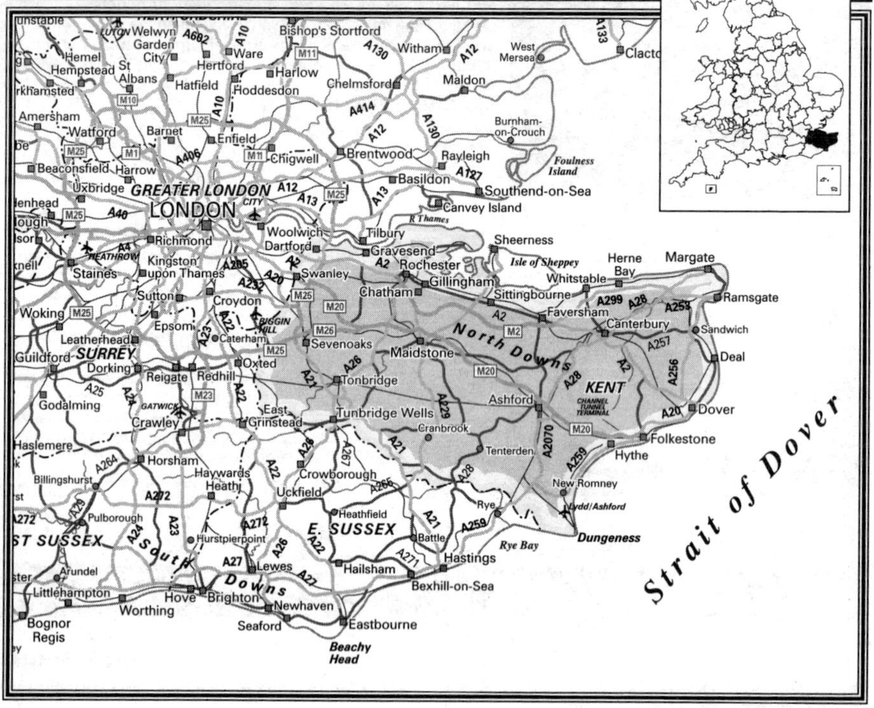

GOUDHURST

Marion Fuller, Three Chimneys Farm Holiday Cottages, Bedgebury Road, Goudhurst TN17 2RA (Tel & Fax: 01580 212175). Set on top of a hill at the end of a one-mile track, on the edge of Bedgebury Forest, Three Chimneys is a haven of tranquillity, yet only an hour from London. The five cottages (and two Bed and Breakfast rooms) are individually and tastefully furnished. The cottages are well equipped and all bed linen is included. Central heating; telephone. There is a tennis court and the forest is perfect for visitors who like to walk or cycle. Goudhurst is centrally placed for visiting the castles and gardens of the South East. **ETC ★★★★**, *KENT TOURISM ALLIANCE AWARD FOR EXCELLENCE 2002/2003.*

e-mail: marionfuller@threechimneysfarm.co.uk

website: www.threechimneysfarm.co.uk

ULCOMBE

Apple Pye Cottage. Welcome to this self-catering cottage situated next to our farmhouse Bed and Breakfast, surrounded by 45 acres of beautiful countryside in the centre of Kent, yet only ten minutes' drive from M20 junction 8. An ideal location for visiting Leeds Castle, Sissinghurst and Canterbury. Channel ports only 45 minutes, and only one hour 15 minutes train ride to London. The cottage sleeps four comfortably. It has a double en suite with shower room, suitable for a wheel chair user, a twin bedroom with shower room. Kitchen/dining/ living room with TV, microwave, electric cooker, washer/dryer, fridge. Outside there is a large patio with barbecue. Ample parking next to cottage. Full central heating and linen included. Sorry no smoking or pets. Terms from £228 to £360. Open all year except Christmas and New Year. **ETC ★★★★** *DISABLED CATEGORY 2.* Contact: **Mrs Diane Leat, Bramley Knowle Farm, Eastwood Road, Ulcombe, Maidstone ME17 1ET (01622 858878; Fax: 01622 851121).**

e-mail: diane@bramleyknowlefarm.co.uk **website: www.bramleyknowlefarm.co.uk**

LANCASHIRE

See also Colour Display Advertisement

CLITHEROE

Rakefoot Farm, Chaigley, Near Clitheroe BB7 3LY (Chipping 01995 61332; mobile: 07889 279063; Fax: 01995 61296). Family farm peacefully situated in the beautiful countryside of the Ribble Valley in the Forest of Bowland, with panoramic views. Ideally placed for touring Coast, Dales and Lakes. Eight miles from M6 Junction 31a. Superb walks, golf and horse riding nearby, or visit pretty villages and factory shops. Warm welcome whether on holiday or business, refreshments on arrival. Bed and Breakfast or Self Catering in 17th century farmhouse and traditional stone barn conversion. Wood-burning stoves, central heating, exposed beams and stonework. Most bedrooms en suite, some ground floor. Excellent home-cooked meals, laundry; pubs/restaurants nearby. Indoor/outdoor play areas, garden and patios. Dogs by arrangement. Bed and Breakfast £17.50 to £25.00 sharing double/twin room; some rooms available with own lounge. Four self-catering properties, three can be internally interlinked. £80 to £507 per property per week. Short breaks available. **ETC ◆◆◆◆** *GUEST ACCOMMODATION*; **ETC ★★★/ ★★★★** *SELF-CATERING. NWTB SILVER AWARD FOR SELF CATERING HOLIDAY OF THE YEAR 2000.*

e-mail: info@rakefootfarm.co.uk **website: www.rakefootfarm.co.uk**

Visits & Attractions

National Football Museum, Preston, Lancashire • 01772 908442

www.nationalfootballmuseum.com

The story of the world's greatest game. In two distinctive halves, it can be enjoyed by supporters of all ages. Shop and restaurant.

See also Colour Display Advertisement

CLITHEROE (near)

Mrs Lund, Spring Head Farm Cottages, Hellifield Road, Bolton-by-Bowland, Near Clitheroe BB7 4LU (01200 447245). Sleep 4-8. Three charming cosy, comfortable cottages in the beautiful Ribble Valley. Furnished to a very high standard. Enjoy the bird song and peace of the countryside. Views to Pendle Hill. Ideal base for visiting Yorkshire Dales, Lake District, West Coast and many market towns. Ground floor of Mallard suitable for wheelchair users. Rates from £180 - £475. Brochure available. **ETC ★★★★**

See also Colour Display Advertisement

HIGH BENTHAM

Woodside & Parkside, High Bentham, Lancaster LA2 7BN. Sleep 6-14. Large stone barn converted into two properties with interconnecting doors so that they can be let separately for 6-8 or let together to accommodate 14. Mainly en suite bathrooms. Parkside has a ground floor bedroom and bathroom. Set in beautiful countryside yet within walking distance of the market town. Pets welcome. Rates from £200. Open all year. Colour brochure available. **ETC ★★★★**, *FARM STAY UK MEMBER*. Contact: **Thomas & Jane Marshall, Knowe Top, Low Bentham Road, Bentham, Lancaster LA2 7BN (Tel & Fax: 015242 62163).**
website: www.riversidecaravanpark.co.uk

LUNE VALLEY

Barbara Mason, Oxenforth Green, Tatham, Lancaster LA2 8PL (015242 61784). Working farm, join in. Sleeps 4 plus cot. Cottage and static caravan on working farm with panoramic views of Ingleborough and surrounding hills. Central for Lakes, dales and coast. Good walking, fishing and horse-riding nearby. Guests are welcome to watch the day-to-day workings of the farm. Our cottage sleeps four in one double and one twin room with lounge, fitted kitchen, ground and first floor shower rooms. The caravan sleeps four in one double and two twin beds, with washbasin, shower, flushing toilet, colour TV. Garden and garden chairs available. Children welcome. One dog welcome.Three-quarters-of-a-mile to nearest pub. Prices from £200 to £270 per week. Caravan from £150 per week.

SOUTHPORT

Mr W.H. Core, Sandybrook Farm, 52 Wyke Cop Road, Scarisbrick, Southport PR8 5LR (Tel & Fax: 01704 880337). Welcome to our small arable farm and 18th century Barn, which has been converted into five superbly equipped holiday apartments. Many of the Barn's original features have been retained and it is furnished in traditional style but also offers all modern amenities. The Barn is situated three-and-a-half miles from the seaside town of Southport and five miles from the historic town of Ormskirk with lots of places to visit in the surrounding area. Families are welcome and cot and high chairs are available. One apartment equipped for wheelchair/disabled guests. Central heating, bed linen and towels are provided free of charge. **ETC ★★★**
e-mail: sandybrookfarm@lycos.co.uk

LEICESTERSHIRE

MOUNTSORREL

Marilyn Duffin, Stonehurst, Bond Lane, Mountsorrel LE12 7AR (01509 413216). This comfortable, modern, well-equipped family house with five bedrooms, a private garden and barbecue, is attached to Stonehurst Family Farm and Museum, to which free admission is given during stay. Teashop and restaurant on farm. All amenities in the village. The farm is 12 minutes from M1 J21A. Open all year. Children and pets welcome. Terms from £225 34£350.

LINCOLNSHIRE

See also Colour Display Advertisement

ALFORD

Rose Cottage, Claythorpe, Alford. A small, old, shepherd's cottage set in farmland a quarter of a mile from the road. The cottage consists of a large living room, small adjoining kitchen with electric cooker, fridge-freezer and microwave, spare room with single bed, bathroom with toilet, washing machine and shower over bath, all on the ground floor. Three bedrooms upstairs - one double and two singles. Gas fired central heating and electricity inclusive. There are several attractive short walks nearby, and the country lanes are ideal for cyclists. Skegness, Cleethorpes, Sutton-on-Sea and Mablethorpe all easily accessible, with the little market towns of Louth, Alford and Horncastle not far away. Village shop and pub four miles. No smoking. Parking available. Short Breaks available from £95. Terms from £175 to £245 weekly. Contact: **Mrs D. Stovin, Aby Grange, Aby, Alford LN13 0DG (01507 450367).**
e-mail: danddstovin@amserve.net

ALFORD (near)

Manor Farm Cottage. Comfortable cottage in rural countryside, midway between the coast and Lincolnshire Wolds. Well equipped including colour TV, washing machine, microwave and freezer. Rose garden including picnic table. Suitable area for pets to exercise. Pets and children welcome. Ample parking space. For further details please contact: **Mrs E.M. Farrow, Manor Farm, Strubby, Alford LN13 0LW (01507 450228). ETC ★★**

See also Colour Display Advertisement

ALFORD (near)

Mrs Stubbs, Woodthorpe Hall Country Cottages, Near Alford LN13 0DD (01507 450294; Fax: 01507 450885). Very well appointed luxury one and three bedroomed cottages, overlooking the golf course, all with central heating, colour TV, microwave, washer, dryer, dishwasher and fridge freezer. Woodthorpe is situated approximately six miles from the coastal resort of Mablethorpe and offers easy access to the picturesque Lincolnshire Wolds. Adjacent facilities include golf, fishing, garden centre, aquatic centre, snooker, pool and restaurant with bar and family room. **ETC ★★★★**
e-mail: enquiries@woodthorpehall.com
website: www.woodthorpehall.com

GRANTHAM

Mr & Mrs C.J. Grindal, Old Moat Barn, Lobthorpe, Grantham NG33 5LS (01476 860350; Fax: 01476 861724). Sleeps 6. Delightful barn conversion in a rural location, convenient for A1. The accommodation comprises an oak-beamed lounge, three bedrooms and fitted kitchen; central heating. There is a lawned garden with patio; ample parking. Stamford nine miles, Lincoln 25 miles, Oakham and Rutland Water nearby. Short Breaks available October to March, please ring for details. Children welcome. Non-smoking. Terms from £200 to £400 per week.

LOUTH

Shepherd's Cottage, Louth. Fall in love with the experience of staying in our charming 16th century self-catering cottage, situated in the grounds of Grimblethorpe Hall, in the heart of the Lincolnshire Wolds. Recently restored with original beams and stonework with a very spacious bedroom, lounge and kitchen/dining area. Facilities include cooker, microwave, fridge/freezer, washer/dryer, linen and bedding, towels and cloths, full central heating, television, video, garage and board games. Electricity inclusive. Fabulous walking and cycling routes nearby, including the Viking Way, and visitors may use the private trout lake. An optional evening meal can be waiting for you on your arrival and occasional picnic hampers are available. Prices from £150 per week; Short Breaks from £95.Contact: **Annie and Robert Codling, Grimblethorpe Hall, Grimblethorpe, Near Louth LN11 0RB (01507 313671/313440; Fax: 01507 313854).**
e-mail: enquiries@ShepherdsHolidayCottage.co.uk
website: www.ShepherdsHolidayCottage.co.uk

See also Colour Display Advertisement

MARKET RASEN

Mrs Julia Merivale, The Gables, Hatton Hall, Hatton, Market Rasen LN8 5QG (01673 858862; mobile: 07702 271041/07801 282529). Beautiful old red brick and pantile barn conversion with gardens and stables. Tastefully decorated with modern facilities and overlooking open countryside. Both cottages are spacious, with fully fitted kitchens, lounge/dining rooms with colour TV and video. Bicycles available for hire. Babysitting and evening meals by arrangement. Terms: £175 to £350 per week. 3-night short breaks available all year. No.1: April-Sep £120, Oct-Mar £100. No.2: April-Sep £200, Oct-Mar £180. **ETC ★★★★★**
e-mail: jmerivale@aol.com
website: www.thegables-hatton.co.uk

See also Colour Display Advertisement

SKEGNESS

The Chestnuts Farm & Country Cottages, Wainfleet Road, Burgh Le Marsh PE24 5AH (Tel & Fax: 01754 810904). 'Farm, Fishing, Friendly and Fun'. Two, three and four bedroom cottages on a real farm situated on the edge of the village of Burgh le Marsh, only five miles from Skegness, yet ideal for a quiet, rural holiday. Children's play area, farm animals - horses, pigs, calves, chickens etc. Cottages have their own private fishing waters. Tennis court, plenty of space, ample parking and gardens. Full colour brochure available. Short Breaks out of season from as little as £70. Please telephone for our current price list. **ETC ★★★**. Contact: **Mrs J Mackinder**.
e-mail: macka@freenetname.co.uk
website: www.thechestnutsfarm.co.uk

Readers are requested to mention this guidebook when seeking accommodation (and please enclose a stamped addressed envelope).

SKEGNESS

Mr and Mrs K. Bennett, Field Farm, Station Road, Burgh-Le-Marsh PE24 5ES (Tel & Fax: 01754 810372). Self-contained one bedroom farmhouse flat on working farm, sleeps two to four, with sofa bed in living area. Fully equipped, fridge freezer, electric cooker, shower room, storage heaters for winter. Features include attractive beams, electric fire, patio doors into large entrance porch. Static caravan sleeps four/six available March to October, fully equipped with fridge, gas cooker, shower, etc. The farm is 250 yards from the A158, with ample safe parking. Conveniently situated between the coast/ Fantasy Island (six miles) and attractive Wolds with its many interesting small towns and "Bomber" country. Abundant fishing lakes. Good migratory bird-watching nine miles. B&B available next door. Terms from £160 to £220 per week. Non-smokers only please. No pets.

SPALDING

The Barn. This attractive converted and refurbished barn is situated in the owners' large water fowl gardens in an area of outstanding beauty six miles from Spalding with its exceptional garden centres, and approximately 30 miles from the coast. Within one mile of local village centre with excellent restaurants and pubs. The accommodation consists of one double bedroom with additional single bed, one twin with additional single, spacious lounge and dining room, fully equipped modern kitchen with cooker, fridge, microwave and washing machine. Central heating throughout. Barbecue and patio furniture. Dog and children welcome, cot available. Bed linen provided. Ample parking. Convenient for people with disabilities. Terms from £50 per night, £200 per week. Contact: **Mr & Mrs A.J. Smith, 110 Quadring Road, Donnington, Spalding PE11 4SJ (01775 821242).**

See also Colour Display Advertisement

STAMFORD

Mrs Harrison-Smith, Midstone Farm House, Midstone, Southorpe, Stamford PE9 3BX (01780 740136). Enjoy a relaxing break in this delightful farmhouse situated in a quiet village close to Stamford and Peterborough. Centrally heated with all modern facilities whilst retaining original features. Close to a nature reserve with many wild flowers and butterflies. Wonderful country views and pleasant gardens. Ideal location for exploring Lincolnshire, Cambridgeshire and Norfolk. Stabling available, golf nearby and cycling. We can arrange a holiday itinerary for you. Brochure on request.
e-mail: midstonehouse@yahoo.co.uk
website: www.SmoothHound.co.uk/stamford

Visits & Attractions

Natureland Seal Sanctuary, Skegness, Lincolnshire • 01754 764345

Famous for its work with abandoned baby seal pups, this conservation centre has aquaria, butterflies, pets' comer. A highlight is feeding time for the seals and penguins.

One FREE child with one full-paying adult at
Butterfly & Wildlife Park
See our READERS' OFFER VOUCHER for details.

When making enquiries or bookings, a stamped addressed envelope is always appreciated

NORFOLK

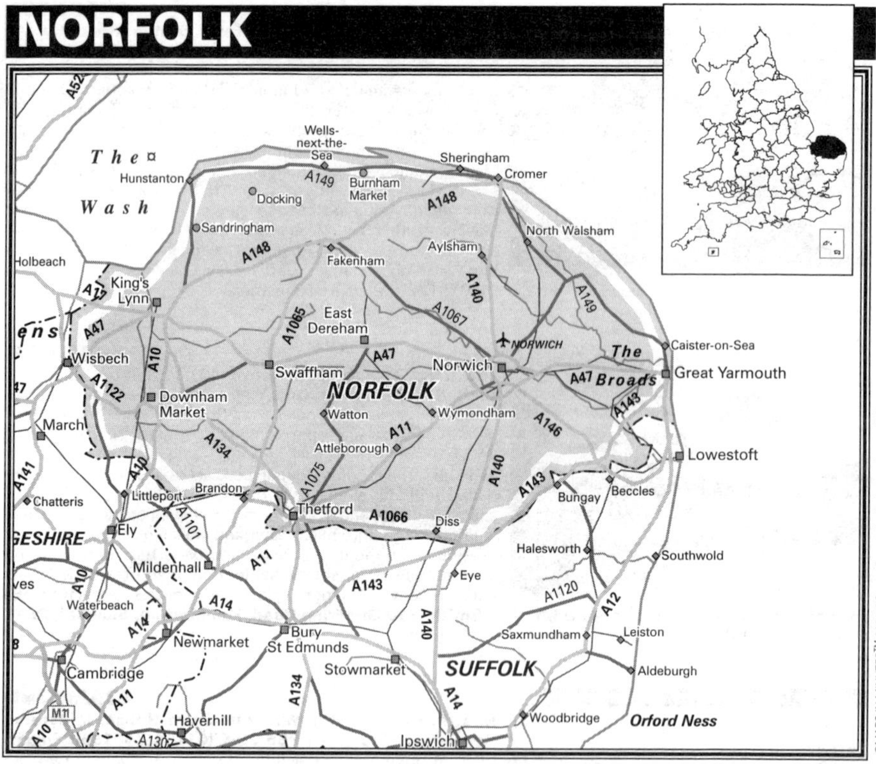

AYLSHAM

The Old Windmill, Cawston Road, Aylsham. Sleeps up to 8. This 19th century cornmill has been renovated by the owners to provide luxurious accommodation for up to eight. One double bedroom with en suite bathroom, further double and twin with shared en suite shower room. Sofa bed is available in lounge. Fully equipped kitchen. Separate utility and cloakroom. Private patio garden and ample parking. The Mill is on the outskirts of the historic market town of Aylsham which is centrally situated for The Broads, the coast and Norwich. Easy access to good pubs and restaurants, beautiful countryside, footpaths and cycle rides. Terms £200 to £750 per week fully inclusive. Regret no pets or smoking. B&B also available in owners' adjoining house. **ETC ★★★★★**. Contact: **Janet and Tim Bower, Old Mill House, Cawston Road, Aylsham NR11 6NB (Tel & Fax: 01263 732118). e-mail: timatmill@aol.com**

BLAKENEY

4 Mariners Hill, Blakeney & Starlings, 82 High Street, Blakeney. Properties sleep 7/6. All year round, house and cottage available to visitors hoping for a holiday that combines true relaxation, comfortable accommodation and splendid scenery. MARINERS HILL is a flint/brick-built house sleeping seven, with spectacular views over the quay and marsh. Small, secluded, walled garden. Well furnished and equipped. Colour TV, washing machine, dishwasher, microwave and fridge/freezer. STARLINGS is a pink-washed cottage with a part covered courtyard. With accommodation for six, it has TV and night storage heaters. Good dinghy sailing and birdwatching at hand, golf courses nearby. For further details please write to: **Mrs A. Suckling, 8 Home Farm, Letheringsett, Holt, Norfolk NR25 7JL (01263 712636).**

CLIPPESBY HALL

Clippesby, Great Yarmouth NR29 3BL

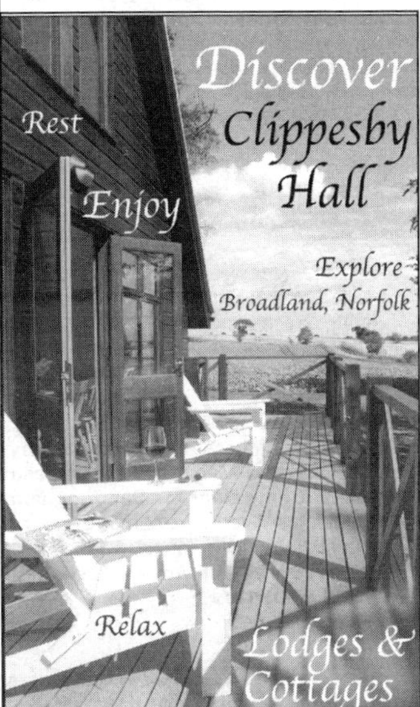

Discover
Clippesby
Hall
Rest
Enjoy
Explore
Broadland, Norfolk
Relax
Lodges &
Cottages

FOR A BROCHURE PLEASE CALL

Tel: 01493 367800

Fax: 01493 367809

e-mail: holidays@clippesby.com

web: www.clippesby.com

See also Colour Advertisement on Inside Front Cover

Parlours, Norwich

Comfortable, recently modernised Victorian house in Norwich city centre sleeping six. Walk to shops, restaurants, places of interest and recreation, ancient and modern. Accommodation comprises front parlour with TV and telephone, dining room, kitchen, utility room, shower room and wc. Upstairs there are two double and one twin bedroom and bath/shower/wc. Linen, heating and electricity included. Paved garden. Street parking. Sorry, no pets. Terms £420 to £560 per week.

Bookings to:

Susan & Derek Wright,
147 Earlham Road, Norwich NR2 3RG
Tel & Fax: 01603 454169
e-mail: earlhamgh@hotmail.com

Also available

Earlham Guest House

B & B from £25 to £80.

www.earlhamguesthouse.co.uk

FHG PUBLICATIONS

publish a large range of well-known accommodation guides. We will be happy to send you details or you can use the order form at the back of this book.

DISS

Walcot Green Farm Cottage. Ken and Nannette Catchpole welcome you to their family-run farm, set amid peaceful countryside close to the pleasant market town of Diss, an ideal base for exploring Norfolk and Suffolk. There are three bedrooms - one single, one single bunk room, and a family room with double and single bed. Linen and towels provided. Fully equipped kitchen and utility room with fridge/freezer, microwave, washing machine, tumble dryer and ironing facilities. Lounge has colour TV, video and music centre. Spacious lawned garden, patio with barbecue and garden furniture. Children welcome; cot, high chair and stair gates available. No pets and no smoking. Heated indoor swimming pool. Details from: **Mrs N. Catchpole, Walcot Green Farm, Diss IP22 3SU (Tel & Fax: 01379 652806).**

See also Colour Display Advertisement

MATTISHALL

The Old Mill. The Old Mill in the heart of Norfolk has been tastefully converted to provide peaceful holidays, away from the rush of modern living. Standing in the owners' delightful grounds, it has one round Victorian-style double bedroom with French doors overlooking the paddock, lounge/diner with TV, kitchen, bathroom, scullery with fridge and microwave. Linen and towels provided. Electricity with £1 coin meter. Village has surgery, chemist, bakery, butcher, Post Office etc. Market town of Dereham four miles, Norwich 12 miles. Convenient for Sandringham, Broads etc. Your privacy respected. Warm welcome. Sorry, no smoking or pets. Open all year. Terms on request. **ETC ★★★ Margaret and Don Fisher, Ivydene, Mill Road, Mattishall, Dereham NR20 3RL (01362 850312).**

WINTERTON-ON-SEA

Church Farm Cottages. Sleep 4/5 plus cot. Five minutes' walk from Winterton's famous sand dunes, Church Farm is a cluster of traditional farm buildings, set in four acres of fields and gardens. Excellent centre for Broads and beach. The main single-storey range of outbuildings recently converted into three very comfortable holiday cottages, each with separate enclosed garden. Original features – flint walls inside and out, Norfolk pantiles, low ceilings - carefully preserved, cosy and atmospheric, as well as clean and well-equipped – continental showers, microwaves, washing machines, etc. Secure car park. Use of more than an acre of play field. Secure bicycle storage. Rates from £175 to £350 per week. Short breaks available. Children and pets welcome. **Mrs Sally Woods, Church Farm, Black Street, Winterton-on-Sea, Norfolk NR29 4AP (01493 393224).**

NORTHUMBERLAND

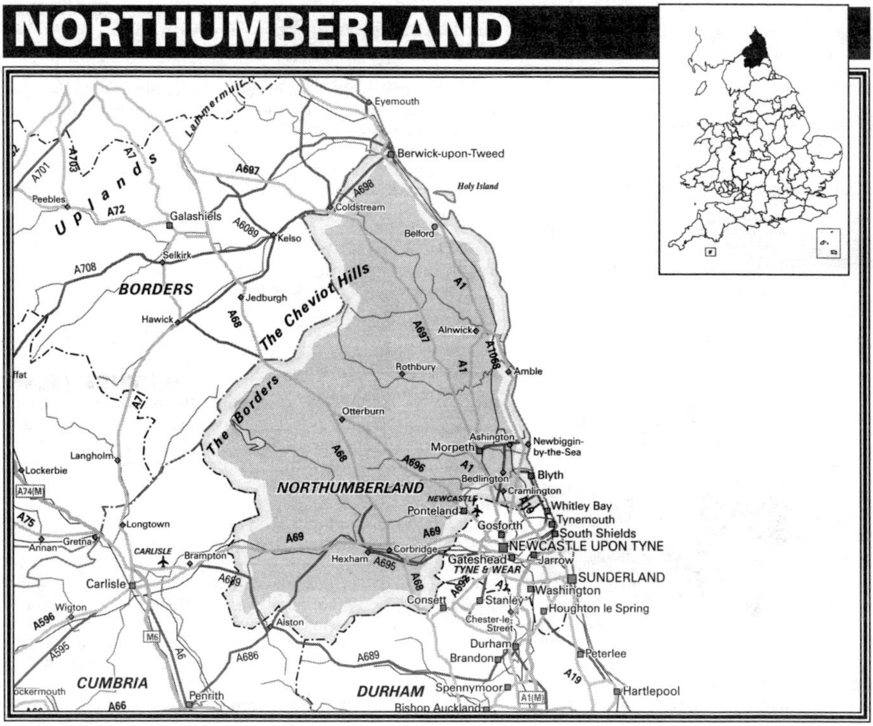

Enjoy a break on the Northumberland Coast

Choose from twelve family-owned and managed cottages along the Northumberland coast.
Three-day short breaks from £70 per cottage during low season.
Beautiful rugged coastline, fishing villages little changed in 100 years, golden beaches, historic castles, wildlife, walks, cycling, fishing, golf, National Park, Kielder Water and Forest.

For details and bookings contact: Heritage Coast Holidays, Unit 6 Greensfield Court, Alnwick, Northumberland NE66 2DE
• 01670 787864 24-hour enquiry line • Tel: 01665 606022 (office hours)
• Fax: 01670 787336 • e-mail: pault@marishal.co.uk

Visit our website• www.northumberland-holidays.com

See also Colour Advertisement

One FREE adult with one paying adult at
Chesters Walled Garden
See our READERS' OFFER VOUCHER for details.

Readers are requested to mention this guidebook when seeking accommodation (and please enclose a stamped addressed envelope).

ALNWICK

Mrs J.M. Gilroy, White House Folly Farm NE66 2LW (01665 579265). Stone-built semi-detached cottage situated in an elevated position with beautiful views, on a working farm just four miles north of the attractive, historic town of Alnwick - famous for its castle. The cottage is well decorated and carpeted throughout and provides a comfortable base for sightseeing, or simply relax in this fascinating area of Northumberland. The cottage has a sittingroom, diningroom, kitchen with washer, dryer, dishwasher, freezer, microwave and payphone, cloakroom, two bedrooms, bathroom. Shops and pubs four miles away in Alnwick and just one mile from bus route. Children welcome, cot and high chair available. Sorry no pets. Enclosed garden, ample parking. Electricity by meter reading. Weekly terms from £150 to £300. Brochure available. **ETC ★★★** *SELF CATERING*.

ALNWICK (near)

Briar, Rose & Clematis Cottages. Sleep 2-4+cot. Quality self-catering cottages in recent barn conversions in a courtyard setting, providing the perfect base for exploring historic Northumberland. All with log-burning stoves and modern facilities, both Rose and Briar Cottages have open plan sitting/ dining room and well-equipped kitchen, with open staircase leading to double bedroom with four-poster and bathroom with over bath shower. Clematis Cottage (shown in photo; sleeps 4 + cot) includes picture windows with views to open countryside. Superb walking area, golf, horse riding, birdwatching and fishing available locally. Within easy reach of Heritage Coast and the Cheviots; Hadrian's Wall (30 miles) and Edinburgh (65 miles) within easy reach. Well-behaved pets welcome in Rose Cottage and Clematis Cottage. Contact: **Graeme and Helen Wyld, New Moor House, Edlingham, Alnwick NE66 2BT (01665 574638).**

e-mail: stay@newmoorhouse.co.uk **website: www.newmoorhouse.co.uk**

BERWICK-UPON-TWEED

Mrs Judith A. King, Kingsway Cottage, East Ord Farm, Berwick-upon-Tweed TD15 2NS (01289 306228). A lovely stone-built, pantile-roofed farm cottage on the edge of the quiet and picturesque Borders village of East Ord. Open views over attractive farmland, a few minutes' walk from the River Tweed and a short distance away from the historic town of Berwick-upon-Tweed. Fully modernised and very comfortable, the cottage has two bedrooms, one twin and one double, as well as attractive living and kitchen areas. Large bathroom with a separate bath and shower. Quality kitchen appliances, colour TV, VCR and gas central heating throughout. Private parking and secure rear garden. Available all year. **ETC ★★★★**

e-mail: jking4kingsway@aol.com

BERWICK-UPON-TWEED

Mrs S. Wight, Gainslawhill Farm, Berwick-upon-Tweed TD15 1SZ (01289 386210). Well-equipped cottage with own walled garden on mixed farm, three miles from Berwick-upon-Tweed, situated between the rivers Tweed and Whiteadder (last farm in England). Ideal position for touring north Northumberland and the Border country. Good beaches, golf, riding nearby. Lovely walks along both rivers; trout fishing. The tasteful interior comprises livingroom with open fire, colour TV, telephone; three bedrooms (linen provided); kitchen with dining area, fridge/freezer, automatic washing machine, microwave oven. Bathroom. Night store heaters. Terms from £250. Pets welcome. **ETC ★★★**

e-mail: susan@gainslawhill.co.uk
website: www.gainslawhill.co.uk

MORPETH

Mr & Mrs A.P. Coatsworth, Gallowhill Farm, Whalton, Morpeth NE61 3TX (01661 881241). Working farm. Sleep 4-6. Relax in our two spacious stone-built cottages. Recently converted and modernised to give you every facility you require. Electric cooker, fridge, freezer, dishwasher, washer/dryer, microwave, colour TV. Located in the heart of Northumberland on a very tidy farm with private gardens. Bolam Lake two miles, Belsay Castle four miles, coast 20 minutes, Hadrian's Wall 30 minutes, to name only a few attractions. All linen, heating, electricity included in price. Sorry, no pets. All children welcome. Brochure on request. Terms £220 to £410.

ROTHBURY

The Granary, Charity Hall Farm, Sharperton, Morpeth NE65 7AG (01669 650219). Sleeps up to 8 plus cot. Located on our 350 acre farm, this exceptional conversion of a former granary building provides the perfect setting for a carefree, country holiday. Spacious, fully equipped and tastefully furnished accommodation, with delightful features such as exposed roof beams, traditional stone flagged and timber floors. Cosy inglenook fireplace with cast iron stove. The views over the Coquet Valley are stunning. There is a large garden for enjoying barbecues and relaxing and a playing field for the more energetic. An excellent location for walking, mountain-biking and exploring Northumberland. Rates from £325 - £720 per week; short breaks from £200. **ETC ★★★★★**
website: www.charityhallfarm.com

WOOLER

Coach House Cottages, Ilderton Glebe, near Wooler. Sleep 4/5. Two cottages converted from a Grade II Listed barn, offering comfortable accommodation in a peaceful location. Ilderton is a hamlet on the edge of the Northumbrian National Park and close to the Cheviot Hills, an ideal spot for walking, bird watching, visiting historic houses and castles. There are beautiful beaches 15 miles away and trips to the Farne Islands and Holy Island. Both cottages have garages, ample parking, one has an open fire, night storage heating and fitted carpets throughout. There is a walled garden with garden chairs. Children and dogs welcome. Electricity, fuel and linen included in rent. Open all year. Terms from £145 to £395 per week. Also Bed and Breakfast available at Ilderton Glebe. **ETC ★★★.** Contact: **Mrs Sale, Ilderton Glebe, Ilderton, near Wooler NE66 4YD (01668 217293).**

Visits & Attractions

Grace Darling Museum, Bamburgh, Northumberland • 01668 214465

Commemorates the rescue by Grace and her father of the nine survivors of the wreck of the Forfarshire. Many relics, including the cable used in the rescue, plus books, paintings etc.

NOTTINGHAMSHIRE

OWTHORPE

Woodview Cottage, Owthorpe. A haven of tranquillity, Woodview Cottage has been lovingly converted from a traditional barn on the family farm to provide cosy accommodation with log-burning stove, beamed ceilings and character furniture. Nestling on the edge of the Vale of Belvoir, surrounded by gardens, with views over patchwork fields and woodland. Located 20 minutes from Nottingham and Leicester. Providing high standards in purpose designed self-catering cottage comprising living/dining room and fully equipped, farmhouse kitchen. One double, one twin bedroom with linen and towels included. Bathroom with separate shower. Cot/highchair available upon request. Ample free car parking. Cottage is shown to the left in the photograph. Sorry, no smoking and no pets. **ETC ★★★★**. Contact: **Judith Morley, Newfields Farm, Owthorpe NG12 3GF (Tel & Fax: 01949 81279).**
e-mail: enquiries@woodviewcottages.co.uk **website: www.woodviewcottages.co.uk**

OXFORDSHIRE

See also Colour Display Advertisement

BANBURY

Anita's Holiday Cottages: The Shippon, The Byre, & The Stables. Sleep 2-8. Top quality barn conversions, superbly finished to a high standard. Fitted kitchens include microwave, cooker, washing machine, dishwasher. Fully heated. Linen included. Suits couples and large parties. Central to the Cotswolds, Oxford and Stratford or for just enjoying the surrounding countryside. Walk to village pub. Non-smoking. No pets and sorry, no children under 5. Ample parking. Close to M40 Junction 12. Short breaks available during low season. **ETC ★★★/★★★★.** For further details please telephone **01295 750731 or 07966 171959.**

PANGBOURNE (near)

"Brambly Thatch" Holiday Cottage, Coombe End Farm, Whitchurch Hill, Near Pangbourne, Reading. Brambly Thatch is an attractive, thatched, 17th century farm cottage, located on a working mixed (dairy and arable) farm, at the southern end of the Chiltern Hills. The cottage is about two miles north of Pangbourne, seven miles north-west of Reading, and about 20 miles south of Oxford. London is within easy reach. With the River Thames, Chiltern beech woods and countryside nearby, there is the chance to go walking, boating, driving or picnicking. One double bedroom, one single bedroom, and bathroom/W.C. upstairs; while downstairs there are the kitchen, main living room, dining room, and third bedroom. Fully equipped kitchen, VCR, colour TV, and telephone. Small garden. No pets, except by special arrangement. Smoking discouraged.Terms from £355 to £425. Contact: **Mr J. N. Hatt, Merricroft Farming, Goring Heath, Reading, Berkshire RG8 7TA (01189 843121).**
e-mail: hatts@merricroft.demon.co.uk

SHROPSHIRE

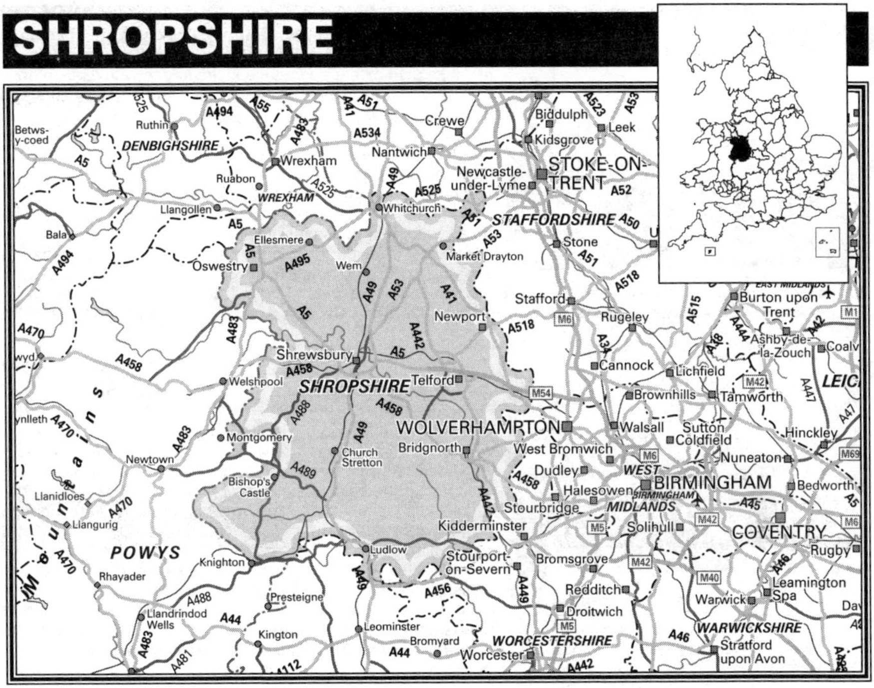

CRAVEN ARMS

Mrs B. Freeman, Upper House, Clunbury, Craven Arms SY7 0HG (01588 660629). Welcome to Horseshoe Cottage which is situated in the beautiful gardens of Upper House (17th century Listed) in Clunbury, a village of archaeological interest in a designated Area of Outstanding Natural Beauty – A. E. Housman countryside. This private self-catering cottage is completely furnished and equipped; being on one level the accommodation is suitable for elderly and disabled persons. Colour TV. Sleeps four; cot available. Children and pets welcome. Ample parking. This Welsh Border countryside is rich in medieval history, unspoilt villages and natural beauty. Enjoy walking on the Long Mynd and Offa's Dyke, or explore Ludlow and Ironbridge. £135 to £170 per week. Please write or phone for further details.

Visits & Attractions

Acton Scott Historic Working Farm, Church Stretton • 01694 781306

A fascinating working farm using heavy horses and 19th century techniques, designed to show agricultural life from years past. Daily demonstrations of farming, butter making and traditional crafts.

A useful index of towns and counties appears at the back of this book on pages 379-382. Refer also to Contents Pages 50/51.

LUDLOW

Hazel Cottage, Duxmoor, Onibury, Craven Arms. Sleeps 4. Beautifully restored, semi-detached, yet private, period cottage, set in its own extensive cottage-style garden with its own drive and ample parking space. Amidst peaceful surroundings and panoramic views of the countryside, it is situated five miles north of historic Ludlow and one-and-a-half miles from the A49. The cottage retains all its original features and fittings with traditional decoration and is fully furnished, with antiques throughout. It comprises a comfortable living room with a Victorian range for coal and log fire; TV, wireless and telephone; dining room with bread oven; fully equipped kitchen, hall, Victorian bathroom; two bedrooms (one double and one twin-bedded) with period washbasins. Electric central heating throughout. All linen included. Tourist information. Open all year. Short Breaks available. No pets. Terms from £90 to £395 per week. **ETC ★★★★. Mrs Rachel Sanders, Duxmoor Farm, Onibury, Craven Arms SY7 9BQ (01584 856342).**

SHREWSBURY

John & Annabel Gill, Courtyard Cottages, Lower Springs Farm, Kenley, Shrewsbury SY5 6PA (Tel & Fax: 01952 510 841). Situated in the Kenley Valley beneath Wenlock Edge with lovely panoramic views, two beautifully restored and converted 19th century barns in large garden overlooking stocked trout pool. Both have lounge, fitted kitchens and bathroom. The smaller conversion is ideal for 2 people while the larger cottage is more suitable for a party of 4. All heating and hot water is included and there is private parking. Electricity is metered. Close by is the historic town of Much Wenlock with its ruined abbey, museum and interesting shops. Shrewsbury, Ironbridge, several famous gardens and local pubs and restaurants are all within easy reach. Prices range from £150 -£350 per week. **ETC ★★★★.**

e-mail: a-gill@lineone.net **website: www.courtyard.bridgnorthshropshire.com**

FHG Holiday and Accommodation guides 2003

Each year FHG Publications produces a large range of attractive holiday accommodation guides for all kinds of holiday opportunities throughout Britain. They are great value for money and are available in most bookshops and larger newsagents at the following prices.

SOMERSET

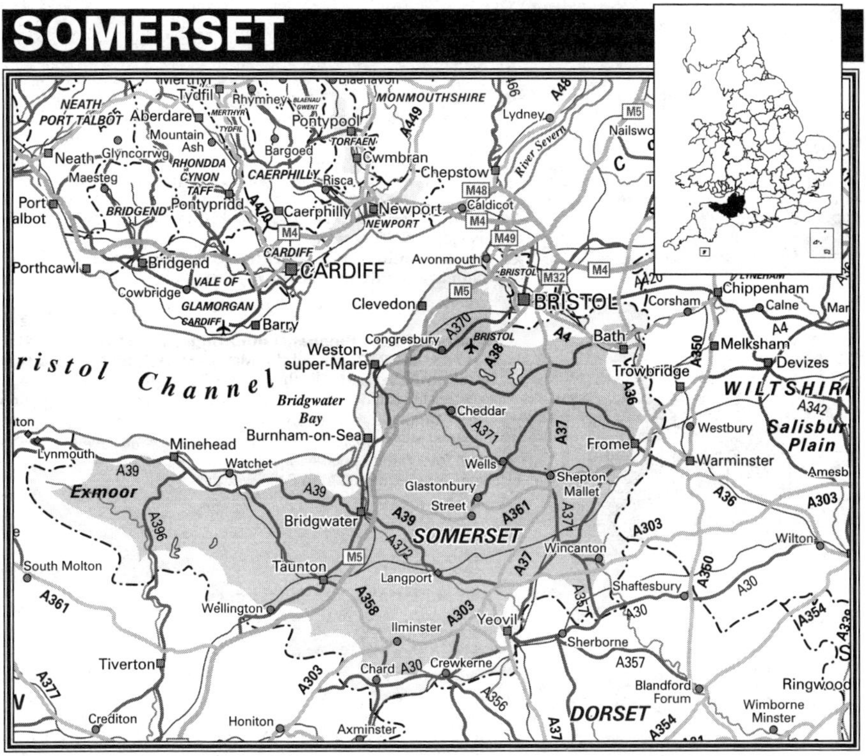

Helpful Holidays
Self catering Cottages & Houses in the West Country
We have a wonderful variety of self-catering farmhouses and cottages, on farms, where you can help or wander the farm, or just picnic in the fields - all over the West Country. All properties are inspected, star rated & frankly described by us in our full colour brochure
Tel: 01647 433535 (24hrs)
www.helpfulholidays.com

See also Colour Display Advertisement

ALLERFORD

The Pack Horse, Allerford, Near Minehead TA24 8HW (Tel & Fax: 01643 862475). Sleep 2-6. Idyllic location for a self-catering holiday in the National Trust village of Allerford alongside the shallow River Aller, overlooking the famous Pack Horse Bridge. Immediate access to Exmoor and the beautiful surrounding countryside. Variety of well-equipped apartments and family cottage arranged around a pretty courtyard. Pets welcome. Stabling available. Ample private parking. Local amenities: Post Office, stores, additional restaurants/pubs etc in nearby Porlock. Terms from £200 to £450 per week. Open all year. Short Breaks available. **SWT ★★★**

e-mail: holidays@thepackhorse.freewire.co.uk

website: www.thepackhorse.net

BATH

Whitnell Farm, Binegar, Emborough, Radstock BA3 4UF (01749 840277). Delightful Manor House just off the B3139 Wells to Bath road. On the edge of a pretty Mendips village overlooking Cheddar Gorge, Wookey Hole. Very central for touring West Country - plenty to do and see. Garden and fields to relax in. Coast 20 miles, Bristol Airport 18 miles. 18-hole golf, fishing, riding. Ideal for a family holiday. Sleeps two to eight persons. Sorry, no pets. Terms from £300 to £450 weekly.

BATH

Ken & Merinda Kendall and Family, Lime Kiln Farm, Faulkland, Near Bath BA3 5XE (01373 834305; mobile: 07779 110014). Two self-contained cottages in a lovingly restored barn just 15 minutes south of Bath, ideally situated for the major tourist attractions of the area including Longleat, Cheddar, and Wookey Hole Caves. Close by there is golf, pony trekking, hiking, theatre and good eating out. The cottages are well-equipped with electric cooker, fridge, freezer, washing machine/dryer, dishwasher and microwave. Linen, duvets and towels supplied. Oil central heating. Patio furniture and barbecue. Ample parking. Non-smoking. **ETC ★★★★★**. B&B also available (**ETC ◆◆◆◆**).

e-mail: lime_kiln@hotmail.com

See also Colour Display Advertisement

CHEDDAR

Sungate Holiday Apartments, Church Street, Cheddar BS27 3RA (01934 842273 or 742264; Fax: 01934 844994). Sleep 2-4. In Cheddar village, close to Cheddar Gorge and the Mendip Hills, this Listed Georgian building has been thoughtfully converted into four non-smoking holiday apartments. Each apartment has lounge with sofa bed, TV, bedroom, bathroom, fully-equipped kitchen plus microwave. Linen supplied. Laundry facilities. Pets welcome with prior approval. Private parking. Swimming and leisure facilities nearby. Competitively priced for a short break, longer holiday or a short-term let. **ETC ★★★**. Bookings: **Mrs Fieldhouse, "Pyrenmount" Parsons Way, Winscombe, Somerset BS25 1BU**.

EXMOOR

Jane Styles, Wintershead, Simonsbath, Exmoor TA24 7LF (01643 831222). Occupying a unique location with breathtaking views within the National Park, five quality stone cottages converted from original farm buildings, offering peace, tranquillity, privacy and all the comforts of home. A special place to recharge your batteries away from the stresses of everyday life. Please telephone, fax or write for a colour brochure. **ETC ★★★★**

website: www.wintershead.co.uk

Leigh Farm Pensford, Near Bristol BS39 4BA

Telephone or Fax: 01761 490281

Leigh Farm is situated in the old mining village of Pensford. 7 miles Bristol and 8 miles Bath. Overlooking the floodlit pool; a 3-bedroomed cottage sleeping 6 plus baby. Terraced bungalow conversion built tastefully in natural stone with original oak beams. One or two bedroomed, with shower room, WC and basin. TV. Night storage heating. Bed linen is not supplied but can be hired. Cot and high chair available. Wander round the ponds where Duck and Moorhen nest. Park and ride for both cities near, and plenty of Tourist Information for your use. Safe floodlit car park.

See also Colour Advertisement

Open all year. No pets. £170-£400 weekly. B&B available. *For brochure contact Josephine Smart.*

EXMOOR

'Inner Lype' & Goosemoor Farm Cottage, Wheddon Cross, Minehead. Sleeps 6 plus cot. Go home relaxed from the perfect break. Enjoy a stay in one of our two detached cottages nestled in the Brendon Hills, Exmoor National Park. Truly peaceful and quiet. A warm welcome awaits you. Comfortable, warm and well-equipped country cottages each in its own setting. Far reaching views over beautiful countryside from both cottages. Many pubs/restaurants nearby serving good food. Close to moorland and coast. Easy access from M5/Taunton. Pets and children welcome. Terms £150 – £400 per week. Open all year. Short Breaks. Many regular visitors. Colour brochure. Contact: **Mrs Mary Howe, Lype Farm, Wheddon Cross, Minehead TA24 7BJ. (Tel & Fax: 01643 841557)**

e-mail: om.howe@virgin.net **website: www.cottageguide.co.uk/innerlype**

EXMOOR (near Selworthy)

Penny & Roger Webber, Hindon Organic Farm, Near Selworthy TA24 8SH (Tel & Fax: 01643 705244). Real Farm – Real Food– Relax. Escape to where the buzzards soar and red deer roam. B&B and Self-catering. Charming cottage and 18th century farmhouse on our 500-acre organic stock farm adjoining heather moors, South West coast path, and thatched village of Selworthy for 'scrummy' cream teas. All within National Trust Estate – wonderful walks and riding, bring dogs and horses. Waymarked farm trail with picnic wood. Organic lamb, Aberdeen Angus beef, free-range pork, bacon, ham, sausages, and more, all available in our farm shop. Free organic produce basket for self-catering accommodation guests; organic breakfasts also available. Minehead three miles, Dunster Castle six miles. Award winners from Exmoor National Park for conservation. **ETC★★★/ ★★★★**

e-mail: info@hindonfarm.co.uk **website: www.hindonfarm.co.uk**

LANGPORT

Mr J. Woodborne, Muchelney Ham Farm, Muchelney Ham, Langport TA10 0DJ (Tel & Fax: 01458 250737). Sleeps 4/5. Self-catering cottages built in traditional style adjoining farmhouse. Double and family bedrooms, en suite. Large kitchen/diningroom. One further bathroom downstairs. Stable cottage has a downstairs bedroom. Electricity by coin meter. Linen included in price. Open all year. Weekly terms from £150 to £395, or from £120 to £285. **ETC ★★★★** and **★★★**

website: www.muchelneyhamfarm.co.uk

PORLOCK

Lucott Farm, Porlock, Minehead. Sleeps 2/10. Isolated farmhouse on Exmoor, with wood burning fireplaces and all modern conveniences. It lies at the head of Horner Valley and guests will delight in the wonderful scenery. Plenty of pony trekking in the area. Ten people accommodated in four double and two single bedrooms, cot; bathroom, two toilets; sittingroom; dining room. Kitchen has oil-fired Aga and water heater. No linen supplied. Shops three miles; sea four miles. Car essential - parking. Open all year, Terms (including fuel) on application with SAE please to **Mrs E.A. Tucker, West Luccombe Farm Cottage, Porlock, Minehead TA24 8MT (01643 862810).**

SHEPTON MALLET

Knowle Farm, West Compton, Shepton Mallet BA4 4PD (01749 890482; Fax: 01749 890405). Working farm. Cottages sleep 2/5/8. Knowle Farm Cottages are converted from the old cowstall and stables, set around the old farmyard now laid out as a pleasant garden. Quiet location at the end of a private drive. Excellent views and plenty of wildlife. All cottages furnished to a high standard - bathroom (bath, shower, toilet, washbasin); fully fitted kitchen (automatic washing machine, fridge/freezer, microwave, full size cooker). Two cottages have kitchen/diner, separate lounge with colour TV, the other two have kitchen, lounge/diner, colour TV. Cot, high chair by prior arrangement. Bed linen supplied, towels by request. Surrounding area full of interesting places to visit. Five miles from Wells and Mendip Golf Clubs; the area also has a wide selection of family attractions, fishing, selection of pubs and restaurants. Around the farm plenty of walks, play area for children. Sorry no pets. Terms from £180 to £450. Car essential, ample parking. Payphone for guests. Open all year. **ETC ★★★**.

TAUNTON

Mrs Joan Greenway, Woodlands Farm, Bathealton, Taunton TA4 2AH (01984 623271). You can be assured of a warm and friendly welcome on our family-run dairy farm. Children are welcome and will enjoy feeding the animals. We are in the heart of beautiful unspoilt countryside within easy reach of the north and south coasts and Exmoor. The cottage sleeps five people and is furnished to a high standard to enjoy a relaxing holiday. Well equipped kitchen with use of washing machine and dryer. Bathroom with bath and shower. Electricity, central heating and bed linen included in the tariff. Terms from £135 to £300 per week. Fishing, golf and horse riding near by. Please write or phone for colour brochure.

WELLINGTON

Mrs A. Toogood, Dunns Farm, Langford Budville, Wellington TA21 0QP (01823 667808). Sleeps 4/6. Dunns is a working farm situated in a beautiful and peaceful area near the Devon/Somerset border. Ideal for exploring the Quantock Hills and the north and south coasts. The West Somerset Steam Railway and Hestercombe Gardens are nearby. Accommodation is in the spacious self-contained wing of our 16th century farmhouse, which has inglenook fireplaces and beamed ceilings. The wing is well equipped with central heating, TV, dishwasher, washing machine and microwave. Electricity is included. Visitors are welcome to join in with the farming activities. Open from April to October. Terms from £180 to £325. Children welcome, sorry, no pets.
e-mail: toogood@tinyonline.co.uk

STAFFORDSHIRE

LEEK

Edith and Alwyn Mycock, 'Rosewood Cottage and Rosewood Flat', Lower Berkhamsytch Farm, Bottom House, Near Leek ST13 7QP (Tel & Fax: 01538 308213). Each sleeps 6. Situated in Staffordshire Moorlands, one cottage and one flat overlooking picturesque countryside. Fully equipped, comfortably furnished and carpeted throughout. Cottage, with three bedrooms (one with four-poster), all on ground floor, is suitable for the less able. An ideal base for visits to Alton Towers, the Potteries and Peak District. Patio, play area. Cot and high chair available. Laundry room with auto washer and dryer. Electricity and fresh linen inclusive. Prices from £150 to £305. **ETC ★★★**

SUFFOLK

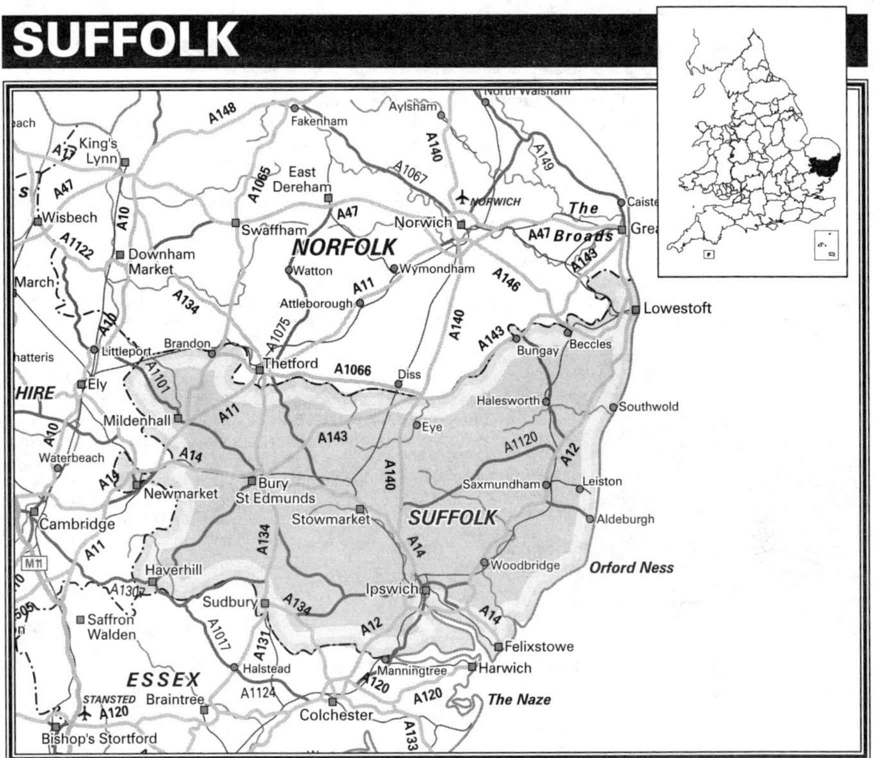
North Walsham
A148
Fakenham
Aylsham
King's Lynn
A17
A47
A1065
East Dereham
A140
A1067
A149
NORWICH
Wisbech
A10
A47
Swaffham
Norwich
The Broads
A47
Caister
Great
A1122
Downham Market
NORFOLK
Watton
Wymondham
A146
A143
March
A134
A11
Attleborough
Lowestoft
A10
A1075
A140
A143
Brandon
Littleport
Bungay
Beccles
Chatteris
Thetford
A1066
Diss
A1101
Ely
HIRE
Halesworth
Southwold
Mildenhall
A11
Eye
A10
A143
A1120
A14
Waterbeach
A140
A12
A14
Bury St Edmunds
Saxmundham
Leiston
Newmarket
Stowmarket
SUFFOLK
Aldeburgh
Cambridge
A134
A14
M11
A11
Woodbridge
Orford Ness
Haverhill
A1307
Ipswich
Sudbury
A134
A14
Saffron Walden
A1017
A12
Felixstowe
A131
Halstead
Manningtree
Harwich
ESSEX
A1124
A120
A120
STANSTED
Braintree
The Naze
A120
Colchester
A133
Bishop's Stortford

ENGLAND

Knights Holiday Homes

at Kessingland on the Suffolk Heritage Coast

THE BEST OF BRITISH SELF-CATERING HOLIDAYS

at the 'Seaview' and 'Alandale' Holiday Parks on the peaceful Suffolk Coast

CHILDREN AND PETS WELCOME
OPEN ALL YEAR

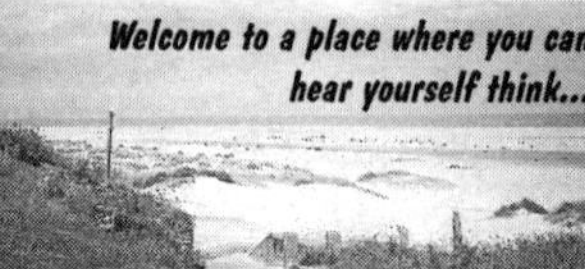

Welcome to a place where you can
hear yourself think...

'Kessingland: Most easterly village in the United Kingdom. First to greet the sun. Once known as the richest village in England because of its prolific fishing. Now known for its peaceful, pleasant surroundings, its beautiful spacious beach and its Suffolk countryside, where you can relax in peace and watch the boats sail by on the North Sea's Herring Pond.'

Seaview Bungalows
These bungalows are situated on a quiet, attractive estate set in nine acres of lawns overlooking the sea. There is a made-up roadway round the estate and parking near your door. Your bungalow has three bedrooms, bathroom and toilet, kitchen and lounge with a sun door opening onto the lawns. A walkway leads immediately from the estate to the promenade and the beach.
SHOPS ARE APPROXIMATELY 450 YARDS AND BUS STOP 300 YARDS.

THE BUNGALOWS
- 1-6 persons
- Colour Television
- Bed linen supplied • Fully equipped kitchens
- Full size cookers and refrigerators
- Cots and Highchairs are available
- Electrically heated - no meters • Parking

THE VILLAGE
- Clean Beach Award
- Mother Hubbard's Cupboard – Kessingland Art Centre and Gift Shop
- Suffolk Wildlife Park
- Shops • Pubs
- Restaurants • Cafes • Bus Service

BROCHURE ◆ CALENDAR ◆ OFFER LETTER ◆ BOOKING FORM from
Knights Holiday Homes, 198 Church Road, Kessingland, Suffolk NR33 7SF Freephone 0800 269067

See also Colour Advertisement

KESSINGLAND

Kessingland Cottages, Rider Haggard Lane, Kessingland. Sleeps 6. An exciting three-bedroom recently built semi-detached cottage situated on the beach, three miles south of sandy beach at Lowestoft. Fully and attractively furnished with colour TV and delightful sea and lawn views from floor-to-ceiling windows of lounge. Accommodation for up to six people. Well-equipped kitchen with electric cooker, fridge, electric immersion heater. Electricity by £1 coin meter. Luxurious bathroom with coloured suite. No linen or towels provided. Only a few yards to beach and sea fishing. One mile to wildlife country park with mini-train. Buses quarter-of-a-mile and shopping centre half-a-mile. Parking, but car not essential. Children and disabled persons welcome. Available 1st March to 7th January. Weekly terms from £50 in early March and late December to £225 in peak season. SAE to **Mr S. Mahmood, 156 Bromley Road, Beckenham, Kent BR3 6PG (Tel & Fax: 020-8650 0539).**
website: www.k-cottage.co.uk

SAXMUNDHAM

Mrs Mary Kitson, White House Farm, Sibton, Saxmundham IP17 2NE (01728 660260). Working farm. Sleeps 4/6 adults; 2/4 children. The flat is a self-contained part of late Georgian farmhouse standing in 130 acres of quiet farmland with a variety of livestock. Fishing on farm. Accommodation in three double bedrooms (two double/two single beds) plus cot; livingroom with TV; shower/toilet on first floor. Entrance hall, kitchen/diner on ground floor. Full central heating. Situated one-and-a-half miles from village shops, etc. Ten miles from coast at Dunwich, Minsmere Bird Sanctuary, Snape Maltings. Linen optional. Pets permitted. Car essential - parking. Available all year. Terms from £150 to £200 per week. SAE, please, for further details.

Terms quoted in this publication may be subject to increase if rises in costs necessitate

EAST SUSSEX

ALFRISTON

Mr and Mrs G. Burgess, Polhills, Arlington, Polegate BN26 6SB (01323 870004). Idyllically situated on shore of reservoir and edge of Sussex Downs within easy reach of the sea. Fully furnished period cottage (approached by own drive along the water's edge) available for self-catering holidays from April to October (inclusive). Fly fishing for trout can be arranged during season. Accommodation consists of two main bedrooms; tiled bathroom. Lounge with colour TV; large well-fitted kitchen with fridge freezer, electric cooker, microwave, washing machine; dining room with put-u-up settee; sun lounge. Central heating. Linen supplied. Most rooms contain a wealth of oak beams. Children and pets welcome. Car essential. Ample parking. Shops two miles. Golf, hill climbing locally. Sea eight miles. Weekly terms from £220 to £295 (electricity included).

WARWICKSHIRE

STRATFORD-UPON-AVON

Richard & Philippa Bluck, Weston Farm, Weston-on-Avon, Stratford-upon-Avon CV37 8JY (01789 750688). Set in beautiful Warwickshire countryside, the quiet hamlet of Weston-on-Avon only four miles from Stratford-upon-Avon, and close to the Cotswolds. Weston Farm's four beautifully converted barns offer an ideal location for relaxing holidays. A superb area for walking and cycling. Private fishing on the River Avon. All linen provided. En suite facilities. Bicycles available. Sorry no pets. Please telephone for a brochure and tariff. **ETC ★★★★**
e-mail: r.bluckwestonfarm@amserve.net
website: www.westonfarm.co.uk

STRATFORD-UPON-AVON

Crimscote Downs Farm Self-catering Accommodation. Sleeps 2 and 4. PARADISE COTTAGE is a romantic hideaway for two people in a newly converted former shepherd's retreat, with views over the downs. It is full of character, with beams and wooden floors; centrally heated throughout. The kitchen is fully equipped with microwave, dishwasher, electric cooker and washing machine. THE DAIRY is ideal for a family visit, with fully equipped kitchen, sitting room and two en suite bedrooms; centrally heated throughout. It has stunning views and is full of character with beams and wooden floors. Terms from £175 to £325. Both cottages are five and a half miles from Stratford-upon-Avon. No smoking. Ample parking. Pets by prior arrangement. Contact: **Mrs J James, The Old Coach House, Whitchurch Farm, Wimpston, Stratford-upon-Avon CV37 8NS (01789 450275).**
website: www.stratford-upon-avon.co.uk/crimscote.htm

WILTSHIRE

See also Colour Display Advertisement

BRADFORD-ON-AVON

Church Farm Country Cottages, Church Farm, Winsley, Bradford-on-Avon BA15 2JH (Tel & Fax: 01225 722246). Working farm. Seven single storey cottages, formerly old cow byres, tastefully converted with exposed beams and vaulted ceilings on a working farm with sheep and horses. Countryside location in an Area of Outstanding Natural Beauty. Enclosed garden with patio furniture. HEATED INDOOR SWIMMING POOL AND GAMES ROOM – NEW FOR 2003. Three cottages sleep two, and four sleep four/five. Ample parking. Pub and shop 500 metres. Bath five miles; close to Longleat, Lacock, Stonehenge and many National Trust properties. Kennet and Avon Canal three-quarters of a mile for boating, cycling and walking. Regular buses. Welcome cream tea. Short Breaks when available. Also 20 pitch rural caravan/campsite with many facilities. **ETC ★★★★**, *WELCOME HOST, GREEN TOURISM AWARD.*

e-mail: stay@churchfarmcottages.com website: www.churchfarmcottages.com

DEVIZES

Colin and Cynthia Fletcher, Lower Foxhangers Farm, Rowde, Devizes SN10 1SS (Tel & Fax: 01380 828795; Fax: 01380 828254). Sleep 4/6. Enjoy your holiday with us on our small farm/marina with its many diverse attractions. Hear the near musical clatter of the windlass heralding the lock gate opening and the arrival of yet another narrowboat. Relax on the patios of our rural retreats - four holiday mobile homes sleeping four/six in a setting close to the canal locks. Bed and Breakfast accommodation in 18th century spacious farmhouse from £22 per person. Self-catering rates from £210 per week. Also available weekly hire with our narrowboat holidays or small camp site with electricity and facilities.

LACOCK (near Bath)

The Cheese House & The Cyder House. Situated on a working farm, both these beautiful self-catering properties were converted in 1994, with great care taken to preserve their natural charm. THE CYDER HOUSE sleeps up to four persons and has the original cyder press on the ground floor, separating the kitchen from the sitting room.There are two single bedrooms and one double, and shower room with wash basin and W.C. Wooden floors throughout, all rooms have either night storage heaters or panel heaters. THE CHEESE HOUSE sleeps up to five persons and consists of an open living/dining room with arch to fitted kitchen. One double and one single bedroom on first floor with shower room with wash basin and W.C, and a further twin-bedded room on the second floor with galleried sitting area with books, TV and games. Both properties have been traditionally furnished with co-ordinating fabrics and attention to detail. Each has parking area and separate garden with seating and barbecue. Sorry no pets. Non-smoking. Short Breaks available. **Sue and Philip King, Wick Farm, Lacock, Chippenham SN15 2LU (01249 730244; Fax: 01249 730072). ETC ★★★★**. *WELCOME HOST, FARM STAY UK MEMBER.*

e-mail: kingsilverlands2@btinternet.com website: www.cheeseandcyderhouses.co.uk

Visits & Attractions

Bowood House & Gardens, Calne, Wiltshire • 01249 812102

website: www.bowood.org

Set in parkland, the magnificent home of the Marquis and Marchioness of Lansdowne, with adventure playground and rhododendron walks (April to mid-June).

Readers are requested to mention this guidebook when seeking accommodation (and please enclose a stamped addressed envelope).

Why Yorkshire?

With ruined abbeys and castles, great houses and gardens framed by high moors and wooded hills, Yorkshire is a place of great natural beauty. This beauty is conserved in three national parks: the Yorkshire Dales, the Peak District and the North York Moors. In contrast to nature, Yorkshire is also home to The West Yorkshire Playhouse, The Yorkshire Sculpture Park and The National Museum of Photography, Film & Television. The Millennium Galleries, the new multimillion MAGNA and The Deep all make it a worthwhile place to visit.

For further information contact the Yorkshire Tourist Board, Tel: **01904 707070** or visit **www.yorkshirevisitor.com**

ENGLAND

EAST YORKSHIRE

See also Colour Display Advertisement

KILHAM

Mrs P.M. Savile, Raven Hill Farm, Kilham, Driffield YO25 4EG (01377 267217). Working farm. Sleeps 8+2 plus cots. With delightful views overlooking the Yorkshire Wolds, ideally situated for touring the East Coast, Bridlington, Scarborough, Moors and York, this secluded and private four-bedroomed farmhouse is set in its own acre of woodland lawns and orchard, with garden furniture, summerhouse and children's play area. Games room in converted Granary in the main farm area 200 yards away. Clean and comfortable and very well equipped including dishwasher, microwave, automatic washing machine and dryer; two bathrooms, payphone, TV and video. Fully centrally heated. Beds are made up for your arrival; cots and high chair available. Three miles to the nearest village of Kilham with Post Office, general stores, garage and public houses. Available all year. Terms from £270 - £380 per week (low season) to £380 - £505 per week (high season). Brochure on request. **ETC ★★★**

NORTH YORKSHIRE

ASKRIGG

Fern Croft, 2 Mill Lane, Askrigg. Sleeps four. A modern cottage enjoying quiet location on edge of village with open fields rising immediately behind. Attractive and compact, this Wensleydale village is an ideal centre for Dales, with facilities for everyday needs, including two shops, Post Office, restaurant and a couple of pubs. Furnished to a high standard for four, ground floor accommodation comprises large comfortable lounge/diner with colour TV and well-equipped kitchen. Upstairs there are two double bedrooms with a double and twin beds respectively, and modern bathroom. Storage heating included, other electricity by meter. Regret no pets. Terms from £125 to £250 weekly. Brochure: **Mr and Mrs K. Dobson (01689 838450).**

ASKRIGG (Wensleydale)

Mrs E. Scarr, Coleby Hall, Askrigg, Leyburn DL8 3DX (01969 650216). Working farm. Sleeps 5 plus cot. Situated in Wensleydale, half-a-mile from Bainbridge and one mile from Askrigg, Coleby Hall is a 17th century gabled farmhouse with stone mullioned windows, the west end being to let. A stone spiral staircase leads to two bedrooms; linen provided. The kitchen is equipped with electric cooker, fridge, crockery, etc., and coal fire. The lounge has an inglenook coal fire and TV. Oil-fired central heating throughout. Coleby has lovely views and is an ideal situation for walking, fishing and driving round the Yorkshire Dales. Children and pets welcome. Terms from £180 per week.
website: www.colebyhall.co.uk

The FHG Directory of Website Addresses on pages 349- 378 is a useful quick reference guide for holiday accommodation with e-mail and/or website details

BURTON IN LONSDALE

Brentwood Farm Cottages, Barnoldswick Lane, Burton in Lonsdale LA6 3LZ (Tel & Fax: 015242 62155). Quality holiday accommodation set amidst splendid open countryside on our family-run working dairy farm. Once a traditional stone barn, our two cottages are the result of a careful conversion project. All fittings and furnishings are of a high standard, with double glazing, central heating, colour TV, video, washing machine/dryer, fridge and freezer, electric cooker, microwave, bed linen and towels. One cottage has been designed to accommodate wheelchair users with assistance. Fishing is available by prior arrangement and golf and bicycle hire available locally. Burton in Lonsdale has a pub serving food, with many shops and eating establishments in nearby Ingleton, Kirkby Lonsdale and Bantham. Non-smoking. Pets by prior arrangement. Credit cards accepted. **ETC ★★★★**, *FARM STAY UK, WELCOME HOST*.

e-mail: info@brentwoodfarmcottages.co.uk **website: www.brentwoodfarmcottages.co.uk**

COVERDALE

Mrs Caroline Harrison, Hill Top Farm, West Scrafton, Leyburn DL8 4RU (01969 640663). Working farm. A warm and comfortable welcome is guaranteed. Relax and unwind in the peace and tranquillity surrounded by panoramic views. The hamlet of Scrafton is in the heart of Yorkshire Dales National Park. BARN OWL COTTAGE sleeps four to six, has a fully equipped kitchen and modern en suite bathrooms and retains much character with original exposed beams and open fireplace. Full central heating, colour TV, dishwasher, washing machine, fridge and deep freeze. Linen provided. Farmhouse Bed and Breakfast also available in one twin and one single room with hospitality tray, TV, lounge, full central heating, log fire, clothes drying facilities. Fishing, horse livery and grazing available. Please telephone for comprehensive brochure.

GRASSINGTON (near)

Mrs Judith M. Joy, Jerry and Ben's, Hebden, Skipton BD23 5DL (01756 752369; Fax: 01756 753370). Properties sleep 3/6/8/9. Jerry and Ben's stands in two acres of grounds in one of the most attractive parts of the Yorkshire Dales National Park. Seven properties; Ghyll Cottage (sleeps eight); Mamie's Cottage (sleeps eight); Paradise End (sleeps six); Robin Middle (sleeps six); High Close (sleeps nine); Cruck Rise (sleeps six); Raikes Side (sleeps two/three). All have parking, electric cooker, microwave, toaster, fridge, colour TV, electric heating and immersion heater; lounge, dining area, bathroom with shower; cots if required. Fully equipped, including linen if requested. Washing machine and telephone available. Ghyll and Mamie's Cottages now have dishwashers. Well behaved pets accepted. Open all year. Fishing and bathing close by. Terms from £90 to £390. SAE, please for detailed brochure. Suitable for some disabled guests.

e-mail: dawjoy@aol.com **website: www.yorkshirenet.co.uk/stayat/jerryandbens**

HARDRAW

Cissy's Cottage, Hardraw, Hawes. Sleeps 4. A delightful 18th century cottage of outstanding character. Situated in the village of Hardraw with its spectacular waterfall and Pennine Way. Market town of Hawes one mile. This traditional stone built cottage retains many original features including beamed ceilings and an open fire. Sleeping four in comfort, it has been furnished and equipped to a high standard using antique pine and Laura Ashley prints. Equipped with dishwasher, microwave and tumble dryer. Outside, a south-facing garden, sun patio with garden furniture, and a large enclosed paddock make it ideal for children. Cot and high chair if required. Open all year. Terms £100-£295 includes coal, electricity, linen and trout fishing. For brochure, contact **Mrs Belinda Metcalfe, Southolme Farm, Little Smeaton, Northallerton DL6 2HJ (01609 881302).**

ENGLAND

HARROGATE

Mrs Hardcastle, Southfield Farm, Darley, Harrogate HG3 2PR (01423 780258). Two well-equipped holiday cottages on a farm in an attractive area between Harrogate and Pateley Bridge. An ideal place to explore the whole of the dale with York and Herriot country within easy driving distance. Riverside walks, village shop and post office within quarter-of-a-mile, and local pub one mile away. Each cottage has two bedrooms, one double and one with bunk beds. Games room. Large lawn for ball games, with garden chairs and barbecue. Pets welcome. Ample car parking. Prices from £170 to £200 low season, £200 to £270 high season.

HELMSLEY (near)

Mrs Rickatson, Summerfield Farm, Harome, York Y62 5JJ (01439 748238). Working farm. Sleeps 6. Enjoy walking or touring in North York Moors National Park. Lovely area 20 miles north of York. Comfortable and well-equipped farmhouse wing with electric cooker, fridge, microwave and automatic washing machine. Sit beside a log fire in the evenings. Linen supplied. Trout stream on farm. Children and dogs welcome. Weekly terms £95 to £230. Mid-week and weekend bookings are possible. For further information phone or write for leaflet.

See also Colour Display Advertisement

NORTHALLERTON

Julie and Jim Griffith, Hill House Farm Cottages, Hill House Farm, Little Langton, Northallerton DL7 0PZ (01609 770643; Fax: 01609 760438). Sleep 2/4. These former farm buildings have been converted into four well-equipped cottages, retaining original beams. Cosily heated for year-round appeal. Peaceful setting with magnificent views. Centrally located between Dales and Moors with York, Whitby and Scarborough all within easy driving distance. Pets welcome; exercise field. Weekly rates from £150 inclusive of all linen, towels, heating and electricity. Short Breaks available. Pub food one mile, golf two miles, shops three miles. Please telephone for a free colour brochure. **ETC ★★★★**

e-mail: info@Hillhousefarmcottages.com

e-mail: dysonbarn@tinyworld.co.uk

RICHMOND

Dyson House Farm, Newsham, Richmond, North Yorkshire DL11 7QP (01833 627365). Sleeps 6. A personal welcome from the owners living in the adjoining farmhouse awaits visitors to the converted barn. Midway between Richmond and Barnard Castle it is the ideal base for touring Swaledale, Teesdale, Cumbria, Durham, York and the surrounding areas where there are numerous museums, castles, antique shops and markets. One double and one twin bedroom and bathroom are on the first floor. The ground floor has a twin bedroom (two steps up), shower room, large lounge, large kitchen/diner, utility and cloakroom. The enclosed patio makes it ideal for children. Two pub/restaurants ten minutes' walk. Dogs welcome, £10 each. Colour brochure available. Terms from £205 – £420 per week. **ETC ★★★★**

website: www.cottageguide.co.uk/dysonhousebarn

Visits & Attractions

World of James Herriot, Thirsk, North Yorkshire • 01845 524234

website: www.worldofjamesherriot.org

Combines history, humour, nostalgia, science and education in a unique tribute to the creator of the famous "vet' novels. Set in the original 'Skeldale House'.

RICHMOND

Mrs Elizabeth Jopling, High Dalton Hall Cottage, Newsham, Richmond DL11 7RG (Tel & Fax: 01833 621450). Recently converted, spacious, luxury stone barn with exposed beams, open fire and breathtaking views over open countryside. The cottage has been renovated and furnished to a high standard and is situated on a working family hill farm midway between Richmond and Barnard Castle. This idyllic rural retreat is perfect for those wishing to relax and unwind yet easily accessible to both the Yorkshire Dales and Teesdale. The cottage sleeps 4-6 people and is open all year. Non-smoking. Prices range from £200 to £350 per week. **ETC ★★★★**

ROBIN HOOD'S BAY (near)

Ken and Nealia Pattinson, South House Farm, Fylingthorpe, Whitby YO22 4UQ (01947 880243). Glorious countryside in North York Moors National Park. Five minutes' walk to beach at Boggle Hole. Super large farmhouse sleeps 10/12. Two spacious detached cottages sleeping four and six. All inclusive and fully equipped. Gardens. Parking. Terms from £120 to £1000.

SCARBOROUGH

Mr & Mrs J. Donnelly, Gowland Farm, Gowland Lane, Cloughton, Scarborough YO13 0DU (01723 870924). Sleep 2/7. Four charming converted stone barns situated within the beautiful North York Moors National Park, enjoying wonderful views of Harwood Dale and only two miles from the coast. The cottages have been sympathetically converted from traditional farm buildings, furnished and fitted to a very high standard, retaining the old features as well as having modern comforts. They are fully carpeted, warm and cosy with central heating and double glazing. Electric fire and colour TV in all lounges. Well-equipped kitchens. All linen and bedding provided (duvets). Large garden with plenty of car parking space. Garden furniture and laundry facilities. Sorry, no pets. Open all year. From £120 to £450 per week. White Rose Award Self-Catering Holiday of the Year runner up 1993.

e-mail: jeff@gfarm.fsworld.co.uk **website: www.gowlandfarm.co.uk**

SEDBUSK (near Hawes)

Mrs A. Fawcett, Mile House Farm, Hawes, Wensleydale DL8 3PT (01969 667481; Fax: 01969 667425). Sleeps 8. Sedbusk is a peaceful village just over a mile from the market town of Hawes, close to the Pennine Way. "Clematis Cottage" is a delightful old stone cottage tastefully restored with beamed ceilings, open fires and Laura Ashley prints. Beautifully maintained, the cottage is very warm and cosy with every comfort. Breath-taking views over Upper Wensleydale. The cottage has a lovely walled south-facing garden. Free trout fishing on the farm. Also charming traditional Dales character cottage in the picturesque village of West Burton, near Aysgarth Falls. Sleeps four plus baby. SAE for terms and prompt reply.

e-mail: milehousefarm@hotmail.com
website: www.wensleydale.uk.com

A useful index of towns and counties appears at the back of this book on pages 379-382. Refer also to Contents Page 50/51.

See also Colour Display Advertisement

SKIPTON

Mrs Brenda Jones, New Close Farm, Kirkby Malham, Skipton BD23 4DP (01729 830240; Fax:01729 830179). Sleeps 5. A supa dupa cottage on New Close Farm in the heart of Craven Dales with panoramic views over the Aire Valley. Excellent area for walking, cycling, fishing, golf and touring. Two double and one single bedrooms; bathroom. Colour TV and video. Full central heating and double glazing. Bed linen, towels and all amenities included in the price. Low Season £250, High Season £300; deposit required. Sorry, no young children, no pets. Non-smokers preferred. The weather can't be guaranteed but your comfort can. *FHG DIPLOMA AWARD WINNER*.
e-mail: brendajones@newclosefarmyorkshire.co.uk
website: www.newclosefarmyorkshire.co.uk

STAITHES

Garth End Cottage, Staithes. Sleeps 5/6. Victorian cottage situated on sea wall in this old fishing village in the North Yorkshire Moors National Park. Excellent walking centre. Small sandy beach with numerous rock pools. Cottage has feature fireplace, beamed ceilings, pine panelled room, well equipped kitchen including microwave. Warm, comfortable, well equipped with central heating, electricity and bed linen included in rent. Two lounges, front one with picture window giving uninterrupted panoramic views of sea, harbour and cliffs. Dining kitchen; bathroom with toilet; three bedrooms - one double, one twin, one single (two with sea views); colour TV. Front terrace overlooking the sea. Sorry, no pets. Terms from £200. **Apply Mrs Hobbs (01132 665501).**

See also Colour Display Advertisement

WEST SCRAFTON

Westclose House (Allaker), West Scrafton, Coverdale, Leyburn DL8 4RM. Stone farmhouse with panoramic views, high in the Yorkshire Dales National Park (Herriot family's house in 'All Creatures Great and Small' on TV). Three bedrooms (sleeps 6-8), sitting and dining rooms with wood-burning stoves, kitchen, bathroom, WC. House has electric storage heating, cooker, microwave, fridge, washing machine, colour TV, telephone. Garden, large barn, stables. Access from lane, private parking, no through traffic. Excellent walking from front door, near Wensleydale. Pets welcome. Self-catering from £400 per week. For bookings telephone: **020 8567 4862**
e-mail: ac@adriancave.com
website: www.adriancave.com/allaker

WHITBY

Nick Eddleston, Greenhouses Farm Cottages, Greenhouses Farm, Lealholm, Near Whitby YO21 2AD (01947 897486). The three cottages have been converted from the traditional farm buildings. The old world character has been retained with the thick stone walls, exposed beams and red pantile roofs typical of North Yorkshire. Set in the tiny hamlet of Greenhouses and enjoying splendid views over open countryside, the cottages offer a very quiet and peaceful setting for a holiday. All the cottages are equipped with colour TV, electric cooker, fridge/freezer, microwave and automatic washing machine. Linen, fuel and lighting are all included in the price. There are ample safe areas for children to play. Sorry, no pets. Prices from £188 to £509 per week. Winter Breaks from £142.

Valley View Farm

Old Byland, Helmsley, York, North Yorkshire YO6 5LG
Telephone: 01439 798221

Four holiday cottages sleeping two, four and six persons respectively. Each with colour TV, video, washer, dishwasher, microwave. Peaceful rural surroundings on a working farm with pigs, sheep and cattle. Winter and Spring Breaks available. Short Breaks from £90 and High Season weeks up to £495. Bed and Breakfast also available (ETC ◆◆◆◆). Please telephone for brochure and further details to: Mrs Sally Robinson.

e-mail: sally@valleyviewfarm.com website: www.valleyviewfarm.com

WHITBY

Mrs O. Hepworth, Land of Nod Farm, Near Whitby YO21 2BL (01947 840325). Sleeps 6 plus cot. This 250-year-old sandstone cottage is an annexe to the main farmhouse, situated on a 50-acre working farm in the North Yorkshire Moors National Park. Whitby is around nine miles away. Goathland & "Heartbeat" Country about the same, villages on the coast, like Staithes and Runswick Bay are closer, around three miles. The cottage looks over farmland, with splendid views to the south and east across the widening valley. Parking for two cars, a private garden and patio area. The cottage consists of a kitchen/diner, lounge with colour TV and electric fire, shower room, and a bathroom. Three bedrooms, two double and one with twin beds. Bed linen and night storage heaters are included in the hire, electricity is on a £1.00 slot meter, (with a £5.00 credit on entry) .We prefer to keep the cottage non-smoking, how ever smoking is permitted in the entrance porch. Prices for 2003 start from £95 to £195 per week, pets £14 a week extra. For availability and prices, please ring or e-mail.

colin@thecottage-ugthorpe.freeserve.co.uk **www.thecottage-ugthorpe.freeserve.co.uk**

YORK

Orillia Cottages, Stockton-on-the-Forest, York. Four converted farmworkers' cottages in a courtyard setting at the rear of the 300-year-old farmhouse in Stockton-on-the-Forest; three miles from York. Golf course nearby, pub 200 yards away serves food. Post Office, newsagents and general stores within easy reach. Convenient half-hourly bus service to York and the coast. Fully furnished and equipped for two to eight, the cottages comprise lounge with colour TV, etc; kitchen area with microwave oven, grill and hob. Bedrooms have double bed or twin beds. Gas central heating. Non-smokers preferred. Children and pets welcome. Available all year. Short Breaks may be available. Terms from £195 to £495 weekly includes heating, linen, etc. Contact: **Mr & Mrs G.Hudson, Orillia House, 89 The Village, Stockton-on-the-Forest, York YO3 9UP (01904 400600).** (B&B also available **ETC ◆◆◆◆**)
website: www.orilliacottages.co.uk

YORK

Wolds View Holiday Cottages, Yapham, Pocklington. Attractive, well-equipped accommodation situated in unspoilt countryside at the foot of the Yorkshire Wolds. Four units, sleeping from three to six, three of which are suitable for wheelchairs. Themed holidays, with transport provided, exploring the villages and countryside nearby; York only 12 miles. Terms from £145 to £540 per week. Short Breaks available. Pets welcome. Category 1,2 and 3 National Accessible Scheme. For further details contact: **E. and M.S.A. Woodliffe, Mill Farm, Yapham, Pocklington, York YO42 1PH (01759 302172).**

YORK

Sunset Cottages, Grimston Manor Farm, Gilling East, York YO62 4HR. Working farm. Six beautiful cottages lovingly converted from the granaries of our family farm. Superbly situated in the heart of the Howardian Hills, on the outskirts of the National Park and only 17 miles north of the historic city of York, Herriot country. With panoramic views, these warm and comfortable cottages retain their original mellow beams and interesting stonework while still providing all the modern comforts you rightfully expect in a well-designed self-catering cottage. Full central heating. Personally supervised by the resident owners, Heather and Richard Kelsey. Sorry, no pets (sheep country). Prices from £175 to £400. **ETC ★★★/★★★★**. Please write, or phone for brochure to **Mr and Mrs R. J. Kelsey, Grimston Manor Farm, Gilling East, York YO62 4HR (01347 888654; Fax: 01347 888347).**
website: www.sunsetcottages.co.uk

ENGLAND

WEST YORKSHIRE

See also Colour Display Advertisement

HOLMFIRTH

Summerwine Cottages, Shepley, Near Holmfirth, Huddersfield. Sleep 2/4. Part of a beautifully converted 17th century farmhouse, set in six acres of Pennine farmland, deep in the heart of 'Summer Wine' country. Sympathetically restored in the mid 1980s, the cottages have continued to be very popular with ramblers, walkers and country loving people who just want to 'get away from it all'. Fully self-contained, each has access via patio doors to a lovely enclosed rose garden. Furnishings and decor are to a high standard and all cottages have TV, video, cooker, washer/dryer, microwave, iron, lounge suite and dining table, etc. Each has central heating, double glazing and off-road parking. Cot, high chair available. Short breaks available. Price range £150 to £325 per week. **ETC ★★★**. For more information please contact: **Mrs Susan Meakin, West Royd Farm, Marsh Lane, Shepley, Huddersfield HD8 8AY (01484 602147; Fax: 01484 609427; mobile: 07711 000233).**

e-mail: summerwinecottages@lineone.net **website: www.summerwinecottages.co.uk**

• • *Some Useful Guidance for Guests and Hosts* • •

Every year literally thousands of holidays, short breaks and ovemight stops are arranged through our guides, the vast majority without any problems at all. In a handful of cases, however, difficulties do arise about bookings, which often could have been prevented from the outset.

It is important to remember that when accommodation has been booked, both parties – guests and hosts – have entered into a form of contract. We hope that the following points will provide helpful guidance.

GUESTS:

- When enquiring about accommodation, be as precise as possible. Give exact dates, numbers in your party and the ages of any children.
- State the number and type of rooms wanted and also what catering you require – bed and breakfast, full board etc. Make sure that the position about evening meals is clear – and about pets, reductions for children or any other special points.
- Read our reviews carefully to ensure that the proprietors you are going to contact can supply what you want. Ask for a letter confirming all arrangements, if possible.
- If you have to cancel, do so as soon as possible. Proprietors do have the right to retain deposits and under certain circumstances to charge for cancelled holidays if adequate notice is not given and they cannot re-let the accommodation.

HOSTS:

- Give details about your facilities and about any special conditions. Explain your deposit system clearly and arrangements for cancellations, charges etc. and whether or not your terms include VAT.
- If for any reason you are unable to fulfil an agreed booking without adequate notice, you may be under an obligation to arrange suitable alternative accommodation or to make some form of compensation.

While every effort is made to ensure accuracy, we regret that FHG Publications cannot accept responsibility for errors, omissions or misrepresentations in our entries or any consequences thereof. Prices in particular should be checked because we go to press early. We will follow up complaints but cannot act as arbiters or agents for either party.

ENGLAND

Caravan & Camping Holidays

CORNWALL

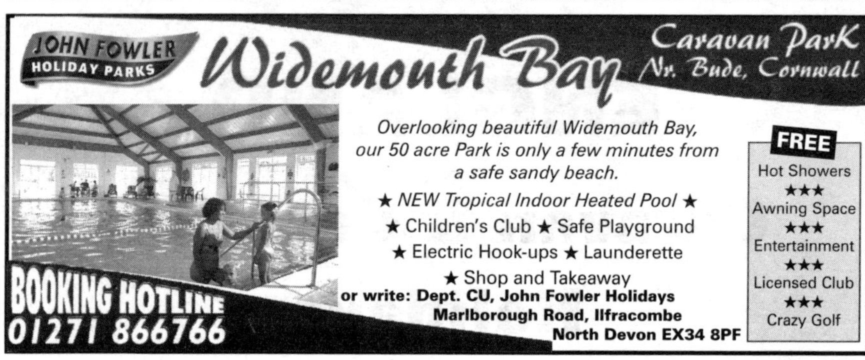

BUDE

Willow Valley Holiday Park, Bush, Bude EX23 9LB (01288 353104). Our camp site, which is only two miles from Bude and the sandy surfing beaches, is set in a beautiful valley. There is a small river meandering through the site which adds to its beauty. We are only a small site, with two pitches on four acres of land and, as these are not arranged in rows but around the edges of the site, there are always plenty of open spaces. We have toilets, showers, dishwashing area and a laundry. We also have a children's adventure playground which is in full view of most pitches, but not set amongst them. Dogs on leads are very welcome and we have seven acres of land in which they can run free. We also have a wide variety of pets on site including chickens, ducks, rabbits and peacocks. Open 31st March to 31st October, but enquiries are welcome anytime. For further details please write or telephone for a brochure and price list.

HELFORD RIVER

Mrs J. Jenkin, Mudgeon Farm, St Martin, Helston TR12 6BZ (Tel & Fax: 01326 231202). Here there are only two modern, spacious eight and six-berth caravans, in a quiet setting on a dairy farm near the Helford River on the Lizard Peninsula. The large grassed site, with easy access by car, is ideal for children. Helford River, including Frenchman's Creek, can be reached by beautiful walks across open fields and wooded countryside. Safe sandy beaches and facilities for boating, sailing and fishing are nearby. Helston is eight miles and has a supermarket, indoor swimming pool, gym and squash courts. The luxury eight-berth has one double and two twin bedrooms; separate toilet; and microwave. The six-berth has one double and one twin bedroom. Both caravans have galley kitchen, lounge, bath/shower, toilet, full sized gas cooker, fridge, colour TV, heaters, duvets and pillows. Bed linen is not provided. Available all year. Rates from £100.00 inclusive.

See also Colour Display Advertisement

ST AUSTELL

Trencreek Farm Holiday Park, Hewaswater, St Austell PL26 7JG (01726 882540). A peaceful, family-run holiday park with self-catering and camping facilities, all with country views and within easy reach of the sea. We can provide two and three bedroom units to sleep up to eight, and fully equipped self-catering tents to sleep six. We have a heated swimming pool, tennis court, and fishing lakes, etc, with kids entertainment in the main season. Children will love our free roaming and friendly animals. One of Cornwall's favourite family holiday parks.

e-mail: trencreekfarm@aol.com

website: www.trencreek.co.uk

CUMBRIA

See also Colour Display Advertisement

AMBLESIDE

Greenhowe Caravan Park, Great Langdale, Ambleside LA22 9JU (015394 37231; Freephone: 0800 071 7231; Fax: 015394 37464). Greenhowe is a permanent Caravan Park with self-contained holiday accommodation. Subject to availability, holiday homes may be rented for short or long periods from 1st March until mid-November. The park is situated in the Lake District half-a-mile from Dungeon Ghyll at the foot of the Langdale Pikes. It is an ideal centre for climbing, fell walking, riding, swimming and water skiing. Please ask about our short breaks. Please telephone for a free colour brochure. ✓✓✓✓ *DAVID BELLAMY SILVER CONSERVATION AWARD, WELCOME HOST, ROSE AWARD WINNERS 1983-2000.*

CONISTON

Mrs E. Johnson, Spoon Hall, Coniston LA21 8AW (015394 41391). Caravans sleep 6. Three 6-berth caravans situated on a 50 acre working hill farm one mile from Coniston, overlooking Coniston Lake. All have flush-toilet, shower, gas cookers, fires and water heaters, electric lighting and fridge plus colour TV. Children are welcome. Pets are allowed free. Available March to October. Pony trekking arranged from farm. Weekly terms on request.

PENRITH

R & A Taylforth, Side Farm, Patterdale, Penrith CA11 0NP (017684 82337). Camping on the shores of Lake Ullswater for tents and motor caravans (sorry, no towing caravans), surrounded by the beautiful scenery of the Lake District. Activities on the lake include swimming, sailing, boating, canoeing and fishing; steamer cruises. Modern toilet block, showers, washing facilities, shaving, hair drying points, washing machines and dryers. Dogs allowed provided they are kept on a lead. Convenient for touring the Lake District National Park. Fresh milk and eggs are available at the farm, with shops and post office in nearby Patterdale; regular bus services. Terms - Adults £4.50 per night; reductions for children; vehicles/motor bikes £1, boats/trailers 50p. Open Easter to November.

SILLOTH-ON-SOLWAY

Mr and Mrs Bowman, Tanglewood Caravan Park, Causeway Head, Silloth-on-Solway CA5 4PE (016973 31253). Tanglewood is a family-run park on the fringes of the Lake District National Park. It is tree-sheltered and situated one mile inland from the small port of Silloth on the Solway Firth, with a beautiful view of the Galloway Hills. Large modern holiday homes are available from March to October, with car parking beside each home. Fully equipped except for bed linen, with end bedroom, central heating in bedrooms, electric lighting, hot and cold water, toilet, shower, gas fire, fridge and colour TV, all of which are included in the tariff. Touring pitches also available with electric hook-ups and water/drainage facilities, etc. Play area. Licensed lounge with adjoining children's play room. Pets welcome free but must be kept under control at all times. Full colour brochure available. **ETC ★★★**, **AA** *THREE PENNANTS*.

Cumbria - The Lake District

With dramatic fells and lakes, changing seas and coasts, quiet valleys, unique towns and villages plus nature that has inspired many a writer, Cumbria is an ideal area in which to spend your holiday. Quality accommodation, a reputation for good food, the best walking in England, along with a wealth of other outdoor activities, ranging from sailing and canoeing to climbing and scrambling, cycling and pony trekking, all add to its appeal. If that sounds too energetic there are also plenty of attractions that celebrate Cumbrian people and history, literary and artistic life. There is something for everyone in Cumbria!

DEVON

HALDON LODGE FARM,

Kennford, Near Exeter EX6 7YG

Tel: (01392) 832312

In an attractive setting, three six-berth holiday caravans and log cabin in a private and friendly park. Fully equipped kitchen, lounge with TV, bathroom, toilet, H/C. Rates from £70 to £195 per week high season; tourers and campers welcome.

Excellent facilities. Open all year. Pets welcome.

Exeter and South Devon beaches 15 minutes, horse riding from a nearby farm. Three well-stocked coarse fishing lakes close by, also the attraction of barbecues and hayrides to a friendly country inn during school holidays.

Personal welcome given by David & Betty Salter.

ASHBURTON

Parkers Farm Holiday Park, Ashburton TQ13 7LJ (01364 652598; Fax: 01364 654004). A friendly, family-run farm site, set in 400 acres and surrounded by beautiful countryside. 12 miles to the sea and close to Dartmoor National Park. Ideal for touring Devon/Cornwall. Perfect for children and pets with all farm animals, play area and plenty of space to roam, also large area for dogs. Holiday cottages and caravans fully equipped except for linen. Level touring site with some hard standings. Electric hook-up. Free showers in fully tiled block, laundry room and games room. Small family bar, restaurant, shop and phone. Prices start from £90 Low Season to £480 High Season. Good discounts for couples. To find us: From Exeter take A38 to Plymouth till you see "26 miles Plymouth" sign; take second left at Alston Cross signposted to Woodland and Denbury. **ETC ★★★**, *AA FOUR PENNANTS, BRITISH FARM TOURIST AWARD. 2000 GOLD AWARD FOR QUALITY AND SERVICE. SILVER DAVID BELLAMY CONSERVATION AWARD. PRACTICAL CARAVAN TOP 100 PARKS 2000.*

e-mail: parkersfarm@btconnect.com **website: www.parkersfarm.co.uk**

BIDEFORD

Mr Chris Fox, Highstead Farm, Bucks Cross, Bideford EX39 5DX (01237 431201). Large and attractive modern caravan on a private farm site with fine sea views nearby. Just off the A39 Bideford/Bude road close to the coast of North Devon and convenient for Clovelly, Bideford and Westward Ho! Luxury accommodation for six adults (sleeping accommodation for up to 11 at extra charge) with bath/shower, separate toilet, fully equipped kitchen including microwave, gas fire and colour TV. Babysitting also available. Pets welcome by arrangement. Linen supplied as extra. Shopping, beaches, local attractions within easy reach. Car essential but good walking country. Open March to October from £95 weekly low season.

Visits & Attractions

Quince Honey Farm, South Molton, Devon • 01769 572401

The world's largest living honey bee exhibition, where the hives can be viewed in complete safety. Ideal for all ages, with fascinating videos and well-stocked shop.

Tuckers Maltings, Newton Abbot, Devon • 01626 334734

England's only working malthouse open to the public. See how barley is turned into malt for brewing beer and sample Devonshire Real Ale. Speciality shop.

See also Colour Display Advertisement

COLYTON

Bonehayne Farm, Colyton EX24 6SG. Working farm. Enjoy a relaxing holiday deep in the tranquil Devon countryside. Bonehayne is a 250-acre family farm. Our six-berth luxury caravan is situated in the farmhouse garden. It is south-facing and overlooks the banks of the River Coly. It is quiet and tranquil and the caravan enjoys lovely surrounding views. Two miles from quaint little town of Colyton; four miles to coast. Children welcome – we have spacious lawns and animals to see. Good trout fishing, woodlands and walks. Laundry rooms, picnic tables, barbecue, deck chairs. Bed and Breakfast also available. Details from **Mrs R. Gould (01404 871396) or Mrs S. Gould (01404 871416)**

e-mail: gould@bonehayne.co.uk

website: www.bonehayne.co.uk

CULLOMPTON

Mrs A. M. Davey, Pound Farm, Butterleigh, Cullompton EX15 1PH (01884 855208). Working farm. Sleeps 7. Enjoy a family break all year round on this family-run 80 acre beef and sheep farm. At Pound Farm, a holiday combines typical English scenery with the traditional beauty of the village of Butterleigh. Our luxury two bedroomed static caravan with decking can accommodate up to seven people. One double bedroom, second bedroom has two single beds with a bunk above, both rooms have electric heating. Dining seating area can be made into a double bed. Kitchen has fridge, electric hob and double oven with grill. Bathroom, flushable toilet and handbasin; shower room with additional washbasin. Lounge has TV with teletext and electric fire. Iron, ironing board, kettle, toaster, all utensils, cutlery and crockery are provided free of charge. Adjacent outbuilding/utility room is ideal for storage of fishing gear and bait. £1 coin meter for electricity. The caravan is set within its own grass and gravelled area, with parking space for two cars. Visitors are free to walk over the farm. Pets welcome. Free fishing on Pound Farm during your stay, no closed season, well stocked with carp, tench, rudd and perch. North and South coast 40 - 60 minutes' drive. Four miles from M5 (Junction 28) Cullompton. Terms from £100 to £200 per week.

HONITON

Francis Wigram, Riggles Farm, Upottery, Honiton EX14 4SP (01404 891229). Working farm. Caravans sleeps 2-6. Two beautifully situated caravans on 300 acre beef, sheep, arable farm six miles from Honiton, with easy access to many lovely beaches, moors and local attractions. Visitors welcome on farm, well behaved pets accepted. Children's play area, table tennis, darts. Linen hire, washing machine and dryer. Caravans set in two peaceful acres near farmhouse. Each is fully equipped for two/six people. Two separate bedrooms and spacious living areas. Own bathroom with shower, flush toilet, washbasin. Gas cooker, heater, colour TV, fridge. Terms from £110 to £235 per week (10% reduction for couples, not school holidays). For brochure please write or telephone.

e-mail: rigglesfarm@farming.co.uk

website: www.braggscottage.co.uk

WOOLACOMBE

Mrs Gilbert, North Morte Farm Caravan and Camping, Dept. FHG, Mortehoe, Woolacombe EX34 7EG (01271 870381). The nearest camping and caravan park to the sea, in perfectly secluded beautiful coastal country. Our family-run park, adjoining National Trust land, is only 500 yards from Rockham Beach, yet only five minutes' walk from the village of Mortehoe with a Post Office, petrol station/garage, shops, cafes and pubs – one of which has a children's room. Four to six berth holiday caravans for hire and pitches for tents, dormobiles and touring caravans, electric hook-ups available. We have hot showers and flush toilets, laundry room, shop and off-licence; Calor gas and Camping Gaz available; children's play area. Dogs accepted but must be kept on lead. Open Easter to end September. Brochure available. **ETC ★★★★**

DORSET

See also Colour Display Advertisement

WIMBORNE

Woolsbridge Manor Farm Caravan Park, Three Legged Cross, Wimborne BH21 6RA (01202 826369). Situated approximately three-and-a-half-miles from the New Forest market town of Ringwood – easy access to the south coast. Seven acres level, semi-sheltered, well-drained spacious pitches. Quiet country location on a working farm, ideal and safe for families. Showers, mother/baby area, laundry room, washing up area, chemical disposal, payphone, electric hook-ups, battery charging. Children's play area on site. Site shop. Dogs welcome on leads. Fishing adjacent. Moors Valley Country Park golf course one mile. Pub and restaurant 10 minutes' walk. **AA** *THREE PENNANTS*, **ETC ★★★**

NORFOLK

See also Colour Display Advertisement

BACTON-ON-SEA

Cable Gap Holiday Park, Coast Road, Bacton NR12 0EW (01692 650667; Fax: 01692 651388). Cable Gap Holiday Park is a friendly family-run caravan park that takes pride in providing first-class facilities. Our caravans have achieved the highest Tourist Board Grading and the coveted Rose Award for many years. You can have a carefree and relaxing time in one of our wide choice of quality caravans, sited only a stone's throw from the beach, some with sea views. Choice of two and three bedroomed caravans, both 12ft and 10ft wide, all equipped to a high standard and including background heating in the main bedroom. Our Deluxe range caravans are centrally heated and double-glazed. A one bedroom caravan is also available. Well behaved pets are welcome in a selected number of vans. We are situated just a few minutes' walk from Bacton Village Centre with local shops, public houses, restaurant and tea rooms, a Post Office, amusement arcade and a fish & chip shop. Bacton Woods is only a few minutes' drive away, an excellent place for a picnic, walking or cycling. **ETC ★★★★★** *HOLIDAY PARK, ROSE AWARD, SILVER DAVID BELLAMY CONSERVATION AWARD.*

e-mail: cablegap@freenet.co.uk **website: www.visitbritain.co.uk**

SHROPSHIRE

CRAVEN ARMS

Mrs S. Thomas, Llanhowell Farm, Hopton Castle, Craven Arms SY7 0QG (01588 660307). Comfortable and well equipped mobile home (30'x10'). Single site with own lawn, located on an upland working family farm. Sleeps four to five in two separate bedrooms, kitchen includes full cooker, fridge and microwave. Lounge area includes colour TV and gas fire. Shower room with all services. Linen included. Local village pubs provide good food. Historic town of Ludlow approximately 14 miles. Booking concessions for two people or less and long lets. 10% deposit required on booking. Prices on application.

SOMERSET

ENGLAND

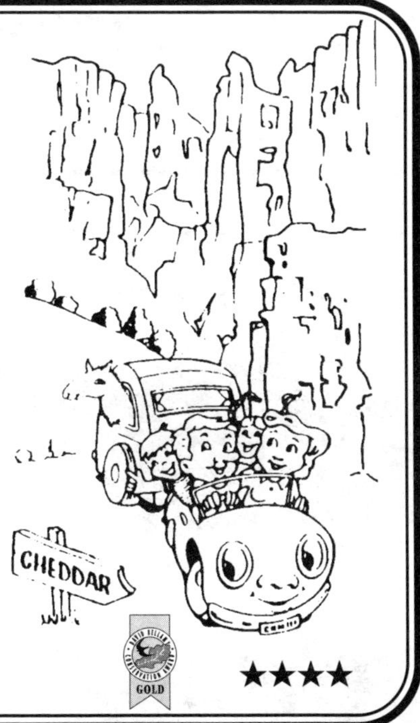

CHEDDAR

Broadway House Holiday Touring Caravan and Camping Park, Cheddar BS27 3DB (01934 742610; Fax: 01934 744950). SELF-CATERING: GENERAL. Cheddar Gorge - "England's Grand Canyon." A totally unique five star caravan and camping family experience. One of the most interesting inland parks in the West Country. A family business specialising in family holidays. A free cuddle with the llama a speciality. Prices include the use of the heated outdoor swimming pool and entrance to the Bar/Family room. Activities on the park include fishing archery, shooting; bike/tandem hire; table tennis, crazy golf, boules, croquet, skate-board ramp; three-acre lake. **ETC ★★★★, AA** *5 PENNANTS*, **RAC** *APPOINTED, DAVID BELLAMY GOLD AWARD.*

e-mail: enquiries@broadwayhouse.uk.com **website: www.broadwayhouse.uk.com**

Visits & Attractions

Dunster Water Mill, Dunster, Somerset • 01643 821759

The West Country's finest working water mill, set alongside the River Avill. See how flour is produced, then visit the Mill Shop where stoneground floor, home-made muesli and other products are available.

Readers are requested to mention this guidebook when seeking accommodation (and please enclose a stamped addressed envelope).

ENGLAND

Activity Holidays

HALDON LODGE FARM,

Kennford, Near Exeter EX6 7YG
Tel: (01392) 832312

In an attractive setting, three six-berth holiday caravans and log cabin in a private and friendly park. Fully equipped kitchen, lounge with TV, bathroom, toilet, H/C. Rates from £70 to £195 per week high season; tourers and campers welcome.

Excellent facilities. Open all year. Pets welcome.

Exeter and South Devon beaches 15 minutes, horse riding from a nearby farm. Three well-stocked coarse fishing lakes close by, also the attraction of barbecues and hayrides to a friendly country inn during school holidays.

Personal welcome given by David & Betty Salter.

ASHBURTON

Parkers Farm Holiday Park, Ashburton TQ13 7LJ (01364 652598; Fax: 01364 654004). A friendly, family-run farm site, set in 400 acres and surrounded by beautiful countryside. 12 miles to the sea and close to Dartmoor National Park. Ideal for touring Devon/Cornwall. Perfect for children and pets with all farm animals, play area and plenty of space to roam, also large area for dogs. Holiday cottages and caravans fully equipped except for linen. Level touring site with some hard standings. Electric hook-up. Free showers in fully tiled block, laundry room and games room. Small family bar, restaurant, shop and phone. Prices start from £90 Low Season to £480 High Season. Good discounts for couples. To find us: From Exeter take A38 to Plymouth till you see "26 miles Plymouth" sign; take second left at Alston Cross signposted to Woodland and Denbury. **ETC ★★★, AA** *FOUR PENNANTS. BRITISH FARM TOURIST AWARD. 2001 GOLD AWARD FOR QUALITY AND SERVICE. SILVER DAVID BELLAMY CONSERVATION AWARD. PRACTICAL CARAVAN TOP 100 PARKS 2000*

e-mail: parkersfarm@btconnect.com **website: www.parkersfarm.co.uk**

TWO adult tickets for the price of ONE at

Cold Harbour Mill Visitor Centre & Museum

See our READERS' OFFER VOUCHER for details.

One FREE child with full paying adult at

The Gnome Reserve & Wild Flower Garden

See our READERS' OFFER VOUCHER for details.

SCOTLAND

Board Accommodation

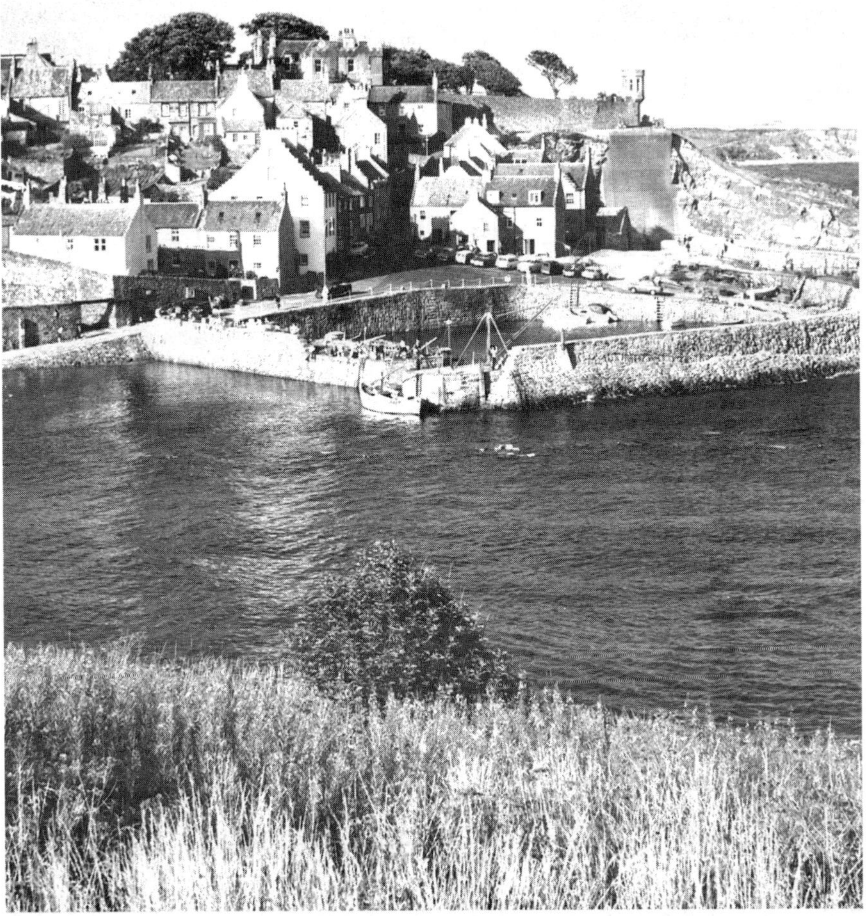

THE FHG DIPLOMA

HELP IMPROVE BRITISH TOURIST STANDARDS

You are choosing holiday accommodation from our very popular FHG Publications. Whether it be a hotel, guest house, farmhouse or self-catering accommodation, we think you will find it hospitable, comfortable and clean, and your host and hostess friendly and helpful.

Why not write and tell us about it?

As a recognition of the generally well-run and excellent holiday accommodation reviewed in our publications, we at FHG Publications Ltd. present a diploma to proprietors who receive the highest recommendation from their guests who are also readers of our Guides. If you care to write to us praising the holiday you have booked through FHG Publications Ltd. – whether this be board, self-catering accommodation, a sporting or a caravan holiday, what you say will be evaluated and the proprietors who reach our final list will be contacted.

The winning proprietor will receive an attractive framed diploma to display on his premises as recognition of a high standard of comfort, amenity and hospitality. FHG Publications Ltd. offer this diploma as a contribution towards the improvement of standards in tourist accommodation in Britain. Help your excellent host or hostess to win it!

FHG DIPLOMA

We nominate

Because

Name ....

Address ....

....

Telephone No..

ABERDEEN, BANFF & MORAY

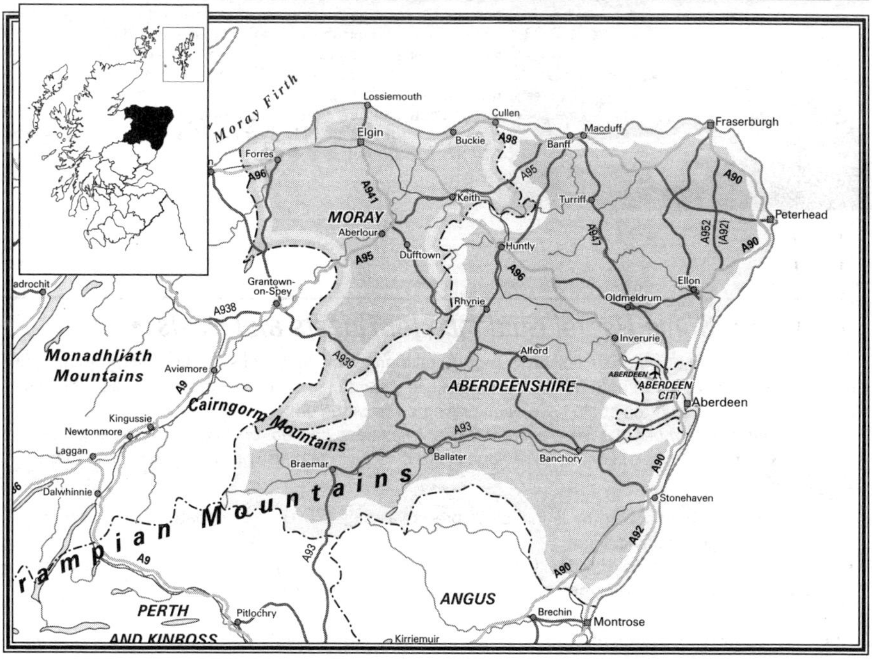

See also Colour Display Advertisement

BANCHORY

Raemoir House Hotel, Raemoir, Banchory AB31 4ED (01330 824884; Fax: 01330 822171). Raemoir House Hotel is part of an idyllic 3,500 acre estate, situated on Royal Deeside and within easy reach of Aberdeen. Timeless and beautiful, the hotel is recognised as the finest in the area. The food is divine. Also self-catering cottages in the grounds with one, two or three bedrooms sleeping up to eight people. A wonderful welcome for you and your pets. **STB ★★★★** *HOTEL*, **AA ★★★** *TWO ROSETTES*, **RAC ★★★** *THREE DINING AWARDS.*

e-mail: relax@raemoir.com

website: www.raemoir.com

HUNTLY

Mrs Alice Jane Morrison, Haddoch Farm, By Huntly AB54 4SL (01466 711217). Family-run farm 15 miles from Moray Coast. The town of Huntly has a castle, leisure centre, swimming pool and golf course with forest walks nearby. Enjoy well-cooked Scottish fayre in a peaceful location. Excellent views from our 19th century farmhouse. Tastefully decorated, spacious bedrooms with electric blanket, tea/coffee making facilities and hairdryer. Central heating throughout, residents' lounge with colour TV; friendly atmosphere. Ideal touring base. Open from April to October. Bed and Breakfast £15 to £16. Evening Meal £10. **STB ★★★** *B&B*

e-mail: alice.morrison@tinyworld.co.uk

KEITH

Mrs Jean Jackson, The Haughs Farm, Keith AB55 6QN (Tel & Fax: 01542 882238). The Haughs is a traditional mixed farm engaged in rotational cropping and cattle and sheep production. The spacious old farmhouse has a light cheerful dining room with excellent views. Ground floor bedrooms, three en suite, all with tea/coffee facilities and colour TV. The farm is situated just half-a-mile outside Keith and off the A96 Inverness road on the Whisky Trail; Falconry Centre eight miles. Open April to October. Bed and Breakfast from £18 to £21; Evening Meal £12.50. **STB ★★★** *GUEST HOUSE,* ***AA*** **◆◆◆◆**

• • *Some Useful Guidance for Guests and Hosts* • •

Every year literally thousands of holidays, short breaks and ovemight stops are arranged through our guides, the vast majority without any problems at all. In a handful of cases, however, difficulties do arise about bookings, which often could have been prevented from the outset.

It is important to remember that when accommodation has been booked, both parties – guests and hosts – have entered into a form of contract. We hope that the following points will provide helpful guidance.

GUESTS:

- When enquiring about accommodation, be as precise as possible. Give exact dates, numbers in your party and the ages of any children.
- State the number and type of rooms wanted and also what catering you require – bed and breakfast, full board etc. Make sure that the position about evening meals is clear – and about pets, reductions for children or any other special points.
- Read our reviews carefully to ensure that the proprietors you are going to contact can supply what you want. Ask for a letter confirming all arrangements, if possible.
- If you have to cancel, do so as soon as possible. Proprietors do have the right to retain deposits and under certain circumstances to charge for cancelled holidays if adequate notice is not given and they cannot re-let the accommodation.

HOSTS:

- Give details about your facilities and about any special conditions. Explain your deposit system clearly and arrangements for cancellations, charges etc. and whether or not your terms include VAT.
- If for any reason you are unable to fulfil an agreed booking without adequate notice, you may be under an obligation to arrange suitable alternative accommodation or to make some form of compensation.

While every effort is made to ensure accuracy, we regret that FHG Publications cannot accept responsibility for errors, omissions or misrepresentations in our entries or any consequences thereof. Prices in particular should be checked because we go to press early. We will follow up complaints but cannot act as arbiters or agents for either party.

ARGYLL & BUTE

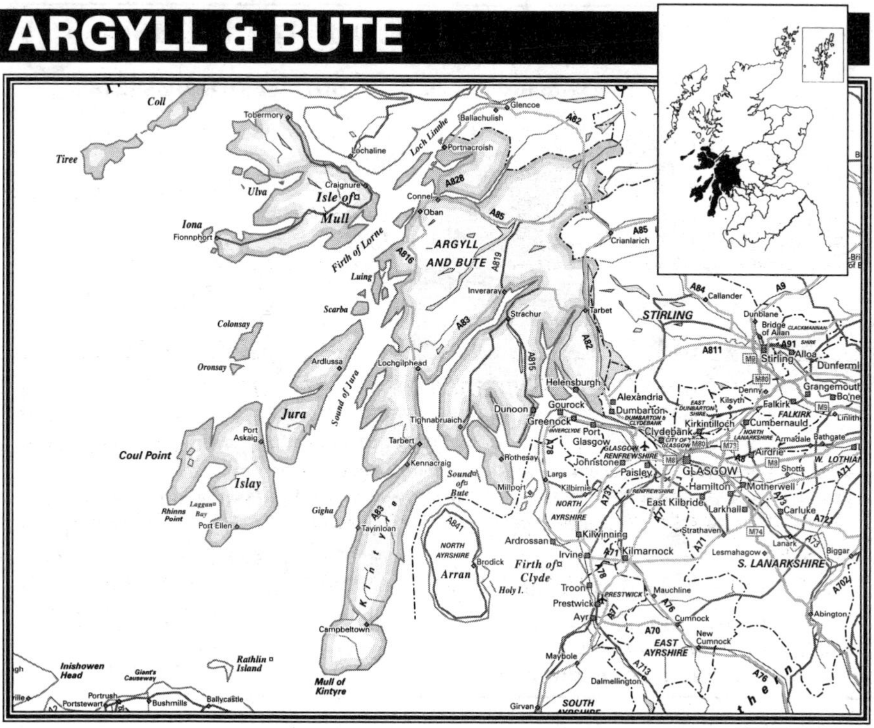

CARRADALE

Mrs D. MacCormick, Mains Farm, Carradale, Campbeltown PA28 6QG (01583 431216). Working farm. From April to October farmhouse accommodation is offered at Mains Farm, five minutes' walk from safe beach, forestry walks with views of Carradale Bay and Arran. Near main bus route and 15 miles from airport. Golf, sea/river fishing, pony trekking, canoeing locally. Comfortable accommodation in one double, one single, one family bedrooms; guests' sitting/dining room with coal/log fire; bathroom, toilet. Heating in rooms according to season. Children welcome at reduced rates, cot and high chair available. Pets by prior arrangement. The house is not suitable for disabled visitors. Good home cooking and special diets catered for. Bed and Breakfast from £17.50. Tea making facilities in rooms. **STB ★★** *B&B*.

Rockhill Waterside Country House

Est 1960

Ardbrecknish, By Dalmally, Argyll PA33 1BH Tel: 01866 833218

17th century guest house in spectacular waterside setting on Loch Awe with breathtaking views to Ben Cruachan, where comfort, peace and tranquillity reign supreme. Small private Highland estate breeding Hanoverian competition horses. 1200 metres free trout fishing. Five delightful rooms with all modern facilities. First-class highly acclaimed home cooking with much home-grown produce. Wonderful area for touring the Western Highlands, Glencoe, the Trossachs and Kintyre. Ideal for climbing, walking, bird and animal watching. Boat trips locally and from Oban (30 miles) to Mull, Iona, Fingal's Cave and other islands. Dogs' Paradise!

Also Self-Catering Cottages.

www.rockhillhanoverianstud.co.uk

See also Colour Advertisement

AYRSHIRE & ARRAN

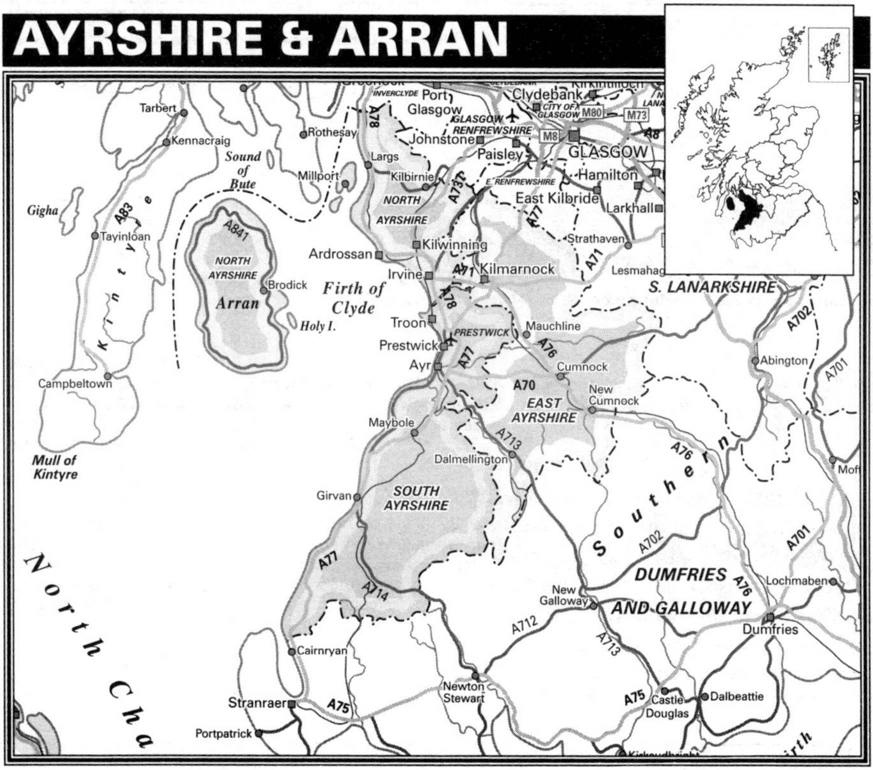

See also Colour Display Advertisement

AYR

Mrs Agnes Gemmell, Dunduff Farm, Dunure, Ayr KA7 4LH (01292 500225; Fax: 01292 500222). Welcome to Dunduff Farm where a warm, friendly atmosphere awaits you. Situated just south of Ayr at the coastal village of Dunure, this family-run beef and sheep unit of 600 acres is only 15 minutes from the shore providing good walks and sea fishing and enjoying close proximity to Dunure Castle and Park. Accommodation is of a high standard yet homely and comfortable. Bedrooms have washbasins, radio alarm, tea/coffee making facilities, central heating, TV, hair dryer and en suite facilities (the twin room has private bathroom). There is also a small farm cottage available sleeping two/four people. Bed and Breakfast from £23 per person; weekly rate £130. Cottage £250 per week. Colour brochure available. **STB ★★★★** *B&B*, **AA/RAC ◆◆◆◆◆**

e-mail: gemmelldunduff@aol.com **website: www.gemmelldunduff.co.uk**

Visits & Attractions

Culzean Castle and Country Park, Maybole, Ayrshire • 01655 884400

website: www.nts.org.uk/culzean.html

Robert Adam's masterpiece set in landscaped gardens. Investigate the Eisenhower connection and visit the Interpretation Centre, swan pond and aviary. Restaurant and tea rooms

A useful index of towns and counties appears at the back of this book on pages 379-382. Refer also to Contents Page 50/51.

KILMARNOCK

Mrs Nancy Cuthbertson, West Tannacrieff, Fenwick, Kilmarnock KA3 6AZ (01560 600258; mobile: 07773 226332; Fax: 01560 600914). A warm welcome awaits all guests at our dairy farm, situated in the peaceful Ayrshire countryside. Relax in spacious well-furnished en suite rooms with all modern amenities, colour TV and tea/coffee making facilities. Large parking area and garden. Situated off the A77 on the B751 road to Kilmaurs, so easily accessible from Glasgow, Prestwick Airport and the south. An ideal base for exploring Ayrshire's many tourist attractions. Enjoy a hearty breakfast with home-made breads and preserves and home-baking for supper. Children welcome. Terms from £20 per person. Brochure available. **STB ★★★** *B&B.*
e-mail: westtannacrieff@btopenworld.com
website: www.SmoothHound.co.uk/hotels/westtannacrieff.htm

KILMARNOCK

Mrs M. Howie, Hill House Farm, Grassyards Road, Kilmarnock KA3 6HG (Tel & Fax: 01563 523370). Enjoy a peaceful holiday on a working dairy farm two miles east of Kilmarnock. We offer a warm welcome with home baking for supper, choice of farmhouse breakfasts with own preserves. Four large comfortable bedrooms with lovely views over Ayrshire countryside, en suite facilities, tea/coffee, electric blankets, central heating; TV lounge, sun porch, dining room and garden. Excellent touring base with trips to coast, Arran, Burns Country and Glasgow nearby. Easy access to A77 and numerous golf courses. Children very welcome. Bed and Breakfast from £20 (including supper). Self-catering cottages also available. **STB ★★★★** *B&B.*

PLEASE NOTE

All the information in this book is given in good faith in the belief that it is correct. However, the publishers cannot guarantee the facts given in these pages, neither are they responsible for changes in policy, ownership or terms that may take place after the date of going to press. Readers should always satisfy themselves that the facilities they require are available and that the terms, if quoted, still apply.

BORDERS

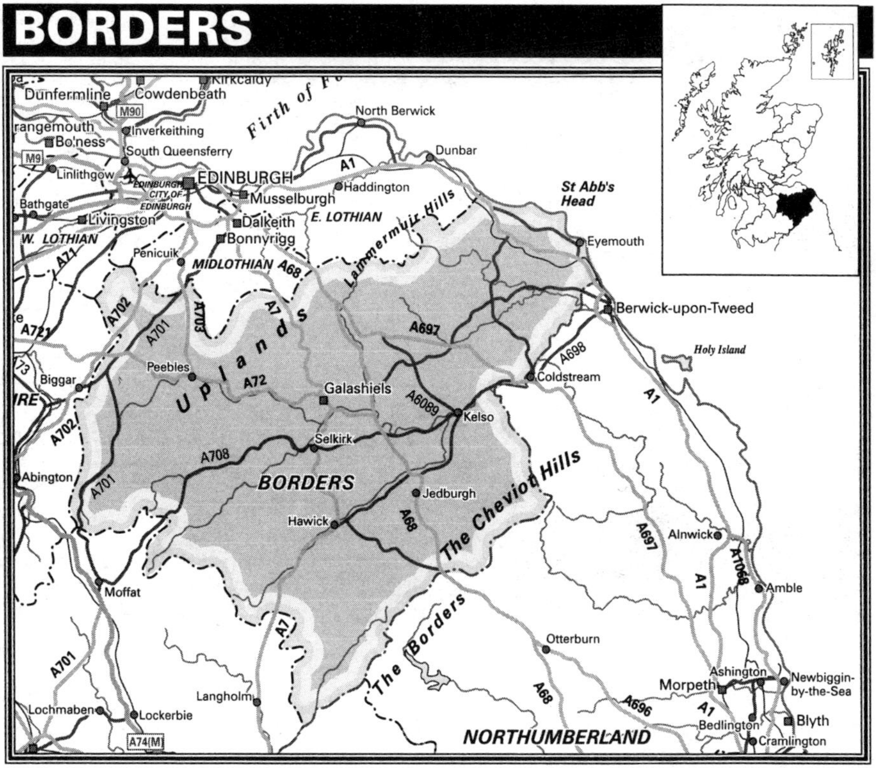

KELSO

Mrs Debbie Playfair, Morebattle Tofts Farm, Kelso TD5 8AD (01573 440364; Fax: 01573 440634). Working farm. Elegant 18th century farmhouse set amongst the Cheviot foothills where a warm welcome awaits you. Three acres of gardens and a woodland with tennis court. Ideally situated for touring the Borders. Accommodation includes two elegantly furnished double rooms en suite and twin room with private bathroom. Beautiful drawing room for guests' own use with TV. The working farm is noted for its pedigree cattle and sheep. Situated seven miles south of Kelso. Fishing, golf and wonderful walking. Bed and Breakfast from £25 per person. Reductions for children. Write or telephone for booking details and directions.
e-mail: debbytofts@aol.com
website: www.scotland2000.com/morebattle

TRAQUAIR

Mrs J. Caird, The Old School House, Traquair, Innerleithen EH44 6PL (Tel & Fax: 01896 830425). The Old School House has been recently modernised. Stands above picturesque Traquair village, with spectacular views of the River Tweed valley. The Southern Upland Way passes close by; perfect walking and riding country. Nearby is Innerleithen Golf Course, historic Traquair House and Kailzie Garden with fishing lake. Salmon and trout fishing on Tweed; horses can be hired or bring your own. Peebles is an attractive Border town with splendid woollen shops and a swimming pool. Edinburgh 35 minutes by car. Children and dogs welcome; stabling available; resident cats, dogs, ponies, hens and sometimes puppies. Log fire; home-cooked evening meals on request.

DUMFRIES & GALLOWAY

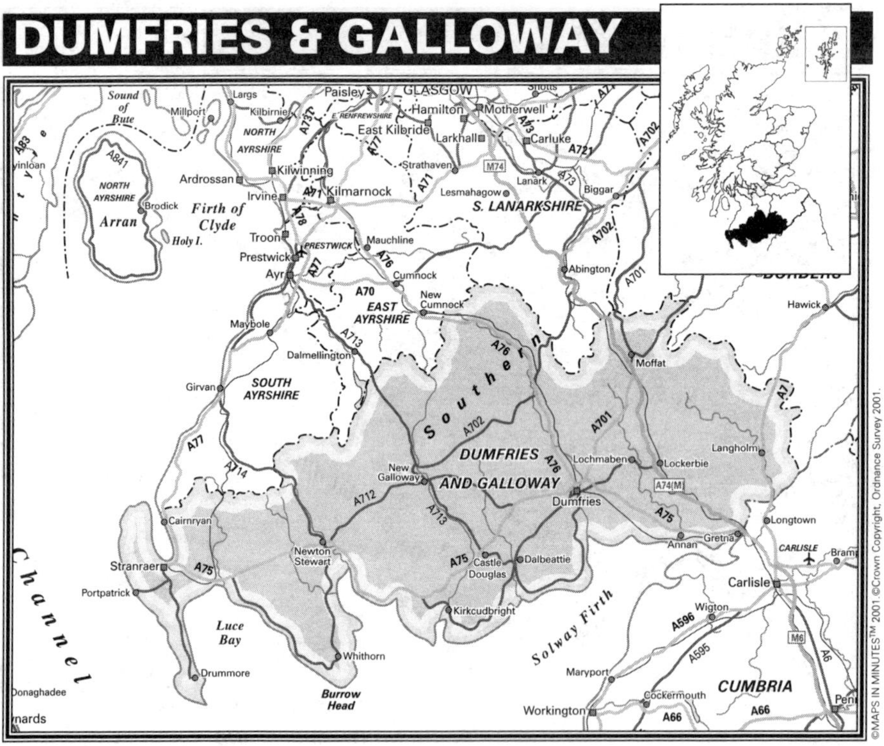

See also Colour Display Advertisement

CASTLE DOUGLAS

Ms Pickup, Craigadam Guest House, Castle Douglas DG7 3HU (Tel & Fax: 01556 650233). Working farm. Family-run, 18th century farmhouse. All bedrooms are en suite. Lovely oak-panelled dining room offering Cordon Bleu cooking, using local produce such as venison, pheasant and salmon. Billiard room. Trout fishing, walking and golfing available. Winner of the Macallan Taste of Scotland 2001. **STB** ★★★★ *B&B*, **RAC** ◆◆◆◆◆ *LITTLE GEM AWARD*, **AA** ◆◆◆◆◆ *PREMIER AWARD.*

website: www.craigadam.com

Visits & Attractions

Shambellie Museum of Costume, Dumfries, Dumfriesshire • 01387 850375

Step back in time and experience Victorian and Edwardian grace and refinement. Set in wooded grounds, it offers visitors the chance to see period clothes in appropriate settings.

Gem Rock Museum, Creetown, Kirkcudbrightshire • 01671 82357

website: www.gemrock.net

Award-winning collection of gems and minerals from around the world.

Audio-visual programmes, Crystal Cave, exhibition workshop, tea rooms and gift shop.

SCOTLAND

CROSSMICHAEL (Galloway)

Mr James C. Grayson, Culgruff House Hotel, Crossmichael DG7 3BB (01556 670230). Culgruff is a former Baronial Mansion standing in its own grounds of over 35 acres, overlooking the beautiful Ken Valley and the loch beyond. The hotel is comfortable, ideal for those seeking a quiet, restful holiday. An excellent position for touring Galloway and Burns country. The hotel is half-a-mile from A713 Castle Douglas to Ayr road, four miles from Castle Douglas and A75 to Stranraer. Many places of interest in the region - picturesque Solway coast villages, gardens, castles (including Culzean), the Ayrshire coast. For holiday activities - tennis, riding, pony trekking, bowls, golf, fishing (salmon, fly, coarse and sea), boating, water ski-ing, windsurfing, swimming etc. Lovely walks. All rooms have washbasins (some en suite), electric blankets, tea/coffee facilities; ample bathroom/toilet facilities. All bedrooms have TVs. Large family rooms available. One of the lounges has colour TV; dining room. Central heating. Cot. Non-smoking accommodation if required. Car advisable, parking. Bed and Breakfast from £12 per person in large family rooms, doubles from £18.50 per person. Open from Easter to October. Restricted October to Easter. Home of author James Crawford.

GRETNA

Mr Gary Beattie, Guards Mill Farm, Gretna DG16 5JA (01461 338358). Modern farmhouse accommodation in separate units on this family-run mixed farm. One double and one family room, both with shower en suite, TV, radio, tea/coffee making facilities and central heating. Convenient for M74/M6. Parking available. Non-smoking. Children welcome. Open March to November. B&B £18 per person sharing. Short breaks available. **STB ★★** *B&B.*

DUNDEE & ANGUS

BRECHIN

Rosemary Beatty, Brathinch Farm, By Brechin DD9 7QX (01356 648292; Fax: 01356 648003). Working farm. Brathinch is an 18th century farmhouse on a family-run working arable farm, with a large garden, situated off the B966 between Brechin and Edzell. Rooms have private or en suite bathroom, TV and tea/coffee making facilities. Shooting, fishing, golf, castles, stately homes, wildlife, swimming and other attractions are all located nearby. Easy access to Angus Glens and other country walks. Open all year. We look forward to welcoming you. **STB ★★★** *B&B.*
e-mail: adam.brathinch@btinternet.com

The FHG Directory of Website Addresses
on pages 349-378 is a useful quick reference guide for holiday accommodation with e-mail and/or website details

SCOTLAND

EDINBURGH & LOTHIANS

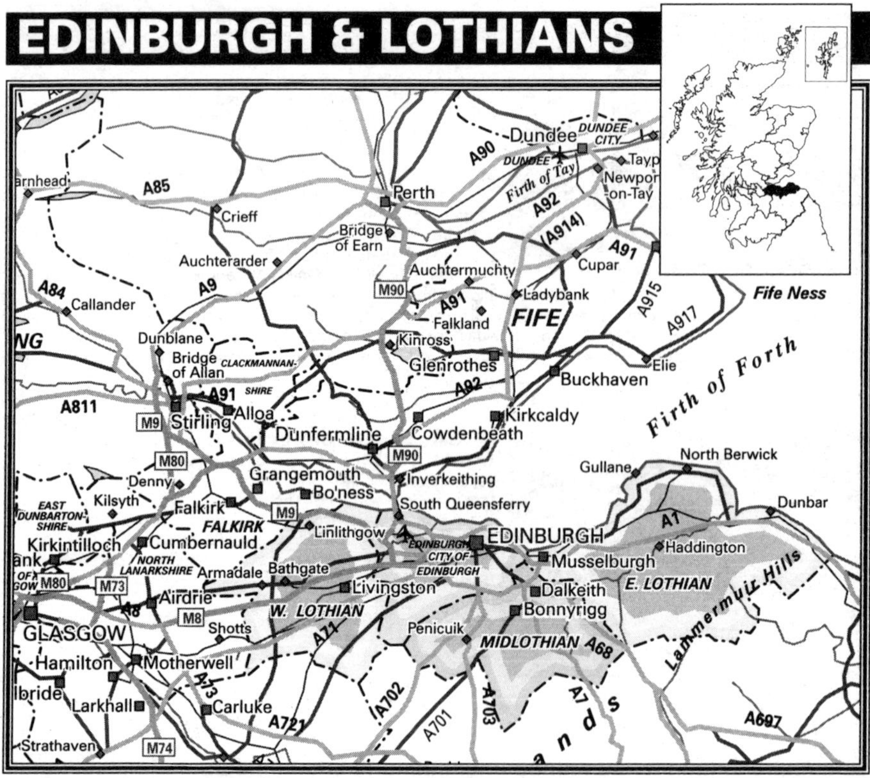

MUSSELBURGH

Inveresk House, Inveresk Village, Musselburgh EH21 7UA (0131-665 5855; Fax: 0131-665 0578). Historic Mansion house and award-winning Bed & Breakfast. Family-run "home from home". Situated in three acres of garden and woodland. Built on the site of a Roman settlement from 150 AD, the remains of a bathhouse can be found hidden in the garden. Three comfortable en suite rooms. Original art and antiques adorn the house. Edinburgh's Princes Street seven miles from Inveresk House. Good bus routes. Families welcome. Off-street parking. Telephone first. Price from £40 per person. Family room £100 to £120.
e-mail: chute.inveresk@btinternet.com
website: http://travel.to/edinburgh

PATHHEAD

Mrs Anne Gordon, "Fairshiels", Blackshiels, Pathhead EH37 5SX (01875 833665). We are situated on the A68, three miles south of Pathhead at the picturesque village of Fala. The house is an 18th century coaching inn (Listed building). All bedrooms have washbasins and tea/coffee making facilities; one is en suite. All the rooms are comfortably furnished. We are within easy reach of Edinburgh and the Scottish Borders. A warm welcome is extended to all our guests – our aim is to make your stay a pleasant one. Cost is from £18 per person; children two years to 12 years £11, under two years FREE.

FIFE

ST ANDREWS

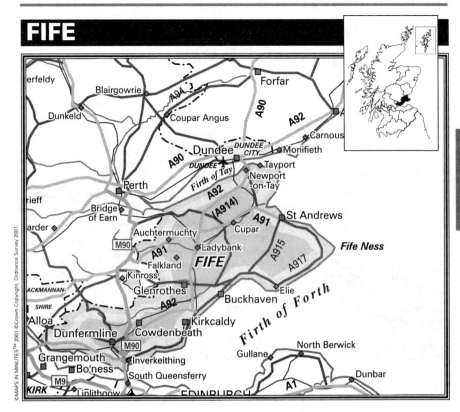

Mrs Anne Duncan, Spinkstown Farmhouse, St Andrews KY6 8PN (Tel & Fax: 01334 473475). Working farm. Only two miles from St Andrews on the picturesque A917 road to Crail, Spinkstown is a uniquely designed farmhouse with views of the sea and surrounding countryside. Bright and spacious, it is furnished to a high standard. Accommodation consists of double and twin rooms, all en suite, with tea/coffee making facilities and colour TV; diningroom and lounge. Substantial farmhouse breakfast to set you up for the day. The famous Old Course, historic St Andrews and several National Trust properties are all within easy reach, as well as swimming, tennis, putting, bowls, horse riding, country parks, nature reserves, beaches and coastal walks. Plenty of parking available. Bed and Breakfast from £23.

STB ★★★★ ***B&B*****, AA ◆◆◆◆**

e-mail: anne@spinkstown.com **website: www.spinkstown.com**

Visits & Attractions

Scotland's Secret Bunker, Near St Andrews, Fife • 01333 310301

website: www.secretbunker.co.uk

An amazing labyrinth built 100ft below ground, from where the country would have been run in the event of nuclear war. The command centre with its original equipment can be seen, AV theatre and two cinemas.

Dunfermline Abbey, Fife

HIGHLANDS

HIGHLANDS (South)

See also Colour Display Advertisement

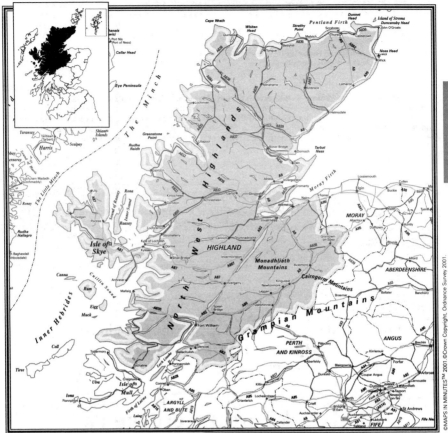

DALCROSS

Mr & Mrs R.M. Pottie, Easter Dalziel Farm, Dalcross, Inverness IV2 7JL (01667 462213). This Scottish farming family offers the traveller a friendly Highland welcome on their 200 acre stock/arable farm, seven miles east of Inverness, between the A96 and B9039. Three charming bedrooms are available in the delightful early Victorian farmhouse. The lounge has log fire and colour TV. Delicious home cooking and baking served, including choice of breakfasts. Ideal base for business or touring. Local attractions include Cawdor Castle, Culloden, Fort George, Loch Ness and nearby Castle Stuart. Telephone Margaret or Bob to book your stay. **STB ★★★★** *B&B*, **AA ◆◆◆◆**

e-mail: stay@easterdalzielfarm.co.uk

website: www.easterdalzielfarm.co.uk

FORT WILLIAM

Norma and Jim McCallum, "The Neuk", Corpach, Fort William PH33 7LR (01397 772244). The Neuk is fully centrally heated and double glazed throughout to ensure maximum comfort of guests. Two family, one twin and one double bedrooms, all en suite and have colour TV and refreshment facilities. Guests' dining room and smoking lounge. Payphone. Situated north-west of Fort William in the village of Corpach offering panoramic views over Mamore Mountains, Ben Nevis and Loch Linnhe. An ideal base for exploring the surrounding area either walking, cycling or motoring. Open all year. Whatever the weather you can always be sure of a warm welcome. Bed and Breakfast from £18 to £40. Evening meal £11. Brochure available.
e-mail: normamccallum@theneuk10.fsbusiness.co.uk
website: www.fortwilliamguesthouse.com

INVERNESS

Mrs E. MacKenzie, The Whins, 114 Kenneth Street, Inverness IV3 5QG (01463 236215). Comfortable, homely accommodation awaits you here 10 minutes' walking distance from town centre, bus and railway stations, Inverness being an excellent touring base for North, West and East bus and railway journeys. Bedrooms have TV and tea making facilities, washbasin and heating off-season. Bathroom has a shared shower and toilet. Two double/twin rooms from £15 per person per night. Write or phone for full details. Non-smoking.

Highland Wildlife

With plenty of space, and not a lot of people, there is an abundance of wildlife to be found in the Highlands, and you don't have to be out walking to see it either! You can watch red kites and ospreys from the comfort of your car, and from many of the hotels along the western seaboard you can also observe local wildlife - anything from red deer, seals, otters, dolphins and a large variety of birds, all from the warmth and comfort of your hotel.

PERTH & KINROSS

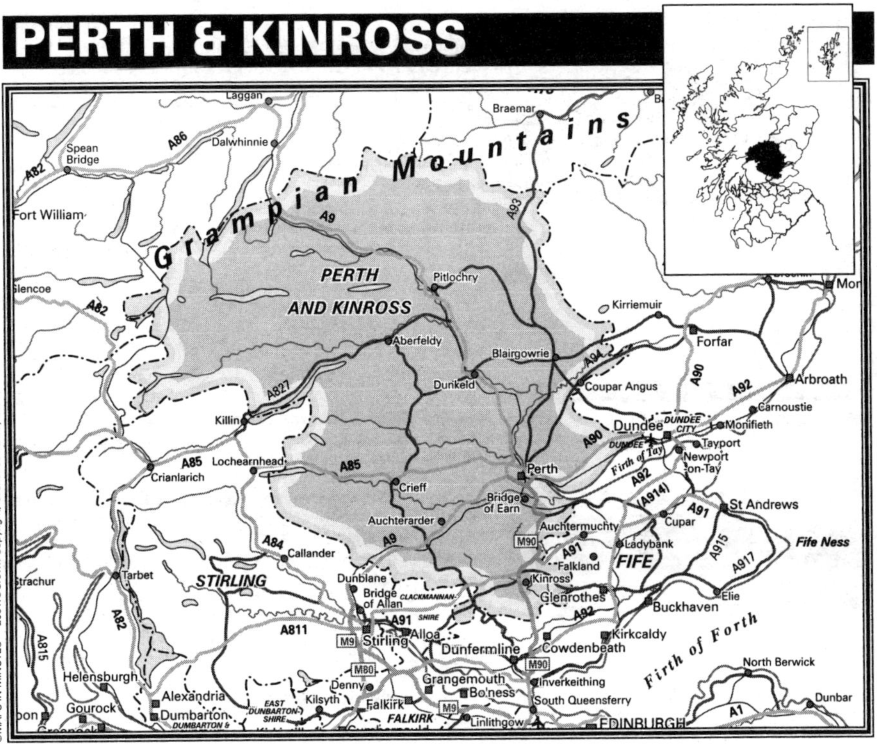

BRIDGE OF CALLY

Mrs Josephine MacLaren, Blackcraig Castle, Bridge of Cally PH10 7PX (01250 886251 or 0131-551 1863). A beautiful castle of architectural interest situated in spacious grounds. Free trout fishing on own stretch of River Ardle. Excellent centre for hill walking, golf and touring – Braemar, Pitlochry (Festival Theatre), Crieff, Dunkeld, etc. Glamis Castle within easy reach by car. Three double, two twin, two family and one single bedroom, all with washbasin; two bathrooms, three toilets and one shower. Cot, high chair. Dogs welcome free of charge. Car essential – free parking. Open for guests from 1st July to 7th September. £25 per person per night includes full Breakfast plus night tea/coffee and home baking at 10pm in the beautiful drawing room which has a log fire. Reduced rates for children under 14 years. Enquiries November to end June to **1 Inverleith Place, Edinburgh EH3 5QE.**

See also Colour Display Advertisement

GLENISLA

Glenmarkie Guest House, Health Spa & Riding Centre, Glenisla PH11 8QB (01575 582295) Quietly situated within one of the most beautiful glens in Perthshire, nestling on the edge of the forest. Our traditional licensed Scottish Guest House is cosy; all bedrooms are en suite, with tea/coffee making facilities. Enjoy bird watching, walking, wildlife, riding lessons, hacks and trekking in breathtaking scenery. Treat yourself to a hot spa or use the beauty facilities offering top-to-toe beauty therapy. Brochures and price list available on request. **STB** ★★★★ *GUEST HOUSE.*
website: www.glenmarkie.freeserve.co.uk

See also Colour Display Advertisement

e-mail: guthrienewmill@sol.co.uk

STANLEY

Mrs Ann Guthrie, Newmill Farm, Stanley PH1 4QD (01738 828281. This 330-acre farm is situated on the A9, six miles north of Perth. Accommodation comprises twin and double en suite rooms and a family room with private bathroom; lounge, sittingroom, dining room; bathroom, shower room and toilet. Bed and Breakfast from £19; Evening Meal on request. The warm welcome and supper of excellent home baking is inclusive. Reductions and facilities for children. Pets accepted. The numerous castles and historic ruins around Perth are testimony to Scotland's turbulent past. Situated in the area known as "The Gateway to the Highlands", the farm is ideally placed for those seeking some of the best unspoilt scenery in Western Europe. Many famous golf courses and trout rivers in the Perth area. **STB** ★★★ *B&B.*
website: www.newmillfarm.co.uk

STIRLING & THE TROSSACHS

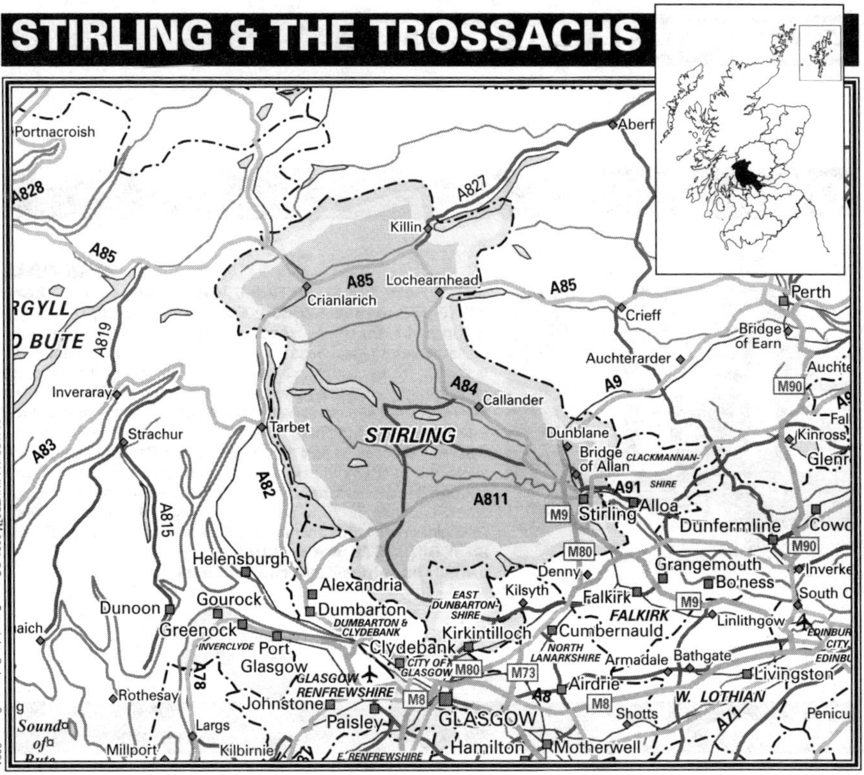

DENNY

Mrs Jennifer Steel, The Topps Farm, Fintry Road, Denny FK6 5JF (01324 822471; Fax: 01324 823099). A modern farmhouse guesthouse in a beautiful hillside location with stunning, panoramic views. Family, double or twin-bedded rooms available, all en suite with tea/coffee, shortbread, TV, and radio. Food a speciality ("Taste of Scotland " listed). Restaurant open to non-residents. A la carte menu and farm meals available most evenings. Easy access to all major tourist attractions. Your enjoyment is our aim and pleasure! Children welcome, pets by arrangement. Open all year. Bed and Breakfast from £20; Evening Meal from £10. **STB ★★** *GUEST HOUSE.*

DRYMEN

Mrs Julia Cross, Easter Drumquhassle Farm, Gartness Road, Drymen G63 0DN (01360 660893). Join us in this quiet rural setting, with spectacular views. Ideal base for touring Loch Lomond and Central Scotland. Situated on the West Highland Way. Accommodation consists of one double, one twin and one family room, all en suite. Children and pets welcome. Bed and Breakfast from £17.50 to £26. Evening Meal from £12.50. **STB ★★★** *B&B.*

e-mail: juliamacx@aol.com

website: http://members.aol.com/juliamacx

SCOTTISH ISLANDS

Orkney

KIRKWALL

Mrs D. Flett, The Albert Hotel, Mounthoolie Lane, Kirkwall KW15 1JZ (01856 876000; Fax: 01856 875397). Situated in Kirkwall town centre close to all local attractions, the Albert Hotel makes an ideal base for your stay in Orkney. The Bothy Bar is a must for the tourist, sit by the cosy fire, enjoy the authentic surroundings whilst sampling our local ales or whiskies, delicious bar menu and snacks served daily. Most Sunday evenings local musicians play traditional music, come along and join in. Enjoy that special occasion and dine in the Stables Restaurant where we serve the best Orkney Beef, Lamb and Seafood. Matchmakers Lounge Bar serves family lunches and bar suppers seven days a week. Lunches 12-2pm, suppers 5-9.30pm, Dinners 6-9.30pm. All major credit cards accepted. Call us for information on Special Break Offers. **STB ★★★** *HOTEL.*
e-mail: enquiries@alberthotel.co.uk

South Uist

GROGARRY

Mrs C. Macaskill, Drimisdale House, Grogarry, Isle of South Uist HS8 5RT (01870 620231; Fax: 01870 620397). Drimisdale House is an old Manse situated one mile from the sea, surrounded by countryside of outstanding beauty. A warm welcome awaits those wishing a relaxing and memorable holiday. The house has a large cosy lounge with peat fire, perfect for relaxing after a day's fishing, birdwatching, golfing or hill walking. All rooms have tea and coffee making facilities and radios. Two single rooms, one double and four twins, two bath and shower rooms. Bed and Breakfast from £16pp double/twin, £17pp single; Dinner, Bed and Breakfast from £24pp double/twin, £25pp single. Traditional home cooking.

PLEASE NOTE

All the information in this book is given in good faith in the belief that it is correct. However, the publishers cannot guarantee the facts given in these pages, neither are they responsible for changes in policy, ownership or terms that may take place after the date of going to press. Readers should always satisfy themselves that the facilities they require are available and that the terms, if quoted, still apply.

SCOTLAND

Self-catering Accommodation

See also Colour Display Advertisement

Islands & Highlands Cottages 2003. We specialise in those places most people only dream about, so allow us to help your dream become a reality and spend your precious vacation in one of our holiday properties. Awesome scenery, breathtaking sunsets, miraculous dawns and an abundance of wildlife. Holiday properties to suit all tastes and pockets. Please send for our brochure or visit our website. **Islands & Highlands Cottages, Bridge Road, Portree, Isle of Skye IV51 9ER (01478 612123; Fax: 01478 612709).**
website: www.islands-and-highlands.co.uk

Ratings You Can Trust

ENGLAND

The English Tourism Council (formerly the English Tourist Board) has joined with the **AA** and **RAC** to create a new, easily understood quality rating for serviced accommodation, giving a clear guide of what to expect.

HOTELS are given a rating from One to Five **Stars** – the more Stars, the higher the quality and the greater the range of facilities and level of services provided.

GUEST ACCOMMODATION, which includes guest houses, bed and breakfasts, inns and farmhouses, is rated from One to Five **Diamonds**. Progressively higher levels of quality and customer care must be provided for each one of the One to Five Diamond ratings.

HOLIDAY PARKS, TOURING PARKS and CAMPING PARKS are now also assessed using **Stars**. Standards of quality range from a One Star (acceptable) to a Five Star (exceptional) park.

Look out also for the new **SELF-CATERING** Star ratings. The more **Stars** (from One to Five) awarded to an establishment, the higher the levels of quality you can expect. Establishments at higher rating levels also have to meet some additional requirements for facilities.

SCOTLAND

Star Quality Grades will reflect the most important aspects of a visit, such as the warmth of welcome, efficiency and friendliness of service, the quality of the food and the cleanliness and condition of the furnishings, fittings and decor.

THE MORE STARS, THE HIGHER THE STANDARDS.

The description, such as Hotel, Guest House, Bed and Breakfast, Lodge, Holiday Park, Self-catering etc tells you the type of property and style of operation.

WALES

Places which score highly will have an especially welcoming atmosphere and pleasing ambience, high levels of comfort and guest care, and attractive surroundings enhanced by thoughtful design and attention to detail

STAR QUALITY GUIDE FOR

HOTELS, GUEST HOUSES AND FARMHOUSES

SELF-CATERING ACCOMMODATION
(Cottages, Apartments, Houses)

CARAVAN HOLIDAY HOME PARKS
(Holiday Parks, Touring Parks, Camping Parks)

Exceptional quality
Excellent quality
Very good quality
Good quality
Fair to good quality

In England, Scotland and Wales, all graded properties are inspected annually by Tourist Authority trained Assessors.

ABERDEEN, BANFF & MORAY

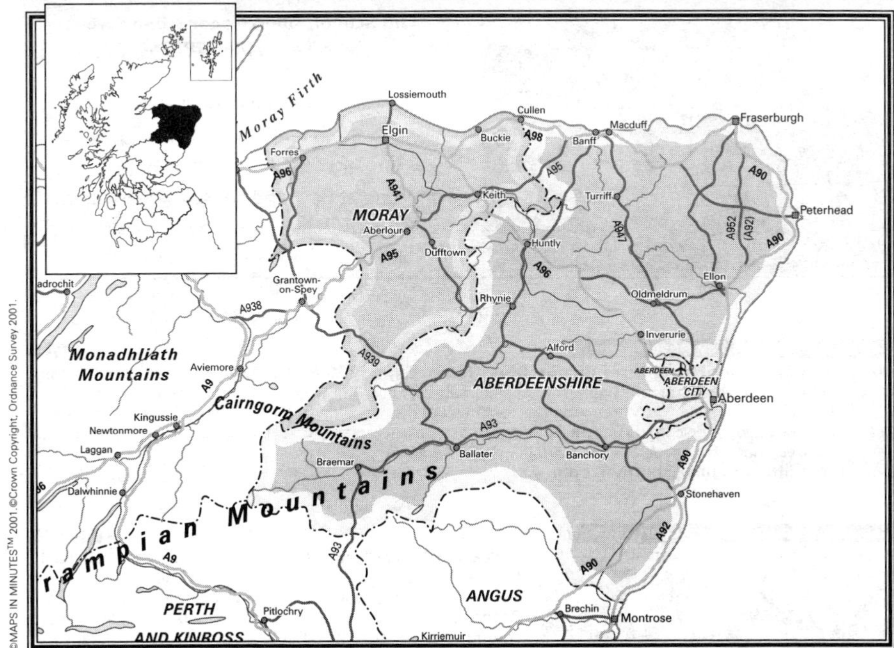

ABERDEEN

Holiday Flat. To suit couple or small family. Clean, comfortable and conveniently located for Aberdeen city centre and attractions. Lounge, double bedroom, bathroom with shower, fully equipped galley kitchen. heating, lighting and all bedding included. Regular bus service to city centre. No smoking and no pets. **STB ★★★** *SELF-CATERING.* ALSO PROPERTY IN WICK. Sleeps up to 6. Close to airport, bus and rail stations. Lounge with DVD, SKY TV, Playstation; dining kitchen, bathroom, en suite double bedroom, twin/double and single/twin; ground floor single. Fully equipped. *ASSC MEMBER.* Details of both properties from: **Donald Campbell, The Old Schoolhouse, Ulbster, Lybster, Caithness KW2 6AA (Tel & Fax: 01955 651297)**
e-mail: ulbster@ntlworld.com **www.visit.ourflat.co.uk** **www.assc.co.uk**

See also Colour Display Advertisement

ABERDEEN

The Robert Gordon University, Business & Vacation Accommodation, Schoolhill, Aberdeen AB10 1FR (01224 262134; Fax: 01224 262144). The Robert Gordon University in the heart of Aberdeen offers a variety of accommodation in the city centre to visitors from June through to August. Aberdeen is ideal for visiting Royal Deeside, castles and historic buildings, playing golf or touring the Malt Whisky Trail. The city itself is a place to discover and Aberdonians are friendly and welcoming people. We offer 2-Star self-catering accommodation for individuals or groups at superb rates in either en suite or shared facility flats. Each party has exclusive use of their own flat during their stay. The flats are self-contained, centrally heated, fully furnished and suitable for children and disabled guests. All flats have colour TV, microwave, bedlinen, towels, all cooking utensils and a complimentary "welcome pack" of basic groceries. There are laundry and telephone facilities on site as well as ample car parking spaces. *ASSC MEMBER.*
e-mail: p.macinnes@rgu.ac.uk **website: www.scotland2000.com/rgu**

Bremners of Foggie

Old School, Aberchirder AB54 7XS
Tel & Fax: 01466 780260
or 01466 780510
website: www.bremnersoffoggie.co.uk

Two and three bedroomed houses to let in quiet country village. Only 20 minutes' drive from coast at Banff and Portsoy. Weekly terms from £150 to £250; electricity extra. Sleeps 6. STB ★★★ SELF-CATERING

See also Colour Display Advertisement

ELGIN

Mrs J.M. Shaw, Sheriffston Farm Chalet, Sheriffston, Elgin IV30 8LA (01343 842695). An "A" frame chalet situated on a working farm. "Habitat" furnished, fully equipped for two to six people, colour TV, bed linen, duvets. Beautiful rural location in Moray – famous for flowers – district of lowlands, highlands, rivers, forests, lovely beaches, historic towns, welcoming people. Excellent local facilities. Moray golf tickets available. From £180 to £300. January to December. **STB** ★★ *SELF-CATERING. ASSC MEMBER*.
e-mail: jennifer_m_shaw@hotmail.com

See also Colour Display Advertisement

FORRES

Tulloch Lodges. Peace, Relaxation and Comfort in beautiful Natural Surroundings. One of the loveliest self-catering sites in Scotland. Modern, spacious, attractive and beautifully equipped Scandinavian lodges for up to six in glorious woodland/water setting. Perfect for the Highlands and Historic Grampian, especially the Golden Moray Coast and the Golf, Castle and Malt Whisky Trails. £235 to £675 per week. **STB** ★★★★ *SELF-CATERING.*. For a brochure contact: **Tulloch Lodges, Rafford, Forres, Moray IV36 2RU (01309 673311; Fax: 01309 671515).** *ASSC MEMBER.*
website: www.tullochlodges.co.uk

See also Colour Display Advertisement

INVERURIE

Mr and Mrs P. A. Lumsden, Kingsfield House, Kingsfield Road, Kintore, Inverurie AB51 0UD (01467 632366; Fax: 01467 632399). 'The Greenknowe' is a comfortable detached and renovated cottage in a quiet location at the southern edge of the village of Kintore. It is in an ideal situation for touring castles, historic sites and distilleries, or for walking, fishing and even golf. The cottage is all on one level with a large south-facing sittingroom overlooking the garden. It sleeps four people in one double and one twin room. A cot is available. Parking adjacent. Open from March to November. Prices from £275 to £475 per week, inclusive of electricity (the cottage is all-electric) and linen. Walkers Welcome Scheme. **STB** ★★★★ *SELF-CATERING. ASSC MEMBER*.
e-mail: kfield@clara.net

See also Colour Display Advertisement

TURRIFF

Forglen Country Cottages. 10 cottages, sleep 6-9. The Estate lies along the beautiful Deveron River and our traditional stone cottages nestle in individual seclusion. Visitors can explore one of the ancient baronies of Scotland. The sea is only nine miles away, and the market town of Turriff only two miles, with its golf course, swimming pool, etc. Places of interest including the Cairngorms, Aviemore, picturesque fishing villages and castles, all within easy reach on uncrowded roads. See our Highland cattle. Six miles of own walks. Terms from £149 weekly. Special winter lets. Children and reasonable dogs welcome. **STB** inspected. For a brochure contact: **Mrs P Bates, Holiday Cottages, Forglen Estate, Turriff, Aberdeenshire AB53 4JP (01888 562918/562518; Fax: 01888 562252).**
website: www.forglen.co.uk

ARGYLL & BUTE

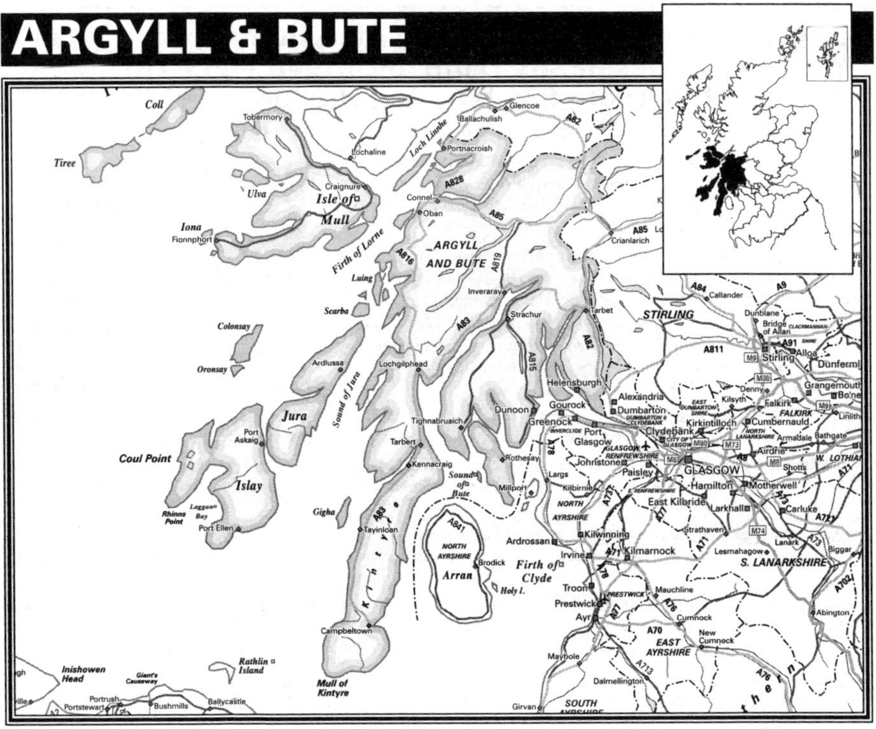

See also Colour Display Advertisement

APPIN

Ardtur Cottages, Appin. Two adjacent cottages in secluded surroundings on promontory between Port Appin and Castle Stalker, opposite north end of Isle of Lismore. Ideal centre for hill walking, climbing etc.(Glencoe and Ben Nevis half hour drive). Direct access across the field to sea (Loch Linnhe). Tennis court available by arrangement. Boat hire, pony trekking, fly fishing all available locally. Accommodation in first cottage is suitable for eight people in one double and three twin-bedded rooms, large dining/sittingroom/kitchenette and two bathrooms. Second cottage accommodates six people in one double and two twin-bedded rooms, dining/sittingroom/kitchenette and bathroom. Everything is provided except linen. Shops one mile; sea 200 yards. Pets allowed. Car essential, parking. Open March/October. Terms from £165 to £375 weekly. SAE, please for full details to **Mrs J. Pery, Ardtur, Appin PA38 4DD (01631 730223 or 01626 834172)**
e-mail: pery@eurobell.co.uk

See also Colour Display Advertisement

INVERARAY

Bralecken House, Brenchoille Farm, Inveraray PA32 8XN (Tel & Fax: 01499 500662). A mid 19th century stone building carefully restored to provide two comfortable houses situated on private upland farm. Each comprises sitting room, fully-fitted kitchen, two bedrooms, bathroom and shower room. Both are completely private or suitable for two families wishing to holiday together. Large parking area and garden. Children most welcome, but regretfully no pets. **STB ★★★** *SELF-CATERING*. Contact **Mr and Mrs Crawford**. *ASSC MEMBER.*

Situated on beautiful Seil Island with wonderful views of surrounding countryside. These lovingly restored cottages (one detached and one attached to the main croft house) retain their traditional character while incorporating all modern facilities. The cottages are near to each other and ideal for two families on holiday together. Seil is one of the most peaceful and tranquil spots in the West Highlands, with easy access to neighbouring Isles of Luing and Easdale.
Oban, the hub for trips to Mull and Iona, is half an hour's drive away over the famous 18th century "Bridge Over The Atlantic".
Wonderful area for hillwalking, cycling, fishing and bird watching.
Short breaks from £35.00 per day.

Kilbride Cottage

KILBRIDE CROFT

Balvicar, Isle of Seil, Argyll PA34 4RD
Contact: Mary & Brian Phillips
Tel: 01852 300475
e-mail: kilbridecroft@aol.com
web: www.kilbridecroft@fsnet.co.uk

Croft Cottage

See also Colour Advertisement

See also Colour Display Advertisement

LOCHGILPHEAD (By)

Ellary Estate Office, By Lochgilphead (01880 770232/770209 or 01546 850223). Properties sleep 6/8. Ellary affords peace and seclusion amidst outstanding scenery, plus complete freedom to pursue holiday pastimes for young and old alike. The range of accommodation is wide - small groups of cottages and chalets on Ellary, and super luxury and luxury caravans at Castle Sween. Cottages accommodate six to eight. All units fully equipped except for linen. The estate, beautiful at all times of the year, is suitable for windsurfing, fishing, swimming, wildlife observation and numerous walks. Further details and brochure on request.
e-mail: info@ellary.com website: www.ellary.com

See also Colour Display Advertisement

OBAN

Cologin Country Chalets. Set in a tranquil glen less than three miles from Oban, our cosy chalets and atmospheric country pub/ restaurant are a winning combination. Enjoy the waymarked forest trails in the hills above our farm, or relax in front of the fire and sample home-cooked local produce in the pub. The attractions of Oban – "Gateway to the Islands" – are minutes away. Pets and children are welcome – we have a playpark, games byre, and 17,000 acres to walk the dog. Disabled access chalets are available. Free fishing on our hill loch; boats and rods provided. Short breaks from £30, weekly lets from £160 to £495. **STB ★★★ to ★★★★** *SELF CATERING.* **Mrs Linda Battison, Cologin House, Lerags Glen, By Oban PA34 4SE (01631 564501; Fax: 01631 566925).** *ASSC MEMBER.*
e-mail: cologin@west-highland-holidays.co.uk website: www.west-highland-holidays.co.uk

See also Colour Display Advertisement

OBAN (By)

Eleraig Highland Lodges, Kilninver, By Oban PA34 4UX (Tel & Fax: 01852 200225). Sleep 4/7. These seven well-equipped, widely spaced chalets are set in breathtaking scenery in a private glen 12 miles south of Oban, close to Loch Tralaig, with free brown trout fishing and boating - or bring your own boat. Peace and tranquillity are features of the site, located within an 1800 acre working sheep farm. Walkers' and bird-watchers' paradise. Children and pets are especially welcome (dogs free). Cots and high chairs are available, also free. Gliding, water skiing and other sports pastimes and evening entertainment are available locally. Car parking by each chalet. Open March to January. From £205 per week per chalet including electricity and bed linen. Colour brochure from resident owners **Anne and Robin Grey. STB ★★** *SELF-CATERING.*
website: www.scotland2000.com/eleraig

Terms quoted in this publication may be subject to increase if rises in costs necessitate

SKIPNESS ESTATE

FARM HOLIDAY GUIDE DIPLOMA
STB ★ SELF-CATERING

This unspoilt, peaceful, West Highland estate with its own historic castle, medieval chapel and way-marked walks has traditional cottages to let all year round. Each cottage has an open fire and television; some cottages have a rowing dinghy in summer. Laundry facilities are available alongside the Seafood Cabin at Skipness Castle. Properties sleep 4 – 10.

All cottages have magnificent views and beautiful surrounding countryside and coastline. Safe, sandy beaches can be enjoyed on the estate, with fishing, pony trekking and golf nearby. Local ferries to Arran, Gigha, Islay, Jura and Northern Ireland. PETS WELCOME. Apply for rates and further details:

Sophie James, Skipness Castle, By Tarbert, Argyll PA29 6XU

Tel: 01880 760207 • Fax: 01880 760208 • e-mail: sophie@skipness.freeserve.co.uk

WEST LOCH TARBERT, ARGYLL – DUNMORE COURT

Five cottages in architect design conversion of home farm on the estate of Dunmore House. Spacious accommodation for 2-8 persons. All have stone fireplaces for log fires. Bird-watching, fishing and walking. Easy access to island ferries. Pets welcome. Open all year. Colour brochure. From £175-£490. STB ★★

Telephone: 01880 820654
e-mail: dunmorecourtsc@aol.com
www.dunmorecourt.com

Contact: Amanda Minshall, Dunmore Court, Kilberry Road, Near Tarbert, Argyll PA29 6XZ

One child (3-16) with 2 full paying adults at
Argyll Wildlife Park
See our READERS' OFFER VOUCHER for details.

10% DISCOUNT on all admissions at
Oban Rare Breeds Farm Park
See our READERS' OFFER VOUCHER for details.

AYRSHIRE & ARRAN

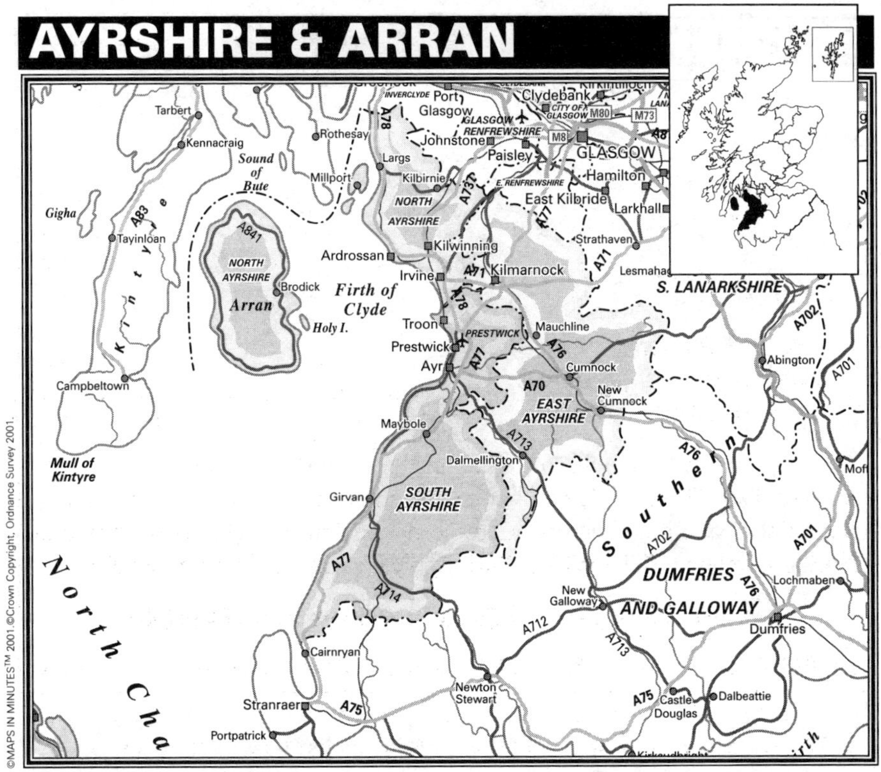

Isle of Arran

See also Colour Display Advertisement

ARRAN

Arran Hideaways, Invercloy House, Brodick, Isle of Arran KA27 8AJ. Choice of properties on the island, available throughout the year. All villages, all dates. STB Quality Assured. Short breaks available. Major credit cards accepted. Please ask for our brochure. On-line booking and availability. Our staff are here to help you seven days a week. **Call 01770 302303/302310.** *ASSC MEMBER.*
e-mail: holidays@arran-hideaways.co.uk
website: www.arran-hideaways.co.uk

KILMORY

Kilbride Farmhouse. Sleeps 5-7 adults, 2 children. Adjacent to a working farm. Located towards the south end of the Isle of Arran, with extensive gardens towards the front and a secluded and enclosed yard to the rear, ideal for family holidays. Kilbride enjoys sea views towards Ireland and Ailsa Craig to the South and towards Campbeltown and those romantic sunsets over Kintyre to the West. The long, sandy beach of Torrylinn is nearby, whilst the hills, golf courses and other attractions are only a short drive away. Accommodation comprises on first floor: two twin rooms, one single, bunk room with bunk-bed, bathroom with shower and bath,W.C. and wash hand basin. Ground floor: sitting room with open fire, sofa and TV/video, kitchen with oil-fired stove, electric hob and oven, microwave, and farmhouse dining table. Shower room/cloakroom. Spacious garage with games table(s). Prices from £510 per week. Enquiries: **Arran Estate Office, Douglas Park, Brodick, Isle of Arran KA27 8EJ (01770 302203, Fax: 01770 302813).**
e-mail: ccff.arran@virgin.net website: www.arranland.net/farmhouse.html

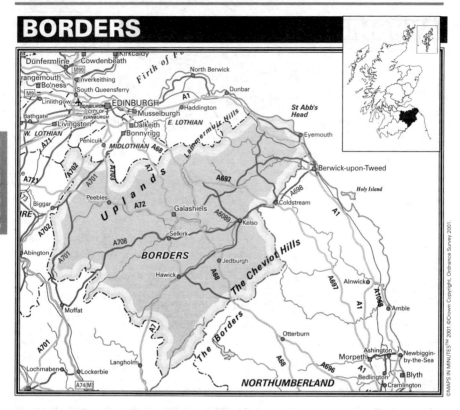

BORDERS

ASHKIRK

Wendy and Chris Davies, Synton Mains Holiday Cottages, Synton Mains Farm, Ashkirk, Selkirk TD7 4PA (Tel & Fax: 01750 32388). Sleep 6+6. Two beautifully renovated, semi-detached farm cottages positioned to one side of a farm steading, located in the heart of the Scottish Borders, an ideal base for touring and sightseeing. Both cottages are well furnished and extremely well-equipped, with double glazing, oil central heating and woodburning stoves. Lawned to front and sides; terrace with patio furniture. One cottage is suitable for disabled, having double bedroom downstairs with en suite bathroom, shower available for wheelchair users. We have our own golf driving range, small private loch for fishing; horse riding and golf available locally. Pets welcome by arrangement. Terms from £170 to £360 per week.

e-mail: Syntonmains@Tinyworld.co.uk

website: www.Syntonmains-holidaycottages.co.uk

See also Colour Display Advertisement

JEDBURGH

Mill House, Letterbox and Stockman's Cottages. Three recently renovated, quality Cottages, each sleeping four, on a working farm three miles from Jedburgh. Ideal centres for exploring, sporting holidays or getting away from it all. Each cottage has two public rooms (ground floor available). Minimum let two days. Terms £190–£330. Open all year. Bus three miles, airport 54 miles. **STB ★★★★** *SELF-CATERING*. **Mrs A. Fraser, Overwells, Jedburgh TD8 6LT (01835 863020; Fax: 01835 864334).** *ASSC MEMBER.*

e-mail: abfraser@btinternet.com

website: www.overwells.co.uk

See also Colour Display Advertisement

KELSO

Edenmouth Holiday Cottages, near Kelso. Unique, quality cottages, recently converted from a traditional farm steading. Magnificent views across the Tweed Valley. Ideal base for fishermen, golfers, walkers, families and couples wanting a relaxing break. Comfortable, well-equipped cottages on ground level. All bedrooms have en suite facilities. Central heating, linen, towels and electricity included in rates. Large grass garden, games room, laundry/drying room, bicycle lock-up. Pets by arrangement. Open all year. Cottages sleep 1 – 8. Parties of up to 18 catered for. Weekly lets from £160 to £420. Short Breaks – 3 nights for 2 people £100. Bed and Breakfast £20pppn. **Mrs Geraldine O'Driscoll, Edenmouth Farm, Near Kelso, Scottish Borders TD5 7QB (01890 830391). STB ★★★** *SELF-CATERING/B&B.*

e-mail: edenmouth.odris@virgin.net

website: www.edenmouth.co.uk

KELSO

Houndridge Holiday Cottages, Houndridge, Ednam, Kelso TD5 7QN (Tel & Fax: 01573 470604). Sleep 4, 6, 7. Houndridge is a special place, three miles from Kelso. Take a walk around our farm and admire the magnificent views of the Cheviots, Eildon Hills and Hume Castle or spot the elusive deer or barn owl. Not only do we have high quality cottages but private 3 star Leisure Club offering many activities including an INDOOR HEATED SWIMMING POOL. You can also play squash, tennis, table tennis, exercise in the well-equipped gym, take a swim or hire a bike. Of course do not forget to tour the beautiful Borders and visit the many attractions, abbeys, houses and gardens. **STB ★★★/★★★★** *SELF-CATERING*

e-mail: houndridge.holiday@virgin.net

website: www.houndridge.co.uk

NEWCASTLETON

Cumbrian/Scottish Borders. Sleep up to 7 plus cot. Superb character cottages set in historic landscape. Conservation farm. Panoramic views. High quality furnishings. Wood burning stoves. Stabling facilities - bring your horse. Great for walking, cycling, riding with forest tracks, bridleways, rivers and wooded valleys. Explore the Lake District, Hadrian's Wall, Solway Coast, historic Carlisle and return to a barbecue on your own patio or relax by the fire. Children and pets welcome. Terms from £250 to £450. Open all year. **STB ★★★★** *SELF CATERING*. Contact: **Jane Gray, Saughs Farm, Bailey, Newcastleton, Roxburghshire TD9 0TT (01697 748000/748346; Fax: 01697 748180).**

e-mail: skylark@onholiday.co.uk

website: www.skylarkcottages.co.uk

PEEBLES

Mrs R. Smith, Chapelhill Farm, Peebles EH45 8PQ (01721 720188; 01721 729734). Three delightful cottages on working farm situated in quiet, peaceful location with superb country views. The popular town of Peebles with its many shops, hotels, pubs and restaurants is less than a mile away. Edinburgh just 30 minutes by car. All cottages have central heating throughout, electric cooker, microwave and washing machine. Heating and bed linen included in price. Garden and garden furniture. Ample parking. Children most welcome. Dogs by arrangement. Many golf courses, beautiful walks, fishing, horse riding, cycling etc. All nearby. Brochures available. Prices from £150-£290 per week. Farmhouse B&B also available. **STB ★★★** *SELF CATERING.*

A useful index of towns and counties appears at the back of this book on pages 379-382. Refer also to Contents Page 50/51.

DUMFRIES & GALLOWAY

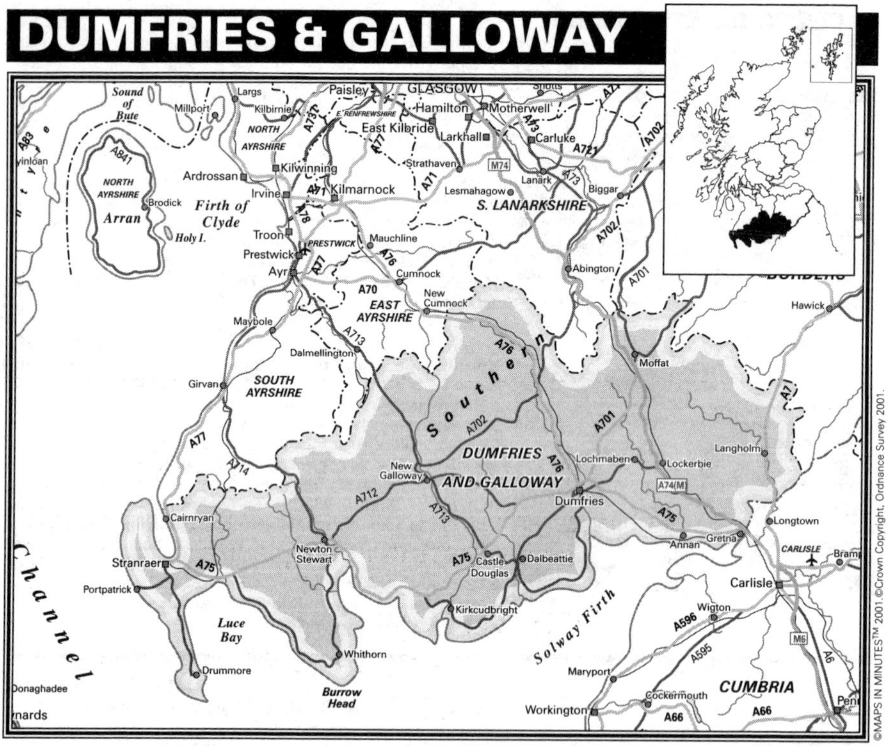

CASTLE DOUGLAS

Cala-Sona, Auchencairn, Castle Douglas. Sleeps 6. A stone-built house in centre of Auchencairn village, near shops, Post Office and garage. To let, furnished. Equipped for six persons. Linen supplied. Two bedrooms (one double bed; two single beds); cot available. Bathroom, bedroom with double bed, livingroom and kitchenette with electric cooker, fridge and geyser. Auchencairn is a friendly seaside village and you can enjoy a peaceful holiday here on the Solway Firth where the Galloway Hills slope down to the sea. Many places of historic interest to visit, also cliffs, caves and sandy beaches. A haven for ornithologists. SAE brings prompt reply. Car essential – parking. **Mrs Mary Gordon, 7 Church Road, Auchencairn, Castle Douglas DG7 1QS (01556 640345).**

PORTPATRICK

Mr A.D. Bryce, "Alinn", Portpatrick DG9 8JW (01776 810277). Sea front situation with unrestricted views of harbour and boats, overlooking small sandy beach with safe bathing. Golf, bowling, tennis and sea angling, scenic cliff walks and ideal country roads for touring. Shops and restaurants nearby. Area is of great historical and archaeological interest and enjoys a mild climate. Self-catering flats, three bedrooms; cottage, two bedrooms. Electric heating,cooking etc. Prepayment coin meter. Terms from £150 to £215 per week. Parking at door. Please write or telephone for further details.

Visits & Attractions

Shambellie Museum of Costume, Dumfries, Dumfriesshire • 01387 850375

Step back in time and experience Victorian and Edwardian grace and refinement. Set in wooded grounds, it offers visitors the chance to see period clothes in appropriate settings.

Gem Rock Museum, Creetown, Kirkcudbrightshire • 01671 82357
website: www.gemrock.net

Award-winning collection of gems and minerals from around the world.
Audio-visual programmes, Crystal Cave, exhibition workshop, tea rooms and gift shop.

DUNDEE & ANGUS

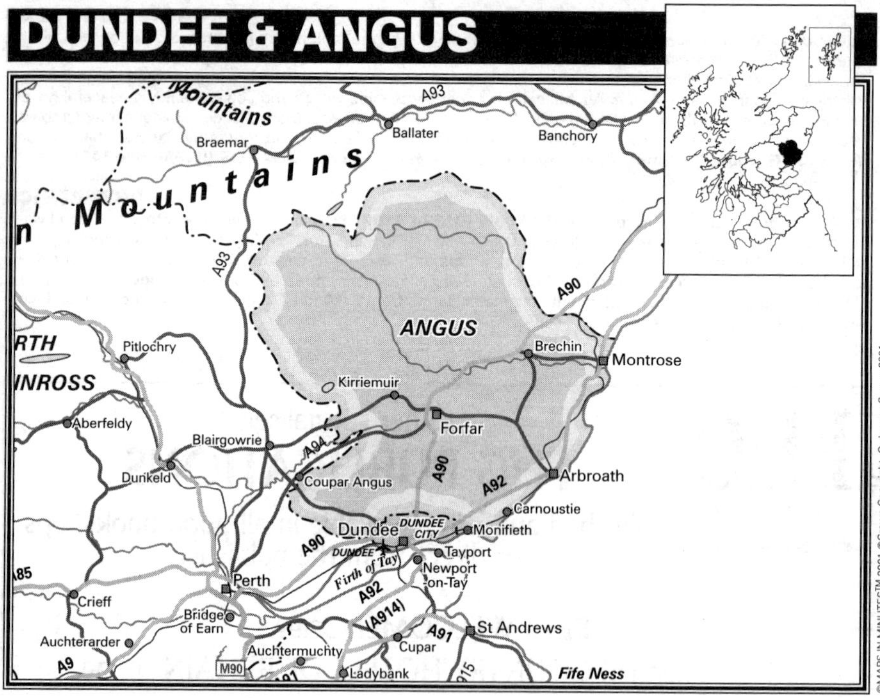

BROUGHTY FERRY

Kingennie Fishings and Holiday Lodges, Kingennie, Broughty Ferry DD5 3RD (01382 350777; Fax: 01382 350400). The four modern Lodges provide luxury self-catering holiday accommodation; all have colour TV and are well insulated and centrally heated. Set in secluded woodland, they enjoy views over the fishing ponds below, where experts and beginners alike can try their skills. GLENCLOVA, sleeping up to seven has been specially designed for disabled visitors, GLENISLA and GLENESK, sleeping four to six, both enjoy lovely views. THE BARD'S NEUK is situated in a quiet secluded corner site. The nearby towns, villages, beaches and countryside around the area provide many fascinating and enjoyable trips all of which can be covered within a day. Pets welcome. Terms from £220 to £465 for Esk, Clova and Isla Cottages; from £363 to £747 for The Bard's Neuk. **STB ★★★★** *SELF-CATERING.*

e-mail: kingennie@easynet.co.uk **website: www.kingennie-fishings.com**

EDINBURGH & LOTHIANS

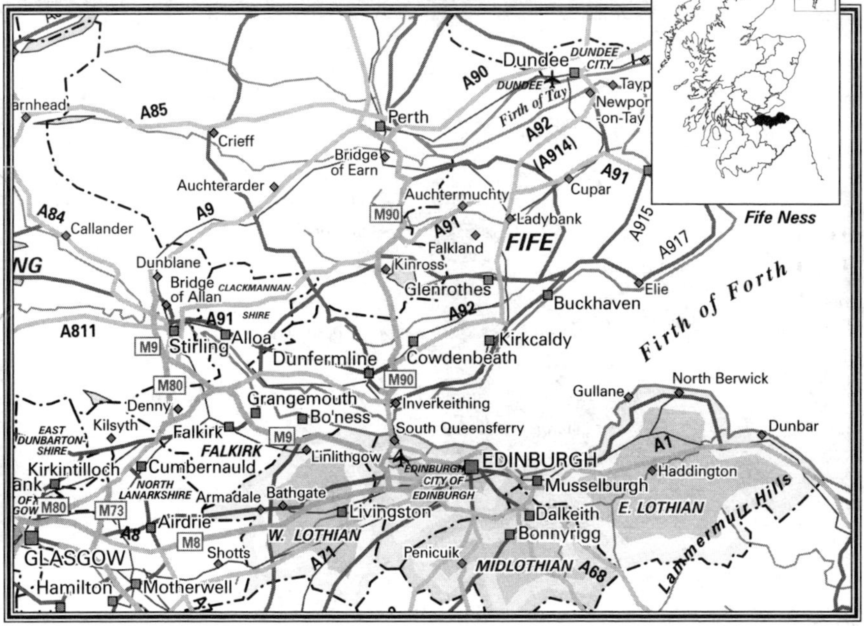

EDINBURGH (near)

Mrs Geraldine Hamilton, Crosswoodhill Farm, By West Calder EH55 8LP (01501 785205; Fax: 01501 785308). 3 properties sleep 4/6. STB AWARD WINNER: SCOTTISH SELF-CATERING OPERATOR OF THE YEAR 2001. Imagine the best of both worlds . . .two stunning cities, Edinburgh and Glasgow, within an hour's drive and . . .midway. . . Crosswoodhill, a haven of rural tranquillity. Situated on the A70, just 18 miles from the heart of historic Edinburgh, our 1700 acre livestock farm is perfectly placed for exploring Fife, the Borders, Rob Roy and Braveheart country. Visit castles, stately homes, museums, galleries, fine shops; enjoy leisure pursuits close by. Or simply relax; it's a perfect place to unwind. Choose between Midcrosswood, a gem of a cottage on the scenic Pentland Hills, Steading Cottage or a self-contained wing of our handsome 200 year-old farmhouse with its own garden. Comfort, charm, warmth, tradition and a friendly welcome await you. All properties are superbly equipped, including colour TV, video, electric cooker, microwave, washing machine, tumble dryer, dishwasher, fridge, freezer, pay-phone, all bed linen and towels. Bath and power shower. Central heating. Extras: home-grown peat/coal for multi-fuel stoves, oil, electricity by meter reading. Dogs by arrangement (sheep country). Own transport essential. From £260 to £590 weekly. Two cottages wheelchair friendly. **STB** ★★★ to ★★★★ *SELF-CATERING. ASSC MEMBER.*

e-mail: cottages@crosswoodhill.co.uk **website: www.crosswoodhill.co.uk**

See also Colour Display Advertisement

ROSEWELL

Hunter Holiday Cottages, Thornton Farm, Rosewell, Edinburgh EH24 9EF (0131 448 0888; Fax: 0131 440 2082). Hunter Holiday Cottages offer a range of cottages in beautiful countryside only eight miles from Edinburgh City Centre. These superior cottages are recently renovated, have all modern facilities and sleep four to ten plus. They provide the ideal base for the perfect Scottish holiday from their location in Midlothian's historic countryside. There is easy access to Scotland's capital and the major routes to the rest of Scotland. For more information visit our website. Also B&B £25 per night. Contact **Margot Crichton**.

e-mail: info@edinburghcottages.com

website: www.edinburghcottages.com

FIFE

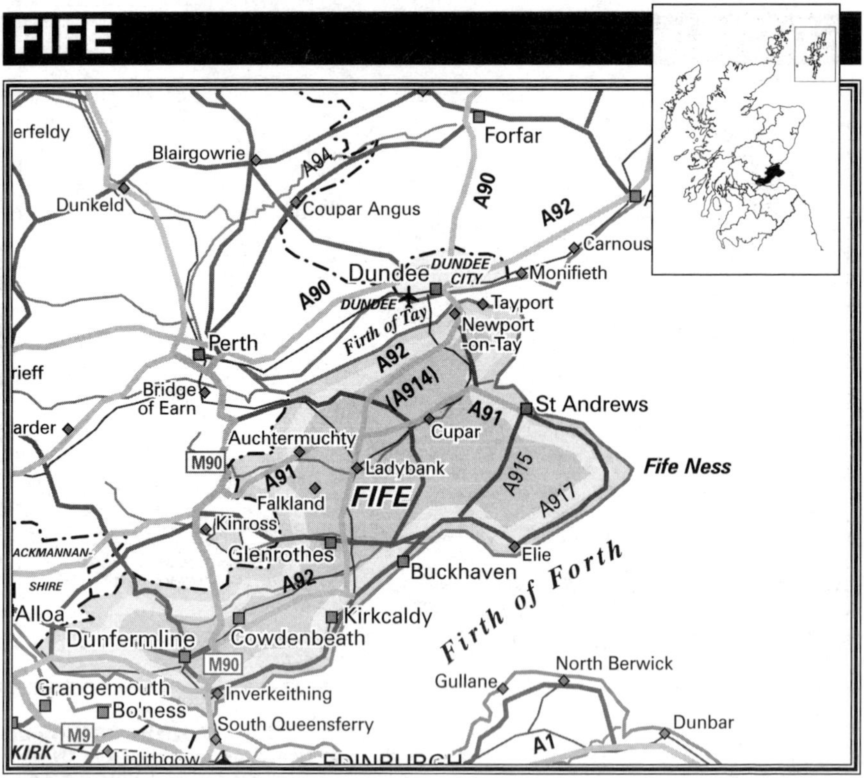

See also Colour Display Advertisement

ANSTRUTHER

Mr & Mrs R. Sparrow, Old Bank House Restaurant & Apartments, 23-25 High Street East, Anstruther KY10 3DQ (01333 310189/310168). Overlooking its own beach just west of the harbour at Anstruther, the Old Bank House is centrally situated in the heart of the town. Wine and dine in our intimate restaurant or drop in for a drink and a selection of Tapas in the cosy bar; games room with pool table, darts and an inviting log fire. Four letting apartments, all with en suite facilities, central heating, telephone and fully equipped kitchens. All linen and towels are supplied, and a laundry service is available on request. Apartment One sleeps 4-8 and overlooks the garden. Apartment Two is for two people and has twin beds, garden and sea view. Apartment Three has disabled access and facilities and sleeps 2-8. Apartment Four sleeps 4-8 persons. In each apartment one child under seven may stay free of charge. Dogs permitted in apartments One and Two only. Breakfast available on request. Terms from £20 per person per night, based on two sharing. *ASSC MEMBER.*

e-mail: ricardosrest@hotmail.com **www.undiscoveredscotland.co.uk/anstruther/oldbank**

HIGHLANDS

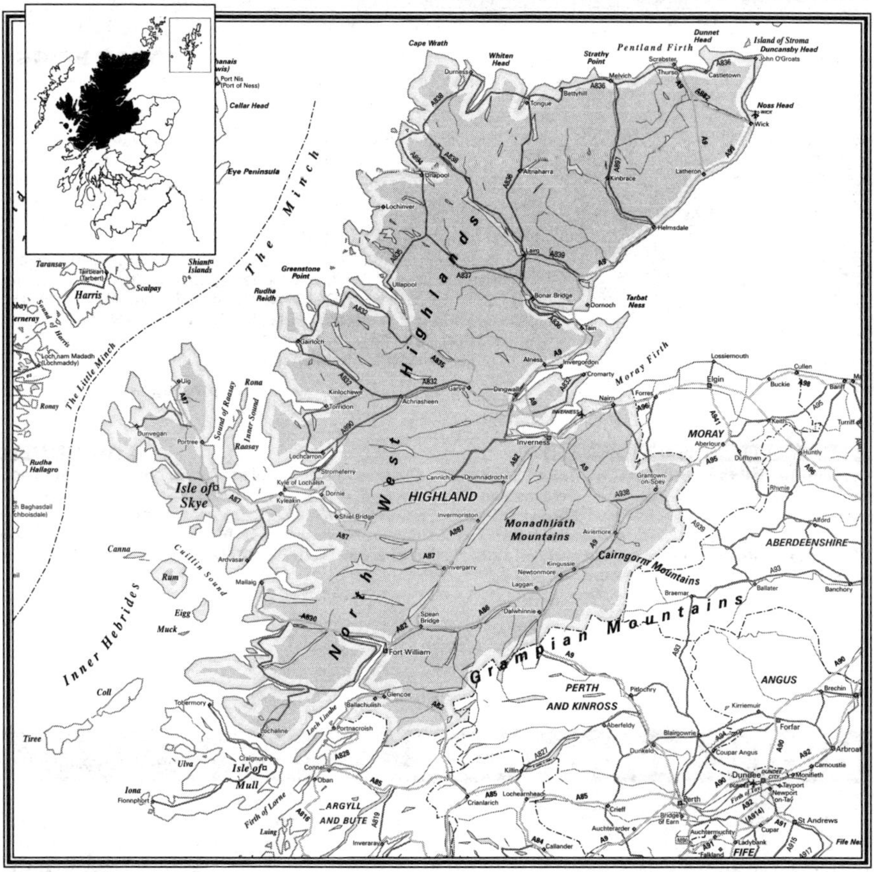

Highland Wildlife

With plenty of space, and not a lot of people, there is an abundance of wildlife to be found in the Highlands, and you don't have to be out walking to see it either! You can watch red kites and ospreys from the comfort of your car, and from many of the hotels along the western seaboard you can also observe local wildlife - anything from red deer, seals, otters, dolphins and a large variety of birds, all from the warmth and comfort of your hotel.

HIGHLANDS (North)

SCOTLAND

BONAR BRIDGE

Achue Croft Cottage. Sleeps 6. Comfortable, relaxing cottage three miles outside Bonar Bridge (40 miles north of Inverness) in a peaceful rural setting. The cottage is on a working farm, with a flock of 240 Cheviots and is ideally placed for touring, walks, golf and fishing or just unwinding. The traditional croft cottage has been extensively renovated and now has all modern conveniences, including central heating throughout, tumble-dryer, washing machine, microwave and dishwasher. It sleeps six in three bedrooms (including ground floor double bedroom with en suite shower and toilet). The double glazed sun lounge has superb panoramic views of open moorland and hills. Children welcome. **STB ★★★★** *SELF CATERING*. Contact **Evelyn Walker Smith, Drumbhan, Airdens, Bonar Bridge IV24 3AS (Tel & Fax: 01863 766144).**
e-mail: smith@drumbhan.freeserve.co.uk

See also Colour Display Advertisement

LOCHINVER

Clashmore Holiday Cottages, Lochinver. Sleeps 2-5. Our three croft cottages at Clashmore are the ideal base for a holiday in the Highlands. They are cosy and fully equipped, with linen provided. Nearby there are sandy beaches, mountains and lochs for wild brown trout fishing. Children welcome, but sorry – no pets. Open all year. Terms from £160 to £340. **STB ★★★** *SELF-CATERING.* Contact: **Mr and Mrs H. Mackenzie, Lochview, 216 Clashmore, Stoer, Lochinver, Sutherland IV27 4JQ (Tel & Fax: 01571 855226).** *ASSC MEMBER.*
e-mail: clashcotts@supanet.com

HIGHLANDS (Mid)

See also Colour Display Advertisement

POOLEWE

Innes Maree Bungalows, Poolewe IV22 2JU (Tel & Fax 01445 781454). Only a few minutes' walk from the world-famous Inverewe Gardens in magnificent Wester Ross. A purpose-built complex of six superb modern bungalows, all equipped to the highest standards of luxury and comfort. Each bungalow sleeps six with main bedroom en suite. Children and pets welcome. Terms from £190 to £425 inclusive of bed linen and electricity. Brochure available. **STB ★★★★** *SELF-CATERING. ASSC MEMBER.*
e-mail: fhg@poolewebungalows.com **website: www.poolewebungalows.com**

ULLAPOOL (near)

Broomview & Sunset. Enjoy peace and tranquillity in the North West Highlands in the comfort of our accommodation. These properties overlook picturesque Loch Broom where panoramic views and spectacular sunsets can be seen. Broomview is on the ground floor. One double en-suite bedroom, one double and one single bedroom both with wash hand basins. Bathroom, utility, spacious, well-equipped kitchen/dining room, lounge with colour TV and video. Sunset is on the upper floor with a double and single bedroom, shower room, utility, kitchen and lounge with colour TV and video. Ideal base for touring. Children welcome. Sorry, no pets. Colour brochure available. Broomview from £250 to £360, Sunset £195 to £285. **STB ★★★★** *SELF-CATERING.* For further information contact: **Mrs Linda Renwick, Spindrift, Keppoch Farm, Dundonnell, By-Garve, Ross-shire IV23 2QR (Tel & Fax: 01854 633269).**

HIGHLANDS (South)

See also Colour Display Advertisement

ARISAIG

Arisaig House Cottages. Luxurious, secluded accommodation in mature woodland. Set in an area of breathtaking coastal and hill scenery, and wonderful sandy beaches. Mountain bike hire, clay pigeon shooting, and fishing on Loch Morar can be arranged. Golf seven miles, swimming pool 13 miles. Day trips to the Small Isles and to Skye. Various properties, sleeping from two to eight persons. Details from: **Andrew Smither, Arisaig House, Beasdale, Arisaig, Inverness-shire PH39 4NR (Tel & Fax: 01687 450399).** *ASSC MEMBER.*
e-mail: enquiries@arisaighouse-cottages.co.uk
website: www.arisaighouse-cottages.co.uk

See also Colour Display Advertisement

CULLODEN (By Inverness)

Blackpark Farm, Westhill, Inverness IV2 5BP (01463 790620; Fax: 01463 794262). This newly-built holiday home is located one mile from Culloden Battlefield with panoramic views over Inverness and beyond. Fully equipped with many extras to make your holiday special, including oil-fired central heating to ensure warmth on the coldest of winter days. Ideally based for touring the Highlands including Loch Ness, Skye etc. Extensive information is available on our website. A Highland welcome awaits you. *ASSC MEMBER.*
e-mail: i.alexander@blackpark.co.uk **website: www.blackpark.co.uk**

See also Colour Display Advertisement

DALCROSS

Easter Dalziel Farm Holiday Cottages, Dalcross IV2 7JL (Tel & Fax: 01667 462213). Three cosy, traditional stone-built cottages in a superb central location, ideal for touring, sporting activities and observing wildlife. Woodland and coastal walks. The cottages are fully equipped including linen and towels. Pets by arrangement. Terms from £135 low season to £430 high season per cottage per week. Recommended in 'The Good Holiday Cottage Guide'. Open all year for long or short breaks. Brochure on request. **STB ★★★** and **★★★★** *SELF CATERING. ASSC MEMBER.*
e-mail: fhg@easterdalzielfarm.co.uk
website: www.easterdalzielfarm.co.uk

See also Colour Display Advertisement

KINCRAIG

Loch Insh Log Chalets, Kincraig PH21 1NU (01540 651272). Just six miles south of Aviemore these superb log chalets are set in 14 acres of woodland in the magnificent Spey Valley, surrounded on three sides by forest and rolling fields with the fourth side being half a mile of beach frontage. Free watersports hire for guests, 8.30-10am/4-5.30pm daily. Sailing, windsurfing, canoeing, salmon fishing, archery, dry ski slope skiing. Hire/instruction available by the hour, day or week mid-April to end of October. Boathouse restaurant on the shore of Loch Insh offering coffee, home-made soup, fresh salads, bar meals, children's menu and evening à la carte. Large gift shop and bar. New children's adventure areas, three kilometres lochside/woodland walk/ interpretation trail, ski slope, mountain bike hire and stocked trout lochan are open all year round. Ski, snowboard hire and instruction available December to April. *ASSC MEMBER.*
e-mail: office@lochinsh.com **website: www.lochinsh.com**

SCOTLAND

NEWTONMORE

Crubenbeg Holiday Cottages, Newtonmore PH20 1BE (01540 673566; Fax: 01540 673509). Rural self-catering cottages in the central Highlands where one can relax and stroll from the doorstep or take part in the choice of many sporting activities in the area. We have a children's play area, a games room, pond stocked with trout for fishing and a barbecue. Pets welcome. **STB ★★★★** *SELF CATERING*.
e-mail: enquiry@crubenbeg.com
website: www.crubenbeg.com

See also Colour Display Advertisement

ONICH

Cuilcheanna Cottages
& Caravans

Cuilcheanna Cottages and Caravans, Onich, Fort William PH33 6SD. Three cottages and eight caravans (6 x 2003 models) situated on a small peaceful site. The cottages are built to the highest standards with electric heating, double glazing and full insulation. Tastefully furnished and fully equipped, each cottage has a large picture window in the main living area which looks out over Loch Leven and Glencoe. Adjacent car parking. Laundry room and phone box on site. Only a short walk from the centre of Onich and an ideal base from which to explore the West Highlands. Paradise for hillwalkers. The caravans also have full facilities. Whether your stay with us is a long one, or just a few days, we shall do our best to ensure that it is enjoyable. Weekend Breaks available, winter rates, off season discounts. *ASSC MEMBER*. For further details please telephone **01855 821526** or **01855 821310**.

LANARKSHIRE

See also Colour Display Advertisement

BIGGAR (Clyde Valley)

Carmichael Country Cottages, Carmichael Estate Office, Westmains, Carmichael, Biggar ML12 6PG (01899 308336; Fax: 01899 308481). Working farm, join in. Sleep 2/7. These 200-year-old stone cottages nestle among the woods and fields of our 700-year-old family estate. Still managed by the descendants of the original Chief of Carmichael. We guarantee comfort, warmth and a friendly welcome in an accessible, unique, rural and historic time capsule. We farm deer, cattle and sheep and sell meats and tartan – Carmichael of course! Children and pets welcome. Open all year. Terms from £190 to £535. 15 cottages with a total of 32 bedrooms. We have the ideal cottage for you. Private tennis court and fishing loch; cafe, farm shop and visitor centre. Off-road driving course. **STB ★★/★★★★** *SELF-CATERING. ASSC MEMBER. FHB MEMBER.*
e-mail: chiefcarm@aol.com **website: www.carmichael.co.uk/cottages**

PERTH & KINROSS

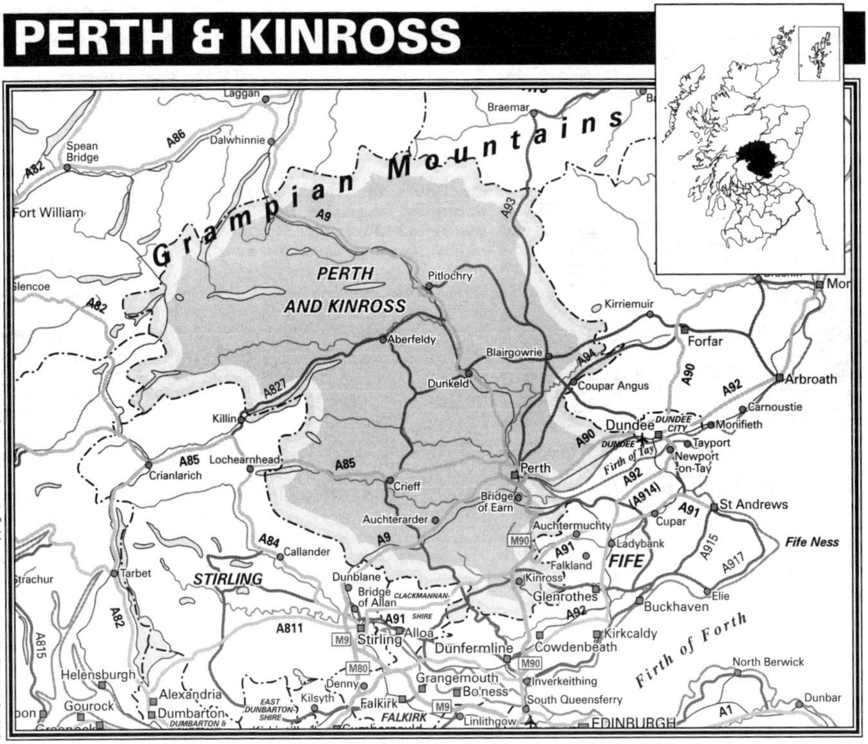

COMRIE

Mrs Pauline Booth, Loch View Farm, Mill of Fortune, Comrie, Crieff PH6 2JE (Tel & Fax: 01764 670677). There is a south-facing lodge and a residential caravan situated separately on the edge of a privately-owned loch at Loch View farm, in idyllic surroundings, with beautiful scenery, two miles from the village of Comrie and six miles from the town of Crieff. Ideally situated for a quiet holiday, away from it all, with fishing, walking and birdwatching in abundance. Also centrally situated for touring. Wallace Lodge sleeps up to eight and is equipped to a very high standard. The residential caravan sleeps four. **STB** ★★★★ *SELF-CATERING.*

See also Colour Display Advertisement

DUNKELD (By)

Laighwood Holidays, Butterstone, By Dunkeld PH8 0HB (01350 724241; Fax: 01350 724212). Properties sleep 2/8. A de luxe detached house, comfortably accommodating eight, created from the West Wing of a 19th century shooting lodge with panoramic views. Two popular cottages sleeping four to six, situated on our hill farm, with beautiful views. Two well-equipped apartments adjoining Butterglen House near Butterstone Loch. Butterstone lies in magnificent countryside (especially Spring/ Autumn), adjacent to Nature Reserve (ospreys). Central for walking, touring, historic houses, golf and fishing. Private squash court and hill loch (wild brown trout) on the farm. Sorry no pets. Terms: House £424 to £660; Cottages and Apartments £165 to £375 per week. **STB** ★★★ **to** ★★★★ *SELF-CATERING. ASSC MEMBER.*
e-mail: holidays@laighwood.co.uk
website: www.laighwood.co.uk

RANNOCH

Mrs N. Robertson, Camusericht Farm, Bridge of Gaur, Rannoch, By Pitlochry PH17 2QD (01882 633219 or 01882 633277). Sleeps 5. Situated in the rugged and romantic hills of Scotland where River Gaur runs into Loch Rannoch: Bothy Cottage. Contains livingroom with multi-fuel stove; kitchenette; shower and toilet; two bedrooms with one single and two double beds. Fully furnished except linen. Children welcome. Tariff £130 per week, excluding electricity. Plenty of swimming and fishing. Also Bed & Breakfast in farmhouse. SAE for further details.

TAYMOUTH

Mr Robin Menzies, Mains of Taymouth Cottages, Kenmore, Aberfeldy PH15 2HN (01887 830226; Fax: 01887 829059). Mains of Taymouth Cottages are set in magnificent Highland Perthshire by the village of Kenmore amidst the finest scenery Scotland has to offer. We are surrounded by lovely walks, good fishing, Kenmore Golf Course is on our doorstep and activities abound from water sports and mountain biking to Highland Adventure safaris. Our five cottages are based around an 18th century courtyard and vary from a cosy two-bedroomed cottage to an extensive luxury four-bedroom with en suite facilities, large garden and sauna. All cottages are traditional stone built and tastefully modernised with full central heating, open fires, dishwashers and all other mod cons you would possibly need. The cottages are in a quiet private setting with easy access to the golf course and restaurant and everything the area has to offer.

e-mail: info@taymouth.co.uk **website: www.taymouth.co.uk**

STIRLING & THE TROSSACHS

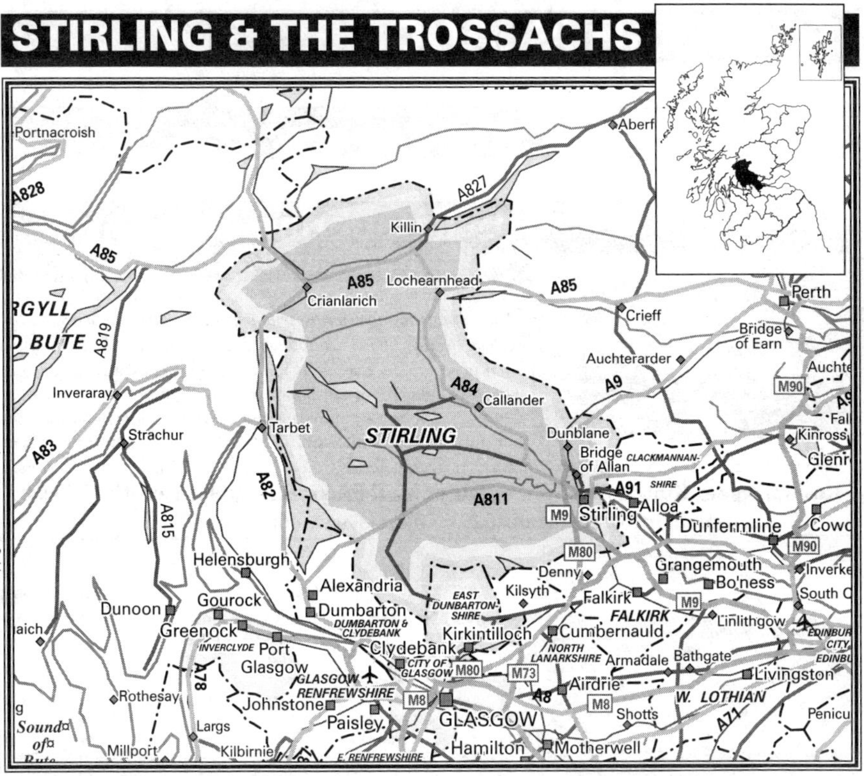

• Hawthorn Cottage •

Luxury Self-Catering Accommodation

Hawthorn Cottage was purpose-built in 2001 to the highest standard. The cottage can sleep up to six people plus a baby and is suitable for the disabled. Prices range from £330 to £510.

Also available at West Drip is a brand new for 2003 residential caravan which sleeps up to 8. Prices from £170 to £230 per week.

Both cottage and caravan are located at West Drip farm (3 miles north of Stirling) and have a quiet and peaceful setting with panoramic views. Sorry no pets.

Scottish Tourist Board ★★★★ Self Catering

For bookings contact: Eleanor Graham, West Drip Farm, By Stirling FK9 4UJ

Tel: 01786 472523 • e-mail: enquiries@westdripfarm.com

www.westdripfarm.com

See also Colour Advertisement

Visits & Attractions

National Wallace Monument, Stirling, Stirlingshire • 01786 472140

website: www.stirling.co.uk/attractions

Against the background of the events of 700 years ago when Scotland first struggled for independence, the story of William Wallace, freedom fighter and national hero. For a superb view, climb the 246 steps of the 220ft high tower

SCOTTISH ISLANDS

Isle of Mull

Scoor House Self-Catering Holidays

Bunessan, Isle of Mull

Scoor House is a former farmhouse, restored and converted to provide four self-catering apartments, with adjoining cottage plus a detached cottage nearby. All have stunning views to the sea and the Hebrides. Each property has a spacious lounge/dining area with kitchenette. There is a utility room with washing machine, tumble dryer and deep freeze. Payphone on premises; cots can be provided. Dogs allowed but must be kept under control. All domestic equipment and bed linen provided. Electricity by meter reading. Open all year. Terms from £100 to £380. *Details from Manageress:*

Rosie Burgess, Kintra, Fionnphort, Isle of Mull PA66 6BT • Tel & Fax: 01681 700509

e-mail: info@scoorhouse.f9.co.uk • www.scoorhouse.f9.co.uk

See also Colour Advertisement

GRULINE

Mrs McFarlane, Torlochan, Gruline, Isle of Mull PA71 6HR (01680 300380; Fax: 01680 300664). Torlochan is situated in the centre of the Isle of Mull, with panoramic views over Loch Na Keal. We are a small working croft where you can relax and enjoy the antics of our animals, which include llamas, sheep, Jersey cows, goats, pigs and varieties of poultry. Pets free of charge. A friendly welcome awaits you, your children and pets. More information and colour brochure available from Diana McFarlane. Terms: Self Catering from £205 per week. Short breaks self catering from £45 per night. Bed and Breakfast from £20 per person. Eagles and wildlife in abundance, spotted from your door, come and see for yourself.
e-mail: diana@torlochan.sol.co.uk
website: www.holidaymull.org/members/torlochan.html

PLEASE NOTE

All the information in this book is given in good faith in the belief that it is correct. However, the publishers cannot guarantee the facts given in these pages, neither are they responsible for changes in policy, ownership or terms that may take place after the date of going to press. Readers should always satisfy themselves that the facilities they require are available and that the terms, if quoted, still apply.

SCOTLAND

Caravan & Camping Holidays

ARGYLL & BUTE

ACHARACLE

Fiona Sinclair, Resipole Farm Caravan & Camping Park, Loch Sunart, Acharacle PH36 4HX (01967 431235; Fax: 01967 431777). On the beautiful Ardnamurchan Peninsula this spacious family-run park is situated on the shores of Loch Sunart. A haven for a wide range of wildlife, the park is centrally positioned for exploring this remote and peaceful area. The superb facilities include an excellent restaurant, slipway for boat launching, a nine hole golf course, and laundry. Luxury Thistle award-winning caravan holiday homes for hire and for sale. Lodges and a beautifully furnished cottage are for hire throughout the year. Touring caravans, motor homes and tents can enjoy the wonderful views down Loch Sunart. Pets are welcome. Calor gas available. Please write or phone for a full colour brochure or visit our website.

e-mail: info@resipole.co.uk. **website: www.resipole.co.uk**

KINLOCHLEVEN

Mrs Patsy Cameron, Caolasnacon Caravan & Camping Park, Kinlochleven PA40 4RS (01855 831279). There are 20 static six-berth caravans for holiday hire on this lovely site with breathtaking mountain scenery on the edge of Loch Leven - an ideal touring centre. Caravans have electric lighting, Calor gas cookers and heaters, toilet, shower, fridge and colour TV. There are two toilet blocks with hot water and showers and laundry facilities. Children are welcome and pets allowed. Open from April to October. Milk, gas, soft drinks available on site; shops three miles. Sea loch fishing, hill walking and boating; boats and rods for hire, fishing tackle for sale. Weekly rates from £195 for vans; 10% reductions on two week bookings. Tourers from £8.25 nightly. Seven and a half acres for campers - rates from £6 nightly.

DUMFRIES & GALLOWAY

NEWTON STEWART

Whitecairn Farm Caravan Park, Glenluce, Newton Stewart DG8 0NZ (01581 300267). Peacefully set by a quiet country road, one-and-a-half-miles from the village of Glenluce with panoramic views over the rolling Galloway countryside to Luce Bay. This family-run park offers a choice of two different caravan types sleeping up to six, all of a high standard and fully equipped except for linen. Amenities include shop, children's play area, launderette, telephone, toilet blocks and shower rooms. Electric hook-ups on touring pitches. Open from March to October, the six acre site offers freedom for children of all ages and dogs are welcome under strict control. Colour brochure available. **STB ★★★★** *HOLIDAY PARK*.

HIGHLANDS (South)

ARISAIG

A. Simpson, Camusdarach, Arisaig, Inverness-shire PH39 4NT (01687 450221). 'Camusdarach' is the ideal base to explore the beautiful scenery of the 'Road to the Isles' and the West Highlands. The grassy site, surrounded by mature trees, has 42 pitches for tents or vans including 11 electric hook-ups. A unique shower/toilet block has sheltered washing-up sinks, a laundry and a separate room with disabled and baby changing facilities. A foot path leads you on the short walk to the fabulous beaches featured in 'Local Hero'. Local shops, restaurants and ferries are within easy reach at Arisaig (four miles) and Mallaig (six miles). Traigh Golf Course is only one mile away. Pitch fees, based on two people with car: tents from £8 per night, caravans from £10 per night, electricity from £2 per night. *ASSC MEMBER*
e-mail: camusdarach@aol.com
website: www.road-to-the-isles.org.uk/camusdarach

SCOTLAND

PERTH & KINROSS

COMRIE

West Lodge Caravan Park, Comrie PH6 2LS (01764 670354). Two to six berth caravans for hire fully equipped with gas cooker, running water, toilet, electric fridge, lighting, colour TV and gas fire. Crockery, cutlery, cooking utensils, blankets and pillows are provided. Sheets and towels can be hired. All caravans have showers. Pitches available for tents, tourers and motor homes. One modern shower block on site, complete with washing machine, tumble dryer, showers and hot and cold running water; shop. Fishing, golf, tennis, bowling, hill-walking and canoeing all within easy reach. Watersports available on nearby Loch Earn. Ideal for touring, 23 miles north of Stirling and 23 miles west of Perth. Terms from £25 to £37 nightly, £100 to £245 weekly; VAT, electricity and gas included. Open 1st April to 31st October. **STB** ★★★★ *SELF-CATERING*.

KILLIN

Cruachan Farm Caravan and Camping Park, Cruachan, Killin FK21 8TY (01567 820302). Family-run site of 10 acres adjacent to farm, set amidst beautiful Highland scenery. Ideal central situation for touring; walking, fishing and golf nearby. Licensed restaurant and coffee shop on site. Children and pets welcome. Open mid-March to October. Terms: (per night) touring caravans £7.50, motor caravans £7, car and tent £7. Holiday caravans for hire, also Lodge House for self catering lets. Reduced rates off season. Brochure available. New amenities for 2003 – loos, showers, indoor wash-up, laundry machines.
e-mail: info@cruachan.killin.co.uk
website: www.cruachan.killin.co.uk

Terms quoted in this publication may be subject to increase if rises in costs necessitate

FHG Diploma Winners 2002

Each year we award a small number of diplomas to holiday proprietors whose services have been specially commended by our readers. The following were our FHG Diploma Winners for 2002.

England

DEVON

Woolacombe Bay Holiday Park, Woolacombe, North Devon EX34 7HW (01271 870343).

LANCASHIRE

Mrs Holdsworth, Broadwater Hotel, 356 Marine Road, East Promenade Morecambe, Lancashire LA4 5AQ (01524 411333).

Peter & Susan Bicker, Kelvin Private Hotel, Reads Avenue, Blackpool, Lancashire FY1 4JJ (01253 620293).

LINCOLNSHIRE

Sue Phillips & John Lister, Cawthorpe Farm, Cawthorpe Bourne, Lincolnshire PE10 0AB (01778 426697).

OXFORDSHIRE

Liz Roach, The Old Bakery, Skirmett, Nr Henley on Thames Oxfordshire RG9 6TD (01491 638309).

SOMERSET

Pat & Sue Weir, Slipper Cottage, 41 Bishopston, Montacute, Somerset TA15 6UX (01935 823073)

Scotland

ARGYLL & BUTE

David Quibell, Rosneath Castle Caravan Park Near Helensburgh, Argyll & Bute G84 0QS (01436 831208)

DUNDEE & ANGUS

Carlogie House Hotel, Carlogie Road, Carnoustie, Dundee DD7 6LD (01241 853185)

EDINBURGH & LOTHIANS

Geraldine Hamilton, Crosswoodhill Farm, West Calder Edinburgh & Lothians EH55 8LP (01501 785205)

FIFE

Mr Alastair Clark, Old Manor Country House Hotel, Lundin Links, Nr St Andrews Fife KY8 6AJ (01333 320368)

HIGHLANDS

N & J McCallum, The Neuk Corpach, Fort William PH33 7LE (01397 772244)

HELP IMPROVE BRITISH TOURISM STANDARDS

Why not write and tell us about the holiday accommodation you have chosen from one of our popular publications? Complete a nomination form giving details of why you think YOUR host or hostess should win one of our attractive framed diplomas and send it to:

FHG Publications, Abbey Mill Business Centre, Seedhill, Paisley PA1 1TJ

WALES

Board Accommodation

ANGLESEY & GWYNEDD

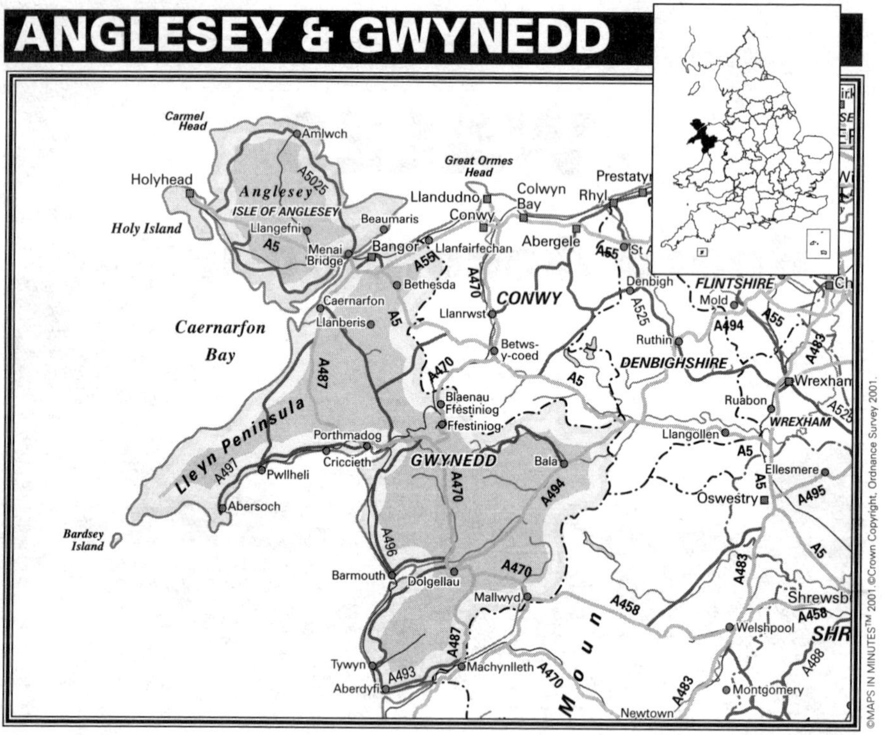

WALES

ANGLESEY

Mrs J Bown, Drws-y-Coed, Llannerch-y-medd, Anglesey LL71 8AD (Tel & Fax: 01248 470473). Welcome to Drws-y-Coed. Enjoy excellent hospitality, food and tranquil surroundings with panoramic views of Snowdonia. Centrally situated to explore Anglesey's coastline and attractions. 25 minutes to the Port of Holyhead. Beautifully decorated and furnished en suite bedrooms with all facilities to make your stay most enjoyable. Inviting spacious lounge with a log fire. The freshly cooked breakfasts are served in the cosy dining room with separate tables. Games room. Interesting historic farmstead and walks on a 550 acre beef, sheep and arable farm. Attractive garden with a gazebo to relax in. Non-smoking establishment. Open all year. Bed and Breakfast £25. **WTB** ★★★★ *B&B,* **RAC** ◆◆◆◆, *WARM WELCOME AND SPARKLING DIAMOND AWARDS, FACM, FARM HOLIDAY GUIDE DIPLOMA, WTB RURAL TOURISM AWARD.*

e-mail: drws.ycoed@virgin.net **website: www.SmoothHound.co.uk/hotels/drwsycoed.html**

BALA

Mrs S.E. Edwards, Bryn Melyn, Rhyduchaf, Bala LL23 7PG (01678 520376). Working farm. Bryn Melyn, Rhyduchaf is situated in the beautiful countryside of Bala, and offers accommodation all year. The house is stone-built and stands on 56 acres of mixed farmland. Home cooking and home produced food makes this a real home from home. Two double and one twin bedrooms, all with washbasins; two bathrooms, toilet; sittingroom; diningroom; central heating. With tea and coffee facilities. Children welcome at reduced rates. Sorry, no pets. A car is necessary to ensure that visitors derive all the pleasure that this region offers. Parking space. Sea 28 miles. Good recreation facilities in the area. Bed and Breakfast from £17–£18 per person. No smoking. Mrs Edwards is a Farm Holiday Guide Diploma winner. **WTB** ★★ *B&B.*

DOLGELLAU

Mr and Mrs J.S. Bamford, Ivy House, Finsbury Square, Dolgellau LL40 1RF (01341 422535; Fax: 01341 422689). A country town guesthouse offering a welcoming atmosphere and good homemade food. Guest accommodation consists of six double rooms, three with en suite toilet facilities, all with colour TV, tea/coffee facilities and hairdryers. The dining room, which is licensed, has a choice of menu - including vegetarian dishes. The lounge has tourist information literature and there are maps available to borrow. Dolgellau is an ideal touring, walking and mountain biking region in the southern area of the Snowdonia National Park. Bed and Breakfast from £20. **WTB** ★★ *GUEST HOUSE,* **AA** ◆◆◆
e-mail: marg.bamford@btconnect.com
website: www.ukworld.net/ivyhouse

TYWYN

Mrs Gweniona Pugh, Eisteddfa, Abergynolwyn, Tywyn LL36 9UP (01654 782385; Fax: 01654 782228). Eisteddfa offers you the comfort of a newly built bungalow on the Tan-y-coed Ucha Farm, situated adjacent to the farmhouse but with all the benefits of Bed and Breakfast accommodation. The bungalow, which has been designed to accommodate disabled guests, is conveniently situated between Abergynolwyn and Dolgoch Falls with Talyllyn Narrow Gauge Railway running through the farmland. Three bedrooms, two en suite and the third with a shower and washbasin suitable for a disabled person. The toilet is located in the adjacent bathroom. Tea/coffee tray and TV are provided in the bedrooms as are many other extras. We also cater for Coeliac Diets. **WTB** ★★★ *B&B.*

WALES

NORTH WALES

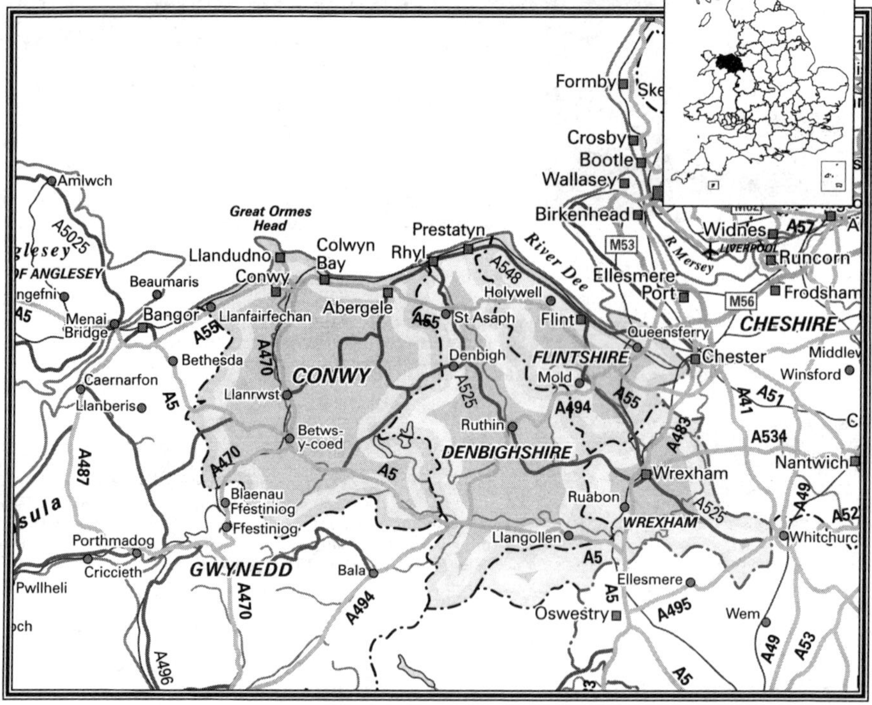

WALES

BETWS-Y-COED

Jim and Lilian Boughton, Bron Celyn Guest House, Lon Muriau, Llanrwst Road, Betws-y-Coed LL24 0HD (01690 710333; Fax: 01690 710111). A warm welcome awaits you at this delightful guest house overlooking the Gwydyr Forest and Llugwy/Conwy Valleys and village of Betws-y-Coed in Snowdonia National Park. Ideal centre for touring, walking, climbing, fishing and golf. Also excellent overnight stop en route for Holyhead ferries. Easy walk into village and close to Conwy/Swallow Falls and Fairy Glen. Most rooms en suite, all with colour TV and beverage makers. Lounge. Full central heating. Garden. Car park. Open all year. Full hearty breakfast, packed meals, snacks, evening meals - special diets catered for. Bed and Breakfast from £22 to £26, reduced rates for children under 12 years. Special out of season breaks. **WTB ★★★** *GUEST HOUSE.*

e-mail: welcome@broncelyn.co.uk

website: http://www.broncelyn.co.uk

See also Colour Display Advertisement

LLANDUDNO

Warwick Hotel, 56 Church Walks, Llandudno, Conwy LL30 2HL (01492 876823). Peacefully situated, yet only five minutes from pier, beach and town centre, this Victorian hotel has 14 guest bedrooms, all en suite, and family accommodation is available. The dining room overlooks the pleasant south-facing garden with sun terrace, and the chef/proprietor is happy to cater for special diets and children's menus. Licensed. Open all year. **WTB ★★★** *HOTEL*, **RAC ★★**

See also Colour Advertisement

WALES

CARMARTHENSHIRE

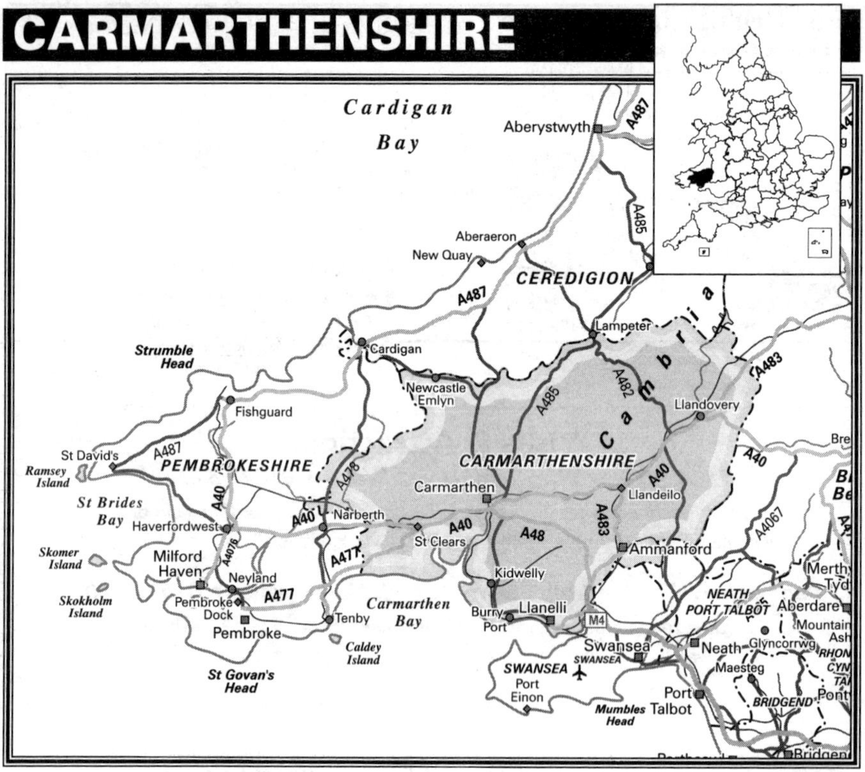

WHITLAND

Mrs O. Ebsworth, Brunant Country House, Whitland SA34 0LX (Tel & Fax: 01994 240421). 'Never enough time to enjoy this to the full, never enough words to say how splendid it was.' – John Carter (Wish You Were Here). Welcome to our 200-year-old farmhouse, centrally situated for touring, beaches, walking or just relaxing. Comfortable spacious bedrooms, all en suite, tea/coffee facilities, TV, hairdryers. Good home cooking, comfortable lounge, separate tables in dining room. No smoking. Open all year except Christmas and New Year. Bed & Breakfast £22 to £27. Evening meal £15.

WHITLAND

Mrs A. Windsor, Forest Farm, Whitland SA34 0LS (01994 240066). Forest Farm is a mixed livestock farm, situated on the A40 (en route to Fishguard for Ireland) in the rolling hillside of the Taf Valley, with beautiful walks around the farm and woodlands and fishing on the River Taf, which runs through the farm (salmon and trout). Within easy reach of the coastal areas (Tenby and Saundersfoot) and shopping areas of Carmarthen and Swansea. Close to several National Trust properties and within easy reach of Oakwood and other pleasure parks. A homely atmosphere, fully centrally heated. TV lounge for guests, diningroom with separate tables – good home-cooked breakfast. Plenty of good restaurants and pubs nearby. En suite bedrooms. Ample parking space. B&B from £20.

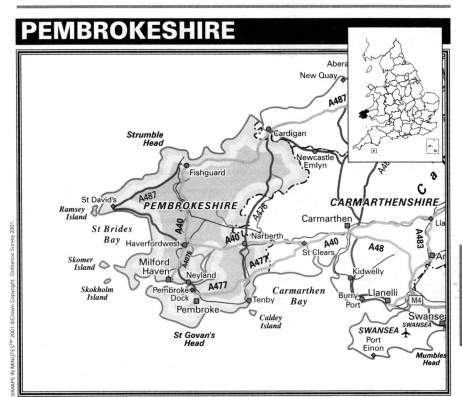

PEMBROKESHIRE

BROADHAVEN

Mrs F. Morgan, Albany Bed & Breakfast, 27 Millmoor Way, Broadhaven, Haverfordwest SA62 3JJ (01437 781051; Fax: 01437 781050. Albany is a friendly, family-run Bed & Breakfast. Three en suite rooms, double, single or twin, all with tea/coffee making facilities, TV, central heating, and access at all times (some rooms have sea views). Parking. Two minutes from sandy beach of Broadhaven and leading to Little Haven. Within walking distance are shop/Post Office, cafe, pub/restaurant and Coastal Path. Windsurfing, swimming, diving and boat trips to Skomer and Grassholm bird islands (puffins, razorbills etc); seal pups in bays September/October. Coastal bus May to September. Nearby are St David's, Tenby, Oakwood etc and sandy beaches. **WTB ★★** *GUEST HOUSE.*
e-mail: holiday@albanybedandbreakfast.co.uk
website: www.albany-bedandbreakfast.co.uk

BROADHAVEN (near)

Sandra Davies, Barley Villa, Walwyns Castle, Near Broadhaven, Haverfordwest SA62 3EB (01437 781254). Our 20 acre smallholding with friendly horses offers peace, tranquillity and walks and overlooks Rosemoor Nature Reserve in Pembrokeshire's National Park. Our spacious house, furnished for the comfort of our guests, has three bedrooms, two of which are en suite, complete with hospitality trays; lounge/dining room with colour TV, coal fire and board games for restful evenings. We are centrally situated for visiting Pembokeshire's many sandy bays, famous bird islands, coastal paths and historic places. Many sport and leisure activities within easy travelling distance. We offer hearty breakfasts, packed lunches, special diets. Private car parking. No smoking. Bed and Breakfast from £21 to £26 en suite. Comfortable two-bedroomed caravan also available for hire. **WTB ★★★** *FARM.*
e-mail: sandra.barleyvilla@btinternet.com **website: www.barleyvilla.co.uk**

HAVERFORDWEST

Mrs Margaret Williams, Skerryback, Sandy Haven, St Ishmaels, Haverfordwest SA62 3DN (01646 636598; Fax: 01646 636595). Our 18th century farmhouse is a working farm set in a sheltered garden adjoining the Pembrokeshire coast footpath. It is an ideal situation for walkers and bird lovers to explore the secluded coves and sandy beaches of the area, or take a boat trip to see the puffins on Skomer Island. The two attractive double rooms, both en suite, look out across horses grazing in the meadow; the guests' lounge has a colour TV and central heating backed up by log fires on chilly evenings. A welcoming cup of tea/coffee on arrival plus hospitality trays in the bedrooms. Skerryback breakfasts are a real treat, the perfect way to start a day of strenuous walking or just relaxing on the nearest beach. Bed and Breakfast £22.50 to £28. **WTB ★★★** *FARMHOUSE* .

e-mail: skerryback@pfh.co.uk **website: www.pfh.co.uk/skerryback**

See also Colour Display Advertisement

HAVERFORDWEST

Mr and Mrs Patrick, East Hook Farm, Portfield Gate, Haverfordwest, Pembroke SA62 3LN (01437 762211). Howard and Jen welcome you to their Georgian Farmhouse surrounded by beautiful countryside, four miles from the coastline and three miles from Haverfordwest. Double, twin and family suite available, all en suite. Pembrokeshire produce used for dinner and breakfast. Dinner £14 per person. Bed and Breakfast from £20 to £22 per person. **WTB ★★★** *FARMHOUSE*.

website: www.easthookfarmhouse.co.uk

HAVERFORDWEST

Mrs M. E. Davies, Cuckoo Mill Farm, Pelcomb Bridge, St David's Road, Haverfordwest SA62 6EA (01437 762139). Working farm. There is a genuine welcome to our mixed working family farm. Quietly set in beautiful countryside surrounded by animals and wild life. Comfortable, well-appointed accommodation. Bedrooms with tea/coffee tray, radio, TV and en suite. Excellent quality food using home and local produce. Families welcome. Deductions for children and Senior Citizens. Open January to December. Pretty flowers, lawns in relaxed surroundings. Personal attention. Unrestricted access. Ideally situated in central Pembrokeshire for coastline walks. Sandy beaches. Bird islands, castles, city of St David's, Tenby. Bed and Breakfast; Bed, Breakfast and Evening Dinner. Terms on application. **WTB ★★★** *FARM, GOLD WELCOME HOST AWARD, TASTE OF WALES.*

MARTINS HAVEN/MARLOES

Mrs Christina Chetwynd, East Hook Farm, Marloes, Haverfordwest SA62 3BJ (01646 636291). Farm on Pembrokeshire Coast Path offering Bed and Breakfast, camping, caravans, cycle hire, sea fishing, bird-watching and walking. Convenient for boat trips to Skomer and Skokholm Islands and next to Marloes Mere Nature Reserve. 110 acres of natural unspoilt beauty. Bedrooms with washbasin, TV and tea/coffee making facilities available. Reception room on site. Transport to Martins Haven for boat trips, diving and Marine Nature Reserve. Bed and Breakfast £18 per person per night. Children welcome.

Visits & Attractions

Marine Life Centre, St David's, Pembrokeshire •01437 721665

All-weather attraction giving a unique insight into the undersea world. Simulation of underwater caves, shipwreck tank and touch tanks; gift shop, refreshments, play areas.

WALES

POWYS

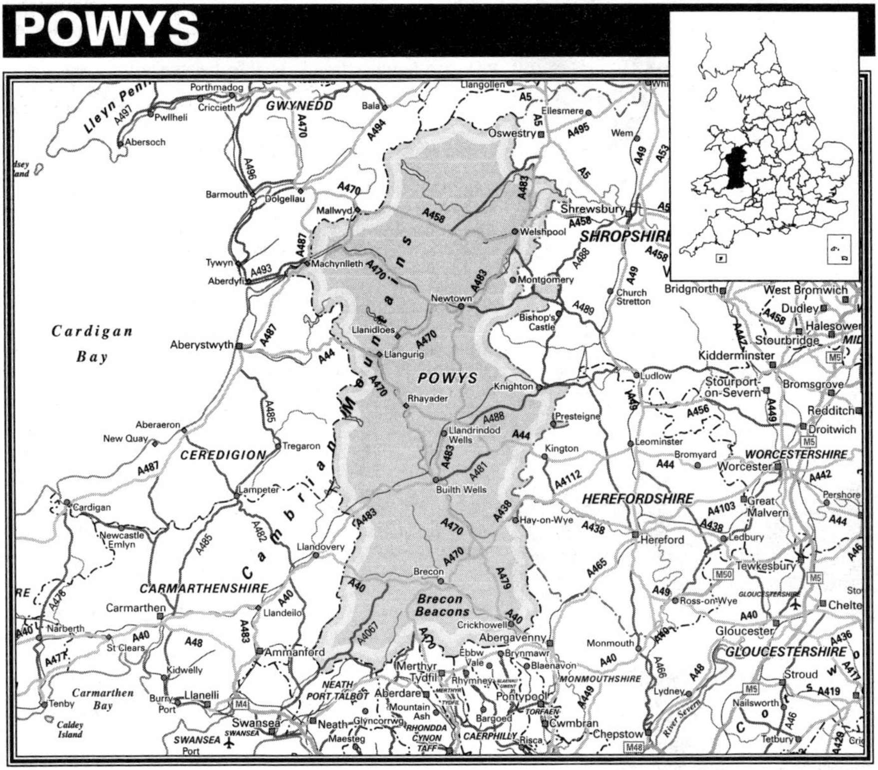

BRECON

Gwyn and Hazel Davies, Caebetran Farm, Felinfach, Brecon LD3 0UL (Tel & Fax: 01874 754460). Working farm, join in. A warm welcome, a cup of tea and home-made cakes await you when you arrive at Caebetran. Visitors are welcome to see the cattle and sheep on the farm. There are breathtaking views of the Brecon Beacons and the Black Mountains and just across a field is a 400 acre common, ideal for walking, bird-watching or just relaxing. Ponies and sheep graze undisturbed, while buzzards soar above you. The farmhouse dates back to the 17th century and has been recently modernised to give the quality and comfort visitors expect today. There are many extras in the rooms to give that special feel to your holiday. The rooms are all en suite and have colour TV and tea making facilities. The dining room has separate tables, there is also a comfortable lounge with colour TV and video. Caebetran is an ideal base for exploring this beautiful, unspoilt part of the country with pony trekking, walking, birdwatching, wildlife, hang-gliding and so much more. For a brochure and terms please write, telephone or fax. "Arrive as visitors and leave as our friends". Winners of the 'FHG Diploma' for Wales 1998 and 1999. *WELCOME HOST.*
e-mail: hazelcaebetran@aol.com

BRECON

Mrs A. Harpur, Llanbrynean Farm, Llanfrynach, Brecon LD3 7BQ (01874 665222). Llanbrynean is a fine, traditional, Victorian farmhouse peacefully situated on the edge of the picturesque village of Llanfrynach, three miles south-east of Brecon. We are in an ideal spot for exploring the area - the Brecon Beacons rise behind the farm and the Brecon/Monmouth canal flows through the fields below. We are a working family sheep farm with wonderful pastoral views and a large garden. The house is spacious and comfortable with a friendly, relaxed atmosphere. We have two double en suite bedrooms and one twin with private bathroom. All have tea/coffee facilities. There is a sitting room with log fire. Bed and Breakfast from £19 per person. Excellent pub food within easy walking distance.

See also Colour Display Advertisement

LLANDRINDOD WELLS

Mrs Ruth Jones, Holly Farm, Howey, Llandrindod Wells LD1 5PP (Tel & Fax: 01597 822402). Tastefully restored Tudor farmhouse on working farm in peaceful location. En suite bedrooms with breathtaking views over fields and woods, colour TV, beverage trays. Two lounges with log fires. Renowned for excellent food. Wonderful area for wildlife, walking, cycling, near Red Kite feeding station. Safe parking. Bed, Breakfast and Evening meal weekly from £215 to £240. Bed and Breakfast from £22 to £26 per day. Brochure on request. **WTB ★★★** *FARM*, **AA ◆◆◆◆**, *TASTE OF WALES TOURISM AWARD, FARM STAY UK MEMBER.*

LLANIDLOES

Mrs L. Rees, Esgairmaen, Y Fan, Llanidloes SY18 6NT (01686 430272). "Croeso Cynnes" a warm welcome awaits you at Esgairmaen, a working farm one mile from Clywedog reservoir where fishing and sailing can be enjoyed, an ideal base for walking, bird watching and exploring nearby forests. The house commands magnificent views of unspoilt countryside, only 29 miles from the coast. One double and one family room, both en suite with tea/coffee making facilities. Central heating. Open April to October. Children and pets welcome. Camping also available. We offer peace and tranquillity.

TWO for the price of ONE at
National Cycle Centre
See our READERS' OFFER VOUCHER for details.

Visits & Attractions

Powis Castle and Garden, Near Welshpool, Powys • 01938 554336

Perched on a rock above gardens of great historical and horticultural importance, the medieval castle contains a superb collection of paintings and furniture and treasures from India.

King Arthur's Labyrinth, Machynlleth, Powys • 01654 761584
website: www.kingarthurslabyrinth.com

A boat ride along a beautiful subterranean river takes you to the Labyrinth, carved from rock, where the tales of King Arthur are re-told. New 'Bard's Quest' challenges you to go in search of the lost legends hidden in the Maze of Time.

WALES

MONTGOMERY

Ceinwen Richards, The Drewin Farm, Churchstoke, Montgomery SY15 6TW (Tel & Fax: 01588 620325). A family-run mixed farm set on hillside overlooking panoramic views of the most beautiful countryside. The Drewin is a charming 17th century farmhouse retaining much of its original character with oak beams and large inglenook fireplace, separate lounge; twin and family rooms, both en suite and all modern amenities with colour TV. Full central heating. Offa's Dyke footpath runs through the farm - a wonderful area for wildlife. Ideal base for touring the many beauty spots around. Good home cooking and a very warm welcome await our visitors. Bed and Breakfast from £23 to £25; Bed, Breakfast and Evening Meal from £35. Featured in The Travel Show. Holder of Essential Food Hygiene Certificate and Farmhouse Award from Wales Tourist Board, 1999/2000 winner of AA Best Breakfast in Wales Award. Open April to October. **WTB** ★★★★ *FARM,* **AA** ◆◆◆◆
e-mail: ceinwen@drewin.freeserve.co.uk

PENYBONT-FAWR

Mrs Anne Evans, Glanhafon, Penybont-Fawr SY10 0EW (01691 860377). Working farm, join in. Secluded farmhouse in the Upper Tanat Valley, ideal for a peaceful break. Glanhafon is a working sheep farm with hill walks on the farm. Bordering the Berwyn Mountains, it is a wonderful area for walking, bird-watching, or touring, with Lake Vyrnwy, RSPB Centre, and Pistyll Falls - one of the seven wonders of Wales- just seven miles away. Many other places of interest within easy reach, including Powys and Chirk Castle, Snowdonia, Erddig and the market towns of Shrewsbury and Oswestry. There are three attractive bedrooms, all en suite, with tea making facilities. Guests' own sittingroom. Ample parking. Children and pets welcome. Open Easter till October. Bed and Breakfast from £18. **WTB** ★★★ *FARM.*

WALES

• • *Some Useful Guidance for Guests and Hosts* • •

Every year literally thousands of holidays, short breaks and ovemight stops are arranged through our guides, the vast majority without any problems at all. In a handful of cases, however, difficulties do arise about bookings, which often could have been prevented from the outset.

It is important to remember that when accommodation has been booked, both parties – guests and hosts – have entered into a form of contract. We hope that the following points will provide helpful guidance.

GUESTS:

- When enquiring about accommodation, be as precise as possible. Give exact dates, numbers in your party and the ages of any children.
- State the number and type of rooms wanted and also what catering you require – bed and breakfast, full board etc. Make sure that the position about evening meals is clear – and about pets, reductions for children or any other special points.
- Read our reviews carefully to ensure that the proprietors you are going to contact can supply what you want. Ask for a letter confirming all arrangements, if possible.
- If you have to cancel, do so as soon as possible. Proprietors do have the right to retain deposits and under certain circumstances to charge for cancelled holidays if adequate notice is not given and they cannot re-let the accommodation.

HOSTS:

- Give details about your facilities and about any special conditions. Explain your deposit system clearly and arrangements for cancellations, charges etc. and whether or not your terms include VAT.
- If for any reason you are unable to fulfil an agreed booking without adequate notice, you may be under an obligation to arrange suitable alternative accommodation or to make some form of compensation.

While every effort is made to ensure accuracy, we regret that FHG Publications cannot accept responsibility for errors, omissions or misrepresentations in our entries or any consequences thereof. Prices in particular should be checked because we go to press early. We will follow up complaints but cannot act as arbiters or agents for either party.

SOUTH WALES

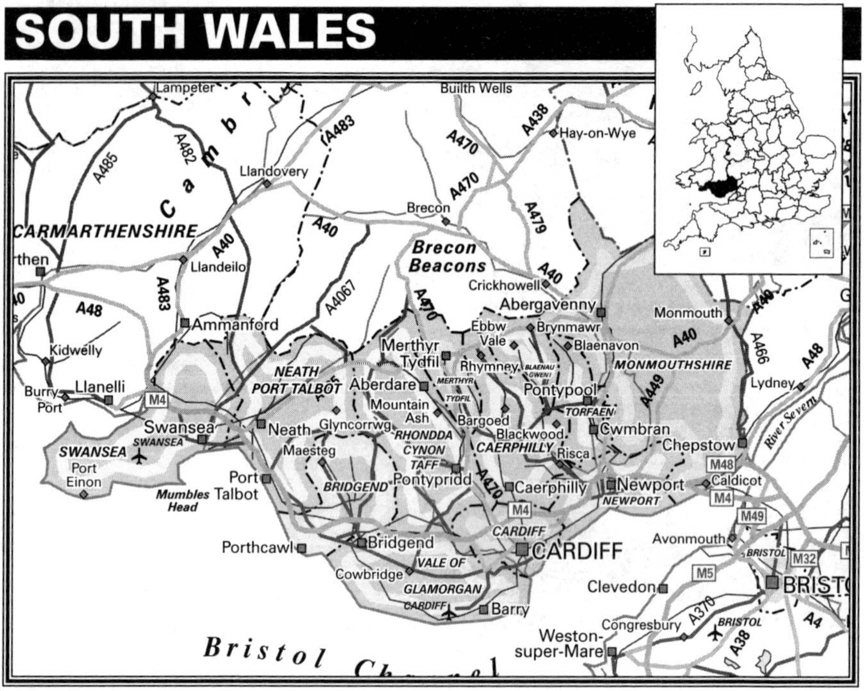

COWBRIDGE (near)

Mrs Sue Beer, Plas Llanmihangel, Llanmihangel, Near Cowbridge CF71 7LQ (01446 774610). Plas Llanmihangel is the finest medieval Grade I Listed manor house in the beautiful Vale of Glamorgan. We offer a genuine warmth of welcome, delightful accommodation, first class food and service in our wonderful home. The baronial hall, great log fires, the ancient tower and acres of beautiful historic gardens intrigue all who stay in this fascinating house. Its long history and continuous occupation have created a spectacular building in romantic surroundings unchanged since the sixteenth century. A great opportunity to experience the ambience and charm of a past age. Guests are accommodated in three double rooms. Bed and Breakfast from £28. High quality home-cooked Evening Meal available on request.

WTB ★★ *GUEST HOUSE, CONSUMER ASSOCIATION'S 'WHICH?' GOOD BED & BREAKFAST GUIDE.*

e-mail: plasllanmihangel@ukonline.co.uk

MONMOUTH

Rosemary and Derek Ringer, Church Farm Guest House, Mitchel Troy, Monmouth NP25 4HZ (01600 712176). A spacious and homely 16th century former farmhouse with oak beams and inglenook fireplaces, set in large attractive garden with stream. An excellent base for visiting the Wye Valley, Forest of Dean and Black Mountains. All bedrooms have washbasins, tea/coffee making facilities and central heating; most are en suite. Own car park. Colour TV. Non-smoking. Terrace and barbecue area. Bed and Breakfast from £21 to £25 per person. Evening Meal by arrangement. We also offer self-guided Walking Holidays and Short Breaks. Separate "Wysk Walks" brochure on request.

WTB ★★ *GUEST HOUSE,* **AA ◆◆◆**

PONTYPOOL

Mr and Mrs Jayne, Mill Farm, Cwmafon, Near Pontypool NP4 8XJ (Tel & Fax: 01495 774588). Caroline and Clive Jayne welcome you to experience complete tranquillity in their 15th century farmhouse situated in 30 acres of gardens, grounds and woodlands. Enjoy the comfort of rooms furnished with antiques, with breakfast until noon. Relax in the indoor heated pool situated in the large comfortable lounge. Ideal centre for walking, touring, visiting historic sites. Bed and hearty Welsh Breakfast £25 per person. Adults only. **AA ◆◆◆◆**

See also Colour Display Advertisement

RAGLAN

Mrs J.E. Thom, The Grange, Penrhos, Raglan NP15 2LQ (01600 780202). Organic mixed farm set in 115 acres, off the beaten track. Enjoy our peace and space and breath-taking views. Lots of places to visit and several good local golf courses (The Rolls of Monmouth is three miles). The countryside is ideal for walking and we are on Offa's Dyke Path. We welcome families, dogs and horses – we have an arena, stabling and farm jumps. Large en suite rooms and superb home-cooked evening meals if required. Bed and Breakfast from £20 to £25. Come and share this beautiful place. **WTB ★★★** *B&B.*

WALES

Visits & Attractions

Rhondda Heritage Park, Trehafod, South Wales • 01443 682036
www.netwales.co.uk/rhondda-heritage

A living testament to the coal mining valleys of the Rhondda, and to the spirit of the people who dug for "Black Gold". Special effects and life-like models bring to life this unique story.

Carreg Cennen Castle, Near Landeilo, South Wales • 01558 822291
website: www.cadw.wales.gov.uk

In a spectacular location in the Brecon Beacons National Park, this 'eagle's nest' of a castle is an adventure below and above ground, with passageways cut into the cliff face leading to natural caves.

Cefn Coed Colliery Museum, Neath. South Wales • 01639 750556

Housed in the buildings of what was once the deepest anthracite mine in the world, giving a vivid portrayal of the working conditions endured by the miners.

Centre for Visual Arts, Cardiff, South Wales • 029 20394040

Wales' largest gallery with regularly changing exhibitions and 'Fantasmic', an interactive gallery with over 100 hands-on exhibits to push, pull, touch and see

THE FHG DIPLOMA

HELP IMPROVE BRITISH TOURIST STANDARDS

You are choosing holiday accommodation from our very popular FHG Publications. Whether it be a hotel, guest house, farmhouse or self-catering accommodation, we think you will find it hospitable, comfortable and clean, and your host and hostess friendly and helpful.

Why not write and tell us about it?

As a recognition of the generally well-run and excellent holiday accommodation reviewed in our publications, we at FHG Publications Ltd. present a diploma to proprietors who receive the highest recommendation from their guests who are also readers of our Guides. If you care to write to us praising the holiday you have booked through FHG Publications Ltd. – whether this be board, self-catering accommodation, a sporting or a caravan holiday, what you say will be evaluated and the proprietors who reach our final list will be contacted.

The winning proprietor will receive an attractive framed diploma to display on his premises as recognition of a high standard of comfort, amenity and hospitality. FHG Publications Ltd. offer this diploma as a contribution towards the improvement of standards in tourist accommodation in Britain. Help your excellent host or hostess to win it!

FHG DIPLOMA

We nominate ....

....

Because

Name ....

Address ....

....

Telephone No...

WALES

Self-catering Accommodation

ANGLESEY & GWYNEDD

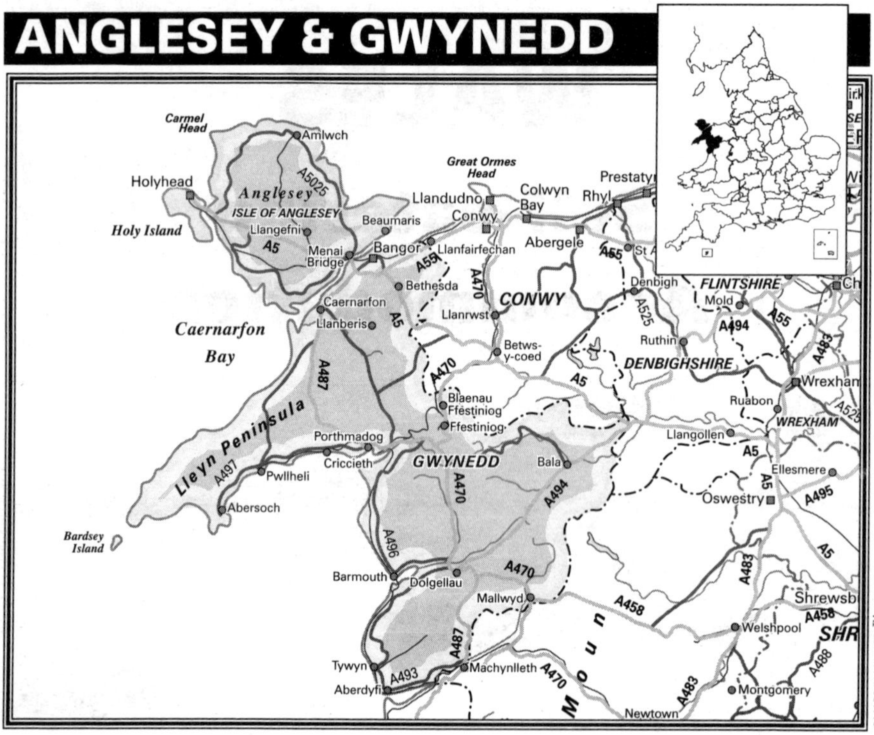

AROUND THE
MAGNIFICENT WELSH COAST

Away from the Madding Crowd • Near safe sandy beaches

A small specialist agency with over 40 years experience of providing quality self-catering, offers privacy, peace and unashamed luxury.

The first Wales Tourist Board Self-Catering Award Winner. Highest residential standards.

Dishwashers, Microwaves, Washing Machines, Central Heating. No Slot meters.

LOG FIRES • LINEN PROVIDED • PETS WELCOME FREE!

All in coastal areas famed for scenery, walks, wild-flowers, birds, badgers and foxes.

Free colour brochure from F.G. Rees "Quality Cottages", Cerbid, Solva, Haverfordwest, Pembrokeshire SA62 6YE

Telephone: (01348) 837871 • Website: www.qualitycottages.co.uk

ABERSOCH

Quality Cottages. Around the magnificent Welsh coast. Away from the madding crowd. Near safe sandy beaches. A small specialist agency offering privacy, peace and unashamed luxury. Wales Tourist Board 1989 Award Winner. Residential standards - dishwashers, microwaves, washing machines, central heating, log fires, no slot meters. Linen provided. Pets welcome free. All in coastal areas famed for scenery, walks, wild flowers, birds, badgers and foxes. Free colour brochure. **S.C. Rees, Quality Cottages, Cerbid, Solva, Haverfordwest, Pembrokeshire SA62 6YE (01348 837871).**
website: www.qualitycottages.co.uk

Semi-detached house sleeping 6 in village in National Park. Walks from the house including path to the summit of Snowdon. Steam railway to village expected to open Spring 2003. Seaside, gardens, historic buildings, lakes, riding, fishing, golf within easy reach.
Three bedrooms; two living rooms; bathroom; new kitchen. Well-equipped. Mountain view, terrace, rough garden. Inn (serving meals) nearby. No *pets*.

High season £160 to £320 per week; low season £70 to £150 per week.

Short Breaks. Open all year.

Bron Eifion

Rhyd Ddu, Beddgelert.

Apply: Mr Paul Johnson, 20 Plasturton Avenue, Cardiff CF11 9HH. Tel: 079 7030 1198

BRYNBRAS CASTLE

Welcome to beautiful Bryn Bras Castle – enchanting castle Apartments, elegant Tower-House within unique romantic turreted Regency Castle (Listed Building) in the gentle foothills of Snowdonia. Centrally situated amidst breathtaking scenery, ideal for exploring North Wales' magnificent mountains, beaches, resorts, heritage and history. Near local country inns/restaurants, shops. Each spacious apartment is fully self-contained, gracious, peaceful, clean, with distinctive individual character, comfortable furnishings, generously and conveniently appointed from dishwasher to fresh flowers, etc. Inclusive of VAT. Central heating, hot water, linen. All highest WTB grade. 32 acres of tranquil landscaped gardens, sweeping lawns, woodland walks of natural beauty, panoramic hill walks overlooking the sea, Anglesey and Mount Snowdon. Mild climate. Enjoy the comfort, warmth, privacy and relaxation of this castle of timeless charm in truly serene surroundings. Open all year, including for Short Breaks. Sleep 2-4 persons.

Regret no young children. Brochure sent with pleasure

Llanrug, Near Caernarfon, North Wales LL55 4RE

Tel & Fax: Llanberis (01286) 870210

E-mail: holidays@brynbrascastle.co.uk Website: www.brynbrascastle.co.uk

WALES

BALA (near)

Rhyd Fudr, Llanuwchllyn, Near Bala. Sleeps 6. Stone farm cottage set in an isolated position with views of five mountain peaks and Bala Lake. Accommodation comprises three bedrooms, plus cot; two sittingrooms; sun room; kitchen; bathroom. Garage. Multi-fuel burning stove and most modern conveniences but no TV. Fully-equipped including washing machine and telephone. Linen not supplied. Mountain stream and lovely walks on the doorstep. Sea, 45 minutes by car; Snowdon, one hour. Steep access - four-wheel drive advisable. Children welcome. Terms from £180. Apply: **Mrs J. H. Gervis, Nazeing Bury, Nazeing, Essex EN9 2JN (0199 289 2331) or Mrs G. E. Evans, Pant-y-Ceubren, Llanuwchllyn, Bala (01678 540252).**

CRICCIETH

Quality Cottages. Around the magnificent Welsh coast. Away from the madding crowd. Near safe sandy beaches. A small specialist agency offering privacy, peace and unashamed luxury. Wales Tourist Board 1989 Award Winner. Residential standards - dishwashers, microwaves, washing machines, central heating, log fires, no slot meters. Linen provided. Pets welcome free. All in coastal areas famed for scenery, walks, wild flowers, birds, badgers and foxes. Free colour brochure. **S.C. Rees, Quality Cottages, Cerbid, Solva, Haverfordwest, Pembrokeshire SA62 6YE (01348 837871).**
website: www.qualitycottages.co.uk

The FHG Directory of Website Addresses

on pages 349 – 378 is a useful quick reference guide for holiday accommodation with e-mail and/or website details

CRICCIETH

Betws-Bach & Rhos-Dhu, Ynys, Criccieth LL52 0PB (Tel & Fax: 01758 720047; 01766 810295). Sleep 2-6 plus cot. A truly romantic, memorable and special place to stay and relax in comfort. Old world farmhouse and period country cottage. Situated just off the B4411 road in tranquil surroundings. Equipped with washing/drying machines, dishwashers, microwaves, freezers, colour TV, old oak beams, inglenook with log fires, full central heating. Snooker table, romantic four-poster bed; sauna and jacuzzi. Open all year – Winter Weekends welcomed. Ideal for couples. Own fishing and shooting rights, wonderful walks, peace and quiet with Snowdonia and unspoilt beaches on our doorstep. For friendly personal service please phone, fax or write to **Mrs Anwen Jones. WTB ★★★★★** *SELF-CATERING.*

e-mail: cottages@rhos.freeserve.co.uk **website: www.rhos-cottages.co.uk**

CRICCIETH

Mrs M. Williams, Gaerwen Farm, Ynys, Criccieth LL52 0NU (Tel & Fax: 01766 810324). Sleeps 7. This 200 acre dairy/mixed farm is situated four-and-a-half miles inland from Criccieth and beaches. An ideal centre for enjoying climbing, fishing, pony trekking and quiet country walks with extensive views of Snowdonia and Cardigan Bay. Within easy reach of various historic places nearby. Accommodation is self-contained in furnished farmhouse, comprising TV/video lounge with inglenook fireplace and oak beams, electric fire; fitted kitchen with electric cooker, automatic washing machine, fridge/freezer and microwave; diningroom; two double bedrooms, one twin-bedded room and one single bedroom, with duvets and bed linen; bathroom/shower with washbasin and toilet. Children most welcome, cot and babysitting available. Pets welcome. Car essential. Electricity provided. Weekly terms from £125 to £320. Short Breaks offered. Please telephone **(01766 810324)**

LLANBEDR

Mrs Beti Wyn Jones, Pensarn Farm, Llanbedr, Gwynedd LL45 2HS (01341 241285). Working farm. Sleeps 4 adults, 2 children. Self-catering, semi-detached cottage in beautiful surroundings, ideal for a peaceful and relaxing holiday. The accommodation consists of modern kitchen, lounge/diner, two bedrooms, bathroom and toilet on ground floor; one bedroom, shower/toilet upstairs. Night storage heaters. Ample parking space and garden. Children and pets welcome. It is situated one mile from the picturesque village of Llanbedr, quarter-of-a-mile off the main Barmouth to Harlech road. Convenient for beach, mountains, golf course, fishing and pleasant walks up the River Artro to the Nantcol and Cwm Bychan Valleys. Terms from £200 to £250 per week.

LLANBEDR

Mrs O. Evans, Werngron Farm, Llanbedr, Merioneth LL45 2PF (01341 241274). Working farm. Pleasant bungalow on working farm, set in own grounds and enjoying open views of unspoilt countryside. Llanbedr two miles, Harlech three, Barmouth 10. Good touring centre for north and mid Wales; within easy reach of sandy beaches, golf course, indoor swimming pool, pony trekking, freshwater and coarse fishing, sea fishing, various tourist attractions and lovely country and mountain walks. Sleeps six, plus cot, in three bedrooms - double, twin and bunks - all with own washbasins. Sittingroom with colour TV; diningroom; well equipped, all electric fitted kitchen; spacious sun lounge; bathroom/shower. Fitted carpets throughout, electric fires, oil central heating. Bed linen provided. Open all year. Terms from £200 to £300 per week plus heating and electricity.

COASTAL HOUSE

35 Corbett Close, Tywyn

Two minutes' walk to sandy beach. Two minutes' walk to pub/bar meals. Fully equipped as own home. Garden front and rear. Garage. Scenic and pleasant walking areas nearby. Tal-y-Llyn Steam Railway walking distance. Pets welcome FREE OF CHARGE. Three bedrooms. Sleeps five. Terms £179-£229 per week.

Enquiries: Mr Ian Weston, 18 Elizabeth Road, Basingstoke, Hampshire RG22 6AX
Tel: 01256 352364; Evenings: 01256 412233
e-mail: ianweston@iname.com

PORTHMADOG

Mrs M. J. Thomas, Pensyflog Farm, Porthmadog LL49 9PW (01766 513055). Spacious country farmhouse on the outskirts of the popular holiday town of Porthmadog and within easy access of a number of good beaches and hill walks. Comfortable accommodation, traditionally furnished, with lots of character and exposed beamed ceilings. Bathroom with overhead shower, separate toilet. Colour TV. Cafes, shops and pubs approximately half-a-mile. Ample parking on tarmac yard. Children welcome.

PWLLHELI

Mrs C.A. Jones, Rhedyn, Mynytho, Pwllheli LL53 7PS (01758 740669). Sleeps 5. Rhedyn is a small farm overlooking the beautiful Nanhoron Valley, and the farm cottage, accommodating four people, is offered for hire between April and November. It is two miles from Llanbedrog and Abersoch, both noted for their safe bathing. Children are made especially welcome. The house has two double bedrooms; bathroom and toilet; combined sitting/diningroom with TV; kitchen with immersion heater, washing machine, microwave oven. Calor gas stove and fridge. Linen supplied. Pets permitted. One mile from shops and two from the sea. Car essential, ample parking. SAE, for further details and terms.
e-mail: katie@rhedyn.freeserve.co.uk
website: www.rhedyn.freeserve.co.uk

One FREE child with each full fare paying adult at

Bala Lake Railway

See our READERS' OFFER VOUCHER for details.

One pet travels FREE with each full fare paying adult at

Llanberis Lake Railway

See our READERS' OFFER VOUCHER for details.

NORTH WALES

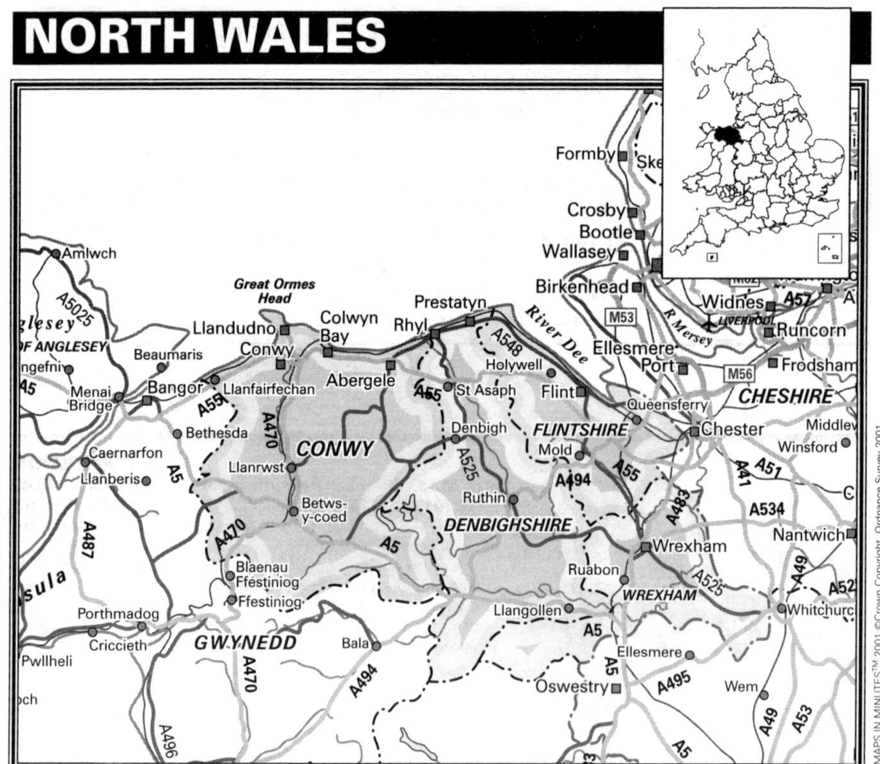

BETWS-Y-COED

Jim and Lilian Boughton, Bron Celyn, Lôn Muriau, Llanrwst Road, Betws-y-Coed LL24 0HD (01690 710333; Fax: 01690 710111). Our cosy 200-year-old converted coach house has been tastefully refurbished and offers accommodation for up to four persons. Upstairs: one double room with space for a cot, and one bunk-bedded room with full length/width bunk beds. All bed linen is provided but not towels. Downstairs: lounge with colour TV and video, and wood-burning stove (ample supply of chopped timber available). Kitchen with fridge, electric cooker, microwave, toaster and water heater. Shower room and toilet. Electric storage heaters fitted throughout. Open all year. Ideal centre for walking, climbing, fishing or simply just relaxing! Terms £150 to £325 per week. Short Breaks available.

e-mail: welcome@broncelyn.co.uk **website: http://www.broncelyn.co.uk**

CEREDIGION

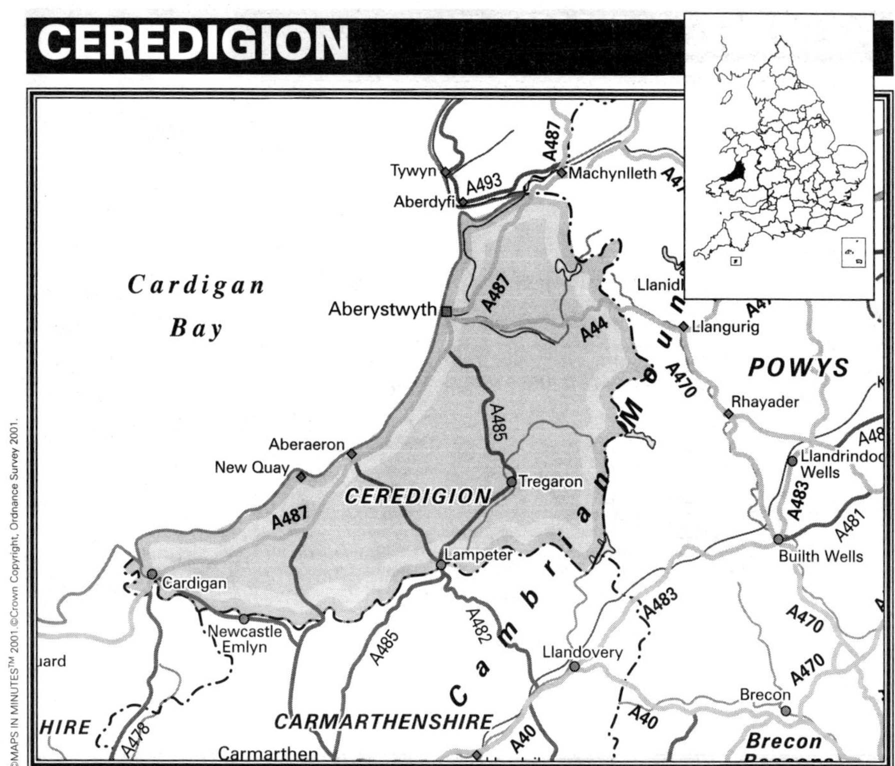

ABERPORTH

Quality Cottages. Around the magnificent Welsh coast. Away from the madding crowd. Near safe, sandy beaches. A small specialist agency offering privacy, peace and unashamed luxury. Wales Tourist Board 1989 Award Winner. Residential standards - dishwashers, microwaves, washing machines, central heating, log fires, no slot meters. Linen provided. Pets welcome free. All in coastal areas famed for scenery, walks, wild flowers, birds, badgers and foxes. Free colour brochure. **S.C. Rees, Quality Cottages, Cerbid, Solva, Haverfordwest, Pembrokeshire SA62 6YE (01348 837871).**
website: www.qualitycottages.co.uk

CARDIGAN (near)

Quality Cottages. Around the magnificent Welsh coast. Away from the madding crowd. Near safe sandy beaches. A small specialist agency offering privacy, peace and unashamed luxury. Wales Tourist Board 1989 Award Winner. Residential standards - dishwashers, microwaves, washing machines, central heating, log fires, no slot meters. Linen provided. Pets welcome free. All in coastal areas famed for scenery, walks, wild flowers, birds, badgers and foxes. Free colour brochure. **S.C. Rees, Quality Cottages, Cerbid, Solva, Haverfordwest, Pembrokeshire SA62 6YE (01348 837871).**
website: www.qualitycottages.co.uk

LLANGRANNOG

Quality Cottages. Around the magnificent Welsh coast. Away from the madding crowd. Near safe sandy beaches. A small specialist agency offering privacy, peace and unashamed luxury. Wales Tourist Board 1989 Award Winner. Residential standards - dishwashers, microwaves, washing machines, central heating, log fires, no slot meters. Linen provided. Pets welcome free. All in coastal areas famed for scenery, walks, wild flowers, birds, badgers and foxes. Free colour brochure. **S.C. Rees, Quality Cottages, Cerbid, Solva, Haverfordwest, Pembrokeshire SA62 6YE (01348 837871).**
website: www.qualitycottages.co.uk

NEW QUAY

Mrs C. Davies, Cwmcynon Farm, Llwyndafydd, Ceredigion SA44 6LE (01545 560426). Working farm. Sleeps 6 plus one child. Cwmcynon is a working farm with beef cattle and sheep. This semi-detached house, which adjoins the owners' residence on a working farm, originally dates from 1808, and provides an ideal base from which to enjoy the surrounding countryside and sandy beaches. All within a fifteen mile radius are golfing, fishing, pony trekking. Within four and-a-half miles are the towns of Aberaeron, Cardigan, Lampeter and New Quay Beach. The nearest pub is half-a-mile away. Terms are from £210 to £290 per week.

PEMBROKESHIRE

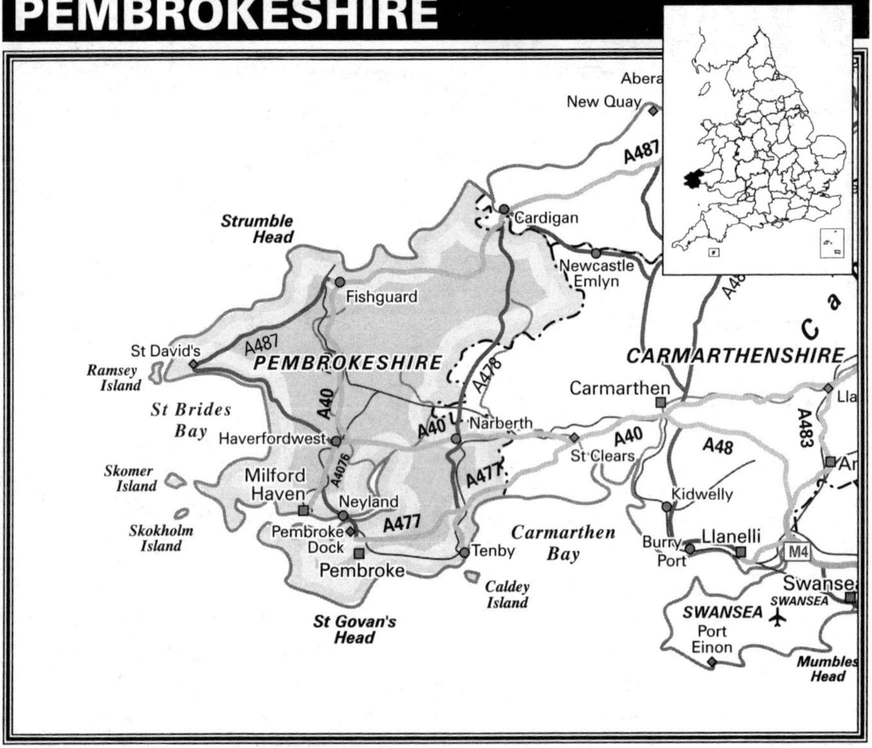

See also Colour Display Advertisement

AMROTH

Carol Lloyd, East Llanteg Farm, Llanteg, Amroth SA67 8QA (01834 831336). Two charming cottages privately situated and ideally located for exploring Pembrokeshire. The resorts of Saundersfoot and Tenby are close at hand with the seaside resort of Amroth and the coastal path just minutes away. Each cottage sleeps four to five adults; cots and high chairs are also provided. All facilities including fully fitted kitchen, central heating and colour television are included. There is ample private parking plus a lawned garden area and patio with garden furniture provided. **WTB ★★★★★** *SELF-CATERING.*
e-mail: john@pembrokeshireholiday.co.uk
website: www.pembrokeshireholiday.co.uk

BOSHERTON

Quality Cottages. Around the magnificent Welsh coast. Away from the madding crowd. Near safe sandy beaches. A small specialist agency offering privacy, peace and unashamed luxury. Wales Tourist Board 1989 Award Winner. Residential standards - dishwashers, microwaves, washing machines, central heating, log fires, no slot meters. Linen provided. Pets welcome free. All in coastal areas famed for scenery, walks, wild flowers, birds, badgers and foxes. Free colour brochure. **S.C. Rees, Quality Cottages, Cerbid, Solva, Haverfordwest, Pembrokeshire SA62 6YE (01348 837871).**
website: www.qualitycottages.co.uk

Readers are requested to mention this guidebook when seeking accommodation (and please enclose a stamped addressed envelope).

AROUND THE MAGNIFICENT WELSH COAST

Away from the Madding Crowd • Near safe sandy beaches

A small specialist agency with over 40 years experience of providing quality self-catering, offers privacy, peace and unashamed luxury.

The first Wales Tourist Board Self-Catering Award Winner. Highest residential standards.

Dishwashers, Microwaves, Washing Machines, Central Heating. No Slot meters.

LOG FIRES • LINEN PROVIDED • PETS WELCOME FREE!

All in coastal areas famed for scenery, walks, wild-flowers, birds, badgers and foxes.

Free colour brochure from F.G. Rees "Quality Cottages", Cerbid, Solva, Haverfordwest, Pembrokeshire SA62 6YE

Telephone: (01348) 837871 • Website: www.qualitycottages.co.uk

Stable Cottage & Granary Cottage, Amroth

The impressive position of these cottages, the wonderful views and beautiful setting, together with an imaginative conversion of an exceptionally high standard, make these properties outstanding. From the cottages and grounds, some nine acres, it is possible to see for many miles over the sea and countryside.

Stable Cottage sleeps 6 • 3 bedrooms • WTB Grade 5 • Terms from £251.

Granary Cottage sleeps 4 • 2 bedrooms • WTB Grade 5 • Terms from £235

Details from **Mrs Green, Furzewood Farm, Amroth, Pembrokeshire SA67 8NQ**

Tel: 01834 814674 • www.coastalcottages.co.uk

See also Colour Advertisement

GOODWICK

Mrs Rosemary Johns, Carne Farm, Goodwick SA64 0LB (01348 891665). Working farm, join in. Sleeps 6. Stone cottage adjoining farmhouse sleeps six in three bedrooms, also a spacious residential caravan for six with two bedrooms, each with its own garden where children can play safely. In peaceful countryside on 350 acre dairy and sheep farm between Fishguard and Strumble Head, three miles from the sea. Within easy reach of many beaches by car, ideal for walking and bird-watching. No linen supplied. Children welcome. Washing machine in cottage. TV, microwave, cots, high chairs. Baby sitting available. You can be sure of a warm welcome and visitors can feed calves and watch the milking.

NEWGALE

Quality Cottages. Around the magnificent Welsh coast. Away from the madding crowd. Near safe sandy beaches. A small specialist agency offering privacy, peace and unashamed luxury. Wales Tourist Board 1989 Award Winner. Residential standards - dishwashers, microwaves, washing machines, central heating, log fires, no slot meters. Linen provided. Pets welcome free. All in coastal areas famed for scenery, walks, wild flowers, birds, badgers and foxes. Free colour brochure. **S.C. Rees, Quality Cottages, Cerbid, Solva, Haverfordwest, Pembrokeshire SA62 6YE (01348 837871).**
website: www.qualitycottages.co.uk

A useful index of towns and counties appears at the back of this book on pages 379 - 382. Refer also to Contents Page 50/51.

WALES

See also Colour Display Advertisement

ST BRIDES

St Brides Bay Holiday Cottages. Sleep 2-11. Cosy cottages and farmhouses near superb beaches and coastal path, around beautiful St Brides Bay in Pembrokeshire. WTB Graded. Pet welcome. Telephone: **0870 7572270.**
website: www.stbridesbaycottages.com

ST DAVID'S

Quality Cottages. Around the magnificent Welsh coast. Away from the madding crowd. Near safe sandy beaches. A small specialist agency offering privacy, peace and unashamed luxury. Wales Tourist Board 1989 Award Winner. Residential standards - dishwashers, microwaves, washing machines, central heating, log fires, no slot meters. Linen provided. Pets welcome free. All in coastal areas famed for scenery, walks, wild flowers, birds, badgers and foxes. Free colour brochure. **S.C. Rees, Quality Cottages, Cerbid, Solva, Haverfordwest, Pembrokeshire SA62 6YE (01348 837871).**
website: www.qualitycottages.co.uk

ST DAVID'S

WALES

Liz Stiles, Swn-y-Don, Tregwynt, Castle Morris, Haverfordwest SA62 5UX (Tel & Fax: 01348 891616). Sleep 2-12. Pembrokeshire Coast – Newport to Little Haven. Charming, individual cottages situated near sandy beaches, rocky bays and spectacular cliff walks. Traditional stone-built cottages or modern properties, many with central heating and wood-burning stoves. All furnished to high residential standards, fully equipped and personally supervised. Watersports, golf, birdwatching and wild flowers. Boat trips to the islands. Explore the Preseli Mountains, castles, cromlechs and Iron Age forts. Visit art galleries and craft workshops, relax in country pubs and quality restaurants. Pets and children welcome.
e-mail: lizstiles@onetel.net.uk
website: www.pembrokeshireholidays.co.uk

SOLVA

Quality Cottages. Around the magnificent Welsh coast. Away from the madding crowd. Near safe sandy beaches. A small specialist agency offering privacy, peace and unashamed luxury. Wales Tourist Board 1989 Award Winner. Residential standards - dishwashers, microwaves, washing machines, central heating, log fires, no slot meters. Linen provided. Pets welcome free. All in coastal areas famed for scenery, walks, wild flowers, birds, badgers and foxes. Free colour brochure. **S.C. Rees, Quality Cottages, Cerbid, Solva, Haverfordwest, Pembrokeshire SA62 6YE (01348 837871).**
website: www.qualitycottages.co.uk

TENBY

Quality Cottages. Around the magnificent Welsh coast. Away from the madding crowd. Near safe sandy beaches. A small specialist agency offering privacy, peace and unashamed luxury. Wales Tourist Board 1989 Award Winner. Residential standards - dishwashers, microwaves, washing machines, central heating, log fires, no slot meters. Linen provided. Pets welcome free. All in coastal areas famed for scenery, walks, wild flowers, birds, badgers and foxes. Free colour brochure. **S.C. Rees, Quality Cottages, Cerbid, Solva, Haverfordwest, Pembrokeshire SA62 6YE (01348 837871).**
website: www.qualitycottages.co.uk

See also Colour Display Advertisement

WHITLAND

Mrs Angela Colledge, Gwarmacwydd, Llanfallteg, Whitland SA34 0XH (01437 563260; Fax: 01437 563839). Gwarmacwydd is a country estate of over 450 acres, including two miles of riverbank. Come and see a real farm in action, the hustle and bustle of harvest, newborn calves and lambs. Children are welcomed. On the estate are five character stone cottages, Tourist Board Grade Four. Each cottage has been lovingly converted from traditional farm buildings, parts of which are over 200 years old. Each cottage is fully furnished and equipped with all modern conveniences. All electricity and linen included. All cottages are heated for year-round use. Colour brochure available. **WTB** ★★★★ *SELF-CATERING*.
e-mail: info@a-farm-holiday.org
website: www.a-farm-holiday.org

POWYS

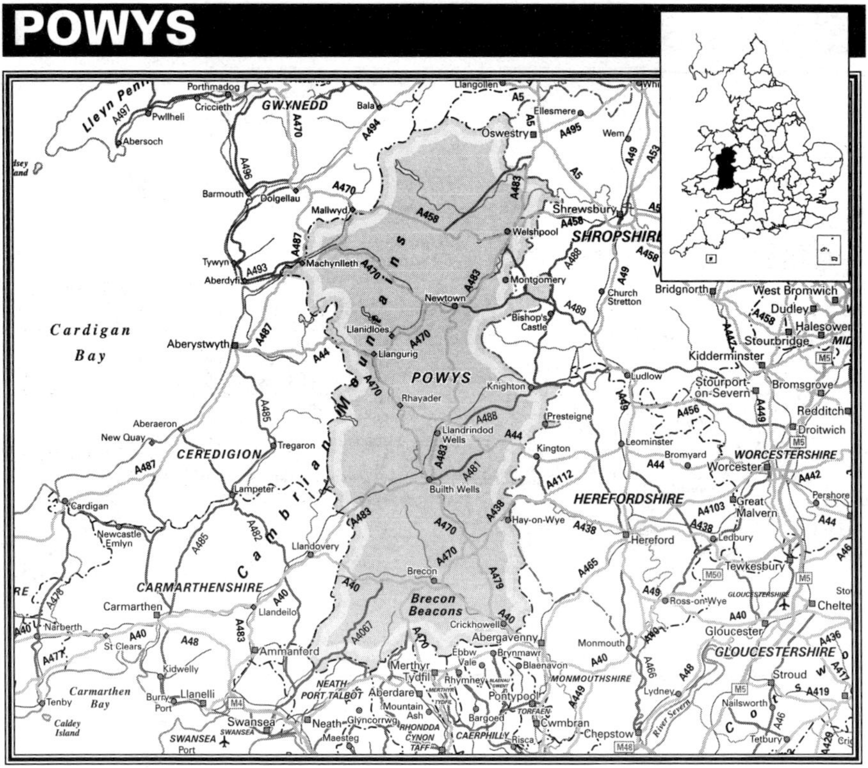

LLANDRINDOD WELLS

Phillip and Patricia Harley, Gaer Cottage, Hundred House, Llandrindod Wells LD1 5RU (Tel & Fax: 01982 570208). Gaer Cottage is a comfortable, well equipped, recently restored Welsh cottage. It has oil-fired central heating throughout. There are large south- facing windows and a conservatory. The kitchen and utility are well stocked with pots and pans for up to eight people. There is a fan oven, microwave, fridge/freezer, dishwasher and automatic washing machine. The lounge is very spacious providing a dining table with seating for eight, comfortable chairs and a bed-settee. There is a TV and video. Upstairs there are two en suite bedrooms; one has a double bed and the other has three single beds, two of which can join together to form a double. Bed and Breakfast available in farmhouse.

e-mail: unwind@gaercottage.co.uk

website: www.gaercottage.co.uk

RHAYADER

See also Colour Display Advertisement

Oak Wood Lodges, Llwynbaedd, Rhayader LD6 5NT (01597 811422). Self-catering log cabins. Luxurious Norwegian log cabins situated at approximately 100ft above sea level with spectacular views of the Elan Valley and Cambrian Mountains. Enjoy pursuits such as watching in the most idyllic of surroundings. Excellent touring centre. Dogs welcome. Short breaks as well as full weeks. Open all year round. Please telephone for more information and brochure. **WTB ★★★★** *SELF-CATERING.*

SOUTH WALES

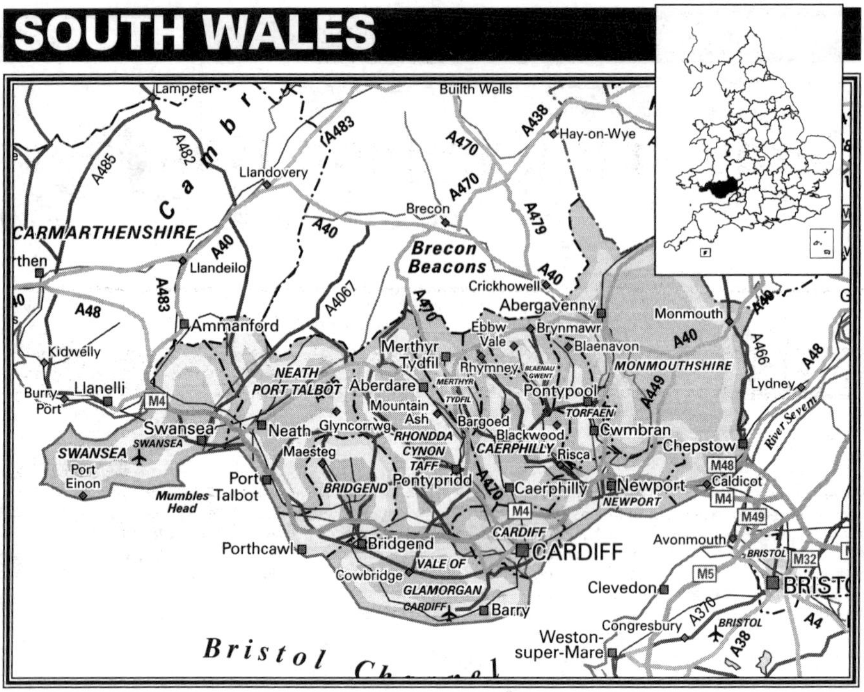

See also Colour Display Advertisement

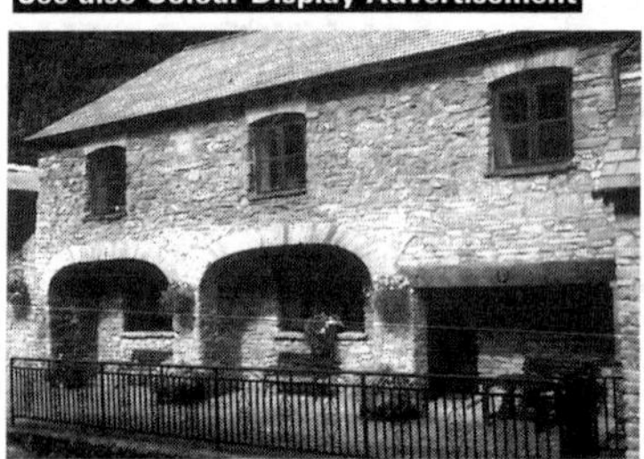

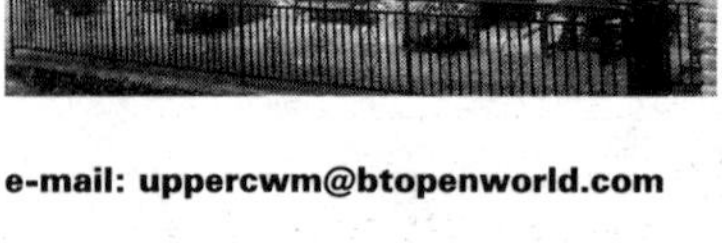

ABERGAVENNY (near)

Mrs Ann Ball, Upper Cwm Farm, Brynderi, Llantilio, Crossenny, Abergavenny NP7 8TG (Tel & Fax: 01873 821236). Come and visit us to relax and explore. The Granary and Coach House are in a beautifully converted barn, midway between Abergavenny and Monmouth. Ideal family self-catering accommodation. Each unit has three bedrooms (two twin/one double), lounge, diner/kitchen with full electric cooker, microwave, refrigerator and toaster. Bathroom has a shower over the bath. Colour TV in lounge. Bedlinen, towels and electricity included in the price. Cot and high chair available. Patio and children's play area. Barbecue. Ample parking. Pets by arrangement only. Superb country area for walking, bird watching or visiting interesting market towns and local castles. Colour brochure. **WTB ★★★★** *SELF-CATERING.*

e-mail: uppercwm@btopenworld.com
website: www.downourlane.co.uk/3htm

Visits & Attractions

Cefn Coed Colliery Museum, Neath, South Wales • 01639 750556

Housed in the buildings of what was once the deepest anthracite mine in the world, giving a vivid portrayal of the working conditions endured by the miners.

Centre for Visual Arts, Cardiff, South Wales • 029 20394040

Wales' largest gallery with regularly changing exhibitions and 'Fantasmic', an interactive gallery with over 100 hands-on exhibits to push, pull, touch and see.

WALES

Caravan & Camping Holidays

NORTH WALES

ABERGELE

Mr and Mrs T.P. Williams, Pen Isaf Caravan Park, Llangernyw, Abergele LL22 8RN (01745 860276). This small caravan site in beautiful unspoilt countryside is ideal for touring North Wales and is situated 10 miles from the coast and 12 miles from Betws-y-Coed. The eight-berth caravans are fully equipped except for linen and towels and have shower, flush toilet, hot and cold water, Calor gas cooker, electric light and fridge. Fresh eggs and milk can be obtained from the farm on which this 20 caravan site is situated. Children especially will enjoy a holiday here, there being ample space and facilities for fishing and pony riding. Pets are allowed but must be kept under control. Open March to October. Terms on application with SAE, please.

CEREDIGION

ABERPORTH

Mrs S. Jones, Manorafon Caravan Park, Sarnau, Llandyssul SA44 6QH (01239 810564). Sleeps 6. Quiet, peaceful site of five caravans and two log chalets, fully equipped including linen (except towels); all caravans six-berth with end bedrooms. All essential facilities provided. Bathroom facilities with hot water on tap in each van; Calor gas cooker, electric lighting and heating. Toilets and washbasins, showers, shaving points. Calor and Camping Gaz sold. Available Easter to October. Children welcome. No dogs. Only half-a-mile from the pleasant Penbryn beach and nine miles from the market towns of Cardigan and Newcastle Emlyn. One-and-a-half-acres for campers and tourers.

Visits & Attractions

Vale of Rheidol Railway, Aberystwyth, Ceredigion • 01970 625819

An unforgettable journey by narrow gauge steam train , climbing over 600 feet in 12 miles from Aberystwyth to Devil's Bridge. There are many sharp turns and steep gradients, and the journey affords superb views of the valley.

REPUBLIC OF IRELAND

Board Accommodation

Co. Cork

BANTRY

Mrs Agnes Hegarty, Hillcrest Farm, Ahakista, Durrus, Bantry (00 353 27 67045). Seaside farm. Charming old-style farmhouse, newly renovated, retaining traditional character. Situated in picturesque peaceful setting overlooking harbour and Dunmanus Bay, quarter-of-a-mile from Ahakista village on the Sheep's Head Peninsula. Magnificent sea and mountain scenery; swimming, fishing, boating and five minutes' walk to the sea. Irish pubs and restaurants close by. Bantry 12 miles, Durrus six miles. Ideal centre for touring the Peninsulas of West Cork and Kerry. Signposted in Durrus. Four guest bedrooms, three with bath/shower en suite, one with washbasin; two are family rooms. Ground floor room available. Tea/coffee making facilities and electric blankets in all bedrooms. Bathroom. Spacious dining room with stone walls; sittingroom with old world fireplace and log fire. Play/games room, antiques, swing, lovely garden with mature trees. Warm hospitality. Fresh farm vegetables and home baking. Babysitting. On new Sheeps Head Way walking route. Bed and Breakfast from 30 to 34 euros; Dinner 22 euros, High Tea 17 euros. 25% reductions for children sharing with parents. Extensive breakfast menu. Award Winner of Farmhouse of the Year 1991/2. Also to let, modern 4-Star seaside cottage for self catering. Fully equipped and in superb location, from 270 to 485 euros per week. Available all year.

e-mail: agneshegarty@oceanfree.net **website: www.ahakista.com**

Co. Galway

ORANMORE

Mrs Cannon, Cartroon Farm, Galway Coast Road, Oranmore (00 353 91 794345). Spacious farmhouse in scenic surroundings overlooking Galway Bay. Situated one mile west of Oranmore and four-and-a-half miles east of Galway City just off N18 and N6 roads. Ideal base for touring Connemara, Burren, Cliffs of Moher and indeed the whole of the West of Ireland. Galway City and Airport eight minutes' drive. Galway Bay Golf and Country Club five minutes, also horse riding, fishing and sailing locally. Dairy farm, other farm animals and domestic poultry also kept. Good food and accommodation in four bedrooms, all en suite. Bed and Breakfast from IR£16 per person; single supplement IR£5; Dinner IR£15.

e-mail: cartroonfarmhouse@eircom.net
website: http://homepage.eircom.net/~cartroonfarmhouse/

REPUBLIC OF IRELAND

Self-catering

Co. Kerry

LAURAGH

Creveen Lodge Caravan and Camping Park, Healy Pass Road, Lauragh (00 353 64 83131; from Ireland 064 83131). Attractive two-storey dormer-style farmhouse attached to proprietors' residence, 200 yards from roadside, with magnificent views of sea and countryside. The 80-acre mixed farm is conveniently situated for fishing, mountain climbing, Derreen Gardens, shops and old Irish pub: 16 miles south of Kenmare. Accommodation for six/eight persons in three double and one single room, all with washbasin; cot. Sittingroom with large stone fireplace, TV; separate diningroom. Kitchen has gas cooker; full oil-fired central heating and storage heating; washing machine and dryer. Everything supplied including linen. Children and pets welcome; high chair, and babysitting arranged. Car essential - parking. Available all year. April May and October 190 euros; June 254 euros; July and August 380 euros per week; rest of the year by 150 euros. Gas and electricity extra.

e-mail: info@creveenlodge.com **website: www.creveenlodge.com**

Ratings You Can Trust

ENGLAND

The English Tourism Council (formerly the English Tourist Board) has joined with the **AA** and **RAC** to create a new, easily understood quality rating for serviced accommodation, giving a clear guide of what to expect.

HOTELS are given a rating from One to Five **Stars** – the more Stars, the higher the quality and the greater the range of facilities and level of services provided.

GUEST ACCOMMODATION, which includes guest houses, bed and breakfasts, inns and farmhouses, is rated from One to Five **Diamonds**. Progressively higher levels of quality and customer care must be provided for each one of the One to Five Diamond ratings.

HOLIDAY PARKS, TOURING PARKS and CAMPING PARKS are now also assessed using **Stars**. Standards of quality range from a One Star (acceptable) to a Five Star (exceptional) park.

Look out also for the new **SELF-CATERING** Star ratings. The more **Stars** (from One to Five) awarded to an establishment, the higher the levels of quality you can expect. Establishments at higher rating levels also have to meet some additional requirements for facilities.

SCOTLAND

Star Quality Grades will reflect the most important aspects of a visit, such as the warmth of welcome, efficiency and friendliness of service, the quality of the food and the cleanliness and condition of the furnishings, fittings and decor.

THE MORE STARS, THE HIGHER THE STANDARDS.

The description, such as Hotel, Guest House, Bed and Breakfast, Lodge, Holiday Park, Self-catering etc tells you the type of property and style of operation.

WALES

Places which score highly will have an especially welcoming atmosphere and pleasing ambience, high levels of comfort and guest care, and attractive surroundings enhanced by thoughtful design and attention to detail

STAR QUALITY GUIDE FOR

HOTELS, GUEST HOUSES AND FARMHOUSES

SELF-CATERING ACCOMMODATION
(Cottages, Apartments, Houses)

CARAVAN HOLIDAY HOME PARKS
(Holiday Parks, Touring Parks, Camping Parks)

★★★★★	*Exceptional quality*
★★★★	*Excellent quality*
★★★	*Very good quality*
★★	*Good quality*
★	*Fair to good quality*

In England, Scotland and Wales, all graded properties are inspected annually by Tourist Authority trained Assessors.

COUNTRY INNS

Other specialised

FHG PUBLICATIONS

Published annually: available in all good bookshops or direct from the publisher.

PETS WELCOME! £7.99

Recommended **COUNTRY HOTELS OF BRITAIN** £5.99

Recommended **WAYSIDE INNS OF BRITAIN** £5.99

Recommended **SHORT BREAK HOLIDAYS IN BRITAIN** £5.99

FHG PUBLICATIONS LTD,
Abbey Mill Business Centre,
Seedhill, Paisley, Renfrewshire PAI ITJ
Tel: 0141-887 0428 • Fax: 0141-889 7204
e-mail: fhg@ipcmedia.com
website: www.holidayguides.com

CUMBRIA

Talkin Village, Brampton, Cumbria CA8 1LE

Tel: 016977 3452 • Fax: 016977 3396

The Blacksmith's Arms offers all the hospitality and comforts of a traditional country inn. Enjoy tasty meals served in the bar lounges, or linger over dinner in the well-appointed restaurant. The inn is personally managed by the proprietors, Anne and Donald Jackson, who guarantee the hospitality one would expect from a family concern. Guests are assured of a pleasant and comfortable stay. There are five lovely bedrooms, all en suite and offering every comfort. Peacefully situated in the beautiful village of Talkin, the inn is convenient for the Borders, Hadrian's Wall and the Lake District. There is a good golf course, walking and other country pursuits nearby.

See also Colour Advertisement

SHROPSHIRE

LUDLOW

The Church Inn, Buttercross, Shropshire SY8 1AW (01584 872174, Fax: 01584 877146). This historic inn has undergone several changes of name over the centuries – it was originally called the "Cross Keys" – but retains the fine old-fashioned traditions of good ale and good food which have ensured its lasting popularity through the ages. Nine cosy en suite bedrooms all with telephone and modem points, provide first-rate overnight accommodation, and a full range of catering, from freshly cut sandwiches to succulent steaks, ensures that appetites large and small will be amply satisfied. Regularly changing guest beers supplement the already extensive range of wines, spirits and ales on offer. The ancient town of Ludlow is an ideal base for exploring the Border counties and the Welsh Marches, and is conveniently located for road and rail links to the Midlands. Children welcome. **ETC/AA/RAC ◆◆◆**, *CAMRA, EGON RONAY.*
website: www.thechurchinn.com

The FHG Directory of Website Addresses

on pages 349–378 is a useful quick reference guide for holiday accommodation with e-mail and/or website details

THE STAR INN, ALFRISTON

The centuries old village of Alfriston is situated on the River Cuckmere, near Polegate, East Sussex.

★ The Star Inn ★

lies at its heart and is known as one of England's oldest inns.

Prince Edward is among the guests who have visited this famous 14th century inn which was once a renowned meeting place for smugglers.

Oak beams and open fires offer mellow reminders of the past and create an intimate atmosphere in the bar. Set in the South Downs, there are many fine walks, and the famous South Downs Way starts right at the door of the inn.

All rooms en suite, with tea/coffee making facilities, colour television and direct dial telephone.

Pets welcome with a charge.
Extra beds for children.

Local attractions
South Downs
Glyndebourne
The English Wine Centre
Herstmonceux Science Centre
Seven Sisters Cliffs
Bluebell Railway
Pevensey Castle
Beachy Head
Local Leisure Facilities
Pool, Sauna, Tennis, Squash,
Horse Riding and Golf Course.

★ THE STAR INN ★

Alfriston, Near Polegate, East Sussex BN26 5TH

Tel: 0870 400 8102 • Fax: 0132 387 0922

e-mail: starinn@macdonald-hotels.co.uk

See also Colour Advertisement on Inside Back Cover

WEST SUSSEX

One of the most attractive features of this delightful South Downs Village, The Horse and Groom presents a variety of options for a rewarding break. Superb walking, cycling and riding terrain is all around, and beautiful beaches can be reached in 20 minutes. Goodwood and Fontwell Park await the racing enthusiast and the city of Chichester and its famous harbour are close by. There are eleven bedrooms, all en suite with TV and beverage-making facilities. A first-rate choice of home-cooked fare is available each lunchtime and evening, augmented by traditional real ales and quality wines. Short Break details available on request.

the Horse & Groom

East Ashling, Chichester PO18 9AX
Tel: 01243 575339 • Fax: 01243 575560
e-mail: horseandgroomea@aol.com
website: www.horseandgroom.sageweb.co.uk

ETC 

WILTSHIRE

THE LAMB AT HINDON

Hindon, Near Salisbury, Wiltshire SP3 6DP
Tel: 01747 820573 • Fax: 01747 820605 • e-mail: lambinnhotel@youngs.co.uk

The fascinating history of this ancient inn is related in its brochure, which reveals among other intriguing facts that it was once the headquarters of a notorious smuggler. No such unlawful goings-on today – just good old-fashioned hospitality in the finest traditions of English inn-keeping. Charmingly furnished single, double and four-poster bedrooms provide overnight guests with cosy country-style accommodation, and the needs of the inner man (or woman!) will be amply satisfied by the varied, good quality meals served in the bar and restaurant. Real ales can be enjoyed in the friendly bar, where crackling log fires bestow charm and atmosphere as well as warmth.

ARGYLL & BUTE

ISLE OF MULL

Argyll Arms Hotel, Bunessan, Isle of Mull PA67 6DP (01681 700240; Fax: 01681 700717). Located on the waterfront of the village of Bunessan, and close to the famous Isle of Iona, the hotel affords its guests spectacular sea and island views. Duncan and Gillie MacLeod invite you to enjoy their friendly and relaxed Scottish hospitality in comfortable accommodation, value-for-money bistro-style food and the unique atmosphere of the Isle of Mull. All bedrooms en suite. Open all year. **STB ★★** *SMALL HOTEL*.
e-mail: argyllarms@isleofmull.co.uk
website: www.isleofmull.co.uk

HIGHLANDS (Mid)

KINLOCHEWE HOTEL

ACHNASHEEN

Kinlochewe Hotel, Kinlochewe, Wester Ross IV22 2PA (01445 760253). This 10-bedroom hotel, surrounded by the magnificent Torridon Mountains, is ideally situated for walking, climbing, birdwatching, or touring the North West of Scotland. The Beinn Eighe Nature Reserve, the Inverewe National Trust Gardens, the spectacular Applecross Peninsula and the Isle of Skye are all within easy reach.The hotel has an excellent reputation for home-cooked food and a varied menu, at reasonable prices. For climbers and walkers, there are over 20 Munros within 20 miles, and guides can be arranged for all levels of experience. Bar meals available. Children welcome. Non-smoking areas.
e-mail: kinlochewehotel@tinyworld.co.uk

SOUTH WALES

NEWPORT (near)

The Inn at the Elm Tree, St Brides, Wentlooge, Near Newport NP10 8SQ (01633 680225; Fax: 01633 681035). A hidden retreat between two cities - Cardiff and Newport – just two miles from the M4 and a different world away. Originally an early 19th century barn, now transformed from a celebrated restaurant to an inn, the Elm Tree keeps the spirit of timeless hospitality alive, but with all the most modern appointments. Comfort epitomised, attention to detail paramount, relaxation assured. The Inn at the Elm Tree is the perfect retreat for a week or weekend, a special night stay, or simply a drink. The Restaurant has a long-standing reputation as one of the most distinguished in the area, using Wales' best natural produce. Bedrooms are all en suite, and individually designed to the highest standards with lots of personal touches and luxuries. **WTB ★★★★★** *INN*, **AA/RAC ◆◆◆◆◆**, *AA ROSETTE, GOOD HOTEL GUIDE.*
e-mail: inn@the-elm-tree.co.uk
website: www.the-elm-tree.co.uk

"Family-Friendly"

Pubs, Inns & Hotels

This is a selection of establishments which make an extra effort to cater for parents and children. The majority provide a separate children's menu or they may be willing to serve small portions of main course dishes on request; there are often separate outdoor or indoor play areas where the junior members of the family can let off steam while Mum and Dad unwind over a drink.

For full details of facilities offered, please contact the individual establishments.

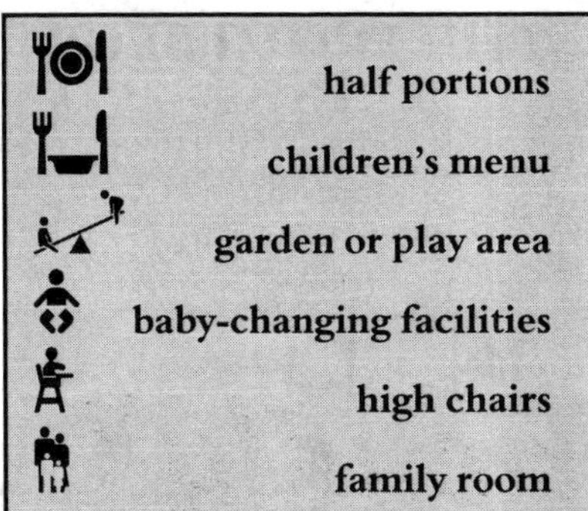

THE CROWN

16 High Street, Amersham,
Buckinghamshire HP7 0DH
Tel: 0870 400 8103
Fax: 01494 331283

BELL HOTEL

Market Square, Winslow
Buckinghamshire MK18 3AB
Tel: 01296 714091
Fax: 01296 714805

THE DOG INN

Well Bank Lane, Over Peover,
Near Knutsford, Cheshire
WA16 8UP
Tel: 01625 861421
Fax: 01625 864800

THE HARBOUR INN

Commercial Road, Porthleven,
Cornwall TR13 9JB
Tel: 01326 573876
Fax: 01326 572124

WATEREDGE INN

Waterhead Bay, Ambleside
Cumbria LA22 0EP
Tel: 015394 32332
Fax: 015394 31878

BLACK BULL INN & HOTEL

1 Yewdale Road, Coniston
Cumbria LA21 8DU
Tel: 015394 41335
Fax: 015394 41168

SUN INN

Main Street, Dent, Sedbergh,
Cumbria LA10 5QL
Tel: 01539 625208

WATERMILL INN

Ings, Near Staveley,
Kendal, Cumbria LA8 9PY
Tel: 01539 821309
Fax: 01539 822309

THE TROUTBECK INN

Troutbeck, Penrith,
Cumbria CA11 0SJ
Tel: 017684 83635
Fax: 017684 83928

RUTLAND ARMS HOTEL

The Square, Bakewell,
Derbyshire DE45 1BT
Tel: 01629 812812
Fax: 01629 812309

YORKSHIRE BRIDGE INN

Ashopton Road, Bamford in the
High Peak, Hope Valley,
Derbyshire S33 0AZ
Tel & Fax: 01433 651361

THE NEW INN

High Street, Clovelly, Near
Bideford, Devon EX39 5TQ
Tel: 01237 431303
Fax: 01237 431636

SITWELL ARMS HOTEL

39 Station Road, Renishaw,
Derbyshire S21 3WF
Tel: 01246 435226
Fax: 01246 433915

THE BRIDGE INN

Lynbridge, Lynton,
Devon EX35 6NR
Tel: 01598 753425
Fax: 01598 753225

WHITE HART HOTEL

Fore Street, Okehampton,
Devon EX20 1HD
Tel: 01837 52730/54514
Fax: 01837 53979

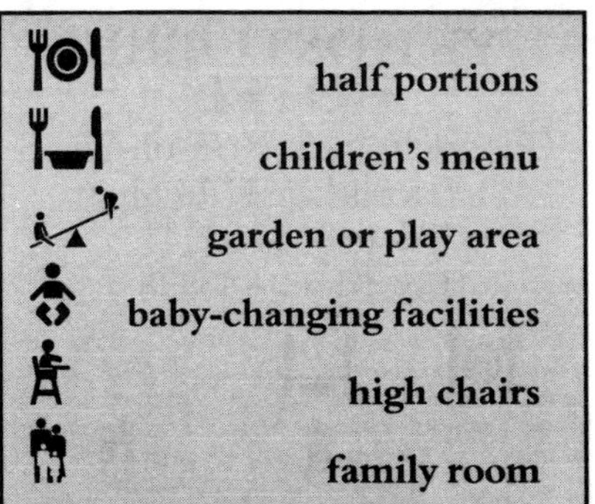

PLUME OF FEATHERS INN

The Square, Princetown,
Yelverton, Devon PL20 6QQ
Tel: 01822 890240
Fax: 01822 890780

BARTON CROSS HOTEL

Huxham, Stole Canon,
Near Exeter, Devon EX5 4EJ
Tel: 01392 841245
Fax: 01392 841942

OLD CHURCH HOUSE INN

Torbryan, Devon TQ12 5UR
Tel: 01803 812372
Fax: 01803 812180

ROYAL SEVEN STARS HOTEL

The Plains, Totnes, Devon
TQ9 5DD
Tel: 01803 862125
Fax: 01803 867925

THE WAIE INN

Zeal Monachorum, Crediton,
Devon EX17 6DF
Tel: 01363 82348
Fax: 01363 82898

THE MARQUIS OF LORNE INN

Nettlecombe, Near Bridport,
Dorset DT6 3SY
Tel: 01308 485236
Fax: 01308 485666

HUNTERS REST INN

King Lane, Clutton Hill,
Bristol, Gloucestershire
BS39 5QL
Tel: 01761 452303
Fax: 01761 453308

THE HARE AND HOUNDS HOTEL

Westonbirt, Near Tetbury,
Gloucestershire GL8 8QL
Tel: 01666 881000/880233
Fax: 01666 880241

YE HOSTELRIE HOTEL

Goodrich, Near Ross-on-Wye,
Herefordshire HR9 6HX
Tel: 01600 890241
Fax: 01600 890838

SARACENS HEAD INN

Symonds Yat East, Ross-on-Wye,
Herefordshire HR9 6JL
Tel: 01600 890435
Fax: 01600 890034

SALISBURY ARMS HOTEL

Fore Street, Hertford,
Hertfordshire SG14 1BZ
Tel: 01992 583091
Fax: 01992 552510

THE WHITE HORSE INN

The Street, Boughton,
Near Faversham, Kent ME13 9AX
Tel: 01227 751343
Fax: 01227 751090

BELL HOTEL

The Quay, Sandwich, Kent
CT13 9EF
Tel: 01304 613388
Fax: 01304 615308

OWD NELL'S CANALSIDE TAVERN

Guy's Thatched Hamlet,
Bilsborrow, Lancashire PR3 0RS
Tel: 01995 640010 • Fax: 01995 640141
e-mail: guyshamlet@aol.com
website: www.guysthatchedhamlet.co.uk

ANGEL AND ROYAL HOTEL

High Street, Grantham,
Lincolnshire GN31 6PN
Tel: 01476 565816
Fax: 01476 567149

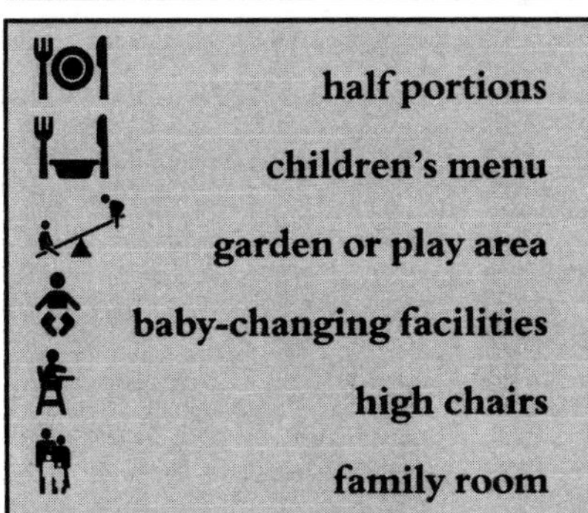

MASONS ARMS

Cornmarket, Louth, Lincolnshire
LN11 9PY
Tel: 01507 609525
Fax: 08707 066450

RED LION HOTEL

Main Street, Redbourne,
Lincolnshire DN21 4QR
Tel & Fax: 01652 648302

THE PLOUGH INN

Norwich Road, Marsham,
Norwich, Norfolk NR10 5PS
Tel: 01263 735000
Fax: 01263 735407

OLD BREWERY HOUSE HOTEL

Market Square, Reepham,
Norfolk NR10 4JJ
Tel: 01603 870881
Fax: 01603 870969

THE OLD RAM COACHING INN

Ipswich Road, Tivetshall St Mary,
Norfolk NR15 2DE
Tel: 01379 676794
Fax: 01379 608399

THE MALTSTERS COUNTRY INN

The Green, Badby,
Near Daventry,
Northamptonshire NN11 3AF
Tel: 01327 702905

THE KNOWESGATE INN

Knowesgate, Kirkwhelpington,
Newcastle-upon-Tyne,
Northumberland NE19 2SH
Tel: 01830 540336
Fax: 01830 540449

RED LION INN

115 High Street, Chalgrove,
Oxfordshire OX44 7SS
Tel: 01865 890625
Fax: 01865 890795

BAT AND BALL INN

28 High Street, Cuddesdon,
Oxfordshire OX44 9HJ
Tel: 01865 874379
Fax: 01865 873363

THE THREE FISHES HOTEL

Pave Lane, Newport,
Shropshire TF10 9LQ
Tel & Fax: 01952 825580

THE TRAVELLERS REST INN

Upper Affcot, Near Church
Stretton, Shropshire SY6 6RL
Tel: 01694 781275
Fax: 01694 781555

THE BOWL INN & LILIES RESTAURANT

16 Church Road,
Lower Almondsbury, Bristol,
South Gloucestershire BS32 4DT
Tel: 01454 612757
Fax: 01454 619910

THE TOM MOGG INN

Station Road, Burtle,
Near Bridgwater, Somerset
TA7 8NU
Tel: 01278 722399
Fax: 01278 722724

THE FRIENDLY SPIRIT

Brook Street, Cannington,
Somerset TA5 2HP
Tel: 01278 652215
Fax: 01278 653636

ANCHOR INN

Exebridge, Near Dulverton,
Somerset TA22 9AZ
Tel: 01398 323433
Fax: 01398 323808

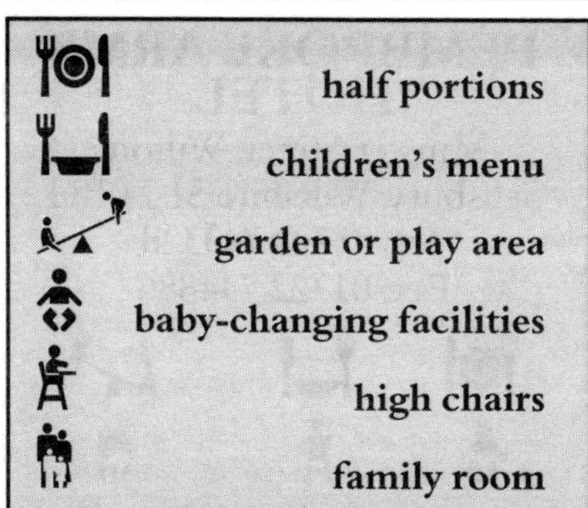

LORD POULETT ARMS

High Street, Hinton St George,
Somerset TA17 8SE
Tel: 01460 73149

APPLE TREE HOTEL

Keenthorne, Nr Nether Stowey,
Bridgwater, Somerset TA5 1HZ
Tel: 01278 733238
Fax: 01278 732693

WHITE HART HOTEL

Sadler Street,
Wells, Somerset BA5 2RR
Tel: 01749 672056
Fax: 01749 671074

YE OLDE DOG AND PARTRIDGE

High Street, Tutbury,
Burton-upon-Trent, Staffordshire
DE13 9LS
Tel: 01283 813030
Fax: 01283 813178

BLACK LION HOTEL & RESTAURANT

The Green, Long Melford,
Suffolk CO10 9DN
Tel: 01787 312356
Fax: 01787 374557

CLARENDON HOUSE

High Street, Kenilworth,
Warwickshire CV8 1LZ
Tel: 01926 857668
Fax: 01926 850669

RED LION HOTEL

Long Compton,
Near Shipston-on-Stour,
Warwickshire CV36 5JS
Tel: 01608 684221

NEW INN

Clifford Chambers,
Stratford-upon-Avon,
Warwickshire CV37 8HR
Tel: 01789 293402

PEMBROKE ARMS HOTEL

Minster Street, Wilton,
Salisbury, Wiltshire SP2 0BH
Tel: 01722 743328
Fax: 01722 744886

VILLIERS INN

Moormead Road,
Wroughton, Swindon,
Wiltshire SN4 9BY
Tel: 01793 814744
Fax: 01793 814119

THE PEAR TREE INN AND COUNTRY HOTEL

Smite, Worcester,
Worcestershire WR3 8SY
Tel: 01905 756565
Fax: 01905 756777

ST QUINTIN ARMS INN

Main Street, Harpham,
Near Driffield,
East Yorkshire YO25 4QY
Tel & Fax: 01262 490329

THE WORSLEY ARMS HOTEL

Hovingham,
North Yorkshire YO62 4LA
Tel: 01653 628234
Fax: 01653 628130

THE WHEATSHEAF INN AND HOTEL

22 High Street, Ingleton, Via
Carnforth, North Yorkshire
LA6 3AD
Tel: 015242 41275

THE SHOULDER OF MUTTON INN

Kirby Hill, Richmond,
North Yorkshire DL11 7JH
Tel: 01748 822772
Fax: 01325 718936

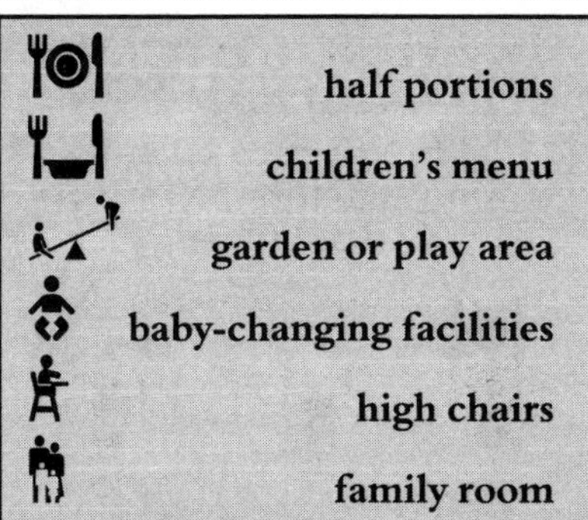

CLOVENFORDS HOTEL

1 Vine Street, Clovenfords, Near Galashiels, Selkirkshire TD1 3LU
Tel & Fax: 01896 850203

MURRAY ARMS HOTEL

Gatehouse of Fleet, Castle Douglas, Kirkcudbrightshire DG7 2HY
Tel: 01557 814207
Fax: 01557 814370

BALLYGRANT INN & RESTAURANT

Ballygrant, Isle of Islay, Argyll PA45 7QR
Tel & Fax: 01496 840277

ANCHOR HOTEL

Kippford, Dalbeattie, Kirkcudbrightshire DG5 4LN
Tel & Fax: 01556 620205

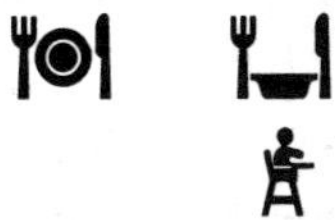

ABERDOUR HOTEL

38 High Street, Aberdour, Fife KY3 0SW
Tel: 01383 860325
Fax: 01383 860808

THE CRUSOE HOTEL

Main Street, Lower Largo, Fife KY8 6BT
Tel: 01333 320759
Fax: 01333 320865

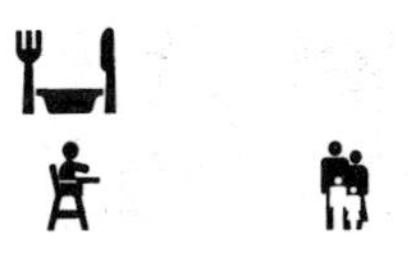

COVENANTERS' INN

Auldearn, Near Nairn, Highland IV12 5TG
Tel: 01667 452456
Fax: 01667 453583

THE ROYAL HOTEL

Melville Square, Comrie,
Perthshire PH6 2DN
Tel: 01764 679200
Fax: 01764 679219

HALF MOON INN

Llanthony, Abergavenny,
Monmouthshire NP7 7NN
Tel: 01873 890611

KING ARTHUR HOTEL

Higher Green, Reynoldston,
Swansea, South Wales SA3 1AD
Tel: 01792 390775
Fax: 01792 391075

DIRECTORY OF WEBSITE AND E-MAIL ADDRESSES

A quick-reference guide to holiday accommodation with an e-mail address and website, conveniently arranged by country and county, with full contact details.

•LONDON

B & B
Mrs Anne Scott, Holiday Hosts (London) Ltd, 59 Cromwell Road, Wimbledon, LONDON SW19 8LF
020 8540 7942
- **e-mail: holiday.hosts@btinternet.com**
- **website: www.holidayhosts.free-online.co.uk**

Guesthouse
MacDonald Hotel, 45-46 Argyle Square, LONDON WC1H 8AL
020 7837 3552
- **e-mail: fhg@macdonaldhotel.com**
- **website: www.macdonaldhotel.com**

Hotel / B & B
Lincoln House Hotel, 33 Gloucester Place, LONDON W1V 8HY
020 7486 7630
- **e-mail: reservations@lincoln-house-hotel.co.uk**
- **website: www.lincoln-house-hotel.co.uk**

Hotel
Gower Hotel, 129 Sussex Gardens, Hyde Park, LONDON W2 2RX
020 7262 2262
- **e-mail: gower@stavrouhotels.co.uk**
- **website: www.stavrouhotels.co.uk**

Hotel
Athena Hotel, 110-114 Sussex Gardens, Hyde Park, LONDON W2 1UA
020 7706 3866
- **e-mail: athena@stavrouhotels.co.uk**
- **website: www.stavrouhotels.co.uk**

B & B / Guesthouse
Barry House Hotel, 12 Sussex Place, Hyde Park, LONDON W2 2TP
020 7723 7340
- **e-mail: hotel@barryhouse.co.uk**
- **website: www.barryhouse.co.uk**

Hotel
Shakespeare Hotel, 22-28 Norfolk Square, LONDON W2 1RS
020 7402 4646
- **e-mail: info@shakespearehotel.co.uk**
- **website: www.shakespearehotel.co.uk**

Hotel
Adria Hotel, 44 Glenthorne Road, Hammersmith, LONDON W6 0LS
020 7602 6386
- **e-mail: george@adria.demon.co.uk**
- **website: www.dalmacia-hotel.co.uk**

Hotel
Dalmacia Hotel, 71 Shepherds Bush Road, Hammersmith, LONDON W6 7LS
020 7603 2887
- **e-mail: george@adria.demon.co.uk**
- **website: www.dalmacia-hotel.co.uk**

B & B
Sohel & Anne Armanios, 67 Rannoch Road, Hammersmith, LONDON W6 9SS
020 7385 4904
- **website: www.thewaytostay.co.uk**

Hotel
Queens Hotel, 33 Anson Road, Tufnell Park, LONDON N7
020 7607 4725
- **e-mail: queens@stavrouhotels.co.uk**
- **website: www.stavrouhotels.co.uk**

B & B
Hanover Hotel, 30 St George's Drive LONDON SW1V 4BN
020 7834 0367
- **e-mail: reservations@hanoverhotel.co.uk**
- **website: www.hanoverhotel.co.uk**

•BERKSHIRE

Guest House

Mrs Sue Chapman, Lyndrick House, The Avenue, ASCOT, Berkshire SL5 7ND
01344 883520

- **e-mail: mail@lyndrick.com**
- **website: www.lyndrick.com**

Inn

Swan Inn, INKPEN, Hungerford, Berkshire RG17 9DX
01488 668326

- **e-mail: enquiries@theswaninn-organics.co.uk**
- **website: www.theswaninn-organics.co.uk**

•CAMBRIDGESHIRE

Guest House

Dykelands Guest House, 157 Mowbray Road, CAMBRIDGE, Cambridgeshire CB1 7SP
01223 244300

- **e-mail: dykelands@fsbdial.co.uk**
- **website: www.dykelands.com**

B & B

J & R Farndale, Cathedral House, 17 St Mary's Street, ELY, Cambridgeshire CB7 4ER
01353 662124

- **e-mail: farndale@cathedralhouse.co.uk**
- **website: www.cathedralhouse.co.uk**

B & B

Mrs Linda Peck, Sharps Farm, Twenty Pence Road, Wilburton, ELY, Cambridgeshire CB6 3PX
01353 740360

- **e-mail: sharpsfarm@yahoo.com**

•CHESHIRE

Hotel

Frogg Manor Hotel & Restaurant, Fullers Moor, Nantwich Road, Broxton, CHESTER, Cheshire CH3 9JH
01829 782629

- **e-mail: info@froggmanorhotel.co.uk**
- **website: www.froggmanorhotel.co.uk**

Please mention the FHG Guide to Coast & Country Holidays when enquiring about accommodation

B & B / Self-Catering

Mrs Angela Smith, Mill House and Granary, Higher Wych, MALPAS, Cheshire SY14 7JR
01948 780362

- **e-mail: angela@videoactive.co.uk**
- **website: www.millhouseandgranary.co.uk**

B & B

Mrs Jean E. Callwood, Lea Farm, Wrinehill Road, Wybunbury, NANTWICH, Cheshire CW5 7NS
01270 841429

- **e-mail: contactus@leafarm.co.uk**

•CORNWALL

Self-Catering

Fiona & Martin Nicolle, Classy Cottages, Cornwall
07000 423000

- **e-mail: nicolle@classycottages.co.uk**
- **website: www.classycottages.co.uk**

Self-Catering

Cornish Traditional Cottages, Blisland, BODMIN, Cornwall PL30 4HS
01208 821666

- **e-mail: info@corncott.com**
- **website: www.corncott.com**

Self-Catering / Caravan & Camping

Ruthern Valley Holidays, Ruthernbridge BODMIN, Cornwall PL30 5LU
01208 831395

- **e-mail: ruthernvalley@hotmail.com**
- **website: www.self-catering-ruthern.co.uk**

Self-Catering

Mr Charles Tippet, Mineshop Holiday Cottages, Crackington Haven, BUDE, Cornwall EX23 0NR
01840 230338

- **e-mail: tippett@mineshop.freeserve.co.uk**
- **website: www.cornwall-online.co.uk/mineshop**

Self-Catering / Caravan & Camping

Willow Valley Holiday Park, Bush, BUDE, Cornwall EX23 9LB
01288 353104

- **e-mail: willowvalley@talk21.com**
- **website: www.caravansitecornwall.co.uk**

Caravan & Camping
Cornish Coasts Caravan & Camping Park, Middle Penlean, Poundstock, Widemouth Bay, BUDE, Cornwall EX23 0EE
01288 361380
- **e-mail: info@cornishcoasts.co.uk**
- **website: www.cornishcoasts.co.uk**

Guest House
Harvey Jay, Wringford Down Motel, CAWSAND, Cornwall PL10 1LE
01752 822287
- **e-mail: ramehols@aol.com**
- **website: www.cornwallholidays.co.uk**

Guest House
Mrs C. Carruthers, The Clearwater, 59 Melvill Road, FALMOUTH, Cornwall TR11 4DF
01326 311344
- **e-mail: clearwater@lineone.net**
- **website: www.theclearwater.co.uk**

Guest House
Miss Fannin, Trevaylor, 8 Pennance Road, FALMOUTH, Cornwall TR11 4EA
01326 316899
- **e-mail: stay@trevaylor.co.uk**
- **website: www.trevaylor.co.uk**

Self-Catering / Caravan Park
Mr Christopher Harvey, St Ives Bay Chalet & Caravan Park, HAYLE, Cornwall TR27 5BH
01736 752274
- **e-mail: stivesbay@dial.pipex.com**
- **website: www.stivesbay.co.uk**

Caravan & Camping
Mrs J. Jenkin, Mudgeon Farm, St Martin, HELSTON, Cornwall TR12 6BZ
01326 231202
- **e-mail: jenkin@mudgeon.fsnet.co.uk**

Self-Catering
Mrs S. Trewhella, Mudgeon Vean, St Martin, HELSTON, Cornwall TR12 6DB
01326 231341
- **e-mail: mudgeonvean@aol.com**
- **website: www.cornwall-online.co.uk/mudgeon-vean/ctb.htm**

Caravan & Camping
Boscrege Caravan & Camping Park, Ashton, HELSTON, Cornwall TR13 9TG
01736 762231
- **e-mail: enquiries@caravanparkcornwall.com**
- **website: www.caravanparkcornwall.com**

Guest House
Greystones Guest House, 40 West End, Porthleven, HELSTON TR13 9JL
01326 565583
- **e-mail: neilvwoodward@hotmail.com**

Self-Catering
Trewalla Farm Cottages, Trewalla Farm, Minions, LISKEARD, Cornwall PL14 6ED
01579 342385
- **e-mail: cotter.trewalla@virgin.net**

B & B
Mrs S. Rowe, Tregondale Farm, Menheniot, LISKEARD, Cornwall PL14 3RG
01579 342407
- **e-mail: tregondale@connectfree.co.uk**
- **website: www.tregondalefarm.co.uk**

Self-Catering
Sue Jewell, Boturnell Farm Cottages, St Pinnock, LISKEARD, Cornwall PL14 4QS
01579 320880
- **e-mail: boturnell-barns@breathemail.net**
- **website: www.dogs-holiday.co.uk**

Caravan & Camping
Tregoad Farm Touring Caravan & Camping Park, St Martins, LOOE, Cornwall PL13 1PB
01503 262718
- **e-mail: tregoadfarmtccp@aol.com**
- **website: www.cornwall-online.co.uk/tregoad**

B & B / Self-Catering
Paul Brumpton, Talehay Holiday Cottages, Pelynt, near LOOE, Cornwall PL13 2LT
01503 220252
- **e-mail: paul@talehay.co.uk**
- **website: www.talehay.co.uk**

Small Hotel / Guest House
Mr G.J. & Mrs P.E. Hope, Seavista Hotel, MAWGAN PORTH, Newquay, Cornwall TR8 4AL
01637 868276
- **e-mail: seavista@btopenworld.com**
- **website: www.seavista.co.uk**

B & B
Mrs Dawn Rundle, Lancallan Farm, MEVAGISSEY, St Austell, Cornwall PL26 6EW
01726 842284
- **e-mail: dawn@lancallan.fsnet.co.uk**

Hotel

White Lodge Hotel, Mawgan Porth Bay, near NEWQUAY, Cornwall TR8 4BN
01637 860512
- **e-mail: adogfriendly@aol.com**
- **website: www.dogfriendlyhotel.co.uk**

Hotel

Mrs M.G. Waldron, Golden Bay Hotel, Pentire Avenue, Pentire, NEWQUAY, Cornwall TR7 1PD
01637 873318
- **e-mail: enquiries@goldenbayhotel.co.uk**
- **website: www.goldenbayhotel.co.uk**

Guest House / Self-Catering

Trewerry Mill Guest House, Trewerry Mill, Trerice, St Newlyn East, NEWQUAY, Cornwall TR8 5GS
01872 510345
- **e-mail: trewerry.mill@which.net**
- **website: www.trewerrymill.co.uk**

Guest House

Mrs C. Lavery, Pensalda, 98 Henver Road, NEWQUAY, Cornwall TR7 3BL
01637 874601
- **e-mail: carol@pensalda.fsnet.co.uk**
- **website: www.pensalda-guesthouse.co.uk**

Self-Catering

Trevose Golf Club, Constantine Bay, PADSTOW, Cornwall PL28 8JB
01841 520208
- **e-mail: info@trevose-gc.co.uk**
- **website: www.trevose-gc.co.uk**

Guest House

Mr & Mrs J.A. Leggatt, Cornerways Guest House, 5 Leskinnick Street, PENZANCE, Cornwall TR18 2HA
01736 364645
- **e-mail: LEGGATT6@aol.com**
- **website: www.penzance.co.uk/cornerways**

Farm / B & B

Mrs Hall, Treen Farmhouse, Treen, St Levan, PENZANCE, Cornwall TR19 6LF
01736 810253
- **e-mail: paulachrishall@treenfarm.fsnet.co.uk**

Caravan & Camping

Roselands Caravan Park, Dowran, St Just, PENZANCE, Cornwall TR19 7RS
01736 788571
- **e-mail: camping@roseland84.freeserve.co.uk**
- **website: www.roselands.co.uk**

Hotel

Boscean Country Hotel, St Just, PENZANCE, Cornwall TR19 7QP
01736 788748
- **e-mail: Boscean@aol.com**
- **website: www.bosceancountryhotel.co.uk**

Hotel / Inn

Mrs J. Treleaven, Driftwood Spars Hotel, Trevaunance Cove, ST AGNES, Cornwall TR5 0RT
01872 552428 / 553323
- **e-mail: driftwoodspars@hotmail.com**
- **website: www.driftwoodspars.com**

B & B

Ted and Jeanie Ellis, Cleaderscroft Hotel, 16 British Road, ST AGNES, Cornwall TR5 0TZ
01872 552349
- **e-mail: tedellis@btinternet.com**

B & B

Mrs Liz Berryman, Polegreen Farm, London Apprentice, ST AUSTELL, Cornwall PL26 7AP
01726 75151
- **e-mail: polgreen.farm@btclick.com**

Hotel

Dalswinton House, ST MAWGAN, near Newquay, Cornwall TR8 4EZ
01637 860385
- **e-mail: dalswinton@bigwig.net**
- **website: www.dalswinton.com**

Self-Catering

Mr & Mrs C.W. Pestell, Hockadays, Tregenna, near Blisland, ST TUDY, Cornwall PL30 4QJ
01208 850146
- **website: www.hockadaysholidaycottages.co.uk**

Self-Catering

Mrs Sandy Wilson, Salutations, Atlantic Road, TINTAGEL, Cornwall PL34 0DE
01840 770287
- **e-mail: sandyanddave@tinyworld.co.uk**
- **website: www.tintagelsalutations.co.uk**

Small Hotel

The Penallick Hotel, Treknow,TINTAGEL, Cornwall PL34 0EJ
01840 770296
- **website: www.penallickhotel.co.uk**

Self-Catering

Mrs Sue Zamaria, Colesent Cottages, St Tudy, WADEBRIDGE, Cornwall PL30 4QX
01208 850112
- **e-mail: welcome@colesent.co.uk**
- **website: www.colesent.co.uk**

•CUMBRIA

Hotel

Anne-Marie O'Neill, Rothay Manor, Rothay Bridge, AMBLESIDE, Cumbria LA22 0EH
015394 33605

- **e-mail: hotel@rothaymanor.co.uk**
- **website: www.rothaymanor.co.uk**

B & B

Malcolm & Margaret MacFarlane, Borwick Lodge, Outgate, Hawkshead, AMBLESIDE, Cumbria LA22 0PU
015394 36332

- **e-mail: borwicklodge@talk21.com**
- **website: www.borwicklodge.com**

Self-Catering

Lakelovers, Belmont House, Lake Road, BOWNESS-ON-WINDERMERE, Cumbria LA23 3BJ
015394 88855

- **e-mail: bookings@lakelovers.co.uk**
- **website: www.lakelovers.co.uk**

Farmhouse B & B

Anne Taylor, Russell Farm, BURTON-IN-KENDAL, Carnforth, Lancashire LA6 1NN
01524 781334

- **e-mail: miktaylor@farming.co.uk**

Hotel

Hazel Thompson, New House Farm, Lorton, BUTTERMERE, near Cockermouth, Cumbria CA13 9UU
01900 85404

- **e-mail: hazel@newhouse-farm.co.uk**
- **website: www.newhouse-farm.co.uk**

Guest House

Dalegarth Guest House, Hassness Estate, BUTTERMERE, Cumbria CA13 9XA
01768 770233

- **e-mail: dalegarth.buttermere@rdplus.net**
- **website: www.dalegarthguesthouse.co.uk**

B & B

Mr & Mrs A. Savage, Swaledale Watch, Whelpo, CALDBECK, Cumbria CA7 8HQ
016974 78409

- **e-mail: nan.savage@talk21.com**

Half Board / Self-Catering / B & B

J. Elwen, New Pallyards, Hethersgill, CARLISLE, Cumbria CA6 6HZ
01228 577308

- **e-mail: info@newpallyards.freeserve.co.uk**
- **website: www.newpallyards.freeserve.co.uk**

Farm

Mrs L. Lawson, Craigburn Farm, Penton, CARLISLE, Cumbria CA6 5QP
01228 577214

- **e-mail: louiselawson@hotmail.com**
- **website: www.craigburnfarmhouse.co.uk**

Self-Catering

Loweswater Holiday Cottages, Scale Hill, Loweswater, COCKERMOUTH, Cumbria CA13 9UX
01900 85232

- **e-mail: mike@loweswaterholidaycottages.co.uk**
- **website: www.loweswaterholidaycottages.co.uk**

Guest House

George & Isobel Kerr, Link House, Bassenthwaite Lake, COCKERMOUTH, Cumbria CA13 9YD
017687 76291

- **e-mail: linkhouse@lineone.net**
- **website: www.link-house.com**

Self-Catering

Mr P. Johnston, The Coppermines and Lakes Cottages, The Estate Office, The Bridge, CONISTON, Cumbria LA21 8HX
015394 41765 (24 hours)

- **website: www.coppermines.co.uk**
- **website: www.lakescottages.info**

Self-Catering

Mrs J. Hall, Fisherground Farm Cottages, Fisherground, ESKDALE, Cumbria, CA19 1TF
01946 723319

- **e-mail: holidays@fisherground.co.uk**
- **website: www.fisherground.co.uk**

Self-Catering

Margaret & William Beck, Brunt Knott Farm, Staveley, KENDAL, Cumbria LA8 9QX
01539 821030

- **e-mail: margaret@bruntknott.demon.co.uk**
- **website: www.bruntknott.demon.co.uk**

Self-Catering
Keswick Cottages, Kentmere, How Lane, KESWICK, Cumbria CA12 5RS
017687 73895
- **e-mail: info@keswickcottages.co.uk**
- **website: www.keswickcottages.co.uk**

Self-Catering
Barrowside & Swinside Cottages, c/o Mrs Walker, 15 Acorn Street, KESWICK, Cumbria CA12 4EA
01768 774165
- **e-mail: info@watendlathguesthouse.co.uk**
- **website: www.watendlathguesthouse.co.uk**

Hotel
Swan Hotel, Thornthwaite, KESWICK, Cumbria CA12 5SQ
017687 78100
- **e-mail: bestswan@aol.com**
- **website: www.swan-hotel-keswick.co.uk**

Guest House
Mr & Mrs Birtwistle, Kalgurli Guest House, 33 Helvellyn Street, KESWICK, Cumbria CA12 4EP
017687 72935
- **e-mail: info@kalgurli.co.uk**
- **website: www.kalgurli.co.uk**

B & B
Val Bradley, Rickerby Grange, Portinscale, KESWICK, Cumbria CA12 5RH
017687 72344
- **e-mail: val@ricor.co.uk**
- **website: www.ricor.co.uk**

Self-Catering
Derwentwater Marina, Portinscale, KESWICK, Cumbria CA12 5RF
017687 72912
- **website: www.derwentwatermarina.co.uk**

Guest House
Linda & Stuart Robertson, Clarence House, 14 Eskin Street, KESWICK, Cumbria CA12 4DQ
017687 73186
- **e-mail: enquiries@clarencehousekeswick.co.uk**
- **website: www.clarencehousekeswick.co.uk**

Guest House
Ian & Janice Picken, Lynwood House (Licensed Guest House), 35 Helvellyn Street, KESWICK, Cumbria CA12 4EP
017687 72398
- **e-mail: info@lynwoodhouse.net**
- **website: www.lynwoodhouse.net**

Caravan & Camping
Linda Lamb, Burns Caravan & Camping Site, St Johns In the Vale, KESWICK, Cumbria CA12 4RR
017687 79225
- **e-mail: llamb@callnetuk.com**

Self-Catering
Liz Webster, Howscales, KIRKOSWALD, Penrith, Cumbria CA10 1JG
01768 898666
- **e-mail: liz@howscales.fsbusiness.co.uk**
- **website: www.eden-in-cumbria.co.uk/howscales**

Self-Catering
Mrs S.J. Bottom, Crossfield Cottages, KIRKOSWALD, Penrith, Cumbria CA10 1EU
01768 898711
- **e-mail: info@crossfieldcottages.co.uk**
- **website: www.crossfieldcottages.co.uk**

Guest House / B & B
Mr & Mrs C. Smith, Mosedale House, MOSEDALE, Mungrisdale, Cumbria CA11 0XQ
01768 779371
- **e-mail: mosedale@northlakes.co.uk**
- **website: www.mosedalehouse.co.uk**

Guest House
Geoff Mason, Knotts Mill Country Lodge, Ullswater, Watermillock, PENRITH, Cumbria CA11 0JN
017684 86699
- **e-mail: knottsmill@cwcom.net**
- **website: www.knottsmill.cwc.net**

Self-Catering / Caravan & Camping
Parkfoot Caravan & Camping Park, Howtown Road, Pooley Bridge, PENRITH, Cumbria CA10 2NA
017684 86309
- **e-mail: park.foot@talk21.com**
- **website: www.parkfootullswater.co.uk**

Self-Catering
Mr & Mrs Dodsworth, Birthwaite Edge, Birthwaite Road, WINDERMERE, Cumbria LA23 1BS
015394 42861
- **e-mail: fhg@lakedge.com**
- **website: www.lakedge.com**

Self-Catering
J.R. Benson, High Sett, Sun Hill Lane, Troutbeck Bridge, WINDERMERE, Cumbria LA23 1HJ
015394 42731
- **e-mail: info@accommodationlakedistrict.com**
- **website: www.accommodationlakedistrict.com**

Guest House
John Dixon, The Beaumont Hotel,
Holly Road, WINDERMERE,
Cumbria LA23 2AF
015394 47075
- **e-mail: thebeaumonthotel@btinternet.com**
- **website: www.lakesbeaumont.co.uk**

•DERBYSHIRE

Self-Catering
Derbyshire Cottages, Contact: Mary
01335 300202
- **e-mail: info@dogandpartridge.co.uk**
- **website: www.dogandpartridge.co.uk**

Farmhouse B & B / Self-Catering
Mrs M.A. Richardson, Throwley Hall Farm,
Ilam, ASHBOURNE, Derbyshire DE6 2BB
01538 308202
- **e-mail: throwleyhall@talk21.com**
- **website: www.throwleyhallfarm.co.uk**

Farm / Board
New House Organic Farm, Kniveton,
ASHBOURNE, Derbyshire DE6 1JL
01335 342429
- **e-mail: b&b@newhousefarm.co.uk**

Inn
Mrs Stelfox, The Dog & Partridge Country
Inn, Swinscoe, ASHBOURNE,
Derbyshire DE6 2HS
01335 343183
- **e-mail: info@dogandpartridge.co.uk**
- **website: www.dogandpartridge.co.uk**

Self-Catering
Cotterill Farm Cottages, Cotterill Farm,
Links Road, BIGGIN-BY-HARTINGTON,
Buxton, Derbyshire SK17 0DJ
01298 84447
- **e-mail: enquiries@cotterillfarm.co.uk**
- **website: www.cotterillfarm.co.uk**

Guest House
Mr & Mrs Hyde, Braemar,10 Compton Road,
BUXTON, Derbyshire SK17 9DN
01298 78050
- **e-mail: buxtonbraemar@supanet.com**
- **website: www.cressbrook.co.uk/buxton/braemar**

Self-Catering
R.D. Hollands, Wheeldon Trees Farm, Earl
Sterndale, BUXTON, Derbyshire SK17 0AA
01298 83219
- **e-mail: hollands@earlsterndale.fsnet.co.uk**
- **website: www.wheeldontreesfarm.co.uk**

Inn
Nick & Fiona Clough, The Devonshire Arms,
Peak Forest, near BUXTON,
Derbyshire SK17 8EJ
01298 23875
- **e-mail: fiona.clough@virgin.net**
- **website: www.devarms.com**

Hotel
The Charles Cotton Hotel, Hartington,
near BUXTON, Derbyshire SK17 0AL
01298 84229
- **e-mail: info@charlescotton.co.uk**
- **website: www.charlescotton.co.uk**

Hotel
Biggin Hall Hotel, Biggin-by-Hartington,
BUXTON, Derbyshire SK17 0DH
01298 84451
- **e-mail: bigginhall@compuserve.com**
- **website: www.bigginhall.co.uk**

Self-Catering
Hartington Cottages,
HARTINGTON, Derbyshire
01298 84447
- **e-mail: enquiries@hartingtoncottages.co.uk**
- **website: www.hartingtoncottages.co.uk**

Self-Catering
Field Head Farmhouse Holidays, Calton,
PEAK DISTRICT, Derbyshire
Contact: Janet Hudson
01538 308352
- **e-mail: info@field-head.co.uk**
- **website: www.field-head.co.uk**

•DEVON

Self-Catering
Toad Hall Cottages,
DEVON
08700 777345
- **website: www.toadhallcottages.com**

Self-Catering
Mr Ridge, Braddon Cottages, Ashwater,
BEAWORTHY, Devon EX21 5EP
01409 211350
- **e-mail: holidays@braddoncottages.co.uk**
- **website: www.braddoncottages.co.uk**

Self-Catering / B & B
Peter & Lesley Lewin, Lake House Cottages
and B&B, Lake Villa, BRADWORTHY,
Devon EX22 7SQ
01409 241962
- **e-mail: info@lakevilla.co.uk**
- **website: www.lakevilla.co.uk**

B & B

Mrs Roselyn Bradford, St Merryn, Higher Park Road, BRAUNTON, Devon EX33 2LG
01271 813805
- **e-mail: ros@st-merryn.co.uk**
- **website: www.st-merryn.co.uk**

Self-Catering

Little Comfort Farm Cottages, Little Comfort Farm, BRAUNTON, North Devon EX33 2NJ
01271 812414
- **e-mail: jackie.milsom@btclick.com**
- **website: www.littlecomfortfarm.co.uk**

Hotel

The Smugglers Haunt, Church Hill, BRIXHAM, Devon TQ5 8HH
01803 853050
- **e-mail: enquiries@smugglershaunt-hotel-devon.co.uk**
- **website: www.smugglershaunt-hotel-devon.co.uk**

Guest House

Mr John Parry, Woodlands Guest House, Parkham Road, BRIXHAM, South Devon TQ5 9BU
01803 852040
- **e-mail: Diparry@aol.com**
- **website: www.dogfriendlyguesthouse.co.uk**

Self-Catering

Little Farm, Southleigh, near COLYTON, Devon EX24 6JE
01404 871361
- **e-mail: littlefarmhols@madasafish.com**
- **website: www.littlefarmonline.co.uk**

Self-Catering/ Caravan /Board

Mrs Ruth Gould, Bonehayne Farm, COLYTON, Devon EX24 6SG
01404 871416 / 871396
- **e-mail: gould@bonehayne.co.uk**
- **website: www.bonehayne.co.uk**

Hotel

The Lord Haldon Country House Hotel, DUNCHIDEOCK, near Exeter, Devon EX6 7YF
01392 832483
- **e-mail: enquiries@lordhaldonhotel.co.uk**
- **website: www.lordhaldonhotel.co.uk**

Farm / B & B

Mrs Karen Williams, Stile Farm, Starcross, EXETER, Devon EX6 8PD
01626 890268
- **e-mail: info@stile-farm.co.uk**
- **website: www.stile-farm.co.uk**

B & B

Culm Vale Guest House, Stoke Canon, EXETER, Devon EX5 4EG
01392 841615
- **e-mail: culmvale@talk21.com**
- **website: www.SmoothHound.co.uk/hotels/culmvale.html**

Self-Catering

Mr F. Wigram, Riggles Farm, Upottery, HONITON, Devon EX14 4SP
01404 891229
- **e-mail: rigglesfarm@farming.co.uk**
- **website: www.braggscottage.co.uk**

Self-Catering

Mr Tromans, Hope Barton Barns, HOPE COVE, Devon TQ7 3HT
01548 561393
- **e-mail: info@hopebarton.co.uk**
- **website: www.hopebarton.co.uk**

Caravan & Camping

John Fowler Holidays, Marlborough Road, ILFRACOMBE, Devon EX34 8PF
01271 866766
- **e-mail: bookings@jfhols.co.uk**
- **website: www.johnfowlerholidays.com**

Farmhouse B&B

Mrs Alison Homa, Mullacott Farm, Mullacott Cross, ILFRACOMBE, Devon EX34 8NA
01271 866877
- **e-mail: alison@mullacottfarm.co.uk**
- **website: www.mullacottfarm.co.uk**

Farm / Self-Catering

Mrs E. Sansom, Widmouth Farm, Watermouth, near ILFRACOMBE, Devon EX34 9RX
01271 863743
- **e-mail: holiday@widmouthfarmcottages.co.uk**
- **website: www.widmouthfarmcottages.co.uk**

B & B / Self-Catering

Mrs Stephens, Venn Farm, Ugborough, IVYBRIDGE, Devon PL21 0PE
01364 73240
- **website: www.SmoothHound.co.uk/hotels/vennfarm**

Guest House / Self-Catering

Mrs M. Newsham, Marsh Mills, Aveton Gifford, KINGSBRIDGE, Devon TQ7 4JW
01548 550549
- **e-mail: Newsham@Marshmills.co.uk**
- **website: www.Marshmills.co.uk**

Self-Catering
Dittiscombe Holiday Cottages, Slapton, near KINGSBRIDGE, Devon TQ7 2QF
01548 521272
- **e-mail: info@dittiscombe.co.uk**
- **website: www.dittiscombe.co.uk**

Guest House / Tea Gardens
Mrs J. Parker, Tregonwell, The Olde Sea Captain's House, 1 Tors Road, LYNMOUTH, Exmoor National Park, Devon EX35 6ET
01598 753369
- **website: www.SmoothHound.co.uk/hotels/tregonwl.html**

Guest House
Tricia & Alan Francis, Glenville House, 2 Tors Road, LYNMOUTH, North Devon EX35 6ET
01598 752202
- **e-mail: tricia@glenvillelynmouth.co.uk**
- **website: www.glenvillelynmouth.co.uk**

Inn
The Crown, Market Street, LYNTON, Devon EX35 6AG
01598 752253
- **website: www.thecrown-lynton.co.uk**

Guest House
John McGowan, The Denes, 15 Longmead, LYNTON, Devon EX35 6DQ
01598 753573
- **e-mail: enquiries@thedenes.com**
- **website: www.thedenes.com**

Hotel
Alford House Hotel, Alford Terrace, LYNTON, North Devon EX35 6AT
01598 752359
- **e-mail: enquiries@alfordhouse.co.uk**
- **website: www.alfordhouse.co.uk**

Farm / B & B
Great Sloncombe Farm, MORETONHAMPSTEAD, Newton Abbot, Devon TQ13 8QF
01647 440595
- **e-mail: hmerchant@sloncombe.freeserve.co.uk**
- **website: www.greatsloncombefarm.co.uk**

Self-Catering
Helen Griffiths, Look Weep Farm Cottages, Liverton, NEWTON ABBOT, Devon TQ12 6HT
01626 833277
- **e-mail: holidays@lookweep.co.uk**
- **website: www.lookweep.co.uk**

Self-Catering
Christine & Mike Grindrod, Serena Lodge, 15 Cliff Road, PAIGNTON TQ4 6DG
01803 550330
- **website: www.serenalodge.com**

Guest House
The Lamplighter Hotel, 103 Citadel Road, The Hoe, PLYMOUTH, Devon PL1 2RN
01752 663855
- **e-mail: lamplighterhotel@ukonline.co.uk**

Hotel / Inn
The Port Light, Bolberry Down, near SALCOMBE, South Devon TQ7 3DY
01548 561384
- **e-mail: info@portlight-salcombe.co.uk**
- **website: www.portlight.co.uk**

Self-Catering
Boswell Farm Cottages, Boswell Farm, SIDFORD, Devon EX10 0PP
01395 514162
- **e-mail: dillon@boswell-farm.co.uk**
- **website: www.boswell-farm.co.uk**

Farmhouse B & B
Mrs Elizabeth Tancock, Lower Pinn Farm, Peak Hill, SIDMOUTH, Devon EX10 0NN
01395 513733
- **e-mail: liz@lowerpinnfarm.co.uk**
- **website: www.lowerpinnfarm.co.uk**

Farm / Board
Mrs Hilary Tucker, Beera Farm, Milton Abbot, TAVISTOCK, Devon PL19 8PL
01822 870216
- **website: www.beera-farm.co.uk**

Hotel
Mr Stevens, The Old Coach House Hotel, Ottery, near TAVISTOCK, Devon PL19 8NS
01822 617515
- **e-mail: eddie@coachhouse1.supanet.com**
- **website: www.the-coachhouse.co.uk**

Hotel / Guest House
Rowan & Carole Ward, Green Park Hotel, 25 Morgan Avenue, TORQUAY, Devon TQ2 5RR
01803 293618
- **e-mail: greenpark.torquay@cwcom.net**
- **website: www.greenparktorquay.co.uk**

Self-Catering
South Sands Apartments, Torbay Road, TORQUAY, Devon TQ2 6RG
01803 293521
- **e-mail: southsands.torquay@virgin.net**
- **website: www.southsands.co.uk**

Self-Catering
Atlantis Holiday Apartments, Solsbro Road, Chelston, TORQUAY, Devon TQ2 6PF
01803 607929
- **e-mail: enquiry@atlantistorquay.co.uk**
- **website: www.atlantistorquay.co.uk**

Guest House
Aveland Hotel, Aveland Road, Babbacombe, TORQUAY, Devon TQ1 3PT
01803 326622
- **e-mail: avelandhotel@aol.com**
- **website: www.avelandhotel.co.uk**

Self-Catering
Ashfield Rise Holiday Apartments, Ruckamore Road, Chelston, TORQUAY, Devon TQ2 6HF
01803 605156
- **e-mail: stay@ashfieldrise.co.uk**
- **website: www.ashfieldrise.co.uk**

Self-Catering
Mrs S. Milsom, Stowford Lodge, Langtree, TORRINGTON, North Devon, EX38 8NV
01805 601540
- **e-mail: stowford@dial.pipex.com**
- **website: www.stowford.dial.pipex.com**

Guest House / Hotel
The Old Forge at Totnes, Seymour Place, TOTNES, Devon, TQ9 5AY
01803 862174
- **e-mail: enq@oldforgetotnes.com**
- **website: www.oldforgetotnes.com**

Hotel
Dartington Hall, TOTNES, Devon TQ9 6EZ
01803 847136
- **e-mail: dhcc.ops@dartingtonhall.com**
- **website: www.dartingtonhall.com**

Guest House
Lynda Hunt, Sunnymeade Country Hotel, Dean Cross, West Down, WOOLACOMBE, Devon EX34 8NT
01271 863668
- **e-mail: info@sunnymeade.co.uk**
- **website: www.sunnymeade.co.uk**

Hotel
Woolacombe Bay Hotel, WOOLACOMBE, Devon EX34 7BN
01271 870388
- **e-mail: woolacombe.bayhotel@btinternet.com**
- **website: www.woolacombe-bay-hotel.co.uk**

Hotel
Crossways Hotel, The Seafront, WOOLACOMBE, Devon EX34 7DJ
01271 870395
- **website: www.s-h-systems.co.uk/hotels/crossway.html**

Farmhouse
Mrs Gozzard, Stokehill Farmhouse, Stokehill Lane, Crapstone, YELVERTON, Devon PL20 7PP
01822 853791
- **e-mail: gozzard@btopenworld.com**
- **website: www.stokehillfarmhouse.co.uk**

• DORSET

Hotel
The Anvil Hotel, Salisbury Road, Pimperne, BLANDFORD, Dorset DT11 8UQ
01258 453431
- **e-mail: info@anvilhotel.co.uk**
- **website: www.anvilhotel.co.uk**

Farm / Self-Catering
Mr M. Kayll, Luccombe Farm, Luccombe, Milton Abbas, BLANDFORD FORUM, Dorset DT11 0BE
01258 880558
- **e-mail: mkayll@aol.com**
- **website: www.luccombeholidays.co.uk**

Hotel
Golden Sovereign Hotel, 97 Alumhurst Road, BOURNEMOUTH, Dorset BH4 8HR
01202 762088
- **e-mail: goldensov@aol.com**
- **website: www.goldensovereign.co.uk**

Guest House
S. Barling, Mayfield, 46 Frances Road, BOURNEMOUTH, Dorset BH1 3SA
01202 551839
- **e-mail: accom@mayfieldguesthouse.com**
- **website: www.mayfieldguesthouse.com**

Hotel / Guest House
Southernhay Hotel, 42 Alum Chine Road, Westbourne, BOURNEMOUTH, Dorset BH4 8DX
01202 761251
- **e-mail: enquiries@southernhayhotel.co.uk**
- **website: www.southernhayhotel.co.uk**

Hotel
Fircroft Hotel, Owls Road, BOURNEMOUTH, Dorset BH5 1AE
01202 309771
- **e-mail: info@fircrofthotel.co.uk**
- **website: www.fircrofthotel.co.uk**

Self-Catering
Westover Farm Cottages, Wootton Fitzpaine, BRIDPORT, Dorset DT6 6NE
01297 560451
- **e-mail: wfcottages@aol.com**
- **website: www.lymeregis.com/westover-farm-cottages/**

Caravan & Camping
Martin Cox, Highlands End Holiday Park, Eype, BRIDPORT, Dorset DT6 6AR
01308 422139
- **e-mail: holidays@wdlh.co.uk**
- **website: www.wdlh.co.uk**

B & B
Mrs Jane Greening, New House Farm, Mangerton Lane, Bradpole, BRIDPORT, Dorset DT6 3SF
01308 422884
- **e-mail: jane@mangertonlake.freeserve.co.uk**
- **website: www.mangertonlake.co.uk**

Hotel
Eypes Mouth Country Hotel, Eype, near BRIDPORT, Dorset DT6 6AL
01308 423300
- **e-mail: eypehotel@aol.com**
- **website: www.eypehotel.co.uk**

Caravan Park
Mr F. Loosmore, Manor Farm Holiday Centre, CHARMOUTH, Bridport, Dorset DT6 6QL
01297 560226
- **website: www.manorfarmholidaycentre.co.uk**

B & B / Self-Catering
Mrs S.M. Johnson, Cardsmill Farm Holidays, Whitchurch Canonicorum, CHARMOUTH, Bridport, Dorset DT6 6RP
01297 489375
- **e-mail: cardsmill@aol.com**
- **website: www.farmhousedorset.com**

B & B
The Old Rectory, Winterbourne Steepleton, DORCHESTER, Dorset DT2 9LG
01305 889468
- **e-mail: trees@eurobell.co.uk**
- **website: www.trees.eurobell.co.uk**

Self-Catering
Lyme Bay Holidays, 44 Church Street, LYME REGIS, Dorset DT7 3DA
01297 443363
- **website: www.lymebayholidays.co.uk**

Farm
Mrs Stephenson, Holly Hedge Farm, Malls Road, Lytchett Matravers, POOLE, Dorset BH16 6EP
01929 459688
- **e-mail: ceri.stephenson@lineone.net**
- **website: www.hollyhedgefarm.com**

Guest House / Self-Catering
White Horse Farm, Middlemarsh, SHERBORNE, Dorset DT9 5QN
01963 210222
- **e-mail: enquiries@whitehorsefarm.co.uk**
- **website: www.whitehorsefarm.co.uk**

FREE or REDUCED RATE entry to Holiday Visits and Attractions see our READERS' OFFER VOUCHERS on pages 55-82

Hotel
The Knoll House, STUDLAND BAY,
Dorset BH19 3AW
01929 450450
• **e-mail: enquiries@knollhouse.co.uk**
• **website: www.knollhouse.co.uk**

Hotel / Guest House
The Limes Hotel, 48 Park Road, SWANAGE,
Dorset BH19 2AE
01929 422664
• **e-mail: info@limeshotel.demon.co.uk**
• **website: www.limeshotel.demon.co.uk**

Farm / Bed & Breakfast
Mrs Justine Pike, Downshay Farm,
Haycrafts Lane, Harmans Cross, SWANAGE,
Dorset BH19 3EB
01929 480316
• **e-mail: downshayfarm@farmersweekly.net**

Self-Catering
Dorset Cottage Holidays, 11 Tyneham
Close, Sandford, WAREHAM,
Dorset BH20 7BE
01929 553443
• **e-mail: enq@dhcottages.co.uk**
• **website: www.dhcottages.co.uk**

Farm B & B / Caravan & Camping
Mrs L.S. Barnes, Luckford Wood House,
East Stoke, WAREHAM, Dorset BH20 6AW
01929 463098
• **e-mail: info@luckfordleisure.co.uk**
• **website: www.luckfordleisure.co.uk**

Caravan & Camping
Mrs Savage, Wareham Forest Tourist Park,
North Trigon, WAREHAM, Dorset BH20 7NZ
01929 551393
• **e-mail: holiday@wareham-forest.co.uk**
• **website: www.wareham-forest.co.uk**

Self-Catering on Working Farm
Josephine Pearse, Tamarisk Farm Cottages,
WEST BEXINGTON, Dorchester,
Dorset DT2 9DF
01308 897784
• **e-mail: tamarisk@eurolink.ltd.net**
• **website: www.tamariskfarm.co.uk**

B & B
Mrs Tory, Hemsworth Farm, Witchampton,
near WIMBORNE, Dorset BH21 5BN
01258 840216
• **website: www.ruraldorset.org.uk/bed**

•DURHAM

Farmhouse B & B
Mrs Carol Oulton, Newlands Hall,
Frosterley in Weardale, BISHOP AUCKLAND
Co Durham DL13 2SH
01388 529233
• **e-mail: carol.oulton@ukonline.co.uk**

B & B
David Turner, Bee Cottage Farmhouse,
Castleside, near CONSETT,
Co Durham DH8 9HW
01207 508224
• **e-mail:**
welcome@beecottagefarmhouse.freeserve.co.uk

•GLOUCESTERSHIRE

Farmhouse
Mrs Ann Cook, Moor's Farmhouse,
32 Beckford Road, ALDERTON,
Gloucestershire GL20 8AL
01242 620 523 / Freephone: 0800 298 9287
• **e-mail: annmoorsfarmhouse@talk21.com**

Farmhouse B & B / Self-Catering
Box Hedge Farm, Coalpit Heath, BRISTOL,
Gloucestershire BS36 2UW
01454 250786
• **e-mail: marilyn@boxhedgefarmbandb.co.uk**
• **website: www.boxhedgefarmbandb.co.uk**

Hotel
Charlton Kings Hotel, London Road,
CHELTENHAM, Gloucestershire GL52 6UU
01242 231061
• **e-mail: enquiries@charltonkingshotel.co.uk**
• **website: www.charltonkingshotel.co.uk**

B & B
Mrs G. Jeffrey, Brymbo, Honeybourne Lane,
Mickleton, CHIPPING CAMPDEN,
Gloucestershire GL55 6PU
01386 438890
• **e-mail: enquiries@brymbo.com**
• **website: www.brymbo.com**

B & B
Mrs C. Hutsby, Holly House, Ebrington,
CHIPPING CAMPDEN,
Gloucestershire GL55 6NL
01386 593213
• **e-mail: hutsby@talk21.com**
• **website: www.hollyhousebandb.co.uk**

Farm / B & B
Mrs D. Gwilliam, Dryslade Farm, English Bicknor, COLEFORD, Gloucestershire, GL16 7PA
01594 860259
- **e-mail: dryslade@agriplus.net**
- **website: www.fweb.org.uk/dryslade**

Guest House
Gunn Mill Guest House, Lower Spout Lane, MITCHELDEAN, Gloucestershire GL17 0EA
01594 827577
- **e-mail: info@gunnmillhouse.co.uk**
- **website: www.gunnmillhouse.co.uk**

B & B
Mrs F.J. Adams, Aston House, Broadwell, MORETON-IN-MARSH, Gloucestershire GL56 0TJ
01451 830475
- **e-mail: fja@netcomuk.co.uk**
- **website: www.netcomuk.co.uk/~nmfa/aston_house.html**

B & B
Mrs Wendy Swait, Inschdene, Atcombe Road, SOUTH WOODCHESTER, Stroud, Gloucestershire GL5 5EW
01453 873254
- **e-mail: malcolm.swait@repp.co.uk**
- **website: www.inschdene.co.uk**

• HAMPSHIRE

B & B
Mrs Arnold-Brown, Hilden B&B, Southampton Road, Boldre, BROCKENHURST, Hampshire SO41 8PT
01590 623682
- **e-mail: aliab@totalise.co.uk**
- **website: www.newforestbandb-hilden.co.uk**

Hotel
The Watersplash Hotel, The Rise, BROCKENHURST, Hampshire SO42 7ZP
01590 622344
- **e-mail: bookings@watersplash.co.uk**
- **website: www.watersplash.co.uk**

Caravan & Camping
Kingfisher Caravan Park, Browndown Road, Stokes Bay, GOSPORT, Hampshire PO13 9BE
023 9250 2611
- **e-mail: info@kingfisher-caravan-park.co.uk**
- **website: www.kingfisher-caravan-park.co.uk**

Campsite
Hayling Island Family Campsites, Copse Lane, HAYLING ISLAND, Hampshire
023 9246 2479, 023 9246 4695, 023 9246 3684
- **e-mail: lowertye@euphony.net**
- **website: www.haylingcampsites.co.uk**

Farm / B & B
John & Penny Harkinson, Fritham Farm, Fritham, LYNDHURST, Hampshire SO43 7HH
023 8081 2333
- **e-mail: frithamfarm@supanet.com**

Guest House
The Penny Farthing Hotel, Romsey Road, LYNDHURST, Hampshire SO43 7AA
023 8028 4422
- **e-mail: stay@pennyfarthinghotel.co.uk**
- **website: www.pennyfarthinghotel.co.uk**

B & B
Mrs P. Farrell, Honeysuckle House, 24 Clinton Road, LYMINGTON, Hampshire SO41 9EA
01590 676635
- **e-mail: skyblue@beeb.net**
- **website: www.newforest.demon.co.uk/honeysuckle.htm**

Hotel
Woodlands Lodge Hotel, Bartley Road, Woodlands, NEW FOREST, Hampshire SO40 7GN
023 8029 2257
- **e-mail: reception@woodlands-lodge.co.uk**
- **website: www.woodlands-lodge.co.uk**

Self-Catering
Jenny Monger, Little Horseshoes, South Gorley, RINGWOOD, Hampshire BH24 3NL
01425 479340
- **e-mail: jenny@littlehorseshoes.co.uk**
- **www.littlehorseshoes.co.uk**

Self-Catering
Mrs Thelma Rowe, 9 Cruse Close, SWAY, near Lymington, Hampshire SO41 6AY
01590 683092
- **e-mail: ronrowe@talk21.com**
- **website: www.tivertonnewforest.co.uk**

B & B
Mrs S. Buchanan, "Acacia", 44 Kilham Lane, WINCHESTER, Hampshire SO22 5PT
01962 852259
- **website: www.btinternet.com/~eric.buchanan**

•HEREFORDSHIRE

Guest House
Brian Roby, Felton House, FELTON, Herefordshire HR1 3PH
01432 820366
- **e-mail: bandb@ereal.net**
- **website: www.SmoothHound.co.uk/hotels/felton.html**

B & B
Mrs Gill Andrews, Webton Court Farmhouse, KINGSTONE, Herefordshire HR2 9NF
01981 250220
- **e-mail: gill@webton.fsnet.co.uk**

Farmhouse B & B
Mrs Jane West, Church Farm, Coddington, LEDBURY, Herefordshire HR8 1JJ
01531 64027
- **e-mail: jane@dexta.co.uk**
- **website: www.dexta.co.uk**

B & B
Mrs S.W. Born, The Coach House, Putley, LEDBURY, Herefordshire HR8 2QP
01531 670684
- **e-mail: wendyborn@putley-coachhouse.co.uk**
- **website: www.putley-coachhouse.co.uk**

Small Hotel
Miss G. Benjamin, The New Priory Hotel, STRETTON SUGWAS, Hereford, Herefordshire HR4 7AR
01432 760264
- **e-mail: newprioryhotel@ukonline.co.uk**
- **website: www.newprioryhotel.co.uk**

•ISLE OF WIGHT

Self-Catering
Island Cottage Holidays, Isle of Wight. Contact: Honor Vass, The Old Vicarage, Kingston, Wareham, Dorset BH20 5LH
01929 480080
- **e-mail: enq@islandcottageholidays.com**
- **website: www.islandcottageholidays.com**

Please mention the FHG Guide to Coast & Country Holidays when enquiring about accommodation

Caravan Park / Self-Catering
Mrs A.J. Coleman, Sunnycott Caravan Park, Rew Street, Gurnard, COWES, Isle of Wight PO31 8NN
01983 292859
- **e-mail: sunnycott2000@sunnycott2000.freeserve.co.uk**
- **website: www.sunnycott.co.uk**

Guest House
Barbara Tubbs, The Hazelwood, 14 Clarence Road, SHANKLIN, Isle of Wight PO37 7BH
01983 862824
- **e-mail: barbara.tubbs@thehazelwood.free-online.co.uk**
- **website: www.thehazelwood.free-online.co.uk**

Caravan & Camping
The Orchards Holiday Caravan & Camping Park, Newbridge, YARMOUTH, Isle of Wight PO41 0TS
01983 531331/350
- **e-mail: info@orchards-holiday-park.co.uk**
- **website: www.orchards-holiday-park.co.uk**

•KENT

Hotel / Guest House
Ashford Warren Cottage Hotel, 136 The Street, Willesborough, ASHFORD, Kent TN24 0NB
01233 621905
- **e-mail: general@warrencottage.co.uk**
- **website: www.warrencottage.co.uk**

Farm
Mrs Lewana Castle, Great Field Farm, Misling Lane, Stelling Minnis, CANTERBURY, Kent CT4 6DE
01227 709223
- **e-mail: greatfieldfarm@aol.com**

Guest House
Mr R.D. Linch, Upper Ansdore, Duckpit Lane, Petham, CANTERBURY, Kent CT4 5QB
01227 700672
- **e-mail: upperansdore@hotels.activebooking.com**
- **website: www.SmoothHound.co.uk/hotels/upperans.html**

Farmhouse B & B
Nicola Ellen, Crockshard Farmhouse, Wingham, CANTERBURY Kent CT3 1NY
01227 720464
- **e-mail: crockshardbnb@yahoo.com**
- **website: www.crockshard.com**

Guest House

Penny Farthing Guest House, 109 Maison Dieu Road, DOVER, Kent CT16 1RT
01304 205563

- **e-mail: pennyfarthingdover@btinternet.com**
- **website: www.pennyfarthingdover.com**

B & B

Bleriot's, 47 Park Avenue, DOVER, Kent CT16 1HE
01304 211394

- **website: www.SmoothHound.co.uk**

Caravan & Camping

Woodlands Park, Biddenden Road, TENTERDEN, Kent
01580 291216

- **e-mail: woodlandsp@aol.com**
- **website: www.campingsite.co.uk**

Self-Catering

Garden of England Cottages, The Mews Office, 189a High Street, TONBRIDGE, Kent TN9 1BX

- **e-mail: holidays@gardenofenglandcottages.co.uk**
- **website: www.gardenofenglandcottages.co.uk**

•LANCASHIRE

B & B

Mrs Melanie Smith, Capernwray House, Capernwray, CARNFORTH, Lancashire LA6 1AE
01524 732363

- **e-mail: thesmiths@capernwrayhouse.com**
- **website: www.capernwrayhouse.com**

•LEICESTERSHIRE

Guest House

Mrs Indge, The Highbury Guest House, 146 Leicester Road, LOUGHBOROUGH, Leicestershire LE11 2AQ
01509 230545

- **e-mail: emkhighbury@supanet.com**
- **website: www.thehighburyguesthouse.co.uk**

Guest House

Mrs Jackson, The Exeter Guest House, Wakerley, OAKHAM, Rutland LE15 8PA
01572 747817

- **website: www.exeterguesthouse.co.uk**

•LINCOLNSHIRE

B & B

Jubilee House, Waring Street, HORNCASTLE Lincolnshire LN9 6DY
01507 527000

- **e-mail: mizpahvilla@aol.com**

Farm / Board

Mrs Evans, Willow Farm, THORPE FENDYKES, Wainfleet, Skegness, Lincolnshire PE24 4QH
01754 830316

- **website: www.willowfarmholidays.fsnet.co.uk**

•NORFOLK

Guest House

Mrs J.A. Bell, Peacock House, Peacock Lane, Old Beetley, DEREHAM, Norfolk NR20 4DG
01362 860371

- **e-mail: PeackH@aol.com**
- **website: www.SmoothHound.co.uk/hotels/peacockh.html**

Self-Catering

Winterton Valley Holidays, 15 Kingston Avenue, Caister-on-Sea, GREAT YARMOUTH, Norfolk NR30 5ET
01493 377175

- **e-mail: info@wintertonvalleyholidays.fsnet.co.uk**
- **website: www.wintertonvalleyholidays.co.uk**

Self-Catering

Blue Riband Holidays, HEMSBY, Great Yarmouth, Norfolk NR29 4HA
01493 730445

- **website: www.BlueRibandHolidays.co.uk**

Farmhouse B & B

Mrs Lynda Mack, Hempstead Hall, HOLT, Norfolk NR25 6TN
01263 712224

- **website: www.broadland.com/hempsteadhall**

Farm / Board

Mrs Davidson, Holmdene Farm, Beeston, KING'S LYNN, Norfolk, PE32 2NJ
01328 701284

- **e-mail: holmdenefarm@farmersweekly.net**
- **website: www.northnorfolk.co.uk/holmdenefarm**

Guest House B & B

Mrs Christine Lilah Thrower, Whincliff, Cromer Road, MUNDESLEY-ON-SEA, Norfolk NR11 8DU
01263 721554

- **e-mail: whincliff@freeuk.com**
- **website: http://whincliff.freeuk.com**

Guest House
Mrs D. Curtis, Rosedale, 145 Earlhay Road, NORWICH, Norfolk NR2 3RG
01603 453743
- **e-mail: drcbac@aol.com**
- **website: www.http://members.aol.com/drcbac**

Guest House / Self-Catering
L.D. Poore, 3 Wodehouse Road, OLD HUNSTANTON, Norfolk PE36 6JD
01485 534036
- **e-mail: st.crispins@btinternet.com**
  or: lesley.cobblerscottage@btinternet.com

Self-Catering
Norfolk Country Cottages, Carlton House, Market Place, REEPHAM, Norfolk NR10 4QN
01603 871872
- **e-mail: info@norfolkcottages.co.uk**
- **website: www.norfolkcottages.co.uk**

•NORTHUMBERLAND

B & B
Eileen Finn, Thornley House, ALLENDALE, Northumberland NE47 9NH
01434 683255
- **e-mail: e.finn@ukonline.co.uk**
- **website: web.ukonline.co.uk/e.finn**

Self-Catering
Catriona Moore, West Fallodon, Embleton, ALNWICK, Northumberland NE67 5EB
01665 579357
- **e-mail: rn.moore@freeonline.com**
- **website: www.wfallodon.freeuk.com**

Self-Catering
Heritage Coast Holidays, 66 Greensfield Court, ALNWICK, Northumberland NE66 2DE
01670 787864
- **e-mail: office@marishalthompson.co.uk**
- **website: www.northumberland-holidays.co.uk**

Guest House
John & Edith Howliston, North Cottage, Birling, WARKWORTH, Morpeth, Northumberland NE65 0XS
01665 711263
- **e-mail: edithandjohn@another.com**
- **website: www.accta.co.uk/north**

•OXFORDSHIRE

Farm / Board
Mrs Katherine Brown, Hill Grove Farm, Crawley Road, MINSTER LOVELL, Oxfordshire OX29 ONA
01993 703120
- **e-mail: kbrown@eggconnect.net**

Guest House
Mandy Buck, Elbie House, East End, Northleigh, near Witney, WOODSTOCK, Oxfordshire OX8 6PZ
01993 880166
- **e-mail: mandy@cotswoldbreak.co.uk**
- **website: www.cotswoldbreak.co.uk**

Inn
Killingworth Castle Inn, Glympton Road, Wootton, by WOODSTOCK, Oxfordshire OX20 1EJ
01993 811401
- **e-mail: wiggiscastle@aol.com**
- **website: www.oxlink.co.uk/woodstock/kilcastle**

•SHROPSHIRE

Farm B & B
Mrs M. Jones, Acton Scott Farm, Acton Scott, CHURCH STRETTON, Shropshire SY6 6QN
01694 781260
- **e-mail: edandm@clara.co.uk**
- **website: http://welcome.to/acton-scott-b&b**

Farm / B & B
Mrs Brereton, Brereton's Farm, Woolston, CHURCH STRETTON, Shropshire SY6 6QD
01694 781201
- **e-mail: joanna@breretonhouse.f9.co.uk**
- **website: www.breretonhouse.f9.co.uk**

Guest House
Ron & Jennie Repath, Meadowlands, Lodge Lane, Frodesley, DORRINGTON, Shropshire SY5 7HD
01694 731350
- **e-mail: meadowlands@talk21.com**
- **website: www.meadowlands.co.uk**

Hotel
Miles Hunter, Pen-y-Dyffryn Country Hotel, OSWESTRY, Shropshire SY10 7JD
01691 653700
- **e-mail: stay@peny.co.uk**
- **website: www.peny.co.uk**

Please mention this publication when enquiring about accommodation

Self-Catering
Mrs Ann Cartwright, Ryton Farm, Ryton, Dorrington, SHREWSBURY, Shropshire SY5 7LY
01743 718449
- **website: www.rytonfarm.co.uk**

Self-Catering
Courtyard Cottages, Lower Springs Farm, Kenley, SHREWSBURY, Shropshire SY5 6PA
01952 510 841
- **e-mail: a-gill@lineone.net**

• SOMERSET

B & B / Self-Catering
Jackie & David Bishop, Toghill House Farm, Wick, BATH, Somerset BS30 5RT
01225 891261
- **website: www.toghillhousefarm.co.uk**

Guest House
Mrs C. Bryson, Walton Villa, 3 Newbridge Hill, BATH, Somerset BA1 3PW
01225 482792
- **e-mail: walton.villa@virgin.net**
- **website: www.walton.izest.com**

Guest House
Jan Wotley, The Albany Guest House, 24 Crescent Gardens, BATH, Somerset BA1 2NB
01225 313339
- **e-mail: the_albany@lineone.net**
- **website: www.bath.org/hotel/albany.htm**

Hotel
Elaine Sexton, Bailbrook Lodge Hotel, 35-37 London Road West, BATH, Somerset BA1 7HZ
01225 859090
- **e-mail: hotel@bailbrooklodge.co.uk**
- **website: www.bailbrooklodge.co.uk**

Self-Catering
T.M. Hicks, Diamond Farm, Weston Road, BREAN, Near Burnham-on-Sea, Somerset TA8 2RL
01278 751263
- **e-mail: trevor@diamondfarm42.freeserve.co.uk**
- **website: www.diamondfarm.co.uk**

B & B
Mrs Alexander, Priors Mead, 23 Rectory Road, BURNHAM-ON-SEA, Somerset TA8 2BZ
01278 782116
- **e-mail: priorsmead@aol.com**
- **website: www.priorsmead.co.uk**

Caravan & Camping Park
Broadway House Holiday Touring Caravan & Camping Park, CHEDDAR, Somerset BS27 3DB
01934 742610
- **e-mail: enquiries@broadwayhouse.uk.com**
- **website: www.broadwayhouse.uk.com**

B & B
Mrs C. Bacon, Honeydown Farm, Seaborough Hill, CREWKERNE, Somerset TA18 8PL
01460 72665
- **e-mail: cb@honeydown.freeserve.co.uk**
- **website: www.honeydown.freeserve.co.uk**

Hotel
Jeff Everitt, Lion Hotel, Bank Square, DULVERTON, Somerset TA22 9BU
01398 323444
- **e-mail: jeffeveritt@tiscali.co.uk**

Farm / Board
Mrs Humphrey, Highercombe Farm, DULVERTON, Exmoor, Somerset TA22 9PT
01398 323616
- **e-mail: abigail@highercombe.demon.co.uk**
- **website: www.highercombe.demon.co.uk**

Self-Catering
Mrs Joan Atkins, 2 Edgcott Cottage, EXFORD, Minehead, Somerset TA24 7QG
01643 831564
- **e-mail: info@stilemoorexmoor.co.uk**
- **website: www.stilemoorexmoor.co.uk**

B & B / Self-Catering
C.R. Horstmann, Court Farm, EXFORD, Exmoor, Somerset TA24 7LY
01643 831207
- **e-mail: colin@courtfarm.co.uk**
- **website: www.courtfarm.co.uk**

Farm B & B / Self-Catering
Penny Webber, Hindon Organic Farm, Near Selworthy, Minehead, EXMOOR, Somerset TA24 8SH
01643 705244
- **e-mail: info@hindonfarm.co.uk**
- **website: www.hindonfarm.co.uk**

Hotel / Self-Catering
Simonsbath House Hotel, Simonsbath, EXMOOR, Somerset TA24 7SH
01643 831259
- **e-mail: hotel@simonsbathhouse.co.uk**
- **website: www.simonsbathhouse.co.uk**

Farm / Self-Catering

Mrs Styles, Wintershead Farm, Simonsbath, EXMOOR, Somerset TA24 7LF
01643 831222
- **website: www.wintershead.co.uk**

Self-Catering

Mrs N. Hanson, Woodcombe Lodges, Bratton, MINEHEAD, Somerset TA24 8SQ
01643 702789
- **e-mail: nicola@woodcombelodge.co.uk**
- **website: www.woodcombelodge.co.uk**

Self-Catering

Inner Lype & Goosemoor Farm Cottages, Wheddon Cross, MINEHEAD, Somerset TA24 7BJ
01643 841557
- **e-mail: om.howe@virgin.net**
- **website: www.cottageguide.co.uk/innerlype**

B & B

Mr P.R. Weir, Slipper Cottage, 41 Bishopston, MONTACUTE, Somerset TA15 6UX
01935 823073
- **e-mail: sue.weir@totalise.co.uk**
- **website: www.slippercottage.co.uk**

Inn

Jackie & Alan Cottrell, The Ship Inn, High Street, PORLOCK, Somerset TA24 8QD
01643 862507
- **e-mail: mail@shipinnporlock.co.uk**
- **website: www.shipinnporlock.co.uk**

Hotel

Mrs Murphy, Farthings Hotel & Restaurant, Hatch Beauchamp, TAUNTON, Somerset TA3 6SG
01823 480664
- **e-mail: farthing1@aol.com**
- **website: www.farthingshotel.com**

Self-Catering

Croft Holiday Cottages, Anchor Street, WATCHET, Somerset TA23 0BY
01984 631121
- **e-mail: croftcottages@talk21.com**
- **website: www.cottageguide.co.uk/croft-cottages**

Guest House

Infield House, 36 Portway, WELLS, Somerset BA5 2BN
01749 670989
- **e-mail: infield@talk21.com**
- **website: www.infieldhouse.co.uk**

Hotel

Braeside Hotel, 2 Victoria Park, WESTON-SUPER-MARE, Somerset BS23 2HZ
01934 626642
- **e-mail: braeside@tesco.net**
- **website: www.braesidehotel.co.uk**

•STAFFORDSHIRE

Farm

Mrs M. Hiscoe-James, Offley Grove Farm, Adbaston, ECCLESHALL, Staffordshire ST20 0QB
01785 280205
- **e-mail: accom@offleygrovefarm.freeserve.co.uk**
- **website: www.offleygrovefarm.co.uk**

Self-Catering

Brookhays, Park Lane, Ipstones, near LEEK, Staffordshire
01335 344132
- **e-mail: KeithLomas@aol.com**

Guest House

Mrs Griffiths, Prospect House Guest House, 334 Cheadle Road, Cheddleton, LEEK, Staffordshire ST13 7BW
01782 550639
- **e-mail: prospect@talk21.com**
- **website: www.touristnetuk.com/wm/prospect/index.htm**

Guest House

Ruth Franks, The Beehive Guest House, Churnet View Road, OAKAMOOR, Staffordshire ST10 3AE
01538 702420
- **e-mail: thebeehiveoakamoor@btinternet.com**
- **website: www.thebeehiveguesthouse.co.uk**

•SUFFOLK

Hotel

The Cornwallis Country Hotel & Restaurant, Brome, EYE, Suffolk IP23 8AJ
01379 870326
- **e-mail: enquiries@thecornwallis.com**
- **website: www.thecornwallis.com**

Farm B & B / Self-Catering

Mr & Mrs Kindred, High House Farm, Cransford, WOODBRIDGE, Suffolk IP13 9PD
01728 663461
- **e-mail: info@highhousefarm.co.uk**
- **website: www.highhousefarm.co.uk**

Hotel
The Crown and Castle, Orford, near WOODBRIDGE, Suffolk IP12 2LJ
01394 450205
- **e-mail: info@crownandcastlehotel.co.uk**
- **website: www.crownandcastle.co.uk**

Hotel / Inn
The Three Tuns Coaching Inn, Main Road, Pettistree, WOODBRIDGE, Suffolk IP13 0HW
01728 747979
- **e-mail: jon@threetuns-coachinginn.co.uk**
- **website: www.threetuns-coachinginn.co.uk**

•SURREY

Hotel
Chase Lodge Hotel, 10 Park Road, Hampton Wick, KINGSTON-UPON-THAMES, Surrey KT1 4AS
020 8943 1862
- **e-mail: info@chaselodgehotel.com**
- **website: www.chaselodgehotel.com**

•EAST SUSSEX

Bed & Breakfast / Guest House
Brighton Marina House Hotel, 8 Charlotte Street, BRIGHTON, East Sussex BN2 1AG
01273 605349
- **e-mail: rooms@jungs.co.uk**
- **website: www.brighton-mh-hotel.co.uk**

Hotel
Jonathan Turner, Dale Hill Hotel, TICEHURST, East Sussex TN5 7DQ
01580 200112
- **e-mail: info@dalehill.co.uk**
- **website: www.dalehill.co.uk**

•WEST SUSSEX

Caravan & Camping
Val & Jeff Burrow, Honeybridge Park, Honeybridge Lane, Dial Post, near HORSHAM, West Sussex RH13 8NX
01403 710923
- **e-mail: enquiries@honeybridgepark.co.uk**
- **website: www.honeybridgepark.co.uk**

B & B
Lady M.R. Milton, Beacon Lodge B&B, London Road, WATERSFIELD, West Sussex RH20 1NH
01798 831026
- **e-mail: beaconlodge@hotmail.com**
- **website: www.beaconlodge.co.uk**

•WARWICKSHIRE

Guest House / B & B
Julia Downie, Holly Tree Cottage, Pathlow, STRATFORD-UPON-AVON, Warwickshire CV37 0ES
01789 204461
- **e-mail: john@hollytree-cottage.co.uk**
- **website: www.hollytree-cottage.co.uk**

Self-Catering
Karen Cauvin, Penshurst Guest House, 34 Evesham Place, STRATFORD-UPON-AVON, Warwickshire CV37 6HT
01789 550197
- **e-mail: karen@penshurst.net**
- **website: www.penshurst.net**

Guest House
Mr J. Worboys, Broadlands Guest House, 23 Evesham Place, STRATFORD-UPON-AVON, Warwickshire CV37 6HT
01789 299181
- **e-mail: broadlands.com@virgin.net**
- **website: www.stratford-upon-avon.co.uk/broadlands.htm**

Guest House
Linhill Guest House, 35 Evesham Place, STRATFORD-UPON-AVON, Warwickshire
01789 292879
- **e-mail: linhill@bigwig.net**
- **website: www.linhillguesthouse.co.uk**

Guest House
Mr & Mrs Learmount, Green Haven Guest House, 217 Evesham Road, STRATFORD-UPON-AVON, Warwickshire CV37 9AS
01789 297874
- **e-mail: susanlearmount@green-haven.co.uk**
- **website: www.green-haven.co.uk**

Guest House / Self-Catering
Mrs Elizabeth Draisey, Forth House/ Copes Flat, 44 High Street, WARWICK, Warwickshire CV34 4AX
01926 401512
- **e-mail: info@forthhouseuk.co.uk**
- **website: www.forthhouseuk.co.uk**

Guest House
Croft Guest House, Haseley Knob, WARWICK, Warwickshire CV35 7NL
01926 484447
- **e-mail: david@croftguesthouse.co.uk**
- **website: www.croftguesthouse.co.uk**

•WILTSHIRE

Farmhouse / Board

Susan Barnes, Lovett Farm,
Little Somerford, near MALMESBURY,
Wiltshire SN15 5BP
01666 823268

- **e-mail: lovettfarm@btinternet.com**
- **website: www.lovettfarm.co.uk**

Guest House

Alan & Dawn Curnow, Hayburn Wyke Guest House, 72 Castle Road, SALISBURY,
Wiltshire SP1 3RL
01722 412627

- **e-mail: hayburn.wyke@tinyonline.co.uk**
- **website: www.hayburnwykeguesthouse.co.uk**

Farm Guest House

Mrs S. Lanham, Newton Farmhouse,
Southampton Road, Whiteparish,
SALISBURY, Wiltshire SP5 2QL
01794 884416

- **e-mail: reservations@newtonfarmhouse.co.uk**
- **website: www.newtonfarmhouse.co.uk**

•WORCESTERSHIRE

Farmhouse B & B

Mrs Jane Hill, Lower Field Farm, Willersey,
BROADWAY, Worcestershire WR11 5HF
01386 858273

- **e-mail: info@lowerfield-farm.co.uk**
- **website: www.lowerfield-farm.co.uk**

Inn

The Crown & Sandys, Main Road,
Ombersley, DROITWICH, Worcester
Worcestershire WR9 0EW
01905 620252

- **e-mail: crown&sandys@evertons.co.uk**

Hotel

Joseph Petitjean, Brockencote Hall,
Chaddesley Corbett, KIDDERMINSTER,
Worcestershire
01562 777876

- **e-mail: info@brockencotehall.com**
- **website: www.brockencotehall.com**

•EAST YORKSHIRE

B & B

Paws-a-While, KILNWICK PERCY,
East Yorkshire YO42 1UF
01759 301168

- **e-mail: paws.a.while@lineone.net**
- **website: www.pawsawhile.net**

•NORTH YORKSHIRE

Guest House

Mr Kingsley, Arbutus Guest House,
Riverside, CLAPHAM, near Settle,
North Yorkshire LA2 8DS
01524 251240

- **e-mail: info@arbutus.co.uk**
- **website: www.arbutus.co.uk**

Guest House

Janet and Steve Frankland, Amadeus,
115 Franklin Road, HARROGATE,
North Yorkshire HG1 5EN
01423 505151

- **e-mail: amadeushotel@btinternet.com**

B & B / Self-Catering

Mrs E.J. Moorhouse, The Courtyard at
Duke's Place, Bishop Thornton,
HARROGATE, North Yorkshire HG3 3JY
01765 620229

- **e-mail: jakimoorhouse@onetel.net.uk**

Guest House

Phil & Carolyn Smith, Inglenook Guest
House, 20 Main Street, INGLETON,
North Yorkshire LA6 3HJ
01524 241270

- **e-mail: inglenook20@hotmail.com**
- **website: www.nebsweb.co.uk/inglenook**

Farm B & B / Self-Catering

John & Felicity Wiles, Sinnington Common
Farm, KIRKBYMOORSIDE, York,
North Yorkshire YO62 6NX
01751 431719

- **e-mail: felicity@scfarm.demon.co.uk**
- **website: www.scfarm.demon.co.uk**

Farmhouse B & B

Mrs Julie Clarke, Middle Farm,
Woodale, Coverdale, LEYBURN,
North Yorkshire DL8 4TY
01969 640271

- **e-mail: julie-clarke@amserve.com**
- **website: www.yorkshirenet.co.uk/stayat/middlefarm/**

Holiday Park

John McCourt, Black Swan Holiday Park,
Rear Black Swan, Fearby, MASHAM, Ripon,
North Yorkshire HG4 4NF
01765 689477

- **e-mail: blackswanholidaypark@fsmail.net**
- **website: www.geocities.com/theblackswan_uk/**

Hotel

Mrs Ella Bowes, Banavie, Roxby Road, Thornton-Le-Dale, PICKERING, North Yorkshire YO18 7SX
01751 474616
- **e-mail: ella@banavie.fsbusiness.co.uk**
- **website: www.SmoothHound.co.uk/hotels/banavie**

Country House Hotel

Hartforth Hall Hotel, Gilling West, RICHMOND, North Yorkshire DL10 5JU
01748 825715
- **website: www.hartforthhall.com**

Farmhouse B & B

Mrs Sandra Gordon, St George's Court, Old Home Farm, Grantley, RIPON North Yorkshire HG4 3EU
01765 620618
- **e-mail: stgeorgescourt@bronco.co.uk**
- **website: www.stgeorges-court.co.uk**

Guest House

Sue & Tony Hewitt, Harmony Country Lodge, 80 Limestone Road, Burniston, SCARBOROUGH, North Yorkshire YO13 0DG
0800 2985840
- **e-mail: tony@harmonylodge.net**
- **website: www.harmonylodge.net**

B & B (Small Hotel)

Mrs M.M Abbott, Howdale Hotel, 121 Queen's Parade, SCARBOROUGH, North Yorkshire YO12 7HU
0800 056 6622
- **e-mail: maria_keith_howdalehotel@yahoo.co.uk**
- **website: www.howdalehotel.moonfruit.com**

Hotel

Ganton Greyhound, Main Street, Ganton, near SCARBOROUGH, North Yorkshire YO12 4NX
01944 710116
- **e-mail: gantongreyhound@supanet.com**
- **website: www.gantongreyhound.co.uk**

Self-Catering

Mr Donnelly, Gowland Farm, Gowland Lane, Cloughton, SCARBOROUGH, North Yorkshire YO13 0DU
01723 870924
- **e-mail: gowlandfarm@hotmail.com**
- **website: www.gowlandfarm.co.uk**

Hotel

Coniston Hall Hotel, Coniston Cold, SKIPTON, North Yorkshire, BD23 4EB
01756 748080
- **e-mail: conistonhall@clara.net**
- **website: www.conistonhall.co.uk**

Self-Catering

Mrs Jones, New Close Farm, Kirkby Malham, SKIPTON, North Yorkshire BD23 4DP
01729 830240
- **e-mail: brendajones@newclosefarmyorkshire.co.uk**
- **website: www.newclosefarmyorkshire.co.uk**

Self-Catering Cottages

Anne Fawcett, Mile House Farm Country Cottages, Mile House Farm, Hawes, WENSLEYDALE, North Yorkshire DL8 3PT
01969 667481
- **e-mail: milehousefarm@hotmail.com**
- **website: www.wensleydale.uk.com**

Self-Catering

Mrs Sue Cooper, St Edmunds, The Green, Crakehall, Bedale, WENSLEYDALE, North Yorkshire DL8 1HP
01677 423584
- **e-mail:stedmundscountrycottages@hotmail.com**
- **website: www.crakehall.org.uk**

Self-Catering

Westclose House (Allaker), WEST SCRAFTON, North Yorkshire c/o Mr A Cave,
020 8567 4862
- **e-mail: ac@adriancave.com**
- **website: www.adriancave.com/allaker**

Self-Catering

June Roberts, White Rose Holiday Cottages, 5 Brook Park, Sleights, near WHITBY, North Yorkshire YO21 1RT
01947 810763
- **e-mail: enquiries@whiterosecottages.co.uk**
- **website: www.whiterosecottages.co.uk**

Self-Catering

Mrs N. Pattinson, South House Farm, Fylingthorpe, WHITBY, North Yorkshire YO22 4UQ
01947 880243
- **e-mail: kmp@bogglehole.fsnet.co.uk**

FREE or REDUCED RATE entry to Holiday Visits and Attractions see our READERS' OFFER VOUCHERS on pages 55 — 82

Inn

Flask Inn, Near Robin's Hood Bay, WHITBY, North Yorkshire YO22 4QH
01947 880305
- **e-mail: flaskinn@aol.com**
- **website: www.flaskinn.com**

Self-Catering

Nick Eddleston, Greenhouses Farm Cottage, Green Houses Farm, Lealholm, near WHITBY, North Yorkshire YO21 2AD
01947 897486
- **e-mail: n_eddleston@yahoo.com**
- **website: www.greenhouses-farm-cottages.co.uk**

Self-Catering

Jill McNeil, Swallow Holiday Cottages, The Farm, Stainsacre, WHITBY, North Yorkshire YO22 4NT
01947 603790
- **e-mail: jillian@swallowcottages.co.uk**
- **website: www.swallowcottages.co.uk**

Hotel

Seacliffe Hotel, North Promenade, West Cliff, WHITBY, North Yorkshire YO21 3JX
01947 603139
- **e-mail: julie@seacliffe.fsnet.co.uk**
- **website: www.seacliffe.co.uk**

Guest House / Self-Catering

Mr Gary Hudson, Orillia House, 89 The Village, Stockton on Forest, YORK, North Yorkshire YO3 9UP
01904 400600
- **e-mail: orillia@globalnet.co.uk**
- **website: www.orilliahouse.co.uk**

B & B / Self-Catering / Holiday Caravans

Mr & Mrs Tyerman, Partridge Nest Farm, Eskdaleside, Sleights, WHITBY, North Yorkshire YO22 5ES
01947 810450
- **e-mail: barbara@partridgenestfarm.com**
- **website: www.partridgenestfarm.com**

Self-Catering

Mrs O. Hepworth, Land of Nod Farm, Ugthorpe, near WHITBY, North Yorkshire YO21 2BL
- **e-mail: colin@thecottage-ugthorpe.freeserve.co.uk**
- **website: www.thecottage-ugthorpe.freeserve.co.uk**

Farm / Self-Catering

Mrs Robinson, Valley View Farm, Old Byland, Helmsley, YORK, North Yorkshire YO6 5LG
01439 798221
- **e-mail: sally@valleyviewfarm.com**
- **website: www.valleyviewfarm.com**

Farmhouse B & B

High Gaterley Farmhouse, Castle Howard Estate, YORK, North Yorkshire YO60 7HT
01653 694636
- **e-mail: relax@highgaterley.com**
- **website: www.highgaterley.com**

•SCOTLAND

•ABERDEEN, BANFF & MORAY

Self-Catering

Willie Bremner, Bremner of Foggie, Old School, ABERCHIRDER, Banffshire AB54 7XS
01466 780260
- **website: www.bremnersoffoggie.co.uk**

Self-Catering

Mrs J. White, Beechgrove Cottages, Tomnavoulin, BALLINDALLOCH, Aberdeenshire AB37 9JA
01807 590220
- **e-mail: jaqui154@msn.com**
- **website: www.beechgrovecottages.co.uk**

B & B

Mrs E. Malim, Invercairn House, BRODIE, by Forres, Moray IV36 2TD
01309 641261
- **e-mail: invercairnhouse@supanet.com**
- **website: www.invercairnhouse.co.uk**

B & B

Mrs H. Massie, Milton of Grange Farm, FORRES, Morayshire IV36 0TR
01309 676360
- **website: www.forres-accommodation.co.uk**

Farmhouse B & B

Mrs Alice Jane Morrison, Haddoch Farm, by HUNTLY, Aberdeenshire AB54 4SL
01466 711217
- **e-mail: alice.morrison@tinyworld.co.uk**

•ARGYLL & BUTE

Inn
Mr D. Fraser, Cairndow Stagecoach Inn, CAIRNDOW, Argyll PA26 8BN
01499 600286
- **e-mail: cairndowinn@aol.com**

B & B
Mrs D. MacCormick, Mains Farm, CARRADALE, Campbeltown, Argyll PA28 6QG
01583 431216
- **e-mail: maccormick@mainsfarm.freeserve.co.uk**

Self-Catering
Mrs Isabella Crawford, Blarghour Farm, Loch Awe-side, By DALMALLY, Argyll PA33 1BW
01866 833246
- **e-mail: blarghour@aol.com**
- **website: www.self-catering-argyll.co.uk**

Self-Catering
David Shaw, Ardbrecknish House, Ardbrecknish, Loch Awe, DALMALLY, Argyll PA33 1BH
01866 833223
- **e-mail: enquiries@ardbrecknish.com**
- **website: www.ardbrecknish.com**

Guest House
A.J. Burke, Orchy Bank, DALMALLY, Argyll PA33 1AS
01838 200370
- **e-mail: aj.burke@talk21.com**
- **website: www.loch-awe.com/orchybank/c2.htm**

Self-Catering
B & M Phillips, Kilbride Croft, Balvicar, ISLE OF SEIL, Argyll PA34 4RD
01852 300475
- **e-mail: kilbridecroft@aol.com**
- **website: www.kilbridecroft.fsnet.co.uk**

Self-Catering
Castle Sween Bay (Holidays) Ltd, Ellery, LOCHGILPHEAD, Argyll PA31 8PA
01880 770232
- **e-mail: info@ellary.com**
- **website: www.ellary.com**

Hotel
Willowburn Hotel, Clachan Seil, by OBAN, Argyll PA34 4TJ
01852 300276
- **e-mail: willowburn.hotel@virgin.net**
- **website: www.willowburn.co.uk**

•AYRSHIRE & ARRAN

B & B
Mrs J. Clark, Eglinton Guest House, 23 Eglinton Terrace, AYR, Ayrshire KA7 1JJ
01292 264623
- **website: www.eglintonguesthouse.co.uk**

Self-Catering
Arran Hideaways, Invercloy House, Brodick, ISLE OF ARRAN
01770 302303
- **e-mail: info@arran-hideways.co.uk**
- **website: www.arran-hideaways.co.uk**

Caravan & Camping

Mr Angus McKie, Braemoor Christian Holiday Village, Torranyard, KILWINNING, Ayrshire KA13 7RD

01274 850286

- **e-mail: info@braemoorchu.com**
- **website: www.braemoorchu.com**

•BORDERS

Guest House

Dunlaverock Guest House, COLDINGHAM BAY, Berwickshire TD14 5PA

01890 771450

- **e-mail: dunlaverockhouse@lineone.net**
- **website: www.dunlaverock.fsnet.co.uk**

Guest House

Mrs Ewen Kenworthy, St Albans, Clouds, DUNS, Berwickshire TD11 3BB

01361 883285

- **e-mail: st_albans@ukf.net**
- **website: www.scotlandbordersbandb.co.uk**

Self-Catering

Mill House, Letterbox and Stockman's Cottages, c/o Mrs A Fraser, Overwells, JEDBURGH, Borders TD8 6LT

01835 863020

- **website: www.overwells.co.uk**

Hotel

The Crook Inn, TWEEDSMUIR, Borders ML12 6QN

01899 880272

- **e-mail: the crookinn@btinternet.com**
- **website: www.crookinn.co.uk**

Self-Catering

Slipperfield House, WEST LINTON, Peeblesshire EH46 7AA

01968 660401

- **e-mail: cottages@slipperfield.com**
- **website: www.slipperfield.com**

•DUMFRIES & GALLOWAY

Guest House / Self-Catering

Mrs E.M. Bardsley, The Rossan, Auchencairn, CASTLE DOUGLAS, Dumfries & Galloway

01556 640269

- **e-mail: bardsley@rossan.freeserve.co.uk**
- **website: www.the-rossan.co.uk**

Self-Catering

Mr Ball, Barncrosh Leisure Co Ltd, Barncrosh, CASTLE DOUGLAS, Dumfries & Galloway DG7 1TX

01556 680216

- **e-mail: enq@barncrosh.co.uk**
- **website: www.barncrosh.co.uk**

Hotel / Guest House

Mrs Nicki Proudlock, Mabie House Hotel, Mabie, DUMFRIES, Dumfries & Galloway DG2 8HB

01387 263188

- **e-mail: niki@mabiehouse.co.uk**
- **website: www.mabiehouse.co.uk**

Self-Catering

Mrs B. Gilbey, Rusko Holidays, GATEHOUSE OF FLEET, Castle Douglas, Dumfries & Galloway DG7 2BS

01557 814215

- **e-mail: gilbey@rusko.demon.co.uk**
- **website: www.ruskoholidays.co.uk**

Self-Catering

Mrs S.M.Finlay, Manor Cottage, Ross Bay, KIRKCUDBRIGHT, Dumfries & Galloway DG6 4TR

01557 870381

- **e-mail: finlay.baycottage@btopenworld.com**
- **website: www.baycottage.net**

B & B

June Deakins, Annandale House, MOFFAT, Dumfriesshire

01683 221460

- **e-mail: june.deakins@virgin.net**
- **website: www.geocities.com/meadowdale/index.html**

B & B

Fiona Corlett, Craigie Lodge, Ballplay Road, MOFFAT, Dumfries & Galloway DG10 9JD

01683 221769

- **e-mail: craigielodge@aol.com**
- **website: www.craigielodge.co.uk**

Caravan Park
A & E Mackie, Galloway Point Holiday Park, Portpatrick, STRANRAER, Dumfries & Galloway DG9 9AA
01776 810561
- **website: www.gallowaypointholidaypark.co.uk**

• DUNDEE & ANGUS

Farmhouse B & B
Rosemary Beatty, Brathinch Farm, by BRECHIN, Angus DD9 7QX
01356 648292
- **e-mail: adam.brathinch@btinternet.com**

Self-Catering
Jenny Scott, Welton Farm, The Welton of Kingoldrum, KIRRIEMUIR, Angus DD8 5HY
01575 574743
- **e-mail: weltonholidays@btinternet.com**
- **website: www.cottageguide.co.uk/thewelton**

• EDINBURGH & LOTHIANS

B & B
Kenneth Harkins, 78 East Main Street, BLACKBURN, By Bathgate, West Lothian EH47 7QS
01506 655221
- **e-mail: cruachan.bb@virgin.net**
- **website: www.cruachan.co.uk**

Guest House
International Guest House, 31 Mayfield Gardens, EDINBURGH, Lothians EH9 2BX
0131 667 2511
- **e-mail: intergh@easynet.co.uk**
- **website: www.accommodation-edinburgh.com**

Guest House
Dorothy Vidler, Kenvie Guest House, 16 Kilmaurs Road, EDINBURGH, Lothians EH16 5DA
0131 668 1964
- **e-mail: dorothy@kenvie.co.uk**
- **website: www.kenvie.co.uk**

B & B
McCrae's B&B, 44 East Claremont Street, EDINBURGH, Lothians EH7 4JR
0131 556 2610
- **e-mail: mccraes.bandb@lineone.net**
- **website: http://website.lineone.net/~mccraes.bandb**

Guest House
D. Green, Ivy House, 7 Mayfield Gardens, Newington, EDINBURGH, Lothians EH9 2AX
0131 667 3411
- **e-mail: don@ivyguesthouse.com**
- **website: www.ivyguesthouse.com**

B & B
Mrs Mary Chase, Jadini Garden, Goose Green, GULLANE, East Lothian EH31 2BA
01620 843343
- **e-mail: marychase@jadini.com**
- **website: www.jadini.com**

• FIFE

B & B
Mrs A. Duncan, Spinkstown Farmhouse, ST ANDREWS, Fife KY16 8PN
01334 473475
- **e-mail: anne@spinkstown.com**
- **website: www.spinkstown.com**

• HIGHLANDS

Self-Catering / Guest House
Mr A. Allan, Torguish Self-Catering & B&B, DAVIOT, Inverness-shire IV2 5XQ
01463 772208
- **e-mail: torguish@torguish.com**
- **website: www.torguish.com**

Guest House B & B
Mrs Sandra Silke, Westwood, Lower Balmacaan, DRUMNADROCHIT, Inverness-shire IV63 6WU
01456 450826
- **e-mail: sandra@westwoodbb.freeserve.co.uk**
- **website: www.westwoodbb.freeserve.co.uk**

Hotel
Allt-Nan-Ros Hotel, Onich, FORT WILLIAM, Inverness-shire PH33 6RY
01855 821210
- **e-mail: fhg@allt-nan-ros.co.uk**
- **website: www.allt-nan-ros.co.uk**

Guest House
Mrs M. Matheson, Thistle Cottage, Torlundy, FORT WILLIAM, Inverness-shire PH33 6SN
01397 702428
- **e-mail: m.a.matheson@amserve.net**
- **website: www.thistlescotland.co.uk**

Hotel
Clan Macduff Hotel, Achintore Road, FORT WILLIAM, Inverness-shire PH33 6RW
01397 702341
- **e-mail: reception@clanmacduff.co.uk**
- **website: www.clanmacduff.co.uk**

Guest House
Mr & Mrs McQueen, Stronchreggan View Guest House, Achintore Road, FORT WILLIAM, Inverness-shire PH33 6RW
01397 704644
- **e-mail: patricia@apmac.freeserve.co.uk**
- **website: www.stronchreggan.co.uk**

Guest House
Norma E. McCallum, The Neuk, Corpach, FORT WILLIAM, Inverness-shire PH33 7LR
01397 772244
- **e-mail: normamccallum@theneuk10.fsbusiness.co.uk**
- **www.fortwilliamguesthouse.com**

Guest House
Gary Clulow, Sunset Guest House, MORAR, by Mallaig, Inverness-shire PH40 4PA
01687 462259
- **e-mail: sunsetgh@aol.com**
- **website: www.sunsetguesthouse.co.uk**

Self-Catering Chalets / B & B
D.J. Mordaunt, Mondhuie, NETHY BRIDGE, Inverness-shire PH25 3DF
01479 821062
- **e-mail: david@mondhuie.com**
- **website: www.mondhuie.com**

Hotel
Loch Leven Hotel, ONICH, By Fort William, Inverness-shire PH33 6SA
01855 821236
- **e-mail: reception@lochlevenhotel.co.uk**
- **website: www.lochlevenhotel.co.uk**

Self-Catering
Mr A. Urquhart, Crofters Cottages, 15 Croft, POOLEWE, Ross-shire IV22 2SY
01445 781268
- **e-mail: croftcottages@btopenworld.com**
- **website: www.scotia-sc.com/335a.htm**

Hotel
Mrs Campbell, Rhiconich Hotel, RHICONICH, by Lairg, Sutherland IV27 4RN
01971 521224
- **e-mail: rhiconichhotel@aol.com**
- **website: www.rhiconichhotel.co.uk**

B & B
Jean Wilson, Tirindrish House, SPEAN BRIDGE, Inverness-shire PH34 4EU
01397 712398
- **e-mail: wpeterwilson@aol.com**
- **website: www.tirindrish.com**

Hotel
Borgie Lodge Hotel, Skerray, TONGUE, Sutherland KW14 7TH
01641 521332
- **e-mail: peter@borgielodgehotel.co.uk**
- **website: www.borgielodgehotel.co.uk**

Self-Catering
Wildside Highland Lodges, By Loch Ness, WHITEBRIDGE, Inverness-shire IV2 6UN
01456 486373
- **e-mail: info@wildsidelodges.com**
- **website: www.wildsidelodges.com**

•LANARKSHIRE

Self-Catering
Carmichael Country Cottages, Carmichael Estate Office, Westmains, Carmichael, BIGGAR, Lanarkshire ML12 6PG
01899 308336
- **e-mail: chiefcarm@aol.com**
- **website: www.carmichael.co.uk/cottages**

•PERTH & KINROSS

Self-Catering
Loch Tay Lodges, Acharn, by ABERFELDY, Perthshire
01887 830209
- **e-mail: remony@btinternet.com**
- **website: www.lochtaylodges.co.uk**

Hotel / Self-Catering
Dalmunzie House Hotel, Spittal of Glenshee, BLAIRGOWRIE, Perthshire PH10 7QG
01250 885224
- **e-mail: dalmunzie@aol.com**
- **website: www.dalmunzie.com**

Hotel
Atholl Arms Hotel, Bridgehead, DUNKELD, Perthshire PH8 0AQ
01350 727219
- **e-mail: enquiries@athollarmshotel.com**
- **website: www.athollarmshotel.com**

Self-Catering
Laighwood Holidays, Laighwood, Butterstone, By DUNKELD, Perthshire PH8 0HB
01350 724241
- **e-mail: holidays@laighwood.co.uk**
- **website: www.laighwood.co.uk**

Self Catering
Mrs Hunt, Wester Lix Holiday Cottages, Wester Lix, KILLIN, Perthshire FK21 8RD
01567 820990
- **e-mail: gill@westerlix.co.uk**
- **website: www.westerlix.co.uk**

B & B
Mrs P. Honeyman, Auld Manse Guest House, Pitcullen Crescent, PERTH, Perthshire PH2 7HT
01738 629187
- **e-mail: trishaatauldmanse@hotmail.com**
- **website: www.guesthouseperth.com**

Hotel
Balrobin Hotel, Higher Oakfield, PITLOCHRY, Pethshire PH16 5HT
01796 472901
- **e-mail: info@balrobin.co.uk**
- **website: www.balrobin.co.uk**

Guest House
Jacky Catterall, Tulloch Enochdhu, by PITLOCHRY, Perthshire PH10 7PW
01250 881404
- **e-mail: maljac@tulloch83.freeserve.co.uk**
- **website: www.econet.org.uk/tulloch**

B & B / Camping (wigwam)
Mrs Ann Guthrie, Newmill Farm, STANLEY, Perth, Perthshire PH1 4QD
01738 828281
- **e-mail: guthrienewmill@sol.co.uk**
- **website: www.newmillfarm.co.uk**

•STIRLING & TROSSACHS

B & B
Mrs Judith Bennett, Mossgiel, Doune Road, DUNBLANE, Stirlingshire
01786 824325
- **e-mail: mossgeil2000@yahoo.co.uk**
- **website: www.mossgiel.com**

•ISLE OF SKYE

Self-Catering
Cottage in HARLOSH, c/o Mrs I. MacDiarmid, 21 Dunrobin Avenue, ELDERSLIE, Renfrewshire PA5 9NW
01505 324460
- **e-mail: irenemacdairmid@yahoo.co.uk**
- **website: www.skyecroft.co.uk**

Guest House / B & B
Fiona Scott, Blairdhu House, Old Kyle Farm Road, KYLEAKIN, Isle of Skye IV41 8PR
01599 534760
- **e-mail: blairdhuskye@compuserve.com**
- **website: www.blairdhuhouse.co.uk**

FREE or REDUCED RATE
entry to Holiday Visits and Attractions
see our
READERS' OFFER VOUCHERS
on pages 55-82

•WALES

Self-Catering
Quality Cottages, Cerbid, Solva, HAVERFORDWEST, Pembrokeshire SA62 6YE
01348 837871
- **website: www.qualitycottages.co.uk**

•ANGLESEY & GWYNEDD

B & B
Mrs M. Billingham, Preswylfa, ABERDOVEY, Gwynedd LL35 0LE
01654 767239
- **e-mail: info@preswylfa.co.uk**
- **website: www.preswylfa.co.uk**

B & B
Mrs J. Bown, Drws-y-Coed, Llannerch-y-medd, ANGLESEY LL71 8AD
01248 470473
- **e-mail: drws.ycoed@virgin.net**
- **website: www.SmoothHound.co.uk/hotels/drwsycoed.html**

Self-Catering / Caravan
Plas y Bryn Chalet Park, Bontnewydd, CAERNARFON, Gwynedd LL54 7YE
01286 672811
- **e-mail: philplasybryn@aol.com**
- **website: www.plasybrynholidayscaernarfon.co.uk**

Self-Catering within a Castle
Bryn Bras Castle, Llanrug, near CAERNARFON Gwynedd LL55 4RE
01286 870210
- **e-mail: holidays@brynbrascastle.co.uk**
- **website: www.brynbrascastle.co.uk**

Guest House
Mrs Manya Ann Parker, Seaspray, 4 Marine Terrace, CRICCIETH, Gwynedd LL52 0EF
01766 522373
- **website: www.seasprayguesthouse.co.uk**

Self-Catering
Anwen Jones, Rhos Country Cottages, Betws Bach, Ynys, CRICCIETH, Gwynedd LL52 0PB
01758 720047
- **e-mail: cottages@rhos.freeserve.co.uk**
- **website: www.rhos-cottages.co.uk**

B & B
Mrs G. McCreadie, Deri Isaf, DULAS BAY, Anglesey LL70 9DX
01248 410536
- **e-mail: mccreadie@deriisaf.freeserve.co.uk**
- **website: www.deriisaf.freeserve.co.uk**

Farm B & B
Judy Hutchings, Tal y Foel, DWYRAN, Anglesey, Gwynedd LL61 6LQ
01248 430377
- **e-mail: hutchings@talyfoel.u-net.com**
- **website: www.tal-y-foel.co.uk**

Caravan & Chalet Park
Catherine Jones, Wernol Caravan & Chalet Park, Chwilog, PWLLHELI, Gwynedd LL53 6SW
01766 810506
- **website: www.wernol.com**

•NORTH WALES

Guest House
Mr M. Wilkie, Bryn Bella Guest House, Llanrwst Road, BETWS-Y-COED, Gwynedd LL24 0HD
01690 710627
- **e-mail: brynbella@clara.net**
- **website: www.bryn-bella.co.uk**

Guest House / Self-Catering
Jim & Lilian Boughton, Bron Celyn Guest House, Lôn Muriau, Llanrwst Road, BETWS-Y-COED North Wales LL24 0HD
01690 710333
- **e-mail: welcome@broncelyn.co.uk**
- **website: www.broncelyn.co.uk**

Hotel
Fairy Glen Hotel, Dolwyddelan Road, BETWS-Y-COED, Conwy, North Wales LL24 0SH
01690 710269
- **e-mail: fairyglenhotel@amserve.net**
- **website: www.fairyglenhotel.co.uk**

B & B
Christine Whale, Brookside House, Brookside Lane, Northop Hall, near CHESTER CH7 4HN
01244 821146
- **e-mail: christine@brooksidehouse.fsnet.co.uk**
- **website: www.brooksidehouse.fsnet.co.uk/**

Hotel
Caerlyr Hall Hotel, Conwy Old Road, Dwygfylchi, CONWY, North Wales LL34 6SW
01492 623518
- **website: www.caerlyrhallhotel.co.uk**

Hotel
Castle Bank Hotel & Licensed Restaurant, Mount Pleasant, CONWY, North Wales LL32 2NY
01492 593888
- **e-mail: contact@castle-bank.co.uk**
- **website: www.castle-bank.co.uk**

Hotel
Golden Pheasant Hotel, Glyn Ceiriog, near LLANGOLLEN, North Wales LL20 7BB
01691 718281
- **e-mail: goldenpheasant@micro-plus**
- **website: www.goldenpheasanthotel.co.uk**

B & B
Pen-y-Dyffryn Country House Hotel, near Rhydycroesau, OSWESTRY, North Wales SY10 7JD
01691 653700
- **e-mail: stay@peny.co.uk**
- **website: www.peny.co.uk**

Hotel
Hafod Country Hotel, TREFRIW, North Wales LL27 0RQ
01492 640029
- **e-mail: hafod@breathemail.net**
- **website: www.hafodhouse.co.uk**

• CARMARTHENSHIRE

B & B
Miss S Czerniewicz, Pant y Bas, Pentrefelin, LLANDEILO, Carmarthenshire, SA19 6SD
01558 822809
- **e-mail: anna@pantybas.fsnet.co.uk**
- **website: www.southwestwalesbandb.co.uk**

• CEREDIGION

Self-Catering
Mr Tucker, Penffynnon, ABERPORTH, Ceredigion SA43 2DA
01239 810387
- **e-mail: tt@lineone.net**
  or: jann@aberporth.com
- **website: www.aberporth.com**

• PEMBROKESHIRE

Self-Catering
John Lloyd, East Llanteg Farm Holiday Cottages, Llanteg, near AMROTH, Pembrokeshire SA67 8QA
01834 831336
- **e-mail: john@pembrokeshireholiday.co.uk**
- **website: www.pembrokeshireholiday.co.uk**

B & B
Sandra Davies, Barley Villa, Walwyns Castle, near BROADHAVEN, Haverfordwest, Pembrokeshire SA62 3EB
01437 781254
- **e-mail: sandra.barleyvilla@btinternet.com**
- **website: www.barleyvilla.co.uk**

Farm B & B
Mrs Margaret Williams, Skerryback, Sandy Haven, St Ishmaels, HAVERFORDWEST, Pembrokeshire SA62 3DN
01646 636598
- **e-mail: williams@farmersweekly.net**
- **website: www.pfh.co.uk/skerryback**

Guest House
Mrs Sandra J. Thompson, Ramsey House, Lower Moor, ST DAVIDS, Pembrokeshire SA62 6RP
01437 720321
- **e-mail: info@ramseyhouse.co.uk**
- **website: www.ramseyhouse.co.uk**

Self-Catering
Lower Moor Cottages, c/o Thelma M Hardman, High View, Catherine Street, ST DAVID'S, Pembrokeshire SA62 6RJ
01437 720616
- **e-mail: enquiries@lowermoorcottages.co.uk**
- **website: www.lowermoorcottages.co.uk**

Farm Guest House
Mrs Morfydd Jones, Lochmeyler Farm Guest House, Llandeloy, Pen-y-Cwm, near SOLVA, St David's, Pembrokeshire SA62 6LL
01348 837724
• **e-mail: stay@lochmeyler.co.uk**
• **website: www.lochmeyler.co.uk**

B & B
Mrs J. S Rees, Pen Mar Hotel, New Hedges, TENBY, Pembrokeshire SA70 8TL
01834 842435
• **e-mail: penmarhotel@jhurton.freeserve.co.uk**

•POWYS

B & B / Self-Catering
Laura Kostoris, Erw yr Danty, Talybont-on-Usk, BRECON, Powys LD3 7YN
01874 676498
• **e-mail: kosto@ukonline.co.uk**
• **website: www.wiz.to/lifestyle/**

Farm
Mrs Ann Phillips, Tylebrythos Farm, Cantref, BRECON, Powys LD3 8LR
01874 665329
• **e-mail: sa.phillips@ukonline.co.uk**

Motel / Caravans
The Park Motel, Crossgates, LLANDRINDOD WELLS, Powys LD1 6RF
01597 851201
• **e-mail: lisa@theparkmotel.freeserve.co.uk**
• **website: www.theparkmotel.freeserve.co.uk**

•SOUTH WALES

Self-Catering
John & Sue Llewellyn, Cwrt-y-Gaer, Wolvesnewton, CHEPSTOW, Monmouthshire NP16 6PR
01291 650700
• **e-mail: john.ll@talk21.com**
• **website: www.cwrt-y-gaer.co.uk**

Hotel
Mark Cottell, Culver House Hotel, Port Eynon, GOWER, Swansea, South Wales SA3 1NN
01792 390755
• **e-mail: info@culverhousehotel.co.uk**
• **website: www.culverhousehotel.co.uk**

Guest House
Green Lanterns Guest House, Hawdref Ganol Farm, Cimla, NEATH, South Wales SA12 9SL
01639 631884
• **e-mail: caren.jones@btinternet.com**
• **website: www.thegreenlanterns.co.uk**

Hotel & Inn
Michael J. Thomas, The Inn at the Elm Tree, St Brides, Wentlooge, NEWPORT, South Wales
01633 680225
• **e-mail: inn@the-elm-tree.co.uk**
• **website: www.the-elm-tree.co.uk**

•IRELAND

Co. Donegal

B & B / Guest House
Nuala Duddy, Pennsylvania House B & B, Curraghleas, Mountain Top, LETTERKENNY, Co Donegal
00-353-74-26808
• **e-mail: pennsylvania.house@indigo.ie**
• **website: www.accommodationdonegal.com**

Index of towns and counties.
Please also refer to Contents pages 50-51

Readers are requested to mention this guidebook when seeking accommodation (and please enclose a stamped addressed envelope).

OTHER FHG TITLES FOR 2003

FHG Publications have a large range of attractive holiday accommodation guides for all kinds of holiday opportunities throughout Britain. They also make useful gifts at any time of year. Our guides are available in most bookshops and larger newsagents but we will be happy to post you a copy direct if you have any difficulty. POST FREE for addresses in the UK. We will also post abroad but have to charge separately for post or freight.

SELF-CATERING HOLIDAYS
in Britain
Over 1000 addresses throughout for self-catering and caravans in Britain.

BED AND BREAKFAST STOPS
Over 1000 friendly and comfortable overnight stops. Non-smoking, Disabled and Special Diets Supplements.

BRITAIN'S BEST HOLIDAYS
A quick-reference general guide for all kinds of holidays.

Recommended
WAYSIDE AND COUNTRY INNS of Britain
Pubs, Inns and small hotels.

Recommended
SHORT BREAK HOLIDAYS IN BRITAIN
"Approved" accommodation for quality bargain breaks.

PETS WELCOME!
The original and unique guide for holidays for pet owners and their pets.

CHILDREN WELCOME!
Family Holidays and Days Out guide.
Family holidays with details of amenities for children and babies.

☐

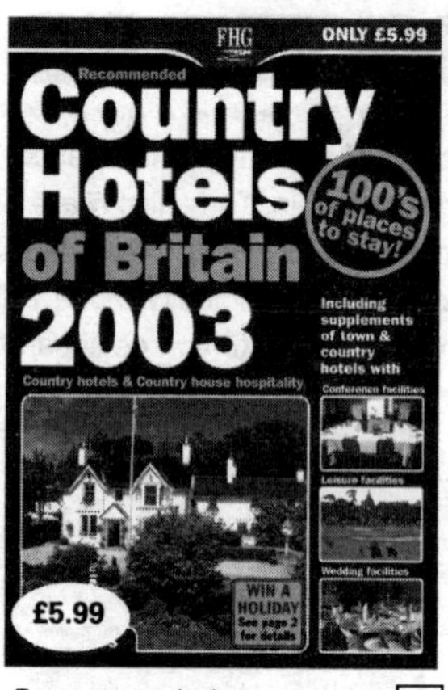

Recommended
COUNTRY HOTELS OF BRITAIN
including Country Houses, for the discriminating.

☐

The GOLF GUIDE –
Where to play Where to stay
In association with GOLF MONTHLY. Over 2800 golf courses in Britain with convenient accommodation. Holiday Golf in France, Portugal, Spain,USA, South Africa and Thailand.

☐

The FHG Guide to **CARAVAN & CAMPING HOLIDAYS,** £4.49
Caravans for hire, sites and holiday parks and centres. ☐

Tick your choice and send your order and payment to

FHG PUBLICATIONS, ABBEY MILL BUSINESS CENTRE,
SEEDHILL, PAISLEY PA1 1TJ
TEL: 0141- 887 0428; FAX: 0141- 889 7204
e-mail: fhg@ipcmedia.com

FHG

Deduct 10% for 2/3 titles or copies; 20% for 4 or more.

Send to: NAME ....

ADDRESS ....

....

....

POST CODE ....

I enclose Cheque/Postal Order for £ ....

SIGNATURE.....................................DATE ....

Please complete the following to help us improve the service we provide. How did you find out about our guides?:

☐ Press ☐ Magazines ☐ TV/Radio ☐ Family/Friend ☐ Other

CONTENTS

NATHANIEL HAWTHORNE

Nathaniel Hawthorne was born in Salem, Massachusetts, USA in 1804. Between 1821 and 1824, he attended Bowdoin College in Brunswick, Maine, along with fellow poet Henry Wadsworth Longfellow and future American President Franklin Pierce. A shy, bookish youth, Hawthorne was writing from a young age, and published his first novel, *Fanshawe,* in 1828. Over the next ten years, he attempted to become a professional writer, supplementing his earnings with a job as a Boston Custom House measurer. In 1842, he married Sophia Peabody and moved to The Manse in Concord, the epicentre of the burgeoning Transcendentalist movement.

Hawthorne's collection of short stories *Mosses from an Old Manse* was published in 1846, and four years later, he published his labour of love, the novel *The Scarlet Letter.* An immediate success, the novel remains widely read to this day, and allowed Hawthorne to devote himself full-time to his writing. Over the rest of his life, he produced six more novels, and a large amount of short stories. Aside from *The Scarlet Letter,* his best-known novel is probably *The Marble Faun,* and his best-remembered short stories include 'My

Kinsman', 'Major Molineux', 'Young Goodman Browne' and 'Feathertop'.

Hawthorne died in 1864, following a long period of illness which included bouts of dementia. Though Hawthorne himself was perpetually dissatisfied with his body of work, he remains lauded as one of the greatest American writers, and *The Scarlet Letter* remains a standard school text in the USA. In 1879, Henry James called Hawthorne "the most valuable example of the American genius."

THE CHRISTMAS BANQUET

Nathaniel Hawthorne

'I have here attempted,' said Roderick, unfolding a few sheets of manuscript, as he sat with Rosina and the sculptor in the summer-house – 'I have attempted to seize hold of a personage who glides past me, occasionally, in my walk through life. My former sad experience, as you know, has gifted me with some degree of insight into the gloomy mysteries of the human heart, through which I have wandered like one astray in a dark cavern, with his torch fast flickering to extinction. But this man, this class of men, is a hopeless puzzle.'

'Well, but propound him,' said the sculptor. 'Let us have an idea of him, to begin with.'

'Why, indeed,' replied Roderick, 'he is such a being as I could conceive you to carve out of marble, and some yet unrealized perfection of human science to endow with an exquisite mockery of intellect; but still there lacks the last inestimable touch of a divine Creator. He looks like a man;

and, perchance, like a better specimen of man than you ordinarily meet. You might esteem him wise; he is capable of cultivation and refinement, and has at least an external conscience; but the demands that spirit makes upon spirit are precisely those to which he cannot respond. When at last you come close to him you find him chill and unsubstantial – a mere vapour.'

'I believe,' said Rosina, 'I have a glimmering idea of what you mean.'

'Then be thankful,' answered her husband, smiling; 'but do not anticipate any further illumination from what I am about to read. I have here imagined such a man to be – what, probably, he never is – conscious of the deficiency in his spiritual organization. Methinks the result would be a sense of cold unreality wherewith he would go shivering through the world, longing to exchange his load of ice for any burden of real grief that fate could fling upon a human being.'

Contenting himself with this preface, Roderick began to read.

In a certain old gentleman's last will and testament there appeared a bequest, which, as his final thought and deed, was singularly in keeping with a long life of melancholy eccentricity. He devised a considerable sum for establishing a fund, the interest of which was to be expended, annually, forever, in preparing a Christmas Banquet for ten of the most miserable persons that could be found. It seemed not to be the testator's purpose to make these half a score of sad hearts merry, but to provide that the stern or fierce expression of human discontent should not be. drowned, even for that one holy and joyful day, amid the acclamations of festal gratitude which all Christendom sends up. And he desired, likewise, to perpetuate his own remonstrance against the earthly course of Providence, and his sad and sour dissent from those systems of religion or philosophy which either find sunshine in the world or draw it down from heaven.

The task of inviting the guests, or of selecting among such as might advance their claims to partake of this dismal hospitality, was confided to the two trustees or stewards of the fund. These gentlemen, like their deceased friend, were sombre humourists, who made it their principal occupation to number the sable threads in the web of human life, and drop all the golden ones out of the reckoning. They performed their present office with integrity and judgement. The aspect of the assembled company, on the day of the first festival, might not, it is true, have satisfied every beholder that these were especially the individuals, chosen forth from all the world, whose griefs were worthy to stand as indicators of the mass of human suffering. Yet, after due consideration, it could not be disputed that here was a variety of hopeless discomfort, which, if it sometimes arose from causes apparently inadequate, was thereby only the shrewder imputation against the nature and mechanism of life.

The arrangements and decorations of the banquet were probably intended to signify that death in life which had been the testator's definition of existence. The hall, illuminated by torches, was hung round with curtains of deep and dusky purple, and adorned with branches of cypress and wreaths of artificial flowers, imitative of such as used to be strewn over the dead. A sprig of parsley was laid by every plate. The main reservoir of wine was a sepulchral urn of silver, whence the liquor was distributed around the table in small vases, accurately copied from those that held the tears of ancient mourners. Neither had the stewards – if it were their taste that arranged these details – forgotten the fantasy of the old Egyptians, who seated a skeleton at every festive board, and mocked their own merriment with the imperturbable grin of a death's head. Such a fearful guest, shrouded in a black mantle, sat now at the head of the table. It was whispered, I know not with what truth, that the testator himself had once walked the visible world with the machinery of that same skeleton, and that it was one of the stipulations of his will, that he should thus be permitted to sit, from year to year, at the banquet which he had instituted. If so, it was perhaps covertly implied that he had cherished no hopes of bliss beyond the grave to compensate for the evils which he felt or imagined here. And if, in their bewildered conjectures as to the purpose of earthly existence, the banqueters should throw aside the veil, and cast an inquiring glance at this figure of death, as seeking thence the solution otherwise unattainable, the only reply would be a stare of the vacant eye caverns and a grin of the skeleton jaws. Such was the response that the dead man had fancied himself to receive when he asked of Death to solve the riddle of his life; and it was his desire to repeat it when the guests of his dismal hospitality should find themselves perplexed with the same question.

'What means that wreath?' asked several of the company, while viewing the decorations of the table.

They alluded to a wreath of cypress, which was held on high by a skeleton arm, protruding from within the black mantle.

'It is a crown,' said one of the stewards, 'not for the worthiest, but for the woefullest, when he shall prove his claim to it.'

The guest earliest bidden to the festival was a man of soft and gentle character, who had not energy to struggle against the heavy despondency to which his temperament rendered him liable; and therefore with nothing outwardly to excuse him from happiness, he had spent a life of quiet misery that made his blood torpid, and weighed upon his breath, and sat like a ponderous night fiend upon every throb of his unresisting heart. His wretchedness seemed as deep as his original nature, if not identical with it. It was the misfortune of a second guest to cherish within his bosom a diseased heart, which had become so wretchedly sore that the continual and unavoidable rubs of the world, the blow of an enemy, the careless jostle of a stranger, and even the faithful and loving touch of a friend, alike made ulcers in it. As is the habit of people thus afflicted, he found his chief employment in exhibiting these miserable sores to any who would give themselves the pain of viewing them. A third guest was a hypochondriac, whose imagination wrought necromancy in his outward and inward world, and caused him to see monstrous faces in the household fire, and dragons in the clouds of sunset, and fiends in the guise of beautiful women, and something ugly or wicked beneath all the pleasant surfaces of nature. His neighbour at table was one who, in his early youth, had trusted mankind too much, and hoped too highly in their behalf, and, in meeting with many disappointments, had become desperately soured. For several years back this misanthrope had employed himself in accumulating motives for hating and despising his race – such as murder, lust, treachery, ingratitude, faithlessness of trusted friends, instinctive vices of children, impurity of women, hidden guilt in men of saintlike aspect – and, in short, all manner of black realities that sought to decorate themselves with outward grace or glory. But at every atrocious fact that was added to his catalogue, at every increase of the sad knowledge which he spent his life to collect, the native impulses of the poor man's loving and confiding heart made him groan with anguish. Next, with his heavy brow bent downward, there stole into the hall a man naturally earnest and impassioned, who, from his immemorial infancy, had felt the consciousness of a high message to the world; but essaying to deliver it, had found either no voice or form of speech, or else no ears to listen. Therefore his whole life was a bitter questioning of himself – 'Why have not men acknowledged my mission? Am I not a self-deluding fool? What business have I on earth? Where is my grave?' Throughout the festival, he quaffed frequent draughts from the sepulchral urn of wine, hoping thus to quench the celestial fire that tortured his own breast and could not benefit his race.

Then there entered, having flung away a ticket for a ball, a gay gallant of yesterday, who had found four or five wrinkles in his brow, and more grey hairs than he could well number on his head. Endowed with sense and feeling, he had nevertheless spent his youth in folly, but had reached at last that dreary point in life where Folly quits us of her own accord, leaving us to make friends of Wisdom if we can.

Thus, cold and desolate, he had come to seek Wisdom at the banquet, and wondered if the skeleton were she. To eke out the company, the stewards had invited a distressed poet from his home in the almshouse, and a melancholy idiot from the street corner. The latter had just the glimmering of sense that was sufficient to make him conscious of a vacancy, which the poor fellow, all his life long, had mistily sought to fill up with intelligence, wandering up and down the streets, and groaning miserably because his attempts were ineffectual. The only lady in the hall was one who had fallen short of absolute and perfect beauty, merely by the trifling defect of a slight cast in her left eye. But this blemish, minute as it was, so shocked the pure ideal of her soul, rather than her vanity, that she passed her life in solitude, and veiled her countenance even from her own gaze. So the skeleton sat shrouded at one end of the table and this poor lady at the other.

One other guest remains to be described. He was a young man of smooth brow, fair cheek, and fashionable mien. So far as his exterior developed him, he might much more suitably have found a place at some merry Christmas table, than have been numbered among the blighted, fate-stricken, fancy-tortured set of ill-starred banqueters. Murmurs arose among the guests as they noted the glance of general scrutiny which the intruder threw over his companions. What had he to do among them? Why did not the skeleton of the dead founder of the feast unbend its rattling joints, arise, and motion the unwelcome stranger from the board?

'Shameful!' said the morbid man, while a new ulcer broke out in his heart. 'He comes to mock us! – we shall be the jest of his tavern friends! – he will make a farce of our miseries, and bring it out upon the stage!'

'O, never mind him!' said the hypochondriac, smiling sourly. 'He shall feast from yonder tureen of viper soup; and if there is a fricassee of scorpions on the table, pray let him have his share of it. For the dessert, he shall taste the apples of Sodom. Then, if he like our Christmas fare, let him return again next year!'

'Trouble him not,' murmured the melancholy man, with gentleness. 'What matters it whether the consciousness of misery comes a few years sooner or later? If this youth deem himself happy now, yet let him sit with us for the sake of the wretchedness to come.'

The poor idiot approached the young man with that mournful aspect of vacant inquiry which his face continually wore, and which caused people to say that he was always in search of his missing wits. After no little examination he touched the stranger's hand, but immediately drew back his own, shaking his head and shivering.

'Cold, cold, cold!' muttered the idiot.

The young man shivered too, and smiled.

'Gentlemen – and you, madam,' – said one of the stewards of the festival, 'do not conceive so ill either of our caution or judgement, as to imagine that we have admitted this young stranger – Gervayse Hastings by name – without a full investigation and thoughtful balance of his claims. Trust me, not a guest at the table is better entitled to his seat.'

The steward's guarantee was perforce satisfactory. The company, therefore, took their places, and addressed themselves to the serious business of the feast, but were soon disturbed by the hypochondriac, who thrust back his chair, complaining that a dish of stewed toads and vipers was set before him, and that there was green ditch water in his cup of wine. This mistake being amended, he quietly resumed his seat. The wine, as it flowed freely from the sepulchral urn, seemed to come imbued with all gloomy inspirations; so that its influence was not to cheer, but either to sink the revellers into a deeper melancholy, or elevate their spirits to an enthusiasm of wretchedness. The conversation was various. They told sad stories about people who might have been worthy guests at such a festival as the present. They talked of grisly incidents in human history; of strange crimes, which, if truly considered, were but convulsions of agony; of some lives that had been altogether wretched, and of others, which, wearing a general semblance of happiness, had yet been deformed, sooner or later, by misfortune, as by the intrusion of a grim face at a banquet; of death-bed scenes, and what dark intimations might be gathered from the words of dying men; of suicide, and whether the more eligible modes were by halter, knife, poison, drowning, gradual starvation, or the fumes of charcoal. The majority of the guests, as is the custom with people thoroughly and profoundly sick at heart, were anxious to make their own woes the theme of discussion, and prove themselves most excellent in anguish. The misanthropist went deep into the philosophy of evil, and wandered about in the darkness, with now and then a gleam of discoloured light hovering on ghastly shapes and horrid scenery. Many a miserable thought, such as men have stumbled upon from age to age, did he now rake up again, and gloat over it as an inestimable gem, a diamond, a treasure far preferable to those bright, spiritual revelations of a better world, which are like precious stones from heaven's pavement. And then, amid his lore of wretchedness, he hid his face and wept.

It was a festival at which the woeful man of Uz might suitably have been a guest, together with all, in each succeeding age, who have tasted deepest of the bitterness of life. And be it said, too, that every son or daughter of woman, however favoured with happy fortune, might, at one sad moment or another, have claimed the privilege of a stricken heart, to sit down at this table. But, throughout the feast, it was remarked that the young stranger, Gervayse Hastings, was unsuccessful in his attempts to catch its pervading spirit. At any deep, strong thought that found utterance, and which was torn out, as it were, from the saddest recesses of human consciousness, he looked mystified and bewildered; even more than the poor idiot, who seemed to grasp at such things with his earnest heart, and thus occasionally to comprehend them. The young man's conversation was of a colder and lighter kind, often brilliant, but lacking the powerful characteristics of a nature that had been developed by suffering.

'Sir,' said the misanthropist bluntly, in reply to some observation by Gervayse Hastings, 'pray do not address me again. We have no right to talk together. Our minds have nothing in common. By what claim you appear at this banquet I cannot guess; but methinks, to a man who could say what you have just now said, my companions and myself must seem no more than shadows flickering on the wall. And precisely such a shadow are you to us.'

The young man smiled and bowed, but drawing himself back in his chair, he buttoned his coat over his breast, as if the banqueting hall were growing chill. Again the idiot fixed his melancholy stare upon the youth, and murmured, 'Cold! cold! cold!'

The banquet drew to its conclusion, and the guests

departed. Scarcely had they stepped across the threshold of the hall when the scene that had there passed seemed like the vision of a sick fancy, or an exhalation from a stagnant heart. Now and then, however, during the year that ensued, these melancholy people caught glimpses of one another, transient, indeed, but enough to prove that they walked the earth with the ordinary allotment of reality. Sometimes a pair of them came face to face while stealing through the evening twilight, enveloped in their sable cloaks. Sometimes they casually met in churchyards. Once, also, it happened that two of the dismal banqueters mutually started at recognizing each other in the noonday sunshine of a crowded street, stalking there like ghosts astray. Doubtless they wondered why the skeleton did not come abroad at noonday too.

But whenever the necessity of their affairs compelled these Christmas guests into the bustling world, they were sure to encounter the young man who had so unaccountably been admitted to the festival. They saw him among the gay and fortunate; they caught the sunny sparkle of his eye; they heard the light and careless tones of his voice, and muttered to themselves with such indignation as only the aristocracy of wretchedness could kindle – 'The traitor! The vile imposter! Providence, in its own good time, may give him a right to feast among us!' But the young man's unabashed eye dwelt upon their gloomy figures as they passed him, seeming to say, perchance with somewhat of a sneer, 'First, know my secret! – then measure your claims with mine!'

The step of Time stole onward, and soon brought merry Christmas round again, with glad and solemn worship in the churches, and sports, games, festivals, and everywhere the bright face of Joy beside the household fire. Again, likewise, the hall, with its curtains of dusky purple, was illuminated by the death torches gleaming on the sepulchral decorations of the banquet. The veiled skeleton sat in state, lifting the cypress wreath above its head, as the guerdon of some guest illustrious in the qualifications which there claimed precedence. As the stewards deemed the world inexhaustible in misery, and were desirous of recognizing it in all its forms, they had not seen fit to reassemble the company of the former year. New faces now threw their gloom across the table.

There was a man of nice conscience, who bore a blood stain in his heart – the death of a fellow-creature – which, for his more exquisite torture, had chanced with such a peculiarity of circumstances, that he could not absolutely determine whether his will had entered into the deed or not. Therefore, his whole life was spent in the agony of an inward trial for murder, with a continual sifting of the details of his terrible calamity, until his mind had no longer any thought, nor his soul any emotion, disconnected with it. There was a mother, too – a mother once, but a desolation now – who, many years before, had gone out on a pleasure party, and, returning, found her infant smothered in its little bed. And ever since she has been tortured with the fantasy that her buried baby lay smothering in its coffin. Then there was an aged lady, who had lived from time immemorial with a constant tremor quivering through her frame. It was terrible to discern her dark shadow tremulous upon the wall; her lips, likewise, were tremulous; and the expression of her eye seemed to indicate that her soul was trembling too. Owing to the bewilderment and confusion which made almost a chaos of her intellect, it was impossible to discover what dire misfortune had thus shaken her nature to its depths; so that the stewards had admitted her to the table, not from any acquaintance with her history, but on the safe testimony of her miserable aspect. Some surprise was expressed at the presence of a bluff, red-faced gentleman, a certain Mr Smith, who had evidently the fat of many a rich feast within him, and the habitual twinkle of whose eye betrayed a disposition to break forth into uproarious laughter for little cause or none. It turned out, however, that with the best possible flow of spirits, our poor friend was afflicted with a physical disease of the heart, which threatened instant death on the slightest cachinnatory indulgence, or even that titillation of the bodily frame produced by merry thoughts. In this dilemma he had sought admittance to the banquet, on the ostensible plea of his irksome and miserable state, but, in reality, with the hope of imbibing a life-preserving melancholy.

A married couple had been invited from a motive of bitter humour, it being well understood that they rendered each other unutterably miserable whenever they chanced to meet, and therefore must necessarily be fit associates at the festival. In contrast with these was another couple still unmarried, who had interchanged their hearts in early life, but had been divided by circumstances as unpalpable as morning mist, and kept apart so long that their spirits now found it impossible to meet. Therefore, yearning for communion, yet shrinking from one another and choosing none beside, they felt themselves companionless in life, and looked upon eternity as a boundless desert. Next to the skeleton sat a mere son of earth – a hunter of the Exchange – a gatherer of shining dust – a man whose life's record was in his ledger, and whose soul's prison-house the vaults of the bank where he kept his deposits. This person had been greatly perplexed at his invitation, deeming himself one of the most fortunate men in the city; but the stewards persisted in demanding his presence, assuring him that he had no conception how miserable he was.

And now appeared a figure which we must acknowledge as our acquaintance of the former festival. It was Gervayse Hastings, whose presence had then caused so much question and criticism, and who now took his place with the composure of one whose claims were satisfactory to himself, and must needs be allowed by others. Yet his easy and unruffled face betrayed no sorrow. The well-skilled beholders gazed a moment into his eyes and shook their heads, to miss the unuttered sympathy – the countersign, never to be falsified – of those whose hearts are cavern mouths, through which they descend into a region of illimitable woe, and recognize other wanderers there.

'Who is this youth?' asked the man with a blood stain on his conscience. 'Surely he has never gone down into the depths! I know all the aspects of those who have passed through the dark valley. By what right is he among us?'

'Ah, it is a sinful thing to come hither without a sorrow,' murmured the aged lady, in accents that partook of the eternal tremor which pervaded her whole being. 'Depart, young man! Your soul has never been shaken; and, therefore, I tremble so much the more to look at you.'

'His soul shaken! No; I'll answer for it,' said bluff Mr Smith, pressing his hand upon his heart, and making himself as melancholy as he could, for fear of a fatal explosion of laughter. 'I know the lad well; he has as fair prospects as any young man about town, and has no more right among us miserable creatures than the child unborn. He never was miserable, and probably never will be!'

'Our honoured guests,' interposed the stewards, 'pray have patience with us, and believe, at least, that our deep veneration for the sacredness of this solemnity would preclude any wilful violation of it. Receive this young man to your table. It may not be too much to say that no guest here would exchange his own heart for the one that beats within that youthful bosom!'

'I'd call it a bargain, and gladly, too,' muttered Mr Smith, with a perplexing mixture of sadness and mirthful conceit. 'A plague upon their nonsense! My own heart is the only really miserable one in the company; it will certainly be the death of me at last!'

Nevertheless, as on the former occasion, the judgement of the stewards being without appeal, the company sat down. The obnoxious guest made no more attempt to obtrude his conversation on those about him, but appeared to listen to the table-talk with peculiar assiduity, as if some inestimable secret, otherwise beyond his reach, might be conveyed in a casual word. And in truth, to those who could understand and value it, there was rich matter in the upgushings and outpourings of these initiated souls to whom sorrow had been a talisman, admitting them into spiritual depths which no other spell can open. Sometimes out of the midst of densest gloom there flashed a momentary radiance, pure as crystal, bright as the flame of stars, and shedding such a glow upon the mysteries of life that the guests were ready to exclaim, 'Surely the riddle is on the point of being solved!' At such illuminated intervals the saddest mourners felt it to be revealed that mortal griefs are but shadowy and external; no more than the sable robes voluminously shrouding a certain divine reality, and thus indicating what might otherwise be altogether invisible to mortal eye.

'Just now,' remarked the trembling old woman, 'I seemed to see beyond the outside. And then my everlasting tremor passed away!'

'Would that I could dwell always in these momentary gleams of light!' said the man of stricken conscience. 'Then the blood stain in my heart would be washed clean away.'

This strain of conversation appeared so unintelligibly absurd to good Mr Smith, that he burst into precisely the fit of laughter which his physicians had warned him against, as likely to prove instantaneously fatal. In effect, he fell back in his chair a corpse, with a broad grin upon his face, while his ghost, perchance, remained beside it bewildered at its unpremeditated exit. This catastrophe of course broke up the festival.

'How is this? You do not tremble?' observed the tremulous old woman to Gervayse Hastings, who was gazing at the dead man with singular intentness. 'Is it not awful to see him so suddenly vanish out of the midst of life – this man of flesh and blood, whose earthly nature was so warm and strong? There is a never-ending tremor in my soul, but it trembles afresh at this! And you are calm!'

'Would that he could teach me somewhat!' said Gervayse Hastings, drawing a long breath. 'Men pass before me like shadows on the wall; their actions, passions, feelings, are flickerings of the light, and then they vanish! Neither the corpse, nor yonder skeleton, nor this old woman's everlasting tremor, can give me what I seek.'

And then the company departed.

We cannot linger to narrate, in such detail, more circumstances of these singular festivals, which, in accordance with the founder's will, continued to be kept with the regularity of an established institution. In process of time the stewards adopted the custom of inviting, from far and near, those individuals whose misfortunes were prominent above other men's, and whose mental and moral development might, therefore, be supposed to possess a corresponding interest. The exiled noble of the French Revolution, and the broken soldier of the Empire, were alike represented at the table. Fallen monarchs, wandering about the earth, have found places at that forlorn and miserable feast. The statesman, when his party flung him off, might, if he chose it, be once more a great man for the space of a single banquet. Aaron Burr's name appears on the record at a period when his ruin

– the profoundest and most striking, with more of moral circumstance in it than that of almost any other man – was complete in his lonely age. Stephen Girard, when his wealth weighed upon him like a mountain, once sought admittance of his own accord. It is not probable, however, that these men had any lesson to teach in the lore of discontent and misery which might not equally well have been studied in the common walks of life. Illustrious unfortunates attract a wider sympathy, not because their griefs are more intense, but because, being set on lofty pedestals, they the better serve mankind as instances and bywords of calamity.

It concerns our present purpose to say that, at each successive festival, Gervayse Hastings showed his face, gradually changing from the smooth beauty of his youth to the thoughtful comeliness of manhood, and thence to the bald, impressive dignity of age. He was the only individual invariably present. Yet on every occasion there were murmurs, both from those who knew his character and position, and from them whose hearts shrank back as denying his companionship in their mystic fraternity.

'Who is this impassive man?' had been asked a hundred times. 'Has he suffered? Has he sinned? There are no traces of either. Then wherefore is he here?'

'You must inquire of the stewards or of himself,' was the constant reply. 'We seem to know him well here in our city, and know nothing of him but what is creditable and fortunate. Yet hither he comes, year after year, to this gloomy banquet, and sits among the guests like a marble statue. Ask yonder skeleton, perhaps that may solve the riddle!'

It was in truth a wonder. The life of Gervayse Hastings was not merely a prosperous, but a brilliant one. Everything had gone well with him. He was wealthy, far beyond the expenditure that was required by habits of magnificence, a taste of rare purity and cultivation, a love of travel, a scholar's instinct to collect a splendid library, and, moreover, what seemed a magnificent liberality to the distressed. He had sought happiness, and not vainly, if a lovely and tender wife, and children of fair promise, could insure it. He had, besides, ascended above the limit which separates the obscure from the distinguished, and had won a stainless reputation in affairs of the widest public importance. Not that he was a popular character, or had within him the mysterious attributes which are essential to that species of success. To the public he was a cold abstraction, wholly destitute of those rich hues of personality, that living warmth, and the peculiar faculty of stamping his own heart's impression on a multitude of hearts by which the people recognize their favourites. And it must be owned that after his most intimate associates had done their best to know him thoroughly and love him warmly, they were startled to find how little hold he had upon their affections. They approved, they admired, but still in those moments when the human spirit most craves reality, they shrank back from Gervayse Hastings, as powerless to give them what they sought. It was the feeling of distrustful regret with which we should draw back the hand after extending it, in an illusive twilight, to grasp the hand of a shadow upon the wall.

As the superficial fervency of youth decayed, this peculiar effect of Gervayse Hastings' character grew more perceptible. His children, when he extended his arms, came coldly to his knees, but never climbed them of their own accord. His wife wept secretly, and almost adjudged herself a criminal because she shivered in the chill of his bosom. He, too, occasionally appeared not unconscious of the chillness of his moral atmosphere, and willing, if it might be so, to warm himself at a kindly fire. But age stole onward and benumbed him more and more. As the hoar-frost began to gather on him, his wife went to her grave, and was doubtless warmer there; his children either died or were scattered to different homes of their own; and old Gervayse Hastings, unscathed by grief – alone, but needing no companionship – continued his steady walk through life, and still on every Christmas day attended at the dismal banquet. His privilege as a guest had become prescriptive now. Had he claimed the head of the table, even the skeleton would have been ejected from its seat.

Finally, at the merry Christmas tide, when he had numbered fourscore years complete, this pale, high-browed, marble-featured old man once more entered the long-frequented hall, with the same impassive aspect that had called forth so much dissatisfied remark at his first attendance. Time, except in matters merely external, had done nothing for him, either of good or evil. As he took his place, he threw a calm, inquiring glance around the table, as if to ascertain whether any guest had yet appeared, after so many unsuccessful banquets, who might impart to him the mystery – the deep, warm secret – the life within the life – which, whether manifested in joy or sorrow, is what gives substance to a world of shadows.

'My friends,' said Gervayse Hastings, assuming a position which his long conversance with the festival caused to appear natural, 'you are welcome! I drink to you all in this cup of sepulchral wine.'

The guests replied courteously, but still in a manner that proved them unable to receive the old man as a member of their sad fraternity. It may be well to give the reader an idea of the present company at the banquet.

One was formerly a clergyman, enthusiastic in his profession, and apparently of the genuine dynasty of those old puritan divines whose faith in their calling, and stern exercise of it, had placed them among the mighty of the earth. But yielding to the speculative tendency of the age, he had gone astray from the firm foundation of an ancient faith, and wandered into a cloud region, where everything was misty and deceptive, ever mocking him with a semblance of reality, but still dissolving when he flung himself upon it for support and rest. His instinct and early training demanded something steadfast; but, looking forward, he beheld vapours piled on vapours, and behind him an impassable gulf between the man of yesterday and today, on the borders of which he paced to and fro, sometimes wringing his hands in agony, and often making his own woe a theme of scornful merriment. This surely was a miserable man. Next, there was a theorist – one of a numerous tribe, although he deemed himself unique since the creation – a theorist who had conceived a plan by which all the wretchedness of earth, moral and physical, might be done away, and the bliss of the millennium at once accomplished. But the incredulity of mankind debarring him from action, he was smitten with as much grief as if the whole mass of woe which he was denied the opportunity to remedy were crowded into his own bosom. A plain old man in black attracted much of the company's notice, on the supposition that he was no other than Father Miller, who, it seemed, had given himself up to despair at the tedious delay of the final conflagration. Then there was a man distinguished for native pride and obstinacy, who, a little while before, had possessed immense wealth, and held the control of a vast moneyed interest which he had wielded in the same spirit as a despotic monarch would wield the power of his empire, carrying on a tremendous moral warfare, the roar and tremor of which was felt at every fireside in the land. At length came a crushing ruin – a total overthrow of fortune, power, and character – the effect of which on his imperious and, in many respects, noble and lofty nature, might have entitled him to a place, not merely at our festival, but among the peers of Pandemonium.

There was a modern philanthropist, who had become so deeply sensible of the calamities of thousands and millions of his fellow-creatures, and of the impracticableness of any general measures for their relief, that he had no heart to do what little good lay immediately within his power, but contented himself with being miserable for sympathy. Near him sat a gentleman in a predicament hitherto unprecedented, but of which the present epoch probably affords numerous examples. Ever since he was of capacity to read a newspaper, this person had prided himself on his consistent adherence to one political party, but, in the confusion of these latter days, had got bewildered and knew not whereabouts his party was. This wretched condition, so morally desolate and disheartening to a man who has long accustomed himself to merge his individuality in the mass of a great body, can only be conceived by such as have experienced it. His next companion was a popular orator who had lost his voice, and – as it was pretty much all that he had to lose – had fallen into a state of hopeless melancholy. The table was likewise graced by two of the gentler sex – one, a half-starved, consumptive seamstress, the representative of thousands just as wretched; the other, a woman of unemployed energy, who found herself in the world with nothing to achieve, nothing to enjoy, and nothing even to suffer. She had, therefore, driven herself to the verge of madness by dark broodings over the wrongs of her sex and its exclusion from a proper field of action. The roll of guests being thus complete, a side table had been set for three or four disappointed office seekers, with hearts as sick as death, whom the stewards had admitted partly because their calamities really entitled them to entrance here, and partly that they were in especial need of a good dinner. There was likewise a homeless dog, with his tail between his legs, licking up the crumbs and gnawing the fragments of the feast; such a melancholy air as one sometimes sees about the streets without a master, and willing to follow the first that will accept his service.

In their own way, these were as wretched a set of people as ever had assembled at the festival. There they sat, with the veiled skeleton of the founder holding aloft the cypress wreath, at one end of the table, and at the other, wrapped in furs, the withered figure of Gervayse Hastings, stately, calm, and cold, impressing the company with awe, yet so little interesting their sympathy that he might have vanished into thin air without their once exclaiming, 'Whither is he gone?'

'Sir,' said the philanthropist, addressing the old man, 'you have been so long a guest at this annual festival, and have thus been conversant with so many varieties of human affliction, that, not improbably, you have thence derived some great and important lessons. How blessed were your lot could you reveal a secret by which all this mass of woe might be removed!'

'I know of but one misfortune,' answered Gervayse Hastings, quietly, 'and that is my own.'

'Your own!' enjoined the philanthropist. 'And, looking back on your serene and prosperous life, how can you claim to be the sole unfortunate of the human race?'

'You will not understand it,' replied Gervayse Hastings, feebly, and with a singular inefficiency of pronunciation, and sometimes putting one word for another. 'None have understood it – not even those who experience the like. It is a chillness – a want of earnestness – a feeling as if what should be my heart were a thing of vapour – a haunting perception of unreality! Thus seeming to possess all that other men have – all that men aim at – I have really possessed nothing, neither joy nor griefs. All things, all persons – as was truly said to me at this table long and long ago – have been like shadows flickering on the wall. It was so with my wife and children – with those who seemed my friends: it is so with yourselves, whom I see now before me. Neither have I myself any real existence, but am a shadow like the rest.'

'And how is it with your views of a future life?' inquired the speculative clergyman.

'Worse than with you,' said the old man, in a hollow and feeble tone; 'for I cannot conceive it earnestly enough to feel either hope or fear. Mine – mine is the wretchedness! This cold heart – this unreal life! Ah! it grows colder still.'

It so chanced that at this juncture the decayed ligaments of the skeleton gave way, and the dry bones fell together in a heap, thus causing the dusty wreath of cypress to drop upon the table. The attention of the company being thus diverted for a single instant from Gervayse Hastings, they perceived on turning again towards him that the old man had undergone a change. His shadow had ceased to flicker on the wall.

'Well, Rosina, what is your criticism?' asked Roderick, as he rolled up the manuscript.

'Frankly, your success is by no means complete,' replied she. 'It is true, I have an idea of the character you endeavour to describe; but it is rather by dint of my own thought than your expression.'

'That is unavoidable,' observed the sculptor, 'because the characteristics are all negative. If Gervayse Hastings imbibed one human grief at the gloomy banquet, the task of describing him would have been infinitely easier. Of such persons – and we do meet with these moral monsters now and then – it is difficult to conceive how they came to exist here, or what there is in them capable of existence hereafter. They seem to be on the outside of everything; and nothing wearies the soul more than an attempt to comprehend them within its grasp.'

Lightning Source UK Ltd.
Milton Keynes UK
UKHW040846141119
353526UK00001B/23/P